Between Law and Culture

Between Law and Culture

Relocating Legal Studies

DAVID THEO GOLDBERG, MICHAEL MUSHENO, AND LISA C. BOWER, EDITORS

University of Minnesota Press
Minneapolis
London

The University of Minnesota Press gratefully acknowledges permission to reprint the following. An earlier version of chapter 2 appeared in *SportCult,* edited by Randy Martin and Toby Miller (Minneapolis: University of Minnesota Press, 1999); copyright 1999 by the Regents of the University of Minnesota. An earlier version of chapter 3 appeared in *Symptoms of Culture,* by Marjorie Garber (New York: Routledge, 1998); copyright 1998 by Routledge; reproduced by permission of Taylor & Francis, Inc./Routledge, Inc., http://www.routledge-ny.com. An expanded version of chapter 8 was published in *The Racial State,* by David Theo Goldberg (London: Blackwell Publishers, 2001); reprinted by permission of Blackwell Publishers. An earlier version of chapter 10 appeared as "Policing Identities: Cop Decision Making and the Constitution of Citizens," by Trish Oberweis and Michael Musheno, in *Law and Social Inquiry* 24, no. 4 (1999); reprinted by permission of the authors. An earlier version of chapter 14 appeared in *Social and Legal Studies: An International Journal* 8, issue 1 (March 1999); copyright 1999, Sage Ltd; reprinted by permission of Sage Publications Ltd.

Published by the University of Minnesota Press
111 Third Avenue South, Suite 290
Minneapolis, MN 55401-2520
http://www.upress.umn.edu

Printed in the United States of America on acid-free paper

Library of Congress Cataloging-in-Publication Data
Between law and culture : relocating legal studies / David Theo Goldberg,
Michael Musheno, and Lisa C. Bower, editors.
p. cm.
Includes bibliographical references and index.
ISBN 0-8166-3380-0 (HC : alk. paper)—ISBN 0-8166-3381-9 (PB : alk. paper)
1. Culture and law. 2. Law—Study and teaching—Sociological aspects.
I. Goldberg, David Theo. II. Musheno, Michael C. III. Bower, Lisa C.
K487.C8 B48 2001
340'.115—dc21 2001000521

The University of Minnesota is an equal-opportunity educator and employer.

12 11 10 09 08 07 06 05 04 03 02 01 10 9 8 7 6 5 4 3 2 1

Contents

Part III. IDENTITIES

Part IV. SEXUALITIES

Acknowledgments

This book grew out of a graduate seminar on justice and identities offered by the three of us through the School of Justice Studies, Arizona State University, in the spring semester of 1997. We are indebted in incalculable ways to the participants in the seminar, visiting presenters and students alike, many of whom are contributors to this volume. It was an extraordinary semester, from which we learned immeasurably—about law and culture and their interface, about silences and frustrations, outbursts and expectations, insight and sensitivity, and above all about learning and teaching, intellectual generosity, and collegiality. These lessons have seen us through the waxing and waning of the editorial process, too.

The burdens of editing and production have been shared equally by all three of us—as too, we trust, the pleasure of the outcome, the text. The only evidence we can offer is that we remain deep friends, even as we have gone on to other interests. Given similar opportunities, we might even consider doing it again. Perhaps happily, those opportunities do not present themselves every day.

We are grateful to the University of Minnesota Press for so graciously seeing the book to publication and especially to our editor, Carrie Mullen, for her warm, engaging, and always magnanimous support. We thank the reviewers for their generously helpful comments, which much improved the manuscript.

Two people warrant special mention. Kay Korman was the wizard of justice studies at Arizona State University. Everyone who had the fortune of working with Kay will know that she turned over every last stone to accommodate needs, fashion greater comfort, reduce (we are tempted to say undermine) bureaucracy (though in a book on law and culture that might raise an eyebrow), and generally make it all magically come together. This project literally might never have seen the light of day without Kay's wand. Reading materials materialized (almost out of whole cloth), visitors arrived and left (mostly on time), misplaced wallets were recovered, folks were fed (and not one fed up), a cello (that's right) was found and rented (not an easy accomplishment in cowboy country) because a practice session could not be missed, and various versions of the manuscript were produced and reproduced, sealed, and mailed—all on deadline and between smiles.

Kim Furumoto, research assistant extraordinaire, read through every manuscript into the early morning hours of her weekends, identifying and then providing missing references and typos, frowning at some of the gaps in argument, and being skeptical of the sometimes too easy formulations in phrasing. She completed all this work between law school courses and graduate seminars, just because she cares and is certainly driven by neither fame nor fortune.

Doug Feremenga, David's research assistant at the University of California, Irvine, and Brian Rowalt, computer specialist at the University of California's Humanities Research Institute, graciously assisted in completing the index.

Michael Musheno thanks his family, Birgit and Micah Musheno, for making home a place of pleasure and work.

We dedicate the book to all those who made it possible.

David Theo Goldberg
Michael Musheno
Lisa Bower
Tempe, Arizona
January 2000

Introduction

Shake Yo' Paradigm

ROMANTIC LONGING AND TERROR
IN CONTEMPORARY SOCIOLEGAL STUDIES

David Theo Goldberg, Michael Musheno, and Lisa C. Bower

Law's Culture

A little over a decade ago there appeared what would become the well-known volume *Feminist Studies/Critical Studies,* edited by Teresa de Lauretis. The volume collected together the proceedings of a conference at the University of Wisconsin, Milwaukee, in the mid-1980s. The preface to the book formulaically acknowledges the various persons and institutions who made the publication possible. What is remarkable, however, is the failure to acknowledge the controversy, the yelling and tears, marking several of the conference panels. The results were astounding to observe, shattering any illusions that sisterhood might be imagined as a local phenomenon and certainly erasing any intimation of its global dimensions. Of course, few men would have been reduced to tears by these sorts of exchanges, suggesting that as late as the mid-1980s some feminists really did believe that acrimonious exchanges, even under the guise of academic "debate," were undesirable. Tears were indications of tears in the fabric of feminism and required concealment so as to present feminist projects as somehow of a whole cloth. Would it have made a difference if the preface or de Lauretis's introduction had referenced these debates? The careful reader of *Feminist Studies/Critical Studies* will notice a tension among the various chapters, one capturing the differences that flared up so dramatically at the conference. Aren't introductions or prefaces that elide controversies, especially when embedded in edited collections, themselves a safer means of revealing the differences within a "marginalized" field as it attempts to establish its validity and vitality? For the appearance of unity among participants and adherents of a field, especially tacit agreement about the field's goals and trajectories, is frequently taken as a sign of a discipline's maturity.

Why introduce a volume mapping the relationship between contemporary sociolegal studies and cultural studies, between law and culture, by invoking heated disagreement within feminist contexts? In the late 1990s such debates seem tired, signaling for some the demise of feminist politics and for others the necessary disaggregation of a singular feminism that for so long celebrated its own voice, conceiving this celebration as its central aim and purpose. Divisions and disagreements long embedded in earlier feminist discourses have erupted to unsettle the fiction of feminism's unanimity. The de Lauretis preface sought to distance itself from the abrasiveness marking its origins, glossing over public displays of heated, often vitriolic disagreement (which nevertheless *were* the primary topic of restroom conversation).

We are suggesting, in comparison, that we turn to face the conflagration, embracing the discomfort engendered by those flames. While often painful, controversies, however, may also be politically and intellectually productive because they frequently signal a discipline's or some scholars' disquietude with the substantive and/or methodological assumptions animating paradigmatic ways of conceptualizing their enterprise. And, of course, they signal moments of "crisis" as well, which must be concealed or at a minimum glossed over, described as anomalous, and certainly referenced as "temporary."

Moments of crisis are a constitutive feature of any enterprise, such as sociolegal studies, that takes seriously the transformative (and therefore) highly unstable nature of law and law's relationship to culture (and vice versa). We suggest that sociolegal scholarship is marked by a permanent instability, a result of movement within (and out of) paradigms as well as a desire to contain that movement. This desire for containment is evidenced by those gestures seeking to cover up the cracks and fissures appearing as paradigms and prevailing frameworks are shaken up, rearranged, and transformed. Even a casual glance at the history of sociolegal studies in the past 100 years reveals the sea-changes effected when methodological or theoretical frameworks are called into question. The emergence of new forms of conceptualization frequently has been aimed to offset the shortcomings of established ones for imagining the relationship between law and society.

In many instances, those introducing such frameworks promised a revolution in sociolegal studies. Each projected revolution promoted itself as one worthy of all who might become its faithful adherents. Moments of discomfort attendant to such destabilizations, as various "paradigm shakers" have promised, are always time-bound and transitional, ultimately to be alleviated by a return to a conceptual unity fantasized as permanent (as if this time the paradigm had been perfected).

Once again the boundaries defining sociolegal scholarship are being rearranged, as key terms—society, culture, power, justice, identity/identities, and the like—have become unsettled. Something is occurring, not to be too vague or mysterious about it, a shift that can be described in part as the legacy of numerous critical interventions. If the *Feminist Studies/Critical Studies* preface failed to foreground controversy, perhaps the time was not right. After all, the 1980s were a peculiar time for feminism, and for critical theories in general, a period of transition. The 1980s signaled the advent of serious criticisms of poststructuralism and antifoundationalism, the emergence of queer theory, and the dramatic rise of critical race theory—the popularizing, indeed commodifying, of cultural studies and a move beyond interdisciplinary work to a recognition of the limitations of disciplinary frameworks in general. All these influences were not yet fully articulated.

At the same time, far too much energy has been normatively and normally expended in repeated attempts to shore up disciplinary frameworks and to avoid the permanence of crisis as a key feature of academic scholarship. The movement now occurring within sociolegal scholarship offers an occasion to consider the state of such scholarship, indeed of all scholarship, as marked by a constitutive instability. In terms of the current crisis, the indicators have circulated for some time now. Sociolegal scholars have struggled for a decade or so over incorporating poststructuralism and its effects on the empirically driven work that for so long has been the signature mark of sociolegal studies, at least as conceived in the United States and in Britain. Tensions running through the annual meetings of U.S.

organizations such as the Law and Society Association have stemmed from this familiar collision between the empirical and the theoretical. Susan Silbey and Austin Sarat (1987) first noted this tension in their now classic article and enjoined sociolegal scholars to be both "empirical" and "critical."

On the other hand, the present tensions are also symptoms of the inability to describe coherently the enterprise known as "sociolegal scholarship," which has rested historically, although certainly precariously, on various methodologies associated with the social sciences. The methodological uprooting of sociolegal studies has been accelerated by the work of scholars traditionally associated with the humanities (broadly defined) and so with disciplines "outside" the law. Bracketing outside in a citational mode, of course, suggests that there is an interior—an agreed set of principles, approaches, and beliefs—that has sustained the work of sociolegal scholarship. This tacit agreement has been thrown into question as a result of various developments. These include the proliferation of text-based analysis; transformations in conceptions of power attendant to the so-called poststructuralist turn; changes in political contexts, including resitings of the political; the increasing sense of law's incoherence and indeterminacy; and the sheer diversity of methodological and theoretical approaches. Scholars with all sorts of disciplinary affiliations—from Stanley Fish to Toni Morrison, Henry Louis Gates to Judith Butler, and John Comaroff to Wendy Brown—now write authoritatively about law.

As the contributions to *Between Law and Culture* attest, sociolegal scholarship can no longer be confined (if it ever really was) to a "social science" model or, indeed, to a post-realist model or perhaps even to any model. In this volume lawyers meet cultural analysts, political scientists bump into social psychologists, sociologists face philosophers, and communications critics engage anthropologists, sometimes along the same keyboard if not in the same person. Disciplinary division gives way to postdisciplinary entanglements of theoretical and empirical work. The theoretical and empirical thus are taken as coconstitutive of the possibilities of each other. Theory without data is empty, to mimic Kant's famous dictum, the empirical without theory is un(in)formed. On its own, theory ultimately lacks a referent and so any body; without theory, data is no more than dazed and confused.

Our purpose in this volume is modest: to attend to yet another difficult moment in sociolegal scholarship by asking what happens to reflections about law and culture when sociolegal and cultural studies meet. At the end of the twentieth century, we have lived through—some would say, we have survived—several decades of deconstructing the subject, disaggregating reason and agency, as well as seemingly dismissing the materiality of lived experience. There is once again emerging now a desire, ardently articulated in professional associations and animating debates in professional journals, to return to conceptual unities, to move beyond crisis, to settle the unsettled if not quite to settle the score. Yet we offer no resolution to the confusion engendered by this breakdown, disaggregation, and disarticulation of disciplinary boundaries. Our aim emphatically is not to offer a solution or to argue for the primacy of one paradigm or discipline over another. We want to resist the romantic longing for closure, to settle the accounting. And yet it is not our goal either merely to resist this seduction, to replace it with its opposite, a plurality of paradigms, a hodgepodge of methodological apparatuses culled from a variety of disciplines, in short, to celebrate the discomfort and confusion that comes with mere paradigmatic diversity.

This curious vacillation between the desire for unity and disaggregation, stability and instability, articulation and disarticulation that seems a constitutive feature if not condition of academic scholarship, including sociolegal studies scholarship, has for us a more localized meaning. Some two years ago, the three of us taught together the interdisciplinary graduate seminar "Justice and Identities," and this volume grew out of that experience. Most of the authors represented here, ourselves included, participated in the seminar as guest speakers and graduate students, at once instructors and instructed. All contributed not simply as visitors or disciples but ultimately and together as (our) teachers, offering the opportunity to reflect on the meaning of "discipline" and "disciplinary" and the "relationship" to these terms for those engaged in the project and prospects of inter-, post-, and transdisciplinary studies concerning the law.

At the outset of the seminar, we stumbled somewhat flippantly on characterizing a dominant tension among theories and theorists along a spectrum between "romantic longing" and "terror." Very quickly this tension ordered a good deal of our critical reference points. Romantic longing represents the desire for conceptual unity, linear models of social change, and the resolution of conflict; terror we usually reserved for texts that offered their antithesis. Initially conceived as mutually exclusive choices—one opted for either romantic longing or terror—this tension became a source both of amusement and discomfort and of dis-ease. Interestingly, it also became for participants in the seminar a marker of "identity" and self-definition. In brief, during the course of the semester, we reinvented larger debates as we enjoyed both components of what might fruitfully be characterized as the sublime. Such vacillation is itself broadly symptomatic of the sorts of historical movements across and within paradigms as described here. Rather than insist on the valorization of this opposition or assume a position in one camp or the other, it seems more fruitful to see how each term—and the position for which it stands—exists as a point on a continuum.

The sublime provides an interesting psychological and conceptual frame for talking about both the romantic longing—that desire for origins and foundations that characterized our conversations in "Justice and Identities" as well as more generally marking sociolegal scholarship—and its antithesis or converse, the discomfort or fear of annihilation that appears in the presence of instability. Romantic longing and the embrace of terror—worlds in which the key terms and signifiers of the political are not secured in advance—stand as components of the sublime. They represent what it means to feel blocked by the fear of losing "count," of being reduced to nothing but counting or interpreting data with little hope of bringing a long series of ideas, concepts, and paradoxes together into some sort of conceptual unity. What writer has not encountered the terror of time slipping away as she hopes for the insight, the grid, the astute editorial insight—the sublime moment—that like the random turn of a kaleidoscope will bring the pattern of argumentation into focus? What student has not yearned for the moment of disciplinary interpellation when (at last) obedience to training and control perversely "pay off," resulting in a state of disciplinary order? And what teacher has not rewarded her disciples when they have coherently demonstrated their internalization of a discipline's key rules and precepts?

Kant's notion of the mathematical sublime suggests that the overload marking all these experiences is followed by a movement in which reason (or theory) celebrates its ability to separate from the confusion of the data at hand, exulting in its own rationality and in the ability to order what the senses insist cannot be ordered. The sublime thus represents a reaction to the anxiety of incompletion, the transcendence apparently achieved in a "sublime moment" suggesting anxiety's attenuation. In the suddenness of the sublime moment, attachments to objects per se are rejected, and an ideal of totality is sought. The move toward totality also becomes a vehicle for consolidating a reassuringly operative, active notion of the self, linked to the exercise of reason. For reason's unity is felt most acutely when, as Kant argues, it is "filled with one great sensation." The price for this sensation is an awareness that is achieved by traversing difficulty, so that it becomes not merely a negative moment but a reassuring one. (One has made the deadline or "mastered" the field, usually by recapitulating its rules and principles, demonstrating once again the power-of-knowledge-as-discipline and disciplehood as a source of agency.) The sublime is conceived in reason's aggrandizement of itself, its own norms and authority, at the expense of a referent, "the real," outside itself. The root of any disciplinary claim to coherence lies in the illusion of reason's capacity to find a point of resolution, to create order out of chaos. The failure to do so creates not merely a source of guilt and anxiety for the individual subject; it transgresses the implicit requirements, the founding rules, of any field in the process of constituting and reconstituting its collective identity.

The scholar's drive, however, is ironically for the moment of containment. Here confusion is apparently resolved in a confrontation that can be managed. The scholar seeks "to identify with" the sheer volume of information or numerical excess with which he or she is confronted, an identification that ultimately is also the guarantee of the self's own integrity as an agent. The moment of contain-ability is a confirmation of the unitary status of the self, a concept now all too easily dismissed as modernist but one that even in these critical times has an uncomfortably familiar resonance. At a general level this may be the condition of scholarly work. Yet it also suggests a continuum rather than the crude opposition we invented at the outset, as though surrogates for steady anchors in the face of casting off the "guaranteed" safety of disciplinary practice and pursuit. On the one hand, conceptions of resolution and unity, progressive theories of law, and theories of identities that can be described and packaged neatly eventuate in experiences of the sublime. Conversely, the terror end of the continuum is conceivable only against the background assumption of the sublime, potentially accessible through the labor of "reason" or "pure theory." One melancholically embraces the moment of containment, anticipating a movement beyond it: The sublime moment releases one from guilt through an identification with the power by which one had formerly been threatened, and by installing reason as the supreme authority, as the ground and effect of the presumption of coherence. Delight is found in the expulsion of the confusion, the excess, that threatens and renders anxious in the assertion of reason's power over its antithesis. At the moment of expulsion, which is followed by illusory aggrandizement (the claim to power of the reasoning self), terror collapses into its opposite, suggesting that the two are mutually constituted rather than antithetical, as we initially fantasized.

The sections and chapters in this volume reveal that what is important here is not whether one embraces romantic longing to confirm a unitary, coherent subject (and identity) or whether one insists on melancholic terror where confusion reigns supreme. What matters is how the symptom that is the sublime is mapped out in a political field of possibilities. The crucial question, then, concerns how one might imagine different meanings of the political by virtue of the romantic longing and terror that attend any effort to represent, for our purposes, the relationship between and among law, identity, space, and culture.

Here there will be no delight that does not perversely also court confusion. Can one apprehend the terror of cognitive exhaustion and live in anxiety and hope without requiring a return to the unity of the self that is defined by a disembodied reason? Can we imagine a kind of politics and social transformation in which the key terms are not known in advance, one that anticipates politics in a future mode? Such a politics of transformation would embrace both hope and anxiety. It would be a politics, as Foucault puts it, of "discomfort." For any attempt to occupy or defend either end of the sublime continuum places us once again in the position of constituting rather than criticizing disciplinary power. Might a theory of "transdisciplinarity" be posited that avoids the former or, at a minimum, avoids the reification of disciplinary boundaries?

This volume aims to query what happens when law, culture, space, and identity are considered simultaneously, as intimately related, as mutually constitutive and constituted. The volume as a whole clearly suggests a shift occurring in the relationship among and between these terms and what they stand for, a movement enjoining a reconsideration of each, as each term is redefined relationally in this engagement. This disciplinary displacement and reworking also suggests a rethinking of the functions of law and the sites and scope of the political as well as the relationships between and among law, culture, space, identities, and political transformations. For, as Derrida notes, "politicization is interminable even if it cannot and should never be total. To keep this from being a truism or a triviality, we must recognize in it the following consequence: each advance in politicization obliges one to reconsider, and so to reinterpret the very foundations of law such as they had previously been calculated or delimited" (Derrida 1992, 28).

Unsurprisingly, a certain resistance emerges not only to rethinking the "foundations of law" but more generally to moving beyond charted territory to embrace confusion and discomfort. A number of questions immediately arise marking interdisciplinary sociolegal scholarship specifically and the academy more generally at the dawn of the twenty-first century. This volume thus mirrors larger debates that, of necessity, it also helps to construct and extend. Looming large as a backdrop are the popular and academic discussions about the relationship between poststructuralism and politics and about the death not of the subject this time but rather of the agent, whoever she may be and wherever she may be found. The achingly familiar question arises concerning how to conceive agency once the subject is viewed as discursively constituted, once liberal choice has been demonstrated as chimerical and, worse yet, as tyrannical, misogynist, colonialist, imperialist, and relentless in its reinscription of various tensions, contradictions, and oppositions. This question can be posed now as one of power at the intersecting points, those spaces of collapse, between state and society, public and private, law and culture. How, then, is power to be differentially articulated at these points of collapse? The law invokes for itself the power of assertion; it states in the name of the state, as state power and state agent. But the law does so—as contributors to part I of this volume demonstrate—always in terms of and by reinscribing culture. There is no abstract law, a language of law transcending culture, purged of all spatiotemporal specificity. There is no law, then, that is not at once political in its assumptions and implications. By the same token, though, resistance too is an assertion, a counterstatement, often legally articulated but in any case equally culturally inscribed and transformatively reproductive. These concerns render problematic any simplistic resistance to theory as well as to empirically driven quantitative and qualitative work. They also question the seemingly endless reiteration of 1960s models of social change, identity politics, and linear progress, tied frequently to arguments about the incontrovertible importance of law's material effects.

The political underpinnings and implications of law's material effects on "everyday people in their ordinary lives" are juxtaposed here to the potential of a cultural politics and the painful reality of nonlinear transformation(s) as constitutive conditions of the political. While perhaps too quickly and simply labeled symptoms of "romantic longing," as we sometimes tended to do in the seminar, this potential intimates at once a failure to comprehend certain terms central to understanding the nature of the social, the legal, and the sociolegal and indeed how such terms have shifted in context and meaning, social implications, and political effects. These are the terms and their relations—culture, identity, space, and sexuality—that this volume is centrally concerned to explore.

To date, the principal questions posed regarding law, culture, and identity have had to do with assimilation, integration, and separatism as responses to the history of segregation. Thus, sociolegal scholars have been concerned to address how law is constrained by cultural identity, giving the lie to liberal claims to legal neutrality. While there are notable exceptions, a prevailing concern, then, has been to assess critically how the application of law has been skewed against those seen not to belong ethnoracially or nationally, to be outside the protective confines of administrative state scope (cf. Sarat and Kearns 1997, 1998). These have been important questions in face of the deeply racially divisive and discriminatory history especially but not only in U.S. experience. Yet even in critically addressing this history, these questions are distinctly delimiting. We are concerned in this volume to broaden the scope and depth of the questions facing the intersection of law, culture, and identity: How is law informed by and through cultural definition and identity, and how is culture shaped and ordered in conception as much as in articulation through and by the authorization of law? What shape(s) does culture assume in and through law?

The central terms with which we are concerned here, then—law, culture, identity, space, and sexuality—are attended to not only in sociolegal studies but also in cultural and postcolonial studies. In a sense, these considerations have always marked the places at which law and culture meet, if often all too silently and unaddressed in the past. What follows, then, is that sociolegal and cultural studies cannot engage and employ such terms without understanding their employment by each other. But it follows equally that the standard terms on which sociolegal studies has tended to rely—such as legal consciousness—cannot be so unproblematically engaged. The notion of "legal consciousness" reinscribes a form of idealism in ignoring how legal sensibilities, understandings, and terms are always already culturally thick. Cultural ordering is already implicated in material and identity formations that sociolegal studies necessarily assumes to make sense on its own terms, inscribed in spatial and sexual relations that at once are denied or silenced or simply ignored. A brief survey of the volume's contributions evidence our concern to loosen paradigmatic holds and in doing so to uncover more subtle constitutive forces operating at the interface of law and culture, sociolegal and cultural studies.

Covering Ground

We accordingly open the volume with a section on culture. Here, David Engel reveals our central concern immediately in arguing that the constitution of identities are clearly revealed in the tensions between injury and (legal) remedy. Injury, remedy, and self are constituted in very localized social settings, where particular conceptions of space and time, community and justice, are engaged. These conceptions shape the meanings of the selves of those who have suffered the injury (or claim to be injured), those who have caused the injury, and those who are in positions to suggest or effect remedies. Law, in the form of judicial bodies and rulings, offers an authoritative forum for mediating these contested meanings and managing the conflicts they represent. But in doing so, law invents notions of community and justice, of social identities and legal entities, to authorize and legitimize remedies and responses in the face of contesting and contested notions of composite selves and injured selves. Injury, in short, is a revealing "measure" for exploring the coconstitutive dynamics of law and culture, of culture through law and law embedded in culture.

While Engel focuses on law's limited and local capacity to shape identity and community in particularistic ways, Rosemary Coombe is more expansive in her claims about law's constitutive powers. Both identify the domain of law in terms of judicial bodies rendering authoritative opinions, and each attends to the symbolic power of law. Engel understands law to effect culture by re/inventing localized notions of self and identity. Coombe, by contrast, considers the national reach of law, its authority enabling and shaping a political economy of mass-mediated and commodifiable signification to produce through intellectual property a restricted if authorized sense of community and culture. She is particularly interested in understanding not just how such commodification through (legally promoted and endorsed) signification reproduces a consensual common sense but also what forms resistance to such commodified selves might assume.

The principal object of analysis by which Coombe chooses to illustrate her argument that law enables and operates through the mass dissemination of stereotypical images is sports and specifically sports trademarks. Here two socially diffuse and penetrating sign systems—the legal and cultural—are sewn together intimately. Consider the importance of "defense" and "offense," rules and representations, judges and rulings, to each respectively. If Coombe and Engel examine the interface of law and culture largely from the point of view of sociolegality, Marjorie Garber inverts the focus. Garber draws attention to the infusion of Christian evangelism, as a normative cultural ordering, into professional and intercollegiate sports in the United States. Focusing on the bundling of Christianity and evangelism with the rhetoric of patriotism and nativist Americanism, she argues that legal claims are subordinated to this incorporation of a particularized religiosity into sports and onto the imagination of sports fans. One could add that this binding of sports and religiosity mediated through law already begins at the school level: witness the case against prayer, specifically to Christ, before high school football games at Salina High School in Texas, recent state high school football champions. Concerned especially to point out the social harms and exclusions of this cultural posturing, legality for Garber seems subordinated, if not submerged, beneath the particularities of cultural thickness and meaningful only within the parameters that such cultural thickness makes possible. Garber's point cuts deep. School district officials in Texas gave up trying to restrict game time public prayer prior to U.S. Supreme Court rulings in 2000 in the face of family resistance and Christian Coalition arguments that it would violate freedom of expression. The god of school prayer and football champions is at once above and beneath the law, advantaging itself through as it is sustained by the gaps in law's reach, reinforcing law's force as it seeks to claim a power beyond it.

In probing the parameters and limits of cultural formation, seeking to scope out the space of possibilities for the emergence of a black cultural formation within a globalizing (and so restrictively universalizing) commercial culture, Herman Gray seeks an analytical terrain that joins Garber with Coombe. In particular, Gray examines the conditions of possibility for the expression of a culture of resistance to the discourses of regulation that are used to appropriating black expressibility strictly for commercial gain. Gray's concern with "discourses of regulation" presumes law as conceived by Coombe but extends outward to include also technologies of surveillance and regulative and so delimiting production strategies constitutive of commercial culture. Thus, Gray is concerned to outline the emergence of a black cultural formation the normative commitments of which are able to negotiate the terrain of regulatory regimes and commercialization without re/producing the (stereo)typical imagery of blackness. His treatment of culture is both local and global, particular to the internally diverse and sometimes contradictory norms and values, sites and signs, of black expressibility, against the critical background of universalizing commodifiability. Like Engel, then, Gray employs identity to shatter notions of holistic community formation, recognizing at once the forces (including law) outside and inside social fields that commensurately shape and fracture it.

If identity formation and transformation are so basic to the making and unmaking of meaning and material implication of law, and yet so often overlooked as necessarily constitutive of law's domain, the same must be said for *space,* both as cultural imaginary and in its materialities. We follow part I of this volume on cultures accordingly with a part on spaces. Coombe, Garber, and Gray treat culture as the imaginative sphere constituting and constituted by and through commodity capitalism. They are especially interested in how commodifying signs, symbols, and normativities pervading contemporary cultural production in sports, music, dance, and the like shape and delimit human imagination. David Harvey also takes up the question of the cultural imaginary. He argues, by contrast, for a utopian imagination that, combined with people's ability at least in part to construct themselves and their built environments, may enable a revitalization of urban existence. Harvey argues accordingly for a human collective engagement elaborated through dialectical utopian movements between the personal and political, time and space, the particular and universal, with the view to reimagining urban living. He nevertheless is fully aware of the dangers of closure prompted by a utopianism that is imagined in spatial abstraction and then built in a specific location.

This latter concern about an abstracted and totalizing utopianism (Le Corbusier may rise to mind here, but also gated communities) underpins the interface between Harvey's intervention and sociolegal critique. Harvey recognizes clearly that process-grounded utopianism likely leads to reification through accumulation of social power in mediating institutions such as courts, a point well established by critical sociolegal studies of law and legal institutions. By contrast, Harvey seeks to emphasize the expansive imaginary that evolves from critical collective engagement, exemplified in particular by the experience of social rights movements. In this, Harvey reiterates a point about the emergent effects of collective critical political action long recognized by sociolegal scholars and activists, namely, that social justice cannot be restricted in its formation to process alone. This common field of *sociolegal* praxis links Harvey's interest in reimagining community as specific to time and space to David Engel's opening notion of "localized settings." But like sociolegal studies also, Harvey conjures the possibilities of communities that are not exclusionary but face up to seemingly unbridgeable differences by struggling through the rapids of sociolinguistic translation.

Harvey offers the contours for rethinking urban space, for understanding how law both shapes and is fashioned as much by sociospatial arrangements as by sociocultural assumptions and expression. Where Harvey proceeds largely at the level of the theoretical and abstract, Lisa Sanchez moves us inside a material urban site by examining the modes of spatial governmentality around street prostitution. Spatiolegal strategies of discipline are invoked to demonize and diminish the presence of female prostitutes in urban zones. Collective community action to "take back the streets" and explicitly to reestablish control over urban zones reinvigorates "citizens" through their combined efforts to enhance "neighborhood livability." Defeated initially in their efforts to push out a more powerfully entrenched, anchored, and organized sex industry, neighborhood activists allied with governmental agencies in the northwestern city Sanchez examines empirically and ethnographically turned to street prostitutes as the target of zoning strategies. Sanchez accordingly demonstrates the exclusionary processes and effects resulting from alliances between neighborhood activists and local government apparatuses. But law is not narrowly unidirectional in such instances, and Sanchez shows that while it is able through zoning regulations and police enforcement practices to enable exclusion, law may also be invoked in just the same setting to constrict aspects of the enforceability of a prostitution-free zoning ordinance.

Thus, like Engel, Sanchez demonstrates the permeability of law and culture, as the boundaries between police and citizen, state apparatus and neighborhood activism, and public and private are blurred through the enactment of processes of enclosure. Sanchez demonstrates the regulatory workings of "spatial anchorage" (Foucault), the grounding of which she shows to flow out of the complex of neighborhood activism, legal mandates, and regulatory en*force*ment mechanisms in terms of which manifest the possessive investment in "citizen police." People of means move into deterio*rated* neighborhoods seeking through political engagement and legal claims to impose norms about livability. Claims regarding space legally collide, ultimately as contestations in the courts between the assertion of property rights and freedom of expression, ultimately manifesting new contestations about the personal and political, space and time, facticity and the normative, and the particular and the universalistic. If it is too strong to say the legal is everywhere here, the political certainly pervades, giving rise to the tension Harvey points to between a frozen utopia of spatial bars and gated access on the one hand and a dialectical utopia of messily negotiated possibilities in critical collective action on the other.

Space and time, as Sanchez demonstrates, are crucial to uncovering the ways in which cultural and legal terms and conditions collide and intersect to produce modes of social exclusion. Rona Halualani extends the point to uncovering the state as a set of institutions regulating belonging and possibility, rights and access, and property and citizenship in racially conceived terms. State speech and codes are shown to structure the meaning and material implications of Hawaiianness. Halualani engages in a critical-historical genealogy conjoined with oral histories to uncover the intersecting legal moralisms and normative legalisms to privilege the economic interests of settlers and foreigners and to separate Kanakas from legal claims to their land. Drawing on critical race theory and employing a culturalist's sensitivity to language, Halualani reveals how racially conceived identities are constructed and structured as regulatory practices in exercising economic power. Formalized identification practices required by state regulation and legal claim clash with indigenous practices of self-identification, evidencing that in the case of Hawaiian dispossession regulatory legal processes in the generic sense indeed are everywhere. By contrast, Halualani argues—and demonstrates through her written intervention—that "performances of proving" are sites of political resistance. Halualani thus offers a countervoice to the more pessimistic conclusions of Engel and Sanchez regarding the depth of discourses of (legal) regulation. Halualani demonstrates that law is never independent of cultural expression, tracing ways that moral claims are "given" legal recognition and how law relies on moral claims making to legitimize its authority.

Where Halualani examines the contested spaces of imposed and self-fashioned identity formation in respect of Hawaiianness, David Theo Goldberg considers the central implication of the state and its legal and administrative institutions in reconceiving whiteness in the United States after abolition. Thus, Goldberg is concerned to interrogate the negotiation of privilege and belonging, of insider and outsider through and in terms of who would count as white. He examines the sociolegal reconstruction of whiteness by way of changing censal categories and a string of important naturalization cases, linking them to the elevation of de jure segregation emerging in the closing decades of the nineteenth and first quarter of the twentieth centuries. Thus, Goldberg seeks to establish the confluence of segregated social space and renegotiated whiteness in and through the law. The law sets the boundaries of who is admissible as white; of who has access, relatively, to privilege, property, and power; and of who acquires status and a modicum at least of security through a racially codified belonging. At the same time, the culture of race alongside spatial delineation establishes who has rights, legal access, and the protection of law.

Goldberg's reflection on race, space, culture, and law raises in a pointed way a theme threaded throughout earlier contributions in the volume concerning sociolegality and social identities. Yuen Huo and Tom Tyler open part III, "Identities," accordingly, by questioning how the boundaried divisions implicated in ethnic identity formation challenge the possibilities of procedural fairness to serve as a medium of social cohesion. Critical culturalists and interpretive sociolegal scholars have focused largely on the conditions that enable the constitution of ethnic identities. Indeed, Sanchez, Halualani, and Goldberg all take up the roles of law in constituting marginalized identities, principally but not only racial, revealing the variety of ways in which the state and legality are deeply implicated in generating sociocultural division, elevation, and marginalization. Huo and Tyler address the corollary question: How might the state and its agents fairly cohere social relations in a just social order in the face of these potentially sharp divisions and conflicts?

Taken together, the chapters making up part III suggest that the state, while necessarily prompting and promoting division and interest group formation, nevertheless simultaneously is driven to employ agents and engage in practices that enable management and conflict. In turn, these processes of mediation are recognized to privilege some, perhaps inevitably given established distributions of resources, power, and voice, while simultaneously managing social arrangements and order. Huo and Tyler find empirical support for the mediating and ordering possibilities of a discourse of procedural fairness provided that people are willing to identify with the imaginary of a national belonging and state institutions beyond what they perceive to be the narrower and narrowing identification within ethnic enclaves. Principles of procedural fairness, on the argument at hand, require also a more substantive cultural imaginary that has institutional agents and other national members caring for the well-being of citizens.

Huo and Tyler's empiricism, like much of social science research, requires a presumptive acceptance of more or less fixed established categories of social identity and identification, including those of ethnoracial belonging. This represents a schematic clash with the understanding of critical culturalists and sociolegal scholars that social identities and the categories of their constructedness are purposeful, malleable, and so mutable, in short, fluid rather than fixed. At the same time, Huo and Tyler challenge critical culturalists and interpretive sociolegal scholars to worry not just about how to represent the complexities of identity formation and the processes of identification in the face of their flux but also about the terms, conditions, and principles of sociolegal justice under the assumptions of fluidity.

Like Huo and Tyler, Oberweis and Musheno are concerned about the implication of social identities for social cohesiveness. Unlike Huo and Tyler, however, they treat identity as only temporarily fixed and always in re/formation as people take up their multiple subject positions differently depending on contexts of place and interaction. Oberweis and Musheno are interested in processes of identification, in particular with how the communicative aspects of policing bind and divide people in local context. In police-public relations, there is some reliance, they find, on crude stereotypical classification schemes like contrasting cops with citizens and blacks being divided from whites. When employing these schemes, police obviously serve as a divisive force in their communities, at the same time generating temporary bonds among uniformed agents of the state and no doubt some community members. Oberweis and Musheno nevertheless reveal through their interpretations of police narratives about their own professional lives particular distinctions among cops that fracture claims to a singular police culture considered necessary perhaps to cohering municipal police agencies. These distinctions play out on the streets as cops connect with some citizens whose categorically constituted identities would place them at the margins of the (local) social order.

Oberweis and Musheno have found that in light of this (sometime) connectivity, cops might "cut breaks" for marginalized subjects as they bestow on them traits that draw the latter more into the mainstream of local culture. Like David Engel's judicial figures, patrolling police are adept at classifying and characterizing people (and events) so as to enforce their connection to the local social order. And like Lisa Sanchez in her focus on the role of citizens as cops under the regime of community policing, Oberweis and Musheno point to the importance of the performance of the cop as citizen for maintaining the legitimacy of municipal policing. Oberweis and Musheno thus do not disagree with Huo and Tyler that closing the divides between urban identities might be crucial to reproducing social order. They nevertheless point to a strategy of particularized differencing as a politics of policing rationality conceived as necessary to gain the allegiances of middle-class communities occupying contemporary urban space.

Oberweis and Musheno accordingly examine the interfacing of law and culture in the identity of state agents and their local relations with community members. Lily Mendoza, by contrast, shifts attention back to a national frame, redrawing our attention to the significance of theorizing as a mode of cultural politics. Mendoza focuses on the processes of national identity formation in the Philippines. Where Huo and Tyler take for granted the formation of a fixed and given national identity, Mendoza's analytical object accordingly is the constitution of a national identity always in the process of being made and remade. She is particularly interested in how Philippine history is understood by intellectuals, including legal scholars, at once living, interpreting, and engaged in its making.

Mendoza's genealogy of national identity formation begins with a critical questioning of canonical Western colonial historical narratives. Philippine intellectuals are as readily fixed, she suggests, in their reactive drive to establish an essentialized "indigenous" identity in opposition to these dominant and dominating narratives. Mendoza articulates a commitment to contrast this with an antiessentializing communicative politics intended to expand political and communicative participation through forging a national discourse on civilization and citizenship predicted on intersecting ethnicities and identities. She elaborates a notion of "translation" as the epistemological tool of a contextualized interdisciplinarity. She argues for such translationality as a means to a larger point, namely, the mutual constitutivity—the hybrid formation—of colonized and colonizing identities, of coloniality and postcoloniality, of dominant and dominated. The modes of translationality thus become means of challenging the exclusionary modes of essentializing identity conditions, whether the colonizing denial of the influence of the dominated on the dominant or the refusal by indigenes to engage the contributions of Western critical culturalism in the cultural politics of national identity formation in the Philippines. Mendoza thus reflects within the politics of postcolonial conditions the sort of critical utopianism called for by David Harvey. In reflecting on the possibilities of a critical culturalism, she challenges also critical sociolegal scholars to think anew the boundaries of international possibility and influence in the constitution and implications of sociolegal formation.

Where Mendoza focuses on the complex of theoretical and international translationality, Deb Henderson looks to the interface between poststructuralists and symbolic interactionists as a theoretical site at which to conceptualize identity formation. Interactionists draw attention to performance as an interactional process that involves the audience in the symbolic processes of identification. Poststructuralists like Judith Butler, by contrast, reformulate the possibility of agency as interior to the repetitive processes of identification. Both thus stress the power of conventions in identity formation and so in identification. Henderson accordingly insists that identity is slippery, and so she sees the destabilizing effects of identity formation and identification most clearly revealed in the ambiguous and ambivalent moments of direct address. It is in direct address that identity is most obviously invoked or presumed—as entrée, as assumption, as interactional and performative "grounds"—and ignored or assumed away. These moments of slippage in turn have no necessary implications, serving in some instances to privilege a person, in others to produce conformity, or yet again to enable evasion by one party or another. Henderson's treatment of identity and the processes of identification, exemplified humorously in terms of the seminar setting for "Justice and Identities," raises epistemological questions about meaning making in the context of researcher-subject interactions, including interactions enabling subjects to identify themselves and to narrate their stories. In that sense, she examines the epistemological commitments underpinning the methodology of subjects' storytelling pursued in the chapters by Sanchez and Oberweis and Musheno.

As Judith Butler makes clear in her own work, and as a good deal of interactionist analysis reveals also, performativity and interaction are enacted perhaps above all else in relation to sexualities. The interface of law and culture clearly bears this out, and we would be remiss in a volume that seeks to stitch them together in their mutual constitutivity to overlook the centrality of sexual identities. We thus close the volume with a section on sexualities.

Carl Stychin accordingly addresses the complex question of how to reconceive sexuality in the struggles over re-visioning national identity in postliberal and postcolonial social formations. Like Lily Mendoza, Stychin thus focuses on the lingering power of colonial effects as powerful interests within national (re-)formations seek to maintain definitional domination, if not hegemony. Stychin's analysis focuses in particular on the conflict between cultural nationalists and gay people in postapartheid southern Africa. He argues that both parties seek to reproduce cultural hegemony through ordering sexual identity even as they stand opposed to each other over what sexual identities deserve legitimation by the postcolonial states of Zimbabwe and South Africa. Both groups ironically turn to "tradition" and selected memories of precolonial sexual practices to authenticate their commitments, thus reifying categorical constructions of sexual identities that Stychin claims are the product of Western colonial projection. Stychin argues that South Africa, unlike Zimbabwe, in drawing on heterogeneity and plurality as encoded in the Freedom Charter (1956) and the logic of universal rights in the creation of a new postapartheid constitution, potentially enables the inclusion of sexual orientation as an effectively (and not simply formally) protected right. Unlike Mendoza, who imagines the processes of translation as providing at least the possibilities for resolving the essentializing tensions between cultural nationalisms and liberal universalisms, Stychin insists that each remains an irreducible, competing source for the constitution of national identities.

While gay people have been included, if formalistically and ambivalently, in the body politic of the new South Africa, Christine Yalda is concerned by contrast with the complexities in establishing a legally sanctioned, performative gay identity in the United States. Yalda reveals the contradictions in U.S. legal decisions concerning the conflation and distinction of *identity* with and from *acts,* always in the interests of enforcing the moral majoritarianism of heterosexuality. Here, as elsewhere in the volume, morality is shown to order legality in the fashioning of authoritative judgments. Law becomes the instrumental means for enforcing these judgments and authorizing those acts expressed in its name. Yalda demonstrates that law, as an authoritative field for managing conflict, represents an important site for engaging in discursive politics. The courts, she shows, not only make material determinations of who gets what but also determine, and perhaps more basically, who is who. She thus reinforces both Engel's and Goldberg's insight that the courts mark the boundaries between legitimate and illegitimate identities in cultural contexts. Lisa Sanchez shows that zoning laws mark some women as street prostitutes, thereby excluding them from certain neighborhoods even though their identities in fact are far more complex and fluid than these identifying constrictions allow and their uses of urban spaces more varied than simply a place to engage in sex work. In the case discussed by Yalda, *Hurley v. Boston,* the U.S. Supreme Court, siding with a veteran's group that organizes Boston's St. Patrick's Day parade, marked the (at least public) performance of Irish-gay identities as illegitimate and so excludable from the parade while insisting that such exclusion fails to amount to an act of sexual discrimination. In effect, the Court declared the public parade a private event.

This legally authorized exclusion of identifiably gay and lesbian people from privately encoded public spheres causes Yalda to question whether the kind of transgressive cultural politics pushed by Rosemary Coombe is always contextually apposite. Oberweis and Musheno reveal, for instance, that some policewomen are able simultaneously to perform as both state agents and lesbians as they acquire the authority, power, and benefits normally reserved for heterosexual policemen. Their inclusion upsets the order of policing—and at least the presumption we usually attach to such identities—in American municipalities. It is a politics of inclusion, of in*corpor*ation, that Yalda settles on as potentially transgressive, as she challenges gay counterparade organizers to be open to including right-wing Christians and gay fascists in their parades rather than to invoke *Hurley* as the grounds for their exclusion. Like David Engel in other cases and contexts, Yalda takes up *Hurley,* then, as a site for a critical cultural reading of conflict and its management, sewing together sociolegal analysis with a critical culturalism.

Paul Passavant likewise looks to case analysis, not so much in contrast but as complementary to Christine Yalda. Rather than explore the sociolegal interiority of a specific case with a view to assessing what it reveals about sociosexual identities and authority, Passavant mobilizes a configuration of legal cases to determine how a society shapes sexual expression. He argues that the U.S. judiciary has shifted the ways it governs sexual expressions from the formal law model of censorship to a social law model embracing a regulatory mode of containment. Two broad considerations underpin this shift. One is a shift in governmentality prompted by a social order more complex economically and more modulated in terms of identity distinctions. The other, relatedly no doubt, concerns the Court's more or less self-conscious strategy to reauthorize its own legitimacy. Passavant compares and contrasts the censorship and containment strategies, noting the normalizing qualities of the latter in a way consistent with the communicative practices of the police as noted by Oberweis and Musheno. Passavant articulates this strategic shift in legal self-consciousness and self-legitimation with the project of reconstructing American national identity. The latter, he notes, relies on ideas of a civilized West, embracing at once norms of decency, a capacity for self-governance and autonomy, and reliance on the rule of law. Passavant insists that the contradiction between this normative need for self-governance and rule of law on the one hand and judicially authorized censorship of sexual expression, on the other entraps the Court in a legitimation crisis. The instrumental wedding of social law and containment strategies enables the Court to continue to govern while functioning as a defining institution of American national identity. This reinvention of order through social law and containment enables the American social order to insist on the toleration of difference while reasserting normalized social identities and sexual practices.

Coming to Terms

Collectively, then, the contributors to this volume exemplify the law as a medium of normative orderings shaped by cultural assumptions and as sites for contestation and normative transformation. And they suggest the thick and complex ways law is implicated in rendering the expression of culture quite literally conceivable. Thus, the usual foci in discussion of legality and cultural identities—on integration in contrast with assimilation, on the normative conditions for coexistence in a diverse or multicultural society—while obviously important, are already thick in their particularistic presumptions, fueled by the intellectual hegemony of philosophical and legal liberalism. This narrowed focus has delimited the broader scope of issues calling for engagement. We have been arguing that these have to do in large part with the cultural thickness of sociolegal conception and application, the implication of law in fashioning social identities, and how their coconstitutivity shapes the grounds of consuming subjectivity and social agency. It is possible to pose these questions, we suggest, only by reading sociolegal and cultural studies in light of, and in some ways against, each other. These counterreadings—laboring against the grain, so to speak—raise anew the concerns about the relation regarding theory and the empirical with which sociolegal studies has long been consumed and so also the problem of methodological paradigms that we suggested at the outset. We reiterate in conclusion what we stated in setting out: The point of the volume, then, is first to recognize the conceptual and methodological crises in the field(s) and second to render them productive by putting them self-consciously and critically into play.

What, in particular, as a consequence can we say about the moments, fleeting or thick, when law and culture meet while holding onto the tensions these meetings generate? Clearly, rather than making the claim that law is everywhere, we are suggesting that there are a multitude of normative orderings, discourses of regulation, as Herman Gray puts it, that swirl around and through individual and national consciousnesses. More deeply, such normative orderings are implicated in various ways, at specific moments and sites, in constituting and in setting limits of possibility as well as ordering regularity for each other. As many of our contributors insist and illustrate, legal institutions and actors, it follows, must think through moral and cultural normativities to make sense of their claims, and to (re-) establish their individual and institutional legitimacy. Further, law and culture meet all too often at the point at which they at once fashion identities and offer media in virtue of which subjects are called to social identification. And this sewing together of the legal and cultural, this constantly renegotiated "need" for each other's terms to make sense of themselves, is enacted always against the backdrop of state formation, of the fabric(ation) of individual identities in relation to national consciousness and culture. It is for this reason too that so many of the contributors are likewise concerned with the specific formation of national identities and so too with thinking the political through processes of inclusion and exclusion, social cohesiveness and containment, and spatial control and sexual normalization, in short, through order and governmentalities. It is to these issues, we are suggesting, that a sociocultural legal studies is now compelled to turn.

References

Derrida, Jacques. 1992. "The Force of Law: The 'Metaphysical Foundation of Authority.'" In Drucilla Cornell, Michael Rosenfeld, and David Gray Carlson, eds., *Deconstruction and the Possibility of Justice* (3–67). New York: Routledge.

Sarat, Austin, and Thomas Kearns, eds. 1997. *Identities, Politics and Rights.* Ann Arbor: University of Michigan Press.

———, eds. 1998. *Law in the Domains of Culture.* Ann Arbor: University of Michigan Press.

Silbey, Susan S., and Austin Sarat. 1987. "Critical Traditions in Law and Society Research." *Law and Society Review* 21: 165.

Part I

Culture

1

Injury and Identity

THE DAMAGED SELF IN THREE CULTURES

David M. Engel

Injury opens a window onto identity. When we say that an individual has suffered an injury, we implicitly refer to a self that is constituted in a particular way and is therefore vulnerable to particular kinds of harm. When we speak of remedies that will make the injured person "whole," we refer to a condition of "wholeness," an imagined self that can be restored through compensation or by other means. Concepts of injury and remedy, therefore, are inseparable from concepts of identity. Because such concepts are socially constructed, they vary significantly across different social settings. Scholars sometimes describe these variations as differences in legal culture. Even within a single social setting, however, one finds multiple perspectives on "culture" and hence on injury, remedy, and identity. The interplay—and sometimes the conflict—between differing perspectives on injury has significant implications for the role and meaning of law.

The construction of injury, remedy, and identity can be usefully studied in specific social locations where one finds distinctive understandings of time and space, self and community, and norm and breach. The occurrence of an injury brings all of these elements into play. This chapter explores injury and identity in three societies: Tibet in the 1940s, Wisconsin in the 1880s, and Thailand in the 1960s. All three cases, as it happens, are set in small towns and involve harm to children. The study of injuries and remedies in these different settings sheds light on how the social environment itself is constructed; and focusing on a particular social environment, in turn, illuminates the ways in which identity is constructed within broader networks of persons and practices that extend beyond the injurer and the person who is injured.

Each of the three sections of this chapter begins with a case study followed by a set of reflections. The first section, introduced by an injury case from Tibet, briefly lays out the basic elements of the chapter as a whole and suggests the deep connections between injury and concepts of time and space, justice and identity. The second section, introduced by a famous nineteenth-century tort case, *Vosburg v. Putney,* explores in greater detail the construction of the social setting and the differing interpretations of an injury that occurs within it. The third section, introduced by a wrongful death case from northern Thailand, focuses on the shaping of identities within different social and cultural environments and the ways in which injuries and remedies depend on understandings of the self who has been harmed and the community of which he or she is a part. The conclusion reviews the common elements of the three case studies and presents a more general theoretical argument about injury, identity, and law.

The Beggar and the Boy

In *The Golden Yoke* (1995), a study of Tibetan "legal cosmology," Rebecca French recounts an incident that took place some fifty years ago in the courtyard of a small Tibetan village near a palace. An old man and a young boy come to the village in the course of their wanderings, seeking food, alms, and a place to sleep. To the villagers, they are familiar figures; the man is ill tempered and has often been seen beating the boy. This day, however, a woman intervenes, and a monk takes the old man's stick to prevent further injury. A crowd gathers in the courtyard, and the monk and the old man begin to debate. The young son of the family lineage holder, who was to be French's informant half a century later, observes the incident from a palace window.

Responding to the monk's reprimand, the old man argues that his abusive behavior toward the boy is not what it seems. They travel together because of the boy's actions in a previous life, and the old man's beatings are a form of karmic retribution for sins the boy committed during that earlier existence. They are not abuse—they are a virtuous act intended to help another being "burn off bad karma." When the monk rejects this explanation as a self-serving excuse and asserts that the beggar is not a man capable of seeing into previous existences, the old man counters by asking how the monk could know that he is not in fact a "famous religious saint" (223).

The old man's argument achieves what French calls a "reality shift." He transforms a mundane assault and battery (to use our own technical terminology concerning injuries) into a broader chain of causes and effects spanning more than one existence, and, in so doing, he silences the crowd and successfully rebukes the monk. As French observes, "The listeners are immediately reminded of the illusory nature of their perceptions and stop judging the incident for what it might only appear to be" (226). It is significant that the audience instantly understands the old man's strategy. Given their shared beliefs about reality and illusion in everyday events, including alleged injuries, the onlookers accept the old man's argument as a conversation stopper. As French explains elsewhere,

> Tibetans accept the presence of several simultaneously operating levels of reality, each giving clues to the next, each crafted of a degree of deceptive illusion except the last, each coexisting with the other in a non-nirvanic space. If all a person knows of the world, legal or otherwise, is illusion, one must attempt to operate within these limitations as a legal actor with the knowledge that there are other levels of Buddhist reality. (62)

The story of the beggar beating the boy, although fragmentary and enigmatic, illustrates the fact that injuries are social and cultural events in which conceptions of justice and identity are forged. The idea of "injury" presupposes a self that can be harmed and an action that is capable of inflicting damage. Within particular social settings, certain understandings of injury and identity may be widely shared, yet alternative understandings are always available and must be acknowledged if not endorsed.

The Tibetan child-beating case occurs within a social setting in which the participants share a religious-based view of everyday life as illusory and impermanent. According to French, events such as injuries could be interpreted in terms of multiple simultaneous realities. Viewed within one "reality frame" (62), the incident involving the beggar and the young boy is a case of child abuse; viewed within another frame, in which concepts of time and causality are expanded to include previous incarnations, it is a story of cosmic justice beyond the power and authority of judge or mediator. Moreover, the two frameworks have profound implications for the identity of the participants. In the first, the child is an innocent victim in need of protection, while the old man is bitter, irresponsible, and reprehensible. In the second, the child is the sinner and the old man a saint.

Here the distinctive construction of time is central to the constitution of the social setting and the people and events in it. The participants in the Tibetan case recognize that each realm of reality contains its own principle of temporal organization. As French puts it, "While each realm has, in a sense, its own time sequence, all the realms in the Tibetan cosmos are ever present: that is, they coexist simultaneously" (72). Thus, the beating incident is understood as occurring simultaneously within the mundane temporal framework of the visible, everyday world and within the temporal framework of unending birth and rebirth that cycles and recycles the "karmic seeds" of existence throughout the various cosmic realms.[1]

The social construction of space also appears to be important in this story, although French's own interpretation does not emphasize the spatial aspect. The beggar and the boy arrive in the village from outside,[2] despite the fact that they are familiar figures within the villagers' world. They pass through the physical space of the village, but they are not rooted in it. They are "wanderers" and have no fixed spatial position. Lacking the positional anchors of a home, a household, and a family, the usual indicia of respectability and social status, the beggar and the boy are liminal figures, readily associated with behavior that falls outside acceptable social conventions and is thus "uncivilized." Lack of a fixed spatial position in Buddhist cosmology can also suggest other, quite different meanings. Holy men may be wanderers. Indeed, the Buddha himself achieved nirvana by leaving his home and family and wandering through the countryside in search of enlightenment. The fact that the beggar and the boy wander unanchored through the physical space of the villagers' world reinforces the ambiguity of their identity and makes it difficult to interpret the injury within a single "reality frame." The beggar may be a scruffy and uncivilized outcast, but he may also be a Buddha-like figure who has shed his attachment to the material world as he progresses toward a higher level of spirituality.

What is a beggar, and what is a boy? The case reduces these basic identity questions to a fundamental ambiguity, and the ambiguity is the point of the story. The meaning of the story depends on a shared worldview in which multiple realities intersect and overlap and the people and events of everyday life are not necessarily what they seem. Given the uncertainty of identity in such a world, justice does not always reside in the punishment of injurers or in judgments requiring them to pay compensation to those whom they have harmed. Sometimes it is more just to allow the karma of both parties to pursue its own laws of cause and effect. In a social setting where the temporal-spatial framework is neither linear nor singular, multiple realities produce multiple interpretations of injury, identity, and justice.

Vosburg and Putney[3]

Seventh grade was not a good year for Andrew Vosburg. He had always been accident prone, but things got worse after he celebrated his fourteenth birthday on December 16,

1888. First, some classmates at Union School in Waukesha, Wisconsin, threw him against a faucet and injured his ankle. The next month, January 1889, he scraped his right knee in a sledding accident. Then, on February 20, 1889, while sitting at his desk in Elizabeth More's classroom, Andrew received the injury that has made his name familiar to generations of first-year law students. After the noon recess, the school bell rang at 1:20 P.M., signaling that classes were about to resume at 1:30 P.M. Ms. More, as was her custom during this ten-minute interval before the afternoon session, began to read to her class. Andrew watched and listened, seated at his desk with his right leg extended into the aisle. At that moment, George Putney, an eleven-year-old classmate, kicked Andrew's leg two inches below the knee, intending, as George later claimed, not to harm Andrew but to get his attention. He certainly succeeded. The blow to Andrew's leg, which was already in a weakened condition because of the sledding accident, soon produced excruciating pain, infection, swelling, illness, several unsuccessful operations, and the very real possibility of amputation. It also led to the filing of one of the most famous of all American tort cases, *Vosburg v. Putney.*[4]

Vosburg is an intentional tort case. The issue is not whether George Putney was negligent or careless but whether he acted intentionally. If so, his contact with Andrew amounted to a battery and exposed him to liability for damages. The case was tried and appealed twice. Both times, George testified that he had not intended to hurt Andrew when he kicked him, and both times the jury supported George's version of the incident, finding explicitly that he did not "intend to do [Andrew] any harm." Nonetheless, both juries found that George had committed an intentional tort—a battery—against Andrew and awarded damages.[5] George Putney appealed both verdicts to the Wisconsin Supreme Court and won both appeals on evidentiary grounds not related to the issue of intent. It is the second opinion, written by Associate Justice William Penn Lyon, that is always reprinted in tort law casebooks. In this opinion, Justice Lyon finds that George did in fact commit a battery, and he draws on concepts of time, space, and social order to explain why George Putney's intent was culpable:

> Had the parties been upon the play-grounds of the school, engaged in the usual boyish sports, the defendant being free from malice, wantonness, or negligence, and intending no harm to plaintiff in what he did, we should hesitate to hold the act of the defendant unlawful. . . . Some consideration is due to the implied license of the play-grounds. But it appears that the injury was inflicted in the school, after it had been called to order by the teacher, and after the regular exercises of the school had commenced. Under these circumstances, no implied license to do the act complained of existed, and such act was a violation of the order and decorum of the school, and necessarily unlawful. (*Vosburg v. Putney,* 403–4)

Since the act of kicking was unlawful at that particular time and place, the intent to commit the act must also have been unlawful, even though George did not intend to harm Andrew and certainly did not intend to inflict the extremely serious injury that ensued. In short, George's liability for Andrew's injury rests not on his intent to inflict harm but on his intent to make physical contact in a way that violated the rules and customs of a seventh-grade classroom in Waukesha, Wisconsin, in 1889.

The school in which this incident occurred exemplifies a cultural space where injuries, identities, and justice norms are shaped within a distinctive temporal and spatial framework. Giddens (1984) urges social scientists to investigate "the modes in which social systems are constituted across time-space," a problem lying "at the heart of social theory" (110). He urges the examination of different "locales" to see how time and space are zoned "in relation to routinized social practices" (119), and he selects the modern school to illustrate the zoning of time-space in a particular locale. In a school, *space* is partitioned not only in terms of the grounds and walls marking its institutional boundaries but also internally in the separate classrooms, corridors, and "regulated spacing of desks" within classrooms (135). All these spatial demarcations enable school authorities to constrain and regulate social interaction according to their own disciplinary worldviews. Similarly, the zoning of *time* within the school reflects an effort to assert disciplinary power within the "school year" and the "school day" as well as within the temporal subunits of school time, such as classes, recess, lunch, and time allotted for travel between classes.

Law—federal, state, and local—is a primary instrument for the zoning of time and space in schools, and law is therefore closely connected to the concepts of order, justice, and identity that prevail within this social setting. As Sally Falk Moore (1978) reminded us more than twenty years ago, however, social fields are not passive spaces where law invariably succeeds in attaining its ends. Rather, social fields are "semi-autonomous"; they create and transform law even as they sometimes bend to its force:

> [The social field] can generate rules and customs and symbols internally, but . . . it is also vulnerable to rules and decisions and other forces emanating from the larger world by which it is surrounded. The semi-autonomous social field has rule-making capacities, and the means to induce or coerce compliance; but it is simultaneously set in a larger social matrix which can, and does, affect and invade it, sometimes at the invitation of persons inside it, sometimes at its own instance. (55–57)

Particular social locales, such as schools, are arenas of interaction where law may play a significant, but not necessarily determinative, role in constructing time and space, justice norms, and the identity of social actors.[6] The instantiation of legal norms helps to account for similarities in practices across social settings, just as the emergence of distinctive localized patterns of interaction helps to account for variations from one social setting to the next.[7] Although concepts of order, justice, and identity may be similar in many schools and school districts in our society, distinctive practices are equally notable and usually reflect social, cultural, historical, or economic variation within different locales. Moreover, as I have already suggested, one may also find competing perspectives and practices even within a single social setting, and these differences may manifest themselves in the form of lawsuits.

Justice Lyon's opinion in *Vosburg v. Putney* illustrates a powerful agent of state law, a Wisconsin Supreme Court justice, attempting to discern and legitimate what he believes to be the appropriate self-regulatory apparatus within a particular social setting. In Lyon's analysis of the encounter between Andrew Vosburg and George Putney, his own reconstruction of the local temporal-spatial framework proves determinative. Lyon observes that the act took place inside the school rather than on the playground. The social setting in question is zoned in such a way that conduct lawful in one space is unlawful in another. Children (especially boys, as it was assumed by the participants in *Vosburg*) are expected to engage in rough activities outside the school building, and George might not have been liable for a battery if he had kicked Andrew while they were still outdoors. Furthermore, although it is not mentioned in Lyon's opinion, both boys were seated at their desks, which were arranged in rows, a spatial configuration characteristic of traditional classrooms. In order to kick Andrew, George had to move outside his assigned space (although Andrew's leg was extended into the aisle), and thus his conduct in itself violated the spatial order on which classroom discipline depended.

Lyon also mentions temporal considerations. The injury, he observes, occurred after the class "had been called to order by the teacher, and after the regular exercises of the school had commenced" (404). Lyon implies that if George had kicked Andrew before class, the case might have been different.[8] The opinion thus places great weight on the fact that the injury occurred within a spatial-temporal zone demarcated by school authorities since judges, as well as school officials, expect particular norms to apply within that zone: "such act was a violation of the order and decorum of the school, and necessarily unlawful" (404). Since the act was unlawful, as defined by norms peculiar to the social setting, George's intent to commit the act exposed him to liability in a court of law even though he intended no harm. Significantly, the court determines what is lawful and unlawful by deferring to the school's concepts of order, despite the fact that this rule system is not itself "legal" in nature. No law authorizes students to kick one another on the playground but not in the classroom or requires them to stay seated at their desks in orderly rows once the bell has rung (compare Macaulay 1986). In this sense, state law is shaped by unwritten local norms, just as the locality that generates such norms is shaped by state law.[9]

Norms within social settings are not necessarily accepted by every actor, nor are the identities they putatively construct. Throughout the *Vosburg* litigation, the parties and onlookers deployed competing images of schools and schoolchildren. We have already seen the stern, orderly, disciplinary image of the classroom underlying Lyon's opinion and the implicit image of the obedient and respectful student that George violated when he kicked Andrew. Running counter to this interpretation of "order and decorum" in the classroom, however, is a gender-based assumption that boys will be boys, that it is unavoidable and even healthy to allow some leeway for physical play among boys (but presumably not among girls or between boys and girls). Thus, George Putney's lawyer, Joseph Quarles, argued in his appellate brief, "The friendly scuffles, the trials of strength among school children . . . were indispensable to their physical growth and development," and the type of contact resulting in Andrew's injury occurs "in every school throughout this broad land nearly every school day in the year" (quoted in Zile 1992, 951). Injecting tort law into the schoolhouse, which Quarles characterized as a self-regulating social field, was risky. He argued that, in the absence of legal intervention, greater latitude would, and should, be given to playful boys:

> The affirmance of this judgment will render every school boy in Wisconsin guilty of assault and battery a dozen times every day. What has heretofore been esteemed healthful sport will take in *[sic]* the sombre complexion of *tort.* All friendly exercise which involves

> "any touching of the person," must be abandoned as *a wrong.* The pastimes of childhood will be visited with penalties and the exuberance of youth repressed by the frowning menace of the law. (Zile 1992, 951)

Quarles's argument was echoed in a series of articles and editorials in the local newspaper, the *Waukesha Freeman,* which viewed the case of *Vosburg v. Putney* as evidence of an alarming rise in litigiousness among local citizens (Zile 1992, 921, 968). When observers see a shift in the balance between self-regulation and external regulation of a social field, they often denounce the perceived change as an increase in litigiousness and an overreliance on law, although law may already play an extensive role in regulating many other aspects of social interaction in that locale.

Within specific social arenas, norms and identities are not static or universally accepted but are contested and transformed as actors invoke different "reality frames." Contests over injuries may bring into play different perspectives on the nature of the self and the traditions and future of the broader community (Greenhouse et al. 1994). In *Vosburg* the issue ultimately became the identity of a "school boy" and the norms that should regulate his conduct in different social contexts. Justice Lyon's perspective was inseparable from contending views expressed within the school, the community of Waukesha, and the society as a whole. Analyzing injuries in specific social settings suggests the importance of connecting particular incidents or interactions to the broader social and legal systems within which they occur. As Giddens (1984) observes, "no strip of interaction—even if it is plainly bracketed, temporally and spatially—can be understood on its own" (142). Broader systems of social and legal order become active primarily within localized arenas and in ways that are shaped significantly by "local knowledge" (Geertz 1983) and actors.

As the Wisconsin Supreme Court considered the case of *Vosburg v. Putney,* then, it confronted a choice between two contending "reality frames," each suggesting a different view of the school, the town, and the identity of a teenage boy. Justice Lyon and his fellow judges were part of the culture of midwestern America in the late nineteenth century. They understood the contending perspectives placed before them and perhaps had a stake in one or the other. By virtue of their formal legal role, however, the justices of the Wisconsin Supreme Court also stood apart from the social context in which the injury occurred. Their position outside and, figuratively, "above" the site of the injury gave their legal pronouncement its peculiar power to legitimate some worldviews while discrediting others. The opinion in *Vosburg v. Putney* is not simply a reflection of the social setting from which this conflict over injury arose; it is also a mythic statement of order, justice, and identity projected back on that setting and meant to change it.

The Runaway Oxcart

Early one April morning in 1969, in the northern Thai province of Chiangmai, a sixteen-year-old village girl named Wandee drove her oxcart to the field to pick corn with her three younger brothers. By 7:30 A.M., as the day became hot, the four children had loaded the cart and prepared to return home. Wandee drove the cart, accompanied by two of her brothers. When they passed the village market, the two oxen bolted ahead out of control. According to Wandee's testimony in the Chiangmai Provincial Court, the animals had halted when they heard the sound of gongs and drums from a funeral nearby. She shook the reins, and they suddenly began to run, excited by the noise and confusion. According to other testimony, however, which Wandee disputed, she lost control of the oxen because of her own carelessness: She had struck them with a stick repeatedly in order to make them go faster. The road was crowded. Before Wandee could stop the oxen, the cart had struck and killed a seven-year-old boy, Samrit, who was standing by the edge of the road in front of the market.

Samrit's father, La, was a farmer and fellow villager. He notified the police immediately of his son's death. They arrested Wandee, but no charges were ever filed. Two months after the accident, La brought a private criminal action against Wandee, for Thai law allows private individuals to prosecute cases in tandem with state prosecutors or alone in cases like this, when the state refuses to prosecute. After hearing testimony from seven witnesses, the judge dismissed La's criminal suit against Wandee.

In 1975, when I read this case file while conducting research in the Chiangmai Provincial Court, I discovered a defense exhibit titled "Record of Costs Paid by the Defendant and Her Father for Merit-making and Funeral of Samrit T——, Child of Plaintiff." The list of expenditures, signed by La and dated five days after Samrit's death, is very detailed: eleven ceremonial trays, costing 220 baht; one straw mat, 11 baht; one pair of shoes, 7 baht; a pair of pants and a hat, 29 baht; tobacco, 12 baht; one kilo of fruit (rambutan), 16 baht; bread, 9 baht; three kilos of curry, 21 baht; eleven containers of milk, 44 baht; seventy-three liters of sticky rice, 95 baht; a casket, 30 baht; liquor, 9 baht; and money for the monks who officiated at the ceremony, 165 baht. The list continues for three full pages. The total amount paid by the defendant's father to Samrit's father in connection with the mortuary rites was 6,960.75 baht, which was then equivalent to about U.S.$350, a very substantial amount of money for a Thai farmer in 1969.

Although the official record of this case leaves many questions unanswered, it tells a story rich with implications concerning injury, remedy, and identity. The payment of costs associated with merit making and funeral expenses for Samrit suggests a frame of reference, a conception of the self, long familiar in northern Thailand. Two incorporeal essences constitute the core of the human personality: *khwan* and *winyan* (Hanks 1963; Heinze 1982). The *khwan* is a spiritual essence that is sensitive and flighty in nature, subject to fright and shock. Illness or injury may cause the *khwan* to fly out of the body, requiring kin to perform a ceremony to recall it and bind it into the body securely. Injurers are often required to pay the costs of such ceremonies; and compensation for injuries, even in the Chiangmai Court, is sometimes referred to as *khaa tham khwan,* or payment to care for the *khwan.*

Injuries causing death are another matter. At the time of death, the *khwan* is irrevocably lost, but the *winyan,* more securely anchored in the body and more centrally involved in regulating all essential aspects of the personality, does not perish. The *winyan* separates itself from the body of the deceased and joins the world of ghosts, both good and evil, who surround the villagers. The *winyan* is also associated with the phenomenon of rebirth, influenced by the store of merit and demerit acquired by the deceased. As the oxcart case illustrates, injuries causing death usually call for the performance of merit-making ceremonies, both to add to the merit of the individual who was killed and to ensure that the *winyan* does not become a malevolent ghost.

Traditionally, Thai villagers tended to distinguish between normal and abnormal deaths (see, generally, Tambiah 1970). Samrit's death was clearly abnormal *(taai hoong)* both because it was associated with a violent accident and because the victim was still young. Abnormal deaths must be handled immediately and with great caution. If the soul *(winyan)* is not guided properly to heaven to await rebirth, it may become a type of ghost *(phii taai hoong)* that endangers the family and potentially the social setting as a whole (Tambiah 1970, 189). To guard against this risk to the community, merit-making ceremonies must be performed by Buddhist monks on behalf of the deceased. The items and expenditures listed in the defendant's exhibit make it apparent that Wandee's father paid the cost of these ceremonies.

It appears that the oxcart case initially triggered a request for a remedy premised on a conception of self that emphasizes *khwan* and *winyan,* the intangible essences of the human personality. This distinctive concept of the self, analogous to the distinctive image of a schoolboy in *Vosburg v. Putney,* is associated with a specific location, the northern Thai village. It is connected to a concept of space that ties the individual to a territorially defined village community of humans and spirits; and it is connected to a concept of time that transcends the individual life span and links the present to past and future incarnations of the human soul. Emphasis on the incorporeal essences that make up the self therefore reflects a "reality frame" that is familiar to many Thai people, especially those who live in village settings. In cases of injury, this conception of the self links the individual to the community as a whole. As Tambiah (1970, 243) points out, when the *khwan* escapes, it flees the village and the community. The ceremony for recalling the *khwan,* which is performed at key moments throughout one's life, thus invites the reintegration of the *khwan,* and hence the individual, into the community in order to restore social order. All villagers have a stake in ensuring that each individual maintains a positive connection to the local society. Similarly, when an individual dies and the *winyan* leaves the body, the entire village has an interest in ensuring that the proper rituals are performed since a malevolent ghost can endanger everyone who lives in that locality. It is assumed, in other words, that each individual and each soul is inextricably connected, throughout this life and future lives, to the entire community of humans and spirits. Because of these shared beliefs about the self and the social setting as a whole, the entire village has a stake in seeing that injurers pay proper compensation for injury.

When La brought a criminal action against Wandee in the Chiangmai Provincial Court, he apparently chose to step outside the framework in which remedies were defined in terms of the incorporeal essences of *khwan* and *winyan.* His decision suggests the availability of alternative conceptions of remedy and hence of injury, self, and community. Since he had received payment for merit making and funeral expenses from Wandee's father two months earlier, it is unclear why he decided to prosecute. Private criminal prosecutions are often brought in order to pressure the defendant to reach a settlement in return for withdrawal of the lawsuit, and La appeared to want a sum that went beyond the customary mortuary expenses. Perhaps he measured his son's loss in other terms or viewed the incident through a different lens. It is notable, however, that La's strategy failed and that his case was dismissed. Probably the judge believed that Wandee and her family had done all that custom required. Since they had satisfied their obligations within the normative framework that defined injuries in terms of *khwan* and *winyan,* the state should not permit La to impose further obligations on them.

The judge's decision in the oxcart case had a paradoxical effect, simultaneously affirming and subverting village-level norms. He may have viewed his task as Justice Lyon did, when the latter approved what he perceived as the appropriate norms of the schoolhouse and the classroom in *Vosburg v. Putney,* although the Thai judge did not allude directly to the norms governing injuries within the village. Instead, the trial court opinion notes La's failure to register his marriage to Samrit's mother at the district office. No one should have been surprised by this omission: At that time, villagers rarely registered their marriages before government officials and usually preferred customary village marriage rituals to the alien procedures of distant bureaucrats. Yet the judge held that the absence of a marriage certificate signaled La's lack of standing to bring a criminal prosecution on his deceased son's behalf. Only Samrit's mother could bring such an action, and the judge dismissed La's case on these grounds. His decision tended to undercut the justice norms of the village concerning marriage even as it reaffirmed village norms concerning remedies for wrongful death.

Like the Tibetan case and *Vosburg v. Putney,* the Thai oxcart case suggests that injuries and remedies can be understood simultaneously through different conceptual frameworks. The availability of numerous religious and cultural frameworks for perceiving and understanding the world has characterized social life in Chiangmai since the beginning of its recorded history. In the late nineteenth century and throughout much of the twentieth, the central Thai government dramatically expanded its legal and political authority. From the villagers' point of view, the central government introduced new concepts of time and space, standards of justice, and conceptions of the self as "citizen of the nation-state." Previously, many social interactions at the village level were subject to the control of "cadastral" religions (Terwiel 1976), which mark out territory in terms of local spirit cults whose authority must be acknowledged for all important events in the life cycle (Engel 1990, 336–42). These religions define social settings temporally as well as spatially since membership in the community links the living to the spirits of the dead. Buddhism blends readily with spirit worship in shaping beliefs about merit and demerit, life and rebirth, humans and ghosts. In the late nineteenth century, when the Thai government attempted to clarify and defend its borders against the neighboring colonial powers and apply its authority throughout every corner of the kingdom, it deployed a gridwork of legal and political units controlled by a legal system emanating from Bangkok (Tambiah 1976; Engel 1978; Winichakul 1994). Within this new spatial-temporal framework, individuals, families, and social relationships acquired new meanings, and different understandings of justice prevailed. Since the Western-style law codes substantially redefined the self in Thai society, it is not surprising that they provided radically new remedies when the self was harmed.

Like the participants in the oxcart case, Thai villagers see the expansion of central government power as unsettling local belief systems. When injuries arise, tension is manifested between concepts emphasizing the incorporeal aspects of the self and those reflecting its material and economic aspects. Remedies associated with injuries to the incorporeal aspects of the self tend to address the web of relationships linking the self to a specific cultural setting. Payment for ceremonial expenses to propitiate the *khwan* soul or to make merit for the deceased person is ultimately intended to reintegrate the individual into the community of villagers and spirits and to ensure community well-being. On the other hand, remedies associated with injuries to the material or economic aspects of the self, such as reimbursement for medical costs or lost wages, are not viewed as having a direct benefit to the village as a whole. It is unlikely that fellow villagers would insist on the necessity of the latter type of remedy in order to protect the community from malign influences or to preserve the fabric of relationships connecting villagers.

Different concepts of remedy grow out of, and reflect, different cultural definitions of the self. Thai village culture has been significantly affected by the processes of globalization over the past two decades as well as the economic crisis of 1997 (the last three years). As farming villages change or disappear entirely, the attendant social transformations may make individuals more conscious of remedy systems other than those concerned with *khwan* and *winyan.* In turn, as they pursue such alternatives, injured persons reinforce new concepts of self, community, and injury. Emphasis on the incorporeal aspects of the self and the local community of humans and spirits may recede in importance. In transformed social settings, new meaning systems may emerge, and, as some fear, a more individualistic, materialistic, and anticommunitarian worldview may become increasingly familiar.

It is important, however, to resist the simplistic conclusion that increased transnational contacts have "westernized" Thai concepts of injury and remedy—whatever that term might mean in a globalized society—or that industrial capitalism inevitably commodifies the self and destroys community. The oxcart case itself suggests that conceptual frameworks based on individualized and material notions of the self were available to Thai villagers long before the pace of globalization accelerated rapidly in the 1980s. The existence of multiple worldviews is not a new phenomenon in northern Thailand. Furthermore, there is some reason to think that incorporeal, communitarian concepts of injury and identity may persist in northern Thailand even in sites far removed from the farming villages with which they are usually associated.[10] Belief systems and the social practices connected with them are not mere epiphenomena that appear and disappear with changing social conditions. Social change certainly has profound effects on beliefs and practices, including those associated with injury and remedy, but the reverse is also true: Beliefs and practices can determine the direction of social and cultural change.

People who live in rural social settings with a strong sense of community do not always share the belief that injuries are essentially incorporeal or that remedies are required for the good of the entire community. Shortly after my research in northern Thailand, I had the opportunity to study a rural American community (Engel 1984). Sander County, Illinois, was experiencing social transformations of its own in the late 1970s, but farmers and other longtime residents spoke clearly and eloquently about injury, identity, and remedy. In a society where the values of interdependence were previously paramount and individuals had to rely on and trust their neighbors, injuries called for sympathy and assistance but not for remediation. My interviewees rarely expressed the view that the injured person acted for the good of the community in seeking compensation from the injurer. On the contrary, longtime residents argued that the reverse was true. They associated claims for remedy, both legal and extralegal, with individuals they perceived as "outsiders" or newcomers to the community, those who did not participate in the fabric of interdependencies that they imagined had once characterized Sander County. Injuries were a common and inevitable part of life in a farming community. The appropriate response to injury, they believed, was to absorb the harm without requesting any compensation from the injurer. Unacculturated outsiders who demanded a remedy and sometimes went to court to enforce their demand were seen as destroying rather than preserving the community.

In Sander County, as in northern Thailand, competing conceptions of self, community, and justice coexisted uneasily and sometimes produced conflict. Old-timers and farmers, moreover, lived with the paradox that the very outsiders whose values, in their view, tended to destroy the community were the same individuals who had been brought into Sander County as assembly-line workers in a large new factory in order to save the community from economic decay. Some of the outsiders believed that injuries could be readily translated into money: lost wages, medical costs, and other expenses. This perception, although inconsistent with the values of many old-timers, was tied to the new industrial, wage-based economy that the old-timers had self-consciously imported into their community. In truth, the boundary between old-timers and newcomers was not clearly defined. Some longtime residents worked in the factory; some newcomers shared the values of the old-timers. Yet nowhere in Sander County did I discover an equivalent to the northern Thai belief that injured persons must demand and receive a remedy in order to preserve the well-being of the community as a whole.

Unlike Thailand, communitarian ideology in American social settings is usually understood as inconsistent with demands for remedies in response to injury. Nor is it easy to find local support for the proposition that the essence of an injury resides in harm to the incorporeal aspects of the self and that the community has an interest in remedying such harm. According to legal historians (e.g., Beckerman 1981), there was once a time when compensation for injuries under the common law resembled the conceptual framework I have described in the northern Thai village context. In thirteenth-century England, even physical injuries were understood primarily in terms of the damage they did to the victim's honor and social status rather than to his or her body. Furthermore, "a wrong was still, in a very real way, an offense against the social group (family or lordship) to which the victim belonged" (Beckerman 1981, 162). The self that was injured was not just the body of the isolated individual but also his or her intangible essence and the system of statuses and reputations within the social setting. Compensation was aimed at readjusting and repairing relations within the community as a whole. This conceptual linking of incorporeal harm, compensation, and community, however, did not last much beyond the thirteenth century. As the royal courts of England assumed jurisdiction over personal injuries, a more individualized and materialistic concept of injury and remedy eventually won out. Vestiges of the earlier common-law understanding—injury harms the incorporeal essence of the self and compensation for injury has a social integrative function—are hard to find in America today, whether one seeks them in specific communities or in the law itself.

When American tort law provides a remedy for injury to the intangible aspects of the human personality, the public may express disapproval or even outrage. Such remedies are viewed as problematic and not socially integrative; they are symptomatic of the destructive use of tort law to cash in on elusive or even imaginary injuries. As Radin (1996) puts it, such intangible injuries challenge the assumption of "commensurability," the understanding that tortious harms can be measured on a scale that converts readily to a dollar figure for purposes of compensation. Contemporary critics on the right oppose compensation for incorporeal harms such as pain and suffering or emotional distress because such injuries cannot be translated readily into market terms; and at least one critic on the left opposes them because he fears that compensation for intangible emotional harms tends to "commodify" the self (Abel 1990, cited in Radin 1996, 203). Furthermore, some scholars (e.g., Chamallas and Kerber 1990) have demonstrated that one particular type of incorporeal harm, emotional distress claims, were historically understood as naturally gendered: They were assumed to be a "women's tort," presumably because of beliefs about fundamental differences between the personalities of men and women and their differing propensity to suffer harm to the intangible, emotional components of the self. Suspicious judges have invented convoluted and essentially incoherent standards to limit and screen such claims. In doing so, they have linked remedies for emotional distress claims to gender identity, to presumptions about women's essential characteristics that supposedly distinguish them from men. The legitimacy of such claims, however, has always been an issue for women claimants and perhaps even more so for men who base their claim on a "women's tort." In the courts and among the public, the suspicion has lingered that this category of claims is especially vulnerable to fraudulent and inappropriate attempts to recover damages.

Even claims for physical harm may, from the perspective of the social settings within which they arise, appear questionable and "unmanly." The case of *Vosburg v. Putney* produced a sense of outrage among some residents of Waukesha. Like many of the old-timers in Sander County, but unlike many of the villagers in northern Thailand, some Waukesha residents believed that the upright citizen would never translate his injury into a demand for compensation. An editorial in the *Waukesha Freeman* expressed this outrage in explicitly gendered terms:

> Naturally enough a great majority of the cases brought into the petty courts, are mere farces arising from drunken sprees, some personal dislike and a desire to cause some one a little expense; yet they all contribute in no small degree to the public tax burden. . . .
>
> It would be a great deal better for everyone if the contestants in these cases had the manhood to settle their insignificant troubles among themselves, and not be thrusting their metaphorical sore heads before the public continually. ("The Tendency to 'Law' It," *Waukesha Freeman,* December 31, 1891, 4, quoted in Zile 1992, 968)

According to this view, injury, remedy, and identity are perceived in terms of gendered images of stoicism and self-reliance. Real men are strong and silent when they suffer pain, and they do not seek compensation from those who injure them. Many voices in the United States today still express this view: It is unmanly and socially destructive to demand compensation for physical harms, and it is fraudulent, or at best unseemly, to seek a remedy for injury to incorporeal, emotional, or psychological aspects of the personality.

Comparison of this particular American perspective on injury and identity to those evident in the Thai oxcart case underscores the fact that such views are culturally contingent and do not reflect universal truths or natural facts about humans or the communities in which they live. In both the Thai and the American examples, however, widely held perspectives coexisted with other meaning systems available to local actors. The plaintiff in the oxcart case, unlike many villagers, did not appear to view injury and identity exclusively in terms of harm to *khwan* and *winyan*. Similarly, tort plaintiffs in American social settings, including Sander County, adopt concepts of self, community, and remedy that differ from the dominant discourses and practices. Although today tort plaintiffs in the United States are often characterized as overreaching, selfish, and unmanly, other perspectives are usually available. For example, some perceive a claim for damages as an effort to curb the injurer's socially destructive behavior as well as an attempt to make the injured person "whole." In a just society, according to this view, injurers should be called to account for their actions, and rights should be vindicated, so that the deterrent effects of legally enforced remedies will produce a safer society for all. Remedy seekers, according to this alternative perspective, are not socially destructive. They reduce the level of risk in society generally and curb the injurious behavior of careless actors.

When injuries occur, competing perspectives on identity come into play, and, as French observes in the Tibetan case of the beggar and the boy, disputes may produce "reality shifts" from one perspective to another. The onlookers in the Tibetan case readily accepted the reality shift urged by the beggar because they believed that multiple realities were simultaneously present in all situations and that humans should not attempt to select one "reality frame" to the exclusion of others. In the Thai oxcart case, the plaintiff's efforts met with less success. The Chiangmai Provincial Court rejected La's attempt to shift from a widely accepted culturally based perspective on injury and identity to one that was less recognized. Today, however, northern Thailand is in a greater state of flux than it was in the late 1960s, and opportunities to invoke competing conceptual frameworks may now be greater than before. In American social settings, on the other hand, injury victims still encounter strenuous resistance when they advocate a perspective that would require injurers to pay compensation. The American media, the public, and even many judges and lawyers are notably reluctant to consider the validity of "reality frames" other than those that characterize personal injury claimants as selfish and socially destructive. Hostility toward claims for remediation is, if anything, increasing, and asserting a claim is often taken as a negative indicator of the claimant's character and identity. If the prevailing ideology in American social settings continues to reject the very conceptual framework that supports injury victims' claims, then it will be the injurers whose worldviews most profoundly shape the communities in which we live.

Conclusion

Identity is inseparable from place and perspective. What is a person? Or, as participants in these three cases asked, what is a boy? The question evokes different answers in different social settings—a Tibetan courtyard, a Wisconsin schoolhouse, a northern Thai village. The question of identity is thrown into sharp relief when a person suffers injury. In what sense has he been harmed? What sort of remedy, if any, could make him whole? Conceptions of injury and remedy reveal which aspects of the person are thought to constitute identity. Within any social setting, however, no single conception of persons and injuries can be found. Injury, therefore, elicits multiple understandings of self and community and brings into play multiple frames of reference and notions of justice. The clash and convergence of meaning systems produce distinctive images of men and women, boys and girls, teachers and students, beggars and saints, and define the responses to injury that are considered appropriate for the actors in particular cultural and social settings.

In the Tibetan case, onlookers readily accepted the coexistence of differing conceptions of beggar, boy, and injury since Tibetan worldviews rested on a belief in multiple simultaneous realities. In the Wisconsin and Thai cases, the reconciliation of contending views proved more difficult. A clash of perspectives led to the filing of a lawsuit, and the courts became involved in the interpretation of injury and identity. The judges in these cases appeared to base their decisions on an analysis of the social arena within which the injuries occurred. They articulated their own view of the relevant temporal-spatial framework and the concepts of self, injury, remedy, and justice they thought appropriate for the locale in question. The Wisconsin Supreme Court, in Justice Lyon's opinion, engages in this analysis explicitly; the Chiangmai Provincial Court, I have suggested, does it implicitly.

Law plays a distinctive role in relation to the social settings in which injuries occur. The judge may act as arbiter, choosing among the contending realities in the locales where conflict arises, but the judge's re-presentation of reality has its own distinctive qualities. This was partially evident in *Vosburg v. Putney,* with its explication of the norms of the playground as well as the classroom. It was fully evident in the runaway oxcart case, where the judge sustained familiar village concepts of remedy while subverting familiar village concepts of marriage and family. The judge is not just an arbiter; the judge tells his or her own story. The judge is a mythmaker. The court projects a version of reality back on the social setting from which the case emerges, and this refashioned version of local truths inevitably redefines them.

Judges, like politicians, understand the power of the myth of the local. They may attempt to legitimate their pronouncements about order and responsibility by relying on romanticized images of schools, families, and communities, selectively rendered and stripped of contestation and ambiguity. Although citizens differ about particular local norms or practices, most would respond to the importance of "local-ness" itself as a value in opposition to intrusions by big government, big business, or "alien" persons into local settings. By using, and inevitably distorting, the norms and practices they discover in local settings, the spokespersons for state law shield themselves from the accusation that they are intruding on the common sense of ordinary people. They legitimate their decisions as mere reflections of a mythic local community. Of course, the law's selectivity and distortion shapes identities in particular ways. Law transforms symbols and images drawn from local settings and redeploys them as authoritative pronouncements that can potentially change the very settings from which they are drawn.

The Thai oxcart case illustrates the transformative potential of state law in relation to local communities. The significance of this case was not simply that the judge reinforced the constraints of traditional village compensation systems and rejected the plaintiff's apparent efforts to escape them. It is equally important that the judge, in dismissing the injury claim, challenged the traditional framework of marriage registration, which controlled the lives of many villagers. By calling into question the relational identities of husband and wife, as well as father and son, the decision may be more significant for its expansion of government control over village-level practices than for its deference toward and protection of such practices.

Although the law can exert a strong influence on the social settings in which conflicts arise, it lacks the power to silence contending voices, and, consequently, its effects may be uncertain or even contradictory. In *Vosburg,* for example, the court endorsed the injury victim's underlying claim by affirming a distinctive and iconic view of orderly classrooms and obedient students. In opposition to this view, however, other voices presented a different perspective emphasizing the virtues of manly self-restraint on the part of injured persons. According to this perspective, the very act of bringing a lawsuit marked the injury victim as someone who had placed himself outside the orderly normative arrangements of the community, just as his attacker, in Justice Lyon's view, had violated the orderly arrangements of the classroom. This latter perspective, quite different from Justice Lyon's, ironically transforms the identity of the injured person into an aggressor and the injurer into an innocent victim of intrusive government.

It is not surprising that the law operates in complex and often contradictory ways in relation to the multiple "reality frames" found in particular social and cultural settings. Legal institutions and actors derive their perspectives from such settings, even as they symbolically separate themselves from local interests and values. Judges and lawyers live in local communities, and common sense tells us that their views must be shaped by the beliefs and meaning systems they themselves have experienced. Indeed, in some ways, the law's connection to local communities is accepted by the public as a source of institutional legitimacy. For example, the essential contribution of the trial jury to our justice system is said to be its capacity to inject community norms and concepts into the decision-making process. Yet judges invariably portray themselves as external, above, and superior to the particularities of place and person. Ultimately, the law must locate itself in a mythical space separate from the space of any particular social locale and must appear neutral, magisterial, and independent. The law simultaneously draws on and distances itself from the play of perspectives that prevail in a specific social and cultural setting. Law's dual character, its involvement in and separation from local communities, gives it certain advantages for local actors. Persons in injury cases whose perspectives are otherwise unlikely to prevail may invoke the law because of its unique capacity to intervene into local settings from "outside" and to acknowledge local identities and practices even as it redefines them.

When the law does intervene in local settings, its invocation by injured persons can lead to social disapproval. In these instances, observers may see the government as a threatening outside force intruding on local autonomy (Greenhouse et al. 1994). They may rhetorically juxtapose "big government" against "community" and "local control." Terms like these are themselves mythic in quality, suggestive of romantic views of communities that are imagined or desired rather than objectively observable. The three case studies in this chapter demonstrate that particular social settings are not the monolithic or harmonious places assumed by advocates of "community" but are cultural spaces where conceptual frameworks overlap and clash, often producing division or conflict. In cases of injury, the state intrudes because local perspectives are divided; its intervention is the *result* of local conflicts and is not, in any simple sense, their cause.

This chapter presents three variations on a theme. What I have written is less a linear argument than a series of iterations, exploring closely related ideas and concepts in significantly different social settings. All three variations explore the diverse strands of a common theme: Concepts of injury and remedy reveal fundamental understandings of the self who has been harmed. Concepts of self, injury, and remedy are constructed differently in different social settings, and such constructions are linked to particular understandings of time and space, community and justice. Within specific social settings, multiple frameworks can be found; and the operation of the legal system in relation to these different frameworks is especially significant. Furthermore, when courts enforce shifts from one conceptual framework to another, they may trigger public outcries against government interference in the lives of local communities.

Some might argue that such shifts, and the changing role of law in relation to them, follow a broader pattern. They would contend that there is a more general and universal evolution in capitalist societies from communitarian, incorporeal concepts of the person to materialistic, commodified, and individualistic concepts. This kind of argument finds some support in the examples I have presented; but it is not very helpful in explaining many key details, such as the differences between Chiangmai and Sander County farming communities in their beliefs about the need for a remedy when injuries arise. Moreover, I believe that much is to be gained by drawing scholarly attention back to the particular social setting itself. A great deal of current sociolegal scholarship rests on broad and essentially meaningless generalizations about "American culture" or the cultures of other countries, as if the boundaries of nation-states somehow demarcate a cultural field within which a single set of norms, practices, and meaning systems prevails. Such generalizations tend to ignore the complex interplay between the perceptions of differently situated individuals and groups, which accounts for so much of our experience of everyday life.

It is essential to maintain an analytic focus on the multiplicity of conceptual systems that, through their overlap and conflict, constitute a cultural field. The arenas of everyday social life are sometimes actual geographic locations but frequently are mythical spaces demarcated by shared beliefs about persons, communities, and social practices. It is difficult to understand, or even to speak of, injury and identity, law and community, without reference to such "real" or mythical locations *within* broader fields such as nation, region, and global society. In specific social and cultural settings, legal meanings and personal identities are forged.

Notes

I am grateful to Anya Engel for her invaluable research assistance and to Jaruwan Engel for her insights and suggestions from beginning to end. Friends and colleagues at the University at Buffalo and at Arizona State University provided helpful comments on earlier versions of this chapter. I would like to thank Lisa Bower, Thomas Burkman, Pablo DeGreiff, David Theo Goldberg, Fred Konefsky, Estelle Lau, Martha McCluskey, Elizabeth Mensch, Frank Munger, Michael Musheno, Suda Rangkupan, and Nancy Staudt. Thanks as always to the Baldy Center for Law and Social Policy and, in particular, to Laura Mangan for support and encouragement and to Anne Gaulin for helping to make the chapter presentable.

1. As French (1995) observes elsewhere (162), children under the age of eight years are not generally viewed as independent, volitional agents but as beings whose actions are shaped by the karma they carry with them from a previous life.
2. So does the monk, for that matter, since he came to the village for a festival.

3. My discussion of this case draws extensively on the extremely detailed historical reconstruction published by Professor Zigurds L. Zile (1992) on the centennial anniversary of the Wisconsin Supreme Court decision.

4. 50 N.W. 403 (Wis. 1891).

5. The jury in the first trial awarded $2,800 in damages. On appeal to the Wisconsin Supreme Court, a new trial was ordered. The second jury awarded $2,500. It is the second trial and judgment, also appealed to the Wisconsin Supreme Court, that is the subject of Justice Lyon's famous opinion.

6. Furthermore, as Harvey (1996) emphasizes, the shaping of these three elements in particular settings is closely interdependent.

7. In a recent study of children with disabilities in the public schools (Engel 1993, 1995), I discovered an enormous range of norms and procedures as I moved from one school to the next. Even within a narrow geographic area, different schools applied the same special education laws in strikingly different ways. As a consequence, the identities of students with disabilities varied greatly from school to school, as did the legally mandated procedures for planning their educations.

8. Actually, the injury occurred during the ten-minute buffer zone between the call to return to class at 1:20 P.M. and the actual resumption of instruction at 1:30 P.M. Perhaps it was significant that Ms. More expected her students to be seated at their desks during this period while she read to them.

9. A number of sociolegal scholars have written about mutually constitutive theory, but one of the more influential studies illustrating its application is Yngvesson (1988). See also Yngvesson (1993) and Greenhouse et al. (1994).

10. See, for example, Muecke (1992) on *khwan* ceremonies in urban settings in Chiangmai.

References

Abel, Richard L. 1990. "A Critique of Torts." *UCLA Law Review* 37, no. 5: 785–831.

Beckerman, John S. 1981. "Adding Insult to Iniuria: Affronts to Honor and the Origins of Trespass." In Morris S. Arnold, Thomas A. Green, Sally A. Scully, and Stephen D. White, eds., *On the Laws and Customs of England: Essays in Honor of Samuel E. Thorne* (159–81). Chapel Hill: University of North Carolina Press.

Chamallas, Martha, with Linda K. Kerber. 1990. "Women, Mothers, and the Law of Fright: A History." *Michigan Law Review* 88, no. 4: 814–63.

Engel, David M. 1978. *Code and Custom in a Thai Provincial Court: The Interaction of Formal and Informal Systems of Justice.* Tucson: University of Arizona Press (Association for Asian Studies).

———. 1984. "The Oven Bird's Song: Insiders, Outsiders, and Personal Injuries in an American Community." *Law & Society Review* 18, no. 4: 551–82.

———. 1990. "Litigation across Space and Time: Courts, Conflict, and Social Change." *Law & Society Review* 24, no. 2: 333–44.

———. 1993. "Origin Myths: Narratives of Authority, Resistance, Disability, and Law." *Law & Society Review* 27, no. 4: 785–826.

———. 1995. "Law in the Domains of Everyday Life." In Austin Sarat and Thomas R. Kearns, eds., *Law in Everyday Life* (123–70). Ann Arbor: University of Michigan Press.

French, Rebecca Redwood. 1995. *The Golden Yoke: The Legal Cosmology of Buddhist Tibet.* Ithaca, N.Y.: Cornell University Press.

Geertz, Clifford. 1983. *Local Knowledge: Further Essays in Interpretive Anthropology.* New York: Basic Books.

Giddens, Anthony. 1984. *The Constitution of Society: Outline of the Theory of Structuration.* Berkeley and Los Angeles: University of California Press.

Greenhouse, Carol J., Barbara Yngvesson, and David M. Engel. 1994. *Law and Community in Three American Towns.* Ithaca, N.Y.: Cornell University Press.

Hanks, Jane Richardson. 1963. *Maternity and Its Rituals in Bang Chan.* Ithaca, N.Y.: Southeast Asia Program, Cornell University.

Harvey, David. 1996. *Justice, Nature and the Geography of Difference.* Cambridge, Mass.: Blackwell.

Heinze, Ruth-Inge. 1982. *Tham Khwan: How to Contain the Essence of Life: A Socio-Psychological Comparison of a Thai Custom.* Singapore: Singapore University Press.

Macaulay, Stewart. 1986. "Private Government." In Leon Lipson and Stanton Wheeler, eds., *Law and the Social Sciences* (445–518). New York: Russell Sage.

Moore, Sally Falk. 1978. "Law and Social Change: The Semi-Autonomous Social Field as an Appropriate Subject of Study." In *Law as Process: An Anthropological Approach* (54–81). London: Routledge & Kegan Paul.

Muecke, Marjorie. 1992. "Monks and Mediums: Religious Syncretism in Northern Thailand." *Journal of the Siam Society* 80, no. 2: 97–104.

Radin, Margaret Jane. 1996. *Contested Commodities.* Cambridge, Mass.: Harvard University Press.

Tambiah, S. J. 1970. *Buddhism and the Spirit Cults in North-east Thailand.* Cambridge: Cambridge University Press.

———. 1976. *World Conqueror and World Renouncer: A Study of Buddhism and Polity in Thailand against a Historical Background.* Cambridge: Cambridge University Press.

Terwiel, B. J. 1976. "Leasing from the Gods (Thailand)." *Anthropos* 71, nos. 1/2: 254–74.

Vosburg v. Putney, 50 N.W. 403 (Wis. 1891).

Winichakul, Thongchai. 1994. *Siam Mapped: A History of the Geo-Body of a Nation.* Honolulu: University of Hawaii Press.

Yngvesson, Barbara. 1988. "Making Law at the Doorway: The Clerk, the Court, and the Construction of Community in a New England Town." *Law & Society Review* 22, no. 3: 409–48.

———. 1993. *Virtuous Citizens, Disruptive Subjects: Order and Complaint in a New England Court.* New York: Routledge.

Zile, Zigurds L. 1992. "*Vosburg v. Putney:* A Centennial Story." *Wisconsin Law Review,* no. 6: 877–996.

2

Sports Trademarks and Somatic Politics

LOCATING THE LAW IN A CRITICAL CULTURAL STUDIES

Rosemary J. Coombe

A lack of juridical context is a curious but significant lacuna in contemporary cultural studies. Although policy concerns were central to the early British school of cultural studies, a disinclination to deal with issues of legality distinguishes most contemporary American scholarship. Despite the immense importance of legal infrastructures in shaping the issues with which cultural studies professes concern—the construction of identity and community, mass-media production and consumption, social textuality and subcultural agency, citizenship and civil society, cultural politics and public spheres, and transnational flows of goods, capital, and people—juridical concerns are rarely central to its interlocutions. Implicitly, it would seem, law is deemed a less than interesting other—a cold, dry, dusty chamber of patriarchal prohibition and regulation rather than a generative force in activities of cultural production.

The location of cultural practice, however, is simultaneously the space of law, and the relationship is both productive and diacritical. The legal status of cultural texts, the ability to exercise power over meaning, and the denial of ambiguity that law effects—as well as the resistances such denials engender—are central to contemporary fields of cultural politics. I will draw on a limited area of juridical discourse—laws of trademark—and a range of cultural activities—examples of cultural politics engaging sports trademarks in the United States—to make my case. Legal regimes, I suggest, provide spaces of governance and accountability as well as means and media for transgression and social transformation. The instances examined are exemplary of the significance of intellectual property laws in wider fields of contemporary cultural politics that we might deem a politics of publicity.[1]

The proliferation of textuality—the accelerated production and circulation of representation—so much discussed as a dimension of postmodernity, is part of a political economy that is integrally dependent on and structured by laws of intellectual property. The cultural forms circulated by mass media incorporate a multiplicity of commodity-texts whose economic value is legally maintained. Our understanding of this textually saturated, hypersignificant world needs to be reintegrated with the regimes of law that regulate it; the relationship between the word and the world is a dialectical space of governance and praxis as well as one of authorship and readership, or production and reception. In overdeveloped societies, we have witnessed a massive expansion of the scope and duration of intellectual property rights since the mid-eighteenth century and an even greater growth and proliferation of legal protections in the twentieth century (capitalist interests are also successfully imposing these laws on others through international trade negotiations and international financial pressures).[2] The rights bestowed by intellectual property regimes (copyright and neighboring rights, registered and common-law trademarks, service and certification marks, publicity, personality and privacy rights, design patents, and associated merchandising rights) play a constitutive role in the creation of contemporary cultures and in the social life of interpretive practice. In consumer cultures, most pictures, texts, motifs, labels, logos, lyrics, trade names, designs, tunes, film footage, photographs, celebrity names and likenesses, and even some colors and scents are governed, if not wholly contained, by regimes of intellectual property.

Intellectual property laws enable the commodification of symbols, imagery, and texts—they create limited monopolies over public representations. The law creates and enforces rights and limitations that shape the relationship between elites who claim proprietary interests in signs and those who seek to appropriate them in the service of alternative agendas—to popularize them, so to speak. It establishes cultural authorities and cultural hierarchies in the public sphere. The legal right to control and contain textuality that intellectual property protections afford has constituted new modes of cultural reproduction, forms of symbolic expropriation, and emergent class configurations.

Legal discourses produce and privilege particular juridical subjects. Power differentials between those who disseminate commodity/signs (signs that are commodities with an exchange value in their own right as well as signifiers in fields of cultural connotation) and those who consume them animate their legal regulation. The recognition and protection of some activities of meaning making as activities of authorship and the delegitimation of other signifying practices as forms of piracy create particular cartographies for cultural agency. Laws of intellectual property construct authors, regulate activities of cultural replication, license copying, and prohibit imitation in the service of maintaining the exchange value of texts. They compel our interest because of their power to achieve particular political effects—legitimating practices of cultural authority that attempt to limit the play of intertextuality in public spheres increasingly dominated by industrial-commercial forms of publicity. Given that such forms of publicity are a major if not primary focus of cultural studies, it is imperative that we attend to the legalities that ensure their predominance and shape their social relations of production. Laws that construct the fiction of the singular, unique, and self-contained work (copyright) or the mark of singular meaning and origin for the commodity (trademark) or that enable celebrities to control publicly recognized indicia of their personalities as their autonomous productions (publicity rights) manage intertextuality as they simultaneously deny it as a source of meaning and value.

It is now critical orthodoxy in cultural studies that mass-media imagery provides symbolic resources for the construction of identity and community, subaltern appropriations, parodic interventions, and counterhegemonic narratives that may challenge social exclusions, assert historically specific trajectories, and comment on social inequalities. The ubiquity of commodified texts in commercial culture makes them particularly available for the signifying activities of others, and the fact that they are everywhere the same seems to invite others to use them to inscribe social difference. The laws that protect texts as expressions of authorial distinction, however, are also at work when they become media for expressions of alterity. Legal regimes of intellectual property shape (although they do not determine) the ways in which cultural signs are re/appropriated. The presence or absence, extent, and enforcement of intellectual property protections are constitutive conditions for cultural production, circulation, and reception—providing incentives to invest in the production and dissemination of texts and regulating their movement while enabling and enjoining alternative forms of reception and interpretation. The culturalist emphasis on the politics of subcultural textual practice is both incomplete and somewhat naive if it fails to incorporate a cognizance of the political economies that enable and constrain textual circulation.

It is important to emphasize that intellectual property laws do not function simply in a rule-like fashion, nor are they adequately portrayed as regimes of rights and obligations. Although such laws are constructed through a rhetoric of rights, I seek to go beyond their self-representations to show how such laws also provide generative conditions and prohibitive boundaries for hegemonic articulations. To the extent that specific legal infrastructures create particular forms of signifying power, such laws also and simultaneously enable, provoke, or invite particular forms of resistance or alternative appropriations. Often, as we will see, these are aw[e]fully appropriate to the forms of legally regulated signification to which they may be seen as forms of response. Drawing exclusively on examples of trademarks in the field of athletics further focuses my discussion. An emphasis on the commodity/sign in sports arenas provokes new perspectives on regimes of corporeal specularity—dominant representations of commodified, racialized, and politicized bodies and struggles to redefine the parameters of the body politic they legitimate. Let me begin by way of a brief discussion of a simple example before moving into more complicated terrain.

Olympics and Monumental Bodies

> Walking down the street in Toronto one day in 1987, pedestrians were surprised to see a message flashing across an electronic billboard—"Lesbians fly Air Canada." The message disappeared overnight. This broadcast by a gay rights group terminated abruptly when the government threatened the group with an injunction to prevent it from using the airline's name.[3]

The tactics of appropriation involved in hegemonic articulations simultaneously invoke and transform fields of power and representation. Bodies politic are signified by symbols that are legally protected. The polysemic power of the nation, the seductive power of the commodity form, and the instrumental power of the state—powers legally bestowed also shape activities that seek to challenge the contours of the body politic configured through such signs. Public propensities to remark on (and put one's own mark on) dominant forms of signifying power are apparent in the case of "official marks"—signs held by public authorities in the name of the public interest. These are often key symbols in national and international cultural lexicons with which subaltern groups seek affirmative association.

Governments bestow the most extensive signifying powers on authorities that control the signs of the nation, the state, and transnational institutional icons. For example, in the United States, there are a group of "national" symbols (ranging from Smokey the Bear to Little League and the Future Farmers of America) that the federal government protects from unauthorized use under the same provisions that penalize desecration of the flag.[4] Rarely, however, are the "public authorities" in control of these marks elected political bodies. More often they are government agencies and nonprofit corporations that are given the discretion to discern discriminating definitions of the public interest. The signs they hold often indicate key institutions of local, national, and transnational legitimacy.[5] The visible and monumental power of these institutions, I have suggested elsewhere, invites others to appropriate their signs in a "politics of direct address" (McClure 1992)—acts of publicity seeking recognition, inclusion, and representation that take the form of struggles over key symbols and their connotative fields of reference. Subaltern groups are likely to mobilize in identifications with signs that promise new forms of legitimacy in the public sphere.

Those who have intellectual property rights in signifiers, however, may attempt to control both the sign's circulation and its meanings. By creating monopolies in fields of representation, the law inserts signifiers into systems of political economy that "reduce symbolic ambivalence in order to ground the rational circulation of values and their play of exchange" (Baudrillard 1981, 146). Signifiers are denied their indeterminacy and polysemy by laws that protect their exchange value. "Owners" of mass-media signifiers may well permit the social production of significance when it mints meanings with potential market value, but they may also prohibit the material circulation of connotations that contest the valences they have propagated. Indeed, most trademark holders have an economic interest in so doing. Unless they "police" their marks, they are in danger of losing them through legal doctrines that deprive holders of their exclusive rights if they lose their distinction and become part of the general vocabulary.

In the case of official marks, however, public authorities are statutorily bestowed with exclusive rights to control particular signifiers without any legal requirement to police their use or fear their loss.[6] This absolute power to prohibit the use of certain symbols may be legitimated by social functions, such as public order and safety. Dangerous confusion is avoided by univocally fixing the referent for a sign like the red cross and restricting its use to a single organization. Consumer confusion provides another rationalization; it is not permissible to suggest government endorsement of one's products. The powers over signification bestowed by such statutes, however, go far beyond those necessary to avoid such harms. Having adopted the sign, authorities are enabled with capacities to singularly dictate the sign's "official" meanings. They may threaten, enjoin, and prosecute those who give the signifier unsanctioned connotations. Such discretionary power to prohibit alternative usages often manifests ideological interests and reveals prejudices about the proper character of the social body.

If official signifiers seldom feature prominently on elite political agendas (a U.S. Senate decision in 1993 not to renew the design patent for the United Daughters of the Confederacy being a rare exception), socially they figure as cultural targets and as resources in struggles for political legitimation. In 1981, for example, a nonprofit group called San Francisco Arts and Athletics (hereafter "the Athletics Group") organized a promotional event to create a more positive image of the gay community. T-shirts, buttons, and bumper stickers financed the Gay Olympics. The United States Olympic Committee (hereafter "the Committee") brought suit to stop the games and to preclude the group from making use of the term "Olympic" (*International Olympic Committee v. San Francisco Arts & Athletics* 789 F. 2d 1319 at 1323 [per Kozinski, J.]). The Committee had exclusive rights to use the word Olympic under the Amateur Sports Act[7] and successfully enjoined the

Athletics Group's use of the term in court appeals culminating in the U.S. Supreme Court's 1987 decision upholding the Committee's exclusive and absolute rights to the word "Olympic."[8]

"Olympic," of course, is a term with a long history of connoting human excellence and achievement. It is recognized transnationally as a humanist symbol and one with which the dispossessed have traditionally sought to identify in aspirations for social affirmation and as a medium for public education. The Committee itself acknowledged the significance of the symbol in achieving social recognition; it had authorized groups of the disabled to hold "Olympic" games to encourage their greater social incorporation. As one dissenting judge remarked, "It seems that the Committee is using its control over the term Olympic to promote the very image of homosexuals that the [Athletics Group] seeks to combat: handicapped, juniors, police, Explorers, even dogs are allowed to carry the Olympic torch, but homosexuals are not."[9] Indeed, the Committee's counsel was a member of a local Olympic Club—an exclusive, segregated, all-male, social club with a history of discrimination against gays and minorities.

Cultural studies alerts us to the practices in which signifiers circulate in social fields and become inflected with new meanings. This story, however, serves as a cautionary reminder that the domains of discourse in which symbols figure as sites for identification may shape and limit their availability for new articulations. If counterhegemonic tactics endeavor to put signifiers into fields of symbolic exchange—which I will define here as activities that refuse the totalizing logic of capitalist production—such practitioners are at a disadvantage when they come up against the interests of proprietors in maintaining the signifier's exchange value. Connotations of Olympic as a festival celebrating human excellence and bodily energy (implicitly linked to a nonreproductive sexuality) encountered the Olympic signifier's status as a commodity. Its exclusionary values were carefully contained to continue the maximum flow of merchandising royalties.

Visible, recognized, and pervasively objectified, the Olympic signifier denotes legitimacy and prestige, while its connotations are legally managed through structures of prohibition. Its status as an official sign of power and value makes it particularly attractive to those who seek political recognition and important to those who seek to preserve contemporary hegemonies. Like other monumental signs, it attracts efforts of appropriation and rearticulation by those who wish to inscribe their own authorial signature on the people, the nation, the state—the body politic. Such acts of subaltern recoding seem to engage the signifiers of power in a fashion appropriate to their mode of signification. This at least is what I will attempt to elaborate in the following discussions of trademarked stereotypes, trademark rumors, and postindustrial publicity relations.

Redskins and Specularized Alterity

As citizens and consumers, commodified signifiers mark us and our sense of social boundaries.[10] Not surprisingly, they also attract the energies of those who would alter those parameters—to highlight and to challenge the implicit inclusions and exclusions that such social distinctions invariably effect. Those concerned with contemporary public spheres (and, to a lesser degree, those who seek to articulate the characteristics of contemporary civil society) suggest that we attend to the quotidian cultural politics that engage commodity/signs.[11] Michael Warner makes perhaps the most global claim for the significance of trademarks in public spheres—as characteristic media forms that interrelate collectivities and imagined national communities: They provide a common discourse that binds the subject to the nation and its markets. As he remarks, "We have brand names all over us" (Warner 1993, 243). Some of "us" and "our" ancestors, however, are in fact brand names: Cherokee®, Oneida®, Pontiac®, Winnebago®, Crazy Horse™, Aunt Jemima®, and Uncle Ben's®. Some of "us" may have national trademarks all over our bodies; others of "us" have bodies and nations that are all over the commercial landscape as trademarks.

Cultural histories of imperialism remind us that the emergence of consumer societies involved the commodified objectification of colonized others and the domestication of social alterity in daily practices of consumption that bound citizen/consumers in imagined communities of belonging.[12] The visual cultures of mass markets are often saturated with signs of social difference; histories of imperialism and colonialism, territorial annexation, and political disenfranchisement are socially inscribed across commercial landscapes. When these icons assume the form of marks used in trade—Gollywogs, black mammies, Indian princesses, Mexican bandits, Hawaiian hula dancers—they may be legally claimed as private properties by those who assert them as marks of their own distinction in commerce.

Trademarks are signifiers that distinguish the goods of one manufacturer, retailer, or service provider from those of others. These may be logos, brand names, characteristic advertising images, or other forms that condense and convey meaning in commerce. The ubiquity of trademarks in national social arenas and their currency both as culture and as private property create generative conditions for struggles over significance; they are simultaneously shared in a commons of signification and jealously guarded in exclusive estates. Their status as trademarks, however, makes them simultaneously appropriate, available, and vulnerable to the claims of those they (mis)represent. To make this case, I will need to summarize some significant features of the evolution of federal trademark laws in the United States before examining some highly publicized contemporary efforts to expunge specific marks from the public sphere.

In the late nineteenth century, indicia of social alterity were routinely appropriated as marks of commercial distinction. These privately held signifiers were publicly circulated to interpellate an American consumer and were then domesticated by individual Americans who consumed the same signs of cultural distinction that the national body politic was simultaneously incorporating. National markets were made possible by mass manufacturing and mass communications but could not be tapped until cultural work was done to standardize American culture and consumption practices.[13] This was partially accomplished through the creation of widely recognized and socially shared marks of trade.[14] The legal protection of imagery as private property provided a means for melding mass production of goods, mass reproduction of cultural forms, and the mass interpellation necessary to transform a mass of immigrants into similar consumers.

The same historical period witnessed the birth of the frontier thesis and preoccupations with American civilization—its distinction from, as well as its annexation and containment of, the savage, the tribal, and the primitive. These processes were linked; the American was constituted in relation to an embodied otherness from which he could be distinguished and whose cultural and corporeal distinctions he would both recognize and consume in domestic rituals of nationality. Images of African Americans, Indian peoples, Hispanic and mestizo subjects, as well as the perceived "tribal" groups colonized by U.S. imperial expansion (e.g., Filipinos, Hawaiians, and "Eskimos"), were mass reproduced and projected on a national scale through the medium of trademarks. More could be said about the legal doctrines that accomplished this; it suffices here to note that national citizens and consumers were similarly bound in newly forged national communities through a specularization of alterity that was simultaneously an establishment of property.

The dynamics of this relationship have been transformed as those whose enforced alterity was historically commodified have turned these objects of property into subjects and sites of politics. Specularizations of alterity have come under the intense scrutiny of civil rights movements since World War II. Peoples historically othered in imperialist social imaginaries protest the continuing circulation of signs that index their former subjugation and contest the propriety of this continuing commodification of colonial desire. The multiple metamorphoses of Aunt Jemima, the abandonment of the Frito Bandito, protests over Sambo's restaurants and Robertson's Golly[wog] are only a few of the struggles in which minority groups have focused attention on commodity/signs. Whether these are commodifications of their cultural heritage or stereotypical signs of their alterity, many find their own representations owned by others.

Of those historically subjugated groups who have demanded an end to the commodification of their cultural difference in North American mass markets, Native Americans have faced the longest struggles. Long after the Frito Bandito has been laid to rest and black mammies and little black sambos have ceased to signify on American commercial terrain (though they have returned as a form of collectible nostalgia), Indians are still a privileged form of alterity in advertising. From Red Man® chewing tobacco, Indian Spirit® air freshener, Indian style™ popcorn, Red Indian® jeans, Warrior boxes, and Indian princesses and Indian heads on everything from butter boxes and baking soda tins to neon beer signs, the corporeality of the "Indian" continues to mark the privileges of the incorporated.

Contesting claims that stereotypical images of themselves be considered primarily the marketing vehicles of others, native peoples come up against commercial indifference, corporate animosity, and public ridicule. The movement to end the use of Native American team names, logos, and mascots in the world of professional sport has been particularly protracted. Dismissed by some as evidence of "political correctness" gone to ridiculous extremes, denied as in any way offensive by many bewildered liberals, and even considered complimentary by some, protests about these signs are greeted with a curious degree of misrecognition. An examination of these controversies reveals a great deal about the trademark as a vehicle for articulatory practice.

The Washington Redskins, Atlanta Braves, Cleveland Indians, Chicago Blackhawks, Kansas City Chiefs, Florida State University Seminoles, and University of Illinois Fighting Illini are nominations that bind fans across ethnic and generational lines. They are also legally protected trademarks that, along with accompanying logos and mascots, provide steady streams of income. Team insignia have become incredibly valuable properties in their own right. The exploitation of merchandising rights (the right to license one's exclusive rights under trademark laws) provides a significant and autonomous source of revenue. It is tempting to reduce the reluctance to abandon such marks to economics and sentiment alone. Significant profits will be lost (or dispersed) if these marks are forgone, and there are now long traditions of fan activity associated with them. The cost of conceiving popularly appealing logos, nicknames, and color combinations is not incidental.[15] Elsewhere I have commented on the peculiarity of legal doctrines deeming public meaning to be the basis for private property (see Coombe 1991, 1998, chapter 1)— to the extent that fans become personally attached to these symbols, the value of such intimacies accrues to the mark's legal holder. To the extent that team owners view public recognition of these symbols as valuable assets in their own right, any prohibition of them is seen as tantamount to an expropriation without compensation.

Neither economics nor emotion, however, fully accounts for the cultural power of such symbols or the almost willful refusal by team owners and fans to entertain native people's concerns. Stereotypical commercial imagery has been abandoned under minority pressures before, despite predictable economic loss and acknowledged social popularity (e.g., the Frito Bandito). The damage to a people's self-esteem effected by public stereotyping has been publicly acknowledged with respect to African, Mexican, and Asian Americans, and offensive trademarks have been withdrawn from commerce. After surveying arguments on both sides of this debate, I will suggest that the financial interests and social sentiments expressed in this controversy are epiphenomena of a deeper convergence of historical, psychosocial, and legal forces.

Native people's opposition to these marks is complex, multifaceted, and far from unanimous in terms of the seriousness accorded the issue or the grounds on which it is (or is not) condemned.[16] Owners of these marks like to quote Indians who do not object to these marks to support their own reluctance to abandon them. Since the 1991 World Series made the "tomahawk chop" famous, for example, the market for "tomahawks" has soared. The Cherokee tribe of North Carolina owns and provides labor for the factory that produces the foam "tomahawks" used at Atlanta Braves games. Chief Jonathan Ed Taylor is quoted as saying that the "Redskin" name (and other usages of Indian symbols)

> gives our people recognition. The most important thing is that it employs my people. It means our people will get work and not stand in welfare lines. Welfare lines are a lot more degrading than using the name Redskins. (cited in Shapiro 1991)

Some might feel less resentment about the exploitation of Indianness if more of the profits made their way back to Indian peoples to serve social needs—implicitly suggesting the political propriety of licensing arrangements to funnel funds back into native communities. Others, of course, might well view this as a form of cultural prostitution.

The most common basis for antagonism is the conviction that the names, logos, mascots, paraphernalia, and related fan activities represent racist stereotypes of Native American cultures. Historic depictions of Indians as bloodthirsty, warlike savages are reproduced and perpetuated in these rituals. Terms like "Redskins" recall a historical period in which there was a bounty on red skins, a genocidal referent that we would tolerate with respect to no other peoples.[17] Concern is also voiced about the negative influence of such symbolism on the self-image of Native Americans and the self-esteem of youth and children. In communities wracked by alarming rates of youth suicide, alcoholism, and chronic unemployment, issues of cultural representation are not insignificant. Indian youth may see few widespread images of their people but monstrous caricatures—cartoon figures with painted faces, grunting and whooping unintelligibly, preparing for battle, and engaged in mock rites divorced from any meaningful context.

A similar range of response characterizes the political sympathy that supporters of Native activists express. Use of such symbols may be seen as disrespectful, demeaning, or discriminatory—an affront to Indian dignity, a mockery of sacred Native American symbols, or quite simply as virulent racism. The racism perceived in the athletic field ranges from the patently obvious to the more subtle and complex. Terms like "Redskins" that have historically figured as racial epithets are more offensive than caricatures that effect a continuation of social stereotyping, while the appropriation of the names of Indian nations and the trivializing of rituals is felt to have the effect of ridiculing them and demeaning their social significance.

Most of the so-called Indianness drawn on in sports arenas recalls the Wild West of Buffalo Bill and Hollywood myth—a stereotypical Great Plains warrior culture now hackneyed to the point that it no longer reflects any particular Indian tradition. This is one reason these marks are regarded as offensive. They reiterate historical stereotypes of the Indian as a monolithic other without internal differentiation in languages, traditions, and ways of life. "The Indian" as a general category has a long history in North America (Berkhofer 1979). Divided into at least 2,000 cultures and more societies at the time of "first contact," the image of the Indian as a singularity is a "white" stereotype that creates its own realities as a result of white power and the necessity of Native Americans to respond to it (Berkhofer 1979). Other aspects of this ensemble of signs are more directly offensive. To the extent that feathers were and are used in highly elaborated systems of political honor and prestige and achieve sacred status in particular contexts, peace pipes are significant in wider systems of meaning, and wampum figures in historical political negotiations of great contemporary import, their appropriation as toys and jokes is more than merely insensitive.

Unlike mascots such as the Irish, Native American mascots were not selected by the ethnic group they supposedly represent, nor, like Vikings, Trojans, Spartans, Buccaneers, Pirates, and 49ers, are they mythic figures of the past—except of course, in popular culture. This perhaps is the most complicated of the injuries effected by such fantasies in sports arenas. They make mythic and imaginary images of Native Americans more visible than they are as living peoples with pressing contemporary concerns, preserving "the crippling myth that Native Americans, their lands, their cultures, their sovereign powers, their very existence, are relics of the past" (Pierson 1992).

Critics of those who oppose the use of these marks make contradictory but telling arguments. Many, like Paul Tagliabue, Commissioner of the NFL, claim to be sensitive to Native American concerns but simply do not find the team names demeaning. Others argue that the use of these names pays a form of tribute to Native Americans by alluding to their bravery and fighting spirit. In athletic competition, aggressiveness, dedication, courage, and pride are prized attributes, and Indians are recognized to embody them. John Cooke, executive vice president of the Washington Redskins (and son of owner Jack Kent Cooke), goes so far as to say that the name "has come to represent the best of the culture—bravery, organization, the whole works. We honor Native Americans. We believe that [it] represents the finest things in Indian culture" (cited in Shapiro 1991). Ted Turner, owner of the Atlanta Braves, claims that "Braves" "is a compliment. Braves are warriors" (cited in

Burkhart 1991). Defenders of the University of Illinois mascot "Chief Illiniwek" say that he honors the tribes that lived in Illinois (the mascot is performed by a student who paints his face and wears "Indian" garb, including a headdress of turkey feathers).[18] Ironically, many who assert that these signifiers are tributes to Native American people simultaneously argue that they do not really refer and were never meant to refer to any particular people; their public meanings have entirely to do with the teams and their time-honored traditions.

There is a paradoxical sense in which all these contradictory assertions are true—in which the use of Native American names and images are both insulting and complimentary, make reference to Indians but refer to no people in particular, and have more symbolically to do with American audiences than with oppressed nations. To comprehend how this might be the case, however, we need to consider the peculiar role of Indians in an American colonial discourse. White views of Indians have been inextricably bound up with an evaluation of their own society and culture and reflect Euroamerican ambivalence toward modernity.[19] Not surprisingly, the figure of the (imaginary) Indian is internally contradictory:

> Encompassing . . . contrasting modes of performance, the Plains warriors performed complex and contradictory roles of enemies and American heroes, of local specimens and national symbols. With or without their permission, Indians participate in the often violent struggle over what and who is or is not American. In the symbolic economy of Wild West violence especially, American Indians are richly polysemic. . . . Indians could signify reckless defiance in face of oppression and tyranny [as they did for Anglo-Americans cross-dressing at the Boston Tea Party] . . . disenfranchised of a continent, American Indians could also signify holders of legitimate entitlement to either repatriation or revenge. From the time of Plymouth, the Indian appeared in the bad conscience of white mythology as a symbol of savage retribution. (Roach 1996, 205)

Such a dramatic field of connotation is particularly apt for the arena of competitive national sport, not least because it reiterates central tropes of American colonialism—the American frontier as a contested space, testing and consolidating a pioneering, male spirit perpetually threatened by races and cultures beyond it.

Homi Bhabha's articulation of the stereotype as a major discursive strategy of colonial discourse helps us to comprehend the effectivity of the trademark and the type of truth it encompasses. The stereotype of the Indian figures as an object of both derision and desire; it is both disparaged and admired. The question of whether Indian trademarks are positive or negative representations ceases to be salient. Instead of subjecting them to judgments of political normativity, Bhabha suggests that we explore stereotypes in terms of the "processes of subjectification" (identities and identifications) that they make possible and plausible (Bhabha 1994, 67). Only then do we have the means to displace rather than dismiss their power.

If colonial discourse fixes otherness in an ideological discourse, it does so in a fashion that demands a continuous and anxious repetition. The force of ambivalence is what gives the colonial stereotype its currency and longevity (Bhabha 1994). Perhaps this is at the heart of the trademark's cultural value—"Indian" trademarks, more obviously than other commodified stereotypes, resonate with an extensive history of national mythmaking in which both the Indian's noble resistance and his ultimate defeat on expanding frontiers are repeatedly imagined and reenacted. Such trademarks may operate more powerfully than others in the political aesthetics of spectator positioning that forge "American" allegiances. (Such sports trademarks have little popularity or presence in either Canada or Australia, interestingly, despite similar histories of "vanquishing" indigenous populations.)

Ideas about modern national foundings—which often stress racial purity or cultural priority—are produced in relation to colonial stereotypes. Recognitions of difference are "disavowed by the fixation on an object that masks the difference and restores an original presence" (Bhabha 1994, 74):

> The . . . stereotype gives access to an "identity" which is predicated as much on mastery and pleasure as it is on anxiety and defence. . . . The stereotype, then, as the primary point of subjectification in colonial discourse, for both colonizer and colonized, is the scene of a similar fantasy and defence—the desire for an originality which is again threatened by the differences of race, colour and culture. (Bhabha 1994, 67)

Bhabha focuses on the scopophilic nature of the stereotype as a site (and sight) of subjectification in which identification with the positivity of whiteness is enabled. This involves a disavowal of one's self as other through the fixation on another's absolute otherness that allows one to identify with "an ideal ego that is white and whole." Such sites of subjectification are evidence of the importance of the visual and auditory imaginary for the histories of societies (Bhabha 1994, 76). If, as I have suggested, a mass of immigrants from diverse cultures were interpellated as (white) "Americans" through the commodified specularization of alterity, there is also a sense in which a national childhood is nostalgically reenacted in national sports arenas. The sentimental attachment that people have to these "Indian" images may be related to the fantasy of purity of (American) origination that they provide in the face of the persistent threat of the disruption of (immigrant, underclass, alien, female?) otherness that they hold at bay. Is it too speculative to suggest that all spectators—regardless of ethnicity, race, gender, sexuality, or generation—become symbolically white, male, and American in these objectifications of the scopic drive?

At any particular moment in the social life of colonial discourse, the differences disavowed and the nature of the subjects produced will be historically specific, but there is little doubt that "the Indian" has figured centrally in racialized enactments of Americanness throughout U.S. history. As theater historian Joseph Roach suggests, from at least the late eighteenth century Native Americans "play a paradoxically central role in the formation of a self-consciously national drama" (Roach 1996, 187). The role is paradoxical because they are permitted entry into this history "only as they are represented by white authors and actors. In such roles they become integral to the self-invention of 'the American people' but only through artistry and imagination" (Roach 1996, 187). The national search for native authenticity rarely involves any but the most superficial dealings with living autochthons; the function of the surrogated aboriginal is always to vanish.

Walter Benn Michaels provides a telling example of this in a recent study of American modernism that traces changing ideas of national identity in literature from the turn of the twentieth century to 1925 (Michaels 1996). American culture, he argues, took on new meanings in this period as a logic of naturalization and assimilation gave way to one of essentialized cultural identities—racially configured. I cannot do justice to his nuanced study here, but I wish to note his assertion that the nineteenth-century stereotype of "the vanishing race" was redeployed in an era in which it was feared that "Nordic" peoples were dying out (by their failure to reproduce themselves at the same rate as "Mediterraneans" and "Asiatics"). The "rhetoric of racial extinction in America was the rhetoric of the vanishing American. To think of Nordics as a vanishing race was inevitably to identify them with the Indians" and to celebrate the Indian's alleged disappearance "as a mark of his racial integrity—better death than cross-breeding" (Michaels 1996, 12). In the aesthetic quest for a pure source for American culture, indigenous peoples were transformed into Nordic ancestors. By virtue of being perceived as vanishing, Indians exemplified what it meant to have a culture (Michaels 1996).

The origin of Americanness was the scene of the Indians' extinction, and this new cultural identity was essentially racial in its contours. Whiteness was rearticulated by an identification with the figure of the Indian, which no longer functioned, as it did at the turn of the twentieth century, as a refusal of American identity in the form of citizenship but came to function "as the assertion of an American identity that could be understood as going beyond citizenship" (Michaels 1996, 45). Indians, unlike aliens and their children who could become Americans, embodied "an Americanism that transcended the state" (Michaels 1996)—a purity and aristocracy of an originary Americanism that those of "dark blood" could not achieve.

This imaginary Indian was always a male Indian, of course; the female Indian posed the potential threat of miscegenation. Michaels explores elite fantasies of carrying on dynasties unthreatened by the deracinating potential of femininity and the eroticizing of relations between men that served as a subliminal model for this racially purified Americanism. Certainly the resemblances and resonances are suggestive, but it would be indulgent and historically irresponsible to map this configuration directly onto contemporary athletic arenas. It does serve, though, to remind us of the complex forces of displacement, projection, and desire that shape the affective life of race so central to the American national imaginary.

To the extent that sports spectacles embody collective social memory, however, it is their performative corporeality that demands consideration.[20] Sports trademarks do not stand as abstract icons in the public sphere but focus a kinetic interpellation of spectators/fans that links bodies in the production of "esprit de corps"—what we might call "team spirit" (Bourdieu 1990). Discussing the performative dimensions of homosocial bonding in sports, Milind Wakankar notes that

> at the core of such collective activity is the establishment of the link between the male body and the mass through physio-psycho-sociological assemblages of series of actions . . . for the effective interpellation of the subject. The proximity of so many uniformed, uniforming, bodies-in-unison initiates a kind of silent communion. . . . Since every action mimes another, collective mimesis sustains the possibility of collective regeneration. As Bourdieu explains, "collective bodily practice, "by" symbolizing the social, contribute to somatizing it and . . . by the bodily and collective mimesis of a social orchestration, aim at reinforcing that orchestration." (Wakankar 1995, 45, 59, citing Bourdieu 1990, 167)

Stereotypical trademarks seem to serve as totemic forms that mark and galvanize bodies in public rituals of homosocial bonding. Not only do fans inscribe these marks on their bodies by donning licensed goods, but they engage in corporeal appropriations of alterity—imitations of and intimations with imaginary indigenes. Surrounding and animating these trademarks are rituals such as the infamous "tomahawk chop," the "war whoop," the smoking of "peace pipes," the beating of "tom-toms," the wearing of "war paint" and war bonnets while on the "warpath," and the assumption of an alleged Indian ferocity in songs, dances, and even the ritual planting of flaming spears. In addition to clothing, fans can cater to their bodily needs with coffee mugs, bath towels, and even toilet paper adorned with trademarked caricatures.

This is certainly not the first instance in U.S. history in which living peoples have been metaphorically erased through appropriations of their alleged alterity in the forging of other identities. Indeed, there seems substantial evidence of such activity in both working-class popular and elite literary culture. Eric Lott's work on antebellum blackface minstrelsy points to the contradictory impulses at work in stereotypicality and the dominant racial subjectivities it enables. Significantly, he also explores bodily caricature in popular cultural practice. Lott denies that the meanings of popular culture are ever simply reflective of relations of political domination. The blackface mask "is less a repetition of power relations than a signifier for them—a distorted mirror, reflecting displacements and condensations and discontinuities" (Lott 1993, 8).

Lott explores the simultaneously transgressive and oppressive dimensions of racial cross-dressing that made possible the "formation of a self-consciously white working class" (Lott 1993, 8) and contributed to ideologies of working-class manhood. Combining fear and fascination with degraded others in a mimicry of potent masculinity, feelings of racial superiority were indulged while class insecurities were assuaged, class resentments were voiced, ethnic conflicts were mediated, and a class identity was articulated (Lott 1993). Among other things, blackface acts elevated the "black Irish" (and later Jews) into white Americans: It was "an 'Americanizing' ritual of whitening through parodic distance" (Lott 1993, 96; see also Rogin 1992). Again, this space of cultural cross-dressing is a largely masculine ideological field.

In these Americanizing rituals, however, black peoples themselves are absent and, in a significant way, erased. From the very beginning of discussions and accounts of the form, the fact of white impersonation was forgotten. The performers became "those amusing darkies" or "the negroes" even in the most serious discussions of blackface and its meaning, as if the originals were in some way lost (Lott 1993, 98). Behaviors that simultaneously involve amnesia and impersonation—erasure and enactment—are not socially unusual. They mark a relation between surrogacy and effigy central to the creation of circum-Atlantic identities. Roach argues that "public enactments of forgetting" or "dramas of sacrificial substitution" (Roach 1996, 3) in spectacles of cultural surrogation were crucial to the self-inventions of modern "cultures." The surrogated double is often alien to the culture that stages it; signs of the socially marginal may provide the cultural idioms through which communities assert identity. What is socially peripheral may well be symbolically central (Stallybrass and White 1986, 5).

As Roach eloquently phrases it, "[T]he relentless search for the purity of origins is a voyage not of discovery, but of erasure" (Roach 1996, 6). What is erased, of course, is both the mixtures, blends, and hybridities in the histories of a people and the contemporary social life of those others whose cultural forms are appropriated in the displacement of memory into more amenable representations. The violence instrumental to the creation of America is forgotten, as is the actual life of indigenous peoples, whose return is nonetheless staged by the performative occupation of their caricatured bodies. Their difference is appropriated, as it were, in effigy:

> a general phenomena of collective memory . . . [t]he effigy is a contrivance that enables the processes regulating performance—kinesthetic imagination, vortices of behavior, and displaced transmission—to produce memory through surrogation. (Roach 1996, 36)

As a noun, the effigy is a pictured likeness or crudely fabricated image, but as a verb, "it means to evoke an absence, to body something forth, especially something from a distant past" (Roach 1996, 36). In sports arenas I suggest that we see

> more elusive but more powerful effigies fashioned from flesh. Such effigies are made by performances. They consist of a set of actions that hold open a place in memory into which many different people may step according to circumstances and occasions . . . performed effigies—those fabricated from human bodies and the associations they evoke—provide communities with a method of perpetuating themselves through specially nominated mediums or surrogates. (Roach 1996, 36)

Blackface minstrelsy "functioned as a dominant cultural figuration of black people that covered up the people themselves" (Lott 1993, 99) and held them captive to representations constructed by others. It took years to loosen the grip of such stereotypes on the popular imagination. Today, indigenous peoples in North America are similarly disguised, dissimulated, and disempowered by representations that have less to do with their culture than with mediated white responses to it, refracted through racist impositions. The enactment of Indianness in athletic arenas, held constant by the totemic power of the trademark form, functions, I suggest, as a contemporary form of whiteface minstrelsy, hence the special disturbance Native peoples voice when African Americans don "Indian" regalia in the contexts of sports events and the hostility expressed at the hypocrisy of another historically oppressed and stereotyped minority engaged in such behavior. This disturbance registers an implicit recognition that the black is not only caricaturing the "Indian" in such moments but also is asserting his "whiteness" in so doing.

Just as blackface minstrelsy had disastrous consequences for black social representation, Native Americans have suffered a continuing erasure in the public sphere as a living people by virtue of the ubiquity of the stereotypes of popular culture. An extended period of Native American political powerlessness and exclusion from the public sphere has enabled stereotypes to become ingrained in American memory. Today, many Native Americans feel that their presence as stereotypical images is stronger and more visible than the conditions of their lives, their poverty, and their political struggles. Legally, Native Americans are again disenfranchised by virtue of this history of powerlessness and representation because laws of trademark privilege dominant public meanings in the allocation of rights. Here, critics of native people's complaints about trademarks unconsciously articulate the law's logic when they assert that whatever the mark might have originally represented, it no longer has this meaning. Such nicknames, mascots, and rituals are not racist, they suggest, because through their longevity they have acquired a separate meaning apart from whatever Indian origins they might have had—they are now primarily and most meaningfully aspects of the traditions of the teams they distinguish. So, for example, John Cooke asserts that the word "Redskins" simply means football in Washington, D.C., and the NFL commissioner can quite plausibly state that "fans don't identify, for example, Redskins with Native Americans."[21]

The legal doctrine of secondary meaning supports these claims. To the extent that a descriptive term has come by extensive use as a mark in commerce to be associated with a particular manufacturer, retailer, or service provider, it will be recognized as a signifier to which he has exclusive rights, by virtue of the fact that the public now associates the term with his wares. For Native peoples, however, these new meanings and their public recognition are products of (and an ongoing source of) the injustices they have historically suffered. Many Native American names, for example, are more prominent because of their mass reproduction as trademarks than are their original referents. People hear the term "Winnebago" used to refer to vehicles more often than they do to refer to a people; they are more likely to know Oneida as a silverware than as a tribal group in Wisconsin and more likely to recognize Pontiac as a brand of car than as a great historical statesman.

To tell Native Americans that these terms no longer refer to them is not to make a mistake of fact but simply to reiterate this injury. It is yet another of the many ways in which Native Americans are reminded of their symbolic status as an invisible, vanquished, and vanishing peoples, whose images serve primarily as effigies in national culture. Victims of the frontier and symbols of its loss in the nation's imaginary, they have figured as a meaningful absence for so long that their contemporary presence struggles to find visibility and voice. Commercial imitations of their embodied alterity mark their continuing colonization in mass-mediated culture, precluding full political engagement in the public sphere.

We know, however, that "in the objectification of the scopic drive there is always the threatened return of the look" (Bhabha 1994, 81). If the powers bestowed by trademark laws serve primarily to protect the entrenched privileges of those who hold proprietary rights in these stereotypes, the economic and symbolic power of the trademark ironically also provides sites for emergent forms of counterpublicity. The very public recognition that makes a trademark so valuable provides public opportunities to effect forms of detournment that American Indian media activists and their supporters have ingeniously exploited. The annual nature of sports spectacles affords regular occasions for counterpublicity as do the accomplishments of teams that bring them to media center stage. At such times, the nicknames, mascots, and other marks of team distinction are pervasive, and anything relating to these teams is news, likely to attract national media coverage. Ironically, then, Native Americans may receive more public attention and media respect (as well as new hostilities) for their grievances and problems at precisely the moments when these stereotypes are most prominent. As Vernon Bellecourt of the National Coalition Against Racism in Sports and Media ruefully acknowledges, unlike so many other Native

American issues, "a story about the offensiveness of the name of a football team will get coverage from coast to coast" (cited in Grow 1982). On occasion, protesters have mimicked the forms of corporeal specularity endemic to sports arenas to make their point. Cross-dressing as "pilgrims" and "Quakers" at sports events for media consumption, Indian activists have appropriated their opponents' practices of embodying alterity in their tactics of counterpublicity. The real challenge for Native activists may be to use the media attention that accrues goodwill for the trademark to dispel old stereotypes and to educate the public about a wider range of Indian social concerns.

A quarter century of protest has failed to erase racist stereotypes in professional sports arenas (although reforms at the level of primary, high school, and college athletics have been effected, state legislatures have shown support, and media sympathy for the issue has grown). Legal grounds are increasingly proffered for challenging the intellectual property rights in such images—including trademark expungement proceedings, defamation suits, passing-off litigation, publicity rights claims, and state civil rights actions—the most ambitious of these being the effort to seek cancellation of federal registration for the "Redskins" trademark. Legal challenges to the use of these marks have thus far failed to induce any professional teams to change their names, but they too serve to keep the issue of racism toward Native Americans in the national spotlight. They also create negative publicity for team owners, a form of pressure that might ultimately yield other dividends for Indian peoples. To be effective, however, pressure on trademark holders who exploit embodied alterity need not necessarily be so direct, as the following discussion of trademark rumors will illustrate.

Trademark Rumors and Corporeal Vulnerability

> FILAR brand sportswear became popular amongst inner city youth who used the expensive goods to mark local hierarchies. Once aware of their products' popularity amongst minority youth, the manufacturer targeted this market with a new jean carrying the trademark "TAG." Amongst gang members, a kill is called a tag. Accusations circulated that the corporation was deliberately promoting violence.[22]

Rumors of corporate promotion of violence through the deployment of trademarks allude to an anxiety at the heart of consumer cultures; they may also constitute a unique form of cultural politics. The nature of corporate power, I will suggest, is both acknowledged and (temporarily) arrested in the rumors that people spread about the meanings of corporate trademarks. Indirectly commenting on corporately disseminated and mass-mediated "culture" in so-called postindustrial societies and registering an anxiety about corporate anonymity, they provoke corporate publicity efforts and may compel companies to assume higher profiles and new social obligations.

As production moves offshore and industrial landscapes become further removed from the "imaginary space of postmodernity," the power of corporations becomes increasingly dematerialized. Corporate presence in the public sphere is reduced to publicity relations and the ubiquitous presence of brand names, company logos, and advertising lingo—different manifestations of the corporate trademark. Rumors, Bhabha suggests, "weave their stories around the disjunctive 'present' or the 'not-there' of discourse" (cited in Barnet and Cavanagh 1994, 200). In the disembodied presence of the corporation and the "not-there" of production, trademark rumors assume significance.

In the distribution of (often functionally indistinguishable) mass-market goods, trademarks have become an increasingly important site for capital investment. In the late twentieth century, the focus of commodity fetishism shifts from products to the sign values that can be made to imbue and surround products with significance. Value lies increasingly in intangibles—well-known brand names, advertising auras, and captivating slogans. Distinctive signifiers may be the most valuable assets a company owns.

Trademarks legally mark a unique source of origin for mass-produced goods, but it is very difficult for consumers to trace them back to any singular location given the complexities of corporate ownership and licensing arrangements. The brand name or logo marks an imaginary moment of contact or manufacture—in its mass-media circulation it conjures up a mysterious source of origin while it magically garners goodwill for its invisible owner.

The most famous marks receive the greatest legal protection; through legal doctrines that permit companies to preclude the "dilution" of the positive valences of their marks, corporations with large market shares are enabled to immunize themselves against oppositional cultural strategies. Attempts to contain tactical appropriations of corporate marks of power are not, however, always successful; clearly this is the case in instances of trademark rumor. Elusive and transitive, anonymous and without origin, rumors belong to no one but are possessed by all. Without identifiable source, they circulate without accountability, making them available for insurgency. Their transitivity also makes them tactically powerful as a subaltern means of communication (Spivak, cited in Guha and Spivak 1988).

> Its intersubjective, communal adhesiveness lies in its enunciative aspect. Its performative power of circulation results in the contagious spreading, . . . the iterative action of rumour, its *circulation* and *contagion,* links it with panic—as one of the *affects* of insurgency . . . uncertainty and panic is generated when an old and familiar symbol develops an unfamiliar social significance as sign through a transformation of the temporality of its representation. (Bhabha 1994, 200, 202)

In rumors, Bhabha suggests, everyday and commonplace forms are transformed in archaic, awesome, and terrifying figurations; the circulation of cultural codes is disturbed by new and awful valences" (Bhabha 1994, 202).

> In the habitus of death and the daemonic, reverberates a form of memory that survives the sign. . . . And then suddenly from the space of the *not-there,* emerges the re-membered historical agency "manifestly directed towards the memory of truth which lies in the order of symbols . . ." by which marginalized or insurgent subjects create a collective agency. (Bhabha 1994, 199–200)

Demonic others figure in many consumer rumors, and the devil seems to assume the image of evil most compelling in the spheres in which it circulates. Ku Klux Klan rumors, for example, circulate among African Americans in postindustrial enclaves; targeting corporate powers by focusing on their trademarks, they register historical legacies of hostility, anger, and distrust of white authorities. Let me repeat one such rumor before exploring the import of such interventions in contemporary public spheres.

A line of sportswear was introduced into inner-city communities in the mid-1980s under the name "Troop." As I have suggested elsewhere, the marketing campaign for the goods capitalized on an incipient male military aesthetic among black youth (Coombe 1993). Reports on community radio stations alerted consumers that the Troop trademark was owned by the Ku Klux Klan, which was deploying the mark to create public perception of an inner-city militia as a means to legitimate and fund the Klan's own paramilitary operations.[23] Troop Sport, however, was a New York firm owned by Korean and American entrepreneurs with production operations based in Asia. No Klan affiliations could be established. This errant rumor (Spivak 1988) captured the public imagination:

> A Chicago variation of the rumor has rap singer L.L. Cool J. ripping off a Troop jacket on the Oprah show and accusing the firm of hating blacks. The singer has never appeared on the talk show. . . . In Memphis, the rumor was that the letters in Troop stood for: To Rule Over Our Oppressed People. And in Atlanta some believed that the words "Thank you nigger for making us rich" were emblazoned inside the tread of Troop's tennis shoes . . . Troop's [black] marketing director . . . [claims] that he has gone to great lengths to disprove the alleged Klan connection. "I went to Montgomery, Alabama to a store and cut open five pairs to prove it wasn't like that." ("Klan Rumor Helped Ruin Sport Clothing Firm," *San Francisco Chronicle,* July 22, 1989)

To counter the rumor, the company affirmed its allegiance to civil rights, and a $200,000 public relations effort enlisted the aid of Operation Push, the National Association for the Advancement of Colored People (NAACP), as well as black musicians and athletes. Black students were awarded scholarships, alliances were forged with black fraternities, and anti-Klan posters were distributed. Soon after, the company filed for bankruptcy. Whatever the primary cause of its business misfortunes, the injuries the rumors did to the company's reputation cannot be denied.

Black response to the Troop marketing strategy—the Ku Klux Klan rumor—although false, served to connote historical truths about black male subordination. The Troop marketing strategy stirred something in the political unconscious of black Americans that surfaced in the form of a fantastic recognition of black social identity. British Knights running shoes and Reebok shoes have also been visited with accusations and beliefs about Klan affiliations (in the Reebok case, support of South African apartheid was an accompanying theme). Like Troop, Reebok publicly disclaimed the Klan affiliation and went to great lengths to repair the company's image, sending representatives out on the road to speak with African American community groups, employing black athletes to speak on its behalf, and declaring its political commitments to human rights and "a responsible corporate America" (Turner 1993, 131).

Although academic folklorists have little to say about the significance of trademarks in "mercantile legends," the following speculation by Gary Alan Fine seems apposite:

> [T]he social-psychological rationale of these attitudes seems based on the separation of the public from the means of production and distribution . . . separating people from the

> means of production under capitalism will result in alienation; this alienation provides a psychological climate in which bogey legends can flourish. (Fine 1985, 80)

Companies at the center of such rumors are usually well known (or at least their trademarks are) and deal almost exclusively in consumer products. The management and production operations of such corporations are more anonymous: "these rumors symbolically mirror the ambivalence between knowledge of the product and ignorance of the individuals who direct the creation and marketing of these products" (Fine 1990, 144).

In conditions of postmodernity, I have elsewhere speculated, demonic others are used to indict systems of consumer capitalism in which the symbols that convey commodities are abstracted from the sources of their production and alienated from social constellations of meaning. Fetishes of evil are addressed and attached to the fetishism of the commodity/sign (see Coombe 1993, 1997). Trademark rumors cannot, however, be reduced to any absolute alienation; to do so is to miss their socially symbolic content. Such rumors seem to articulate a local awareness of historical and contemporary subject positionings in the political economy of capital accumulation. Rumors attach to specific goods with specific advertising strategies that may assume particular local meanings in the context of such histories. Contemporary Ku Klux Klan rumors, for example, continue a tradition of inner-city urban folklore that focuses on the imperiled black body and its markings by and for the purposes of others.[24] They serve both as reminders of black bodily experience and as acts of collective self-recognition in black communities.

It is perhaps not incidental or accidental that so many of these rumors focus on sportswear and sporting goods, given the significance of athletics as a potential field of upward mobility for black youth and as the domain from which so many symbols of status aspirations are drawn. I have explored the Troop rumor in more detail elsewhere as evidence of an anxiety about white enmity consequent on the experience of having local black signif(y)ing practices appropriated and projected back on the community by anonymous forces of white capital.[25] The Knights and Reebok rumors also register anxieties in the black public sphere. Certainly the rage for athletic footwear in the 1980s concerned many in black communities. Some black leaders accuse athletic-wear companies of stoking confrontational violence by inspiring lust for their goods. In 1990, for example, the Reverend Jesse Jackson urged black consumers to boycott products manufactured by Nike because the company had shown so little corporate responsibility toward the black community.

Although it is the world's largest athletic footwear manufacturer, Reebok's vision of American corporate responsibility did not seem to include the provision of any manufacturing jobs in the African American communities that constituted so great a share of its market. Like other corporations, it has adopted strategies of flexible capital accumulation, shifting the place(s) of its production operations to take advantage of low-wage labor and legislative regimes that impose the least onerous regulatory constraints on its operations. The effects of global capitalist restructuring have been particularly grave for African Americans, whose neighborhoods have been left economically devastated by its attendant spatial transformations (Dawson 1994).

Like Troop and other athletic-wear companies, Reebok's manufacturing operations are located in China and Southeast Asia (see Barnet and Cavanagh 1994). Reebok typifies a pattern of disinvestment in black communities that grew throughout the 1980s—providing only low-wage service-level jobs without benefits or security and only to those youth able to commute to their retail outlets. Their shoes might retail for $50 to $150, but they may be produced (largely by women and children) in minimal-wage sweatshop conditions, subcontracting arrangements, or export-processing zones to increase profit margins. These conditions of production or, indeed, any places of manufacture for the consumer goods with which African Americans mark status distinctions have no visible presence in black communities. This makes rumors of demonic production and distribution more compelling than they might be if African Americans had any role in the goods' manufacture.

These rumors focus on the racial body and its surveillance and susceptibility in the United States. They remark a suppressed subaltern truth by pointing to the bodily vulnerability of those whom American industry has controlled, contained, and ultimately discarded as redundant, given contemporary economic conditions. Rumor, then, may be seen as a form of resistance—one of the few "weapons of the weak" in a society where culture is commodified and controlled from indeterminate sources. The "folk idioms of late-twentieth-century life" are resources with which marginalized consumers contest "ubiquitous billboards, glossy advertisements, coupons, and television commercials" (Turner 1993). Moreover, rumors spread in a fashion that mimics the mode in which the trademark itself makes its way into the public sphere. The nature of signifying power shapes the form of the appropriations it engenders. If mass media provide a surplus of anonymous, fleeting signifiers characterized by a dearth of meaning and an excess of fascination, they also seem to invite tactics of counterpublicity with similar characteristics. Traveling anonymously and without clear meaning, authority, or direction, rumors colonize the media in much the same way as the trademark does. Such forms of counterpublicity reproduce patterns of commercial speech. The anonymous signs of mass-mediated corporate capital provoke anonymous others to mimic the mass circulation of commodity/signs with any means of mass reproduction accessible—graffiti, billboard defacement, sandwich boards, T-shirts, bumper stickers, talk shows, and hot lines are typical mediums used to repeat rumors—seizing the authority of the mass media to legitimate African American knowledge of their perceived bodily excess and real corporeal vulnerability.

Such subaltern forms of counterpublicity inevitably provoke corporate response; anonymous appropriations compel corporate actors to assume greater public presence. They may provoke some companies to make more political commitments—Troop Sport and Reebok were pushed into overt political engagement and greater solidarity with African American communities and concerns. Corporate authorities often seek black authorities to validate their own benign intentions and in so doing publicly affirm the specificities of their consumer base (which may involve the provision of education and employment opportunities as well as more obvious incidents of spin doctoring).

Such rumors may be seen as political in their significance if not in their intent. As Bhabha remarks, "What articulates these sites of cultural difference and social antagonism, in the absence of the validity of interpretation, is a discourse of panic that suggests that psychic affect and social fantasy are potent forms of political identity and agency for guerrilla warfare" (Bhabha 1994, 203). The massive investments that manufacturers make to counter the influence of rumors also suggest that they are not ineffective interventions in the public sphere (cited in Turner 1993).

The Celebrity and the Sweated Body

Trademark rumors are an indirect and subaltern means of calling corporations into account by posing a threat to the exchange value of the commodity/sign. If such rumors indirectly challenge dominant regimes of commodity fetishism, more direct oppositions to the political economy of the commodity/sign are emergent. While manufacturers have only reluctantly been dragged into the public sphere by the proliferation of rumors, others with economic interests in maintaining the value of their trademarks have been more directly challenged. For years, laws protecting publicity rights have enabled the famous to capitalize on their celebrity and license the use of their names and likenesses in commerce. Certainly many professional athletes now recognize that endorsement contracts and product merchandising arrangements afford a longer term of predictable revenue than the salaries they are likely to command as players. The commodified names and images of the famous increasingly serve as trademarks in consumer markets. These postmodern authors are only now being called into account for the global production practices on which the value of their trademarks are consolidated.

The economic value of the commodity/sign has long been realized on the backs of Third World women, but only recently has this phenomenon emerged as a political issue in North American public spheres. The great numbers of sports and entertainment figures who "lend" their names to lines of sportswear and athletic equipment provide a unique opportunity to effect a form of articulatory praxis that connects the economic value of the commodity/sign achieved through the marketing of fame to the economic exploitation of those who produce the goods to which it is attached. The recent controversies attaching to the labor conditions under which goods bearing Kathie Lee Gifford's name suggest that new tactics for interrogating commodity fetishism are emergent.

The law recognizes rights of commercial exploitation of personality only to the extent that the public associates the name, image, likeness, or other attribute with a particular individual. The celebrity is effectively capitalizing on public recognition (as in the law of trademark proper, she is deemed to own the meanings the public bestows on her image as proprietary value). Only to the extent that such recognition is positive, however, are corporations likely to extend endorsement privileges, and such public figures may also be under contractual obligations to monitor their behavior (and their press) so as not to tarnish their public image. Precisely because the trademark in such instances is the persona of a prominent individual, a singular target of cultural authority is available for alternative assertions and associations.

Few were impressed when Gifford, who made $5 million for her Wal-Mart "sportswear" line in 1995 alone, claimed that she was simply unaware that the clothing was produced by underage girls in Honduran sweatshops (and, it soon appeared, in New York City). When at first she appeared unconcerned with the girls who worked in these conditions (engaging in an angry tirade against the labor activist who "outed" her and threatening to sue him), public opinion was not entirely sympathetic. Having consolidated her fame propounding Christian virtues, traditional family values, and a devotion to child welfare, charges of hypocrisy were inevitable. As one television commentator put it, "[T]hey hit her slam bang right where she lives" (Rook 1996). As one caller to a national talk show declared, "Kathie Lee is responsible. That's how she makes her money, on the name Kathie

Lee . . . when you're making money on your name, you're responsible for what's sold under that name" (Rook 1996).

Not unsurprisingly, Gifford realized (with the assistance of Howard Rubenstein Associates) that the ongoing marketing value of her persona would be better served by a more overt show of concern for those whose labor commanded 31 cents an hour in the production of goods bearing her smiling face and her dedication to children's charities. Her decision to "do the right thing" and take up the cause of workers in the garment industry may be greeted with some cynicism. However, there is no denying the political boost that this gave to labor activists in North America and abroad. As one editorial suggests, "Like it or not, Gifford's association with the sweatshops will probably do more to target outrage than a lifetime's worth of published investigative reports about the abuses" (*San Francisco Chronicle,* June 11, 1996, A22).

"Here's the difference between Kathie Lee and normal shit," says Jim Dwyer, the *Daily News* columnist who broke the sweatshop story that sent Frank Gifford scurrying to West Thirty-eighth Street with crisp bills the next morning. "Last year, I did a column on kids working in a sweatshop in Sunset Park, Brooklyn. They were working 80 hours a week, no minimum wage, no overtime, terrible conditions. It got no attention at all. Zip. Zero. Now we have Kathie Lee. It's five weeks later, and $40,000 in fines and $20,000 in back wages have been paid by the owners, and there's a national forum about the issue. . . . All because of one celebrity, who is famous for *what?*" (cited in Lippert 1996).

Testifying before congressional human rights subcommittees, helping to ensure participation at a Fashion Industry Forum organized by Secretary of Labor Robert Reich, pressing other celebrities into assuming responsibility for the conditions under which their clothing lines are produced, and building public support for greater numbers of inspectors to monitor factory conditions, Gifford's activities suggest hidden political possibilities for a renewed social realism in the hyperreality of celebrity. With the cooperation of her football hero husband, still a player in professional sports arenas, she was uniquely situated to publicize and put pressure on those who benefit from the legal protection of celebrity and extend more concrete protections to others. There is no guarantee that celebrities like Michael Jordan—who pitches Nike products produced by children in conditions that are alleged to involve forced labor, coerced overtime, and physical abuse—will do any more than shrug their shoulders and hope that "Nike will do the right thing, whatever that might be."[26] On the other hand, every public assertion of lack of concern has a price in terms of the merchandising value of the celebrity persona, even in the eyes of the corporations that exploit their publicity values. It is too early to tell what the ultimate consequences of these articulatory practices will be, but the legal protection of the celebrity form has provided a new site for rendering authorities accountable, publicizing the neocolonial conditions that underlie postmodern authorship, and exposing the lie of a "postindustrial" society.

Conclusion

Practices of authorial power and appropriation, authorized meanings and alternative renderings, and owner's interests and other's needs cannot be addressed simply in terms of dichotomies like domination and resistance, however. Romantic celebrations of insurrectionary alterity—too popular in cultural studies—cannot capture the dangerous nuances of cultural appropriation in circumstances where the very resources with which people express alterity are the properties of others. Acts of transgression, though multiply motivated, are also shaped by the juridical fields of power in which they intervene. Law provides means and forums for both legitimating and contesting dominant meanings and the social hierarchies they support.

Law is not simply an institutional forum or legitimating discourse to which social groups turn to have preexisting differences recognized; more crucially, it is a central locus for the control and dissemination of those signifying forms with which social meanings are made and remade. The signifying forms around which political action mobilizes and with which social rearticulations are accomplished are attractive and compelling precisely because of the qualities of the powers legally bestowed on them. Such mobilizations and new articulations may have political consequence when they "provoke a crisis within the process of signification and discursive address" (Bhabha 1990).

The law creates spaces in which hegemonic struggles are enacted as well as signs and symbols whose connotations are always ever at risk. Legal strategies and legal institutions may lend authority to certain interpretations while denying status to others. The recodings, reworkings, and reactivations of commodified texts celebrated in many variants of cultural studies are possible only given the contingent fixities enabled by the law's proprietary guarantees. Had intellectual property laws not protected such texts in the first instance, they would not have acquired the posterity that makes them such ideal candidates for parodic and polemic redeployments. Law's productive power as well as its sanctions and prohibitions, then, must be kept continually in mind.

The constitutive power of law is not simply the provision of instruments and forums through which social groups may seek to have their differences legitimated or their needs addressed (although it may be experienced in this fashion). Law also generates many of the signs and symbols—the signifying forms—with which difference is constituted and given meaning. It provides those unstable signifiers whose meanings may be historically transformed by those who wish to inscribe their own authorial signature on the people, the nation, the state—the official social text. It invites and shapes activities that legitimate, resist, and potentially rework the meanings that accrue to these forms in public spheres. Such processes of institutionalization and intervention are both ongoing and unstable, effecting unanticipated disruptions and destabilizations.

Social struggles focusing on sports trademarks serve to illustrate the importance of the commodity/sign in contemporary public spheres—its modalities of signification and significance—bespeaking their allure as visual symbols of power, their capacity to interpellate subaltern subjects, and their service as sites for transgressive articulations. They enable us to see how trademarks figure in the making of imagined communities—bodies politic—and in the making and remaking of minority subjects—the racialized bodies of contemporary body politics. They remind us of the creative activities of those marginal to centers of symbolic authority who are marked by a relationship to signs they do not author but often alter in their struggles for recognition and voice. They may also attest to an emergent receptivity to articulatory practices that reconnect the postmodern, the postindustrial, and the postcolonial with the practices of bodily exploitation they avoid and obscure. Contemporary means of publicity may, ironically, provide both new inclinations and new capacities to challenge the very commodity fetishism that gives them their force.

Notes

1. With the exception of the discussion of Kathie Lee Gifford and Michael Jordan, these examples are drawn from Coombe (1998), a work that deals with the effects of copyright, design patents, trademarks, rights of publicity, and merchandising in shaping North American cultural politics.

2. See discussions in Coombe (1996a, 1996c).

3. The story circulates in Toronto, and I first heard it from sociologist Mariana Valverde in the form quoted. I later learned from a friend of one of the organizers that the sign had been conceptualized as part of a citywide progressive art exhibit by Public, a nonprofit arts organization. Before it was broadcast, lawyers advised the group of their potential liability and the likelihood of injunction. A decision was made not to convey the message, but the story circulates as if the event had taken place—an apocryphal rumor that bespeaks a truth about gay and lesbian citizenship in Canada. Given the significance I attribute to rumor, it seems an especially apt anecdote.

4. In Canada, "Section 11 of the Trade Marks Act now prohibits the use in connection with a business, as a trademark or otherwise, of any mark adopted contrary to ss. 9 and 10 of the Trade Marks Act . . . no penalty is provided in the statute for the adoption and use of any such marks and s.107 of the Criminal Code, therefore, becomes applicable" (Fox 1972).

5. In Canada there are over 3,000 of these signs. Listed under Section 9 of the Trade Marks Act R.S.C. 1985, c.T-13, are sixteen categories of prohibited marks, including a category that includes "any . . . mark . . . adopted and used by any public authority in Canada as an official mark for wares and services, in respect of which, the Registrar . . . has given public notice of its adoption and use." It is impossible to know how many marks are so protected in the United States because the costs of doing searches are so exorbitant as to preclude a complete compilation. In early editions of his treatise (see, e.g., McCarty), McCarty includes a list of many federally protected names, characters, and designs but specifies that the list is neither complete nor exhaustive.

6. In Canada, for example, "Section 9 supports public order and as such places the Crown and public authorities in a position of virtual invulnerability. An official mark is virtually unexpungeable" (Hughes 1992).

7. 36 U.S.C. §371–396 (1988). In particular, Section 110 of the act, set forth in 36 U.S.C. §380 (1988), provides that without consent of the USOC, "any person who uses for the purpose of trade, to induce the sale of any goods or services, or to induce the sale of any goods or services to promote any theatrical exhibition, athletic performance, or competition—. . . the words "Olympic," "Olympian,". . . tending to cause confusion, to cause mistake, to deceive, or to falsely suggest a connection with the [USOC] or any Olympic activity shall be subject to suit in a civil action by the [USOC] for the remedies provided in [the Lanham Act] and that "the [USOC] shall have exclusive right to use . . . the words, "Olympic," "Olympian," [etc.] subject only to lawful uses of these words established prior to 1950.

8. Moreover, it was determined that there were no defenses available to anyone who used the term without authorization. *San Francisco Arts & Athletics, Inc. v. United States Olympic Committee,* 107 S. Ct. 2971 (1987).

9. *International Olympic Committee v. San Francisco Arts & Athletics,* 789 F. 2d 1319 at 1323 (per Kozinski, J.).

10. The historical discussion of U.S. trademark law is drawn from Coombe (1996b), in which I discuss further examples, outside of sports arenas, of instances in which the boundaries of national frontiers are negotiated in commercial idioms.

11. For examples, see Garnham (1993), Polan (1993), and Warner (1993). I use the term

"commodity/sign" to reflect the fact that the trademark is both a commodity with an exchange value in its own right and a sign that condenses a relationship between a signifier, a signified, and a referent (linking, e.g., a logo, a lifestyle, and a product, respectively).

12. See McClintock (1995). For discussions of images of alterity in advertising and with respect to consumer goods, see Stedman (1982), Van Nederveen (1992), O'Barr (1994), and Turner (1994).

13. Jowett (1982). Although I recognize the political difficulties involved in the use of the term "American" to refer to things pertaining only to the United States, the term was the indigenous term of national belonging in the period under examination. I have chosen to avoid using quotation marks around the term in every instance that I evoke it on the basis that I evoke it only insofar as it figures in national rhetoric and do not endorse a political position in so doing.

14. See Strasser (1989) and Tedlow (1990). For an informative hagiography, see Marquette (1966).

15. A report in *USA Today* estimated a cost of $25,000 to $100,000 in marketing and research efforts. See Mihoces (1993).

16. For an excellent survey of the arguments, citing a wealth of press reports, see Kelber (1994), and Pace (1994). Ward Churchill (1994) is one of the more prolific of indigenous activists, arguing that the commercialization of native culture undermines Indian political self-determination. His writings on the topic are collected in his *Indians Are Us? Culture and Genocide in Native North America.* My own understanding of the issue was greatly enlightened by Indian activists and supporters who attended the conference "The Commercial Appropriation of Tradition: Legal Challenges and Legal Remedies," which I co-organized with Nell Newton and Peter Jaszi at the Washington College of Law, American University, April 15–18, 1992. I thank Vernon Bellecourt, Johnny Bearcub-Stiffarm, Sam Deloria, Robert Gough, Michael Haney, Ted Jojola, and Charlene Teeters as well as Brian St. Laurent for the education. Collected background readings from the conference are available from Nell Newton at the University of Denver Law School.

17. Shuman (1996), citing Giago. See also Giago (1995).

18. Ritter (1995). Illinois Governor Jim Edgar deemed the mascot an "honored symbol" in 1995. The U.S. Department of Education determined that the mascot did not create an environment hostile to American Indians and thus did not violate federal civil rights legislation.

19. See also Slotkin (1973), Pearce (1988), Truettner (1991), Francis (1994), Root (1996), and Ziff and Rao (1997).

20. "Kinesthetic imagination is a faculty of memory [that] . . . inhabits the realm of the virtual . . . its truth is the truth of stimulation, of fantasy (although its social effects may be tangible indeed)" (Roach 1996).

21. Cited in Kelber (1994). Some fans see these team names as more properly attributes of their *own* familial, regional, or gender identities than as anything belonging to Indians. Indeed, some journalists have suggested that these symbols are now primarily American: "The United States is a melting pot, a unique blend of people from all over the world. Among the ways we celebrate this diversity is by learning the customs and history of all ethnic groups. Indian words and symbols belong to all of us as much as the music, dance and dress of Scotland and other cultures. No disrespect intended" (McEwen 1995).

22. Rumor reported to me by an anthropology graduate student at the Cultural Anthropology Meetings in 1994.

23. I am grateful to Kathleen Pirrie Adams for her insights into this issue.

24. Apologists for slavery in the eighteenth and nineteenth centuries often claimed that Africans had been visited with an ancient, if not biblical, "curse" that "marked" them for slav-

ery. See discussion in Roberts (1994). Hortense Spillers (1987) remarks, "We might well ask if this phenomenon of marking and branding actually 'transfers' from one generation to another, finding various symbolic substitutions in an efficacy of meanings that repeat the initiating moments." Elizabeth Alexander (1994) discusses embodied memories as consolidating "group affiliation by making blackness an unavoidable, irreducible sign which, despite its abjection leaves creative space for group self-definition and self-knowledge." Ku Klux Klan rumors, I believe, are instances of this memory and creative self-recognition.

25. See Coombe (1997). In summary: in the fashion in which it targeted black male consumers, the Troop advertising campaign was designed to mark a *difference.* The pseudomilitary character of the product might be seen to mark young black men (while inviting them to brand themselves) as recruitable subordinates. If, as Michelle Wallace suggests, slavery and its aftermath have left blacks feeling exiled from their own bodies and black culture continually reincorporates the "negative" or "racist" imagery of the dominant culture, then black male youth's adoption of a military aesthetic may be seen as a form of signifying: It employs figurative rhetorical strategies that repeat and imitate elements of dominant culture while critically marking a difference. The conversion of the signs of military conscription into a subcultural aesthetic of resistance was deployed by Troop Sport as a source of profitable distinction in the market. The appropriation and projection back on blacks of their own signifying by anonymous forces of capital—an inversion of their inversion—created that affect of panic to which Bhabha alludes.

26. As quoted in Brewer (1996), in a discussion of labor conditions in Southeast Asia, where many sporting goods manufacturers have their products made.

References

Alexander, Elizabeth. 1994. "Can You Be BLACK and Look at This? Reading the Rodney King Video(s)." *Public Culture* 7: 77–96.

Barnet, Richard, and John Cavanagh. 1994. *Global Dreams: Imperial Corporations and the New World Order.* New York: Simon & Schuster.

Baudrillard, Jean. 1981. *For a Critique of the Political Economy of the Sign.* St. Louis: Telos Press.

Berkhofer, Robert F., Jr. 1979. *The White Man's Indian: Images of the American Indian from Columbus to the Present.* New York: Vintage Books.

Bhabha, Homi. 1990. "DissemiNation: Time, Narrative, and the Margins of the Modern Nation." In *Nation and Narration* (291–322). London: Routledge.

———. 1994. *The Location of Culture.* London: Routledge.

Bourdieu, Pierre. 1990. "Programme for a Sociology of Sport." In *In Other Words: Essays towards a Reflexive Sociology* (156–67). Stanford, Calif.: Stanford University Press.

Brewer, Caroline. 1996. "Disney, Others Profit by Exploiting Child Labor." *The Bergen Record,* June 18, N11.

Burkhart, Dan. 1991. "Turner Won't Change Braves' Name, but Wouldn't Mind Stopping the Chop." *Atlanta Journal,* December 3, F8.

Churchill, Ward. 1994. *Indians Are Us? Culture and Genocide in Native North America.* Toronto: Between the Lines Press.

Coombe, Rosemary J. 1991. "Objects of Property and Subjects of Politics: Intellectual Property Laws and Democratic Dialogue." *Texas Law Review* 69: 1853–80.

———. 1993. "Tactics of Appropriation and the Politics of Recognition in Late Modern Democracies." *Political Theory* 21: 411–33.

———. 1996a. "Authorial Cartographies: Mapping Proprietary Borders in a Less-Than Brave New World." *Stanford Law Review* 48: 1357–1366.

———. 1996b. "Embodied Trademarks: Mimesis and Alterity on American Commercial Frontiers." *Cultural Anthropology* 11: 202–24.

———. 1996c. "Left Out on the Information Highway." *Oregon Law Review* 75: 237–47.

———. 1997. "The Demonic Space of the 'Not There': Trademark Rumors in the Postindustrial Imaginary." In James Ferguson and Ahkil Gupta, eds., *Culture, Power, Place: Critical Explorations in Anthropology* (249–74). Durham, N.C.: Duke University Press.

———. 1998. *The Cultural Life of Intellectual Properties: Authorship, Appropriation, and the Law.* Durham, N.C.: Duke University Press.

Dawson, Michael. 1994. "A Black Counterpublic? Economic Earthquakes, Racial Agendas, and Black Politics." *Public Culture* 7: 195–223.

Fine, Gary Alan. 1985. "The Goliath Effect: Corporate Dominance and Mercantile Legends." *Journal of American Folklore* 98: 63–84.

———. 1990. "Among Those Dark Satanic Mills: Rumors of Kooks, Cults and Corporations." *Southern Folklore* 47: 133–46.

Fox, Harold G. 1972. *The Canadian Law of Trademarks and Unfair Competition.* Toronto: Carswell.

Francis, Daniel. 1994. *The Imaginary Indian: The Image of the Indian in Canadian Culture.* Vancouver: Arsenal Pulp Press.

Garnham, Nicholas. 1993. "The Mass Media, Cultural Identity, and the Public Sphere in the Modern World." *Public Culture* 5: 251–65.

Giago, Tim. 1995. "Indian-Named Mascots Like Those in World Series Assault Self Esteem." *The Buffalo News,* October 26, 3.

Grow, Doug. 1992. "The Way to Redskins Owner's Heart Is through His Wallet." *Star Tribune,* September 11, 3B.

Guha, Ranajit, and Gayatri C. Spivak, eds. 1988. "Subaltern Studies: Deconstructing Historiography." In *Selected Subaltern Studies.* New York: Oxford University Press.

Hughes, Roger. 1992. *Hughes on Trademarks.* Toronto: Butterworths.

Jowett, Garth. 1982. "The Emergence of Mass Society: The Standardization of American Culture 1830–1920." *Prospects* 7: 207–28.

Kelber, Bruce C. 1994. "Scalping the Redskins: Can Trademark Law Start Athletic Teams Bearing Native American Nicknames and Images on the Road to Racial Reform?" *Hamline Law Review* 17: 533–88.

Lippert, Barbara. 1996. "How Does She Do It?" *New York Magazine,* July 22, 34–39.

Lott, Eric. 1993. *Love and Theft: Blackface, Minstrelsy and the American Working Class.* New York: Oxford University Press.

Marquette, Arthur F. 1966. *Brands, Trademarks and Goodwill: The Story of the Quaker Oats Company.* New York: McGraw-Hill.

McCarty, J. Thomas. 1984 & 1990 Supp. *Trademarks and Unfair Competition,* Vol. 2 (2d ed.) 869–72.

McClintock, Anne. 1995. *Imperial Leather: Gender, Race, and Sexuality in the Colonial Contest.* London: Routledge.

McClure, Kirsty. 1992. "The Subject of Rights." In Chantal Mouffe, ed., *Dimensions of Radical Democracy: Pluralism, Citizenship, Community* (108–27). London: Verso.

McEwen, Bill. 1995. "Great Scot! Nicknames Have Worth." *The Fresno Bee,* October 24, C1.

Michaels, Walter Benn. 1996. *Our America: Nativism, Modernism and Pluralism.* Durham, N.C.: Duke University Press.

Mihoces, Gary. 1993. "Trying to Get Handle: Possible Merchandise Bonanza Hinges on Selection." *USA Today,* September 17, 6C.

Nederveen Pieterse, Jan. 1992. *White on Black: Images of Africa and Blacks in Western Popular Culture.* New Haven, Conn.: Yale University Press.

O'Barr, William. 1994. *Culture and the Ad: Exploring the World of Otherness in the World of Advertising.* Boulder, Colo.: Westview Press.

Pace, Kimberly A. 1994. "The Washington Redskins Case and the Doctrine of Disparagement: How Politically Correct Must a Trademark Be?" *Pepperdine Law Review* 22: 7–55.

Pearce, Roy Harvey. [1953] 1988. *Savagism and Civilization: A Study of the Indian and the American Mind.* Reprint, Berkeley and Los Angeles: University of California Press.

Pierson, Don. 1992. "Redskins Nickname Will Be Protest Target." *Chicago Tribune,* January 19, C2.

Polan, Dana. 1993. "The Public's Fear: or, Media as Monster in Habermas, Negt, and Kluge." In Bruce Robbins, ed., *The Phantom Public Sphere* (33–41). Minneapolis: University of Minnesota Press.

Ritter. 1995. *The Tennessean,* December 12.

Roach, Joseph. 1996. *Cities of the Dead: Circum-Atlantic Performance.* New York: Columbia University Press.

Roberts, Diane. 1994. *The Myth of Aunt Jemima: Representing Race and Region.* New York: Routledge.

Rogin, Michael. 1992. "Blackface, White Noise: The Jewish Jazz Singer Finds His Voice." *Critical Inquiry* 12: 426.

Rook, Susan. 1996. *Talk Back Live.* Cable News Network, Inc., June 4 (transcript no. 415).

Root, Deborah. 1996. *Cannibal Culture: Art, Appropriation, and the Commodification of Difference.* Boulder, Colo.: Westview Press.

Shapiro, Leonard. 1991. "Offensive Penalty Is Called on Redskins: Native Americans Protest the Name." *Washington Post,* November 3, D1.

Shuman, Mark. 1996. "Native Voice." *The Denver Post,* January 28.

Slotkin, Richard. 1973. *Regeneration through Violence: The Mythology of the American Frontier.* Middletown, Conn.: Wesleyan University Press.

Spillers, Hortense. 1987. "Mama's Baby, Papa's Maybe: An American Grammar Book." *Diacritics* 17, no. 2: 65–81.

Stallybrass, Peter, and Allon White. 1986. *The Politics and Poetics of Transgression.* Ithaca, N.Y.: Cornell University Press.

Stedman, Raymond William. 1982. *Shadows of the Indian: Stereotypes in American Culture.* Norman: University of Oklahoma Press.

Strasser, Susan. 1989. *Satisfaction Guaranteed: The Making of the American Mass Market.* New York: Pantheon Books.

Tedlow, Richard. 1990. *New and Improved: The Story of Mass Marketing in America.* New York: Basic Books.

Truettner, William H. 1991. *The West as America: Reinterpreting Images of the Frontier.* Washington, D.C.: Smithsonian Institution Press.

Turner, Patricia. 1993. *I Heard It through the Grapevine: Rumor in African-American Culture.* Berkeley and Los Angeles: University of California Press.

———. 1994. *Ceramic Uncles and Celluloid Mammies: Black Images and Their Influence on Culture.* New York: Anchor Books.

Wakankar, Milind. 1995. "Body, Crowd, Identity: Genealogy of a Hindu Nationalist Ascetics." *Social Text* 14, no. 4: 45–73.

Warner, Michael. 1993. "The Mass Public and the Mass Subject." In Bruce Robbins, ed., *The Phantom Public Sphere* (234–56). Minneapolis: University of Minnesota Press.

Ziff, Bruce, and Pratima Rao, eds. 1997. *Borrowed Power: Essays on Cultural Appropriation.* New Brunswick, N.J.: Rutgers University Press.

3

Two-Point Conversion

Marjorie Garber

Hail Mary. A last-second pass, usually thrown toward several receivers in an area near or across the goal line in the hope (and with a prayer) that one of them will catch it.

—*THE PRO FOOTBALL FAN'S COMPANION*

The emblem of St. Lawrence, one of the most famous of Christian martyrs, is the gridiron. Little did this early deacon of Rome know how pertinent that symbol would become in the last decade of the twentieth century, when football, its coaches, its players, and its stadiums have become major purveyors of public prayer. But these days, the contest is not between the Christians and the lions. Instead the Christians *are* the Lions—and the Bears, and the Panthers, and the Jaguars, and the Saints. And—as we will see—the Patriots.

Viewers tuning in at the end of the football playoff games in January 1997 might be pardoned for thinking that they had inadvertently pushed the wrong button and wound up on Reverend Jerry Falwell's Christian television station. First, a Jacksonville Jaguars quarterback informed a sideline reporter that God was responsible for the team's victory. How did he account for his Cinderella team's success? "Thanks be to God," he said. "There's a bunch of guys on this team that really love the Lord." Then the New England Patriots' Keith Byars, on another network, began his postgame recap with "Thanks be to God from whom all blessings flow" before himself flowing seamlessly, as if it were not a change of subject, into a detailed analysis of passes, tackles, and punts. Not to be outdone, Patriots' owner Bob Kraft came out as a Jew, confiding genially to a television interviewer that coach Bill Parcells had told him he had "something Kraft would appreciate" in his pocket. That something turned out it was a "chai," the Hebrew letter that means "life," a pendant given Parcells by a friend from New Jersey that he had kept pocketed during the Patriots' lopsided 28–3 victory over the Pittsburgh Steelers. Kraft appreciated the gesture, he said—even though the charm was upside down.

A photograph of a benignly bemused Parcells holding his "chai" in one vast hand was featured on the sports page of the *Boston Globe,* which described the "Hebrew 'chai' symbol" as one of Parcells's many "superstitions," noting that baseball player Wade Boggs, formerly of the Boston Red Sox and now of the hated New York Yankees, draws a "chai" symbol "with his bat in the dirt prior to every at bat" (Cafardo 1997). (It is perhaps unnecessary to note that Boggs, like Parcells, is not Jewish.)

Although I reveled, briefly, in this moment of ecumenical team spirit (what might be called "'chai' society"), I was struck by the term "superstition." I wondered whether Red Barber would have called it a "superstition" if a Jewish professional ballplayer like Hank Greenberg or Sandy Koufax had—against all probability—drawn a cross in the dirt with his bat each time he stepped up to the plate. Certainly the word "superstition" is not routinely spoken by television sportscasters on those occasions when I have glimpsed a baseball player, often wearing a cross around his neck, make the sign of the cross before stepping into the batter's box.

As for Parcells, when asked whether (in view of the active discussion of religious faith on the part of players on both teams) he thought God would favor one side or the other, he replied judiciously, "No disrespect to anyone, but it usually works better when the players are good and fast" (Eskenazi 1997).

But players' piety has attracted more attention than the coach's realism. "God has certainly played an important role on this football team," announced Jaguars quarterback Mark Brunell to a reporter (Vega 1997). Brunell added,

> There's a lot of guys on this team who love Jesus. That's what's been exciting to me: to get to know these guys and play with them, but more importantly, to just get the chance to develop the friendship and closeness that you don't see in a lot of football teams right now.
>
> I think there's probably 10 or 15 very committed guys on this football team who love God and I firmly believe that's the reason for our success this year.
>
> God has had His hand on this football team, and the Bible says that He's looking around for people who are going to give glory to him and who are going to give Him credit. And this football team is doing that, and I think that's the reason for our success this year.
>
> [Note: The following weekend, the Jaguars lost to the New England Patriots.] [1]

Of course, the Jaguars are far from the only ostentatiously devout squad in the league. Members of the Fellowship of Christian Athletes are active in professional as well as high school and after-school sports programs. The other successful 1996 NFL expansion team, the Carolina Panthers, was praised by hometown fans in Charlotte, North Carolina: "This is the Bible Belt, and we've got a praying team," said a waitress at a soul food restaurant near the stadium. Fundamentalist preacher Joseph R. Chambers viewed the Panthers as an affirmation of "conservative values" by "a conservative city that loves the churches on every corner" (Nossiter 1997).

Former Green Bay Packer Reggie White has been an ordained minister since his college days at the University of Tennessee. During his years in the NFL, he moved from team to team on what is sometimes referred to as the Reggie White Traveling Ministry before settling with the Packers. "This guy," said a teammate, "is like God in pads. He's the most revered athlete I've ever been around" (Don Beebe, quoted in Blaudschun 1997). Some critics took issue with his religious fervor when he declared that God had ordained the Packers' NFC championship victory because that was the role He had cast for them, but in general the media and the fans have shared his teammates' respect. "He rapidly converts the doubters," one sportswriter observed. No one, as far as I know, quoted Psalm 37: "I have seen the wicked in great power, and flourishing like a green bay tree" (Psalm 37:36).

On the eve of Super Bowl XXXI, White requested airtime during the postgame ceremonies to say a public prayer before the assembled crowd and perhaps on national television—if the Packers won. Asked about the precedent of giving a microphone to someone to espouse his private views, White professed surprise: "A lot of people ask me questions about football and religion," he said. "I don't see the problem. Most of you guys [sportswriters and media critics], when we get down in the end zone and pray or get together and pray on the field, you have a real problem when it comes to that" (quoted in Smith 1997). Other members of the Packers' "God squad" framed their desire for public prayer in terms of rights. "I think it's our right," said receiver Don Beebe. "That's our field. We play football on that field."

The NFL director of communications remarked that if anyone else wanted to say a prayer to the crowd from the platform after the game, there was not much the league could do about it, but another league official expressed concern that football fans might find themselves unwittingly and unwillingly listening to a televised sermon ("Some Packers Say They Plan to Pray Publicly," *New York Times,* January 24, 1997, B13). Is this a First Amendment issue? Or is the public to be protected from intrusive, perhaps even coercive, prayer?

After Green Bay's Super Bowl victory, jubilant fans displayed banners of coach Mike Holmgren, quarterback Brett Favre, star player (and minister) Reggie White, and legendary former coach Vince Lombardi, labeled, respectively, "the father, the son, the holy, and the ghost." "It's a spiritual thing for me," said one woman who had waited hours (with 60,000 others of the faithful) at bitter-cold Lambeau Field for the Packers' return. "This is God's team" (quoted in Romell 1997).

The present trend for highly visible postgame prayer huddles in the NFL began with a December 1990 game between the New York Giants and the San Francisco 49ers at Candlestick Park. "Guys from both teams just wanted to make a statement," said 49ers tight end—and evangelical Christian—Brent Jones, who led a group of kneeling players at midfield. The game, which was televised on *Monday Night Football,* set a trend in public piety. It is worth noting that the NFL first opposed the idea, citing a league rule against opposing players "fraternizing" on the field, but an NFL official reversed the ruling after contemplating "the public relations fiasco that would follow a crackdown on prayer." Former 49er Bubba Paris, now an ordained minister and Bible teacher, noted that "you find more Christians on teams with more black players" ("Having a Prayer: Christians Are Making a Statement in the NFL," *San Francisco Chronicle,* January 22, 1997, D1). By "Christians" here, Paris and many others mean "evangelical" or "Pentecostal" or "born-again" Christians, who are often more comfortable with public demonstrations of faith than are mainline Protestants or Roman Catholics.

Indeed, Christianity and sports have long been regarded in certain parts of the United States as not only compatible but boon companions. It is no accident that the Super Bowl is played on a Sunday.

"Your Son is our quarterback and You are our coach," intoned the Catholic archbishop of Miami before a Miami Dolphins football game in the 1970s. "We sometimes get blitzed by heavy sorrows or red-dogged by Satan," announced the archbishop, to the irreverent pleasure of a staff member for the *National Catholic Reporter.* "Teach us to run the right patterns in our life so that we will truly make a touchdown one day through the heavenly gates, as the angels and saints cheer us on from the sidelines" (Kinsolving 1971, quoted in Higgs 1995). Opinions differ as to which position is the most appropriate for the Heavenly Superstar.

If Jesus played football,
he'd be an end.

begins a poem by Bill Heyen ("Until Next Time," quoted in Higgs 1995).

After his shower, he'd appear to us
to pose with us for pictures by his side.

Or, as the country music song has it, "Drop-kick me Jesus through the goalposts of life."

Some have suggested that He plays other sports. Baseball star Brett Butler testified, "I believe that if Jesus Christ was a baseball player he'd go in hard to break up the double play and then pick up the guy and say, 'I love you'" (Swan 1990, cited in Higgs 1995).

The Christian sports connection is not exclusively high or low church, Catholic or Protestant. The football stadium at Notre Dame is presided over by a huge library mural known as *Touchdown Jesus.* In the chapel of the University of the South in Sewanee, Tennessee, is a stained-glass window displaying a figure in the vestments of an Episcopal bishop, holding a football in one hand and the Book of Common Prayer in the other. At his feet is a baseball, and a baseball bat is propped against the frame.[2] The Episcopal Cathedral of St. John the Divine contains a sports bay, dedicated in 1928 to such worldly athletes as Hobey Baker, Walter Camp, and Christy Mathewson, that mingles these football and baseball heroes with biblical scenes like Jacob wrestling with the angel (Willis and Wettan 1977).[3]

It is in the evangelical churches and movements, however, that sports and religion have been most directly linked in the twentieth century, through the rise of what is now quite frankly described as "sports evangelism." So-called muscular Christianity, of the sort touted by baseball player turned evangelist Billy Sunday, loudly refuted the idea that Jesus was a weakling, a man of sorrows, a loser. "I press toward the mark for the prize of the high calling of God in Christ Jesus" (Philippians 3:14) has been described as the verse that has become "the keystone of muscular Christianity" (Higgs 1995; see also McNeille 1948). Athletic skill was a kind of Christian witness, while cheering crowds blended their enthusiasm for sports and—and as—religion.

Christian evangelists in the early and middle parts of the century deliberately made use of sporting events and sports celebrities to attract crowds and especially to win over young men to the cause. The athlete and preacher Gil Dodds ran six laps around the assembled faithful to kick off Billy Graham's revival movement in 1947. Graham himself underscored the disturbing and by now virtually inevitable association of sports, religion, and patriotism, remarking during the Vietnam War, "People who are carrying the Viet Cong flag around the country are not athletes. If our people would spend more time in gymnasiums and on playing fields, we'd be a better nation!" (Martin 1992, cited in Higgs 1995).

Today members of the Fellowship of Christian Athletes bear witness to their faith at sporting events and clinics—sometimes to the dismay of the parents of Little Leaguers inadvertently made to attend a religious rally. It is part of what Frank Deford (1976) called "sportianity" in a *Sports Illustrated* article rather pointedly called "Endorsing Jesus."

"Athletics," declared evangelist and educator Oral Roberts, "is part of our Christian witness. . . . Nearly every man in America reads the sports pages, and a Christian school cannot ignore these people. Sports are becoming the No. 1 interest of people in America."

Sports evangelism, in fact, is a booming business these days. An article suitably titled "From Muscular Christians to Jocks for Jesus," published in *Christian Century* in 1992, noted that "the press and public have struggled to make sense of the increasing number of elite athletes who proclaim their faith in Jesus" (Mathisen 1992, quoted in Higgs 1995). Robert Higgs's *God in the Stadium* reported on the Annual Sports Outreach America conference on sports evangelism. For 1995 Super Bowl Sunday, Higgs reports (quoting Harvey 1995), the Sports Outreach program distributed a twelve-minute video of religious testimony offered by NFL players that was "shown on huge screens set up in churches for this purpose and for presentation of the game." It does not take much to see that "sports evangelism" on television is a version of televangelism, and indeed, as Higgs points out, conservative ministers like Falwell, Roberts, and Pat Robertson are vociferous sports boosters, following in the evangelical footsteps of Billy Sunday and Billy Graham.

This has led to some lively exchanges between church and state or, at least, between religion and law. Irritated at the theatrical display that had become common practice among players who scored touchdowns, in 1995 the National Collegiate Athletic Association (NCAA) tried to enforce a "no-gloating" rule prohibiting self-congratulatory victory demonstrations in the end zone. But it soon found itself on the receiving end of a lawsuit from the Reverend Jerry Falwell's Liberty University, whose team customarily knelt in gratitude to thank God for enabling them to score. Liberty's evangelical Christians sued on the grounds that the prohibition violated the 1964 Civil Rights Act and was a form of religious discrimination. The NCAA, fearing that it would be targeted as an enemy of gridiron prayer, revised its ruling to allow players to pray if they did so discreetly: "Players may pray or cross themselves without drawing attention to themselves," wrote Vince Dooley, chairman of the NCAA Football Rules Committee, in a memo to coaches. "It is also permissible for them to kneel momentarily at the conclusion of a play, if in the judgment of the official the act is spontaneous and not in the nature of a pose" (Chandrasekaran 1995; Hoppe 1995; "N.C.A.A. Clarifies Rule to Permit Prayers," *New York Times,* September 2, 1995, A26). How this distinction would be regulated in church, much less on the football field, was never explained.

As Wendy Kaminer (1996) suggests, "Secularists are often wrongly accused of trying to purge religious ideas from public discourse. We simply want to deny them public sponsorship." But "new Christian advocacy groups, modeled after advocacy groups on the left, are increasingly portraying practicing Christians as citizens oppressed by secularism and are seeking judicial protection. The American Center for Law and Justice (ACLJ) founded by Pat Robertson, is one of the leaders in this movement, borrowing not only most of the acronym but the tactics of the American Civil Liberties Union in a fight for religious 'rights.'"

It is not clear how the public (or, for that matter, sports officialdom) would have responded had Reggie White's or Mark Brunell's evangelical energies been put at the service of a different faith—say, Islam. Some small indication might be found in the NBA's suspension of pro basketball player Mahmoud Abdul-Rauf, who had refused to stand during the national anthem. Abdul-Rauf, a member of the Denver Nuggets, claimed that paying homage to anything but God was idolatry and that the American flag was a symbol of oppression. While he was supported by the American Civil Liberties Union (ACLU) and the NBA players' union, some veterans groups called his behavior treasonous (Herrmann 1996; Nance 1996). The dispute was resolved when Abdul-Rauf decided to stand and pray silently during the playing of the anthem, but the entire matter made Muslim groups, members of the fastest-growing religion in the United States (some five million strong), nervous about public perception.

Star status may make a difference. Houston Rockets star Hakim Olajuwon's Muslim religion requires him to pray five times a day—a schedule that is willingly accommodated by his coach and fans. When the city of Houston staged a victory parade for its NBA champs in 1994, 500,000 people waited in the heat of a Texas June for Olajuwon to arrive from his daily devotions. "We're all aware of his prayer schedule this year," said a spokesperson for the mayor a year later, when the parade was planned around the star center's needs.

But Olajuwon differs from Abdul-Rauf in another way: He has not linked his own Muslim faith to a critique of the United States and its symbols. The designation "America's team," borne proudly in football by the Tom Landry–led Dallas Cowboys and then claimed by the 1996 Green Bay Packers, seemed to blend patriotism with religion and, specifically, with Christianity.

When columnist Rick Reilly (1991) complained in *Sports Illustrated* about the intrusiveness—and coerciveness—of public praying during and after pro football games, his critique of "50-yard-line religious sales pitches" was answered in *Commonwealth,* a journal edited by Roman Catholic laypeople. "Once upon a time people who thought as Reilly does were content to confine their arguments to cases of coercion in the strict, juridical sense," wrote R. Bruce Douglass, an assistant professor of government at Georgetown University, in *Commonwealth* (cited in Steinfels 1991). The issue used to be whether public money was used to underwrite the exercise of religion, but now public expressions of piety by individuals were under attack. "Just who is it," asked Douglass, "that is being intolerant to whom?" Reilly had argued that "imposing one's beliefs on a captive audience is wrong, irreligious, even" and suggested that the NFL ought to outlaw public displays of prayer by players in the huddle or the locker room. At the very least, he thought, television should refuse to broadcast them. As things stood, stadiums full of fans, and millions more watching at home, were subjected to the spectacle of public prayer whether they liked it or not. "It would be just as inappropriate," he said, "for Jewish players to conduct services at the far hash mark or for Muslim players to place prayer rugs under a goalpost and face Mecca." He also had harsh words for players who prayed for results, like the New York Giants team that knelt and prayed as an opposing kicker tried for a last-second field goal. "Is praying for somebody to blow it very Christian?" Reilly asked.

But in a set of moves very like the self-justifications of economic social Darwinism, not only are gridiron victories ascribed to God, they are taken as evidence that the winners are somehow particularly virtuous, or devout, or Christian. The 1997 Super Bowl pregame show clinched this point by showing a clip from Kenneth Branagh's film version of Shakespeare's *Henry V* in which the young king rallies his forces, "we few, we happy few, we band of brothers." Later he will exult in victory: "Take it, God,/For it is none but thine." Though Fox TV did not show this latter moment, the implied parallels were clear—and disturbing. Despite the fact that Grantland Rice's famous 1941 rhyme declared,

When the One Great Scorer comes to write against your name—
He marks—not that you won or lost—but how you played the game

cynical sports journalists are increasingly confronted with public declarations of decisions by the Divine Referee. "This was Jesus Christ working through my players," declared the new coach of the University of Oklahoma football team to ABC-TV after they beat arch-rival Texas in overtime. "What role did God play—or not play—in the eight Oklahoma losses this season?" wondered a writer who identified himself "not as an atheist journalist, but as a Bible-reading Christian" (quoted in Steinfels 1991).

At the same time, evangelical Christianity's receptiveness to the repentant sinner has allowed drug- and sex-abusing athletes to proclaim, publicly, their reformation. At the end of Dallas Cowboys receiver Michael Irvin's five-game suspension for pleading no contest to cocaine possession, he marched to the end zone, knelt, and prayed. No sportswriter present could recall any previous occasion on which Irvin had engaged in public prayer. This is the evangelical obverse of *Catch-22;* the more errant the sinner, the greater God's victory in winning him over. But if theatricalized displays like step-strutting are banned as unsportsmanlike, what is the place of ostentatious prayer? When the private becomes public, becomes uniform, becomes customary, has a line been crossed? And what kind of line? A goal line? A foul line?

Another Super Bowl video staple, the clever commercial, spoke directly to this question when it pictured a locker room full of players being prayed with, or prayed at, first by the coach and then by a politically correct sequence of multicultural clerics, each in distinctive garb. As the praying droned on and the players yawned, they reached for a snack to keep them awake. The sponsor was Snickers, the candy bar. This may be the only way in which snickering at religious display is permitted to a public audience today.

"It seems a feeble pluralism that cannot encompass a bit of postgame prayer," observed *New York Times* "Beliefs" columnist Peter Steinfels, reporting on the "delicate and slightly unsettling moment" when television cameras in the locker room of new NBA champions the Chicago Bulls caught the victors holding hands and reciting the Lord's Prayer (Bayless 1996). Where the intrusive glance of the camera has sometimes had to tilt away to avoid disclosing the physical nakedness of the athlete, the camera in the Bulls locker room offered a glimpse of another kind of intimacy. Was this a kind of voyeurism? Or a kind of exhibitionism?

These are questions to which we will want to return.

At public universities and schools where taxpayers' funds are used, the issue of locker room prayer has attracted some critical attention. The former coach of the University of Colorado football team, Bill McCartney, was accused of giving priority in hiring, recruiting, and playing time to athletes who shared his Christian faith (Monaghan 1985, 1992; see also Fried and Bradley 1994). The ACLU argued that injecting religion into a state-sponsored program violated the constitutional mandate for government neutrality. The worst-case scenario is the succinctly named "no pray/no play" rule. In 1994, students at Memphis State University alleged that the coaches were "attempting to convert the student-athletes to Christianity, to be saved, to be part of the Born-Again movement," and that if they failed to attend coach Ray Dempsey's mandatory prayer meetings, they would not get to play. As an attorney in the case observed, financial constraints often limit the student-athlete's capacity to protest: "It is clear that personnel on athletic scholarships are not going to complain" (Farrell 1984). "No pray/no play" is clearly a violation of First Amendment rights. But what about peer pressure and the emotional prestige of the coach?

Coaches often function in loco parentis for athletes, occupying what one observer called, nicely, "the fatherly/motherly position" (Cross 1973, cited in Fried and Bradley 1994). (I think the observer in question may have meant "fatherly for young men" and "motherly for young women," but the conflation of the two seems entirely appropriate.) The coach is omniscient, omnipotent, nurturing, law giving, and punishing, the male version of the phallic mother. Who would displease such a figure, the true parent, the chosen leader, the fulfillment and apotheosis of the family romance?

A high school football coach in Florence, Arizona, resigned because the principal sent him a memo saying that "there should be no prayer at any school organized events." Coach Tom Shoemake said that he had prayed with his teams before and after games for twenty years ("Not a Prayer," *Boston Globe,* October 16, 1992).

And then there is peer pressure, the emphasis on being a "team player." While an athlete is technically free to leave the locker room during a team prayer, the social costs are so high that the exercise of this "freedom" is unlikely. Much of the case law that exists deals with high school and elementary school team prayer in situations that, by the fact of the relative youth of the students, are often held to be more coercive. However, the argument that *televised* prayer is coercive to at-home viewers has also been persuasively made.

In a Texas case *(Doe v. Duncanville Independent School District),* the court, Jane Doe, and her father, John Doe, protested the mandatory prayers conducted by the coach of a girls' basketball team at practice and at the end of games. (The visual image conjured by the court's words is striking: "the girls on their hands and knees with the coach standing over them, heads bowed," as they recited the Lord's Prayer in the center of the court.) Such prayers had been recited at basketball games for over twenty years when the suit was brought. Prayers were also regularly said at pep rallies, at awards ceremonies, before all home football games, and when teams boarded buses for away games. When Jane Doe elected not to participate in the team prayer, her coach made her stand outside the prayer circle. Other students asked her, "Aren't you a Christian?"; a spectator at a game shouted, "Well, why isn't she praying? Isn't she a Christian?"; and her history teacher called her "a little atheist." The Does sued.

The U.S. Court of Appeals held up a lower court's ruling enjoining the school district's employees from leading, encouraging, promoting, or participating in prayer "with or among students during curriculum or extracurricular activities, including before, during and after school related sporting events." Furthermore, noting the "pervasive nature of past school prayer," the school district was instructed to advise students, in writing, that "under the First Amendment of the United States Constitution, prayer and religious activities initiated and promoted by school officials are unconstitutional, and that students have a constitutional right not to participate in such activities." The claim that prayer accomplished the purpose of stirring up "school spirit" was not held to be persuasively secular.

We may notice that the plaintiff in *Doe* is female. It is not clear whether she was, in fact, "a little atheist," as her history teacher suggested. "Atheist" seems to function here as the "natural" or inevitable opposite to "Christian." It is tempting to remember W. S. Gilbert's mocking verse from *Iolanthe:* "every boy and every gal / That's born into the world alive / Is either a little Liberal, / Or else a little Conservative!" Since "Doe" is a pseudonym that defies religious or ethnic stereotyping, it is also not possible to detect, immediately, whether Jane Doe was Jewish or Muslim, a Buddhist or a Jain. In other team prayer cases, however, the religious identifications of the plaintiffs are more manifest. In two particularly indicative instances, they are Jewish.

Max Berlin was a senior at Crestview High School in Okaloosa County, Florida, and a member of the football team. His sister Tammy was a sophomore at the same school. Through their parents, the Berlins sought an injunction to prevent the school from offering an invocation, through the public address system, before each home football game. They also filed a motion to prevent the football coaches from leading their teams in prayer before or after the game.

The invocation specifically asked for "sportsmanlike spirit" among players and spectators and for blessings on the players, "for we are all winners through Jesus Christ, our Lord." Such an invocation had been offered at Crestview High and other schools in the area for more than thirty years, and the superintendent of schools acknowledged to the court that the invocation was, in the court's words, "in keeping with the customs, expectations, and religious traditions of the vast majority of the residents of Okaloosa County, who are Christians" (1988 WL. 85937 [N.D. Fla.]). He also suggested in a public statement that opposition to the invocation was an opposition to "wholesome values." Mrs. Berlin testified that what was offensive to her in the invocation was the reference to Jesus Christ and that she had felt an animosity from the crowd when she remained seated during the invocation. Tammy Berlin testified that when she walked around rather than standing for the invocation, she was treated as an outsider.

After noting that the school district had instructed its football coaches not to pray with their teams before or after games and not to encourage others to do so (thus rendering part of the motion moot), the judge denied the motion for a preliminary injunction. The invocation could continue, for the time being; the team prayer had to stop.

The Berlins' suit was based on a sense of their own minority status as Jews and on the ways in which the "customs, expectations, and religious traditions of the vast majority of the residents of Okaloosa County, who are Christians," could all too easily slide over into a definition of "wholesome values" that seemed to exclude Jews from wholesomeness (and, indeed, from good "values"). The high school football field became an outdoor church, and Tammy Berlin, like Jane Doe, seemed to be regarded as a little atheist—or worse—because she did not observe its protocols. In another case that turned on religion and sports, however, the entire team was Jewish—and its "customs, expectations, and religious traditions" were resisted, and in fact briefly outlawed, by the "secular" regulating agency.

A class action on behalf of male members of the Orthodox Jewish faith was brought against the Illinois High School Association (IHSA), to which all the public schools and almost all the private schools in the state belonged. At issue was the association's rule, newly passed, that prohibited, for safety reasons, the wearing of yarmulkes when playing basketball.

This was, for me, a completely fascinating case. The plaintiffs were two private Jewish secondary schools whose teams routinely wore yarmulkes attached with bobby pins. Orthodox Jewish men cover their heads at all times (except when unconscious, underwater, or in imminent danger of loss of life) as a sign of respect to God. One of the teams had been part of the association for three years, the other for eight, and during this time players had worn yarmulkes on the court without incident, until 1981, when a problem arose. That year the association refused to let them play in the championship elimination tournament, held in a prestigious and high-profile location (the University of Illinois basketball fieldhouse) unless they took off their yarmulkes.

The basketball rule book instructed referees to prevent players from wearing any equipment that might cause harm to another player, like forearm guards, plastic or metal braces, headwear, and jewelry. Barrettes made of soft material were legal, as were two-inch-wide headbands. The Jewish high schools sought, and the judge granted, an injunction that would allow them to play in the tournament, as the court pointed out not only that there were First Amendment considerations but also that "no rational distinction appeared to exist between a soft barrette attached to the hair with bobby pins or clips and a yarmulke similarly attached" (*Menora et al. v. Illinois High School Association et al.* 527 F. Supp. 637).

After the court entered its preliminary injunction order, and while the action remained pending, the National Federation of State High School Associations, of which the Illinois group is a member, sent out a questionnaire to basketball coaches and officials in forty-four states, including Illinois, asking, among other things, whether they approved of the rule permitting soft barrettes. Over 10,000 responses were received; 8,766 said that the rule was satisfactory, 1,476 that it was not. Nevertheless, in April 1981 the federation changed its rule. The chairman of the Basketball Rules Committee claimed that it was difficult for officials to distinguish between "hard" barrettes and "soft" barrettes and therefore that *all* barrettes should be barred.

The court was neither persuaded nor amused. It noted that there was no information presented about injuries that had occurred as the result of wearing either soft barrettes or yarmulkes. "It taxes credulity," wrote District Judge Shadur, "that the change in the rule was not at least in part responsive to the pendency of this litigation." Furthermore, the judge noted, "under any possible interpretation, for safety and all like purposes a yarmulke is the functional equivalent (although not of course the religious equivalent) of a soft barrette, not a hard barrette" (*Menora et al. v. Illinois High School Association et al.* 527 F. Supp. 642).

There were other disturbing developments. When the results of the questionnaire were submitted, a "typographical error" (the quotation marks are Judge Shadur's) altered the number of "yes" votes approving soft barrettes from 8,766 to 1,766, an "error" that was caught only when the court's law clerk asked for a copy of the actual document, the "only one not so delivered by IHSA counsel." Describing the behavior of the federation's Basketball Rules Committee as "clearly disingenuous," the judge observed dryly, "Obviously a six-to-one vote from more than 10,000 knowledgeable basketball coaches and officials in favor of retaining the rule permitting soft barrettes (functionally equivalent to yarmulkes in all respects as to safety) has a devastating effect on the 'compelling necessity' of a new rule to serve IHSA's stated purpose of prohibiting yarmulkes to assure safety."

Nor was this the end of the matter. As the judge quite emphatically went on to note, "It is most troublesome to encounter what appears to be a pretextual basis for the adoption of the current rule."

The claim of those who pushed for a rule change was safety. Slips and falls, the judge agreed, are common to the game of basketball, as are minor injuries. But in fact the federation did not have on record a single instance of a slip, fall, or injury resulting from either "a yarmulke having come loose and fallen on a basketball court" or "a bobby pin or clip" having fallen. Indeed, in testimony that covered more than 1,300 interscholastic games and many more that were noninterscholastic, no one had ever mentioned a single instance of slippage or injury "from either yarmulkes or their associated bobby pins or clips." Though yarmulkes had fallen onto the basketball court an average of one or two times a game, they had always been promptly picked up.

And, persevered the judge, other things do fall to the basketball court during play, like players' eyeglasses, whether or not they are secured by elastic bands. Likewise, the judge continued, "foreign objects such as paper and coins are unfortunately thrown by fans onto the basketball court from time to time during basketball games, and paper is from time to time left on the court as a result of the incomplete cleaning up of paper detached from pompons left by cheerleaders." All these would be fully as hazardous as a fallen yarmulke. But "IHSA rules do not prohibit persons wearing glasses from playing IHSA interscholastic basketball. Nor do IHSA rules ban attendance at games or cheerleader participation during games." No, indeed: The Illinois group that sponsors the state tournament, the Elite Eight, at the basketball fieldhouse of the University of Illinois does not ban eyeglass wearers or cheerleaders or fans. But it did—or it wished to—ban the wearing of yarmulkes for *safety* reasons. Whose safety is being threatened here—and by whom?

Thus, to summarize: During the course of the litigation, IHSA changed its view from "yes" to "no" on soft barrettes (and thus on yarmulkes) despite the total absence of any demonstrated safety hazard and the presence of an overwhelming six-to-one vote. It claimed "compelling interests" when none—apparently—existed as sufficient reason to override the First Amendment rights of the players who covered their heads for reasons of religious faith. Moreover, the court had "real questions as to the total candor" of those involved in changing the rules in the middle of the legal game. "IHSA's argument involves an impermissible sleight of hand: It falsely equates basketball safety with prohibiting yarmulkes," declared the ruling. "In basketball terms IHSA loses by too many points to make keeping score worthwhile" (*Menora et al. v. Illinois High School Association et al.* 527 F. Supp. 646).

With this final slam dunk, the judge blew the whistle on the IHSA, at least on the yarmulke question. But it may be worth noting that this same organization, the IHSA, has been adamant in its support of football prayer. "The IHSA doesn't have a rule against prayer on the field and shouldn't and never will," said the executive director in November 1996. It is "as appropriate as jumping up and down and yelling 'We're No. 1' and cheering." But precisely who is it who comes out number one in this kind of religious demonstration? Ecumenicism? Or "Christianity"? Who is to be the judge of what is "appropriate" in the realm of religious cheerleading?

Sigmund Freud's "Group Psychology and the Analysis of the Ego" sets forth his general sense that "libidinal ties" link group members, especially in "artificial" (by which he means organized and regulated) groups; his chief examples, in an essay published in 1921, are the Church and the army, both pertinent models for today's professionalized and proselytizing sports teams, whether they are literally pros or just part of a highly developed and well-funded "amateur" sports program.

> It is to be noticed that in these two artificial groups each individual is bound by libidinal ties on the one hand to the leader (Christ, the Commander-in-chief) and on the other hand to members of the group. How the two ties are related to each other, whether they are of the same kind and the same value, and how they are to be described psychologically—these questions must be reserved for subsequent enquiry.

While it would not be especially helpful to "apply" this Freudian analysis uncritically to, say, the Jacksonville Jaguars or the Green Bay Packers, it is worth noting that "leader" and "group" ties are terms perfectly appropriate to the relationship of the team to its coach, captains, and God on the one hand and to itself ("team spirit") on the other. (We might recall professional football player Rich Griffiths's testimony, "I don't do it for Coach Coughlin or for anyone else. I do it for a superior person.")

Robert Higgs (1995) notes that "in its early days football was viewed as a substitute for war and as a training ground for war," citing as the three "staunchest promoters of the football-war metaphor" West Pointer (and first NCAA president) Palmer Pierce, Douglas MacArthur, and Teddy Roosevelt. "If athletes are soldiers of sorts," remarks Higgs, "then the effort of the FCA [Fellowship of Christian Athletes] and other proselytizing groups has been to make them Christian soldiers." Today's vocal and demonstrative Christian Athletes thus combine the two "artificial groups" that seemed to Freud the most obvious examples of his "group psychology."

What Freud (1921) calls, in a wonderful phrase, "the narcissism of minor differences" accounts for the enmity that once made the New York Yankees and the Brooklyn Dodgers such bitter rivals:

> Of two neighboring towns each is the other's most jealous rival; every little canton looks down upon the others with contempt. Closely related races keep one another at arm's length; the South German cannot endure the North German, the Englishman casts every kind of aspersion upon the Scot, the Spaniard despises the Portuguese. We are no longer astonished that greater differences should lead to an almost insuperable repugnance, such as the Gallic people feel for the German, the Aryan for the Semite, the white races for the coloured.

Within groups, however, the opposite occurs:

> But when a group is formed the whole of this intolerance vanishes, temporarily or permanently, within the group. So long as a group formation persists or so far as it extends, individuals in the group behave as though they were uniform, tolerate the peculiarities of the other members, equate themselves with them, and have no feeling of aversion towards

> them. Such a limitation of narcissism can, according to our theoretical views, only be produced by one factor, a libidinal tie with other people.

And what about "team spirit"? Here Freud, again tendentiously, writes of the "desexualized, sublimated homosexual love for other men, which springs from work in common." For mankind as a whole, as for the individual,

> love alone acts as the civilizing factor in the sense that it brings a change from egoism to altruism. This is true both of sexual love for women, with all the obligations which it involves of not harming the things that are dear to women, and also of desexualized, sublimated homosexual love for other men, which springs from work in common.

In other words, men in groups, to use Lionel Tiger's famous phrase, come to love one another, in the process turning their egotism into altruism. Diana Fuss (1996) has commented trenchantly on the effort Freud expends to keep the two kinds of love ("sexual" and "desexualized") apart. His view turns on the question of "identification," the "earliest expression of an emotional tie with another person," distinguishing between wanting to *be* and wanting to *have* another person. (Unsurprisingly, Freud's early example is that of the boy who takes his father as his ideal; his later example is the "tie with the leader." For both "father" and "leader" here, we may, for our purposes, read "coach" or "captain.") The "mutual tie between members of a group" takes the form, says Freud, of an identification based on some perceived common quality—a quality that is *not* based on erotic feelings. "Freud's theory of identification," argues Fuss, "appears as a theoretical *defense* against any eventuality of a nonsublimated homosexual love as the basis of a homosocial group formation. By extracting identification from desire, insisting that a subject cannot identify with another person and desire that person at the same time, Freud is able to conceptualize homosexuality and homosociality as absolutely distinct categories." For Fuss, the supposed distinctness of these categories—like the distinctness of supposed desire and identification—is itself a symptom of their tendency to become both confused and undecidable.

Yet what is most fascinating about Freud's own argument, as Fuss herself notes, is his observation that what he calls "homosexual love" is "far more compatible with group ties" than is heterosexual love, "even when it takes the shape of uninhibited sexual impulsions." He himself calls this "a remarkable fact, the explanation of which might carry us far." "That the locker room can be an erotic environment is undeniable," observes former sports writer Brian Pronger in *The Arena of Masculinity* (1980), a book about sports and homosexuality. Can the eros of physical sexuality and the eros of religious faith be compared? Or identified? "Men who love football love men," says Mariah Burton Nelson in *The Stronger Women Get, the More Men Love Football* (1994).

On- and off-court physical contact between celebrated "straight" male athletes—like the "customary smooching" between best friends Isiah Thomas and Magic Johnson noted by *Sports Illustrated* (June 27, 1988) under the photo caption "Kiss and Make Up"—has been used, through an elementary paradoxical logic, to shore up the *heterosexuality* of men's sports, analogous to the ostentatious wearing of earrings and necklaces that might be deemed, on less monumental males, overt signs of gay identity and display. It takes a "real man"—which is to say, a heterosexual man—to wear all this expensive jewelry in public. By touching and indeed crossing the line between stereotypical "gay" and stereotypical "straight" costume and practice, male athletes affirm their manliness. As Lionel Tiger (1969) noted, "Men such as war heroes, politicians, sports heroes, who have established themselves as virile, may indulge in public tenderness more easily than persons in less evidently virile occupations, such as poetry, teaching, hairdressing, etc."

Mariah Burton Nelson (1994) comments on a photograph of three Texas high school football players, in full football regalia, backs to the camera, holding hands. "Were these same young men to hold hands in a different setting—on a city street, say, or on a beach, without their football uniforms—they would be thought to be gay. They might be taunted by other men—football players, perhaps. Yet in this picture, their handholding projects a solemn, unified sort of group power." "Together," she concludes, "they fall in love—with power, with masculinity. They also fall in love with each other."

What's love got to do with it?

"Language has carried out an entirely justifiable piece of unification in creating the word 'love' with its numerous uses," writes Freud (1921). "In its origin, function, and relation to sexual love, the 'Eros' of the philosopher Plato coincides exactly with the love-force, the libido of psychoanalysis." Indeed, says Freud, "when the apostle Paul, in his famous epistle to the Corinthians, praises love above all else, he certainly understands it in this same 'wider' sense."

Recall here Nelson's description of team bonding: "a solemn, unified sort of group power"; "together, they fall in love." Respected folklorist Alan Dundes (1980) wrote some years ago what he characterized as "a psychoanalytic consideration of American football" in which he pointed out that language like "end" ("tight end," "split end"), "penetration," "go through a hole," and so on was a kind of "folk speech" that suggested "ritual homosexuality." "I have no doubt," said Dundes, "that a good many football players and fans will be skeptical (to say the least)." Even a gay player like David Kopay declined to agree that being able to hold hands in the huddle and "pat each other on the ass" was an overt sign of homosexuality. But Dundes stuck to his argument: "The unequivocal sexual symbolism of the game, as plainly evidenced in folk speech, coupled with the fact that all of the participants are male, makes it difficult to draw any other conclusion."

Easy for him to say. For the average fan, player, or coach, what is difficult is to draw this conclusion or even to entertain the possibility of a subliminal (homo)erotics of male sport. And what is even more difficult is explaining the difference between a cultural practice and a sexual identity. No one—or virtually no one—claims that football players are, as a class, subliminally or overtly gay or that they are drawn to football because it affords them an opportunity to pat each others' bottoms or put their hands (expecting the ball) between each others' legs. Reading America's passion for football as a cultural symptom does not threaten anyone's identity, sexuality, future, or faith. Or does it?

Spectatorship in sport, like film spectatorship, has certain mirroring and compromising effects. Laura Mulvey's famous formulation about the "determining male gaze" in cinema, "woman as image, man as bearer of the look," becomes interestingly complicated when the lookers and the looked-at—in and out of what has been dubbed the "looker room"—are male. More than thirty years ago, televised sports was characterized by one shrewd observer as "Male Soap Opera" (Moon 1963, cited in Tiger 1969). Sociologist Lionel Tiger (1969) offered an evolutionary view: "Perhaps we can regard sport spectatorship as a phenomenon bearing the same relation to hunting and male bonding as love stories do to reproductive drives and mate selection." The need to keep identification apart from desire—to insist that you want to *be* Brett Favre and not *have* Brett Favre—produces all-male spectatorship in a very curious space: the displacement of the *permission* to desire onto a nominally desexualized erotic object—Jesus or God—that legitimizes and sacralizes (which is to say, heterosexualizes) male-male love. By the emotional logic of this position, as long as *someone else* is doing it "wrong," you can be sure you are doing it right. A group of "insiders" depends for its cohesiveness on identifying certain "outsiders" who are either to be permanently excluded for their own good (like women) or, if they meet certain standards, to be converted from error to truth. And in this latter category—the category of the potential convert—we find the usual suspects: homosexuals and Jews. Gay men love other men the "wrong" way. This gives other men permission to love each other—in a way that they can secure as different.

When a Coach Coughlin or a Coach Landry (or, indeed, a "God in pads" like Reggie White) leads a team in prayer, the term "love" circulates freely in the huddle. And the idea that God (or Jesus) is the real captain or quarterback and that the Landrys and Coughlins and Whites are merely apostles is familiar, as we have seen, from the way they think and speak. Coach Bill McCartney, late of the University of Colorado, took this erotics of football from the locker room to the bleachers, with remarkable—and disquieting—effect.

Since 1990, an all-male, all-Christian organization called the Promise Keepers, founded by Coach McCartney, has been holding its rallies in stadiums across the country. Linked to other right-wing groups espousing causes from the teaching of creationism in the schools to the denunciation of abortion and homosexuality, supported by evangelical and politically conservative ministers Jerry Falwell and Pat Robertson, the Promise Keepers gets much of its emotional mileage out of the pep-rally scenario of coach and fans. *New York Times* columnist Frank Rich, formerly assigned to the paper's theater beat, accurately gauged the level and nature of Promise Keepers' appeal when he made a field trip to New York's Shea Stadium, home of the New York Mets (1996). There he found "some 35,000 standing, waving guys shouting their love to Jesus at a decibel level unknown even in Shea's occasional brushes with a pennant race. During a marathon rally of sermonizing, singing, and praying, the men also repeatedly sobbed and hugged each other—or, more joyously, slapped high-fives while repeating the chant, 'Thank God I'm a man!'" The Promise Keepers whom Rich met were, he thought, "more motivated by a Robert Bly-esque hunger to overcome macho inhibitions and reconnect with God than by any desire to enlist in a political army. But an army PK most certainly is. Its preachers sound more like generals and hard-charging motivational cheerleaders than clergy. Every music cue, crowd maneuver and sales pitch for PK paraphernalia is integrated into the show with a split-second precision that suggests a Radio City religious pageant staged by George Patton." In the Promise Keepers, Freud's two characteristic groups, the Army and the Church, come together.

Other media observers have seen the atmosphere at Promise Keepers rallies as "equal parts religious revival, inspirational pep talk and spiritual support group" (Niebuhr 1995). "As a man," said one of the nearly 50,000 who attended a session at the Thunderdome in

St. Petersburg, Florida, "you get trained for your job, you get trained for athletics. But who trains you to be a Christian man?" (Niebuhr 1995). Roaming among book exhibits that feature works like *What Makes a Man* and *Strategies to a Successful Marriage* as well as copies of Promise Keepers' own magazine, *New Man,* sporting T-shirts that declared (in a faint echo of muscular Christianity's defensiveness) "Real Men Love Jesus," the audience (congregation? fans?) testified to the pleasure of meeting in all-male groups. "In our church, there are more women than men," reported one Florida man. "To see this, it's awesome."

For some Americans, and other world citizens too, the Promise Keepers became visible on the national scene only in October 1997, when they held a rally on the Washington Mall. But the movement began in Boulder, Colorado, with a conference of 4,200 Christian men in the university's football stadium. On this rock—or boulder—McCartney built his church. The following year, there were 22,000; the year after that, 50,000. Founder Bill McCartney quit his $350,000 job as Colorado's football coach and went into the Promise Keeping business full time. He called the movement an opportunity for men to "walk in Christian masculinity." The Promise Keepers went national (72,000 men in the Silverdome in Pontiac, Michigan; 52,000 at RFK stadium in Washington, D.C.; 13 cities in the summer and fall of 1995) and planned expansion overseas. Participants, who paid $55 apiece for the privilege of attending, bought Promise Keepers books, tapes, T-shirts, and caps; did "stadium waves"; sang; prayed; held hands; and embraced ("New Men for Jesus," *The Economist,* June 3, 1995, 21).

This fellowship of men, who often embrace one another and speak in a rhetoric of love, is part of a movement that is, officially, anti-gay. Any gay men who show up are candidates for double conversion—to born-again Christianity and to heterosexuality—with counselors on hand to assist in making the change. Coach McCartney, whose movement is dedicated to "uniting men through vital relationships to become godly influences in their world," drew administrative and student ire when he was at the University of Colorado for publicly denouncing homosexuality as "an abomination of almighty God" and for endorsing Colorado's proposed amendment that would have barred laws protecting homosexuals from discrimination. The university's president, the American Civil Liberties Union (ACLU), student groups, and Representative Pat Schroeder all deplored McCartney's use of his university role for political and ideological ends: The conservative group called Colorado for Family Values had listed him as a board member and identified him as Colorado's football coach. A student leader commented that McCartney was "spreading gay hatred and bigotry and gay bashing at an institution of higher education" and asked rhetorically, "You tell me if that is good Christian values and what we should be teaching at a university."

One might think that Coach McCartney's departure from coaching was hastened by the restrictions the state university placed on his role. But he himself claims that he founded the movement—and turned away from coaching—because he suddenly realized that his wife was unhappy. Although he tells this story at every rally, with his wife by his side (sometimes he kisses her on stage to punctuate his story), he does not usually report that his unmarried daughter "gave birth to two children, both fathered by players on McCartney's teams." (Since McCartney had, when at the University of Colorado, criticized homosexuals as people who do not reproduce and want equality with people who do, it is perhaps possible to see this family "expansion team" as consistent with, rather than a violation of, his own beliefs.)

It is fascinating to imagine what the church and the media's response might be to stadiums full of *women,* 50,000 strong, chanting in concert and declaring themselves dedicated to social change. "Mass hysteria" is the phrase that comes to mind. One has only to think of all that file footage on women and girls weeping and screaming at the sight of the Beatles—or, for that matter, the young Frank Sinatra. One of Freud's examples of "group psychology" is in fact "the troop of women and girls, all of them in love in an enthusiastically sentimental way, who crowd round a singer or a pianist after his performance. It would certainly be easy for each of them to be jealous of the rest; but, in the face of their numbers and the consequent impossibility of their reaching the aim of their love, they renounce it, and, instead of pulling out one another's hair, they act as a united group, do homage to the hero of the occasion with their common actions, and would probably be glad to have a share of *his* flowing locks. Originally rivals, they have succeeded in identifying themselves with one another by means of a similar love for the same object" (1921). When a woman's version of the Million Man March was organized, it attracted relatively few participants—and almost no media attention. Was this because the event was so decorous, with so little in the way of "acting out"? (Janofsky 1997). Would anyone take a group of 50,000 sobbing, praying, and embracing women seriously as a sign of moral progress? Or would they be regarded as symptoms of cultural crisis, of *lack* of moral strength and emotional self-control?

If you find this scenario hard to imagine, try replacing the 50,000 singing and chanting heterosexual men with 50,000 gay men. "We're number one" in this context would surely be taken as a sign of group narcissism, as a decadent conspiracy, and as a desperate plot against the moral fiber of the nation—even if they prayed, and especially if they embraced each other.

Ruminating on the peculiarities of "normality" in human sexual life, Sigmund Freud had, on one memorable occasion, rather witty recourse to the figure of conversion. "In general," he remarked, "to undertake to convert a fully developed homosexual into a heterosexual does not offer much more prospect of success than the reverse, except that for good practical purposes the latter is never attempted" (1920). For Freud the Jew, the concept of conversion—forced conversion—was, we can presume, already heavily freighted. "The conversion of the Jews" was a long-term project for Christianity, a project so proverbially formidable that the poet Andrew Marvell could equate it with eternity ("And you should, if you please, refuse/Till the conversion of the Jews"), so ideologically desirable and hotly contested that it formed a central tenet of Protestant Evangelism in England from the time of the French Revolution to the end of the nineteenth century. "In the vocabulary of a Christian," wrote Lewis Way, a member of the London Society for Promoting Christianity amongst the Jews, in 1831, "conversion does not stand opposed to *toleration* but to *persecution*" (quoted in Ragussis 1995). In the vocabulary of football, conversion is a way of scoring points: the "extra point" earned by a kick after a touchdown or the "two-point conversion" scored by running or passing. Modern-day evangelicals, from the Promise Keepers to the more mainline Protestant denominations, have their own kind of two-point conversion: point one, the conversion of the homosexuals; point two, the conversion of the Jews.

When the 14,000 delegates to the Southern Baptist Convention met in New Orleans in June 1996, they affirmed their support for a major campaign to convert American Jews to Christianity. (Delegates called on the same occasion for a boycott of Disney because of its alleged pro-gay stance in producing the TV series *Ellen* and allowing benefits for same-sex partners of Disneyland employees [Niebuhr 1996]. Both points of the "two-point conversion" were thus expressly on the agenda.) Lawyer Leonard Garment wrote eloquently in the *New York Times* that the resolution was "the latest in a centuries-old line of conversion efforts whose history is so distasteful as to make the Baptists' action profoundly offensive" (1996). "In the simple conversionist view," Garment explains in a tone that is carefully, passionately, dispassionate, "Christianity is the natural, necessary culmination of Jewish history. It makes Judaism unnecessary and obsolete. The persistence of Jews who choose to remain Jews poses a challenge to this idea of inevitability. Thus, the argument goes, intensive conversion efforts must be made." Moreover, he noted, the Baptists' mission is specifically targeted at Jews. Their resolution "does not declare that the growing Muslim population in the United States is in special need of spiritual improvement. Only the Jews merit this honor." That persistent and defining evangelical activity, the conversion of the Jews, long regarded as the millenarian missionary moment, was, it seemed, once again at hand.

The evangelism resolution itself had an oddly defensive-aggressive tone, demonstrating perhaps that, as the sports truism goes, the best defense is a good offense. "There has been an organized effort on the part of some either to deny that Jewish people need to come to their Messiah, Jesus, to be saved; or to claim, for whatever reason, that Christians have neither right nor obligation to proclaim the gospel to the Jewish people," it declared. This latest mission to the Jews was thus somehow both anticonspiracy ("an *organized* effort *on the part of some*") and a matter of civil rights (refuting the "claim, *for whatever reason,* that 'Christians *have neither right nor obligation* to proclaim the gospel to the Jewish people'"). What might appear to Jews intrusive and unwelcome spiritual bullying is summarily redefined as a courageous act of conscience. In this latest confrontation between Christians and lions, it was the Lion of Judah who was subject to attack.

We might note that the rise of "muscular Christianity" took place at about the same time as the physician Max Nordau's call, in Germany, for the appearance of a "new Muscle Jew." Sports were part of the regimen recommended by turn-of-the-century Zionists for rebuilding the bodies and spirits of Jews worn down by ghetto life. German-Jewish gymnastic competitions and Nordau's invitation to the playing fields of Berlin and Vienna were part of a systematic plan for incorporating healthy minds and bodies and overcoming the perceived divide between "muscle Jews and nerve Jews"—a view held both by political and by medical commentators (Jastrowitz 1908, cited in Gilman 1991). ("They have been little inducted, during their pilgrimages, into the public games of the countries in which they have been located," wrote a sympathetic American observer in 1882 in a book called *Diseases of Modern Life.*)[4] Thus, the Jewish Olympic athlete was perceived as something of an anomaly.

But the key distinction here, of course, is that modern Judaism is emphatically not a missionary or an evangelical religion. As anyone knows who has contemplated becoming a Jew, the rabbis ordain a period of intensive study, and in general converts are discouraged unless they can prove a sustained and informed interest in the faith. "I don't want to speculate why Jews don't evangelize,"[5] said a Southern Baptist spokesman, "but if your religion is so great, why aren't you on the street evangelizing?" This perceived "exclusiveness" has been held (like so much) against the Jewish religion from time to time. "Unlike that of proselytizing religions," writes James Carroll, "the Jewish ethic boils down to the injunction: Let other people be other people" (1997). Carroll, a columnist and essayist, suggests that Jews have been so hated in history "because they have refused to make an absolute of group identity, thereby calling into question, by their very existence, the rigid intolerance of groups that do exactly that." What is completely out of the question, in any case, is the idea of a football field full of persons "called" to Judaism or a sudden onset of faith. Jewish athletes may be heroes, loners, or role models—but they are not, by the very nature of the Jewish faith, agents of conversion.

We noticed in our discussion of Freud's "Group Psychology" that the narcissism of small differences made neighbors into rivals and that "the libidinal constitution of groups," as he put it, the (carefully desexualized and spiritualized) "love" that is often expressed by team members for one another, is a way of overcoming rivalry, of turning "egoism" into "altruism"—or at least into points on the board. "We're number one" is, when you stop to think about it, a slightly paradoxical chant, numerically speaking. "Identification" produces group identity, which produces "love."

What makes a group a group, though, or a team a team turns out to be as much rivalry or aggression as love. As Freud (1930) remarks with deceptive matter-of-factness in *Civilization and Its Discontents,* "It is always possible to bind together a considerable number of people in love, so long as there are other people left over to receive the manifestations of their aggressiveness." (Are you listening, sports fans?)

"In this respect," he continues, with equal urbanity, "the Jewish people, scattered everywhere, have rendered most useful services to the civilizations of the countries that have been their hosts; but unfortunately all the massacres of the Jews in the Middle Ages did not suffice to make that period more peaceful and secure for their Christian fellows. When once the Apostle Paul had posited universal love between men as the foundation of his Christian community, extreme intolerance on the part of Christendom towards those who remained outside it became the inevitable consequence."

Let us return then, briefly, to the Promise Keepers. What are the promises the Promise Keepers promise to keep?

With Robert Frost's refrain ("I have promises to keep, And miles to go before I sleep") and J. L. Austin's speech-act theory in mind, I had blandly (and as it turned out, blindly) assumed that a promise was a kind of ethical, and indeed largely secular, declaration or assurance made by one person to another. I had imagined that all these men in football stadiums who wept and shouted that they had been bad husbands and bad fathers were promising to reform their conduct toward their (absent) wives and children. And so they may, in part, be doing. But *promise* is also a religious term. The rainbow, I was taught as a child, was God's promise to humankind that there would never be another Flood. And America, I was also taught, was the Land of Promise, to which my (as it happens, Jewish) ancestors came to find freedom and opportunity.

In today's majoritarian religious parlance, however, it seems that *promise* is a word with what has become an increasingly specific Christian meaning. "The word *promise* in the New Testament" says Cruden's concordance to the Bible, "is often taken for those promises that God made to Abraham and the other patriarchs of sending the Messiah. It is in this sense that the apostle Paul commonly uses the word *promises.*" Jesus, in short, is the promise. Romans 4:13: "For the promise, that he should be the heir of the world, was not to Abraham, or to his seed, through the law, but through the righteousness of faith." Galatians 3:16: "Now to Abraham and his seed were the promises made. He saith not, And to seeds, as of many; but as of one. And to thy seed, which is Christ." Promise equals eternal life through Jesus Christ.

Now, this understanding of the "promise" as not—despite what one might at first think—an equal-opportunity opportunity, so to speak, but rather a specifically *Christian* notion brings with it a number of potentially dangerous side effects. Look what happens, for example, to the question not only of the Promised Land (the state of Israel, the place of the Messiah) but also of the Land of Promise (the United States of America). It becomes, as Pat Robertson, Mississippi Governor Kirk Fordice, and others have been all too quick to claim, a "Christian nation" (Smothers 1996). One of the fastest-growing movements in the United States today is the extreme right-wing cluster of organizations known as "Christian patriots," a Christian Identity group whose commitment is to Jesus Christ as savior, to the promise of salvation, and to the idea that Christianity alone can offer eternal life. "The *end* of Christian patriotism," writes sociologist James Aho, "is the preservation of 'Christian values' and 'Americanism,' as the patriots understand them" (1990).[6] And if we understand "promise" as *code* for Christianity and even, especially, messianic and evangelical Christianity, then the promise of the Promise Keepers can be understood as an appropriation, and a naturalization, of born-again Christianity as the American experience.

This is one reason why Jacques Derrida (1994) describes Francis Fukayama's book *The End of History and the Last Man* (1992) as a "neo-evangelistic" gospel, preaching the "good news." ("We have become so accustomed by now to expect that the future will contain bad news with respect to the health and security of decent, democratic political practices that we have problems recognizing *good news* when it comes. And yet, the *good news* has come.") Here is Derrida's swift and devastating analysis: If one takes into account the fact that Fukayama associates a certain Jewish discourse of the Promised Land with the powerlessness of economic materialism or of the rationalism of natural science; and if one takes into account that elsewhere he treats as an almost negligible exception the fact that what he with equanimity calls "the Islamic world" does not enter into the "general consensus that, he says, seems to be taking shape around 'liberal democracy'" [p. 211], one can form at least an hypothesis about which angle Fukayama chooses to privilege in the eschatological triangle. The model of the liberal State to which he explicitly lays claim is not only that of Hegel, the Hegel of the struggle for recognition, it is that of a Hegel who privileges the "Christian vision." In other words, "The end of History is essentially a Christian eschatology," the imagination of postwar America and the European Community as a "Christian State."

It may be of more than passing interest that the place where the Southern Baptist Convention gathered in New Orleans to adopt its "Resolution on Jewish Evangelism" was the

Louisiana Superdome, home of the New Orleans Saints. In a cordoned-off third of the stadium, slated in a few months to play host to Super Bowl XXXI, the assembled faithful heard their newly elected president, Tom Eliff, urge them to "step up to the plate and be the people of God He expects us to be" (quoted in Toalston 1996). (On another occasion, one of the leaders of the Southern Baptists' mission to the Jews predicted that in the End Days of the world, "it'll be the bottom of the ninth, and the Jews will be batting clean-up for Christ.")[7] The Superdome is a football, not a baseball, field, but the month was June, after all, and God (as we have already seen) is, in evangelist-speak, the Utility Infielder to end all utility infielders, a team player—and team leader—in all organized sports. ("We're scoring baskets for Jesus," declared the emcee of a Promise Keeper's event in Colorado's Folsom Stadium, another football venue [quoted in Woodward and Keene-Osborn 1994].) And—I want to suggest—it is neither an accident nor a mere matter of convenience that this act of spiritual cheerleading emanated from a football stadium.

What does it mean to claim that the Dallas Cowboys—or now the Green Bay Packers—are "America's Team"? Is part of what makes "America's Team" American the fact that the players and coaches are overtly, manifestly, even ostentatiously Christian? The oppositional, ecstatic, and zealous nature of sports spectatorship and sports fandom ("Kill the ump"; "throw the bums out") raises the temperature of the crowd even as it lowers the level of nuance and subtlety. The twin phenomena—of exhibitionistic, often televised moments of prayer by players and coaches and of the religious faithful convened for evangelical purpose in football stadiums around the country, exhorted to action by coaches who are now ministers or ministers who are now coaches—reflect each other with uncanny and disturbing symmetry. Winning, it may turn out, converting points for "our" team, the chosen team, the team that *deserves* to win, is once again the "only thing" that counts.

The football rule book contains a number of sounding phrases that mark infractions on the field, from "out of bounds" to "unsportsmanlike conduct" to "palpably unfair acts," like a player coming off the bench to tackle the ball carrier. "Encroachment," defensive or offensive holding, illegal motion, and falling or "piling on" are other sins of the gridiron, as is "prolonged, excessive, premeditated celebration" (Hickok 1995). Once upon a time, before the modern era of illuminated stadiums and luxury boxes, it was also possible for a game to be "called on account of darkness." The high visibility of evangelical and salvific Christianity in sports and its close ties with a competitive rhetoric of patriotism and Americanism suggest that this may be the moment to call for a time-out on proclamations of holiness in the huddle—time to rethink the troubling implications of public prayer on the field and organized team prayers in the locker room.

Notes

1. When reporter Michael Vega asked players for their favorite Bible verses, they had them ready, as if they were plays to be audibled from the huddle.

"Philippians 4:13," said guard Rich Tylski. "That's been my favorite Scripture ever since I became a Christian in high school." "Colossians 3:23," said tight end Rich Griffith. "It has to do with 'Everything you do, do with all your heart as for the Lord and not for men.' So everything I do, I try to do it for God. I don't do it for Coach Coughlin or for anyone else. I try to do it for a superior person." As for Brunell's favorite, it was Jeremiah 29:11: "For I know the plans I have for you, declares the Lord, plans to prosper you and not to harm you, but to give you hope for the future."

Said Jaguars' team chaplain Don Walker, "When Coach Coughlin put this team together, he didn't just stop with excellent athletes, he went looking for young men with values and character . . . some good guys." "What he ended up getting were good guys who are walking and looking after God." "From the very beginning," the chaplain observed, "I think there was a very strong core group, spiritually, within this team, and it has grown and progressed. There's a very, very positive atmosphere spiritually in this team and there's almost positive peer pressure to consider walking in faith. There's just a tremendous sense of prayer on this team." (Notice the interesting qualification, "*almost* positive peer pressure." Is that "almost pressure"—or "almost positive"?)

2. Described by W. Brown Patterson, dean of the college at the University of the South. Quoted in Higgs (1995, 238).

3. The chapel's racing runners would seem to illustrate St. Paul's instruction to the Corinthians, "Know yet not that they which run in a race run all, but one receiveth the prize? So run that ye may obtain" (1 Corinthians 9:24)—rather than Ecclesiastes, "the race is not to the swift" (Ecclesiastes 9:11) or even Paul's more temperate—or marathon-like—"let us run with patience the race which is set before us" (Hebrews 12:1).

4. Benjamin Ward Richardson (1882, cited in Gilman 1991).

5. Larry Lewis, former president of the Home Mission Board that supervises the Southern Baptist Convention's U.S.-based missionaries. Quoted in Goldberg (1997).

6. Since, according to the logic of these groups, only the Anglo-Saxon peoples have fulfilled all of God's promises in the Bible, they alone are His chosen people. Thus, Gordon "Jack" Mohr, the cofounder of a group called the Christian Patriot Defense League and a member of the Christian Identity movement, can claim that Talmudism is Satan worship, that Jews are born evil, and that the real Israelites, the ones to whom God promised a chosen future, are white Aryans. Mohr's book on this topic is called *Exploding the 'Chosen People' Myth.* In it, he suggests, among other things, that Jews cannot be converted because the "Jewish character" is inherited from "2,500 years of legacy." "Judah," in fact, say some Christian Identity believers, was the homeland of the Aryan people known as the Jutes, who lived in northern Germany. Under the headline "Adolf Hitler was Elijah," a brochure distributed by the Socialist Nationalist Aryan Peoples Party declared that the "message of Identity" was that Aryans are, "to the exclusion of all others, representative of the only Covenant agreeable to our God." Jews are "vipers," "murderous," "mongrelizing" international bankers, rightly opposed by the prophet Hitler. A color brochure from Mythos Makers, Aryan Nations (reproduced in Aho's appendix), advertises—among other items—a Mythos baseball jersey (50 percent cotton, 50 percent polyester) bearing the logo "White Pride World Wide." Such extremist groups, often overtly and proudly anti-Semitic, "Aryan," and racialist, are far from the mainstream of American Christian opinion. But whether Jews and homosexuals are cast out forever or capable of being "saved" and "converted" to the majority's faith makes less difference than the fact that self-appointed experts have determined their right to coax and coach them into conformity.

7. The Reverend Phil Roberts (quoted in Goldberg 1997).

References

Aho, J. A. 1990. *The Politics of Righteousness: Idaho Christian Patriotism.* Seattle: University of Washington Press.

Bayless, S. 1996. "God's Playbook." *New York Times,* December 1, E7.

Blaudschun, M. 1997. "No Doubt White Is on a Mission." *Boston Globe,* January 22, F5.

Cafardo, N. 1997. "Parcells Plays to Audience." *Boston Globe,* January 7, C5.

Carroll, J. 1997. "Critics of Albright's Conversion Ignore the Essence of Judaism." *Boston Globe,* February 18, A11.

Chandrasekaran, R. 1995. "A Reverse in the End Zone: After Liberty's Challenge, NCAA Clarifies Rule, Allows Praying after Touchdowns." *Washington Post,* September 2, C1.

Cross, H. M. 1973. "The College Athlete and the Institution." *Law and Contemporary Problems* 30: 150, 168–69.

Deford, F. 1976. "Endorsing Jesus." *Sports Illustrated,* April 26, 54–69.

Derrida, J. 1994. *Specters of Marx.* New York: Routledge.

Dundes, A. 1980. "Into the Endzone for a Touchdown: A Psychoanalytic Consideration of American Football." In *Interpreting Folklore,* 199–210. Bloomington: Indiana University Press.

Eskenazi, G. 1997. "Jaguars and Patriots Put It on the Line: Expect a Shootout." *New York Times,* January 12, H3.

Farrell, C. R. 1984. "Memphis State Coach Is Accused of Imposing Religious Beliefs on Players." *The Chronicle of Higher Education* 29, no. 6: 26.

Freud, S. 1920. "The Psychogenesis of a Case of Homosexuality in a Woman." In James Strachey, ed. and trans., *The Standard Edition of the Complete Psychological Works of Sigmund Freud.* Vol. 18. London: The Hogarth Press and the Institute of Psycho-Analysis, 1955.

———. 1921. "Group Psychology and the Analysis of the Ego." In James Strachey, ed. and trans., *The Standard Edition of the Complete Psychological Works of Sigmund Freud.* Vol. 18. London: The Hogarth Press and the Institute of Psycho-Analysis, 1955.

———. 1930. *Civilization and Its Discontents.* In James Strachey, ed. and trans., *The Standard Edition of the Complete Psychological Works of Sigmund Freud.* Vol. 21. London: The Hogarth Press and the Institute of Psycho-Analysis, 1955.

Fried, G., and L. Bradley. 1994. "Applying the First Amendment to Prayer in a Public University Locker Room: An Athlete's and Coach's Perspective." *Marquette Sports Law Journal,* no. 301 (spring).

Fukayama, F. 1992. *The End of History and the Last Man.* New York: Maxwell Macmillan International.

Fuss, D. 1996. *Identification Papers.* New York: Routledge.

Garment, L. 1996. "Christian Soldiers." *New York Times,* June 27, A23.

Gilman, S. 1991. *The Jew's Body.* New York: Routledge.

Goldberg, J. 1997. "Some of Their Best Friends Are Jews." *New York Times Magazine,* March 16, 43.

Harvey, M. 1995. "Super Bowl Sunday Stokes Creative Fires of Clergy Nationwide." *Johnson City Press,* January 28, 7.

Herrmann, A. 1996. "A Legal Leg to Stand On." *Chicago Sun-Times,* March 14, 8.

Hickok, R. 1995. *The Pro Football Fan's Companion.* New York: Macmillan.

Higgs, R. J. 1995. *God in the Stadium: Sports and Religion in America.* Lexington: The University Press of Kentucky.

Hoppe, A. 1995. "Football Prayers." *San Francisco Chronicle,* September 6, A15.

Janofsky, M. 1997. "At Mass Events, Americans Looking to One Another." *New York Times,* October 27, A21.

Jastrowitz, M. 1908. "Muskeljuden und Nervenjuden." *Judishe Turnzeitung* 9: 33–36.

Kaminer, W. 1996. "The Last Taboo." *The New Republic,* October 14, 28–32.

Kinsolving, L. 1971. "Exploiting Athletes in Religion Questioned." *Johnson City Press,* January 12, 10.

Martin, W. 1992. *A Prophet with Honor: The Billy Graham Story.* New York: William Morrow.

Mathisen, J. A. 1992. "From Muscular Christians to Jocks for Jesus." *Christian Century,* January 1–8, 11–15.

McNeille, J. T. 1948. "The Christian Athlete in Philippians 3:7–14." *Christianity in Crisis: Q Christian Journal of Opinion,* August 2, 106–7.

Monaghan, P. 1985. "Religion in a State-College Locker Room: Coach's Fervor Raises Church-State Issue." *Chronicle of Higher Education* 32, No. 3: 37–38.

———. 1992. "U. of Colorado Football Coach Accused of Using His Position to Promote His Religious Views." *Chronicle of Higher Education* 32, no. 12: A35, A37.

Moon, B. 1963. "For the Sake of Argument: The Case against Christian Unity." *Maclean's Magazine,* October 5, 30–36.

Nance, R. 1996. "Abdul Rauf to Stand, Pray during Anthem." *USA Today,* March 15, 1C.

Nelson, M. B. 1994. *The Stronger Women Get, the More Men Love Football.* New York: Harcourt Brace.

Niebuhr, G. 1995. "Men Crowd Stadiums to Fulfill Their Souls." *New York Times,* August 6, A1.

———. 1996. "Baptists Censure Disney for Gay-Spouse Benefits." *New York Times,* June 13, A14.

Nossiter, A. 1997. "North Carolina's Faith in Football." *New York Times,* January 11, N6.

Pronger, B. 1980. *The Arena of Masculinity: Sports, Homosexuality and the Meaning of Sex.* New York: St. Martin's Press.

Ragussis, M. 1995. *Figures of Conversion: "The Jewish Question" and English National Identity.* Durham, N.C.: Duke University Press.

Reilly, R. 1995. "Save Your Prayers Please." *Sports Illustrated,* February 4, 86.

Rice, G. 1941. "Alumnus Football." *Only the Braves: and Other Poems.* New York: A. S. Barnes.

Rich, F. 1996. "'Thank God I'm a Man.'" *New York Times,* September 25, A21.

Richardson, B. W. 1882. *Diseases of Modern Life.* New York: Bermingham and Co.

Romell, R. 1997. "Packer Pride: Jubilant Hordes Jam Homecoming." *Milwaukee Journal Sentinel,* January 28, 5A.

Smith, T. W. 1997. "White Wants Pulpit between Hash Marks." *New York Times,* January 23, B13, B14.

Smothers, R. 1996. "For Mississippi's Governor, Another Fight over Power." *New York Times,* July 10, A10.

Steinfels, P. 1991. "Beliefs." *New York Times,* June 22, A10.

Swan, G. 1990. "Religion's a Hit in Baseball Clubhouses." *Greenville Sun,* August 25, B1.

Tiger, L. 1969. *Men in Groups.* New York: Random House.

Toalston, A. 1996. "SBC Challenges Disney, Church Arsons, Moves Ahead with 21st Century Thrust." *Baptist Press News Service,* June 13.

Vega, M. 1997. "Jaguars' Leap of Faith." *Boston Globe,* January 9, C7.

Way, L. 1831. *Jewish Repository I.* London.

Willis, J. D., and R. G. Wettan. 1977. "Religion and Sport in America: The Case for the Sports Bay in the Cathedral Church of Saint John the Divine." *Journal of Sport History* 4, no. 2 (summer): 189–207.

Woodward, K. L., and S. Keene-Osborn. 1994. "The Gospel of Guyhood." *Newsweek,* August 29, 60.

4

Prefiguring a Black Cultural Formation

THE NEW CONDITIONS OF BLACK CULTURAL PRODUCTION

Herman Gray

At the dawn of the twenty-first century, I would venture to say that black intellectuals, filmmakers, musicians, choreographers, playwrights, and novelists are profoundly shaping the imagination of American culture. What may distinguish this moment is the recognition by the cultural dominant of the sheer influence and pervasiveness of black presence in mainstream American culture. This recognition and influence approaches, in the language of Raymond Williams, the rudiments of an institutional formation (Williams 1982). The institutionalization of black cultural production, especially the social reach of its cultural influence, appears in a post–civil rights period of global corporate consolidation. Even as American culture travels widely and corporate ownership and administrative control over the making of culture becomes more concentrated, a new generation of artists, filmmakers, scholars, cultural critics, and novelists are now members, even leaders, of the nation's major cultural and social institutions. For perhaps the first time, a small but highly visible cohort of black culture workers enjoy access to dominant institutional resources, especially the forms of legitimization, prestige, and recognition that such institutions bestow.

A complex and often contested terrain of discourse, representation, and politics typifies these conditions of black cultural production. These cultural struggles bear directly on questions of power, in particular, the relationship of dominant national institutions to forms of black cultural productions and expressivity that remain outside mainstream institutions and those that operate beyond the recognition and support of these dominant institutions. For example, locally and regionally based organizations and communities of musicians, painters, dancers, and writers in Los Angeles, Detroit, Brooklyn, Kansas City, Chicago, and the San Francisco Bay Area nurture and develop artists, some of whom also enjoy national prominence. No less significant are those artists and cultural workers who form local and regionally based operations that produce, train, and reproduce black expressive forms and practices in local lodges, high schools, community theaters, and churches. With very few exceptions, these organizations, networks, and institutions seldom appear on the radar screen of national media. It is as if these levels of cultural production and practice exert little if any direct influence on the national cultural and intellectual imagination. Against the enormous public profile and cultural influence of a place like New York City and the organizational resources of sites like the Lincoln Center, for example, local and regional activities can go almost completely unrecognized.

Bringing these smaller-scale and often more marginal organizations and their activities into sharper focus complicates institutional conditions and relations of black cultural production (especially any claim to a coherent and fixed conception) of a black cultural formation. The controversy surrounding the 1995 Whitney Museum Exhibition on Black Masculinity illustrates, for example, the depths of cultural debates surrounding the production and exhibition of artistic representation of black expressive culture within mainstream arts institutions as well as the tension between local and national, marginal and dominant cultural institutions. As the polemic surrounding the Whitney Exhibition shows, the political differences and multiple claims on blackness trouble the ease with which such cultural performances can be viewed as expressions of oppositional black cultural politics.

By the same token, such performances do provide the occasion for a critical interrogation of what the exhibition means, the mainstream institutional spaces from which it was staged, the circumstances through which it derived its legitimacy, and how it came to be constituted as a discursive intervention in black image making. These issues were made all the more vexing and complex by the racial, sexual, generational, and gender-based disputes surrounding the exhibition.[1]

My point is simply this. The successful acquisition and "occupation" of institutional spaces and the cultural claims that emanate from them complicate rather than simplify the very notion of black cultural politics. As examples like the Whitney Museum Exhibition on Black Masculinity demonstrate, presenting black cultural expressions within dominant mainstream cultural spaces like the Whitney Museum generates, within black cultural discourse anyway, highly contentious political disputes about black cultural practices and images.

Against this backdrop, I view the institutional recognition and legitimation of black cultural production (and the media celebrations that have accompanied it) in political terms. That is, I see this recognition and legitimation as an instance in which black cultural production functions as a cultural site of political disputes over representation, meaning, and the valuation of blackness as a cultural expression (Powell 1997; Taylor 1998). I regard the recognition, even the subsequent incorporation, of black cultural production by dominant cultural institutions as very much a strategic move by dominant mainstream cultural institutions. Such a move does, nonetheless, express (if only momentarily) something of a challenge to the historic pattern of exclusion and deformation of black images by these very same institutions. Moreover, black artist, intellectuals, and critics have helped to transform these sites of cultural production. Thus, I also see this development as *one* strategy by which black cultural producers negotiate and navigate the uneven terrain of an American national imaginary that still remains deeply ambivalent about black cultural presence.

Moving onto the terrain of dominant institutions while retaining the focus on the conceptual and political idea of a black cultural formation is potentially productive. Such an emphasis helps us move beyond binary conceptions of cultural politics that rely on categories that posit oppositional as located either inside or outside of mainstream social institutions and the legitimacy that they confer. By centering black cultural production and the contemporary strategies through which black cultural producers negotiate the contemporary cultural and institutional landscape, I aim to map the discursive, political, and social conditions that structure the cultural and social spaces of black cultural production.

Black Cultural Formation

The right to represent blackness (in the United States), who has a rightful claim on a particular version of blackness as representative, or indeed the need to delimit what constitutes blackness no longer defines the terms of black cultural production and of black critical discourse. Most immediately, this means that the still entrenched language of positive/negative images, vexing polemics about the commodification of blackness, and the endless search for authenticating narratives have come under productive critical scrutiny (Hall 1989, 1992; Mercer 1994; Harper 1996). Black representation produced in the United States has also come in for some rather sustained critical interrogations from black cultural critics, especially in England, for its purported hegemonic tendencies (Gilroy 1994). Despite the characteristics and specificity of the local circumstances in which they are generated, U.S. black cultural productions are nonetheless globally pervasive (Gilroy 1993; Lipsitz 1994). That black American cultural representations sustain their global appeal, circulating, borrowing, aligning, and, yes, appropriating a wide array of traditions, formations, memories, and desires is deeply disturbing and problematic for some members of the black Atlantic Diaspora. Black American cultural representations involve complex texts, discourses, and narratives that are typically expressed in multiple and overlapping sites and media. Black cultural producers in the United States deliberately mix and match, spill and cross aesthetic, geographic, technological, and social borders, exemplifying what Dick Hebdige (1987) calls a cut n' mix aesthetic.

Since the mid-1980s, black Americans working in film, television, and music video have experienced a precarious but nonetheless sustained cycle of image making in documentary and narrative film and television (Guerrero 1993; Watkins 1998). These forms of cultural production and the representations they generate are heavily influenced by developments in black popular culture, notably music, fashion, vernacular language, and sport.

Of course, black popular music remains one of the richest and most controversial sources of black self-representation and expression. Black American musicians continue to invent and stretch the complex terrain on which to articulate black imagination and creative possibility. In particular, black composers and performers in jazz, rock, pop, and rap continue to generate musical styles that unsettle and destabilize the music industry's racialized pattern of musical production, marketing, and definition.

Black critical and intellectual discourse in cultural studies, literary criticism, feminist theory, film studies, critical race studies, and African American studies has opened and in some cases consolidated institutional spaces and discursive communities from which to identify, evaluate, and legitimate black cultural production and self-representation. Black scholars and critics are engaged in the routine and necessary discursive work of generating and sustaining cultural communities. Indeed, this critical work has been enabled by and built on the commercial success and critical recognition of black writers, especially in the areas of black women's fiction and biography and memoir. These genres have themselves become forms in which black writers have made crucial interventions in the area of black self-representation.[2]

In some cases, black cultural achievements are enabled by the significant (and often very public) leadership by blacks of prestigious and high-profile cultural organizations and institutions. This leadership has been central to the visibility, circulation, and legitimization of black cultural production in the United States, especially in its national life and public culture.[3]

I am especially interested, then, in the insights that these complex conditions of production and representation offer for understanding the contemporary politics of black cultural production, the shifts in cultural imagination and desire, and the strategies deployed to achieve cultural legitimacy and visibility. In broad terms, these cultural developments, the social condition of their appearance, and their attendant institutional sites may actually prefigure what I call a *cultural formation.* I use this idea of cultural formation as a staging arena from which to explore the institutional character, cultural features, and political implications of these recent cultural developments.

By cultural formation, I intend something similar to the sociological and cultural characteristics identified by labor historian Michael Denning to describe the cultural and artistic significance of radical popular front cultural expressions in America of the 1930s, 1940s, and 1950s. In *The Cultural Front* (1996), Denning suggests that in literature, photography, theater, intellectual production, and cinema, a radical and progressive sensibility—structure of feeling, really—defined the cultural and artistic products of the period. The pervasiveness and impact of this influence amounted to what Denning terms the "laboring" of American culture. Anchored by a progressive labor movement and rooted in local as well as national organizations like art houses, coffee shops, academic departments, bookstores, and union locals, the cultural formation to which he refers expressed a distinctive cultural sensibility. It helped give a distinctive similitude to the organizing and political work of the popular front. In addition to Denning's suggestive example, my conception of culture is indebted to the work of Raymond Williams and Antonio Gramsci. Both recognized the centrality and relationship of culture to the consolidation and institutionalization of a progressive historical bloc (Denning 1996). Both avoided the reductionist and mechanical conceptions of art and culture that characterized classical Marxist analysis of ideology and culture, particularly in relationship to material life and progressive movements for social change.

Insofar as black cultural production in the United States is concerned, it is tempting to use the concept of cultural formation (even if only loosely) to describe two earlier historical moments: the Harlem Renaissance in the 1920s and the Black Arts movement in the 1960s. Harold Cruse's important but largely neglected *The Crisis of the Negro Intellectual* (1967) offers a negative, but no less critical, example of why our present might be productively characterized by a term like "cultural formation." Indeed, for Cruse the failure of the Harlem Renaissance as a cultural movement was the absence of a viable institutional and economic infrastructure. Accordingly, there was too little organizational stability, institutional legitimacy, and economic autonomy with which to shield these movements from the predictable shifts of interests, economic support, and connection to material experiences of working-class blacks. Unable to sustain themselves financially, to maintain autonomy socially, and to root themselves in the day-to-day experiences of those for whom they sought to speak and represent, according to Cruse these moments of cultural possibility simply withered.

Are we perhaps at the threshold of what we might call, following Denning's formulation, a "racing" (i.e., an explicit darkening, blackening, or coloring) of American culture at least in terms of the operation of its dominant institutions of cultural production and legitimation? Using his conception of black cultural projection, Merlman seems to think that African Americans have been able effectively to project, as it were, black cultural achievements and a worldview into the mainstream of American society (Merlman 1995). Cornel West, Eric Michael Dyson, and others also suggest as much in the realm of popular culture. I am interested in black cultural production at century's end not as empirically representative evidence that definitively confirms (or disproves) the presence of a new black cultural formation. My aim, rather, is to map the social, economic, technological, and political features of such a possible formation and to assess its political and cultural effects. I pursue this mapping and interrogation by way of two highly visible and, I think, suggestive examples: the emergence of a critical group of highly visible critical black (public) intellectuals and the formation of the Jazz at Lincoln Center program in New York City. I believe that these institutional expressions of black cultural production are more than accidental but perhaps less than planned and coordinated.

The Sociological Production of Contemporary Black Expressive Culture

Black cultural expression is shaped by the flexible conditions of production, new technologies of communication and circulation, regulatory state policies, expanding means and sites of representation, competing claims of ownership and authenticity, and contested discourses of judgment and evaluation. By now it is rather axiomatic that regardless of genre, venue, or medium, contemporary black cultural production in the United States is, for the most part, produced, mediated, and circulated through commercially mediated sites such as television, video, music, film, publishing, and theater. Black cultural (popular and artistic) productions cross the boundaries of high/low, popular/elite, and commercial/noncommercial and operate in dialogue with one another as well as those social and cultural circumstances in which black folk live.

Thus, social conditions, political struggles, and cultural discourses directly and indirectly structure black expressive culture. A partial list of these relevant structuring conditions include the racialization of U.S. society; continuing debates about race, identity, multiculturalism, immigration, citizenship, and nation; shifts in the structure of the economy; transformations in the geographic distribution, circuits, and flows of racialized populations; and the social organization and cultural redefinition of public space. Disputes among blacks about difference, class, community, mass collective action, authenticity, and, of course, representation constitute the discursive field within which black expressive culture and representation is constituted, negotiated, and enacted (Kelley 1997).

I use "blackness" here to refer to both social location and cultural meaning. In discursive terms, I use "blackness" as a cultural trope and social category over which competing claims are made and registered (Gray 1995). The material and discursive come together when blackness appears as the object of cultural disputes where conflicting claims are waged, registered, and then used in the service of different interests. In this conception, the empirical, political, and moral veracity on which such claims rest are shifting and unstable, depending on the historical and structural conditions within which they circulate and are registered. The deployment of various moral, rhetorical, and political strategies in the name of blackness (or against it) are designed to construct social identifications in order to win the political allegiance and popular sentiments of social subjects on whose behalf such claims are made. Thus, for example, black cultural critics sometimes use scholarly and professional legitimacy to contest damaging claims of white racists or the exaggerated claims of unrepenting black isolationists, both of which may be couched in the rhetoric of science. On the other hand, black neonationalists and Afrocentrists might just as easily use rhetorical and moral appeals to a noble and glorious past as a corrective to claims that point to the absence of black contributions to world history and civilization. Liberal policymakers sometimes use the trope of blackness in political appeals directed at the state to call attention to the excessive and punitive sanctions aimed at specific populations (e.g., Latino, Asian, and Caribbean immigrants; black teenage mothers; and single parents). Finally (black) neoconservative scholars and liberal individualists mobilize specific conceptions of blackness to attack the political rhetoric of black solidarity rooted in racial kinship as the basis to enlist political support and to advocate social policies against the distribution of social resources based on race. These kinds of public narratives make some implicit claim to black representation; as such, how blackness is constituted in cultural representation is crucial to the formation of common sense about the meaning of blackness and the identification and organization of interests that it structures. Commercial media like network television, cinema, popular music, music video, digital technologies, and virtual reality, as well as venues of artistic production such as theater, art galleries, and the concert hall, are all necessary sites for the organization, presentation, and circulation of these competing claims on blackness.

This is precisely why such structuring conditions are so important, for there are very real political and legal stakes in how representations are produced, framed, and potentially deployed to construct political projects (Hunt 1999). Whether publishing, television, cinema, the university, law schools, or the courtroom, black cultural production and representation is variously shaped by industrial shifts, organizational restructuring, state regulation, and economic imperatives that continue to transform the social conditions of production, circulation, and reception. In the case of commercial network television in the United States, to take an obvious example, structuring factors contribute to the enabling conditions (and constraints) within which the black television market/audience is constructed as a profitable (or ignored as an unprofitable) commodity by the television industry. As existing structuring conditions give way to new ones—including new ownership structures, new markets, different pricing structures, and different delivery systems—the visibility, position, and meaning of the black television audience to networks also change.

These shifting institutional conditions are only the most visible signs of the significant transformations in the communications industry. Different sectors of the communication industry (e.g., music, television, and cinema) are constantly packaging, arranging, and vying to extend and exert control over the terms and circumstances in which their products circulate and take on value. This process involves the industry's assignment of differential value to distinctive audiences that in turn constructs (from the industry perspective) various audiences as markets that are easily combined, segmented, aggregated, and disaggregated so that they fit the commodity logic that structures the modern media industry (Watkins 1998). But, as S. Craig Watkins demonstrates in his very careful analysis of black film cycles of the 1980s, these processes are mutually constitutive rather than determined beforehand (Watkins 1998). Social and political interests both outside of and within black communities also make and register equally significant and meaningful claims on blackness, many of which operate squarely within the logic expressed by the media. Specifying blackness as the subject of different social positions, competing cultural claims, conflicting political interests, and shifting market imperatives highlights the strategic necessity (in matters of cultural politics anyway) of thinking about the processes and relations of black cultural production in institutional terms.

Materially and institutionally, the organizational and economic relationships that now characterize vertically and horizontally integrated culture/media/entertainment/information-based global corporations parallel the cultural and political relations of representation. Black cultural expression is increasingly caught in and thus mediated by (and mediates) the new so-called media synergy—multiple levels of intertextual and organizational complementarity and exchange. As with workers, commodities, and information, black cultural images circulate across different media, countries, markets, and genres. As central as they are to the operations of various political, legal, organizational, discursive, and technological structures, the movement of black images and representation is never free of cultural and social traces of the condition of their production, circulation, and use. As Stuart Hall notes, blackness is never innocent or pure in some original and authentic sense (Hall 1992).

In this movement and circulation, representation of the black social body, like the physical body, is the object of administrative management, legal regulation, social control, and even cultural fascination by the state, the news media, and the entertainment industry. One need only look at network and cable television programming in the United States (and in much of the Western industrialized world) to get a sense of the extent of this cultural fascination and legal regulation at work. Network television news, talk, reality, and sports are very often the primary (some would argue preferred) genres through which the disciplining effects of racial discourse and fascination with black representation are expressed culturally. Dick Hebdige, John Fiske, and John Caldwell, for example, identify the pervasiveness of technologies of image surveillance mobilized around the black body (Hebdige 1988; Fiske 1994; Caldwell 1998). Examples abound: the low-tech home video cameras used to record the Rodney King beating in Los Angeles, courtroom cameras, hidden security cameras found in department stores, car-mounted camcorders used by the police, and news cameras used by local news units that literally cover the social body in search of the big story. I would want to include large-scale technologies of observation and regulation, such as the domestic use of high-powered aerial searchlights that were perfected by the Los Angeles Police Department's gang division in black and Latino communities like Compton, Watts, and South Central Los Angeles (Davis 1992). The U.S. Immigration Service also relied on high-tech surveillance hardware, like infrared cameras, night-vision lenses, and heat-seeking radar, to police the U.S. border with Mexico.

Discourses about race in the United States are not just the products of structuring influences alone. Discourses about race are produced in the very representations and logic of commonsense racial knowledge produced and constituted in representations like television news and entertainment. Law and legal discourse are crucial here both as a subject of media representation, as in shows about the law and courtrooms, and as a structuring force for representation, as in the legal conditions that structure a whole range of guiding logics in television, from laws regulating the structure of the industry to statutes protecting speech and guarding against censorship. In matters of race and representation, law and legal discourse are especially crucial because they are the structuring scene or site in which organizing narratives about fairness, civility, propriety, transgression, and responsibility are framed. Transgressions and conflicts that are seen as racial encourage viewers to ask, Is it fair? Is it right? Is it legal? Is it good? These are all judgments that are inscribed in the very representational logic through which public narratives about racial conflict are presented. Scholars in critical race theory and critical legal studies have worked to make visible the complex racial, gender, and class operations in legal discourse, knowledge production, and legal practices. But when rendered in televisual representations of the law (especially at work), television works hard to render invisible the deeply systemic processes of racialization, gender subordination, and class inequalities that are central to the very structure of legal practice and the law. Instead, the narrative focus is on the occupational hazards (or glories) of the legal profession, the character defects of individual criminals, or the fetishization of the technical machinations of the criminal justice system. Black musicians (especially hip-hoppers) and image makers (especially music videographers) have consistently commented on and made visible the centrality of race to the operation of the criminal justice system and the law. Through vernacular practices of the street, these culture workers seek to articulate their experience of themselves as racial(ized) subjects of the state. As the objects of media narratives about crime, the criminal justice system, and the legal profession, commercial media, especially television, work hard to produce (counter) stories that sustain a naturalized and commonsense understanding of crime, criminals, and the legal system.

When linked to a technology of representation like television, the discourse of regulation that underwrites this commonsense understanding of crime and the legal system operates through the production of the black body as spectacle. Discursively, this operation depends on the production of the black body as the site of pleasure and adoration, fear and menace. In crime discourse in the 1980s, the black male (youth) body signified menace and the loss of civility in the public sphere. This narrative of loss was expressed most explicitly by media and politicians and to the steady expansion of the coercive arm of the state (e.g., prison and police) and the privatization of key functions of regulation (private police), incarceration (prisons), and surveillance (private security forces). Television represented the public sphere as the site of an increasing but necessary regulation and surveillance that depended on race, even though it was overtly expressed as moral panics and political disputes over immigration, gangs, welfare, and crime. Culturally, the multiply inflected meaning of black (self) representation in this discourse of regulation can be seen in the various media constructions of black male criminality, gansta rappers, and male youth (Reeves and Campbell 1994; Gray 1995; Kelley 1997; Watkins 1998). The electronic mass media (especially news, sport, and music video) is the preeminent site where competing claims about black masculinity are waged. Black youth, the sectors of the black middle class, preachers, moral entrepreneurs police, politicians, black feminists, queer activists, and, yes, even scholars all wage claims on behalf of "the" commonsense definition of black masculinity (as, among other things, dangerous and menacing).

Cultural constructions of menace are not limited to black heterosexual men, youth, or gansta rappers, either. In a discourse of regulation erected on the rhetoric of traditional values (Stacey 1996), black gay men threaten the social body in another way, for they generate a kind of masculine anxiety that cuts across race (Harper 1996). This articulation of blackness and heterosexual masculinity, this traversal of blackness by an anxious heterosexual black masculinity, produces an odd alliance. This articulation produces a conception of hyperheterosexual manliness that appears in popular and political discourse and cultural representation as a renewed claim by heterosexual men (of all races) on women, children, family, community, and nation. Hence, in the media discourse of regulation (where fear and menace are the key touchstones of a society seen as out of control), the black male gay body operates symbolically to signify the erosion of morality and threats to manhood. Recent examples are not difficult to come by. North Carolina Senator Jessie Helms used the documentary film *Tongues Untied* by the late Marlon Riggs as the basis of a nasty frontal assault in the culture wars on gays and lesbians, the National Endowment for the Arts and Humanities, and public broadcasting. This anxious masculinity also finds expression by protonationalists, religious leaders, and popular musicians within the black social body. Black British filmmaker Issac Julian's documentary film exploration of Diaspora music in the United States, England, and the Caribbean titled *The Darker Side of Black* and Marlon Riggs's *Black Is, Black Ain't* explicitly set out the terms of black assaults on black homosexual masculinity within black popular culture.

In network television news, national political ad campaigns, and Hollywood cinema, while the physical body of black women has often been present, her subjectivity has not (especially as the primary subject of narrative cinema). In the discourse of regulation, the black body has more often than not functioned symbolically to signal the erosion of family, the deleterious consequence of single-parent households, and the purported threat to a patriarchal moral order. In this discursive universe, women's sexuality and sexual behavior should be strictly confined to the nuclear family and used only in the service of motherhood and (for some cultural nationalist) reproduction. (Here the black welfare queen/client of the Reagan/Bush presidencies is the most obvious example.) In the production of female heterosexuality (anchored by European myths of beauty and sexuality), black women's experiences have been rendered almost uniformly invisible. Indeed, through their very absence, black women function discursively to consolidate and condense representations that equate beauty and desire with a persistent and pronounced semiotic slide toward whiteness (or of late hybridity). In the moral economy of contemporary American discourses of gender, sexuality, and race, black women's bodies operate culturally to mark the boundaries of female (hetero) sexuality, motherhood, family, desire, and beauty.

These discourses of regulation and the moral panics that they helped to mobilize worked for a time in the 1980s to consolidate a neoconservative hegemonic bloc. This bloc routinely used media images of black men and women, the poor, and immigrants to represent social crisis. Gendered and racialized images of poverty and disenfranchisement became the basis for a barrage of public policies and legislation intended to shore up this hegemonic position and to quiet the moral panics constructed around race in general and blackness in particular. Typical examples are the erosion of moral standards, the disappearance of the work ethic (e.g., the 1996 Welfare Bill), the loss of law and order (e.g., the 1995 Crime Bill), the decay of Western civilization (e.g., the culture wars of the 1980s), and the assaults on whiteness and masculinity (California, Florida, and Texas propositions on affirmative action). In short, politically and culturally, the image of blacks, the poor, and immigrants anchored a moral panic about the diminution and erosion of American civic and public life and fueled public policy positions on citizenship, nation, community, and family.

The link between media representations of blackness (along with sexuality and immigration) and policy proscriptions for reimagining and consolidating a traditional vision of the American nation is of course contradictory and has been actively challenged. This challenge, at the level of expressive culture and representation, is discursive and a potentially counterhegemonic force that circulates through mass commercial forms like television, music, literature, and film. Generated from within black artistic, intellectual, and popular spheres, these representations might in one sense be seen as a rejoinder to the various conservative attempts to demonize, regulate, define, and contain blackness within a right-wing discourse. In some cases, these black representations share much with discourses of regulation, especially on matters of culture, crime, sex, and family. But black claims and counterclaims provide the basis for a cultural assertion of black self-representation that is also deeply engaged with the cultural politics of difference within black cultural discourse as well as broader American debates about national identity, citizenship, and the public sphere.

The remainder of my discussion is devoted to the terms of this engagement from the perspective of an emerging black cultural formation. I now turn to two specific cases of black cultural production and the social and cultural terms that structure them.

Institutional Seizure: Jazz at Lincoln Center

After a three-year period of offering modest programs and a concert series, in 1991 the Lincoln Center for the Performing Arts established a full-time jazz program and appointed its first artistic director, trumpeter Wynton Marsalis. Although controversial, this appointment began a new period of visibility, funding, and institutional recognition for jazz in one of the nation's premier cultural institutions. With long-established departments in classical music, opera, and dance, Lincoln Center added jazz to its funded programs. Even though it was not institutionally on par with its existing cultural departments in dance, opera, and classical music, the establishment of the jazz program was a key move toward recognition and legitimization. In addition to regular concert offering, jazz at the center would be included in the center's regular funding allocation and program offerings. The expectation was also that the jazz program would become a regular part of the center's highly visible education series. This stability and visibility would generate national press attention and attract high-caliber players who would be presented in one of the nation's most prestigious performance venues—Alice Tully Hall, a 1,100-seat concert auditorium.

The establishment of the jazz program at Lincoln Center was met with often celebratory, though at times contentious, media attention and public interest in jazz. The program also produced critical debate in the national jazz press (especially the New York press) about the future and direction of jazz. In the aftermath of the program's establishment, there was a noticeable proliferation of philanthropic, public, and corporate funding for jazz as well as a modest increase in research and training opportunities in conservatories, institutes, and universities. These developments signal a significant advance in the institutional recognition and cultural legitimization of jazz, especially among cultural gatekeepers, philanthropists, and critics. I contend that Marsalis and his colleagues used the installation of the jazz program at Lincoln Center as a conscious attempt to establish an institutional base for the development of a black cultural front, at least in the case of jazz. In other words, I view the activities at Lincoln Center as a decided move, on the part of Lincoln Center administrative personnel, musicians, and advisers, to institutional recognition and legitimacy for jazz in a major national cultural institution. Discursively and organizationally, Lincoln Center constitutes an arena within which to produce a dominant way of seeing and defining jazz. To be sure, the details of the organizational decisions and institutional moves, which culminated in the establishment of the jazz program, were riddled with controversy. By far the most glaring was the installation of Marsalis as director, his choice of critic Stanley Crouch and writer Albert Murray as advisers, and the appointment of Rob Gibson as administrator. These problems were compounded by the selection of musicians and programs. Together these developments fueled debate and contributed to disputes in the jazz community (including musicians and members of the press) about the merits and political efficacy of institutionalizing jazz at a place like Lincoln Center in the first place (Gray 1997). The available evidence and press accounts indicate that once the opportunity presented itself, Marsalis and his advisers *seized* the moment to *secure* a place for jazz in the national culture at one of the most prestigious cultural institutions in the nation. They did this discursively, so to speak, through a series of polemical but effective moves. Marsalis and his colleagues *defined* and then *advocated* on behalf of what they considered classical works; as director of the jazz program, Marsalis *staged* performances, *commissioned* compositions, and *employed* musicians. In short, by selecting the music, narrating its history, setting its direction, and defining its aesthetic underpinnings, Marsalis and his advisers actively constructed a black musical canon from within the institutional space of Lincoln Center. Marsalis accomplished this discursive work by making claims on the music's tradition and setting the terms in which the music would be represented from a dominant cultural space. Like them or not (and there were plenty of those who did not like them), Marsalis and Lincoln Center's definitions were necessarily exclusive and exclusionary, as is true of any canonical project. As part of their project of institutionalization and legitimization, Marsalis and his colleagues wrote and commissioned program notes and otherwise saturated the jazz press, media, and general public with their collective take on the music's history, significant composers and performers, and cultural status in American music. This too was the source of heated exchanges and disagreements in the press and among musicians.

Such moves and choices were controversial to be sure, particularly among musicians and members of the jazz press. There were suspicions of cronyism from black journalists, accusations of racism from whites, and charges of cultural elitism and musical conservatism from musicians, all aimed at Marsalis and his Lincoln Center supporters. These polemics—the responses and counterresponses in the press—seemed simply to bolster the intellectual and political will and, some even argued, the personal arrogance of leaders of the jazz program.

Regardless of the particular positions involved in the debates that followed, the effects of this project are culturally important and politically emblematic of the constitutive power and cultural effects of thinking about black cultural production in terms of a concept like cultural formation. This significance can be more fully appreciated when the Lincoln Center program is placed within the context of developments in the political economy of jazz, the racial politics of ownership claims, and aesthetic debates about what constitutes jazz, who decides, and where it is headed. Most journalists, critics, and musicians who object to the direction and choices of the Lincoln Center jazz program might favor a more ecumenical approach to the conception of the music, its key practitioners, and its classical repertory. Nonetheless, many of these same critics see the necessity for establishing something of an institutional beachhead for jazz in the nation's cultural institutions.

Developments at Lincoln Center take on added importance, for example, with the realization that many of the traditional performance venues like small clubs have been replaced by corporate sponsorships, national franchises, and megafestivals (Watrous 1995; Santoro 1996). New forms of public cultural and financial support for the music have appeared in the form of foundation support, juried competitions, degree programs, research institutes, and repertory programs at conservatories and colleges. While jazz still does not sell in the kinds of numbers that would make it as profitable to the recording industry as rock or other forms of popular music, the music does have a measure of cultural prestige associated with it, owing to its status as art music.

It would surely be an overstatement to attribute the renewed interest in jazz or the sudden flow of cultural prestige that the music and a select cadre of its key players have enjoyed solely to the Lincoln Center program. However, it would not be an overstatement to suggest that some of the recognition, appreciation, and response to the music is directly attributable to the growing institutional legitimacy and recognition of jazz by Lincoln Center and similar programs.

Elsewhere I have addressed the vexed question of the politics of canon formation and aesthetic choices surrounding the Lincoln Center program. There is little doubt but that the jazz program is organized on the basis of debatable social assumptions about the tradition and future direction of jazz (Watrous 1994). I do want to suggest, however, that the quest for institutional legitimacy and cultural recognition is an expression of one form of counterhegemonic black culture. Legitimacy and national recognition is one of the social consequences of the emergence of a black cultural formation that has sought some measure of stability and cultural influence in the cultural life of the American national imagination. In a cultural and political climate of social retrenchment, the erosion of public funding for the arts, and neoconservative assaults on the arts and culture, the Lincoln Center jazz program is emblematic of the strategic seizure of the cultural and institutional space. As merely one trajectory of a larger black cultural formation, Marsalis and his associates at Lincoln Center, as cultural entrepreneurs, have successfully established a viable program with institutional, organizational, and financial support. Regardless of the historicity of their claims on the music, by linking such claims to a powerful institution of legitimization and recognition like Lincoln Center, they have in effect carved out a salient cultural space from which to make such claims. In the end, Marsalis and his supporters have effectively consolidated and institutionalized their conception of jazz. As a result, popular media coverage, critical cultural debate, institutional legitimacy, as well as crucial financial support have all congealed around Marsalis, Crouch, and Murray's particular conceptions of the music, its seminal texts, and key performers. There is no doubt but that such a move has produced a legitimate social and cultural space for "jazz" in the nation's dominant and most prestigious cultural institutions. In the ongoing wars of maneuver in matters of culture, this is no small accomplishment.

Public (Relations) Intellectuals and Public Culture

Is it merely accidental that at around the same time Lincoln Center began its push to establish the jazz program, Harvard University moved to resurrect its African American studies program by hiring Henry Louis Gates, Jr., as its director? (Similar moves to strengthen African American studies also occurred at Columbia University, New York University, and the University of California, Berkeley.) And what of the recent fascination with black public intellectuals that has generated a steady barrage of media appearances, talk show experts, and books by black intellectuals and writers? I suggest not, for in terms of my argument about the conditions of possibility for the emergence of black cultural formation, these developments can be understood not as accidental but as a moment of historical conjuncture, even articulation, in which all these events must be seen in relationship to one another. Indeed, what links them and makes them more than coincidental is the fact that they appear to be occurring at prestigious cultural institutions like Lincoln Center, Harvard University, Columbia University, Princeton University, *The New Yorker* magazine, the *New York Times,* the Whitney Museum, and the Public Theater.

In a two-year period between 1995 and 1996, *The New Yorker* magazine featured significant profiles of black cultural producers and intellectuals. In a January 1995 article, Michael Berube considered the emergence of a "new generation" of public intellectuals whose impact on American public life and culture was, to say the least, significant (Berube 1995). Among those included in the profile were Cornel West, Eric Michael Dyson, bell hooks, Derrick Bell, Manning Marable, and Patricia Williams.

A short time later, Henry Louis Gates, Jr., chair of the African American Studies Department and director of the Center of African American Studies at Harvard University and a contributor to *The New Yorker,* edited a special issue of *The New Yorker.* Devoted to recent developments in black arts and letters, this issue included articles by Patricia Williams, John Edgar Wideman, and Anna Devere Smith on topics ranging from Dennis Rodman to Supreme Court Associate Justice Clarence Thomas. Similar profiles of black intellectual and cultural producers were featured around the same time in national publications like the *New York Times Sunday Magazine, The Atlantic,* and the *Village Voice* (Boynton 1995).

While admittedly a limited case example, when seen together these developments are at the very least indicative and suggestive of the point that I have been making with respect to the growing discursive labors and effects of black artists, intellectuals, and entertainers on the public life of America's national culture. (This point is perhaps more clearly grasped in the case of popular culture, where black entertainers, athletes, and spokespersons are more visible and, on occasion, more influential.) It is undoubtedly true that alone none of these examples add up to very much. Discursively and in terms of a network of social relations, however, the various institutional sites from which they operate analytically demand more than a passing glance or casual dismissal. I point to these intellectual interventions as a discursive accomplishment (including the institutional networks and their public recognition) as evidence that black intellectual, artistic, and popular self-representations are increasingly central to the discursive reconstitution or rewriting of American public culture.

Since I am interested in the discursive and institutional conditions of possibility of this potential cultural formation, a number of structural characteristics are worth identifying (Giroux 1997; Goldberg 1997). First, there appears to be a very strong relationship between key black cultural producers and the media (Reed 1995). Many of the most influential and visible of an emerging group of black intellectuals regularly appear on, write for, and are otherwise featured in national news venues. Television talk shows, magazine programs, and feature news segments along with documentary films seem especially keen on having at least one articulate and professionally accomplished black intellectual or culture worker serve as commentator and/or talking head. After all, these intellectuals, critics, and artists are extraordinarily accomplished and professionally successful, and, most important, many of them make good copy. Second, most are products of a post-1960s civil rights/black power generation that gained access to and excelled in America's elite colleges and universities. They are now well into the prime of their careers—many have tenured academic positions and directorships at prestigious universities and colleges. By any measure, all are at the top of their game and thus in the position to watch over important "cultural gates" and to make consequential decisions that shape the lives and careers of young faculty, emerging writers, and funding organizations (DuCille 1996). I regard it as more than symbolic that three of the most prestigious professional academic associations—American Studies Association, American Sociological Association, and Modern Language Association—have in recent years had black presidents. (The association presidents include Houston A. Baker, Modern Language Association; Mary Helen Washington, American Studies Association; and William Julius Wilson, American Sociological Association.) Like Marsalis at Lincoln Center, as advisers, foundation board members, and editorial board members of book publishers and professional journals, members of this generation of visible black (and often public) intellectuals occupy institutional positions in which they, at the very least, help to decide the shape, direction, and definition of black representation (especially at the level of national culture).

Cultural Politics

Something interesting, exciting, and perhaps even consequential is happening at various sites and levels of black representation and American national culture. But do these developments add up to anything remotely approaching a cultural formation? If so, does it exert influence in the realm of American arts and letters? In other words, what difference do these developments make for the remaking of American national identity and cultural imagination? Will the presence of visible and influential black scholars, artists, curators, and filmmakers in dominant and prestigious cultural institutions such as Lincoln Center and the Public Theater or professional organizations like the Modern Language Association or the American Studies Association matter at all?

Despite notable institutional incursions and the important contributions of critical black cultural studies of black representation, critics, academics, culture makers, and black audiences continue to express a good deal of worry about the images and representations that circulate in our name (Reed 1995; Early 1996; Boyd 1997). In popular music, for example, a critical scholar like Paul Gilroy has expressed concerns about the ethical, cultural, and political future of black self-representation with popular expression that are preoccupied with bodily pleasures of sex, drugs, and material acquisition (Gilroy 1994). Ironically, black image makers create many (if not most) of the most commercially successful and popular of these representations. These preoccupations involve a switch from what Gilroy terms ethically based visions of black freedom, guided by (and grounded in) collective struggle, to popular cultural expressions that glibly equate (political) freedom with individual (market) choice, beautiful bodies, a nostalgic glorious past, romanticized racial unity, and immediate sexual pleasure. For Gilroy, the possibility of these values forming the basis of a sublime black sensibility is as scary as it is dangerous. In his view, no matter how pervasive, these representations and popular sensibilities lack political vision and are underwritten by cultural (and market) values steeped in individualism, hedonism, short-term pleasure, social irresponsibility, isolation, and withdrawal from collective black struggle. These images are made under very specific discursive conditions and social relations. Such circumstances set the limits of possibility for imagining, producing, and circulating different kinds of representations. This may be the real political challenge of thinking through and evaluating the effects of a black cultural formation as an emergent possibility. What may be a cause for worry are not so much the images alone as the cultural frameworks and social conditions out of which they are generated and the cultural desires to which they respond. Together these conditions structure the assumptions through which such desires are made representable and culturally meaningful. If this is so, then I want to go further than simply to announce and inventory the conditions of possibility for an emergent black cultural formation. In my estimation, what is required is to sustain the challenging (and often vexing) work of critically interrogating the conditions of cultural production and evaluating the politics that it proposes and enacts. For example, while there are a multiplicity of cultural practices and products circulating in the name of blackness that establish important beachheads in which to seize and hold ground, we must also grapple with the fact that canonical projects are also traditional and conservative, exclusionary and limiting.

One key intellectual strategy for thinking through these challenges is the transdisciplinary practice of cultural studies. Intellectual practices such as critical black cultural studies play an important role in the global relations and movements that I have been describing. It is the primary intellectual and academic practice that maps, describes, evaluates, and legitimates the self-representation of the black cultural production (especially among and within various formations of the black Diaspora). Very much like the critical practices it maps, critical black cultural studies challenges and in some cases unsettles various territorial boundaries (e.g., disciplines, geographies, ideologies, and genres) that maintain deep and enduring investments in political and analytic stories of the purity, separation, and authenticity of cultural forms and practices. Similarly, as an intellectual practice, it aims for identifying a range of knowledges capable of operating both inside and outside official institutions and knowledges. That is to say, in addition to interrogating official sites of power, forms of legitimation, and cultural practice, critical cultural studies encourages an interrogation of the spaces and places where the vernacular, the popular, and, sometimes as an expression of both, the commercial often reside. It encourages an interrogation of what sociologist Avery Gordon (1997) calls the haunting traces that, while seeming absent, are socially and culturally very present. Thus, together critical black cultural studies and the cultural forms and practices that it takes as its object of analysis are constitutive and therefore central to the narration, evaluation, and representation of different cultural and political possibilities. As such, they are very much a part of the politics of cultural formation and representation with which I am concerned.

Economic, Technological, and Global Restructuring

In addition to its cultural meanings and political effects, black cultural representations are also profitable economic commodities that circulate within a global capitalist economy. In the midst of discursive skirmishes within blackness about racial kinship, identity politics, and institutional legitimacy, the commodification of blackness and its global circulation via commercial mass media continues to pose especially vexing questions. Those liberal left critics who are most skeptical of negative moral influence, market values generated by the logic of commodification, represent the cultural obstacle that prevents black collective mobilization. For others (cultural traditionalists) who are most invested in totalizing nationalist discourses of authenticity and the central role of culture in the discursive constitution of the black nation, the rapid global circulation and commodification of blackness weakens traditions, historical forms of association and community, identity, and nation. (This latter position is doubly ironic since it is economic, technological, and global conditions that account for black presence in the New World. These factors helped to structure the very conception of nation, identity, and self that black cultural representations aim to express [Gilroy 1993].)

Indeed, the wave of black popular culture that exploded in the American (and British) cultural imaginations beginning in the late 1970s was, in part, enabled by a global culture industry. Film, television, and the recording industry were each profoundly impacted by developments in technology, alternative delivery systems, changing formats, mergers, buyouts, new markets, and deregulation (*The Economist* 1997). For black popular culture circulating in this shifting commercial environment, this structural uncertainty and rapid transformation was especially significant. As the global reach of media conglomerates became greater and more precise and as the markets on which they depended became more differentiated, black cultural productions gained a measure of access to wide global circulation. In the context of structural changes in the global entertainment industry and driven by the preeminent search for something new and different, black cultural expression came to occupy some of the nooks and crannies of the global and domestic cultural marketplace.

The new global structure that now defines the modern culture and entertainment industry is not just the only game in town but, it seems, the only game on the planet. This new global structure still does not so much dictate the content of black cultural production as establish the very terms within which such products (including those that are counterhegemonic) are produced, financed, and exhibited globally. One would want to ask, then, How are counterhegemonic and alternative expressions and representations in black culture imagined, produced, and sustained? Any response to such a query must of necessity make visible or at the very least offer a cartography of institutional and social spaces necessary to produce and sustain black self-representation under conditions of global transnational media conglomerates.

George Lipsitz suggests that, in matters of culture, it is important to recognize, account for, and challenge the cultural appropriation and economic exploitation of people around the world directly at the points of production. He also encourages cultural analysts and critics to explore just how exploited and dominated communities negotiate, make do with, and, where possible, oppose these processes, structures, and social relations at the point of commercial consumption. Like Stuart Hall, Lipsitz recognizes that commercial culture is an important site of cultural politics because it is where popular meanings are made, loyalties enlisted, and identifications articulated. These processes are important, moreover, because these are the social points of articulation required for the political work of constructing new formations, alliances, and identifications globally. In other words, by focusing on consumption and the commercial routes through which cultural products circulate, Lipsitz imagines the possibility of a counterhegemonic cultural politics that operates on the ground of global capitalism without conceding that such terrain is always already on the side of capital (Lipsitz 1994). This is an important insight for understanding these powerful new organizing structures, the social logic on which they are based, and the conditions of possibility for different forms of counterhegemonic practice. This is the critical challenge we face.

Notes

1. Among the most contentious issues surrounding the exhibition was the representations of black masculinity, the appointment of Thelma Goldman as the show's curator, her selection of participating artists, its corporate underwriting, and its staging by a nationally recognized dominant arts institution like the Whitney Museum.

2. And such contributions are celebrated and legitimated through commendations like the awarding of the 1993 Nobel Prize in Literature to Toni Morrison and the publication (under the general editorship of Henry Louis Gates, Jr.) of the *Norton Anthology of African American Literature* (1997).

3. George Wolf's tenure at the Public Theater, Wynton Marsalis's leadership of the jazz program at Lincoln Center, and Henry Louis Gates, Jr.'s appointment to revive the African American Studies Department at Harvard University are only three of the most highly visible and controversial examples.

References

Berube, Michael. 1995. "Public Academy." *The New Yorker,* January 9, 73–80.
Boyd, Todd. 1997. *Am I Black Enough for You?* Bloomington: Indiana University Press.
Boynton, Robert. 1995. "The New Intellectuals." *The Atlantic Monthly,* March, 56.
Caldwell, John. 1998. "Televisual Politics: Negotiating Race in the L.A. Rebellion." In Sasha Torres, ed., *In Living Color: Race and Television in the United States* (161–95). Durham, N.C.: Duke University Press.
Cruse, Harold. 1967. *The Crisis of the Negro Intellectual.* New York: Morrow.

Davis, Mike. 1992. *City of Quartz.* London: Verso.
Denning, Michael. 1996. *The Cultural Front: The Laboring of American Culture in the Twentieth Century.* London: Verso.
DuCille, Ann. 1996. *Skin Trade.* Cambridge, Mass.: Harvard University Press.
Early, Gerald. 1996. "Black Like Them." *New York Times Book Review,* April 24, 7.
Fiske, John. 1994. *Media Matters.* Minneapolis: University of Minnesota Press.
Gates, Henry Louis. 1997. *Norton Anthology of African American Literature.* New York: W. W. Norton.
Gilroy, Paul. 1993. *The Black Atlantic.* Cambridge, Mass.: Harvard University Press.
———. 1994. "After the Love Has Gone: Bio-Politics and Ethno-Poetics in the Black Public Sphere." *Public Culture* 7, no. 1: 49–77.
Giroux, Henry. 1997. "In Living Color: Black, Bruised, and Read All Over." In *Channel Surfing: Race Talk and the Destruction of Today's Youth* (137–73). New York: St. Martin's Press.
Goldberg, David T. 1997. "Whither West? The Making of a Public Intellectual." In *Racial Subjects: Writing on Race in America* (109–29). New York: Routledge.
Gordon, Avery. 1997. *Ghostly Matters: Haunting and the Sociological Imagination.* Minneapolis: University of Minnesota Press.
Gray, Herman. 1995. *Watching Race: Television and the Struggle for Blackness.* Minneapolis: University of Minnesota Press.
———. 1997. "Jazz Tradition, Institutional Formation, and Cultural Practice: The Canon and the Street as Frameworks for Oppositional Black Cultural Politics." In E. Long, ed., *From Sociology to Cultural Studies* (351–79). London: Blackwell.
Guererro, Edward. 1993. *Framing Blackness: The African American Image in Film.* Philadelphia: Temple University Press.
Hall, Stuart. 1989. "New Ethnicities." In D. Morley and K. Chen, eds., *Stuart Hall: Critical Dialogues in Cultural Studies* (441–50). London: Routledge.
———. 1992. "What Is This 'Black' in Black Popular Culture?" In Gina Dent, ed., *Black Popular Culture: A Project by Michele Wallace* (21–37). Seattle: Bay.
Harper, Phillip Brian. 1996. *Are We Not Men.* Oxford: Oxford University Press.
Hebdige, Dick. 1987. *Cut n' Mix.* London: Comedia.
———. 1988. *Hiding in the Light.* London: Comedia.
Hunt, Darnell. 1999. *OJ Simpson Facts and Fictions: New Rituals in the Construction of Reality.* Cambridge: Cambridge University Press.
Kelley, Robin D. G. 1997. *Yo Mama's dis Funktional: Fighting the Culture Wars in Urban America.* Boston: Beacon Press.
Lipsitz, George. 1994. *Dangerous Crossroads.* London: Verso.
Mercer, Kobena. 1994. *Welcome to the Jungle.* London: Routledge.
Merlman, Richard. 1995. *Representing Black Culture.* New York: Routledge.
Powell, Richard. 1997. *Black Art and Culture in the 20th Century.* New York: Thames and Hudson.
Reed, Adolph. 1995. "What Are the Drums Saying Booker? The Current Crisis of the Black Intellectual." *Village Voice,* April 11, 35.
Reeves, Jimmie, and Richard Campbell. 1994. *Cracked Coverage: Television News, the Anti-Cocaine Crusade, and the Reagan Legacy.* Durham, N.C.: Duke University Press.
Santoro, Gene. 1993. "Young Man with a Horn." *The Nation,* March 1, 280–84.
———. 1996. "All That Jazz." *The Nation,* January 8–15, 34–36.
Stacey, Judith. 1996. *Rethinking Family Values: In the Name of the Family.* Boston: Beacon Press.

Taylor, Clyde R. 1998. *The Mask of Art: Breaking the Aesthetic Contract—Film and Literature.* Bloomington: Indiana University Press.

The Economist. 1997. "Ted Turner's Management Consultant." March 22, 96.

Watkins, S. Craig. 1998. *Representing: Hip-Hop Culture and the Production of Black Cinema.* Chicago: University of Chicago Press.

Watrous, Peter. 1994. "Old Jazz Is Out, New Jazz Is Older." *New York Times,* March 31, C11–12.

———. 1995. "Is There a Mid-Life Crisis at the JVC Festival?" *New York Times,* July 8, Arts and Leisure section, 13.

Williams, Raymond. 1982. *The Sociology of Culture.* New York: Schocken Books.

Part II

Spaces

5

The Spaces of Utopia

David Harvey

A map of the world that does not include Utopia is not even worth glancing at.

—OSCAR WILDE

The Baltimore Story

I have lived in Baltimore City for most of my adult life. I think of it as my hometown and have accumulated an immense fund of affection for the place. But Baltimore is, for the most part, a mess. Not the kind of enchanting mess that makes cities such interesting places to explore, but an awful mess. And it seems much worse now than when I first knew it in 1969. Or perhaps it is in the same old mess except that many people then believed they could do something about it. Now the problems seem intractable.

Too many details of the mess would overwhelm. But some of its features are important to know. There are some 40,000 vacant houses (in a housing stock of 304,000 units) within the city limits (compared to 8,000 in 1970). The concentrations of homelessness (despite all those vacant houses), of unemployment, and, even more significant, of the employed poor (trying to live on less than $200 a week without benefits) are everywhere in evidence. The soup kitchen lines get longer and longer, and the charity missions of many inner-city churches are stretched beyond coping. The inequalities—of opportunities as well as of standards of life—are growing by leaps and bounds. The massive educational resources of the city (Baltimore City has some of the finest schools in the country, but they are all private) are denied to most of the children who live there. The public schools are in a lamentable state (two and a half years behind the national average in reading skills according to recent tests). Some of the finest medical institutions in the world are out of bounds to people who live within their shadow (unless they have the privilege to clean the AIDS wards for less than a living wage or have a rare disease of great interest to elite medical researchers). Life expectancy in the city, in the immediate environs of these internationally renowned hospital facilities, is among the lowest in the nation and comparable to many of the poorer countries in the world (63 years for men and 73.2 for women). The affluent (black and white) continue to leave the city in droves seeking solace, security, and jobs in the suburbs (population in the city was close to a million when I arrived and is now down to around 600,000). The suburbs, the edge cities, and the exurbs proliferate (with the aid of massive public subsidies to transport and upper-income housing construction) in an extraordinarily unecological sprawl (long commutes, massive ozone concentrations in summer, loss of agricultural land). Developers offer up this great blight of suburban conformity (alleviated, of course, by architectural quotations from Italianate villas and

Doric columns) as a panacea for the breakdown and disintegration of urbanity first in the inner city and then, as the deadly blight spreads, the inner suburbs.

There has been an attempt of sorts to turn things around in the city. Launched in the early 1970s under the aegis of a dedicated and quite authoritarian mayor (William Donald Schaeffer), it entailed formation of a private-public partnership to invest in downtown and Inner Harbor renewal in order to attract financial services, tourism, and so-called hospitality functions to the center city. It took a lot of public moneys to get the process rolling. Once they had the hotels (Hyatt got a $35 million hotel by putting up only half a million dollars of its own money in the early 1980s), they needed to build a convention center to fill the hotels and get a piece of what is now calculated to be an $83 billion-a-year meetings industry. In order to keep competitive, a further public investment of $150 million was needed to create an even larger convention center to get the big conventions. It is now feared that all this investment will not be profitable without a large "headquarters hotel" that will also require "extensive" public subsidies (maybe $50 million). And to improve the city image, a quarter of a billion dollars went into building sports stadiums for teams (one of which was lured from Cleveland) that pay several million a year to star players watched by fans paying exorbitant ticket prices. This is, of course, a common enough story across the United States (the National Football League—deserving welfare clients—calculates that $3.8 billion of largely public money will be poured into new NFL stadiums between 1992 and 2002).

This is what is called "feeding the downtown monster." Every new wave of public investment is needed to make the last wave pay off. The private-public partnership means that the public takes all the risks and the private take all the profits. The citizenry wait for benefits that never quite materialize. An upscale condominium complex on the waterfront does so poorly that it gets $2 million in tax breaks in order to forestall bankruptcy while the impoverished working class—close to bankruptcy if not technically in it—get nothing.

There is, of course, a good side to the renewal effort. Many people come to the Inner Harbor. There is even racial mixing. People evidently enjoy just watching people. And there is a growing recognition that the city, to be vibrant, has to be a twenty-four-hour affair and that megabookstores and a Hard Rock Cafe have as much to offer as Benetton and the Banana Republic. Here and there, neighborhoods have pulled themselves together and developed a special sense of community that makes for safer, more secure living without degenerating into rabid exclusionism. Some of the seedier public housing blocks have been imploded to make way for better-quality housing in better-quality environments. But none of this touches the roots of Baltimore's problems.

One of those roots lies in the rapid transition in employment opportunities. Manufacturing jobs accelerated their movement out (mainly southward and overseas) during the first severe postwar recession in 1973–75 and have not stopped moving since. Shipbuilding, for example, has all but disappeared, and the industries that stayed have either "downsized" (Beth Steel employed 30,000 in 1970 compared to less than 5,000 now making nearly the same amount of steel) or demanded public subsidies to stay (General Motors—another deserving welfare client—received a massive Urban Development Action Grant in the early 1980s to keep its assembly plant open). Service jobs have materialized to replace perhaps as many as a quarter of a million jobs lost in manufacturing. But many of these are low-paying (with few benefits), temporary, nonunionized, and female. The best many households can hope for is to keep their income stable by having two people work longer hours at a lower individual wage. The general absence of adequate and affordable day care means that this does not bode well for the kids. Poverty entraps and gets perpetuated, notwithstanding a campaign (based in the churches) for a "living wage" that struggles to improve the lot of the working poor and protect the many thousands now being pushed off welfare into a stagnant labor market.

The income inequalities grow remarkably along with geographic disparities in wealth and power. For a while, the inner suburbs drained wealth from the central city, but now they too have "problems," though it is there, if anywhere, that most new jobs are created. So either the wealth moves further out to exurbs that explicitly exclude the poor, the underprivileged, and the marginalized or it encloses itself behind high walls in suburban "privatopias" and urban "gated communities." The rich form ghettoes of affluence and undermine concepts of citizenship, social belonging, and mutual support. Six million of them in the United States now live in gated communities as opposed to one million ten years ago (Blakeley 1997). And if communities are not gated, they are increasingly constructed on exclusionary lines so that levels of segregation (primarily by class but also with a powerful racial thread) are worse now in Baltimore than ever.

The second major root of the mess lies in institutional fragmentation and breakdown. City Hall, caught in a perpetual fiscal bind buttressed by the belief that slimmer government is always the path to a more competitive city, reduces its services whether needed or not. The potential for cooperation with suburban jurisdictions is overwhelmed by competitive pressures to keep taxes down, the impoverished and marginalized out, and the affluent and stable in. The federal government decentralizes, and the state, now dominated by suburban and rural interests, turns its back on the city. Special tax-assessment districts spring up so that neighborhoods can provide extra services according to their means. Since the means vary, the effect is to divide up the urban realm into a patchwork quilt of islands of relative affluence struggling to secure themselves in a sea of spreading squalor and decay. The overall effect is division and fragmentation of the metropolitan space, a loss of sociality across diversity, and a localized defensive posture toward the rest of the city that becomes politically fractious if not downright dysfunctional.

The prospects for institutional reform seem negligible. A tangled mix of bureaucratic and legal inflexibilities and rigid political institutional arrangements create a pattern of urban governance that is ossified in the extreme. Exclusionary communitarianism, narrow vested interests (usually framed by identity politics of various sorts—predominantly racial at the populist level, though in Baltimore there is a good deal of ethnic rivalry thrown in), corporate profit hunger, financial myopia, and developer greed all contribute to the difficulties. New resources are built into the social, political, and physical landscape of the metropolitan region so as to exacerbate both the inequalities and the fragmentations (most particularly those of race). There is, it seems, no alternative, except for the rich to be progressively enriched and the poor (largely black) to be regressively impoverished.

In the midst of all this spiraling inequality, thriving corporate and big money interests (including the media) promote their own brand of identity politics, with their multiple manifestos of political correctness. Their central message, repeated over and over, is that any challenge to the glories of the free market (preferably cornered, monopolized, and state subsidized in practice) is to be mercilessly put down or mocked out of existence. The power of these ideas lies, I suspect, at the core of our current sense of helplessness. "There is," as Margaret Thatcher insisted in her heyday on the other side of the Atlantic, "no alternative" (unfortunately, even Gorbachev agreed). The effect is to create an overwhelming ideology of what can best be called "free-market Stalinism." Those who have the money power are free to choose among name-brand commodities (including prestigious locations), but the citizenry as a whole are denied any collective choice of political system, of ways of social relating, and of modes of production, consumption, and exchange. If the mess seems impossible to change, then it is simply because "there is no alternative." It is the supreme rationality of the market versus the silly irrationality of anything else. And all those institutions that might have helped define some alternative have either been suppressed or—with some notable exceptions, such as the church—been browbeaten into submission. We the people have no right to choose what kind of city we shall inhabit.

But how is it that we are so persuaded that "there is no alternative"? Why is it, in Roberto Unger's (1987a, 37) words, that "we often seem to be (such) helpless puppets of the institutional and imaginative worlds we inhabit"? Is it simply that we lack the will, the courage, and the perspicacity to open up alternatives and actively pursue them? Or is there something else at work? Surely it cannot be lack of imagination. The academy, for example, is full of explorations of the imaginary. In physics, the exploration of possible worlds is the norm rather than the exception. In the humanities, a fascination with what is called "the imaginary" is everywhere apparent. And the media world that is now available to us has never before been so replete with fantasies and possibilities for collective communication about alternative worlds. Yet none of this seems to impinge on the terrible trajectory that daily life assumes in the material world around us. We seem, as Unger (1987a, 331) puts it, to be "torn between dreams that seem unrealizable and prospects that hardly seem to matter." To be sure, the ideology and practices of competitive neoliberalism do their quietly effective and insidious work within the major institutions—the media and the universities—that shape the imaginative context in which we live. And they do so with hardly anyone noticing. The political correctness imposed by raw money power has done far more to censor opinion within these institutions than the overt repressions of McCarthyism ever did. "Possibility has had a bad press," Ernst Bloch (1988, 7) remarks, adding that "there is a very clear interest that has prevented the world from being changed into the possible." Bloch, interestingly, associated this condition with the demise, denigration, and disparagement of all forms of utopian thought. That, he argued, meant a loss of hope, and without hope alternative politics becomes impossible. Could it be, then, that a revitalization of the utopian tradition will give us ways to think the possibility of real alternatives? In this chapter, I set out to explore that possibility.

The Figure of the City

The figures of "the city" and of "utopia" have long been intertwined. In their early incarnations, utopias were usually given a distinctively urban form, and most of what passes for urban and city planning in the broadest sense has been infected (some would prefer "inspired") by utopian modes of thought. The connection long pre-dates Sir Thomas More's first adventure with the utopian genre in 1516. Plato, after all, connected ideal forms of government with his closed republic in such a way as to fold the concepts of city and citizen into each other. The Judeo-Christian tradition defined paradise as a distinctive place where all good souls would go after their trials and tribulations in the temporal world. From this, all manner of metaphors flowed of the heavenly city, the city of God, the eternal city, and the shining city on a hill (a metaphor dearly beloved by President Reagan). But if heaven is a "happy place," then that "other" place, hell, the place of "the evil other," cannot be far away. The figure of the city as a fulcrum of social disorder, moral breakdown, and unmitigated evil—from Babylon, Sodom and Gomorrah, to Gotham—also has its place in the freight of metaphorical meanings that the word "city" carries across our cultural universe. Dystopias take on urban forms such as those found in Huxley's *Brave New World* or Orwell's *1984*. The word "police" derives from the Greek "polis," which means "city." And if Karl Popper were to depict Plato as one of the first great enemies of "the open society," then the utopias that followed could just as easily be cast as oppressive and totalitarian hells as emancipatory and happy heavens.

It is hard to untangle the grubby day-to-day practices and discourses that affect urban living from the grandiose metaphorical meanings that so freely intermingle with emotions and beliefs about the good life and urban form. I cannot possibly hope to untangle such meanings here. But it is important to recognize their emotive power. So I provide a few illustrative connections to help consolidate the point that urban politics is fraught with deeply held, though often subterranean, emotions and political passions in which utopian dreams have a particular place.

"City air makes one free," it was once said. That idea took shape as serfs escaped their bonds to claim political and personal freedoms within the self-governing legal entities of medieval cities. The association between city life and personal freedoms, including the freedom to explore, invent, create, and define new ways of life, consequently has a long and intricate history. Generations of migrants have sought the heavenly city as haven from rural repressions. The "city" and "citizenship" tie neatly together within this formulation. But the city is equally the site of anxiety and anomie. It is the place of the anonymous alien, the underclass (or, as our predecessors preferred it, "the dangerous classes"), an incomprehensible "otherness" (immigrants, gays, the mentally disturbed, the culturally different, the racially marked), pollution (moral as well as physical), and terrible corruptions—the place of the damned that needs to be enclosed and controlled—making "city" and "citizen" as politically opposed in the public imagination as they are etymologically linked.

This polarization of positive and negative images has its geography. Traditionally, this registers as a division between secular and sacred space within the city. Later, the supposed virtues of the countryside and the small town were often contrasted with the evils of the city. When, for example, the rural army of reaction was assembled on the outskirts of Paris in 1871 poised to engage in the savage slaughter of some 30,000 communards, they were first persuaded that their mission was to reclaim the city from the forces of Satan. When President Ford denied aid to New York City in 1975 in the midst of its fiscal crisis ("Ford to City: 'Drop Dead!'" read the famous newspaper headline), the plaudits of virtuous and God-fearing small-town America were everywhere to be heard. In contemporary America, the image of the respectable God-fearing suburbs (predominantly white and middle class) plays against the inner-city as a hellhole where all the damned (with plenty of underclass racial coding thrown in) are properly confined. Imaginings of this sort take a terrible toll.

When, for example, it was proposed to disperse some 200 families from the inner city of Baltimore to the suburbs as part of a "Movement to Opportunity," the suburbanites rose up in wrath to stop the program, using a language that sounded as if representatives of the devil were about to be released from their inner-city prison and let loose as a corrupting power in their midst. Religion does not always have to play this way, of course. It also powers many an organization that seeks to defend the poor, improve communities, and stabilize family life in the crumbling inner cities.

None of these imaginaries are innocent. Nor should we expect them to be. What distinguishes the worst of architects from the best of bees, Marx (1977, 283–84) long ago observed, is that architects erect a structure in the imagination before realizing it in material form. When, therefore, architects, planners, urban designers, engineers, and urbanists of all sorts find themselves asked to help solve a wide range of social, political, and economic problems, they have to do battle with a wide range of emotive meanings held by themselves as well as by others. But Marx's metaphor prods us further. While the figure of the architect is useful to understand the role of the imagination in the labor process, it can just as easily be reversed. Everyone who engages in any kind of labor process is an architect of sorts. So if the future of humanity lies in cities and if the qualities of urban living in the twenty-first century will define the qualities of civilization, so all of us who labor will be architects of that future. That labor process has very special dialectical qualities. In changing the world, we change ourselves. That dialectic is fundamental to understanding both the history of and the prospects for urban futures. As we collectively produce our cities, so we collectively produce ourselves. Projects concerning what we want our cities to be are, therefore, projects concerning who we want or, perhaps even more pertinently, who we do not want to become. Every single one of us has something to think, say, and do about that.

How our individual and collective imagination works is, therefore, crucial to defining the labor of urbanization. Critical reflection on our imaginaries entails, however, both confronting the hidden utopianism and resurrecting it in order to act as conscious architects of our fates rather than as "helpless puppets" of the institutional and imaginative worlds we inhabit. If, as Unger (1987b, 8) puts it, we accept that "society is made and imagined," then we must also accept that it can be "remade and reimagined."

Utopianism as Spatial Play

Any project to revitalize utopianism must first consider how and with what consequences it has worked as both a constructive and a destructive force for change in our historical geography.

Consider Sir Thomas More's *Utopia.* More's aim, and this is characteristic, was social harmony and stability (in contrast to the chaotic state of affairs in England at that time). To this end, he excluded the potentially disruptive social forces of money, private property, wage labor, exploitation (the workday is six hours), internal (though not external) commodity exchange, capital accumulation, and the market process (though not a marketplace). The happy perfection of the social and moral order depends on these exclusions. All this is secured by way of a tightly organized spatial form. Utopia is an artificially created island that functions as an isolated, coherently organized, and largely closed space economy (though closely monitored relations with the outside world are posited). The internal spatial ordering of the island strictly regulates a stabilized and unchanging social process. Put crudely, spatial form controls temporality—an imagined geography controls the possibility of social change and history.

Not all forms of temporality are erased. The time of "eternal return," of recurrent ritual, is preserved. This cyclical time, as Gould (1987) remarks, expresses "immanence, a set of principles so general that they exist outside of time and record a universal character, a common bond, among all of nature's rich particulars," including, in this instance, all the inhabitants of utopia. It is the dialectic of social process that is repressed. Time's arrow, "the great principle of history," is excluded in favor of perpetuating a happy stationary state. No future needs to be envisaged because the desired state is already achieved. In Bacon's *New Atlantis,* a utopian text written shortly after that of More, the king decided that society had achieved such a state of perfection that no further social change was needed. In Bacon's case, technological change is not only possible but actively sought. But its implantation is tightly regulated by the wise men of Salomon's House (an institution interpreted as a forerunner of the Royal Society). The effect is to progress toward the technological perfection of an already perfected social order. More, on the other hand, evokes nostalgia for a mythological past, a perfected golden age of small-town living, a moral order, and a hierarchical mode of social relating that is nonconflictual and harmonious. This nostalgic strain is characteristic of much utopian thinking (even that projected into the future and incorporating futuristic technologies). And this, as we will see, has very important consequences for how, if at all, such schemes get translated into material fact.

There are many ways to understand More's text and the many utopian schemas that were subsequently produced (such as those of Bacon and Campanella, the latter's *City of the Sun*). I isolate here just one aspect: the relationship proposed between space and time, between geography and history. In effect, as Lukerman and Porter (1976) point out, these forms of utopia can be characterized as "Utopias of spatial form" since the temporality of the social process, the dialectics of social change—real history—are excluded, while social stability is assured by a fixed spatial form. Louis Marin (1984) considers More's Utopia as a species of "spatial play." More, in effect, selects one of many possible spatial orderings as a way to represent and fix a particular moral order. Marin thus interprets all utopics as spatial play. This is not a unique thought. Robert Park (1967), a leading figure in the influential Chicago School of sociology, wrote a compelling essay in 1925 on the city as "a spatial pattern and a moral order" and insisted on an inner connection between the two. But what Marin opens up for us is the idea that the free play of the imagination, "utopics as spatial play," became, with More's initiative, a fertile means to explore and express a vast range of competing ideas about social relationships, moral orderings, political-economic systems, and the like.

The infinite array of possible spatial orderings holds out the prospect of an infinite array of possible social worlds. And what is so impressive about subsequent utopian plans when taken together is their incredible variety. Feminist utopias of the nineteenth century (Hayden 1981) look very different from those supposed to facilitate easier and healthier living for the working class, and all sorts of anarchist, ecologically sensitive, religious, and other alternatives define and secure their moral objectives by appeal to some very specific spatial order. The staggering range of proposals—and of spatialities—testifies to the extraordinary capacity of the human imagination to explore sociospatial alternatives (Kumar 1987, 1991). Marin's notion of "spatial play" neatly captures the free play of the imagination in utopian schemes. Reversion to this utopian mode appears to offer a way out of Unger's dilemma.

Unfortunately, matters are not so simple. Imaginative free play is inextricably bound to the existence of authority and restrictive forms of governance. What Foucault (1986) regards as "a panopticon effect" through the creation of spatial systems of surveillance and control (polis = police) are also incorporated into utopian schemes. This dialectic between imaginative free play and authority and control throws up serious problems. The rejection, in recent times, of utopianism rests on an acute awareness of its inner connection to authoritarianism and totalitarianism (More's Utopia can easily be read this way). But rejection of utopianism on such grounds has also had the unfortunate effect of curbing the free play of the imagination in the search for alternatives. Confronting this relationship between spatial play and authoritarianism must, therefore, lie at the heart of any regenerative politics that attempts to resurrect utopian ideals. In pursuing this objective, it is useful to look at the history of how utopias have been materialized through political-economic practices: It is here that the dialectic of free play of the imagination and authoritarianism comes to life as a fundamental dilemma in human affairs.

Materializations of Utopias of Spatial Form

When Ebenezer Howard read Edward Bellamy's utopian novel *Looking Backward* in 1888, he did so at one sitting and was "fairly carried away" by it. The next morning, he

> went into some of the crowded parts of London, and as I passed through the narrow dark streets, saw the wretched dwellings in which the majority of the people lived, observed on every hand the manifestations of a self-seeking order of society and reflected on the absolute unsoundness of our economic system, there came to me an overpowering sense of the temporary nature of all I saw, and of its entire unsuitability for the working life of the new order—the order of justice, unity and friendliness. (cited in Fishman 1982, 32)

It is easy to recognize such sentiments walking the streets of Baltimore today. But Howard reacted to his reading of Bellamy in a particular way. He proposed to build new towns as a means to materialize much of what Bellamy had envisioned. Thus was the "new towns" movement born, a movement that has been one of the most practical and important interventions in urban reengineering in the twentieth century. Sufficient accounts of this movement and its consequences—both good and bad—exist elsewhere, and it is not my purpose to go over that history (see, e.g., Fishman 1982; Hall 1988). I merely wish to emphasize how the spatial order of the new towns was clearly articulated and meant to achieve social harmony and justice. It was a practical and concrete version of utopics as spatial play.

Howard was not the only one to think in such a fashion. All the great urban planners, engineers, and architects of the twentieth century set about their tasks in a similar way.

While some, such as Le Corbusier and Frank Lloyd Wright, mainly set up the imaginative context, a host of practitioners set about realizing those dreams in bricks and concrete, highways and tower blocks, cities and suburbs, building versions of the Villes Radieuse or Broadacre City, whole new towns, intimate-scale communities, urban villages, or whatever. And even when critics of the authoritarianism and blandness of these realized utopian dreams attacked them, they usually did so by contrasting their preferred version of spatial play with the spatial orderings that others had achieved.

When, for example, Jane Jacobs (1961) launched her famous critique of modernist processes of city planning and urban renewal (damning as she did so Le Corbusier, the Charter of Athens, Robert Moses, and the great blight of dullness they and their acolytes had unleashed on postwar cities), she in effect set up her own preferred version of spatial play by appeal to a nostalgic conception of an intimate and diverse ethnic neighborhood in which artisan forms of entrepreneurial activity and employment and interactive face-to-face forms of social relating predominated. Jacobs was in her own way every bit as utopian as the utopianism she attacked. She proposed to play with the space in a different way in order to achieve a different kind of moral purpose. Her version of spatial play contained its own authoritarianism hidden within the organic notion of neighborhood and community as a basis for social life. The apparatus of surveillance and control that she regarded as so benevolent because it provided much-needed security struck others, such as Sennett (1970), as oppressive and demeaning. And while she placed great emphasis on social diversity, it was only a certain kind of controlled diversity that could really work in the happy way she envisaged.

This brings us to perhaps the most intriguing of Marin's categories: that of "degenerate utopias." The example that Marin used was Disneyland, a supposedly happy, harmonious, and nonconflictual space set aside from the "real" world "outside" in such a way as to sooth and mollify, to entertain, to invent history, and to cultivate a nostalgia for some mythical past, to perpetuate the fetish of commodity culture rather than to critique it. Disneyland eliminates the troubles of actual travel by assembling the rest of the world, properly sanitized and mythologized, into one place of pure fantasy containing multiple spatial orders. The dialectic is repressed, and stability and harmony are secured, through intense surveillance and control. Internal spatial ordering coupled with hierarchical forms of authority preclude conflict or deviation from a social norm. Disneyland offers a fantasy journey into a world of spatial play. And in its later incarnations, as at Epcot, it offers a futuristic utopia of technological purity and unsurpassed human power to control the world (Disney moved, as it were, from More to Bacon for his inspiration). All this is degenerate, in Marin's view, because it offers no critique of the existing state of affairs on the outside. It merely perpetuates the fetish of commodity culture and technological wizardry in a pure, sanitized, and ahistorical form. But, and this is where Marin's idea becomes problematic, Disneyland is an actual built environment and not an imagined place of the sort that More and Bacon produced. This immediately raises the question: Can any utopianism of spatial form that gets materialized be anything other than "degenerate" in the sense that Marin has in mind? Perhaps utopia can never be realized without destroying itself. If so, then this profoundly affects how any utopianism of spatial form can function as a practical social force on political-economic life.

Generalizing from Marin, it can be argued that we are surrounded by a whole host of degenerate utopias of which Disneyland is but the most spectacular exemplar. When "the malling of America" became the vogue, pioneers such as Rouse explicitly recognized that Disney had invented a formula for successful retailing. The construction of safe, secure, well-ordered, easily accessible, and above all pleasant, soothing, and nonconflictual environments for shopping was the key to commercial success. The shopping mall was conceived of as a fantasy world in which the commodity reigned supreme. And if homeless old folks started to regard it as a warm place to rest, youths found it a great place to socialize, and political agitators took to passing out their pamphlets, then the apparatus of surveillance and control (with hidden cameras and security agents) made sure nothing untoward happened. As Benjamin (1969) remarked on the Parisian arcades of the nineteenth century, the whole environment seemed designed to induce nirvana rather than critical awareness. And many other cultural institutions—museums and heritage centers, arenas for spectacle, exhibitions, and festivals—seem to have as their aim the cultivation of nostalgia, the production of sanitized collective memories, the nurturing of uncritical aesthetic sensibilities, and the absorption of future possibilities into a nonconflictual arena that is eternally present. The continuous spectacles of commodity culture, including the commodification of the spectacle itself, play their part in fomenting political indifference. It is either a stupefied nirvana or a totally blasé attitude (the fount of all indifference) that is aimed at (Simmel [1971] long ago pointed to the blasé attitude as one of the responses to excessive stimuli in urban settings). The multiple degenerate utopias that now surround us—the shopping mall being paradigmatic—do as much to signal the end of history as the collapse of the Berlin Wall ever did. They instantiate rather than critique the idea that "there is no alternative," save those given by the conjoining of technological fantasies, commodity culture, and endless capital accumulation. But how could it happen that the critical and oppositional force given in utopian schemes so easily degenerates in the course of materialization into compliance with the prevailing order? There are, I think, two basic answers to this question. Let me unpack them by a closer look at what is now held out as one of the leading candidates to transform our urban futures, the movement called "the new urbanism."

Duany (1997), one of its leading lights, "feels strongly that urbanism, if not architecture, can affect society." Getting the spatial play right, in the manner proposed by the new urbanism, will, he argues, help rectify matters. His proposals evidence a nostalgia for small-town America, its solid sense of community, its institutions, its mixed land uses and high densities, and its ideologists (such as Raymond Unwin). Bring all this back in urban design, and the quality of urban living and of social life will be immeasurably improved. This argument is buttressed by appeal to a long line of critical commentary (Kunstler 1993) on the "placelessness" and the lack of "authenticity" in American cities (soulless sprawling suburbs, mindless edge cities, and collapsing and fragmenting city cores fill in the pieces of this dyspeptic view). The new urbanism does battle with such monstrous deformities (Katz 1994). How to recuperate history, tradition, collective memory, and the sense of belonging and identity that goes with them becomes part of its holy grail. This movement does not, therefore, lack a critical utopian edge.

The new urbanism offers something positive as well as nostalgic. It does battle with conventional wisdoms entrenched in a wide range of institutions (developers, bankers, governments, transport interests, and so on). It is willing to think about the region as a whole and to pursue a much more organic, holistic ideal of what cities and regions might be about. The postmodern penchant for fragmentation is rejected. It attempts intimate and integrated forms of development that bypass the rather stultifying conception of the horizontally zoned and large-platted city. This liberates an interest in the street and civic architecture as arenas of sociality. It also permits new ways of thinking about the relation between work and living and facilitates an ecological dimension to design that goes beyond superior environmental quality as a consumer good. It pays attention to the thorny problem of what to do with the profligate energy requirements of the automobile-based form of urbanization and suburbanization that has predominated in the United States since World War II. Some see it as a truly revolutionary force for urban change in the United States today.

But there are problems with materializing this utopian vision. The movement presumes that America is "full of people who long to live in real communities, but who have only the dimmest idea of what that means in terms of physical design" (Kunstler 1996). Community will rescue us from the deadening world of social dissolution, grab-it-yourself materialism, and individualized selfish market-oriented greed. But what kind of "community" is understood here? Harking back to a mythological past of small-town America carries its own dangerous freight. The new urbanism connects to a facile contemporary attempt to transform large and teeming cities, so seemingly out of control, into an interlinked series of "urban villages" where, it is believed, everyone can relate in a civil and urbane fashion to everyone else. In Britain, Prince Charles has led the way on this emotional charger toward "the urban village" as the locus of urban regeneration. Leon Krier, an oft-quoted scion of the new urbanism, is one of his key architectural outriders. And the idea attracts, drawing support from marginalized ethnic populations, impoverished and embattled working-class populations left high and dry through deindustrialization, as well as from middle- and upper-class nostalgics who think of it as a civilized form of real estate development encompassing sidewalk cafes, pedestrian precincts, and Laura Ashley shops.

The darker side of this communitarianism remains unstated. The spirit of community has long been held as an antidote to threats of social disorder, class war, and revolutionary violence (More pioneered such thinking). Well-founded communities often exclude, define themselves against others, erect all sorts of keep-out signs (if not tangible walls), and internalize surveillance, social controls, and repression. Community has often been a barrier to, rather than facilitator of, social change. The founding ideology of the new urbanism is both utopian and deeply fraught. In its practical materialization, the new urbanism builds an image of community and a rhetoric of place-based civic pride and consciousness for those who do not need it while abandoning those who do to their "underclass" fate. Most of the projects that have materialized are "greenfield" developments for the affluent. They help make the suburb "a better place to live" (Langdon 1994) and do nothing to help revitalize decaying urban cores. Scully (1994), a skeptical ally of the movement, doubts if the new urbanism can ever get to the crux of urban impoverishment and decay.

This happens because the "new urbanism" must, if it is to be realized, embed its projects in a very restrictive set of social processes. Duany (1997) has no interest in designing projects that will not get built. His concern for low-income populations is limited by a minimum price for new housing units in a place like Kentlands, not too far from Baltimore, of

$150,000 (close to ten times the median income in Baltimore). His interest in the suburbs arose quite simply because this is where most new projects can be built. Suburban growth, he argues, is "the American way," buried deep "in our culture and our tradition," and while he objects strongly to the accusation that he is "complicit" with power structures and that he panders to popular taste, he also insists that everything he does is designed to create spectacular projects that outperform all others on a commercial basis. This means "faster permits, less cost, and faster sales." His version of the new urbanism operates strictly within such parameters.

But who is at fault here? The designer, Duany, or the conditions of the social process that define the parameters of his projects? In practice, most realized utopias of spatial form have been achieved through the agency of either the state or capital accumulation, with both acting in concert being the norm in the West. It is either that, or else moving "outside" mainstream social processes (as seemed possible at least in the nineteenth century, with the United States being a favored target for utopian idealists such as Cabet, Robert Owen, and multiple religious movements). Those who took such an outsider path typically suffered a kind of meltdown of their principles, however, as they were absorbed within the mainstream of capital accumulation and the developmental state (something similar happened to the Israeli kibbutz).

The failure of realized utopias of spatial form can just as reasonably be attributed to the processes mobilized to materialize them as to failures of spatial form per se. There is a fundamental contradiction at work here. Utopias of spatial form are typically meant to stabilize and control the very processes that must be mobilized to build them. In the very act of realization, therefore, the historical process takes control of the spatial form that is supposed to control it. This contradiction requires further scrutiny.

On the Utopianism of Social Process

If materialized utopias went wrong because of the social processes mobilized in their construction, then the focus switches to questions of process. Can we think of a utopianism of process rather than of spatial form?

The question appears strange because the word "utopia" is usually attached to some place that is no place as well as a happy place. The qualities of place are important, and this means evocation of spatial form as a container of social processes and as an expression of moral order. Idealized versions of social processes, on the other hand, typically get expressed in purely temporal terms. They are typically bound to no particular place whatsoever. They typically make no reference to place at all and get specified outside the constraints of spatiality altogether. Idealized schemas of process abound. But we do not usually refer to them as utopian. I want to break with that convention and consider the utopianism of temporal process alongside the utopianism of spatial form.

We can identify a rich and complicated history of utopics as divergent temporal unfoldings. One obvious candidate is Hegel, whose guiding spirit is rendered material and concrete by a dialectics of transcendence (a dialectics that unfolds on the logic of "both-and"). Things in themselves move history as they become things for themselves. The end state of history is, interestingly, expressed as a spatialized metaphor. The ethical or aesthetic state is the teleological end point of the unfolding of the World Spirit. Marx sometimes followed this line of thinking, though it was not the World Spirit but active class struggle that assumed the guiding role. As classes in themselves become classes for themselves, so history was moved onward toward the perfected state of a postrevolutionary classless communistic society where even the state ultimately withered away. In both cases (and I obviously simplify), the stationary state as spatial form (which is unspecifiable in advance) is arrived at through a particular conception of historical process. Whereas More gives us the spatial form but not the process, Hegel and Marx give us their distinctive versions of the temporal process but not the ultimate spatial form.

There is, of course, plenty to protest in such teleologies. Both William Blake and Kierkegaard, for example, insisted that the dialectic should be understood as "either-or" rather than "both-and," and the effect of that is to make history a succession of existential or political choices that have no necessary guiding logic or any clearly identifiable end state (Clark 1991). In detail, we find Marx in his political histories and later writings often drawn to a dialectics of "either-or" rather than the "both-and" of Hegelian transcendence. His hesitation in supporting the Paris Commune on the grounds that the time was not yet ripe and his sudden switch to support it up to the hilt had everything to do with his double sense of a dialectic that could be "both-and" or "either-or." Marx clearly recognizes the potential consequences of either making a revolution or not in a given place and time, and with this the teleology gives way to a much more contingent sense of historical unfolding, even if the motor of history still remains class struggle. This distinction within the dialectic of "both-and" and "either-or" is, as we will see, no trivial matter.

In order to sustain his views, Marx had to deconstruct a quite different and even then dominant utopianism of process that relied on the rational activities of "economic man" in a context of perfected markets. Since this has been by far the most powerful utopianism of process throughout the history of capitalism, we need to pay close attention to it. Adam Smith articulated the argument most precisely. His reflections on the theory of moral sentiments—he was in the first instance a moral philosopher rather than an economist—led him to propose a utopianism of process in which individual desires, avarice, greed, drives, creativity, and the like could be mobilized through the hidden hand of the perfected market to the social benefit of all. From this, Smith and the political economists derived a political program to eliminate state interventions and regulations (apart from those that secured free-market institutions) and curb monopoly power. Laissez-faire, free trade, and properly constituted markets became the mantras of the nineteenth-century political economists. Give free markets room to flourish, and all will be well with the world. And this, of course, is the ideology that has become so dominant in the advanced capitalist countries these last twenty years. This is the system to which, we are again and again told, "there is no alternative."

Marx mounted a devastating attack on this utopianism of process in *Capital.* In the second chapter, he concedes the Smithian fiction of a perfected market. Then, with a relentless and irrefutable logic, he shows the inevitable consequences to be

> in proportion as capital accumulates, the situation of the worker, be his situation high or low, must grow worse. . . . Accumulation of wealth at one pole is, therefore, at the same time accumulation of misery, the torment of labour, slavery, ignorance, brutalization and moral degradation at the opposite pole.

Marx's brilliant deconstruction of free-market utopianism has largely been suppressed in recent times. The free-market juggernaut—with its mantras of private and personal responsibility and initiative, deregulation, privatization, liberalization of markets, free trade, downsizing of government, and draconian cutbacks in the welfare state and its protections—has rolled on and on. For more than twenty years now, we have been battered and cajoled at almost every turn into accepting the utopianism of process of which Smith dreamed as the solution to all our ills. We have also witnessed an all-out assault on those institutions—trade unions and government in particular—that might stand in the way of such a project. Margaret Thatcher proclaimed that there is no such thing as society, only individuals and their families, and set about dismantling all those institutions—from trade unions to local governments—that might stand in the way of her utopian vision. With the fall of the Berlin Wall, Fukuyama (1992) put a Hegelian gloss on all this. We are now at the end of history. Capitalism and the free market are triumphant worldwide. The end of history is here (a sad thought if Baltimore is anything to go by). It may seem strange to view the likes of Margaret Thatcher and Newt Gingrich as Hegelians, but the free-market triumphalism that they espoused in their heyday was nothing other than Smithian utopianism of process attached to a very Hegelian kind of teleology ("progress is inevitable, and there is no alternative"). In many respects, as Frankel (1987) points out, the most effective utopians in recent times have been those of a right-wing persuasion, and they have espoused primarily a utopianism of process rather than a utopianism of spatial form. The odd thing, however, is the failure to attach the negative epithets of "utopian" and "teleological" to this right-wing assault on the social order.

The effective consequences are close to those that Marx's deconstruction depicts. Income inequalities have risen rapidly in all those countries that have given themselves over most energetically to the utopianism of the market. Globally, the World Bank (1995) reports that a billion of the 2.3 billion wage workers in the world are struggling to survive on less than a dollar a day. Such a condition would not be so bad if other systems of support (such as self-sufficient peasant agriculture) were available, but in many instances these have also been destroyed through market penetration, environmental degradation, and the like. Global income differentials have also widened (United Nations Development Program 1996): "Between 1960 and 1991 the share of the richest 20% rose from 70% of global income to 85%—while that of the poorest declined from 2.3% to 1.4%." By 1991, "more than 85% of the world's population received only 15% of its income," and "the net worth of the 358 richest people, the dollar billionaires, is equal to the combined income of the poorest 45% of the world population—2.3 billion people." Such income polarization is as astounding as it is obscene. If this is the end of history, then it is a rather desperate and dystopian ending for most of the world's population.

The consequent polarization in income and wealth also has its geographic forms of expression: spiraling inequalities between regions (that left, e.g., sub-Saharan Africa far behind as East and Southeast Asia surged ahead) as well as escalating contrasts between affluent neighborhoods and impoverished shantytowns or, in the case of the United States, between impoverished inner cities and affluent and exclusionary suburbs. All this renders hollow the World Bank's extraordinary utopian claim that international integration, coupled with free-market liberalism and low levels of government interference, is the best way to deliver growth and rising living standards for workers. This claim reads all the more oddly since the repressive and strongly interventionist political regimes in Taiwan, South Korea, and Singapore were then cited as models of free-market liberalism (more than 65 percent of the housing stock in Singapore is state produced and owned, and the whole economy is orchestrated from top to bottom by state power). Now such economies are in financial difficulty; it is claimed that they suffered from too much government intervention.

This brings us to a key issue. The materialization of a utopianism of process requires that the process come to ground someplace, that it construct some sort of space within which it can function. How it gets framed spatially and how it produces space become critical facets of its tangible realization. Much of my own work in the last twenty years (Harvey 1982, 1989) has been about trying to track exactly such a process, to understand how capital builds a geographic landscape in its own image at a certain point in time only to have to destroy it later in order to accommodate its own dynamic of endless capital accumulation, strong technological change, and fierce forms of class struggle. The history of creative destruction and of uneven geographic development in the bourgeois era is simply stunning. Much of the extraordinary transformation of the earth's surface the last 200 years reflects precisely the putting into practice of the free-market utopianism of process and its restless and perpetual reorganizations of spatial forms.

But the manner of this spatial materialization has all manner of consequences. As free-market capital accumulation plays across a variegated geographic terrain of resource endowments, cultural histories, communications possibilities, and labor quantities and qualities (a geographic terrain that is increasingly a differentiated product of capital investments in infrastructures and built environments), so it produces an intensification of uneven geographic development in standards of living and life prospects. Rich regions grow richer, leaving poor regions ever poorer (Baltimore provides a simple example). Circular and cumulative causation embedded within the utopianism of the market process produces increasing differentiations in wealth and power rather than a gradual progress toward homogeneity and equality. There is, the old adage goes, "nothing more unequal than the equal treatment of unequals," and that is exactly how the free market operates.

Community and/or state power has led the way in trying to counteract some of the more egregious consequences of free-market utopianism (spiraling income inequalities, uneven geographic developments, externality effects on the environment, and the like). But the free play of this utopianism of process can be assured if, as Marx and Engels pointed out in the *Communist Manifesto,* the state becomes "the executive committee of the bourgeoisie." Decolonization after 1945 and the subsequent internationalization and liberalization of global markets have brought the whole world much closer to that norm, though the uneven pace at which this has occurred (a product of political and social struggles) has affected how the utopianism of process has been materialized in different places and times. Geopolitical struggles between places are integral to the problem.

The upshot of this argument is that the purity of any utopianism of process inevitably gets upset by its manner of spatialization. In exactly the same way that materializations of spatial utopias run afoul of the particularities of the temporal process mobilized to produce them, the utopianism of process runs afoul of the spatial framings and the particularities of place construction necessary to its materialization. The destruction of Baltimore as a living city in the last twenty years, under conditions of greater freedoms of the market, exactly illustrates the nature of the problem.

Toward a Spatiotemporal Utopianism

The obvious resolution to this problem is to construct a utopianism that is spatiotemporal rather than either spatial or temporal. It has been, after all, many years since Einstein taught us that space and time cannot meaningfully be separated. There are more than a few hints within the social sciences that the separation of space from time, though sometimes useful, can often be misleading (see Harvey 1996, part III). And if space and time are viewed as social constructs (implying the rejection of the absolute theories of space and time attributable to Newton and Descartes), then the production of space and time must be incorporated into any revitalized utopianism.

The history of utopianisms of spatial form and temporal process taken separately is, however, instructive. From the former, the idea of imaginative spatial play to achieve specific social and moral goals can be converted into the idea of potentially endless spatial plays. Experimentation with different spatial forms is a way to explore the wide range of human potentialities (different modes of collective living, of gender relations, of production-consumption styles, in the relation to nature, and so on). This is how Lefebvre (1991) sets up his conception of the production of space. He sees it as a privileged means to explore alternative and emancipatory strategies. But Lefebvre is resolutely antagonistic to the traditional utopianisms of spatial form precisely because of their closed authoritarianism. He fashions a devastating critique of Cartesian conceptions, of the political absolutism that flows from absolute conceptions of space, and of the oppressions visited on the world by a rationalized, bureaucratized, technocratically and capitalistically defined spatiality. For him, the production of space must always remain as an endlessly open possibility. But the effect is to leave the spaces of any alternative frustratingly undefined. Lefebvre refuses specific recommendations (though there are some nostalgic hints that they got it right in Renaissance Tuscany). He refuses to confront the underlying problem: that to materialize a space is to engage with closure (however temporary), which is an authoritarian act. The history of all realized utopias points to this issue of closure as both fundamental and unavoidable, even if disillusionment is the inevitable consequence. If, therefore, alternatives are to be realized, the problem of closure (and the authority it presupposes) cannot endlessly be evaded. To do so is to embrace an agonistic romanticism of perpetually unfulfilled longing and desire. And this is, in the end, where Lefebvre leaves us.

Consider the matter now from the standpoint of process-oriented utopias. The supposedly endlessly open and benevolent qualities of some utopian social process, like market exchange, have to crystallize into a material world somewhere and somehow. Social and material structures (walls, highways, territorial subdivisions, institutions of governance) are either made or not made. The dialectic of either-or is omnipresent. Once such structures are built, they are often hard to change (nuclear power stations commit us for thousands of years). Struggle as we might to create "flexible landscapes," the fixity of structures tends to increase with time, making the conditions of change more rather than less sclerotic. A total reorganization of materialized organizational forms like New York City or

Los Angeles is much harder to envisage let alone accomplish now than a century ago. Free-flowing processes become instantiated in structures, in institutional, social, cultural, and physical realities, that acquire a relative permanence, fixity, and immovability. Materialized utopias of process cannot escape the question of closure, either. The utopianism of the free market necessarily produces a social order akin to free-market Stalinism coupled with a world of accelerating income inequalities instantiated in the physical landscape as massively uneven geographic development of both life chances and human potentialities.

Closure of any sort contains its own authority because to materialize any one design, no matter how playfully construed, is to foreclose, in some cases temporarily but in other instances relatively permanently, on the possibility of materializing others. We cannot evade such choices. The dialectic is "either/or," not "both/and." What the materialized utopianism of spatial form so clearly confronts is the problematics of closure, and it is this that the utopianism of the social process so dangerously evades.

This difficulty has its ramifications for how to write about alternative possible worlds. Consider the works of Roberto Unger, who, like Lefebvre, is deeply committed to the exploration of liberatory alternatives but equally anxious to avoid the errors of traditional utopian formulations. Unger focuses on social processes and institutional/personal transformations. His critique of existing institutions and behaviors is strong and powerful, but the alternatives always remain unspecified even if the objective of finding a more open way of social relating is well-enough articulated. Unger avoids utopianism by refusing closure around any one particular set of institutional arrangements. Like Lefebvre, he lapses into the frustrating romanticism of keeping choices endlessly open. The harsh "either/or" of the dialectic is evaded in favor of the softer and more comforting politics of Hegelian transcendence. The antiauthoritarianism of liberatory political thought here reaches some sort of limit. There is a failure to recognize that the materialization of anything requires, at least for a time, closure around a particular set of institutional arrangements and a particular spatial form and that the act of closure is in itself a material statement that carries its own authority in human affairs. What the abandonment of all talk of utopia on the left has done, is to leave the question of valid and legitimate authority in abeyance (or, more exactly, to leave it to the moralisms of the conservatives—both of the neoliberal and the religious variety). It has left the concept of utopia, as Marin observes, as a pure signifier without any meaningful referent in the material world. And for many contemporary theorists, that is where the concept can and should remain: as a pure signifier of hope destined never to acquire a material referent.

How, then, can a stronger utopianism be constructed that integrates social process and spatial form? I have argued that this cannot be done without facing up to the problems of authority and closure, that fragmentation and dispersal cannot work, and that the bitter struggle of the "either-or" perpetually interferes with the gentler and more harmonious dialectic of "both-and." These insights are fundamental. But they need a stronger and more positive elaboration.

Beginnings

It is one thing to clear away the underbrush of wrong or partial thinking and quite another to propose alternatives. It is tempting to leave matters the way that Lefebvre and Unger do:

endlessly open but frustratingly incomplete. But in chiding such thinkers for lapsing into romanticism, I tacitly insist on some sort of closure, however tentative or tendentious. I also impose a critical restriction. The history of utopianism demonstrates how easily the perfection enunciated by some individual or social sect becomes a restrictive dogma enforced by charismatic leaders or dominant institutions: Followers must obey the rules unquestioningly (even unto death in some cases) in order to achieve the happy state. Between the Scylla of endlessly open noncommitment and the Charybdis of charismatic and fanatical closure, the best that I can offer is an invitation to a conversation about the hard work of tangible social transformation that has as its objective the construction of a far more egalitarian, openly democratic and creatively transformative society than that which is evident today, coupled with the analytic recognition that this cannot be achieved within the existing social framework of production, consumption, and, given my starting point, urbanization.

This conversation has to address spatiotemporal dynamics openly and directly. We need, for example, to cut the connection between "Utopia" and the "City" (with all its emotive freight, both positive and negative) and construct a subtler "utopianism of urbanization," construed as a fluid and evolving set of socioecological processes in relation to malleable spatial forms. The problem for that utopianism is to describe a politically emancipatory and ecologically sane mix of spatiotemporal shifts in ways of life, rather than acquiesce to those imposed by uncontrolled capital accumulation, backed by class privilege and gross inequalities of political-economic power. This provides a broad canvas on which to paint new thoughts and possibilities. But questions can be more specifically framed than that. I propose, then, to end by recognizing some basic steps through which a more dialectical utopianism must pass if it is to gain any kind of momentum.

THE PERSONAL IS POLITICAL

By changing our world, we change ourselves. How, then, can any of us talk about social change without at the same time being prepared, both mentally and physically, to change ourselves? Conversely, how can we change ourselves without changing our world? That relation is not easy to negotiate. Foucault (1984) rightly worried that the "fascism that reigns in our heads" is far more insidious than anything that gets constructed outside. And in a touching letter to the Icarians preparing to emigrate from France to found their utopia in the New World in the wake of the failed revolution of 1848, Marx (cited in Marin 1984) argued that they were "too infected with the errors of their education and the prejudices of today's society to be able to get rid of them in Icarie." The personal is political. But that does not mean, as feminists and ecologists have discovered to their cost, that virtually *anything* personal makes for good politics. Nor does it mean, as is often suggested in some radical (and broadly utopian) alternative movements (such as deep ecology), that all that is necessary for social change to occur is a fundamental transformation in personal attitudes and behaviors. While social change begins and ends with the personal, there is much more at stake here than individualized personal growth. But by the same token, we have also seen what happens when utopianism leaves no space for the private and the personal (including doubt, anger, and despair as well as certitude, altruism, hope, and elation). It is on that contradiction that many a worthy-seeming political project has foundered.

THE POLITICAL PERSON IS A SOCIAL CONSTRUCT

To insist on the personal as political is to confront the question of the political person as grounding for political action. Persons must be understood here as social constructs rather than preformed, absolute, and immutable entities. But how should "social construction" be understood? Adam Smith (cited in Marx 1977, 483) considered that "the understandings of the greater part of men are necessarily formed by their ordinary employments" and that "the uniformity of (the labourer's) stationary life naturally corrupts the courage of his mind." If this is only partially true—as I am sure it is—it highlights how the struggle to think alternatives inevitably runs up against the consciousness that attaches to daily routines and ordinary employments.

Classical utopianism is helpful here, for it permits us to imagine entirely different systems of property rights and living and working arrangements, all manifest as entirely different routines and employments. This imagined reorganization (including its social relations, forms of reproductive work, technologies, and forms of social provision) makes possible a radically different consciousness (of social relations; of rights, duties, and obligations; of the relation to nature; and the like), and from that consciousness an alternative politics of possibility (like the inspiration that Howard drew from Bellamy) can arise.

But there is something in between the utopian imagination and a consciousness attached to ordinary employments. We are not entirely helpless puppets of the social processes that flow around us. We can put ourselves at risk, find time (however little) to experience something different, and thereby open ourselves somewhat to possibilities beyond those dictated by our ordinary employments. It takes a conscious effort to do so, and we can never go outside the processes that so effectively and perpetually socialize and resocialize us into the existing state of things. But we can take charge to some degree of our own social construction and in so doing gain experiences that point to alternatives.

THE POLITICS OF COLLECTIVITIES

The individual cannot go it alone. Some sort of collectivity must arise as an institutionalized agent of political action. Individuals need to create and draw on solidarities and support networks. This means political organization of some sort. There is, of course, no lack of such organization already available to us. Civil and political society is full of organizational forms to facilitate and promote social relating. Unfortunately, many are retrograde and reactionary, designed to consolidate advantages already accrued and to keep others from sharing in those privileges. As Davis (1990) points out, home-owner associations dedicated to the protection of their property values, privileges, and lifestyles dominate the contemporary urban and suburban scene in the United States, and they typically react with violence and anger when threatened by social programs or even the activities of the state or developers. Such territorial expressions of collective governance preclude the search for alternatives.

Traditional utopianism attacks this condition. Communitarianism as a utopian movement gives precedence, for example, to ideals of citizenship and collective identifications over the private pursuit of individual advantage and the "rights talk" that attaches thereto. This founds many a utopian dream (from Thomas More to Fourier and contemporary religious movements like those for a Christian Base Community).

But in practice, distinctive communities are painstakingly built by social practices, including the exercise of authoritarian powers and conformist restrictions. They are not just imagined (however important the imaginary of them may be). And it is not always easy to define the difference between them and the exclusionary and authoritarian practices of, say, home-owner associations. Etzioni (1997), a leading proponent of the new communitarianism, actively supports the principle of closed and gated communities. Collective institutions can also end up merely improving the competitive strength of territories in the high stakes game of the uneven geographic development of capitalism (Putnam 1993). For the privileged, community often means securing and enhancing privileges already gained. For the underprivileged, it all too often means "controlling their own slum."

But spatiotemporal utopianism cannot avoid the issue of collective action and the notion of "community" that is often associated with it. It is important, of course, to view community as a process, not a thing. The tangible struggle to create and sustain institutions—to mobilize collective powers such as churches, unions, neighborhood organizations, local governments, and the like—has long proven central to the pursuit of alternatives to the selfishness of market individualism. But the remaking and reimagining of "community" will work in progressive directions only if it is connected en route to a broader sense of insurgent politics. The embeddedness and organized power that communities and other political collectivities offer form a crucial basis for political action, for transforming the personal into the political, even though organizational coherence requires democratically structured systems of authority, consensus, and "rules of belonging."

Although community "in itself" can have meaning as part of a broader politics, community "for itself" almost invariably degenerates into regressive exclusions and fragmentations (miniutopias of spatial form). Means must be found to reach out across space and time to shape more universal processes of historical-geographic change.

MILITANT PARTICULARISM AND POLITICAL ACTION

The theory of "militant particularism" argues that all broad-based political movements have their origins in particular struggles in particular places and times (see Harvey 1996, chapter 1). Many struggles are defensive—for example, struggles against plant closures, the siting of noxious facilities, violence against women, environmental degradations, attacks on indigenous cultural forms, and the like. A widespread politics of resistance now exists to neoliberalism and capitalism throughout the world. But some forms of militant particularism are proactive. In the West, this typically means struggles for specific group rights that are universally declared but only partially conferred (the rights of slaves, labor, women, gays, the culturally different, animals and endangered species, the environment, and the like).

The critical problem for this vast array of struggles is to shift gears, transcend particularities, and arrive at some conception of a universal alternative to that social system that is the source of their difficulties. Capitalism (coupled with modernism) successfully did this vis-à-vis preexisting modes of production, but the oppositional movements of socialism, communism, environmentalism, feminism, and even humanism and multiculturalism have all constructed some sort of universalistic politics out of militant particularist origins. It is important to understand how this universalization occurs, the problems that arise, and the role that utopianism plays.

Dialectics here is useful. It teaches that universality always exists *in relation to* particularity: Neither can be separated from the other even though they are distinctive moments within our conceptual operations and practical engagements. The notion of justice, for example, acquires universality through a process of abstraction from particular instances and circumstances but becomes particular again as it is actualized in the real world through social practices. But the orchestration of this process depends on mediating institutions (those, e.g., of law and custom within given territories or among specific social groups). These mediating institutions "translate" between particularities and universals and (like the Supreme Court) become guardians of universal principles and arbiters of their application. They also become power centers in their own right. This is, very broadly, the structure set up under capitalism with the state and all its institutions (now supplemented by a variety of international institutions such as the World Bank and the International Monetary Fund, the United Nations, and the General Agreement on Tariffs and Trade and the World Trade Organization) being fundamental as "executive committees" of capitalism's systemic interests. Capitalism is replete with mechanisms for converting from the particular (even personal) to the universal and back again in a dynamic and iterative mode.

No social order can, therefore, evade the question of universals. The contemporary "radical" critique of universalism is sadly misplaced. It should focus instead on the specific institutions of power that translate between particularity and universality rather than attack universalism per se. Clearly, such institutions favor certain particularities (such as the rights of ownership of means of production) over others (such as the rights of the direct producers) and promote a specific kind of universal.

But there is another difficulty. The movement from particularity to universality entails a "translation" from the concrete to the abstract. Since a violence attaches to abstraction, a tension always exists between particularity and universality in politics. This can be viewed either as a creative tension or, as so often happens in the wake of revolutions, as a destructive and immobilizing force in which inflexible mediating institutions come to dominate. It is here that critical engagement with the static utopianism of spatial form (particularly its penchant for nostalgia) and the loosening of its hold by appeal to a utopianism of spatial-temporal transformation can keep open prospects for further change. The creative tension within the dialectic of particularity-universality cannot be repressed for long. Mediating institutions, no matter how necessary, cannot afford to ossify. The utopian vision that emerges is one of sufficient stability of institutional and spatial forms to provide security and continuity, coupled with a dynamic negotiation between particularities and universals so as to force mediating institutions to be as open as possible. At times, capitalism has worked in such a way (consider how, e.g., the law gets interpreted and reinterpreted to confront new socioeconomic conditions and problems). Any radical alternative, if it is to succeed as it materializes, must follow capitalism's example in this regard.

Translations and Aspirations

All this presupposes an ability to translate political aspirations across the incredible variety and heterogeneity of socioecological and political-economic positions. For James Boyd White (1990, 257–64), translation means

> confronting unbridgeable discontinuities between texts, between languages, and between people. As such it has an ethical as well as an intellectual dimension. It recognises the other—the composer of the original text—as a center of meaning apart from oneself. It requires one to discover both the value of the other's language and the limits of one's own. Good translation thus proceeds not by the motives of dominance and acquisition, but by respect. It is a word for a set of practices by which we learn to live with difference, with the fluidity of culture and with the instability of the self.
>
> We should not feel that respect for the other obliges us to erase ourselves, or our culture, as if all value lay out there and none here. As the traditions of the other are entitled to respect, despite their oddness to us, and sometimes despite their inhumanities, so too our own tradition is entitled to respect as well. Our task is to be distinctively ourselves in a world of others: to create a frame that includes both self and other, neither dominant, in an image of fundamental equality. This is true of us as individuals in our relations with others, and true of us as a culture too, as we face the diversity of our world. . . . This is not the kind of relativism that asserts that nothing can be known, but is itself a way of knowing: a way of seeing one thing in terms of another. Similarly it does not assert that no judgments can be reached, but is itself a way of judging, and of doing so out of a sense of our position in a shifting world.

This, in itself, has its own utopian ring. It is not hard to problematize such an argument, as Said (1978) did so brilliantly in *Orientalism,* as the power of the translator (usually white male and bourgeois) to represent "the other" in a manner that dominated subjects (orientals, blacks, women, and so on) are forced to internalize and accept. But that historical understanding itself provides a hedge against the kinds of representational repressions that Said and many feminists have recorded. This links us back to how the personal is always political. As White notes, "To attempt to 'translate' is to experience a failure at once radical and felicitous: radical, for it throws into question our sense of ourselves, our languages, of others; felicitous, for it releases us momentarily from the prison of our own ways of thinking and being." The act of translation offers a moment of liberatory as well as repressive possibility.

Translation offers the possibility of more common understandings. There are two compelling reasons for wanting this. First, as Zeldin (1994, 16), among others, remarks, we know a great deal about what divides people but nowhere near enough about what we have in common. Zeldin takes us away from nostalgic histories (that so often ground utopian thought) in order to show how, in the long history of humanity, meaningful conversations between, for example, even women and men have scarcely yet begun. The same is even more true across cultures and across the socioeconomic barriers that are increasingly etched even within a limited space of a metropolis like Baltimore. But the second compelling reason is this: Without translation, cooperation and collective forms of action become impossible, and all potentiality for an alternative politics disappears. The fluid ability of capitalists and their agents to translate among themselves using the basic languages of money, commodity, and property (backed, where necessary, with the theoretical language of a reductionist economics) is one of their towering class strengths.

THE UTOPICS OF SPACE-TIME TRANSFORMATION

The spatiotemporal utopianism to which I aspire requires the perspective of a long historical-geographic revolution. Perhaps this is the most difficult of all barriers to surmount in articulating its meaning. Utopias are usually located far away in space or in time. A radical break or disjunction lies in between: Some remarkable bloodless revolution has occurred in sentiments and practices. But, as Marx well understood, struggle and force are the midwives of historical-geographic transformations. How can the process of getting from here to there be informed by utopian dialogue? If change is not predetermined, then how can we consciously guide unpredictable spatiotemporal struggles down happier paths toward happier states? And how do we confront the difficulty that force, authority, and closure of some sort is inevitably implicated, and how can we stop that force degenerating into terror (the bane of all too many revolutions)? These are, I suspect, the most difficult of all questions to talk about openly.

I reflect on them by appeal to the idea that space and time (and space-time) are social constructs (though in what sense continues to be a matter of debate). Contemporary financial markets, for example, define a spatiotemporality of nanoseconds in cyberspace. Political horizons stretch to the next election and are based on the geopolitical practices of, for example, thinking locally and acting nationally or globally within some territorial structure (such as the global organization of nation-states). Multinational firms have a quite different spatiotemporal purview to most if not all households. Climatic change works according to its own spatiotemporal logic even though it is partially powered by accumulating anthropogenic action. I list these situations in order to illustrate the wide range of spatiotemporalities to be found in the world around us. Different processes (financial markets, climatic change, household reproduction) define quite different dimensionalities and scales of time and space. These are often in contradiction to one another, and resolving such contradictions sometimes poses acute problems (e.g., how can financial markets behave in such a way as to confront climate change through global warming?). Such contradictions, I argue, provide points of leverage to change social trajectories.

Classical utopianism unfortunately extricated itself entirely from such a contradictory world by presuming stationarity in absolute space and time. The move toward a spatiotemporal utopianism must drop that presumption and confront the problem of dynamics in a relationally constructed space-time.

The history of materialized utopianism provides clues as to what this might mean. Consider, for example, how free-market utopianism was put into place globally after World War II. In this, the United States had an all-powerful but specifically situated and particularistic role. It saw the dismantling of empires and decolonization, the shaping of the proper mediating international institutions (managed to ensure its own particular interests became the universal norm), and the opening of international trade as absolutely essential to the creation of a new world order in its own image. Its self-image was as a beacon of freedom, individual rights and democracy in a troubled world, as a model society to which everyone aspired, as a "shining city on a hill" doing battle, as Ronald Reagan framed it, with an "Evil Empire" of communism as well as with the dark forces of ignorance, superstition, and irrationality. A secularized and more open spatiotemporality had to be imposed on the world within which capital investments could more easily flow, along with movements of information, people, commodities, and the like. States had to be built up as facilitators of freely functioning capital markets (executive committees for capital accumulation). This meant an attempt (often abortive) to impose (with a good deal of militarism and violence) a particular conception of "political democracy" (voting between political parties on a four- or five-year cycle) as a universal principle (as if there are no other possible ways of being free and democratic). The world's spaces were forced open through often violent struggles and then reshaped by the power of U.S. policies (including those of satellite states and international institutions). Many of those who engaged on this project (of both left and right political persuasions, including many nongovernmental organizations) deeply believed that they were involved in a struggle to create a happier, more open, and freer world. They pursued with utopian conviction policies of development, aid, secular and military assistance, and education as means toward a humanistically powered enlightenment around the world.

While this caricatures somewhat, it captures something important about the spatiotemporal utopianism of U.S. internationalism over the last half century (a view subsequently given a Hegelian gloss in Fukuyama's "end of history" thesis). It illustrates the possibility of a spatiotemporal utopianism and gives a sense of what might be involved. By calling it a spatiotemporal utopianism, we can better understand how it worked, why and how it went wrong, and how its internal contradictions might form the seedbed for some alternative.

Scrutiny of the internal contradictions in this project is helpful in this regard. Marx correctly insisted that the seeds of revolutionary transformation must be found in the present and that no society can launch on a task of radical reorganization for which it is not at least partially prepared. On this basis, we can hope to "grow" an alternative spatiotemporal utopianism out of existing spatiotemporal processes and their internal contradictions. Let me list some of these contradictions:

1. Free-market utopianism has produced substantial wealth and empowerment for the few and disillusionment, repression, misery, and degradation for the rest. It has done so at the international as well as at the metropolitan scale (witness the description of Baltimore with which I began). Its utopian claims respecting equality and well-being sound increasingly hollow. The innumerable social and political movements that have sprung into being in opposition to neoliberalism provide the social and political basis for the search for an alternative.

2. The "success" of free-market utopianism was predicated on a preparedness to exercise authority and, where necessary, to resort to means of violence and repression as a necessary path to a more general enlightenment (in this it could not avoid the problems of the classical utopian forms). The trauma of the Vietnam War and subsequent revelations about covert operations around the world as well as internally (e.g., the suppression of the Black Panthers) tarnished the utopianism of the project and made it appear more and

more as an exercise in the power politics of Manifest Destiny as seen by an elite few in the United States rather than as a mass movement for global enlightenment. Political freedoms seemed hollow when reduced to freedoms of the market and little else.

3. The spatial libertarianism of the market undermined territorial structures and powers. The countereffect is a return to territoriality and national identity as a basis for politics (mostly but not always of a reactionary sort).

4. The spatiotemporal horizons of capitalism have converted the whole planet into "one large gasoline station" for resource extraction. Indiscriminate resource use and habitat destruction have promoted a whole series of environmental difficulties that require urgent attention. The concept of "sustainability," though easily coopted, points to spatiotemporal horizons quite different from those of capital accumulation.

Increasing class polarization, alienation from the secular modernist project, and so-called liberal politics, national separatist movements, and environmental issues constitute a broad swath of disaffection from the spatiotemporal utopianism led by the United States after World War II. The current rejection of all utopianism can best be read as the collapse of specific utopian forms, both East and West. Should we try to reignite the powerful spirit of utopianism once more, or just let it die an ungainly and unmourned death?

Dialectical Utopianism

Marx was a violent opponent of utopianism as he knew it. He savaged the utopias of spatial form and thoroughly deconstructed Adam Smith's utopianism of social process. Yet Marx passionately believed in the emancipatory potential of class struggle as *the* privileged process that would lead to a happier life. And both he and Engels argued in the *Communist Manifesto* that there are historical moments when oppositional forces are in such an undeveloped state that "fantastic pictures of future society" come to represent "the first instinctive yearnings" for "a general reconstruction of society." The literature produced by the socialist utopians of the early nineteenth century contains a powerful and important critical element. In attacking "every principle of existing society," they provided "the most valuable materials for the enlightenment of the working class." Furthermore, "the practical measures proposed" were helpful as landmarks in the struggle to abolish class distinctions. The danger, Marx and Engels argued, is that we will come to believe "in the miraculous effects" of some utopian science. Their own science of historical and dialectical materialism should be sufficient, they held, to set free the elements of the new society from within the womb of a collapsing bourgeois order.

But by what process can a city like Baltimore be revitalized, and by what mode of analysis can the elements of some new society be detected in the midst of the mess that now prevails? It is difficult to construct any solid sense of how change can occur in such conditions. The steps through which we must pass can be identified—the crucial moments of passage from the personal to the political and back again, from the particular to the universal and back again, from process to form and back again. Within such a dialectics lie clues to transformative possibilities and actions. Furthermore, the urbanization processes at work in Baltimore are deeply resonant of that interlinkage between spatial pattern and moral order that Robert Park long ago identified as central to understanding any urban condition. To break open that tight connection between spatial form and social process must clearly be a powerfully constitutive political aim. To liberate the spatial form–moral order connection from its existing constraints requires, however, a different kind of utopianism, a genuinely spatiotemporal and dialectical utopianism that can simultaneously embrace Lefebvre's emancipatory concerns for the production of space and Unger's drive to overthrow and refashion institutional arrangements. But Park (1967, 3) also wrote (in a passage that echoes Marx's observations on the labor process),

> The city and the urban environment represent man's most consistent and, on the whole, his most successful attempt to remake the world he lives in more after his heart's desire. But if the city is the world which man created, it is the world in which he is henceforth condemned to live. Thus, indirectly, and without any clear sense of the nature of his task, in making the city man has remade himself.

While we can reasonably aspire to intervene in that process of "remaking ourselves" and perhaps even to acquire some "clear sense of the nature of [our] task," we cannot leap outside the dialectic and imagine that we are not embedded and limited by the institutional worlds, the built environments, and the material conditions we have already created. But, as Marx infers by appeal to the metaphor of architect and bee, we cannot evade the question of the imagination either. To repeat Unger's formulation, "if society is imagined and made then it can be re-imagined and re-made." And it is here that the case for a nonmiraculous dialectical utopianism becomes compelling, not as a total solution but as a moment in which we gather our intellectual, critical, and imaginative powers together to give possibility a much grander press than currently exists.

References

Bacon, F. 1901. *New Atlantis.* In *Ideal Commonwealths.* London: Colonial Press.
Bellamy, E. 1888. *Looking Backward.* New York: Ticknor.
Benjamin, W. 1969. *Illuminations.* New York: Schocken Books.
Blakely, E. 1997. *Fortress America: Gated Communities in the United States.* Cambridge, Mass.: MIT Press.
Bloch, E. 1988. *The Utopian Function of Art and Literature.* Cambridge, Mass.: MIT Press.
Campanella, T. 1901. *City of the Sun.* In *Ideal Commonwealths.* London: Colonial Press.
Clark, L. 1991. *Blake, Kierkegaard, and the Spectre of the Dialectic.* Cambridge: Cambridge University Press.
Davis, M. 1990. *City of Quartz: Excavating the Future in Los Angeles.* London: Verso.
Duany, A. 1997. "Urban or Suburban?" *Harvard Design Magazine,* winter/spring, 47–63.
Etzioni, A. 1997. "Community Watch." *The Guardian,* June 28, 9.
Fishman, R. 1982. *Urban Utopias in the Twentieth Century.* Cambridge, Mass.: MIT Press.
Foucault, M. 1984. "Preface" to G. Deleuze and F. Guattari, *Anti-Oedipus: Capitalism and Schizophrenia* (xi–xiv). London: Athlone.
———. 1986. "Of Other Spaces." *Diacritics* 16, no. 1: 22–27.
Frankel, B. 1987. *The Post-Industrial Utopians.* Oxford: Polity Press.
Fukuyama, F. 1992. *End of History and the Last Man.* New York: The Free Press.
Gould, S. 1987. *Time's Arrow, Time's Cycle.* New York: Penguin.
Hall, P. 1988. *Cities of Tomorrow.* Oxford: Basil Blackwell.

Harvey, D. 1982. *The Limits to Capital.* Oxford: Basil Blackwell.
———. 1989. *The Urban Experience.* Baltimore: The Johns Hopkins University Press.
———. 1996. *Justice, Nature and the Geography of Difference.* Oxford: Basil Blackwell.
Hayden, D. 1981. *The Grand Domestic Revolution: A History of Feminist Designs for American Homes, Neighborhoods, and Cities.* Cambridge, Mass.: MIT Press.
Jacobs, J. 1961. *The Death and Life of Great American Cities.* New York: Vintage.
Katz, P. 1994. *The New Urbanism: Toward an Architecture of Community.* New York: McGraw-Hill.
Kumar, K. 1987. *Utopia and Anti-Utopia in Modern Times.* Oxford: Basil Blackwell.
———. *Utopianism.* Milton Keynes: Open University Press.
Kunstler, J. 1993. *The Geography of Nowhere.* New York: Simon and Schuster.
———. 1996. *Home from Nowhere: Remaking Our Everyday World for the 21st Century.* New York: Simon and Schuster.
Langdon, P. 1994. *A Better Place to Live: Reshaping the American Suburb.* Cambridge, Mass.: MIT Press.
Lefebvre, H. 1991. *The Production of Space.* Oxford: Basil Blackwell.
Lukerman, F., and P. Porter. 1976. "The Geography of Utopia." In D. Lowenthal and M. Bowden, eds., *Geographies of the Mind: Essays in Historical Geosophy* (226–49). New York: Oxford University Press.
Marin, L. 1984. *Utopics: Spatial Play.* London: Macmillan.
Marx, K. 1977. *Capital. Volume 1.* New York: Viking.
Marx, K., and F. Engels. 1952. *The Manifesto of the Communist Party.* Moscow: Progress Publishers.
More, T. 1901. *Utopia.* In *Ideal Commonwealths.* London: Colonial Press.
Park, R. 1967. *On Social Control and Collective Behavior.* Chicago: University of Chicago Press.
Putnam, R. 1993. *Making Democracy Work: Civic Traditions in Modern Italy.* Princeton, N.J.: Princeton University Press.
Said, E. 1978. *Orientalism.* New York: Vintage.
Scully, V. 1994. "The Architecture of Community." In P. Katz, *The New Urbanism: Toward an Architecture of Community* (221–30). New York: McGraw-Hill.
Sennett, R. 1970. *The Uses of Disorder: Personal Identity and City Life.* New York: Knopf.
Simmel, G. 1971. "The Metropolis and Mental Life." In D. Levine, ed., *On Individuality and Social Form* (324–49). Chicago: University of Chicago Press.
Unger, R. 1987a. *False Necessity: Anti-Necessitarian Social Theory in the Service of Radical Democracy.* Cambridge: Cambridge University Press.
———. 1987b. *Social Theory: Its Situation and Its Task.* Cambridge: Cambridge University Press.
United Nations Development Program. 1996. *Human Development Report, 1996.* New York: Oxford University Press.
White, J. 1990. *Justice as Translation: An Essay in Cultural and Legal Criticism.* Chicago: University of Chicago Press.
World Bank. 1995. *World Development Report: Workers in an Integrating World.* New York: Oxford University Press.
Zeldin, T. 1994. *An Intimate History of Humanity.* New York: HarperCollins.

6

Enclosure Acts and Exclusionary Practices

NEIGHBORHOOD ASSOCIATIONS, COMMUNITY POLICE, AND THE EXPULSION OF THE SEXUAL OUTLAW

Lisa E. Sanchez

Practices of enclosure and exclusion have played a key role in maintaining dominant economic and property relations in American society. The circumscription of feminine bodies and sexualities into private spaces and monitored public spaces has been enabled by cultural and legal strategies that fluctuate with historical and material conditions and prevailing political tides. Drawing from ethnographic research on commercial sex in one northwestern U.S. city, this chapter focuses on a new form of spatial regulation, the "prostitution-free-zone ordinance," which utilizes trespass law to exclude those identified as prostitutes from public spaces and city streets. The study highlights the generative and legitimating role that currently popular rhetorics of community and "quality of life" and new strategies of community policing have played in the enactment and enforcement of the "exclusion law." The author interprets the exclusion law as a strategy of spatial governmentality that seeks to enclose a boundary around the public spaces that privileged, propertied residents have claimed as their own, in turn producing the figure of the prostitute as the symbolically sacrificed outlaw of the normalized community.

Located in the Pacific Northwest of the United States, the city of Portland, Oregon,[1] has been hailed as an urban development and growth management success (Kunstler 1993; Walljasper 1997). Well known for its handsomely revitalized commercial districts and its unique blend of urban and natural landscape, Portland's "green cathedrals of spruce and fir" line its parking lots and frame office towers, while fountains and outdoor sculptures animate the town squares and rehabilitated warehouses of a newly refashioned downtown (Walljasper 1997, 11). But this description, a testimony to successful urban planning and slow-growth policy, portrays only one dimension of urban life in Portland: Less familiar but significant features of the urban landscape are the decrepit strip malls, empty buildings, and adult entertainment clubs of Portland's east side. In the less widely traveled subsections of the east side, neon-lit outlines of female bodies advertising "fantasy booths" and "live-nude modeling shows" take the place of the patches of green and picturesque statues downtown, and pubs advertising lap dancing replace the west side's chic storefronts and quaint brick coffeehouses.

The growth of high-tech electronics, software, and light industry energized the economic growth and urban revitalization that characterizes Portland's downtown and west side. In comparison, the economically depressed communities of east Portland have suffered from the effects of deindustrialization (Sanchez 1998). While public and private funds for regentrification projects have flowed into older downtown business districts and the west side, little energy and investment has been channeled into rebuilding the economies and communities of the east side.[2] The effects of deindustrialization are not limited to a decline in blue-collar industries and full-time employment for the working class. More important, east side residents lack a stable economic base and the public and private financial support needed to rebuild their economy.

During this twenty-year period of uneven development and expanding economic polarization, the declining economies of the east side have been bolstered by numerous adult businesses. A few key legal decisions and a laissez-faire stance regarding regulations for locating and managing adult enterprises have fueled their growth. Among the most important of these legal decisions was a 1989 Ninth Circuit Court ruling that overturned a city ordinance that prohibited full nudity in commercial spaces (Sanchez 1997, 1998).[3] Although there were a handful of topless dance bars in Portland prior to the ruling, the decision encouraged local bar owners to feature "all nude" dancing. In subsequent years, the circuit court's decision spawned large-venue strip clubs, while a number of neighborhood taverns and pubs converted to "strip pubs."

In the 1990s, a number of legal decisions that struck down proposed zoning ordinances and business regulations contributed to expanded growth in legal adult entertainment. As a result, the number of all-nude strip clubs in the Portland metropolitan area increased from ten in 1989 to about eighty in 1995 and continued to increase in the late 1990s (Sanchez 1997, 1998). With the increase in strip bars and adult video stores, businesses such as escort services, private dancer businesses, and gentlemen's tanning salons increased steadily during the same time period (Sanchez 1997, 1998). The rapid increase in legal adult businesses enhanced related enterprises, such as alcohol sales and the state-run gaming industry, which currently draws most of its revenues from video poker machines located in pubs and strip bars east of the river.

Not all commercial sex businesses and practices fit within the definition of legal sex work, however. Working the boundaries of legally sanctioned sex services, some women serve an ancillary street market in paid sex. Historical changes in the practice and regulation of commercial sex in Portland suggest that just as the boundaries between licit and illicit sex markets and practices are themselves murky, so too is the enforcement of those boundaries. Until the early part of the twentieth century, Portland officials made no attempt to regulate in-house prostitution (Rosen 1982; Rubin 1984),[4] and in the 1980s prostitution was practiced regularly in massage parlors almost without incident. Over time, the enactment and enforcement of laws and city ordinances prohibiting prostitution and prostitution promotion reconfigured the boundaries between licit and illicit commercial sex and determined which sex workers would be targeted for enforcement. While Portland's regulations appear at times rigid and punitive and at other times flexible and moderate, such regulations have never resulted in the eradication of prostitution and other forms of commercial sex. The enactment and enforcement of laws regulating commercial sex are a fluctuating form of regulatory governance, one that shapes the contours of commercial sex markets and practices and manages the spaces where these practices take place.

Although legal adult businesses have been permitted to operate almost without legal sanction since 1989, the recent growth and transformation of commercial sex in Portland have created conflict. Public protests in front of strip bars and other adult businesses have become commonplace. While such conflicts have underlying moral currents, they have surfaced primarily as concerns about property values and struggles over land use decisions. Perhaps the most striking example of conflict over land use is embodied in a few "suspicious fires" that took place on the premises of adult businesses located in high-income suburban areas and politically active districts. One of the most dramatic incidents involved a 1996 "Mambo Strip Club" fire in inner northeast Portland (local newspaper 1996). Located in a prominent section of the historic Hollywood district, the Mambo Strip Club stood unapologetically next to a Victorian art theater that was a favorite venue for Portlanders. Once the best-known location in town for street prostitution, the Hollywood area had been gentrified between 1994 and 1996 after politically active locals successfully lobbied city government to restore the theater district. With increased street patrol in the Hollywood district, street prostitution all but disappeared from the area by 1996.

Hollywood residents took pride in the gentrification project and in the erosion of both licit and illicit sex markets in their neighborhood. In the less-than-impartial sentiments of one Hollywood resident, "Hollywood [has made a comeback] after twenty years of being down in the sewers" (citizen testimony at a city council meeting, August 1997). For Hollywood residents, the rise in property values in the fashionable new Hollywood area raised the stakes in the struggle to maintain control over commercial land uses. Not surprisingly, then, the "postgentrification" debut of the Mambo Strip Club angered area residents, particularly because the club owner initially received a permit to open a Latin nightclub, then converted the dance club into a strip bar after only three months of operation. The fire occurred about four months after the club's transformation into a strip bar. Following an investigation by the local fire marshal, it was attributed to an electrical short in an accounting office upstairs from the club, but many people were suspicious about the source of the fire and the subsequent investigation. The owner of the club never rebuilt, and the land next to the theater remains fenced off.

The debate surrounding the fire symbolized tensions among the Portland citizenry about land use decisions and the power of the adult sex industry. While the liberationist factions of the Portland business and legal community have supported the expansion and deregulation of legal adult sex businesses, other residents associate the loosely regulated sex industry with a decline in Portland's "quality of life." With the onset of community policing and the growing strength of Portland neighborhood associations in the mid-1990s, residents were better situated to influence the city council and the police, but their influence had little bearing on the ongoing growth and deregulation of legal adult businesses.

Given the community policing emphasis on crime prevention and residents' lack of success in persuading city government to tighten the regulatory reins on legal adult businesses, community activists eventually turned their attention to illicit commercial sex, instigating a crackdown on street prostitution. By 1995, increased citizen participation in policymaking resulted in the enactment of the prostitution-free-zone ordinance (city ordinance 137816). Reversing the zoning logic that has historically confined legal adult businesses *inside* a set spatial boundary, the prostitution-free zone maps out so-called high-vice areas and *excludes* those caught soliciting for prostitution from those areas. According to the 1995 city ordinance, people arrested for prostitution or prostitution procurement within 500 feet of the zone are excluded from that area for ninety days (ordinance 137816).

If convicted, they are excluded for an additional year; if the police find them in the area during that time, they can be arrested for trespassing (ordinance 137816).

Enforcement of the zoning ordinance, commonly referred to as the "exclusion law," is a spatial form of governance, one that seeks to draw a boundary between the life spaces of privileged, propertied residents and the visibly sexual/sexualized body of the prostitute. Public representations of the targeted population of street prostitutes produce the figure of the prostitute as the "symbolically sacrificed outlaw" of the normalized community (Young 1996) and the privileged as law-abiding citizens.

Discipline and Governmentality: On the Production of Identities, the Manipulation of Bodies, and the Government of Space

> A whole history remains to be written of spaces—which would at the same time be the history of powers . . . —from the great strategies of geo-politics to the little tactics of the habitat, institutional architecture from the classroom to the design of hospitals, passing via economic and political installations. . . . Anchorage in space is an economico-political form which needs to be studied in detail. (Foucault 1980, 149)

In Portland, conflicts over public space are rooted in antiquated, if unwitting, attempts to redefine citizenship rights vis-à-vis property ownership.[5] The moral content of these conflicts and the proprietary quality of the regulatory strategies established to address them are encoded in a discourse of "neighborhood livability," known in other places as "quality of life." These regulatory discourses and strategies resonate with new techniques of governmentality and with older strategies of enclosure.

Foucault (1991) used the term "governmental rationality" or "governmentality" to describe the tactics, technologies, and institutions that are peculiar to neoliberal nation-states. Developed in the late eighteenth century against prior forms of sovereignty as obedience to a divine or earthly sovereign, governmental rationality is a form of administrative governance focused on the "welfare of the population," its health, longevity, wealth, and so on (Foucault 1991, 100). According to Foucault, the legitimacy of the state under this logic of governance lies in the rational administration of the knowledge and science of the *population* itself.

In advanced capitalism, governance is not the exclusive domain of the state, and it is not imposed strictly from the top down. The central questions of government concern both the rational enactment of law and policy and the question of how to elicit the desired forms of self-governance—how to govern oneself, how to govern others, how to be governed, and how to organize and legitimate the system of governance; these are the questions of government that are at the heart of modern Western nation-states. From this perspective, governmentality describes those activities that aim to shape, guide, or affect the conduct of self and other.

Governmental regimes are characterized by a perplexing array of technologies for monitoring and managing populations.[6] In the current era of technology and global capitalism, these include regional, national, and global health, social security, and criminal records; sophisticated police surveillance technologies; and geographic profiling systems. While each of these technologies lies squarely in the domain of population management and social control, other strategies, designed to manipulate the boundaries between public and private space, may be more insidious because they appear to be unrelated to social control, but they accomplish the task with remarkable efficiency. For example, architectural structures and zoning codes organize the social landscape and manipulate public space uses even as they appear to be purely objective or aesthetic (Davis 1992; Soja 1992; Dumm 1993; Caldeira 1996). As some scholars have pointed out, gated communities create "new enclosures," utilizing architecture and security devices to enclose private and public space for the residence, leisure, and consumption of those who live within the walls of the community (Davis 1992; Caldeira 1996). At the same time, these new enclosures have been restructured to displace poor and homeless residents, many of whom service the more privileged (Davis 1992).

Elsewhere, I have used the term "spatial governmentality"[7] to describe strategies that manipulate the spatial order of a community or region. Techniques of spatial governmentality effect social order by *managing populations in place.* They rely on the managerial logic of government to order and regulate public and private spaces and to manage the flow of bodies into and out of these spaces. They include civil ordinances and zoning codes that govern public and commercial land uses and criminal codes that establish and police boundaries between public and private space (e.g., trespass, vagrancy, and so on). They include urban planning and architectural strategies as well as the new "communitarian" strategies, such as the currently popular "quality of life" discourses and ordinances. Regimes of spatial governmentality thus join modern technological advances, population management systems, and discourses of citizenship, community, and property with techniques of sociospatial control, producing enclosed spaces and zones of exclusion.

The spatial economy of the new enclosures, like the spatial economy of commercial sex in Portland, illustrates how economic development and population flows may be effectively managed and directed toward select regions of a city. It is in the manipulation of the boundaries between public and private space and in the reformulation of the relationship between citizenship and property that spatial governmentality finds its closest link with the enclosure movements of early capitalism (Thompson 1976; Pateman 1988; Collier, Maurer, and Suárez-Navaz 1995; Yuval-Davis 1997). As land and property were reorganized following the imperatives of capital, the displaced and disenfranchised began to congregate in public spaces where they were soon perceived as a threat to the burgeoning social order (Chambliss 1975; Thompson 1976; Boal 1997). And it was in the effort to resolve these threats—that is, to make the city streets safe for the landed elite and merchant class—that modern disciplinary strategies and carceral spaces, such as prisons, social service programs, and psychiatric institutions, emerged as solutions for controlling displaced populations.

Until the nineteenth century, the spatial logic of enclosure was also used to contain feminine bodies in the "protected" domain of the private sphere (Burt and Archer 1994). The institutionalization of cultural codes of "proper place" and feminine conduct, such as separate spheres doctrine and the common-law practice of coverture,[8] was crucial to controlling reproduction and sexuality. Women involved in prostitution operated in and through public markets and public places. Although prostitution in the United States was not a distinct criminal offense until the late nineteenth century (Rosen 1982; Rubin 1984), women suspected of prostitution were subject to arrest under laws affecting public space uses, including those prohibiting vagrancy, night walking, public indecency, and disorderly conduct (Chambliss 1975; Hobson 1987; Pateman 1988). Women in prostitution thus stood outside culturally accepted spatial orders and norms of conduct, yet they were central to the construction of these cultural conventions.

The links between early enclosure movements, modern disciplinary regimes, and late modern governmental technologies may appear tenuous, but only when couched within a master narrative of progress. Regimes of social control do not simply succeed or replace one another, erasing established histories and social structures. Rather, postdisciplinary society engages the logic of enclosure and utilizes the carceral spaces and regimented practices that developed under industrial capitalism. Governmental regimes increase the effectiveness of disciplinary institutions by organizing the built environment to be selective and exclusive. Such regimes enhance the state's capacity to identify, locate, and monitor high-risk groups and suspicious individuals and to channel them into carceral spaces (like prisons and mental institutions) and disciplinary programs (like probation and social service agencies). Masking their power and moral/exclusionary content behind the sterile rhetoric of science and technology, governmental regimes extend the possibilities of social regulation by reaching further into the lived spaces of the social world and by encouraging the ordinary citizen to monitor and police the moral and spatial boundaries of community.

Constituting the Inside and Outside of Community

> The most serious political consequence of the desire for community, or for copresence and mutual identification with others, is that it often operates to exclude or oppress those experienced as different. (Young 1990, 234)

Just as disciplinary and governmental regimes rely on identity categories to manage populations, they also rely on a discourse of community to justify enforcement strategies and to specify spaces of contact between offenders and state agents. A resurgent nostalgia for community, engendered by the atomizing effects of liberal individualism on the one hand and the bureaucratic domination of welfare capitalism on the other, characterizes late capitalist political economies. Along with the grassroots move toward "the local," some social theorists have idealized community, linking it to contemporary notions of the "just society" (Braithwaite 1989).

The desire for community, embodied in the currently popular quality-of-life discourses and community movements, has reshaped cultural norms about place, space, and identity, enabling some to appropriate public space and to blur the boundaries between private property and customary common space. Conventional notions of community evoke images of connectedness, mutual identification, belonging, and shared place. But "community" expresses the longing or aspiration for these ideals as much as it defines any tangible locality of like-minded or similarly situated individuals (Anderson 1991). While community may be constituted in copresent, real-time interactions, it is also formed in imagined social spaces defined by shared interactions and identities. Community is formed constitutively: The act of defining some as "deviant" or "suspect" is simultaneously an act of self-definition and a declaration of group membership (Herbert 1996; Young 1996). As community members make and remake their own identities and those of others, they simultaneously constitute and enclose community.

In Portland, community may still mean shared geographic and sociopolitical space, but it also is constituted through the circulation of rumors and claims-making processes. Local discourses of community, which assume entitlements to land and property, are reflected in the language of neighborhood associations and community police. Grounded in a logic of difference and exclusionary morality, these discourses and regulatory strategies have significantly altered the meaning of citizenship and community in Portland, extending moral authority and proprietary power to a select group of people who represent themselves as legitimate property owners and established residents.

Over the last twenty-three years, ninety-four neighborhood association districts comprised primarily of home owners, community activists, and businesspeople have formed to preserve the local ethics of property and land use in Portland. Initially designed to foster broader citizen participation in planning programs intended to enhance "neighborhood livability" (ONA report, November 1975), the Office of Neighborhood Associations (ONA) has become the primary center for community activism. The meaning of neighborhood livability has shifted from an initial concern with urban planning to a current focus on crime prevention. The ONA now describes the neighborhood associations as "legal entit[ies]" governed by "citizen-written bylaws" (ONA report, August 1997). The ONA has established seven district offices to "support and stimulate [community] activism" in smaller residential enclaves. Covering an area divided into four residential zones and five police precincts, the ONA has mapped its own vision of the social landscape onto the city. The ONA constructs boundaries around the "natural features" of the environment and the "common identity [and] interest[s]" of the people living within those boundaries (ONA handbook, November 1975). A 1974 city ordinance describes its vision of community quite explicitly: "*Membership* shall be open to all residents, property owners, business licensees and representatives of nonprofit organizations located within the boundaries of the neighborhoods. *Boundaries* shall reflect the common identity or social communication of the people in the area."

Although Portland neighborhood associations have existed for over twenty years, they have gained power by forming liaisons with the Police Bureau, which adopted community-oriented policing (COPs) in 1992. Under COPs, citizens are considered "active co-producers of public safety," and police serve as "primary diagnosticians and treatment coordinators" (Bayley and Shearing 1996, 588). Portland's strategies are preventative, focusing on "high visibility" conduct. These strategies—"looking for people and vehicles that get out of place," spotting people that "don't belong in certain places at certain times," "looking for transients and signs of violations," and "getting people to move along" (police interviews, March 1997)—reflect the "territoriality" of community policing (Herbert 1996).

To facilitate cooperative alliances between residents and police officers, community police are required to attend neighborhood association meetings to discuss crime risk prevention strategies with area residents (neighborhood association meeting and police interviews, August 1997). During these meetings, police officers teach residents to "recognize and report suspicious activity" and encourage them to organize around issues such as prostitution, drug dealing, and youth gangs (ONA report, August 1997; neighborhood association meeting, August 1997). Implicitly invoking the "broken windows" approach to crime prevention (Wilson and Kelling 1982; Kelling and Coles 1996), residents are further encouraged to "clean up" the symbols of disorder thought to contribute to crime (e.g., poor street lighting, abandoned cars and houses, littered vacant lots, and broken windows).

The newly forged bonds between Portland citizens and police officers are captured in the first sentence of the eighth edition of the 1995 Portland Community Policing Information Packet, which reads, "*The police are the public and the public is the police.*" This same slogan was used in early nineteenth-century England[9] to garner public support for the establishment of the first full-time professional police force. Alliances between local citizens and police officers constitute Portland's citizenry anew, as boundaries among residents, neighborhood associations, city officials, and police officers become intangibly blurred. In dialogue, these residents and police officers construct an inside and outside of community that reinscribes the language of ownership and exclusion. This new community, a "citizen-state coalition," is a quasi-legal alliance of official and self-appointed social control agents who promote their own interests and those of state and city government.

The alliances between citizens and state officials are constituted both in concrete, co-present relationships and in the imagination. Neighborhood associations are comprised of comparatively small residential cliques that have some face-to-face interaction within their own district but less communication across districts.[10] Constructing themselves as a para-legal arm of city government and as representatives of their communities, neighborhood associations are imagined communities, buttressed by the power of publicity and the legitimacy of the state. If the citizen-state coalition imagines itself as a body of "concerned citizens," how does it imagine the other? The citizen-state coalition creates a criminal element or suspect other about which to direct its concerns. Citizen groups did not form to confirm the harmony and tranquility of their neighborhoods. They maintain a problem-solving orientation. In order to constitute themselves as concerned citizens and active problem solvers, they required a problem external to their geographic enclaves and own separate identities. Against the powerful resistance of legal adult business owners, the legitimacy and popularity of the state-promoted gaming industry, and the elusiveness of organized, criminally active networks, women in prostitution have offered an easy target for problem solving and community "clean-up" efforts.

The Legal Geography of Commercial Sex: Locating the Body of the Prostitute

> In criminal justice policy, in criminological theory, and in the practices of criminal law can be found, first, an imagined community; second, an identifiable subject which represents a threat to the community; third, a desire to inflict violence upon that subject in the name of the community. (Young 1996, 9)

The Portland citizen-state coalition presently focuses on policing identities and public spaces. The everyday practices of Portland police officers reveal not only the contradictory logic through which the identity of the prostitute is constructed but also the role that women suspected of prostitution play in the symbolic economy of intrusion and impurity. The spatial organization of street prostitution in Portland and the administrative logic of prostitution policing suggest how this works.

There are five street spaces used for solicitation in Portland, including about a five-mile stretch of road in southeast Portland, and a couple of smaller, more concentrated solicitation spaces in northeast Portland and downtown. Each area is patrolled by a different precinct within the Portland Metropolitan Police Bureau, and each precinct conducts periodic "prostitution missions." Prostitution detail and street patrol officers handle the day-to-day enforcement of prostitution and prostitution procurement, and officers from the Drugs and Vice Division investigate pimping and promoting and compelling prostitution. Police officers can arrest women at their discretion for prostitution procurement if they have been spotted flagging down cars, hitchhiking, lingering at phone booths and street corners, or walking the street alone in a "high vice" area (police interview, August 1997). If a woman makes an explicit offer to exchange sex acts for money, she can be charged with prostitution (police interview, March 1997).

I have intentionally chosen the feminine subject to describe the target of police officers' enforcement practices. Many officers interpreted the law prohibiting *prostitution procurement* in explicitly gendered terms, but they did not perceive their actions and assessments as unfair or as unlawful gender discrimination. In everyday conversation, police officers rationalized their enforcement practices, claiming that "women *walking* the street" were more visible and more likely to be the subject of a "citizen complaint" (field interviews, March and August 1997). One officer went as far as to say, "Prostitution procurement applies just to the girls whereas the guy gets a prostitution charge" (police interview, March 1997). Although the procurement ordinance is worded in gender-neutral terms, most officers refrain from enforcing the law against male customers because men's solicitation practices, for example, *driving* up and down the same street in a privately owned car, are understood as more elusive than women's solicitation practices.

Officers viewed gendered enforcement practices as innocuous; after all, customers get a prostitution charge. But prostitution procurement charges are more frequently used because prostitution is presumably harder to prove. Procurement, on the other hand, is thought to be an easier charge to prove, but only if the subject of the charge is a woman. In addition to treating women's conduct as disproportionately actionable, officers often rely on a woman's prior prostitution record as evidence of her guilt. The police department claims gender neutrality and supports their claim by publicizing arrest statistics from prostitution missions, which target both female solicitors and male buyers of commercial sex for *prostitution.*[11] However, the majority of prostitution arrests are for *prostitution procurement.* The same women often are arrested repeatedly for prostitution procurement, while the majority of men who pay for sexual services are never arrested. Predictably, the police department rarely publishes statistics on daily arrests for prostitution procurement in the local news.

Hence, for Portland police officers, the meaning of "suspicious activities" is derived from their understanding of gender, sexuality, public space, and socioeconomic status. While male customers *driving* the boulevards are arguably just as "visible" as women *walking* the streets, police officers implicitly locate men's activities within a "normal" range of masculine conduct; their actions are naturalized as expressions of masculine (hetero)sexual desire. As one officer stated, "It's a quick, easy deal [for men who have a] high sex drive" (field interview, August 1997). Moreover, male customers are privileged because of the mobility and privacy that property ownership (in this case, ownership of a car) signifies. While some officers believe that they have to catch a man "in the act" to enforce the law against male customers, their enforcement practices more accurately reflect the power differential between women, who are socially and economically marginalized, and male customers, who have the status and resources to contest the legality of enforcement. Under the eye of the local legal regime, women engaged in prostitution have learned to downplay their solicitation activities by soliciting in less visible locations and dressing to blend in with other women on the streets. Although most local residents never notice these street prostitutes, police officers and citizen groups represent them as a highly visible and potentially dangerous group of individuals who are magnets for ancillary criminal activities, such as drug dealing, theft, rape, and robbery.

The language that officers use to describe their enforcement practices makes explicit their un-self-consciously gendered construction of commercial sex practice. Male customers are viewed as nameless, faceless bodies, but the bodies of the women are inscribed with a prostitute identity. This is not just a matter of semantics. Police surveillance and record-keeping practices are directed specifically at women. For example, the precincts and the Drugs and Vice Division keep the names, addresses, telephone numbers, birth dates, and criminal records of women with prior prostitution convictions on file, and prostitution detail officers carry these records with them while on patrol. During a ride-along, one detail officer proudly described himself as the best person for the job because he was the "most knowledgeable" officer on the force—he had a "great memory for names, faces, and birth dates" (field interview, August 1997). When asked if he uses the same techniques to monitor male customers, he noted the futility of keeping records on the customers, stating that "to do Johns, you have to have decoys." In other words, customers can be arrested only sporadically, during preplanned prostitution missions. Continuing, the officer added, "If I stop a man just because he has a prostitute in his car, he would deny it and say that he was only giving the girl a ride" (August 1997). By contrast, the officer claimed that the women could not deny it: "Even if they deny it, they know I know what they're doing" (August 1997).

In keeping with these identity-based practices, the precincts and the Drugs and Vice Division keep a file of mug shots of women who have been convicted of prostitution and prostitution procurement within the last ten years. Although the police encourage citizens to take photographs of male customers soliciting for prostitution, the men's photographs are not kept on file. Police officers believe that the act of taking a man's photograph alone will deter him from further involvement in prostitution (police interviews, March and August 1997; neighborhood association meeting, August 1997). Presumably, male customers are not thought of as a threat to the community but as men behaving in mischievous but predictably masculine ways.

Zoning Out: Enforcing the Prostitution-Free-Zone Ordinance

Under the current regime of community-oriented policing and the new prostitution-free zone, women in prostitution are effectively excluded from public streets and commercial spaces. The prostitution-free-zone law has been celebrated by the citizen-state coalition as the most important tool for the police to "protect the public" and an opportunity for the community to "take back their neighborhoods and business districts plagued by drug dealing and prostitution" (local newspaper, March 27, 1997). The new ordinance, also referred to as the "Portland experiment," has been used in other cities and is considered an innovative legal strategy that brings citizens and city government together.

Supporters of the prostitution-free-zone ordinance claim that the new law focuses on citizen concerns rather than punishment. As one deputy district attorney put it,

> The ordinances do not focus on the person, but on a *geographic* area. . . . Their purpose is not retribution or deterrence, which are the typical goals of punishment. Instead, the ordinances try to fix neighborhood crime problems. (quoted in local newspaper, March 27, 1997, my emphasis added)

In the more common sentiments of a local resident, "If [people] are doing drugs or prostitution, they shouldn't be allowed there. I understand it's their constitutional right to be around, but it's making life totally unbearable for people who live there" (quoted in newspaper, April 25, 1997). Expressing concerns with "neighborhood livability" rather than moral conduct, supporters of the prostitution-free-zone ordinance assume that prostitutes do not live in the area and diffuse the potential for political charges of moral reformism—the law does not punish; it simply excludes. Framing prostitution as a problem of *geography* rather than one of *status* or even *conduct,* legal practitioners have circumvented entanglement in the thorny legal questions raised by a law that effectively amounts to a status offense.

Although the exclusion law has been in effect since 1995, it has recently come under fire from a few lawyers, judges, and community members. One defense attorney claimed that the ordinance was "the rough equivalent of banishment" (quoted in newspaper, April 1997). But the ordinance also raises constitutional questions regarding double jeopardy and freedom of travel, and it contradicts federal criminal procedure statutes, requiring criminal prosecutions to focus on a person's conduct rather than her status. The ordinance bans people from some city spaces regardless of the reason for occupying them, and it does so on arrest, that is, prior to their being convicted of a crime.

In April 1997, a circuit court judge ruled that the exclusions violated the Fifth Amendment ban on double jeopardy since the ordinance excludes a person from a part of the city and then prosecutes the person for the same crime. Since the ruling, 200 to 300 cases have been dismissed, but as of 1998 the constitutionality of the ordinance had yet to be challenged in the State Supreme Court. However, the city council, the prosecutors office, and the Police Bureau have devised patchwork remedies in response to recent criticisms. As a temporary measure, the assistant police chief ordered officers to stop issuing exclusions and arrests simultaneously, and those who live or work in the spaces from which they were excluded can now obtain passes allowing them access to those locations by a specific route (local newspaper, August 1997). As a long-term solution to the double-jeopardy problem, the district attorney has drafted an amendment to the prostitution-free-zone ordinance that requires conviction before exclusion. Offenders can still be excluded from the zone after conviction and are subject to trespass charges if they are found in the area within a year of their conviction, whether or not they are engaged in prostitution or prostitution procurement when they are questioned.

Ultimately, the legal questions raised by the prostitution-free-zone ordinance will have to be resolved by the State Supreme Court. In the meantime, police officers continue to enforce the law, and prosecutors are busy directing law enforcement to "get the numbers needed to justify the law" (deputy district attorney, quoted at city council meeting, August 1997). In 1997, the city council voted to establish a new prostitution-free zone on West Burside Boulevard after local residents and business owners complained that the Hollywood Street prostitution-free zone had diverted prostitution activities westward into their neighborhood. At the meeting, which I attended, city council members, prosecutors, and police officers discussed how to shield the ordinance from attack. A deputy district attorney, strategizing the best location for conducting prostitution missions, which supply the so-called magic numbers needed to justify the law, stated,

> There is no magic number. . . . We need to make our ordinance more defensible relative to attack. We need to focus on prostitute numbers not John numbers. Johns are not an accurate predictor of the amount of prostitution occurring in an area. Johns will go wherever the prostitutes go. (quoted at city council meeting, August 1997)

To this, a city council member added, "We can't attack adult businesses because we'll be challenged" (city council meeting, August 1997).

The emotionally charged meeting, heavily publicized by the local television stations and newspapers, featured impassioned testimonials by community members concerned about the effects of prostitution on property values, routine business dealings, and criminal activities. Revealing the implicitly gendered and class-stratified logic of this public discourse, the citizen-state coalition has targeted the body of the prostitute for enforcement. By displacing disempowered individuals from the public spaces that they have claimed as their own, the citizen-state coalition sends a symbolic message: They are working with *the* community to "clean-up *their* neighborhoods" and "keep criminals out."

Portland police officers take pride in their role in the Portland experiment. The fervor with which many officers enforce the exclusion law was perhaps best expressed by one detail officer who referred to the law as "a great tool" and to himself as "the big hammer":

> I'm the big hammer; I get them off the street. They feel it's *their* street so they can do what they want. I'm not hands on—I don't talk to them. Even if they didn't do anything, I just get them off *my* street. (field interview, August 1997)

While the Freudian connotations of this particular officer's statements are obvious, his language also illustrates how the territorial logic of community is inscribed in the discourse of community policing. Representing himself as a "tool" of the state, the officer's claim to ownership of public city streets constructs the geographic battle lines of this conflict as a struggle over real and imagined entitlements to community property and land use decisions. Mirroring the strategies used to enclose land for private use in seventeenth- and eighteenth-century Western capitalism and the urban planning strategies of the new enclosures, the Portland citizen-state coalition seeks to privatize public space for the use and comfort of propertied, privileged residents.

The body of the prostitute is a discursive object around which the community constructs itself and colonizes city space. The threat to the community is perceived as coming from outside, and the subject who represents a threat to the community is thought to be deserving of its violence. The designation of women in prostitution as dangerous women who threaten the health, well-being, and quality of life of the general population positions them outside the normative structures of legitimate community. The exclusion law expels the visibly sexualized bodies of these women both literally and symbolically, enabling the community to constitute itself as the collective victim of these outlaws. Hence, what the citizen-state coalition imagines as proactive, grassroots community activism has a dark underside: The symbolically sacrificed outlaw, embodied in the prostitute, is a "victim of [the] desire for community" (Young 1996, 9).

The Phenomenology of Exclusion

> Perhaps the most disturbing aspect of the power of governmentality is that it takes the "freedom . . . and the soul of the citizen, [reorganizing] the life and the life-conduct of the ethically free subject." (Gordon 1991, 5)

While the prostitute's marked body is central to the discourse of community, her voice is significantly absent. Thus, we may inquire about how the prostitution-free-zone ordinance has impacted the lives of these women. According to some police officers with whom I spoke, the exclusion law is an effective method of addressing citizen concerns with minimal cost to those who are subjected to the law. Although the law creates additional legal penalties for trespass and exclusion, officers claimed that the law is not punitive. After all, I was told, these are just misdemeanor charges. Failing to draw a distinction between public space and private property, one officer claimed that the ordinance was "no different than getting excluded from [Wal-Mart] after being caught shoplifting" (police interview, August 1997). However, the consequences of dealing with frivolous arrests on a repetitive basis are both restrictive and punitive.

I was able to observe the consequences of the prostitution-free-zone ordinance during a ride-along with a detail officer. At a bus stop on Southeast Eighty-second Street, the officer spotted "Kelly," a woman he recognized from previous prostitution arrests. Kelly appeared to be waiting for the bus rather than soliciting for prostitution. Kelly had been excluded from the Eighty-second Street zone less than a year before and was technically "trespassing" in the public space of Southeast Eighty-second Street. During the arrest, Kelly became distressed, claiming that she was waiting for the bus to pick up her five-year-old daughter at the babysitter's house. Kelly worried that she would compromise the relationship she had recently reestablished with her mother. She would have to tell her mother that she had been arrested so her mother could pick up her daughter from the babysitter's house. Kelly also worried that she would miss her appointment at the methadone clinic, potentially causing her to become "drug sick"[12] and to get expelled from her methadone program, risking a relapse into heroin use.

When I saw Kelly in the parking lot of a grocery store on Southeast Eighty-second Street two weeks later, I asked her about this experience.

> I was really upset. It was like your whole day flashed in front of your face and that feeling knowing you're going to jail makes me wanna run. But I know I can't do that. . . .

> I begged and pleaded with the cop because I had my daughter at a friend's house and I was really upset because my mom has a hard time trusting me, partly because of all this drug thing and jail. . . . Also I'm on methadone and if I go to jail for a certain amount of time, I am kicked off the program and then that would mean that the criminal stuff starts all over again because you can't stay sick. Anybody that is sick will tell you that they would do anything that it takes to get well. (interview, August 1997)

About a month after her arrest, the same detail officer spotted Kelly in a parking lot located within the boundaries of the prostitution-free zone and issued her a ticket for trespassing. Although Kelly admitted that she still solicited "dates"[13] on Southeast Eighty-second Street, on this particular occasion she was on her way to go shopping. According to Kelly, the officer knew that she had only nine days left to complete her prior trespass conviction, but he still issued her a trespass ticket. Although Kelly was not arrested that day, she had to go to court and pay an additional fine for trespassing.

Having had numerous conversations with Kelly, the ongoing micromanagement of her life seemed unreasonable. Kelly's prior prostitution record and her sporadic involvement in prostitution have led to repetitive arrests, requiring her presence in court and the payment of numerous fines. In addition to the financial constraints and the logistical problems of court dates, probation, drug rehabilitation, and restitution, Kelly has four children to support. The state placed Kelly's children under her mother's custody, but Kelly lives with her mother and cares for her children on a regular basis. Kelly also is monitored by child social services. Although Kelly understood that she was excluded from the area of Southeast Eighty-second Street, she has always "lived" at the boundaries of the prostitution-free zone. Routine activities such as grocery shopping, waiting for the bus, socializing, and meeting with friends all take place at those boundaries. Although Kelly could obtain passes to gain access to the zone, the task of obtaining a pass to authorize each activity that takes place in the zone would be daunting under any circumstances.

Conclusion

> When policing moves from surveillance to monitoring, a move is made from the correction of individuals to the control of populations. Rights become anachronistic. (Dumm 1993, 188)

Governmental regimes have increased the efficiency with which the specific identities and spaces of our twentieth-century populations can be monitored and managed. Strategies of control, developed at the level of social policy, extend and reinforce the boundaries between "legitimate citizens" and "outsiders," raising important questions about administrative justice in the governmental state.

In Portland, community policing strategies and contemporary zoning laws, like the prostitution-free-zone ordinance, allow the state to manage identities, bodies and populations by outlawing the visible presence of some bodies in some spaces and by "directing the flow of population into certain regions [and] activities" (Foucault 1991, 100). The placement and displacement of people inside or outside the normative and sociospatial boundaries of community and the organization of spaces as legitimately including some people and excluding others highlight the coercive effects of spatial governmentality on twentieth-century American lives.[14] The prostitution-free-zone ordinance excludes women in prostitution from public space and from public view. Contrary to what the name of the law suggests, the prostitution-free-zone ordinance is applied precisely when women are *not* engaged in prostitution. The law thus criminalizes one's imposed status and presumed propensity to commit crime over any actual sexual exchanges. Mirroring early statutes prohibiting vagrancy and night walking, contemporary enforcement strategies designed to regulate the activities of prostitutes and would-be prostitutes are like status offenses, making it illegal to *be identified* as a prostitute and to occupy visible public spaces. The additional trespass charges and exclusions used in Portland reify identity, constructing a legal identity that becomes the basis for long-term exclusion from the community.

Early enclosure movements integrated ownership and identity in the body of the citizen. In late capitalism, the logic of enclosure has reemerged in technologies of spatial governmentality that unite population management strategies with identitarian discourses of citizenship, community, and property. The prostitution-free zone is a unique illustration of spatial governmentality, one that can be linked to modern techniques of government and to antiquated strategies of enclosure. It replays the kinds of spatial conflicts that characterized early and industrial capitalism but extends the logic of enclosure and exclusion beyond the overt containment of early enclosure acts and beyond the creatively hostile architectural tricks of the new enclosures. Applying the logic of enclosure directly to the population rather than to land, property, or architectural structure, the exclusion law zones *people out of place,* using a rhetoric of community that appears rational and impersonal even as it is deeply exclusionary and moralistic.

The resurgence of the ideal of community comes at a critical point in our history, one foreshadowed by the remoteness of the bureaucratic state and marked by a growing sense of disillusionment with the legitimacy of administrative justice. Enforcement of the prostitution-free-zone ordinance relies, in important ways, on a legitimating discourse of community, iterated in Portland as "neighborhood livability." Although the effort to make the neighborhood safe is an admirable goal in the abstract, such efforts foreground property ownership as the primary means for confirming citizenship and the primary criteria for making rights claims.

In forging new bonds between citizens and the state, community discourses restore individual and community support for state action while simultaneously increasing the state's capacity to manage and monitor its population. In comparison, strategies of spatial governmentality operate beneath the contemporary/popular rhetoric of community and remain largely unintelligible as a form of power. Such strategies involve the populace in the systematic governance of self and other and in the policing of boundaries between the inside and outside of community. Both "totalizing" and "individualizing" (Foucault 1991; Gordon 1991), the logic of spatial governmentality gives "legitimate" citizens a stake in managing their own affairs and monitoring their communities. Interpreted through the proprietary lens of a privatized, consumer-oriented society, such practices are generally understood as legitimate claims to social and economic rights and privileges.

Recent efforts to involve the Portland community of property owners and residents in local problems extend authority to a privileged group and broaden the scope of the state's surveillance powers. These strategies, in turn, reinscribe the discursive and spatial boundaries that constitute the community and insulate it against invasion by those imagined as suspects, criminals, and strangers. *If the police are the public and the public is the police,* then which members of the community are the *police* and which are the *policed*? Enforcing the prostitution-free-zone ordinance against those who are most marginalized is the height of governmentality. The citizen-state coalition has developed the necessary apparatus to privatize a public life space that privileged, propertied residents claim as their own. Fine-tuning the science of identity and spatiality to include new techniques of enclosure and exclusion, the privileged community maintains their own comfortable existence by managing the visibility of those identified as prostitutes.

In the Portland experiment, policing has moved from surveillance to monitoring to geographic intelligence—in the language of one district attorney, the ordinance does not "focus on the person but on a geographic area." Under this logic of spatial governmentality, individuals, even populations, melt into air, and space takes on a life of its own. In comparison to seventeenth-century enclosure movements, which merely enclose private property, contemporary strategies of spatial governmentality enclose both public and private space. Less tangible than the gated communities and fortified enclaves of yesterday's urban ethnography, the Portland enclosure is an enclosure without walls.

The inscription of the prostitute identity is an act of violence in which citizen, state, and community collude. This violence is reflected in the community's intolerance of women in prostitution and embodied in a new regulatory technique that has as its life force the power of exclusion and as its cloak the luster of the aesthetically pleasing community. For the women who are subjected to the law, the minute details of everyday life become stringently monitored as the interior and exterior spaces of their lived existence become increasingly micromanaged. As Portland's sacrificial outlaws, they are subjected to the literal and symbolic violence of the normalized community. That violence kills the time and keeps the place of these socially excluded women.

Notes

This chapter is part of a six-year ethnographic study involving sex trade participants and their affiliates, police officers, and community groups. The data are drawn from recorded and unrecorded conversations in the work environments and social settings of the participants. In addition, data were drawn from city council meetings, neighborhood association meetings, media reports, and the official documents and statistics of the Portland Police Bureau and the Office of Neighborhood Associations.

1. In previous articles on commercial sex in Portland, I used "Evergreen" as a pseudonym for the city where I conducted this research. The names of all participants and specific adult businesses have been altered to protect the identities of those who participated in the study.
2. This is particularly true of southeast Portland, which is the only area of the city that was excluded from the federally funded Model Cities Program, the results of which much of the recent hype over the city's success in planning and development is based (report of the ONA, November 1975).
3. Reasoning that full nudity was allowed in other public places, such as in art classes and at some river beaches, the presiding judge ruled that the prohibition against full nudity in bars and clubs discriminated against business establishments selling alcohol (Portland newspaper, May 1990).

4. The 1913 passage of the "Tin Plate Ordinance," which attempted to intimidate landlords from renting rooms to those involved in prostitution by requiring them to post their name on a tin plate in front of the house, illustrates that house prostitution was common enough to evoke regulatory efforts.

5. See the discussion in Yuval-Davis (1997) regarding the historically and culturally varied criteria for defining citizenship. Yuval-Davis defines citizenship broadly, as full membership in a community, focusing on the rights and exclusions of specific citizens and noncitizens rather than on the legal definition of inclusion or exclusion from membership in the nation.

6. Following Foucault, other scholars have focused on the management and manipulation of populations and the statistical representation of risk (see, e.g., Reichman 1986; Simon 1987, 1988, 1993; O'Malley 1992; Deflem 1997; Sanchez 1997, 1998; Ewick 1998; Merry 1998; Perry and Sanchez 1998; Valverde 1998). As Jonathan Simon aptly puts it, the statistical representation of risk has shifted the primary concerns of government from the threat of the dangerous classes to the aggregate pathologies of industrial and postindustrial society (Simon 1988, 1993).

7. See Sanchez (1997, 1998). The notion of spatial governmentality that I am invoking in this chapter has developed in dialogue with scholars in a collective research project undertaken at the University of California, Irvine, under a research initiative titled "Law as Regimes of Culture" organized by Richard Perry.

8. Coverture was the common-law doctrine in which a married woman's legal identity was subsumed within that of her husband. See, for example, the discussion in Hartog (1993).

9. The first professional police force in Britain was established in 1829 under the passage of the Metropolitan Police Act (Silver 1967).

10. On average, the groups range in size from approximately ten to thirty members, although some districts have as many as fifty members, and a "hot issue" can bring a larger crowd to any association meeting (ONA report, August 1997).

11. While a few male prostitutes are arrested annually in Portland, I am focusing on women who solicit for prostitution because the majority of solicitation charges are brought against women.

12. Participants in this study use the term "drug sick" to describe withdrawal from heroine, methadone, or other drugs.

13. The women I interviewed commonly refer to an act of prostitution as a "date" and to their customers as "dates."

14. See, for example, Rubin (1984), Musheno (1995), and Thomas (1995) discussing methods of displacing and excluding sexual outlaws. See also Goldberg (1993) and Calavita (1998) for similar discussions regarding displacements and exclusions based on race and immigration status.

References

Anderson, Benedict. 1991. *Imagined Communities: Reflections on the Origin and Spread of Nationalism.* New York: Verso.

Bayley, David H., and Clifford D. Shearing. 1996. "The Future of Policing." *Law and Society Review* 30: 585–606.

Boal, Iain A. 1997. "The Long Theft: Enclosures and Planetary Capitalism in Historical Perspective." Paper presented at the Conference on Globalization and Governmentality, University of California, Irvine, April.

Braithwaite, John. 1989. *Crime, Shame, and Reintegration.* New York: Cambridge University Press.

Burt, Richard, and John Michael Archer, eds. 1994. *Enclosure Acts: Sexuality, Property, and Culture in Early Modern England.* London: Cornell University Press.

Calavita, Kitty. 1998. "Immigration, Law and Marginalization in a Global Economy: Notes from Spain." *Law and Society Review* 32, no. 3: 529–66.

Caldeira, Teresa P. R. 1996. "Fortified Enclaves: The New Urban Segregation." *Public Culture* 8: 303–28.

Chambliss, William. 1975. "The Law of Vagrancy." In William Chambliss, ed., *The Criminal Law in Action,* 33–41. New York: John Wiley & Sons.

Collier, Jane F., Bill Maurer, and Liliana Suárez-Navaz. 1995. "Sanctioned Identities: Legal Constructions of Modern Personhood." *Identities* 2, nos. 1–2: 1–27.

Davis, Mike. 1992. *City of Quartz: Excavating the Future of Los Angeles.* New York: Vintage Books.

Deflem, Mathieu. 1997. "Surveillance and Criminal Statistics: Historical Foundations of Governmentality." *Studies in Law, Politics and Society* 17: 149–84.

Dumm, Thomas L. 1993. "The New Enclosures: Racism in the Normalized Community." In Robert Gooding-Williams, ed., *Reading Rodney King/Reading Urban Uprising.* New York: Routledge.

Ewick, Patricia. 1998. "Punishment, Power and Justice." In Bryant Garth and Austin Sarat, eds., *Justice and Power in Sociolegal Studies.* Evanston, Ill.: Northwestern University Press.

Foucault, Michel. 1980. "The Eye of Power." In Colin Gordon, ed., *Power/Knowledge: Selected Interviews and Other Writings, 1972–1977,* 146–65. New York: Pantheon Books.

———. 1991. "Governmentality." In Graham Burchell, Colin Gordon, and Peter Miller, eds., *The Foucault Effect,* 87–104. Chicago: University of Chicago Press.

Goldberg, David Theo. 1993. *Racist Culture: Philosophy and the Politics of Meaning.* Oxford: Blackwell Publishers.

Gordon, Colin. 1991. "Governmental Rationality: An Introduction." In Graham Burchell, Colin Gordon, and Peter Miller, eds., *The Foucault Effect: Studies in Governmentality,* 1–51. Chicago: University of Chicago Press.

Hartog, Hendrik. 1993. "Abigail Bailey's Coverture: Law in a Married Woman's Consciousness." In Austin Sarat and Thomas Kearns, eds., *Law in Everyday Life.* Ann Arbor: University of Michigan Press.

Herbert, Steve. 1996. *Policing Space: Territoriality and the Los Angeles Police Department.* Minneapolis: University of Minnesota Press.

Hobson, Barbara Meil. 1987. *Uneasy Virtue: The Politics of Prostitution and the American Reform Tradition.* New York: Basic Books.

Kelling, George L., and Catherine M. Coles. 1996. *Fixing Broken Windows: Restoring Order and Reducing Crime in Our Communities.* New York: The Free Press.

Kunstler, James. 1993. *The Geography of Nowhere: The Rise and Decline of the American Manmade Landscape.* New York: Simon and Schuster.

Merry, Sally Engel. 1998. "The Kapu on Women Going Out to Ships: Spatial Governmentality on the Fringes of Empire." Paper presented at the annual meeting of the Law and Society Association, Aspen, Colorado, July.

Musheno, Michael. 1995. "Legal Consciousness on the Margins of Society: Struggles against Stigmatization in the AIDS Crisis." *Identities* 2, nos. 1–2: 101–22.

O'Malley, Pat. 1992. "Risk, Power and Crime Prevention." *Economy and Society* 21: 252–75.

Pateman, Carole. 1988. *The Sexual Contract.* Stanford, Calif.: Stanford University Press.

Perry, Richard, and Lisa Sanchez. 1998. "Transactions in the Flesh: Toward an Ethnography of Embodied Sexual Reason." *Studies in Law, Politics and Society* 18: 29–76.

Reichman, Nancy. 1986. "Managing Crime Risks: Toward an Insurance Based Model of Social Control." *Research in Law, Deviance and Social Control* 8: 151–72.

Rosen, Ruth. 1982. *The Lost Sisterhood: Prostitution in America: 1900–1918.* Baltimore: The Johns Hopkins University Press.

Rubin, Gayle. 1984. "Thinking Sex: Notes for a Radical Theory of the Politics of Sexuality." In Carol Vance, ed., *Pleasure and Danger: Exploring Female Sexuality.* New York: Routledge and Kegan Paul.

Sanchez, Lisa E. 1997. "Boundaries of Legitimacy: Sex, Violence, Citizenship and Community in a Local Sexual Economy." *Law and Social Inquiry* 22, no. 3: 543–80.

———. 1998. *Sex, Violence, Citizenship and Community: An Ethnography and Legal Geography of Commercial Sex in One American City.* Ph.D. diss., University of California, Irvine.

Silver, Allan. 1967. "The Demand for Order in Civil Society: A Review of Some Themes in the History of Urban Crime, Police, and Riot." In David J. Bordua, ed., *The Police: Six Sociological Essays,* 1–24. New York: John Wiley & Sons.

Simon, Jonathan. 1987. "The Emergence of a Risk Society: Insurance, Law, and the State." *Socialist Review* 95: 61–89.

———. 1988. "The Ideological Effects of Actuarial Practices." *Law and Society Review* 22: 771–800.

———. 1993. "For the Government of Its Servants: Law and Disciplinary Power in the Work Place, 1870–1906." *Studies in Law, Politics and Society* 13: 105–36.

Soja, Edward. 1992. "Inside Exopolis: Scenes from Orange County." In M. Sorkin, ed., *Variations on a Theme Park: The New American City and the End of Public Space,* 94–122. New York: Hill and Wang.

Thomas, Kendall. 1995. "Beyond the Privacy Principle." In Dan Danielson and Karen Engle, eds., *After Identity: A Reader in Law and Culture.* New York: Routledge.

Thompson, E. P. 1976. *Whigs and Hunters: The Origin of the Black Act.* New York: Pantheon Books.

Valverde, Mariana. 1998. "Governing Out of Habit." *Studies in Law, Politics and Society* 18: 217–42.

Walljasper, Jay. 1997. "Portland's Green Peace: At Play in the Fields of Urban Planning." *The Nation,* October, 11–15.

Wilson, James Q., and George L. Kelling. 1982. "Broken Windows: Police and Neighborhood Safety." *Atlantic Monthly,* v. 249, no. 3 (March): 29–38.

Young, Alison. 1996. *Imagining Crime: Textual Outlaws and Criminal Conversations.* London: Sage Publications.

Young, Iris Marion. 1990. *Justice and the Politics of Difference.* Princeton, N.J.: Princeton University Press.

Yuval-Davis, Nira. 1997. *Gender and Nation.* London: Sage Publications.

7

Purifying the State

STATE DISCOURSES, BLOOD QUANTUM, AND THE LEGAL MIS/RECOGNITION OF HAWAIIANS

Rona Tamiko Halualani

These instructions in applying for a lease of Hawaiian Home Lands were issued by the State of Hawai'i, Department of Hawaiian Home Lands:[1]

> Eligibility Requirements
>
> To be eligible to apply for a Hawaiian Home Lands homestead lot lease, you must meet the following requirement:
>
> > A native Hawaiian, that is, a person with at least 50% Hawaiian ancestry; **Note: Native Hawaiian qualification is based on biological (natural) ancestry.
>
> Please submit the following items to the department.
>
> 1. Application for Lease of Hawaiian Home Lands
> 2. Kumu 'Ohana Worksheet (See Figure 52 on next page); **Note: Completed Kumu 'Ohana must be supported by documented evidence to prove at least 50% Hawaiian ancestry.
> 3. Necessary documents to prove 50% Hawaiian ancestry and at least 18 years old.

Sometimes an applicant may be confused by the State Department of Hawaiian Home Lands (hereafter DHHL) request for more documentation. Usually if a request is made for more documentation, it is because a question regarding a person's application or genealogy has been raised. For example, the document presented may refer to the applicant as "Part-Hawaiian," "Caucasian-Hawaiian," "Hawaiian-Chinese," or "Portuguese-Hawaiian." Often an applicant will interpret such statements to mean the individual is 50 percent Hawaiian. In fact, because the percentage of Hawaiian is not specified, additional documentation will be required to identify the full-blooded Hawaiian ancestor(s). Regarding variation in names or single names, if a document shows a variation in names, such as the difference between a name on a birth certificate and a marriage certificate, more documentation will be requested to explain the difference.

Blood Quantum

She entered the same space as her ancestors had in 1850. She approached a neutral commission officer, filled out a form, and followed the "equitable" procedures of the state administration, as required for access to a Hawaiian homestead. Her participation in these state actions remembers the historical (mis)recognition of Hawaiians by law and governance. In 1850, by way of the Kuleana Act, Hawaiians became eligible for fee simple kuleana land ownership, but only if they filed a claim with a land commission, proved their ownership of the claimed plot through land surveys, and understood the concept of Western land ownership. Only 20 percent of the Hawaiian population at the time received lands. Today, Hawaiians continue to file claims for Hawaiian homesteads to the DHHL. They must prove their blood heritage to be "no less than one-half part of the blood of the races inhabiting the Hawaiian Islands previous to 1778" (Hawaiian Homes Commission Act 1921, Title 2, Section 201, Line 7). Such a process has failed Hawaiians. Many claims are delayed or denied because of insufficient proof of "Hawaiianness" (MacKenzie 1991; Yamamoto, Haia, and Kalama 1994). Two acts instituted by Western colonial administrations (first British and then U.S. authority in the 1800s) and now carried out by a localized state power (the State of Hawaii) link Hawaiians together in a legacy of proving who they are according to Western terms (i.e., a homogeneous, consistent, and pure identity).

Blood quantum policies and the formal recognition of Hawaiians being "no less than one-half part of the blood of the races inhabiting the Hawaiian Islands previous to 1778" (Hawaiian Homes Commission Act 1921, Title 2, Section 201, Line 7) have dominated the sociolegal sphere of Hawai'i (see MacKenzie 1991; Trask 1993a; Hasager and Friedman 1994).[2] This has led to many debates over whether current blood quantum mandates accurately represent the mixed and interracial makeup of Hawaiians and Hawaiians who have been trapped in the administrative mess of lost or inaccurate birth certificates, census records, and unrecognized hānai (adopted) family relations. As Hawaiians—both in Hawai'i and those who migrated to the mainland—struggle to locate formal proof certifying their blood heritage so as to gain access to homestead lands and social services, the construction of blood as a racializing device has slipped by unnoticed. We take for granted the predetermined-in-the-blood identity, always assuming its natural origins and rarely uncovering how blood and "Hawaiianness" have been sutured together.

In this chapter, I analyze how a discursive and performative mechanism of blood ushers in a revisioned identity economy of "Hawaiianness." I argue that the spheres of federal and state governance and law (mis)recognize Hawaiian identity through a racializing blood discourse, intertwined with historically contingent material and economic demands. These forces write over and (mis)recognize indigenous forms of subjectivity, wholly misreading an indigenous blood metaphor. Consequently, a hierarchy of subject positions for Hawaiians and haole (foreigner) sovereign residents is continually reproduced. Guided by the theoretical concept of articulation from cultural studies, my project in this chapter is to trace this governmental/legal production of "Hawaiianness" politically—through its historically situated inscription, logics, rhetorical claims, and communicative expressions found within the 1921 congressional hearings before the Committee on Territories, U.S. Senate, when the Hawaiian Homes Commission Act (and the 50 percent blood rule) was formalized as policy.

Drawing on Goldberg's (1993) field of racialized discourse and Hall's (1979) theory of articulation in critical terms of racial structures and economic relations, I unveil the embedded framework through which race via blood economizes identity for Hawaiians. This task requires a process of remembering and walking through the archives, a site where "blood" can be traced from indigenous reality to colonialist weapon. Informed by several excellent sources, namely, Parker (1989), MacKenzie (1991), and Kame'eleihiwa (1992), I briefly trace how "blood" shifted from an indigenous Hawaiian self-definition to a colonialist technology legislated as policy by the Hawaiian Homes Commission Act. This act marks the origin of legislated Hawaiian blood quantum (or 50 percent blood requirements). Thus, I critically analyze transcripts from the 1921 congressional hearings before the Committee on Territories, U.S. Senate. It is here that we find the historical locus in which the Hawaiian Homes Commission Act was debated and finally approved. In this arena, Hawaiian identity is historically excised, scientifically and legally blooded, and stripped of legal voice and self-representation.

Within the realm of cultural studies, the concept of articulation reveals how identity is constructed and operates in relation to history, context, and power. Informed by Laclau (1977) and Hall (1980) in response to a trend of economically reductive analyses of power, articulation is defined as a practice in which noncorresponding meanings are linked in terms of a variety of relationships: through difference, similarity, contradiction, juxtaposition, and essence. These constructed yet naturalized linkages are attached to particular historical conditions, social structures, and social groups. Meanings therefore do not naturally and necessarily correspond to one another; rather, they are conjoined into complex structures of unity (Hall 1980). These structures of meaning inform larger structures of power. By invoking the concept of articulation, I uncover the operations of hegemony and examine how meanings, identities, and subject positions are configured for social members.

History, context, and power shed light on how some structures of meaning, in fact, may become normatively established as necessarily corresponding. For example, since the passage of the 1920 Hawaiian Homes Commission Act, "Hawaiian" identity and factual parentage of 50 percent blood quantum are continually signified as necessarily equivalent. Thus, it is this articulation of a necessarily corresponding structure between meanings—tying together "blood relations" and "Hawaiianness"—that needs to be analyzed in the context of Hawaiians. I present this analysis, then, as a critical-historical genealogy with the following questions in mind: How did the contemporary legal identification of "Hawaiianness" as "blood quantum" historically come into being? What were/are its operations of identification in the everyday life and legal encounters of Hawaiians?

In analyzing the structural formations shaping formal-legal identity for and in the name of Hawaiians, I refer to the "nation-state" or "colonial administration" as the larger national bodies (e.g., British, U.S.) that historically colonized and imposed their sovereignty over Hawai'i and its people in the mid-1700s. The designation—the "state"—refers to the power of the State of Hawaii, a consolidated localized force exerting control over Hawai'i and Hawaiians, as enabled by U.S. federal power. The state, through administrative bodies, localized state-issued policy mandates, and normative rules, undoubtedly has inherited the authority of the colonial administration established through historical conditions, thus exacting a tight hold over Hawaiians.

Law and governance, therefore, name the historically specific moments and practices—from the late 1700s to the early 1900s—through which British and then U.S. policy confronts and disintegrates an indigenous Hawaiian system and subjectivity. This becomes a pressured confrontation that writes out the Kanaka (Hawaiian) through the structural exclusion of "prehumanity." Hawaiians are constructed as a soon-to-be-blooded group existing outside Western moral/political jurisdiction through several discursive tools of excision: the doctrine of discovery, the sovereign resident position, the legal principles of ultimate land use and alienation, and the incorporation of land commissions. Tools such as these structurally (unspokenly) normalize "rightful" haole (foreigner) citizenry and install a legacy of (mis)recognized identity for Hawaiians. (Mis)recognition again specifies how particular practices and identities are politically appropriated and distorted from and toward a position of dominance. Thus, while surely there is more than one way to recognize "Hawaiianness" within and outside Hawaiian community, there are identity forms that more closely resonate with and serve a lived Hawaiian collective memory and its political interests. To be (mis)recognized is to externally mimic and speak for and in the name of one's subjectivity, inscribing it as "native" and "natural." Understanding the historicization of the legal (mis)recognition of Hawaiians—the shift from an indigenous Hawaiian metaphor of blood to a contrasting Western technology of blood and from a particular Hawaiian social structure grounded in land use (ʻāina) to Western formal policy and governance based on land ownership/citizenship—reveals the complicated nature of the legal (mis)-recognition of Hawaiians and the encoded stakes in current political struggles. Our analytical movements should be to note the dominant framings of Hawaiian identity and uncover the cultural material useful for identity remakings.

A Critical Genealogy of Hawaiian Identity and Land

Raced identities, specific to time and space, are created through articulated structures, namely, the "fits between different instances, different periods and epochs, indeed different periodicities, e.g., times, histories" as well as different moments within/out a structure" (Hall 1979, 326). By analyzing the variant combination of elements within a historically specific structure, we play with the possibility of temporarily witnessing the processes of power and identity construction, in all their moving forms. Lisa Lowe (1996) opens up the past in this way. She exposes the invisible race-ing of Asian American "immigrants" and links it to present strategies of Asian Pacific American movements and actors. In the same spirit, the race-ing of Hawaiians—as an inferior race "in the blood" and in contradistinction from sovereign residents of Hawaiʻi (as national subjects of somewhere else), American citizens, "Oriental" labor, and Indian "aliens"—can be seen, though just for a moment, through several historical/political collisions and cataclysmic formation shifts. These include a uniquely noncapitalist Hawaiian social formation unified and stratified through religious ideology; the formal Western structures of governance, law, and commerce directed by Great Britain, France, and the United States; and, specifically, unrelenting American moral, political, and economic aggression.

The Western representation of land as a natural right and capitalist duty for all "humanity" has conveniently written out Kānaka (Hawaiians) as pureblooded "abject aborigines," or a near-extinct population proven to be "unenterprising, apathetic, thriftless" and "indigent."[3] They, the Hawaiians, would historically be located "outside of," "before," and "incompatible" with humanity. The moral vision of Western imperialism thus could be magically reconciled with driving economic incentive, piercing contradictions concealed. Dominant societies would push Christ, progress, and justice to the (selectively) natural few. The late 1800s would be the dawning of formal policy and law, its installed authority swift and merciless for Hawaiians.

Hawaiian subjectivity begins well before Captain Cook's arrival and the written word. It is captured in Hawaiian oral memory and genealogy (Malo 1951; ʻIʻi 1959; Kamakau 1962; Pukui, Haertig, and Lee 1972; Kameʻeleihiwa 1992) as a moving world centered on ʻāina (life through land). ʻĀina was not a mere physical space; it translates in Hawaiian as the act of living through land. ʻĀina was a way of life revolving around a spiritual understanding of land as the natural, deified force of Lono, God of Fertility and Love, or Kāne, God of Agricultural Growth. Land was therefore the physical manifestation of a greater nonmaterial power. You could not "own" it. You were blessed to have its sacred presence in your life (Kelly 1984; Parker 1989; MacKenzie 1991; Kameʻeleihiwa 1992). Through the land, these Akua, or Gods, among others, watched over and cared for Hawaiians, bestowing rich soil and conditions for the bountiful production of food for a thriving Kānaka (Hawaiian) population. The population, estimated by Stannard (1989) to have been at least 800,000 to one million at the time of contact, dropped to less than 40,000 by 1890.[4]

Collectively, within their own inherited social positions, Hawaiians were culturally summoned to both live through and work the land in specialized labor. Assigned different duties, the overall goal was to tend the land carefully so that it would bear enough food for all people (Malo 1951; Parker 1989; MacKenzie 1991; Kameʻeleihiwa 1992). The Gods ruled over and emanated from the land, which is why Hawaiians culturally never understood or expressed the principle of ownership. In their language, you could not commercially own or hold title to a greater religious being. You could temporarily possess land but never truly materialize a larger structure of mana (spiritual power). The Mōʻī, a supreme chief, held the land in their honor as a God-appointed (blessed) "trustee" (Parker 1989; MacKenzie 1991; Kameʻeleihiwa 1992). "Trustees" were those deemed to be of divine blood kinship. Particular relations were honored and elevated because they were closer to the Gods in birthright and so held great mana (power, status). They were our Aliʻi Nui (Hawaiian leaders/royalty).

From an indigenous Hawaiian perspective, then, blood was understood in terms of performative kinship relations. "Blood" symbolized divine status as destined leaders of the Hawaiian Lāhui (nation) and the relative closeness to (and thus favor of) the Akua (Gods). Through the practice of blood via Niʻaupiʻo matings, or incestuous relations among the higher social classes (chiefly incest), a higher social class of Hawaiians could increase and preserve their mana (power, status). To engage in incestuous relations was also performatively to be of Hawaiian divinity, such as with half-sibling matings and "uncle-niece" and "aunt-nephew" matings, which "bridged the generation gap" (Kameʻeleihiwa 1992, 41). Traditional Hawaiian genealogies, in this context, demonstrated the "rightfulness" of certain Aliʻi Nui (Hawaiian royalty) to care for the Hawaiian people. Higher, close-to-Akua (Gods) status was established through a lived blood metaphor. Blood less signified a biological substance and percentage amount than served as a performative indicator and producer of the collective honor and mana (power, status) of a family. This would mark the difference between an indigenous practice of blood and an imposed state policy of blood.

While claims to the purity of a family line appear in traditional Hawaiian texts (e.g., Malo 1951; Kamakau 1961), genealogies serve a cultural function. They bring into being an identity of "who one is" through those before and after her/him. For example, we typically think of genealogies as family maps proving "predetermined" descendancy. Rather, Hawaiian genealogies articulate from whom someone descends (top down, in response to a question, "Where are you from?") as well as how one's line ascended relations (how certain members could rise up potentially climbable, suddenly mobile family ranks) (Kame'eleihiwa 1992). As a metaphor, blood is double sided, seemingly positioning genealogies as purely factual and indisputable tables of parentage while symbolically encoding them as to-be-performed relations via Ni'aupi'o matings (chiefly incest) and chantings. Genealogies were not givens (ends in themselves), guaranteed, or even valued for their accuracy as fixed truths. They were to be, within a certain social class, re-created and reconstituted time and time again (Kame'eleihiwa, 1992). They would move. If you were Ali'i (chiefs), you could move through them. Genealogical practices ritually served to create and preserve a variety of Hawaiian epic stories and make real certain social relations, some of which were historically privileged (Kame'eleihiwa 1992). For Hawaiians, these rich stories—their stories and crafted life tales—represent sense-making models for everyday experiences and social relations.

With a genealogically divine status, the Mō'ī was granted responsibility for a moku, a large land division equivalent to the size of an island, which typically was an independent kingdom. The Mō'ī (king) and Ali'i, or royal chiefs positioned underneath the Mō'ī, politically protected those within their designated area in times of war, while religious priests made certain that all Akua (Gods) were respected with the appropriate ceremonies and sacrifices. To do so was to demonstrate their mana and secure more of the same. A leader who provided for his people was considered a "favorite" of the Akua (Gods).

Lower in the social hierarchy were the maka'āinana (people of the land, commoners) who worked and cultivated ahupua'a, which were land units that extended from mountaintop to coast, encompassing terrains for wet- and dryland farming and inshore fishing (allowing for the gathering of taro, breadfruit, sweet potato, and fish). On these land units, the commoners were entitled to use all food and water resources of the land. Use was a privilege granted by the Akua (Gods). The konohiki, a type of land supervisor, managed the maka'āinana (commoner) labor in order to ensure organized and timely cultivation. Hawaiians religiously made sense of this status hierarchy; they believed that each Hawaiian, in different social roles, worked and lived in interdependence. Although the social hierarchy structurally formed disproportionate power relations between the chiefs and maka'āinana (commoner), there was a perpetual give-and-take. If the Mō'ī (king) and/or Ali'i (chiefs) failed to care for the maka'āinana (commoners) or abused their power, the maka'āinana could move their labor and loyalty to another chief's lands, a considerable loss to the Mō'ī. If the Hawaiians neglected their work or the konohiki (land supervisor) abused their power, the Ali'i (chiefs) could banish them from the land (Parker 1989; MacKenzie 1991; Kame'eleihiwa 1992).

In a cultural frame different from a market-driven society, 'āina (land) was not a capitalist-centered system with commercially valued land. Instead, productivity was always a spiritually infused offering by the Akua (Gods). Land productivity therefore meant the amount of food cultivated to feed a bustling population and the social and cultural use of land by the larger Hawaiian community. They would use and practice the land. Land use was ensured as long as proper respect was given to the Gods and social groups performed their designated labor. Archival sources describe the land base at this time—a time marked by the greatest amount of warfare in the islands—as richly fertile and expansive, thus affirming the deep structure and organization of Hawaiian ʻāina (land). However, Hawaiian life was not perfect. There were limits within this organized social system. Only the Mōʻī (king) and Aliʻi Nui (Hawaiian chiefs, royalty) could materially attain and control land through conquest or inheritance (especially in the case of ruling chiefs with distinguished lineage). The makaʻāinana (commoners) would be able to live on land but never materially make claim to it.

In a non-Western culture motivated by deeply held religious and cultural practices, religiosity constituted the lived relations of Hawaiian society. It stood as the primary force in reproducing a secure, fully functioning social formation. Scholars like Buck (1993, 26) highlight the difference between capitalist and noncapitalist formations; religion ideologically united an indigenous culture. Hawaiian religious practices "sanctified social relationships, maintained the hierarchical divisions between sacred rulers and the less-sacred ruled, and ideologically resolved structural contradictions." The religious ideology of Akua (Gods) and mana (power) therefore framed and motivated the social structure and the economic practices of food and resource production. Buck identifies this "naturalization" of power-vested relations in "precontact" Hawaiʻi as "hegemonic." It was a cultural hegemony that should be recognized for largely reconstituting a Hawaiian social hierarchy, even among destabilizing pressures of continual warfare among competitive Aliʻi (chiefs) and grievances by several makaʻāinana for being abused by their Aliʻi or konohiki (Malo 1951; Kameʻeleihiwa 1992). The hegemony of the early Hawaiian everyday would be politically transformed and historically subsumed under a larger struggle for existence at all, only when it is thrown "in crisis" by British contact and colonization in the 1700s (followed by residency by French, Russian, and American haole citizens) (Mercer 1994).

Structurally, the cultural economy secured through Hawaiian religious practices and strong leadership gradually dissolved sometime around 1778 at the mark of Western intrusion, from the time Western goods and its exchange value came to dominate social relations (Buck 1992; Kameʻeleihiwa 1992). Meanwhile, local government power amid the constant influx of haoles (foreigners) maintained the Hawaiian Kingdom, at least for a while (e.g., the number of haole [foreigner] residents grew from a total of five in 1790 to 200 in 1817; Vancouver 1798, 122; Kotzebue 1821, 333; Parker, 1989) .

After the Hawaiian islands were unified into one kingdom in 1810 by the great King Kamehameha, land tenure changed to ensure political stability (Malo 1951; Parker 1989; MacKenzie 1991; Kameʻeleihiwa 1992). Tactically, to retain the loyalty of those around him and establish Hawaiʻi as a Lāhui (Hawaiian nation) capable of strong foreign relations with national powers, Kamehameha granted land parcels to lower Aliʻi (chiefs) and foreigners who served as political advisers (Kameʻeleihiwa 1992). These haoles (foreigners) presumed a natural right to land—to which they were entitled—before any formal institution of Hawaiian law and through sovereign ideologies back at home—to pass land on to their heirs and families.

Immediately after his father's death, Liholiho (Kamehameha II) assumed the throne, as haole (foreign) residents and Aliʻi (chiefs) continued to push for the formalization of land inheritance within the frame of Hawaiian land tenure (Parker 1989; MacKenzie 1991; Kameʻeleihiwa 1992). Soon after it became law, in 1825, a young Liholiho and the Council of Chiefs, heavily influenced by Britain's Lord Byron, adopted a formal policy—the Law of 1825—allowing Ali'i to transfer retained lands (on the king's death) to their heirs (Parker 1989; MacKenzie 1991; Kame'eleihiwa 1992). As mentioned earlier, this right had already been assumed ideologically (and not yet formally recognized by Hawaiian leaders) ten years earlier by foreign-born residents. Haoles from Britain, France, Russia, and America believed that they "naturally" had individual rights of property and ownership to land they occupied. In fact, even in the face of expulsion from Hawaii, many haoles blatantly conducted business with one another, leasing, selling, and buying titles to land that was formally held by Ali'i (chiefs, royalty) (Kotzebue 1821, 1:333; Parker 1989). Thus, residency, for Westerners, ideologically exceeded mere use and leasing of land. It encompassed a superior right to the New World (and its perpetually producing resources) based on the assumed natural order of humanity. Through the reigning mandates of their imperial homelands, haole (foreign) residents called on intermingling natural rights and discovery discourses together with their national identities to claim privatized rights before, outside of, and thereby over indigenous structures.

Dating back to sixteenth-century Europe, natural rights and the doctrine of discovery constructed an unspoken racializing hierarchy of developed white nations and primitive peoples (Hall 1979; Goldberg 1993; Parker 1989; Kame'eleihiwa 1992; McClintock 1995). Stepping onto virgin lands in the 1700s, European Christian nations brought with them their religious virtue and "developed" forms of law and politics, aspects that "naturally" impelled these nations to name their own supremacy over "savage tribal peoples." Written over by the laws of nature, Hawaiians were located as an unchanging, inferior "prehumanity" whose heathenist ways—the puzzling oversight of God (for how could you overlook the splendor of the Christian God?) and the lack of individuated, competitive modes of land production—proved their differentiation from all human groups. Natural distinctions such as these ideologically positioned haoles as superior and worthy not only of land but also of land ownership, privileges that would not be afforded to Hawaiians.

The material inequalities between haoles (foreigners) and Hawaiians and the glaring, intrusive presence of westerners paradoxically conflicted with their proclaiming of Christian morality and its promised salvation: Christ would save, liberate, and nourish all human life. This conflict was suppressed and smoothened out, however, by differentiating between "humanity" and those who were "nonhuman" or "prehuman." The Western-exclusive membership of Christianity (and its rights) was naturally justified as being reserved solely for "humanity": for able, civilized citizens who could live and work according to the word of God. Those without rights, privileges, and the land and wealth they afforded were clearly and naturally "not human." Thus, while Hawaiians were indigenously installed into social positions because of religious ideology (Akua, mana), Western contact ushered in a much larger religiosity coarticulated with brazen world imperialism, a sweeping formation that racialized and excluded "natives" in the same moment it created and normalized white citizen-subjects.

Living without contradiction, European settlers and later (after 1820) American residents represented Hawaiians as "uncivilized" and "lazy," for they could not produce land and lacked any proper modes of governance that facilitated citizenship (individual labor). Hawaiians, it seemed, could not sustain their society (Parker 1989; MacKenzie 1991; Kame'eleihiwa 1992; Trask 1993). Hiram Bingham, an American Calvinist missionary and later instigator of the 1893 overthrow of the last Hawaiian monarch, Queen Lili'uokalani, harshly expressed the savage inferiority of Hawaiians in

> the appearance of destitution, degradation, and barbarism, among the chattering, and almost naked savages, whose heads and feet, and much of their sunburnt swarthy skins, were bare, was appalling. Some of our number, with gushing tears, turned away from the spectacle. Others with firmer nerve continued their gaze, but were ready to exclaim, "Can these be human beings! How dark and comfortless their state of mind and hearts! How imminent the danger to the immortal soul, shroud in this deep pagan gloom! Can such beings be civilized? Can they be Christianized?" (Bingham 1847, 81)

It was primarily within this locus—a combination of religious doctrine, backed by the law of nations, the justification for New World discovery and conquest, and the citizenship ideal of "capitalist virtue" (the fusion of moral living and economic production)—that the "Hawaiian" is excised out of temporal existence, residing only in the popular imagination as "before time" or "pre-European/Cook time" (Fabian 1983; Duncan 1993; Duncan and Ley 1993).

Capitalist virtue resonated throughout Christian European nations and a similarly structured early America. It captured the ideal citizen-subject, one who claimed to live according to a pure Christian faith of truth, community, chastity, and benevolence to others. The citizen would pray and work the land so that the land-as-Western capitalist machine would always produce more salable goods—agricultural products and livestock—in excess of itself. This was true, right, and good; this was the Christian life. Capitalist virtue therefore inscribes a private resident subject in Hawaii, a self-interested subject who individually worked the land through an intimate, predestined relationship between nature and God. In the contradictory form of capitalist virtue, man, a godly subject, was encouraged to exercise the interdependence of the human-land connection and actively draw out the innermost naturalness of the land. Virtue in this sense required work and ability, for land was a limited, often unmanageable, and thus unguaranteed resource. With the onus to proving their Christian goodness, subjects set out to exert the highest form of control and dominance (termed "ultimate use") over nature. Parker (1989) traces the concept of ultimate use to European philosophical discourse. Thus, Sir Thomas More (*Utopia,* 1516) argues in the natural law tradition,

> When people holdeth a piece of ground void and vacant to no good or profitable use: Keeping others from the use and possession of it, which notwithstanding, by the law of nature, ought thereof to be nourished and relieved. (*quoted* in Parker 1989, 3)

In the 1830s, haole (foreign) residents pressed Ali'i (chiefs) to incorporate a land law embodying this principle of ultimate use.[5] Hawaiians accordingly would receive land five times as much as they cultivated. As a result, any undeveloped land would be placed on the market (Parker 1989; *Polynesian,* July 8, 1848). This furnished a means for privatizing a major proportion of Hawaiian land while also setting into place a commercial economy based on the practice of private ownership and market competition among individual farmers. A formal discourse of law therefore installed a white citizen position as normative while differentially marking Hawaiians as outside the scope of Christian principles and the societal good. Their tribalistic rituals and lack of land production and economic sustenance placed them outside legal citizenry, their identities and practices (mis)recognized through Western colonialism.

Land and its Christianized encoding reproduced a different structural formation and promised what would become a consumer message: The Western system of land would save and cure the inferior Hawaiians. Through capitalist virtue, Kānaka (Hawaiians) could be remade through the promotion of Christian behavior. Land reform would create a class of independent Hawaiian farmers who could support larger families and thus reverse their massive depopulation. They were told that land would save them.

A New World order and its accompanying natural rights discourse therefore collapse into, collide with, and racially restructure a Hawaiian social formation. After 1820, residents clamored for the necessary transition from usufruct (the granted use of land held in title by the Ali'i, who could revoke land tenure at any time) to the Western ideal of fee simple ownership (the absolute, unrestricted ownership of land). Haoles (foreigners) engaged in practices that partly dissolved the local native structure, such as intermarriage between haole (foreign) men and Hawaiian women combined with the invocation of the doctrine of discovery (see Hall 1979).

As new marriage and love moved throughout Hawaii, haole (foreign) residency refashioned itself. Private residents (British, French, and American) amplified their identity rights and privileges by invoking the doctrine of discovery and the authority of their national governments (their homelands). These dominant discourses constructed a special form of residency, one in which haole (foreign) residents could call on the law of nations (which ideologically authorized a nation's exclusive jurisdiction over new territories discovered by its representatives). Here they would claim privileged status in Hawai'i (with complete rights, uses, and authority) and compel their home governments to overrule local affairs of Hawaiian land tenure (Parker 1989). Thus, a new identity position was created, that of the sovereign resident who had absolute power over indigenous tenets.

Writing Over 'Āina as an Individual Private Right: A Legal-Economic Alliance

Ali'i submission to colonial power, however, would be coerced through the rapid disintegration of Hawaiian land tenure from the inside. By the late 1800s, several haoles (foreigners) occupied influential positions within the Hawaiian government. Others established commercial outfits like plantation farms for agriculture and sugar. These occupations would center a new cultural world for Hawaii. In the 1900s, with the acquisition of millions of acres of Hawaiian land, these plantations prospered into commercial industries that required enormous amounts of labor (e.g., the legally disenfranchised and excluded "alien" Chinese, Portuguese, Japanese, and Pilipino immigrant labor that settled in Hawaii), even more land, and a political structure that enabled its continued success. Rapidly and deeply, Hawai'i (and Hawaiian society) became a forum for foreign interests, at the expense of indigenous Hawaiians.

Bettleheim (1972) and Hall (1979) suggest that a noncapitalist formation, such as the traditional Hawaiian social order, changes through a dissolution-conservation dynamic, the partial dissolving and restructuring of an indigenous structure, which eventually holds and activates, in just the right moment, conserved capitalist structural material. Indeed, pressures inside Hawaiian governance—the growing economic dependence on trade, the tight-knit relation between land property and financial profit, and the increasingly invoked sovereign resident identity position—chipped away at the once secure local native structure during Kamehameha I's rule. I stress that an indigenous and sovereign Hawaiian identity is gradually extracted by a sovereign resident position that seems more "native" in its widening access to Hawaiian land entitlements and protection from national governments. Western law, the final thread, draws together the brewing-beneath-the-surface predominant forms: an aggressive colonialist political order, capitalist relations, and racially bound citizenship. Through the codification of equalized rights to land and the formal recognition of a private resident, the law unifies the economic and political aspects of an emerging nation-state.

The coarticulated forces of formal law, policy, and commerce overwhelmed Hawaiian society. In 1845, pressured by influential foreigners and interested in empowering Hawaiians, Kamehameha III agreed to establish a land commission to approve privatized land claims by Hawaiians and residents. He strongly reminded all vested interests that Hawaiian land tenure would still formally guide this commission. In 1848, the Ka Māhele (division) mandated the equal division of the Hawaiian kingdom lands among the king, chiefs, government, and Hawaiian people. The king claimed and divided approximately 2.5 million acres of all Hawaiian lands, 1.5 million of which were designated as "Government Lands" of the kingdom of Hawai'i (Revised Laws 1925, supra note 29, 2152–76; also in MacKenzie 1989, 7; Parker 1989). The leftover 984,000 acres of the king's allotments were set aside as the lands of the institution of the monarchy; these were the "King's Lands" (or "Crown lands") (Parker 1989; MacKenzie 1991; Kame'eleihiwa 1992). After the king's share, the Ali'i (chiefs) were assigned the remaining 1.6 million acres of the kingdom, which were privatized and awarded to 245 chiefs. Only portions of these lands could be claimed by chiefs and native tenants, and money payment made for titles would revert back to the government. Hawaiians were framed here as private tenants who, when occupying any of the lands allotted to the chiefs (1.6 million acres), possessed ownership rights and thus were formally obligated individually to cultivate these lands. Such a concept was strange to Hawaiians. This new structure conflicted with their Akua-centered communal land structure based on specialized labor and reciprocity; and, as newly native tenants, Hawaiians could assume their rights by first applying to a land commission board for a fee simple title claim through the Kuleana Act.

Finally, in July 1850 (the same month when the Kuleana Act passed), as pressure mounted, the Hawaiian government granted allodial (fee simple) ownership to foreign residents regardless of citizenship, as long as there was no political intervention on the part of their governments. As defined in the Kuleana Act of 1850, native tenants could be awarded fee simple titles to individual richly fertile plots of land (kuleanas) that were to be taken out of the chiefs' lands. Formally designed to provide for maka'āinana (commoners), the Kuleana Act minimally benefited Hawaiians, as only 26 percent (7,500 maka'āinana males) of the total native male population actually received claimed lands and less than 1 percent of the total land was transferred in title to Hawaiian commoners (MacKenzie 1991, 8). A whopping 74 percent of native males thus remained landless.

The Kuleana Act foretold the legal future of Hawaiians: containment under the procedural hands of the law. For example, the notion of a land commission for native tenants operated under the premise that a tenant identity and land rights existed only through and after legal recognition. The act itself, while posing as an equitable procedure of law, necessitated completion in order for a Hawaiian (male) to gain the right to land. Completion seemed a difficult (almost designed to be unlikely) feat, for potential tenants first had to understand English, the often ambiguous and all-too-specific letter of the law, and the complex nature of an entirely new land system through which use was reframed as an individual entitlement, given certain conditions and duties. Most Hawaiians, however, did not know English, nor could they take hold of these massive changes. They dismissed the Kuleana grant as a form of betrayal against their Ali'i Nui chiefs, who they feared would punish them for accepting the new policy. This refusal reflected how difficult it was for Hawaiians to break from an interdependent, albeit imperfect, hegemonic order in which food and basic needs were for the most part guaranteed to one tiered by relatively autonomous yet cooperating power outlets (governance, citizenship, commerce, and religious institution). Suddenly, sustenance, a responsibility that in Kānaka (Hawaiian) eyes called for interdependent, organized labor, was based, in the Western way, on individual ability and competition. To Hawaiians, the prospects seemed dismal (Parker 1989; MacKenzie 1991).

Complicating the supposedly neutral procedural nature of law, native applicants were required to present surveys of the land plots being claimed. However, surveys were conducted mostly by haole (foreign) missionaries, for only they could read and write in English. Surveyors and census enumerators politically held the advantage of English in record keeping, which would later haunt Hawaiians in their search for seemingly accurate documents. The surveys were also expensive and, again, reflected the dominant ultimate use land law in which many surveyors reported only the amount of land cultivated and not the totality held (Parker 1989; MacKenzie 1991). Moreover, all land applications were to be filed and documented (proven) within a brief period of four years, a time substantially less than it took for Hawaiians to understand the whirlwind of legal technicalities, save enough money to pay for a survey, and find a fair surveyor for a kuleana plot. As a result, only a small number of claims were filed by maka'āinana (commoners), the entitled beneficiaries of the act (approximately 7,000 applications by 20 percent of the total Hawaiian "male" population) (Parker 1989; MacKenzie 1991). Some maka'āinana (commoners) surrendered their land plots to chiefs, fleeing 'āina (land) for the bustling urban life. No longer able to survive in this alien land system, many Hawaiians entered the growing cities as wage laborers in a cash economy. Also, as telling indication of the power imbalance created by this act, it is through the Kuleana Act and the formalization of fee simple ownership for haoles that a whole island—Ni'ihau—was purchased by a haole. Revealingly, the indigenous inhabitants of Ni'ihau failed to file any claims for their land portions (Parker 1989).

The new law would gender landowners as well. The foreign land tenure system framed landowners as either white residents or native males, excluding Hawaiian women from applying for their land rights (especially those who held large amounts of land through inheritance). Hawaiian women who intermarried also became concerned with maintaining family plots for their mixed children, who would later have to prove (with great difficulty) their percentage of Hawaiian blood for land claims. Ironically, the haole (foreign) husbands of Hawaiian women could file for a land claim (originally the Hawaiian woman's) more easily than his native wife. Thus, the political power gained by Hawaiian women in traditional Hawaiian history, especially among ruling female Ali'i (royalty), was overturned through the incorporation of Western policy. In this context, the practice of intermarriage between haole men and Hawaiian women structurally endorsed white male authority in the islands and triggered a struggle among white and native masculine power, pushing Hawaiian women out to domestic private labor traditionally reserved for certain stratified groups of Kānaka (Hawaiian) women (for the domestication of Natives and its intensified effect for native women, see McClintock 1995).[6]

This backdrop of structured disadvantage (wherein Hawaiians are always a few steps behind haole applicants in the land tenure process) underlying the supposed blank slate of process and procedure displaces a Kanaka (Hawaiian) subject with that of a private tenant/citizen subject, a position that had historically been practiced by haoles outside and within Hawaii. Land commissions seem to ensure a systematically neutral process that equalizes all applicants (and identities). However, such neutrality appears in its true form if one looks more closely. In particular, the apparently nondiscriminating, up-for-grabs private citizen position discriminates against indigenous Hawaiians via the very neutrality of its embedded procedural mechanisms. For example, standardized language, the privileging of written records over oral genealogical memory, as well as a presupposed capital-centered land economy dislocate Hawaiians outside the legal process and the purview of formal identity and rights recognition.

If, as Maivan Clech Lam (1989) brilliantly argues, the law can be propped open through its unspecified ambiguity, then Hawaiians also experience its flip side: the ambiguously practiced specificity of the law in federal and state courts. This occurs when Hawaiians try legally to require the U.S. government to sue the State of Hawai'i for a breach of the Hawaiian Homes Commission trust. Here they face the mysterious vagueness and selective interpretation behind a legally specified obligation assigned to the State of Hawaii. The law, in different moments, can wield its specificity vaguely or tightly, depending on the legal-cultural work it takes to reproduce particular power interests. Certainly, through Lam's (1989) work, we can see how procedural truth, the selective deployment of legal interpretation, and the writ of law more obviously speak to haole (foreign) interests.

This critical genealogy reveals the intricate process by which an indigenous Hawaiian structure based on social stratification and a communal land system is disintegrated through the vehicles of law and governance as wielded by colonial power and an emerging U.S. nation-state. Haole residents presume their absolute natural right to Hawai'i by practicing their legal and citizen rights from "home." In so doing, private ("white") sovereign residency is normalized while a Hawaiian subject position is racially marked and structurally excised through its constructed difference: signs of prehuman, non-Christian ways and the absence of a capitalist system of land production. When foreign authorities promoted capitalist virtue (the fusion of capitalist incentive and Christian ideology) and codified laws of ultimate use, fee simple ownership, and equitable land commissions with open and fair application procedures, they structurally and unspokenly excluded Hawaiians from those very principles and rights. Ironically, through a formal recognition of ownership rights to all residents in the Kuleana Act, U.S. law and policy racially homogenize citizenship and legal membership to only haole (foreign) residents (the true "natives"). This historical move foreshadows the pivotal moment in 1921, when blood is signified as a state technology that renders Hawaiian identity inferior and produces an idealized (white) American citizenry.

The Hawaiian Homes Commission Act: Blooding a Race

It is said that "if you couldn't take the blood out of the Hawaiians, surely you could homestead them." Land, that pure manifestation of tradition and civilization, would morally proselytize the "wretched." It would make them over. It would build a nation. In the 1920s, as a result of the Hawaiian Homes Commission Act, government homesteading programs were created and designed to "rehabilitate a population-in-need" and place Hawaiians on land parcels. Programs such as these, however, intensely racialized the Hawaiians as "pre-dated savages," in line with the structured discourses of travel, geography, and discovery by legislatively inscribing a pre-formative Hawaiian identity of 50 percent blood quantum. For example, in the Hawaiian Homes Commission Act, "native Hawaiians" are simultaneously designated a right to land and identified:

> The Congress of the United States and the State of Hawaii declare that the policy of this Act is to enable Native Hawaiians to return to their lands in order to fully support self-sufficiency of native Hawaiians in the administration of this Act." (Hawaiian Homes Commission Act 1921, Title 1A, Section 1101)
>
> The term "native Hawaiian" means any descendant of not less than one-half part of the blood of the races inhabiting the Hawaiian Islands previous to 1778. (Hawaiian Homes Commission Act 1921, Title 2, Section 201, Line 7)

Through quantum technology, U.S. federal power determines Hawaiian agency and who is allowed to speak as a "Hawaiian," all the while reviving the Western moral project. With the church at an arm's reach, the nation-state frames itself as the preeminent legal-moral authority. Its new promise, "homesteading," would offset the natural inferiority of Kānaka (Hawaiians) and assimilate them into American citizenship and its dominant capitalist system.

Historically, only after Hawaiians had been invisibly racialized as dark and strange, living through incomprehensible rituals and ways, were they legally (mis)recognized through the discursive device of blood. Such bloody work was articulated through the Hawaiian Homes Commission Act of 1921. To quantum blood is to divide, assign, and regulate a parental and racial identity and render it "factual and known" among a social group. This quantum construction would extend the historical writing over Kānaka (Hawaiians) by formal law and policy and establish the colonial state as measuring, slicing, and controlling the (mis)identified Hawaiian body.

Blood, in this shifting historical juncture, comes to signify both an archaic, almost extinguished "prehumanity," rearticulated as a biological given and at the same time a social indication of potential citizenship in the newfound American territory. The Hawaiian Homes Commission Act is the generative site for imposing a racial identification on Hawaiians in terms of blood economy along with an economy of material resources and speaking practices (or, rather, communicative positions). As a legal-cultural production (that continues to produce a "Hawaiian" subjectivity), the congressional hearings surrounding the Hawaiian Homes Commission Act—through which the merits and injustices of a bill are debated in the presence of an appointed panel of all white senators—exemplifies a field of racialized discourse. This is a historically specific formation constitutive and reflective of racialized logics, principles, and expressions that define and justify a raced identity, thus reifying it into existence (Goldberg 1993). I critically engage these hearings, examining the discursive racialization of Hawaiians (and their speaking practices) and their contemporary political effects.

As provocatively demonstrated by Hall (1979), Gilroy (1987, 1993), Goldberg (1993), and Lowe (1996), discourse racially produces subjects through the power-vested reproduction of logics, expressions, rhetorical claims, and systematic exclusions; and, when backed by political governance, regulation, and the eyes of the law, this discourse more forcefully frames the kinds of cultural narratives, speaking practices, and performances of those who are suppressed (Yamamoto et al. 1994).

The racial discourse around the Hawaiian Homes Commission Act of 1921 speaks to the historically specific legal exclusions of Hawaiians in relation to land. I will illustrate how the act identified Hawaiians and who would be authorized to speak as a "Hawaiian." At the time, Hawai'i stood as an annexed territory with special status federal jurisdiction. The territorial government oversaw impressive modes of commerce (plantations), military arsenals, and practice sites. The distinction—resident—still reflected a majority of landowning white haoles with more rights and land than Hawaiians. "Pure" Hawaiians during this period drastically decreased in number from between 80,000 and 100,000 in the late 1700s to 23,000 in 1921 (Parker 1989; MacKenzie 1991; Kame'eleihiwa 1992). At this historical moment, it became necessary after decades of colonially dissolving and re-forming one system and conserving another now to preserve the economic/national interests consolidated during the formal writing over of Hawaiian identity since the 1800s. The Hawaiian Homes Commission Act expresses the capitalist preservation of an emerging U.S. nation-state, again rearticulating the sovereign resident position via the (white) American citizen. Citizenship and legal rights were not bestowed naturally on indigenous Hawaiians who, by degree or percentage, were either doomed to predestined extinction or cast as potential citizens.

The Hawaiian Homes Commission Act

In 1898, not long after (but deeply reminiscent of) the 1893 illegal overthrow of Queen Li'uokalani's rule, the United States held Hawai'i as a territory. (This was achieved through U.S. resolution and without the consent of Hawaiian inhabitants.) As such, the United States exercised complete authority over the island territory and on July 9, 1921, signed into law an act "designed to rehabilitate the Native Hawaiians." The bill was created by longtime Hawaiian royalist/sovereignty leader and Hawai'i congressional delegate Prince Jonah Kuhio Kalaniana'ole, who wanted to secure federal aid for his dying, landless people. Prince Kuhio strongly believed that federal support would rekindle a spirit of Hawaiian self-sufficiency and self-determination.

Before the bill's passage, the thriving sugar and ranching interests, which leased richly fertile crown lands (approximately 26,000 acres) for their plantations, faced a hard-hitting blow. Their lease contracts were to be terminated. As it turned out, the official lease expiration date came due just as the Hawaiian Homes Commission Act (HHCA) hit the congressional floor for debate (Murakami 1991). The implications were serious. All leased plantation lands could be reverted to general homesteading purposes for "native Hawaiians." The commercial interests (C & H Sugar, Dole Pineapple) panicked. They had enjoyed years of cheap rent on the best available land, and now that would all change.

Several commercially vested senators began to propose various resolutions that would allow sugar planters and ranchers to maintain their leaseholds. It was, after all, their money on the line. One was House Resolution 13500 (e.g., amendment to the Organic Act, HCR 28), which united commercial venture with "federal rehabilitation" by exempting all sugarcane lands from homesteading. Dominant sugar and rancher leases could continue, and Hawaiians could be reformed through land. The money made from the leases would be placed into a revolving fund that would subsidize the government administration of Hawaiian homesteads. It was perfect: politicians and business interests in merry union.[7]

After the revised version of HHCA was approved, it set aside 200,000 acres of land (out of the 1.5 million acres of government and crown lands) specifically for homesteading by native Hawaiians (Murakami 1991). The HHCA defined a "native Hawaiian" as a descendant "of not less than one-thirty-second part of the blood of the original races which inhabited the islands at the time of their discovery by Captain Cook" (Report of H.R. 13500, 8). A later amendment further restricted the quantum to "1/2 part of the blood."

If qualified, a native Hawaiian could obtain a 99-year lease for $1.00 a year for residential, pastoral (for ranching purposes), and agricultural lots (Murakami 1991). Ultimately, HHCA's goal was to distribute land to qualified Hawaiians and to create a formal commission—the Hawaiian Homes Commission or later the Department of Hawaiian Homelands—to administer homesteads.

Legal Morality and Blood Technology: Dying Namesakes and "Potential Citizens"

Homesteading, a government-endorsed practice, replaced Christianity as the dominant institution in legitimizing the prevailing moral project of the United States. Hawaiians would be rehabilitated through U.S. law, thus presupposing that some "normal" state (whiteness) need be restored or at the very least compensated. For "Hawaiians," homesteading counterbalanced an absence that was naturalized as biologically and scientifically true—they were naturally inferior and foreign to American life.

How does a blood technology become a part of legal-governmental discourse? It does so as unquestionable, a priori fact, for science was the new God. Blood classifications provided greater certainty and rhetorical leverage than its previous expression: the natural rights ideology. These blood identifications (e.g., purebloods, mixed bloods) negatively valorize and suppress Hawaiians but in guised fashion. Blood work affords an image of unmediated, objective science and an institutionalized claim to knowledge, without indicting national power structures and its gendered and racialized particularizing of citizens. With newly afforded power, scientific classifications and descriptions, all the while operating as social-cultural productions of difference, are legally appropriated as verifying reference sources.

Thus, in scientized fashion, blood fixed the nature of Kānaka (Hawaiians) and so accounted for their diminished landholdings as compared to haoles (foreigners). Blood could specify difference in the same moment it wiped away the structured dispossession of Hawaiians, a process of historical forgetting achieved just as a moral claim of rehabilitation emerged. By this logic, blood economizes land allotments in line with citizenship. Those of pure Hawaiian blood, undeniably the racially different, would fail to productively use (exploit) land and embody capitalist virtue. For example, on the first day of the congressional hearings, both proponents and opponents of the bill referred to pure Hawaiians as "wholly abject, thriftless, unproductive aborigines." The purebloods were referenced primarily in relation to their inability to hold land (e.g., Hawaiians would often alienate lands). The aftereffects of Western colonialism were reappropriated as raced effects of "those inferior Hawaiians." Historically and materially speaking, distinctions of blood come after the Western upheaval of Hawaiian society but discursively function as always signifying "coming before."

It was not just the work of blood that racialized Hawaiians. The myth of extinction as discursive device articulated their inferiority as a naturally patterned demise. They would die sooner rather than later. It was again the law of nature. In the hearing testimonies, a myth of extinction helps to shape and ironically to bring about the eventual demise of pure Hawaiians. As discussed in Goldberg's (1997) work on census counts and Jaimes's (1992) critique of federal identification policy and Indian blood quantum, predictions of cultural extinction and depopulation work in line with economic interests but through factual probability. In the officially approved write-up of the HHCA, it was estimated that from 1826, when 142,650 pure Hawaiians were recorded, the full-blood population count decreased to about 22,600 in 1919 (Report to Accompany H.R. 13500, 2). Undeniably, Hawaiians had been dying (via forced genocide) since the late 1700s with the arrival of Cook and his men. In terms of population counts, the demise seems strikingly consistent, gradual, and not as severe, considering the growing number of part Hawaiians.

I stress that while it is feasible to conclude that pure Hawaiians were dying out while mixed bloods slightly increased in number, the representation and deployment of these figures are infused with suspicious power interests. The early missionary censuses, the first recorded population counts, are likely to be accurate estimates of Hawaiian converts only, thus undercounting Hawaiian society. In terms of the U.S. official census, census enumerators (who in this context were those who spoke English and not necessarily fluent Hawaiian) recorded their own interpretations of race with no set criteria for determining "pure" or "part" Hawaiian. They relied on their "common sense judgments and perceptions" of indiscriminate, socially fluctuating markers of race, such as skin tone and physical appearance (e.g., body size, facial attributes) (Goldberg 1997, 38). These evaluative marks recorded in population counts blur the specific, fixed biological criteria distinction, if any, between what constitutes pure and part "Hawaiianness," at the same time concealing the sociohistorical constructedness around these classifications. The classifications themselves are fictions-in-process.

Accurately counting Hawaiians quickly shifted to charting their extinction cycle, then to yearly projections specifying when all Hawaiians would disappear: "It is estimated that by the year ——, all pure Hawaiians will vanish." An extinction discourse therefore positions Hawaiians as a dying population that only the nation-state could save. Their saving would constitute HHCA's driving moral purpose. In a so-called moral act, the congressional senators and witnesses—with charts and counts in hand—argued that it was the government's duty to breathe life back into the Kanaka (Hawaiian) "race" through homesteading. The means to do so: a federally created administrative body that would protect and serve the indigenes. This new administrative body was positioned as an official agency that efficiently and justly restored Hawaiian life on homestead lands.

However, the smooth-running administration operated through a striking irony. It structurally executed the demise of pure Hawaiians through its performative procedures. The official body (first named the Hawaiian Homes Commission and later the Department of Hawaiian Home Lands) developed a neutral and lengthy process of application, including proof of identity claim to land. Each claim required verification, evaluation, and distribution. Such a procedure took (at the very least) anywhere from five to fifteen years, thus working in conjunction with and even exceeding the time and rate of theorized extinction. The procedural nature of the homelands administration therefore made real the possibility that most pure Hawaiians would die out before actually gaining land. True to form, approximately 30,000 Hawaiians have died while waiting for a Hawaiian homestead (Parker 1989; MacKenzie 1991; Murakami 1991). The myth of extinction is less a projection of what will happen based on factual population counts and cycles than it symbolizes a discursive reality brought into being (perhaps more expeditiously) through governmental policy and administration. I emphasize that the demise of Hawaiians in this sense is planned, sealed, and delivered via a resurfacing neocolonial administration.

The opponents of HHCA or those against the "rehabilitation" of Hawaiians have practiced other discursive moves to safeguard their own dominant subject positions through racializing "Hawaiians." Their main argument: Hawaiians were not dying out. In fact, they were increasing (in terms of the part Hawaiian population). One witness, A. G. M. Robertson, a representative of the Parker Ranch on Hawai'i (a ranch that acquired a great deal of Hawaiian land through the formalization of fee simple ownership and the Kuleana Grants), differentiated between a declining sector of Hawaiians and a redeveloping one:

> aboriginal Hawaiians of the pure blood are dying out . . . according to the census . . . in 1900 the pure Hawaiian population was nearly 30,000, while in 1919 it was . . . 22,600, a decrease of over 7,000; whereas, those who were part Hawaiians in 1900 numbered only 7,835, and in 1919 had increased to 16,600, an increase of about 9,000, more than offsetting the decrease in the aboriginals of the pure blood, and the total increase is substantially just as much. . . . So that it can not be said, and it is not true to say, the Hawaiian race as defined, in this bill is a dying race, because the figures show that it is an increasing race. (testimony of A. G. M. Robertson, 14)

Robertson repeatedly argued that though the "pure bloods" were dying out, an increase in "part bloods" (specifically one thirty-second of Hawaiian blood) illustrates that a majority of the beneficiaries of the HHCA (any Hawaiian with at least one thirty-second blood) were growing and thriving. Thus, they would not need any form of rehabilitation. By selectively reading zero-sum population counts across equalized time frames (revealing how already constructed factual data are overlaid with vested evaluation and interpretation), Robertson was attempting to exclude a large segment of potential Hawaiian beneficiaries (all nonpure Hawaiians) from land claims. Consider Robertson's exchange with Senator Smoot:

> SENATOR SMOOT: I do not see that the figures show that. On page 6 of your brief it says that the Hawaiian population in 1872 was 49,044 of the pure blood, and in 1900 the Hawaiians of unmixed race had decreased to 29,834, while the part Hawaiians had increased only from 1,487 in 1878 to 7,835 in 1900. Instead of 50,000, the total in 1872, in 1900 there is only about 37,000.
> MR. ROBERTSON: Yes, Senator; I say, comparing the 1900 figures with 1919 figures, it shows an increase.
> SENATOR SMOOT: No, even that shows a decrease. In 1872 there were 50,000 Hawaiians and part Hawaiians, while in 1919 there were only 39,000.
> MR. ROBERTSON: I was talking about comparing the figures of 1900 with those of 1919, which show an increase.
> SENATOR SMOOT: Yes of a very few, but I have no doubt in my own mind . . . the Hawaiian race is dying out.
> MR. ROBERTSON: Yes; the pure bloods. . . . I do not deny that the Hawaiians of the pure blood are decreasing, but I do deny that the Hawaiians as defined in this bill are decreasing. (14–15)

In comparing "intact categories" across two frames of time, Robertson works hard to differentiate between pure Hawaiians and part Hawaiians, a differentiation serving to write out the majority of potential Hawaiian homesteaders. Eventually, the congressional representatives negotiated with Robertson and other like-minded opponents to the act to restrict further the definition of Native Hawaiian to mean "not less than 1/2 part of the blood." In itself, this unveils the blood distinction to be socially constitutive and politically motivated. For one brief memorable moment, Robertson's attempt to deny Hawaiians their own ʻāina (land) through population counts again represents a means through policy and law to ensure U.S. control over Hawaiian lands through two conjoined paths: administratively setting into place the extinction of pure bloods and dismissing the moral/cultural imperative to assist part Hawaiians.

Throughout the HHCA congressional hearings, the internal differentiating of "Hawaiianness" based on blood percentage morally situates U.S. policy and law while also redrawing the race lines around abstract citizenship. Most crucially here, Hawaiians become racialized while citizenship remains white. My historical genealogy of Hawaiian identity and land unveils how land already elevated one kind of subject (sovereign resident) over another (Kānaka). As U.S. law and policy entered the picture in the 1900s, the land that had been historically collected needed to be preserved in its name. Homesteading emerged as this act of preservation, framing the nation as the saving grace of a dying race, thus rehabilitating and reforming the Hawaiian race as its necessary moral duty.

Marking Hawaiʻi as a territory, the United States ceded to federal control Hawaiʻi's government and crown lands. These transferred lands were then held and controlled by a formal trust relationship. In a trust, Hawaiians became the trusts/wards/beneficiaries of the trustee. For Hawaii, its status as a territory and the established trust relationship guaranteed federal monies and promised citizenship via incorporation into the United States through the Hawai'i Organic Act. All residents of Hawaii, including indigenous Hawaiians, were deemed citizens of the United States with the customary rights and privileges, save voting power for the territorial presidential cabinet (a decision that remained firmly in the hands of the United States).

Citizenship, however, was assigned discursively with particularized gradation to some inhabitants over others, that is, more so to haole residents than to Hawaiians. This "degradation" (Goldberg 1993) specifies a discursive mechanism tailor-made for indigenous peoples. In the HHCA hearings, Hawaiians are not quite "abstract citizens." They are identified more or less as "potential citizens." As potential citizens, Hawaiians are marked—via factual blood percentage—as more or less assimilable to a just, democratic meritocracy. Purebloods who are inherently/biologically constructed never to be true citizens ("pure bloods are apathetic, thriftless, and unindustrious," Report to Accompany H.R. 13500, 14) instead come to symbolize namesakes or true exemplars of a nation's legal morality in assisting a dying population. The United States, no longer politically beholden to an explicit religious morality, would frame itself as the preeminent moral authority of its time through the mechanisms of policy and law. However, its morality would not be inscribed by way of the usual mythic reproduction of American opportunity and liberty. Rather, the U.S. nation recognizes in part a historical injustice done to Hawaiians—the transfer of lands from Hawaiians to foreigners—without naming its own complicity in the act. By way of the HHCA, the United States emerges instead as the bearer of justice (of righting a historical wrong it instituted). American justice therefore can be elevated only through a process of historically erasing earlier decades of colonialism and land dispossession (Lowe 1996). Seen in this way, a legal and moral image of the nation that could save the Hawaiians is achieved through forgetting its own efforts in dispossessing them (e.g., a persistent history of foreign pressure on Hawaiian leaders, economic takeovers of land, and imperialist disintegration of the indigenous social order).

For example, in the hearings, one of the congressional senators calls attention to the hugely imbalanced materialities between Hawaiians and haoles:

> SENATOR NUGENT: What I had in mind was this: It was stated here at the last hearing that there were thousands of natives there that had no roof over their heads and no way of making a living except by hiring out to other people. It would seem to be a rather serious situation of affairs if one company could acquire 500,000 acres of land under those conditions.

Senator Nugent begins to recognize the dire consequence of the resident-centered Kuleana Act and dominant colonial modes of land tenure. However, such flashes of rethinking dominant memory are minimized through the racializing of pure Hawaiians as non-citizen-like, as marked by their low survival rate, decreasing family size, and failure to retain and productively use land. The official HHCA report (Report to Accompany H.R. 13500) concludes that "all previous systems of land distribution, when judged practically by the benefits accruing to the native Hawaiians from the operation of such systems" were "ineffective" (5). Neutralizing language of procedurality and administrative technicality effaces the nation's political acts in repressing a Hawaiian identity under that of the private resident, a discursive move that would continue to serve the U.S. nation and State of

Hawai'i for years to come. As the political state is neutralized, pure Hawaiians are named and blamed in the concluding report for their material inequalities:

> Your committee thus finds that since the institution of private ownership of lands in Hawai'i the native Hawaiians, outside of the King and the chiefs, were granted have held but a very small portion of the lands of the Islands . . . but a great many of these lands have been lost through improvidence and inability to finance farming operations. . . . The Hawaiians are not business men *[sic]* and have shown themselves unable to meet competitive conditions unaided. In the end the speculators are the real beneficiaries of the homestead laws. (Report to Accompany H.R. 13500, 6)

While there is an explicit understanding that Hawaiians have not received due land (granted via the Constitution of 1840 and the Ka Māhele), the blame would be located not in haole (foreign) aggression and colonialism but in the inferior-blooded nature of Hawaiians themselves. This is established via a rigid pureblood signifier, undergirded by scientific authority, that identifies Hawaiians as primordial noncitizens. Hawaiians were thought to belong to a different time and space. They were discursively constructed as never being able to hold land or survive in a modern nation. Thus, their lack was explained as a reflection of their limited racial ability and character. Pure Hawaiians, deemed tragic in the blood, were not citizens or were less like citizens. (However, they were deemed a people that could still be saved through national legal morality.)

Part Hawaiians, however, are positioned as potential citizens (more like a citizen):

> The part Hawaiian, the part Caucasian, the part Chinese, the part Portuguese are a virile, prolific, and enterprising lot of people. They have large families and they raise them—they bring them up. These part Hawaiians have had the advantage, since annexation especially of the American viewpoint and the advantage of a pretty good public school system and they are an educated people. They are not in the same class with the pure bloods. (testimony of A. G. M. Robertson, 15)

As "virile, prolific, increasing, enterprising, intelligent people," part Hawaiians are described as not in need of rehabilitation like the "aboriginals" (Robertson, 15). The recombination of a population increase of part Hawaiians and the representation of "Hawaiian blood . . . as easily absorbed (1/8 Hawaiian looks like a white man)" unmarks Hawaiians as resembling "potential citizens." This identification contrasts with the hegemonic one-drop rule in racial classification of the 1900s (in which mixed-race progeny always took on the "nonwhite" label and the raced identity of the nonwhite parent) (Goldberg 1997). In Hawaii, where a mixed Hawaiian child is raced as either "part Hawaiian" or "Caucasian," one drop of white blood remakes "part Hawaiian blood" into revealing degrees of American assimilability and entitlement and, ultimately, degrees of national exemption from having to distribute any land entitlements to them. Witnesses and senators generally characterize part Hawaiians as "men of education, men who have been in college and have traveled; men who are wealthy" (testimony of A. G. M. Robertson, 16)—a group gendered on patriarchal grounds to have been absorbed quickly and passed the mythic tenets of American equality, freedom, and justice. Hawaiians are citizens, yes, but potentially so.

Those instances in which part Hawaiians still suffer from material inequalities (lack of land ownership, loss of land) question the ability of the individual in an equal meritocracy and not the racial hegemony of the United States. The whitening of Hawaiian blood thus furnishes living evidence of Hawaiian self-sufficiency (their inherent Americanization), thereby forgoing the moral and material imperative for federal aid to this sector of the population.

By contrast, today in state hearings, blood quantum and mixed-blood "Hawaiianness" are deployed to deny Hawaiians political voice. For example, in one case, tourism and business developers countered Hawaiian resistance to development in their traditional villages (like Miloli'i, Hawaii). They argued that Hawaiian residents had no basis for opposition because they were merely "halfbreeds" and "mixed racially" (Elkholm-Friedman and Friedman 1994). Thus, in one context, a mixed-blood construction promises rights, privileges, and opportunities in the name of the potentially assimilable Hawaiian citizen, and in another, it precludes part Hawaiians from claiming any identity right to things "Hawaiian" (land, cultural artifacts). In the latter case, the inscription of Hawaiian blood purity ("pure Hawaiianness") is delimited as the only authoritative grounds for making indigenous claims of entitlement; and, if restricted only to those proven to be of pure blood, according to the declining state/census patterns for the Native Hawaiian population (in which the 1994 count for pure Hawaiians in Hawai'i was approximately 8,244), soon no "Hawaiian" will be able legally to voice an identity claim of "Hawaiianness" (Office of Hawaiian Affairs 1996). This represents an example of how legal identities ("purebloods" and "part-bloods") construct particular identity positions and speaking authority for raced groups.

Blood quantum ultimately highlights the sheer flexibility of U.S. federal power: how the essential binaries ("black-white") of race, its gradations (pure, mixed-blood quantum), and the liberality of assigned whiteness can still bolster a racially homogeneous (white) American polity through the fixed negativity of race ("Negroes") and a loosened and diluted raced identity (quantumed Native Americans, Hawaiians). In this light, the blood-quantumed racial characterization of Hawaiians safeguards the national capital by securing its possession of Hawaiian lands and legislatively writing out purebloods through administrative extinction, excluding mixed Hawaiian progeny as potential citizenry, and outlining who has the discursive authority to claim "Hawaiianness" (which appears to be those who have already passed). All the while, the nation-state, head up high and myths in place, refashions itself as the legal-moral adjudicator of justice and rehabilitation.

The dominant expressions of "citizens" and "aliens" in the HHCA congressional hearings, however, exposes the unscientific, politically subjective, and conceptually open identifications of the government. This can be seen when the congressional participants work hard to distinguish between "Hawaiians," "Indians," and "Orientals." One witness (among many others), A. G. M. Robertson, who strongly opposed the HHCA, adamantly rejected the argument that the HHCA was constitutional in its likeness to the Indian reservation program (which had been activated at the time). He argued,

> The Hawaiians are not Indians. The status of the Hawaiians is diametrically opposed to that of the Indians on the mainland. The Indians have been regarded as aliens. They

> get their rights, such as they have, by treaties between them and the federal government. They have no right to vote, unless under subsequent circumstances they become naturalized. As I understand it, they are aliens and not citizens; and their inherent character is by no means that of the Hawaiians. The Indians were a roving, nomadic race of people. They did not take to civilization the way the Hawaiians did. (testimony of A. G. M. Robertson, 30)

Around this time, Native American Indians, whose history of land dispossession parallels that of the Hawaiians, had already received some land allotments (homesteads) through the Dawes Act while many non-Indians were granted a majority of fee simple (ownership) titles to Indian land through the General Allotment Act (Parker 1989). Thus, it is curious that two indigenous groups, who have strong ties to the land and are similarly constructed through a rhetoric of "barbaric prehumanity," are in the end identified differently from each other: Hawaiians as "citizens" and Indians as "aliens." The colonial fetish with a geographic paradise and the supposed inherent generosity of Hawaiian people ("Hawaiianness at heart," or what I term "normative benevolence") perhaps redeems (and elevates) Hawaiians over Native American Indians, who are remembered as "barbaric, unassimilable," and "forever alien" savages in frequent political confrontations.[8] Both identifications (the seemingly positive and negative), however, work in line with dominant interests. They are articulated in keeping with context-specific economic interests of the nation-state. A more assimilable Hawaiian race exempts the nation from assigning a relatively modest range of island land areas as available homesteads. A dangerous Indian race with land claims spanning much of the U.S. mainland necessitates federal governance over all regions, restricted Indian access to homesteads, and increased surveillance over Indians via the Bureau of Indian Affairs and federal control over tribal councils.

As the Hawaiians are identified as citizens (with their newly educated status and [forced] religious conversion), "Orientals" are racialized as "alien immigrants." Rhetorically justified through their foreign origins, "Orientals" and particularly the Japanese in Hawai'i are framed as serious economic threats to the U.S. nation in terms of their unassimilability or, rather, their wage accumulation and land acquisitions (as citizens, they could purchase land) as well as community growth (e.g., Japanese held a high intramarriage retention rate). The congressional senators discussed the increase in Japanese laborers and how those born in Hawai'i had claimed citizenship and thus a right to own land. At the time in California, there existed heated debate over a state ruling preventing any Japanese from holding lands (Senator Nugent's comments, 34). Indeed, Lowe's (1996) analysis of the legal signification of the "alien immigrant" as sublating the contradictions between the political state (myths of liberty, justice, and equality and the regirding of a white citizenship) and the needs of capital (the need for cheap, economic labor) can be traced throughout these HHCA hearings. Several parties attempt to define "Orientals" and the Japanese in Hawai'i legally in the same manner as mainland United States: as "aliens" located outside the purview of law and rights (as illustrated in one testimony stating, "You can legislate against aliens and discriminate against them any way you want, but not so as to citizens," 34–35). Thus, as the legal discourse goes, the more "pure" a Hawaiian is (100 percent), the less she or he is a self-determined, independent American citizen with rights and privileges; the more "mixed" a Hawaiian is (30 and 50 percent, respectively, and below); the less she or he is entitled to make a cultural claim to Hawaiian land, artifacts, and practice (for the amount of "Hawaiianness" is practically nothing); and the more she or he (as an assimilable citizen) absolves the political state from recognizing its own colonial shadow.

The Legacy of HHCA

The HHCA was approved in 1921. Afterward, a previously (mis)recognized Hawaiian identity was further restrained at the hands of the U.S. federal government and the State of Hawaii. The definition of "Native Hawaiian" was amended from one thirty-second to one-half Hawaiian blood (because of pressure from heavily vested plantation owners and ranchers). This created two distinct legal (and vernacular) identities for Hawaiians: "Native Hawaiians" (at least 50 percent Hawaiian blood) and "Hawaiians" (less than 50 percent Hawaiian blood) (Parker 1989; MacKenzie 1991; Murakami 1991; Trask 1993b). Later, after statehood in 1959, the HHCA Section 204 was amended to allow the commission to "dispose of such (homestead) lands by lease or license to the general public." Thus, non-Hawaiians could gain and lease designated Hawaiian homestead areas. Such an amendment represented a clear violation of the letter of the HHCA act (Hansen 1971).

Other violations became routine. For example, former mayor of Maui Elmer F. Cravalho, who is non-Hawaiian, "received 15,000 acres from the Commission in 1966 which he lease(d) for about $1.60 per acre" (Hansen 1971, 6). The commission has consistently misappropriated and traded homestead land legally set aside for Hawaiians to business interests (e.g., development projects like the Sea Life Park in Waikiki, shopping centers, auto dealerships, hotels, multinational corporations), state outfits (e.g., airports, the University of Hawaii, wastewater treatment centers, freeway constructions), and national needs (military bases, bombing practice sites). The commission defends its actions by claiming the need for revenue to fund its administrative operations and improvements made on the land (to pay for the construction of roads, utilities on undeveloped land parcels). The justification seems to be that the general revenue furnished by non-Hawaiian leases largely supports the administration of Hawaiian Home Lands (Hansen 1971).

The administrative corruption continued when, on statehood in 1959, the State of Hawaiʻi assigned to the State Department of Hawaiian Home Lands (DHHL) administrative control over the homesteads and yet remained within the Hawaiian Homes Commission. The commission members are not elected by Hawaiians; all are appointed by the governor. This commission, with apparently no legal accountability to Hawaiians, who lack a voting say in matters of the commission, "is the specific state entity obliged to implement the fiduciary duty under the HHCA on behalf of eligible Native Hawaiians" (as ruled *Ahuna v. Department of Hawaiian Home Lands,* 64 Haw. 237, 338).

Perhaps the most tragic consequence of the HHCA was its violent yet unseen invasion of Hawaiian consciousness. Suddenly we Hawaiians find ourselves thinking, speaking, and recognizing ourselves within the confines of blood limits. As one example, Lei illustrates the pains of blood quantum racialization administration by the state.

Two years ago, Lei peered over the overwhelming amount of instructions before her. She had agreed to help her father apply for a Hawaiian homestead lease but seemed puzzled as to where to begin.

"I remember a few names," her father kept repeating. "The stories." He gazed outward.

She remembered her father's stories about the Kalia line—especially his grandma and grand-aunts—their family parties, their graceful dancing, and the special coddling of all the grandkids. She clung to his every word, wanting to drown herself in them. The days of yesterday. To reside for a long while in his soft, sweet, pained smile, to join him in gleamful love. "Dad, who was my grandmother?"

With the flip of a page (a document, a record), the stories stopped. For both of them, two different generations, they became fleeting memories. In that moment, they did the unthinkable. They had forgotten, instead becoming consumed with percentages, names, dates, locations, and interpretations—matching, verifying, and identifying the identified.

Crackled papers, edges bent; identifying forms spread all over. "DHHL requires that we completely fill out this sheet." It was a family map worksheet. Strangely, though, it looked different from the genealogies she had heard long ago. The tales with moving actions. The passion, rage, and reunion of Akua (Gods) and Ali'i (chiefs) in love and war. These would not meet the page.

Their routine became one of locating at least 50 percent blood percentage somewhere through his mother and father's lines. They still had no concrete proof of how much "Hawaiian" they were. "Remember," her father continually warned, "all documents must be original and consistent. The rest will be thrown aside by DHHL." That would mean differences in spelling, variations in our family names, and inconsistent information throughout the birth and death certificates and census records. He repeated these words, acting and talking like someone else. They were not alone.

His jargon confused her—"originals," "proof," "documentary"—this language would dominate their frame for the next two years. His attention was straightly focused, his expression deadpanned. Her father had the clarity of sight, but with clouded vision. He rarely looked up from the stack.

Spaces away, she and her father entered its place: uniform, clean, wall to wall stripped of any life or personal touch, a slab of pale white paint enclosing four perfectly lined tables with adjoining chairs. A worker scurried over, straightening out the tabletop, discarding the pencil eraser marks and papers, and wiping the surface with a glossy polish. This office—the place of the DHHL—generically held us. No greetings or meetings. The front clerk approached them, eyes downward; he would retrieve what was needed and proceeded on to those behind them.

From the DHHL office to the State Archives, they finally located the family names linked to the Kalia line. They requested official documents for each of the names they had—especially for her great grandmother, Leialoha Kalia. She smiled, remembering the one remaining photograph of Leialoha, her great grandma. A larger woman with delicate features and gentle eyes, she wore a long mu'umu'u. Leialoha was present.

She was "NONEXISTING," though, on their request for her 1883 birth certificate. All the requested names would read the same: "NONE FOUND/NONEXISTING." How could that be? She had heard about her so many times before—a generous woman who lived next door to her father. As a child, he would run over there, melting in her spoil, tugging her mu'u-mu'u. But now he could not find her. Where was she?

Only later they discovered why she could not be found, her absence in the documents. All birth records for that island were destroyed in a fire, a tragic loss of certifying documents not recognized by the Department of Hawaiian Homelands. Past mishaps were never compensated for by this administrative body. Instead, the hands of administration would remake them. Like neutral, blank slates, records could be redrafted as real. In the 1980s, the State Department of Health issued new birth certificates for those "Hawaiians" who could not be traced, who could not be found, who were missing. The new records, though, formally re-created and changed their existence.

The new retold; the old—the census records—told too much. After additional hours in different libraries and the State Archives in Hawaii, her father brought home copies of old census records. Before 1900, there existed Hawaiian census records (instituted as a result of haole-foreign insistence), but these were recorded in the native Hawaiian language. They could not translate these. They were left with the U.S. official census records. Beginning in 1900 (after annexation), the official U.S. census was conducted every ten years, its categories finite, discernible, and bounded, bounding the names and subjectivities within its columns: the names, the relationship of each person to the head of the family, race, age, and number of children living. Glancing over them, how could they not tell them what they needed to know?

The records teased them, promising them a glance at Lei and her family. There, deep within the cursive, was the name "Kalia." Chills ran up her spine; this was it at long last. Dad blurted out, "She's not here." Her name was missing. She was not reflected in the census column "Number of Children Living" during a time when she would have been at least five years of age. Their tracking led them nowhere and everywhere.

They later discovered why Grandma Leialoha was missing. Census enumerators in Hawai'i had been those who spoke pidgin English and not Hawaiian. Usually, these were either Chinese or Portuguese male recorders. Thus, when each recorder went from home to home, from Hawaiian to Hawaiian, names were written down as he heard them and not necessarily as the family's actual spelling. Also, family relations became a matter of guesswork and perception. If a husband and wife lived with several young children, it was assumed they were directly kin related. Erased from this recorded assumption was the fact that in the Hawaiian family it was common for friends, neighbors, and distant relatives to live with one another. It was the Hawaiian way to open their homes up, especially to those who could no longer be provided for in their original homes and families. Family dispersal was a way to survive in poor economic times. These details would not come from the supposedly truth-bearing cursive. They were forever disintegrated in the translation and muddled through the precision of an administrative census instrument.

The identity possibilities, then, became endless. Either they did not find any trace of her or they found her in multiple places (as multiple names). Their days and nights were spent guessing, theorizing, and debating. Names would fill the air, names now severed from their lives. The stories and private memories had faded away as quickly as Dad's gleam. Their home was shadowed by an altogether different presence. Someone else had been there, rummaging through their Hawaiian selves and histories, someone holding hostage their Grandma Leialoha.

Proving "Hawaiianness"/Disproving the State

The process of proving one's "Hawaiianness"—painful, shamed, and still unspoken—reveals the tragic consequences of a historically extended legal (mis)recognition. This refers to a memory about how formal law and governance not only wrote over Hawaiian identities in the 1700s but also formalized into existence an identity in the (legal) making.

In the pivotal moment when the U.S. Senate Committee of Territories codified the 1920 HHCA, leasing "to native Hawaiians the right to the use and occupancy of a tract or tracts of Hawaiian homelands" while defining "native Hawaiian" as first "one 1/32 blood" to "one half part blood," it already identifies "Hawaiianness," complete in name but materially "unsubstantiated" for those named. A "Hawaiian" must tangibly produce a formalized title (a documented identity-on-paper with material effects) through a process of filing and proving an identity claim (materially proving an identity that is presumed to be nonexistent). A Kānaka is named, led through a maze of proving such a name, and all the while watched over by the U.S. administrative agency and the State of Hawaii, eyes always affixed to our document faces. Indeed, it had been the localized state that was with us all along—the State of Hawaii, protected by the armor of a purely procedural administration, intervening in and controlling a once private practice through which Kānaka (Hawaiians) reclaimed (and re-constituted) their moʻolelo (histories), through which they in earlier times re-created their mana (power).

Administratively, the notion that all names must match and culminate into a consistently uniform (regularized) identity presupposes the centrality of dominant European forms of rationality, language standards, and social relations over a specific cultural context. Also, at its core, native women are overwritten by the patriarchal inscriptions of Hawaiian identity—the male directed family relations—and the expectation of formalized marriage. (Many Hawaiian women did not marry their haole male counterparts, even in the event of a child offspring; according to some oral histories, many haole men refused to marry Hawaiian women because they were "too dark" or because sexual relations were expected in power-imbalanced situations of plantation life, in which haoles were the plantation managers and Hawaiians the workers.) The administrative requirement of procedurally proving one's identity, therefore, as its premise presumes that "Hawaiianness" does not yet exist and determines what it should look like in the end (e.g., verifiable matches across time, cultures, and socioeconomic conditions).

Yet the most tragic consequence of the DHHL process is the fragmenting of a Hawaiian consciousness into one obsessed with surface traces of identities at the expense of telling the stories of our genealogies, at the expense of historically relating to one's ancestors and their struggles beyond the documents. The state's surveilling gaze has become our own, imposing its watchful eyes, its administrative instruments, into the sacred cultural practice of genealogies and their rich narrative forms. It does so by requiring identity verification and the public display of private genealogies. Hawaiians are thus pressured to invoke the very racial categories administered for them by the state. This necessitates blood quantum identity for attaining formal recognition and land claims. On the flip side, a necessary blood identity seems culturally authentic as Hawaiians adopt the discourse of "purebloods" and "mixed bloods" and move through the proper state conditions and rules for claiming homestead land.

When a Hawaiian is required by policy and law to establish a homogeneous, coherent, and consistent identity (one demanding that relatives' names and birth/marriage dates match, that family relations are fully known, and that all family information coincides), it resembles the "tribal rolls" that have plagued Native Americans.[9] The predominant encoding of Hawaiianness all too frequently involves recovering family genealogies mainly in terms of proving blood quantum and gaining resources (predominantly thinking of what will fulfill state requirements for blood ties). This abruptly transforms a private practice of claiming Hawaiian identity for the purposes of symbolically and publicly establishing Hawaiian sovereignty—for example, as foreign pressure increased up to 1893, when Queen Lili'uokalani's monarchical rule was illegally overthrown, Hawaiian-language newspapers published genealogies so as to proclaim their title to the kingdom and seek out new leadership (Kame'eleihiwa 1992)—into a structurally appropriated means of racially containing Hawaiians.

This appropriation pressures Hawaiians into partaking in what I call "structured genealogies" or "performances of proving." In the spirit of naming these processes—a spirit inspired by such critical works as Jaimes's (1992) critique of federal identification policies of blood quantum for Native American Indians and Goldberg's (1997) tracing of a principal racializing technology, the U.S. census—I expose population counts, census records, and the politics surrounding identity certification and documentation (the performativity of it all) of 50 percent Hawaiian blood quantum as politically imposed practices. These are practices originating from federal and state authority and cloaked by "procedure" that stand as a built-in safeguard while claiming to proffer fairness and equality.

Genealogical practices and their cultural political force throughout Hawaiian history have been reduced to a unidimensional, state-surveilled requirement for the completion of an already predetermined legislative identity. Recently, this illustration of power reappeared in the Office of Hawaiian Affairs, a state agency created in 1978 to aid in the betterment of native Hawaiians. It designed a program titled "Operation Ohana Registry," or the agency's enrollment program, through which Hawaiians share their genealogical information and records. The state thus emerges yet again as the centralized unit for publicly gathering, holding, and surveilling private ohana (family) histories. This rupture of Hawaiian genealogies is, among other aspects, a devastating consequence of the state appropriation of all things Hawaiian, most especially our histories and names.

Conclusion

The encroaching and surveilling nature of the modern nation-state identifies "Hawaiianness" in terms of racializing blood constructions. These dominant structures of meaning and identification slip by "unnoticed," without drawing attention to their forceful yet somewhat guised incorporation of prevailing notions of law and governance. Law and governance are violent technologies of struggle and identification that exceed the textuality of identity representations (McClintock 1995). Legal constructions of "Hawaiianness," while impenetrable, are backed up by militarization, law courts, and state administrations. Thus, legal signifiers add an intense, violent dimension to "Hawaiian identity" positionings from the popular gallery. These signifiers demand a political determination and sense of creativity among Hawaiians whose identities, in addition to being mapped, are surveilled, blooded, and (mis)recognized. These forces—colonizing law and policy—mystified through a moral spirit, "capitalist virtue," and the ideal of (white) citizenship powerfully cover in their writing a dynamic, cultural world and an indigenously performed subjectivity.

The writing over of "Hawaiianness" through law and governance historically takes time. It takes effect through the careful disintegration and restructuring of one social formation into another (a Hawaiian society dissolved by Western imperialism) via legal principles of land tenure and property-like principles such as ultimate use and individual, private land ownership. It would take the uniting of religious ideology with economic incentive (the hailed capitalist market of freedom) to produce a new hierarchy of identities: the raced Hawaiians as "prehuman, soon-to-be extinct" aborigines who are strange to modernity; the sovereign resident (the haole) who claims supreme authority, rights, and privileges as a "native" to Hawaii, an identity position politically endorsed and recognized by national governance at home and in Hawaii; and emerging Western legal practices like the seemingly equal land-application process, due process and procedure, and individual protection by law. As Hall (1979) theorizes, in specific contexts like Hawaii, race and capitalist relations enable one another; they coalesce in articulation as a structure created in dominance via the sublating/reconciling power of the law (Lowe 1996) with foreigners normalized into a legal system and Kānaka (Hawaiians) violently excised.

Law was magical, for it could refashion itself in several guises and live in different spaces. In the 1920s, law and science conjoined into a blood technology of naming Hawaiians, an institutionalized practice of pre-forming "pureblooded" Hawaiians as excessively savage (soon-to-be-extinct) and unassimilable, and "mixed bloods" as "not Hawaiian at all" and "not yet a citizen" (but with potential). In this way, Hawaiian-ness and indigenous rights are economized, regulated, and surveilled (by establishing and delimiting quantum, it can watch over what it has framed) while citizenship remains white. Tragically, Hawaiians are forever affected. Their communicative positions and speaking authority are determined in line with blood quantum. "Mixed bloods" are not truly Hawaiian and thus have no identity right or claim to things Hawaiian (sovereignty, sacred lands and artifacts, and cultural practices like hula and chanting); and the authentic Hawaiian—the "pureblood"—is deemed, according to the population counts and certified records, as "gone"/ extinct and since-passed.

Hawaiians face the consequences of this blood work every day, enduring the performances of proving for the State Department of Hawaiian Home Lands so as to qualify for homestead access, loans and services, and scholarships. Through their performances of proving, Hawaiians draw attention to the closed doors and pre-formative assumptions of legislated, administrative identity. They stumble on obstacles and shortcomings of the state, which ironically are revealed only through these performances: lost certificates, inaccurate census bureau records with misspelled names (taken by non-Hawaiian-speaking enumerators), unrecognized family relations, and an administrative system that refuses to contextualize certification with the cultural ways of the Hawaiians (hanai relations, name changes, the politics of intermarriage between haole men and Hawaiian women). Through the rummaging of our sacred histories, we illustrate both the state gaze over our identities and a way to perform its limits. Performances such as these may constitute the critical locus for contesting the blood racialization of "Hawaiianness": a place where Hawaiians can performatively challenge both the historical memory of the "savage" and the legal (mis)recognitions of their subjectivities.

Notes

This chapter is an earlier version of material presented in an upcoming book, *In the Name of Hawaiians: Native Identities and Cultural Politics* (University of Minnesota Press, 2002).

1. I was able to retrieve the full set of administrative documents required of Hawaiians to be granted a land lease (e.g., the actual application; Loa'a Ka'Aina Ho'opulapula [Directions for Applying for Hawaiian Home Lands]). I speak to the private memory of proving "Hawaiianness" by sharing some painful remembrances from my family and many others. Several generous Hawaiians detailed their performances of proving in oral histories and private memory interviews I conducted. Out of deep respect and Aloha to my ancestors and their genealogies, I have altered the family names in this story about proving "Hawaiianness." We, Kanaka Maoli (indigenous Hawaiians), are nothing without our names and the power of naming who we are.

2. Within the last five years, the Office of Hawaiian Affairs (OHA) has debated two related legislative measures (HCR 183 HD1, HR 120 HD1) that request the State Department of Hawaiian Home Lands (the main administrative body for distributing Hawaiian homesteads) to examine the feasibility of blood quantum mandates (Office of Hawaiian Affairs 1997). More specifically, the DHHL would have to seriously consider the possibility of decreasing and/or eliminating blood quantum requirements altogether. Such an issue remains a heated one within Hawaiian communities. Decreasing blood quantum would indeed allow many Hawaiians long denied a homestead to finally attain what is rightfully theirs. However, this possibility quickly risks a set of new problems: (1) more divisiveness among Hawaiians as 50 percenters compete with lesser than 50 percenters, (2) increased access to a still-limited pool of available land, and (3) exemption of the state from facing its colonialist roots and restructuring its administrative policies.

3. I rely on several excellent archival sources to trace out this historical genealogy, namely, Malo (1951), Barrere (1969), Parker (1989), MacKenzie (1991), and Kame'eleihiwa (1992). We are indebted to these scholars for their English translations, attention to historical/cultural detail, and passion to keep working through the past.

4. David Stannard's (1989) arguments are key to demonstrating the devastating population collapse of the Lāhui (Hawaiian Nation). In other historical accounts (e.g., Kuykendall 1938; Day 1955; Kuykendall and Day 1961; Daws 1968), the politics of population counts is made known as either an extremely low 1778 population estimate and/or an inflated total for Hawaiians in the mid-1800s, thus attempting to guise the Western-influenced decimation of a native people and its extension through Western trade, religious conversion, the expropriation of 'āina, and the forced incorporation of Western formal policy and law.

5. As discussed in Parker (1989) and MacKenzie (1991), indigenous Hawaiian practices of tending the land were dramatically different from Western practices encoded in formal law. Unlike ultimate use, Hawaiians would often let land lay fallow for a long period of time, which would allow for the accumulation and storing of rich nutrients and increased arability. To haoles, such a practice was unproductive; for Kānaka, it was pono (right) for 'āina (land) to be blessed, favored, and granted. Popular rhetoric at the time represented the Hawaiian social

order as inherently immoral. Missionaries and sovereign residents argued that a new land tenure could liberate—by God and justice—the maka'āinana from cruel Ali'i (royalty) exploitation and their corruptive greed.

6. I stress that Hawaiian women have resisted this positioning; they have channeled their political power into hula, chanting, genealogies, and language reclamation projects and, most impressively, are rising as the most vehement and confrontational leaders of the Hawaiian sovereignty movement (see Kame'eleihiwa 1992; H. K. Trask 1993; M. B. Trask 1992, 1993).

7. Many speculate that HHCA was a mere ruse for the continued domination of commercial interests in the islands (Parker 1989; MacKenzie 1991). Homesteading Hawaiians onto land intensely racialized them. For example, they were channeled into certain identifiable/identifying spaces (e.g., designated, arid homestead lands—Anahola, Keaukaha, Nanakuli) and types of labor (e.g., farming, grazing). Several legal scholars, lawyers, and Hawaiian activists (Parker 1989; MacKenzie 1991) point out how most homestead lands were of poorer quality than government lands (which were ceded on statehood) and plantation lands (for Dole Pineapple, C & H Sugar). Some homesteads were purely lava rock, trapping the Kanaka who was promised an immediate homesteading survival opportunity.

8. It is interesting that the legal imagination historically remembers (and visualizes) the Hawaiian as peaceful and weak (and not as the political warriors of King Kamehameha's time) and the Indian as violent and uncontrollable.

9. I can only theoretically suggest the presence of tribal rolls for Hawaiians, meaning that I do not have concrete, written proof of these master references. Instead, I make this allegation based on the living proof of private testimonies by Hawaiians (my private memory interviews with Hawaiians in both the mainland and Hawaii). It is rumored that a master file of names and dates of Hawaiian family information exists in the State Department of Health. All Hawaiians' applications for land leases must match this reference. To fail to do so is not only to fail to gain access to land once used by all Hawaiians but also to be denied state recognition as a Hawaiian.

References

GOVERNMENT DOCUMENTS

Hearings before the Committee on Territories. United States Senate. 1921. Sixty-sixth Congress, Third Session on H.R. 13500. A Bill to Amend an "Act to provide a government for the Territory of Hawaii." Approved April 30, 1900, as Amended to Establish an Hawaiian Homes Commission, and For Other Purposes. Washington, D.C.: U.S. Government Printing Office.

Revised Laws, 1925, supra note 29. Hawaii. Sixty-sixth Congress House of Representatives, Report No. 839. (Rehabilitation of Native Hawaiians) (To Accompany H.R. 3500).

"What Inheritance for Hawaiians?" (1997, May) *Ka Wai Ola O OHA,* 14, no. 5): 5.

OTHER SOURCES

Barrere, D. B. 1969. *The Kumuhonua Legends: A Study of Late 19th Century Hawaiian Stories of Creation and Origins.* Pacific Anthropological Records No. 3. Honolulu: Bishop Museum Press.

Bettleheim, C. 1972. "Theoretical Comments." In A. Emmanuel, ed., *Unequal Exchange* (12–34). London: New Left Books.

Bingham, H. 1847. *Residence of Twenty-One Years in the Sandwich Islands; or the Civil, Religious, and Political History of Those Islands.* Hartford, Conn.: Hezekiah Huntington.

Buck, E. 1993. *Paradise Remade: The Politics of Culture and History in Hawai'i.* Philadelphia: Temple University Press.

Daws, G. 1968. *Shoal of Time: A History of the Hawaiian Islands.* Honolulu: University of Hawai'i Press.

Day, A. G. 1955. *Hawaii and Its People.* New York: Meredith Press.

Duncan, J. 1993. "Sites of Representation: Place, Time, and the Discourse of the Other." In J. Duncan and D. Ley, eds., *Place/Culture/Representation* (39–56). Routledge: London.

Duncan, J., and D. Ley. 1993. "Introduction: Representing the Place of Culture." In J. Duncan and D. Ley, eds., *Place/Culture/Representation* (1–21). London: Routledge.

Elkholm-Friedman, K., and J. Friedman. 1994. "Big Business in Small Places." In U. Hasager and J. Friedman, eds., *Hawai'i: Return to Nationhood* (222–53). IWIGIA (International Work Group for Indigenous Affairs). Document 75. Copenhagen: Nordisk Bogproduktion.

Fabian, J. 1983. *Time and the Other: How Anthropology Makes Its Object.* New York: Columbia University Press.

Gilroy, P. 1987. *There Ain't No Black in the Union Jack.* Chicago: University of Chicago Press.

———. 1993. *The Black Atlantic: Modernity and Double Consciousness.* Cambridge, Mass.: Harvard University Press.

Goldberg, D. T. 1993. *Racist Culture: Philosophy and the Politics of Meaning.* Oxford: Blackwell.

———. 1997. "Taking Stock: Counting by Race." In *Racial Subjects: Writing on Race in America* (27–58). New York: Routledge.

Hall, S. 1979. "Race, Articulation and Societies Structured in Dominance." *Sociological Theories,* 305–45.

———. 1980. "Encoding, Decoding." In S. Hall, D. Hobson, A. Lowe, and P. Willis, eds., *Culture, Media, Language* (128–39). London: Hutchinson.

———. 1996. "Introduction: Who Needs 'Identity'?" In S. Hall and P. DuGay, eds., *Questions of Cultural Identity* (1–17). London: Sage.

Hansen, D. 1971. *The Homestead Papers: A Critical Analysis of the Management of the Department of Hawaiian Home Lands.* Honolulu: State Press.

Hasager, U., and J. Friedman. 1994. *Hawai'i: Return to Nationhood.* IWIGIA (International Work Group for Indigenous Affairs). Document 75. Copenhagen: Nordisk Bogproduktion.

Hawaiian Homes Commission Act. 42 Stat. 108. Reprinted in 1 *Haw. Rev. Stat.,* 167–205 (1985, 1989 Supp.).

Hawaiian Voices on Sovereignty. 1993. *He Alo A He Alo: Face to Face.* Honolulu, Hawai'i: Hawai'i Area Office of the American Friends Service Committee.

I'i, J. P. 1959. *Fragments of Hawaiian History.* Translated by Mary Kawena Pukui. Honolulu: Bishop Museum Press.

Jaimes, M. A. 1992. "Federal Indian Identification Policy: A Usurpation of Indigenous Sovereignty in North America." In *The State of Native America: Genocide, Colonization, and Resistance* (123–38). Boston: South End Press.

Kamakau, S. M. 1961. *Ruling Chiefs of Hawai'i.* Honolulu: The Kamehameha Schools.

Kame'eleihiwa, L. 1992. *Native Land and Foreign Desires: Pehea La E Pono Ai?* Honolulu: Bishop Museum Press.

Kelly, M. 1984. "Statement." *Hearings on the Report of the Native Hawaiians Study Commission before the Senate Committee on Energy and Natural Resources,* 98th Congress, 2nd Session, 104.

Kotzebue, O. 1821. *A Voyage of Discovery into the South Sea and Bering's Straits, for the Purpose of Exploring a North-East Passage, Undertaken in the Years 1815–1818.* 3 vols. London. Reprint ed. in 2 vols. 1967. Amsterdam and New York.

Kuykendall, R. S. 1938. *The Hawaiian Kingdom, 1778–1854: Foundation and Transformation.* Honolulu: The University of Hawai'i Press.

Kuykendall, R. S., and A. G. Day. 1961. *Hawaii: A History: From Polynesian Kingdom to American State.* Englewood Cliffs, N.J.: Prentice Hall.

Laclau, E. 1977. *Politics and Ideology in Marxist Theory.* London: New Left Books.

Lam, M. C. 1989. "The Kuleana Act Revisited: The Survival of Traditional Hawaiian Commoner Rights in Land." *Washington Law Review* 64: 233–88.

Lowe, L. 1996. "Immigration, Citizenship, Racialization: Asian American Critique." In *Immigrant Acts: On Asian American Cultural Politics* (1–36). Durham, N.C.: Duke University Press.

MacKenzie, M. A. 1991. *Native Hawaiian Rights Handbook.* Honolulu: Native Hawaiian Legal Corporation and Office of Hawaiian Affairs.

Malo, D. 1951. *Hawaiian Antiquities.* Translated by Nathaniel B. Emerson. Honolulu: Bishop Museum Press.

McClintock, A. 1995. *Imperial Leather: Race, Gender, and Sexuality in the Colonial Context.* New York: Routledge.

Mercer, K. 1994. "1968: Periodizing Politics and Identity." In K. Mercer, ed., *Welcome to the Jungle: New Positions in Black Cultural Studies* (287–308). New York: Routledge.

Murakami, A. 1991. "The Hawaiian Homes Commission Act." In M. MacKenzie, ed., *Native Hawaiian Rights Handbook* (43–76). Honolulu: Native Hawaiian Legal Corporation and Office of Hawaiian Affairs.

Office of Hawaiian Affairs. 1996. *Native Hawaiian Data Book.* Honolulu: Office of Hawaiian Affairs.

———. 1997. *Legislative Action Report: 1997 Session of the Nineteenth Legislature.* Honolulu: Office of Hawaiian Affairs.

Parker, L. S. 1989. *Native American Estate: The Struggle over Indian and Hawaiian Lands.* Honolulu: University of Hawai'i Press.

Pukui, M. K., Haertig, E. W., and C. A. Lee. 1972. *Nana I Ke Kumu (Look to the Source).* Honolulu: Hui Hanai.

Stannard, D. E. 1989. *Before the Horror: The Population of Hawai'i on the Eve of Western Contact.* Honolulu: Social Science Research Institute, University of Hawaii.

Trask, H. K. 1993. "Neocolonialism and Indigenous Structures." In *From a Native Daughter: Colonialism and Sovereignty in Hawai'i* (131–43). Monroe, Me.: CommonCouragePress.

Trask, M. B. 1993a. "The Blood Quantum Issue." *Ka Lahui Hawai'i Papers.*

———. 1993b. "An Interview with Mililani Trask." In He Alo A He Alo, ed., *Hawaiian Voices on Sovereignty: Face to Face* (113–24). Honolulu: The Hawai'i Area Office of the American Friends Service Committee.

Vancouver, C. G. 1798. *A Voyage of Discovery to the North Pacific Ocean and round the World . . . in the Years 1790, 1791, 1792, 1793, 1794, and 1795.* 3 vols. London.

Yamamoto, Eric K., Moses Haia, and D. Kalama. 1994. "Courts and the Cultural Performance: Native Hawaiians' Uncertain Federal and State Law Rights to Sue." *University of Hawai'i Law Review* 16, no. 1: 1–83.

8

States of Whiteness

David Theo Goldberg

Under the shadow of [U.S.] statutes and the constitution, the legislatures and courts of the states have built up a mass of race distinctions which the federal courts and Congress, even if inclined to do so, are impotent to attack.

—STEPHENSON (1909/10, II: 37)

Some States have allowed facts other than physical characteristics to be presumptive of race. If one was a slave in 1865, it is to be presumed that he was a Negro. The fact that one usually associates with Negroes is proper evidence to go to the jury as tending to show that the person is a Negro. If a woman's first husband was a white man, that fact is admissible evidence as tending to show that she is a white woman.

—STEPHENSON (1909/10, II: 41)

The [San Francisco] Board of Education is determined in its efforts to effect the establishment of separate public schools for Chinese and Japanese pupils . . . for the higher end that our children [sic] should not be placed in any position where their youthful imprecisions may be affected by association with pupils of the Mongolian race.

—QUOTED IN STEPHENSON (1909/10, VIII: 700)

Racial distinction is adopted as a state practice very early in modern colonial regimes. More or less formalized racial differentiation and identification as well as racist subordination and subjection, however, "elevate" to the level of coherent and designed state projects only by the closing decades of the "enlightened" eighteenth century, though they are clearly in evidence centuries earlier.

Principles and practicalities of governance; racial conceptions and theories; social, political, and economic conditions; as well as legal articulations and disciplinary reflections weave together to produce specific expressions and manifestations of racial states. The late nineteenth-century complex of material conditions and racial conceptions is illustrative. The slave emancipations by the latter part of the century almost throughout the European sphere of influence sat uneasily with the discovery in various colonial sites of precious metals like gold and diamonds and the attendant push for cheap sources and control of local and migrant labor. Labor demands and the threat of job competition in the wake of abolition and industrialization, alongside fears about spatial pollution and moral (not to mention biological) degeneration, existed in tension with the civilizing missions, calling forth often uneasy alliances between church, capital, and state. As the panics over moral and physical degeneration evidence, the shifting intellectual tensions between naturalistic and historicist presumptions—between claims to inherent inferiority and cultural difference in racial othering—cut across these materialities. Segregationism is one outcome, prevalent at least formally across a wide swath of settler states at the close of the nineteenth century, of the intersection between such sociodiscursive forces.

Thus, social and political imposition as well as legal definition are in considerable part behind defining blacks or whites as "a people" (Haney-Lopez 1996; Hickman 1997), as a group with a more or less coherent identity. Blacks or whites form social collectives—for instance, in the United States, South Africa, Britain, or Australia—the *racial* underpinnings for which are very largely state mediated and managed, fabricated and fictioned, displayed and displaced. Racially conceived states are invariably molded in the image of whiteness, to reflect the interests of whites. But "*being* black" should not be thought of as simply reactive, in either a forced or resistant sense. Blacks, like Jews, are formative in creating themselves as "a people" before and through and after state imposition and resistance. Black folk fashion an identity in relation but not reducible to the identity created "for" them informally in social culture and more formally through state formation. Black identity—as social identity more or less generally—is one created and re-created for itself in negotiation with the definition and meanings of blackness extended to it by broader social forces and relations. In turn, the sense of a more or less self-fashioned social identity diffused throughout the group influences the more formal state definitions over time.

Segregating States

Segregationism manifested more or less at the same moment in the American South and in South Africa in British and French colonial cities.[1] Formalized segregation was a dominant response, in theory and policy, to the interactive conditions of labor demands and political imperatives, changing demographies and legalities, political realities and moral paranoias, shifting discursive terms, and disciplinary presumptions. It was a locally specific, if internationally sustained, reaction to the perceived threats of population proliferation, economic and sexual competition, fear of lost authority (however nebulous), and the challenges of social heterogeneity. Segregationism, then, responded to these concerns with the force of sociospatial imposition promoted, if not sometimes prompted, by legal imperative.

CARCERALITIES OF STATE FORMATION

These newly emergent forms of racial confinement that came to be identified as segregationism were social spaces, state enabled and sustained, mandated and managed, surrounded symbolically and materially by racially conceived and created sanitizing boundaries. In their interiorities, they are, as Michael Taussig has so provocatively put it in another context, magical and implosive maps of anarchy and containability, "freedom and imprisonment." We may think of them as terrains of repressive liberty, spaces in which the inhabitants are left largely to do whatever they find personally profitable or appealing as long as such acts and their material implications, if not quite so straightforwardly their symbolism, are confined within quite strict spatial constraints.

The power of race is magnified here by the fact that it is so obviously everywhere and nowhere. The boundaries of such spaces are visibly identifiable through race as seams of the social fabric. The extent and degree of their material effects are evident to all and yet causally ungraspable. That the causes seem so invisible, so ethereal, makes the racial nature of the spaces seem less real too. Responsibility for their production and reproduction evaporates with historical memory behind the veil that comes to be called color blindness. Their boundaries in any case are "a cordon that with money and influence could be broached any time despite its brutal disposition" (Taussig 1997, 56–57) and indeed from both sides of the divide.

These late modern states of confinement differ, as Taussig rightly insists, from that of the panopticon, both actually and metaphorically. *Panoptical carcerality* rests on an internalized gaze promoted by initially placing the all-seeing social eye at the institutional center. By contrast, the *carcerality of containment* encircles the source of anarchic difference and more or less abandons the spatial internalities to their self-chosen excesses. If panopticism is predicated on the presumption of the self-internalized logic of control, it necessarily fails where increasing numbers of the subjected population explicitly and self-consciously reject the presupposition. The logic of containment is a response to the rejection by the subject population to the given premises of racial rule. It seeks thus to cut off any consequent anarchic influence and implication from effecting or influencing those outside the spaces of confinement. The sought amputation nevertheless is anyway and necessarily incomplete and partial.

The state is deeply implicated in reproducing, if not always initiating, the segregating spatial presuppositions of confinability. De jure segregation enabled the containability that flows from spatial segregation, the latter at once materializing the former. The strategy of containment is implicit within and hidden behind the legal formalities of segregation, though its material possibilities were pursued self-consciously only in the wake of segregation's formal demise.

FORMALIZING SEGREGATION

There is a significant shift in the United States from the pre–Civil War to the post-Reconstruction state conceptions of race. As both Gotanda and Crenshaw indicate, where prior to the Civil War race was taken as a marker of material *status* distinctions, the post-Reconstruction segregationist interpretation marked race in terms of *formal* differentiations constructed by governmental apparatuses (Crenshaw 1995; Gotanda 1995). This change in racial signs is clearly evidenced in U.S. Supreme Court rulings. Thus, in *Dred Scott v. Sanford* (1857), Chief Justice Taney could insist that, because black people were almost universally considered by whites to be inherently inferior, "negroes" were clearly diminished in material and legal status. "Status race" mixes presupposition and perception with material conditions, the former taken to legitimate relative standing as regards the latter, the latter reinforcing the former.

By the late nineteenth century, by contrast, the state had become much more self-consciously instrumental in its creation of racial categories—as evidenced, for instance, in census counts (Goldberg 1997)—leaning increasingly on the claimed neutrality and objectivity of formal racial distinctions. These formal racial distinctions were taken as proof that the state is neutral in its formal treatment of the differentiated groups, considering the groups de jure equal even if de facto dramatically unequal.

> A statute which implies merely a legal distinction between the white and colored races—a distinction which is founded in the color of the two races, and which must always exist so long as white men are distinguished from the other race by color—has no tendency to destroy the legal equality of the two races.[2]

Not only do material elevation and devaluation in reality hide behind formal equality in the law, but the status differentiations marked by race—in particular, the presumption that whiteness is (a) property (Harris 1995)—are promoted and sustained by the claim to formal equality:

> If he be a white man, and assigned to a colored [de facto third-class] coach, he may have his action for damages against the company for being deprived of his so-called "property" [i.e., his "reputation" of belonging to the dominant race, in this case the white race," and so "belonging" in the first-class carriage]. On the other hand, if he be a colored man, and be so assigned, he has been deprived of no property, since he is not lawfully entitled to the reputation of being a white man.[3]

Nowhere in the decision does the Court resort explicitly to status differentiations to sustain racial distinction. Formal distinction is assumed the basis for racial groups identifiable from all others having access, equally, to their own racial railway carriages:

> The power to assign to a particular coach obviously implies the power to determine to which race the passenger belongs, as well as the power to determine who, under the laws of a particular state, is to be deemed a white, and who a colored, person.[4]

Formal equality of course is supposed to veil substantive inequality and thus may be said to legitimate it. The legal consciousness the Supreme Court helps to promote, sustain, and diffuse as the national common sense becomes instrumental in the reproduction of a broad though always challenged consent in the racial status quo. Thus, the judiciary is implicated in ideologically legitimating in the name of the state the differential quality of social facilities to which each group has access: first-class carriages or schools or university classes in the case of whites, third-class facilities literally in the case of blacks. Yet the judiciary serves not only an ideological function. Through its coercive instrumentality, it helps initially to make possible, to promote and extend, the racially differentiated quality of such social facilities.

This process of formalizing racially segregated space, first and foremost instrumentally and then ideologically, is born out also in colonial cities in the first decades of the twentieth century. Urban spaces like Dakar and Johannesburg, Leopoldville and Algiers, were formally divided between native and European cities. It is revealing to conceive of this conscious division of urban space, alongside the policy of indirect rule that dominated at least British colonial policy at this time, as means of institutionalizing and extending racial segregation for settler colonial societies.

Cultivating Whiteness

In the colonies, all Europeans presumptively were more or less white. This presumption is revealed by the contrast of the moralizing phrase "he's gone native." The "gone" in "gone native" is of course ambiguous. Literally, it meant that the person referenced had become native, had assumed the codes and mores, the lifestyle, of the indigenous. More extensively, though, it also indicates a moral judgment expressed about the person having "gone," having abandoned Europeanness or whiteness. This identification of Europeanness and whiteness reveals that whiteness here is considered a state of being, desirable habits and customs, projected patterns of thinking and living, governance and self-governance. Thus, in claiming the person gone in this latter sense, the judgment is expressed not only that he or she was lost but also that the person had lost his or her way (of being), indeed, had lost his or her mind, and so had become irrational.

Now if all Europeans were supposed prima facie white in colonial settings, it was not quite so "at home." Working-class English, for instance, migrated to the colonies and became white where they might not be so fully regarded in English cities like Manchester, Birmingham, or London. The transformative logic at work here mirrored that of the European immigrant experience to the United States. As Malcolm famously remarked, the first word that nonblack immigrants learned on disembarking in America was "nigger." Colonies elevated the European proletariat to the property of whiteness by making at least the semblance of privileges and power, customs, and behavior available to them not so readily agreeable in their European environments.

The urban English working class at "home" in the latter half of the nineteenth century, however, were quite explicitly identified with immigrants and degraded races. Thomas Carlyle led the way in equating the English urban working classes with degraded West Indian slaves (Goldberg 2000). By the end of the century, there was widespread equation of Britain's urban poor as much with "savage tribes" of Africa as with East European immigrants, most notably "Hottentots," "Bushmen," and "pygmies" (Bonnett 1998). In 1902, Rider Haggard captured a widespread bourgeois sentiment in bemoaning the effects of migrations from countryside to city, from the rural sites of "real" Englishness to cosmopolitan degeneracy, as leading to "nothing less than the deterioration of the race" (Haggard 1902). Built into whiteness accordingly is a set of elevated moral dispositions, social customs, and norms from which the working class, like immigrant and black "stocks," are taken to be morally degenerated (Bonnett 1998). Whiteness, then, is deemed definitive and protective of the well-bred national stock, defended against the perceived internal threat of working-class mores, tastelessness, and lack of social standing as much as from foreign invasion, whether continental[5] or colonial.

This "motility" of racial characterization and identification, as Ann Stoler (1997) puts it, reveals at once the racial mobility of the European working and immigrant classes. Racial motility makes evident accordingly not simply the clichéd constructedness of whiteness but more pressingly the relative lack of fixity in racial derogation and elevation. Working and immigrant classes might be devalued from or promoted into the relative privileges, powers, and properties associated with normative middle-class whiteness according to the political, economic, and cultural demands and interests of place and time. Built into this racial motility as an inherent presumption, then, are an implicit critique of racial naturalism and the embrace of racial historicism. In principle, anyone could assume the standards of whiteness, though in fact not quite. Whether or not would depend on one's group history, legacy, education, and capacity for self-determination. John Stuart Mill initiates the polite liberal Victorian embrace of historicism, from status to formal race and from color-bound degradation to race-neutral indifference and status as well as property maintenance in the name of formalized colorblindness (Goldberg 2000).

THE RACIAL URBAN

Embedded in these shifts—from status differentiations to formal(ized) racial divisions, from racial rule imposed from the northern metropoles to the viciousness of its local settler variety, from slave-driven to proletarianizing economies—is the relative shift in focus from race as a largely rural to race as a prevailingly urban concern. Racial concerns now lie less with agricultural labor supplies and stock theft, with skirmishes over slave rebellions and wars over broad territorial claims or control. Rather, they are directed to urban ecologies, migrant and immigrant influx into cities, town turf, manufacturing and mining labor supply, protection of skilled white workers, school access, housing stock, and a sense of social elevation. The concerns over race increasingly become those about the nature and discipline, aesthetics and morality of public space, about who can be seen where and in what capacity. Thus, the moral panic over miscegenation was driven not simply by the disturbed imaginary of mixed sex, with the feared moral degeneracy of black bodies consorting with white, though it was clearly that. Increasingly, such panic was expressed as anxiety regarding mixed offspring, and so the makeup and look, the peopling of and demographic power over public space.

These transformations in concern are reflected clearly in the dramatic emergence of intellectual and academic interests in the disciplines of urban sociology and anthropology in the first decades of the twentieth century, initially fashioned around questions of race and culture. The change in comprehending race from biology to culture is exemplified in the work of Franz Boas in the early decades of the century. Boas claimed to show a shift in shape and size of skulls in the offspring of immigrants moving from the European countryside to American cities as a function of changing environment and diet.[6] This reconceptualizing of race as culturally conceived accompanies the transition from a colonial to a metropolitan set of foci by the 1920s. The new racial urbanism, its intellectual variant reflecting significant social shifts, is exemplified most clearly in the work of Robert Park and the Chicago School. From this point on, the mainstream social science of race increasingly attends to questions of urban poverty and its effects on urban ecologies alongside the individualizing social psychology of intelligence and attitudinal testing. At the same time, racism is identified as a concern about pathological individual prejudice.[7]

No longer a product of or reducible to a social setting considered the outside of white space—colonies, plantations, or rural counties rather than cities—those deemed racially other were to be conceived and comprehended in different terms than before. Where black people in particular had been the object of scientific fascination, considered as different in their very physical constitution, as natural products of naturally different and distinguishable environments, they could—indeed should—now be observed close at hand. Blacks became viewed as products of urban arrangements the determining conditions of which were not unrelated to the very conditions producing the observers' metropolitan ecologies also. The focus thus shifted, slowly and imperceptibly at first, but by the 1930s quite evidently, from measuring bodies and heads to the racial mappings, sociologically and psychologically, of urban spaces. Not unrelatedly, the colonial condition in Africa, Asia, and the Americas came under fire more or less at the time the governance of colonial cities was called increasingly into question. Here "urbanity" assumed the general "measure" of civilization, standing for fine breeding, well-mannered gentility and cultivation, and the capacity for rational deliberation. Those not white or not capable of being considered or made white failed for the most part by default.

RESTATING WHITENESS

It is clear, then, no matter for the moment the specific differences between national experiences, that from the later nineteenth century on there is something distinctively new in the manifestation of whiteness. The decades leading up to and the decades following the close of the century mark a qualitative shift in the production and conception of whiteness. From roughly the sixteenth century to abolition in the later nineteenth century, Europeans and those of European descent were self-elevated as (relatively) privileged and powerful, (more) civilized and superior, whether as a function of blood or historical progress. Superiority and power, civilization and privilege, were taken as givens, as mostly unquestioned, a simple fact of racially predicated life. The state of course had a role, looming increasingly large across time, in enabling and establishing, maintaining and managing, the possibility of this mania. The state was instrumental in defining and refining, projecting and policing, who should count in the class of the privileged, propertied, and powerful and who could not, in defining whites and blacks (or more generally and negatingly nonwhites), their possibilities and prohibitions. But there is a sense in which the state was taking itself simply to codify the nature of things, making explicit what was in any case taken for granted, as the state of being. Thus, Justice Taney could write in 1857, well along the way of this project and with just a hint of self-doubt, that

> [Negroes] had for more than a century before been regarded as beings of an inferior order, and altogether unfit to associate with the white race, either in social or political relations; and so far inferior that they had no rights which the white man was bound to respect; and that the negro might justly and lawfully be reduced to slavery for his benefit. . . . This opinion was at that time fixed and universal in the civilized portion of the white race. It was regarded as an axiom in morals as well as in politics, which no one thought of disputing or supposed to be open to dispute; and men in every grade and position in society daily and habitually acted upon it in their private pursuits, as well as in matters of public concern, without doubting for a moment the correctness of this opinion.[8]

By the mid- to late nineteenth century, in the aftermath of slavery, whiteness had very clearly begun to be challenged—in colonial and settler societies, if not yet quite so emphatically and more slowly in the metropoles. With abolition and the changed conditions it represents, with the tearing apart of the world that slave-based colonization reflected and the increasingly assertive resistance to racial subjection and domination, confidence in the positions of whites, in their givenness, waned. In the face of these challenges, whiteness no longer could be so safely assumed, white superiority so easily taken as a given of nature. Whiteness, in short, needed to be renegotiated, reaffirmed, projected anew. To be sustained, it had to be reasserted; to survive, inevitably in altered form as the conditions for its sustainability had altered, it had to be insisted on. Its re*state*ment required commensurably altered terms. It is from this point on—from the point at which labor needs shift, racial conceptions transform, capital formation and modes of accumulability alter, moral dispositions and cultural conceptions turn—that state racial design is reconceived.

From this point on, then, whiteness explicitly and self-consciously becomes a state project. To say that it is a state project is not to say that the state had been absent from earlier racial manifestations, nor that whiteness was now a product only of state definition. Rather, it is to say that from this moment the state explicitly, deliberatively, and calculatingly takes the lead in *orchestrating* the various instrumentalities in the definition and materialization of whiteness. From the closing decades of the nineteenth century, the making of whiteness flows in and through and out of the state.

This reformation of whiteness is factored around the state(d) project to manufacture people—indeed, peoples—in the mold of whiteness. Being white was considered to carry certain properties. It was not only that one either naturalistically had them or not but also that they could be manifested—discovered or developed—in one, depending on one's breed, one's national geographic origins, one's breeding. In the long wake of slavery and the demise of slave labor, in and for the sociospatial sake of segregation, whiteness had to be made—explicitly, by design—much more self-consciously as a project of the state, and once made, it had constantly to be restated, maintained, and remade.

Slavery gave way to segregated space. Segregated space was more nebulous at its social boundaries than slave space. Thus, segregated boundaries had to be established and enforced as much through definition of identity as directly through marking space on the ground itself. Add immigrants and migrants, miscegenation and intermarriage, and the borders become even more porous. With the remaking of whiteness through segregation and segregation through the renegotiation of whiteness came the well-documented transformation of ethnic immigrants like the Irish and Jews, and the working class generally, into whites (Roediger 1991; Saxton 1992; Allen 1994; Ignatiev 1995; Sacks 1995).

Under colonialism, racial rule in the colonies was about managing heterogeneity, while in the metropoles it was about maintaining and securing homogeneity. In the closing decades of the nineteenth century, heterogeneity in the metropoles—including American towns and cities—was becoming palpable and so undeniable. Thus emerged a shift to reestablishing and reimposing the artifice of homogeneity in the name of whiteness. This growing heterogeneity—the product of migrations from south to north and east to west—alongside the increasing authority of historicism as an assumption about racial otherness undercut the easiness with which white superiority and natural homogeneity could be assumed.

Homogeneity thus was reestablished symbolically, categorically, through the cohering artifice of whiteness, the refashioning of who could belong and who does not. Whiteness became not just a racial but the national identity, and, as Balibar has made clear, race gave to nation both its specificity and its globality, both its criteria of exclusion and exclusivity and its universal connectivity (Balibar 1990). This culture of racial manufacture and remaking is revealed most clearly in the spectacle of racial contrast of Europeanness and Africanity, of civilization and presumptive primitivity recirculated between world fairs and international expositions in "European space" as the nineteenth century closed. Here Europeans, and perhaps especially those of European descent, could find themselves in the mirror of their negation, of what they took themselves not to be.

RACIAL BORDERS

More broadly, then, modern colonial and settler states were involved initially in shaping the ebb and flow of migration and its conditions from European metropoles to the colonies and in policing the counterflow in more restrictive terms, especially in the case of permanent residential settlement. As Hegel indicated in 1821, colonial migration was seen as a solution to Europe's perceived overcrowding and overproduction problems (Hegel 1821, Addition to #248: 278). By the end of the nineteenth century, metropolitan states had become concerned to restrict countermigrations identified precisely in ethnoracial terms not just from the colonies but from the southern and eastern peripheries of Europe to the opportunity filled centers of "the West" as well. The overriding concern was to preserve the artifice of homogeneity, pseudobiological as much as cultural.

This concern with polluting the body politic, as I have elsewhere called it (Goldberg 1993, chapter 8), is exemplified by the English immigration restrictions imposed the day after war was declared on Germany in 1914.[9] The Aliens Restriction Act of 1914, extended after the war by the Aliens Restriction Act (Amended) of 1919, denied entry to Britain to anyone deemed by the home secretary to be contrary to "the public good." Targeted were Germans obviously but also Austro-Hungarians, Turks, and increasingly Africans first from German colonies and then more generally, including Afro-Caribbeans. The British restrictions were modeled on the Natal Act of 1897, which devised a method "to place certain restriction on immigration" pioneered by the colonial regime of Natal, then a colony in Southern Africa, later a province in the Union of South Africa. "Racially neutral on its face," the act necessitated "knowledge of a European language which an immigration officer judged to be sufficient" (Dummett and Nicol 1990, 118 ff.). It was designed to exclude all but Englishmen, and its rationale, mimicking the formalizing logic of "separate but equal," was widely adopted throughout the colonies, as it would later be in Britain itself.

Concerns with racial hygiene, eugenic population formation, and "well-bred races" (Voegelin 1998) underpin also the terms of the increasingly restrictive immigration laws in the United States. The Immigration Restriction Act of 1924 limited European immigration to 2 percent of already present national stocks as evidenced by the 1890 census count. The act thus privileged northern and western Europeans over those from eastern and southern Europe, especially Jews, even as it studiously avoided reference to any specific European national or racial groups. It was not so careful with those of Asian heritage, however, explicitly extending the existing exclusion of Chinese, formalized in the Congressional Act of 1882 forbidding the naturalization of "Chinamen," to extend also to all Japanese immigration.

A series of U.S. naturalization cases between 1890 and 1925 bear out in fascinating if painful detail the judiciary's struggle over racial admission and belonging and thus explicitly over the scope and character of whiteness. The courts found themselves torn between preserving the conceit that in 1790 "the United States were a more or less homogenous people who . . . had come from what has been termed 'Northern Europe'"[10] and the interpretation of laws obviously at odds with rapidly expanding heterogeneity. That national admittance is filtered in the name of naturalization already predisposes the process to racially fashioned principles. The naturalization cases grapple openly and tortuously with whom are to count as white and therefore naturalizable as American citizens. The language of exclusion is explicitly and for the most part unapologetically racial, the significance heightened against the background of America's imperial expansionism at the time.

In 1790, Congress had delimited citizenship to "free white men." This was extended in the wake of the post–Civil War amendments in 1870 to "aliens of African nativity and to persons of African descent." The prevailing deliberations in the wake of this amendment and the increasing heterogeneity effected by rapidly expanding immigrant populations thus concerned whether those outside the western European frame should count as white. Court after court pained over initial congressional intent in its naturalization restrictions to free white men and did so explicitly in the context of prevailing scientific theories of race. Significantly, there is almost no troubling of who might qualify as African or of African descent. I have found but one contentious court claim to naturalization on the basis of invoking African heritage and significantly no court appeals by the immigration and naturalization apparatuses of the state that an already naturalized citizen should have their naturalization revoked because of a misrepresented claim to African descent. Africans or those of African descent apparently could be assumed self-evidently—"naturally"—classifiable as such. The District Court of Eastern New York troubled briefly in 1938 over whether to grant naturalization to a man "half African and half Indian by his mother and fully Indian by his father" on the basis of his being "of African descent." The court ruled that because the petition would be denied were the man one-quarter white and three-quarters Indian, the same logic must be applied in this case.[11] While the 1870 amendment resulted in increased Afro-Caribbean naturalization, the courts nevertheless continued to reveal and reify the degraded status of people of African descent. "To refuse naturalization to an educated Japanese Christian clergyman and accord it to a veneered savage of African descent from the banks of the Congo would appear illogical . . . yet the courts of the United States have held the former inadmissible and the statute accords admission to the latter."[12] The artifice of homogeneity was refashioned first and foremost through the reinvention of whiteness.

In an 1894 challenge to Japanese exclusion from citizenship, the Massachusetts Circuit Court ruled that the 1790 Congress intended to exclude "the Mongolian race." Later language identified "the Mongolian race" as "Asiatic" or "Oriental." By white was meant only "the Caucasian."[13] Japanese, as too Koreans and Filipinos[14] and "the race of people commonly known as Hindus,"[15] did not qualify as members of "the free white race."[16] In 1919, however, the California District Court reversed the exclusion of a Hindu man, citing similar instances in Georgia, southern New York, northern California, and the state of Washington.[17] The Supreme Court nevertheless closed this line of cases, ruling in 1923 that a Hindu, even one of "high caste [and] although of the Caucasian or Aryan race, is not a white person within the meaning of the naturalization laws."[18] That the Court resorted to the narrowed restriction of legal significance ("within the meaning of the naturalization laws") reveals neither simply the well-noted making of "whiteness by law" (Haney-Lopez 1996) nor additionally law's imperiousness (Dworkin 1988). It makes evident equally the self-conscious implication of the state in fabricating and fashioning racial homogeneity, in re-creating the artifice of a national community by whitening out[19] those deemed not to fit the presumptive national profile.

At the same time, there are court rulings that render this teleological homogeneity much more troubled and ambiguous. In an interesting example of judicial race resistance, if not quite race traitorhood, in 1910 the Massachusetts Circuit Court, acknowledging the dramatic extent of race mixture, refused to allow that there is any such thing as "a European or white race" or indeed any "Asiatic or yellow race which includes . . . all the people of Asia." To its credit, the court refused "to deny citizenship by reason of their color to aliens," though it limited the refusal to those "hitherto granted it." In the context of its decision, the court nevertheless affirmed the definition of whiteness by negation, characterizing as white any person "not otherwise classified as . . . Africans, Indians, Chinese, and Japanese." Whites were left "as a catch-all word to include everybody else." Armenians thus were to count among whites, actually on the evidentiary authority of the most prominent anthropologists of the day,[20] as were Persians, whether living in Persia or having long migrated to India.[21]

Syrians, it seems, were the courts' ultimate poltergeist. Determined both by the Massachusetts District Court in 1909 and by the Oregon District Court in 1910 to be white,[22] the South Carolina District Court objected in 1913. Explicitly denying citizenship to Syrians, the court ruled generally that "all inhabitants of Asia, Australia, the South Seas, the Malaysian Islands and territories, and of South America, who are not of European, or mixed European and African descent" would be "exclude[d] from naturalization." Whites were characterized principally on "geographic" grounds as any "fair-complexioned people of European descent." They explicitly included Celts, Scandinavians, Teutons, Iberians, Latins, Greeks, Slavs, Magyars, Lapps, Finns, Basques, and Albanians; "mixed Latin, Celtic-Iberian and Moorish inhabitants of Spain and Portugal"; as well as "Greek, Latin, Phoenician, and North African inhabitants of Sicily," "mixed Slav and Tartar inhabitants of South Russia," and "all European Jews . . . of Semitic descent." Alongside Syrians, whites excluded Chinese, Japanese, Malays, and American Indians, exclusions already noted in 1910 by the *Balsara* court.[23] The South Carolina District Court twice reaffirmed exclusion of Syrians in 1914, citing *Shahid* as precedent. The court rejected the related claims that the decision should turn on perceptual criteria of skin color or other morphological considerations and that whiteness be defined as being of *Caucasian* descent. The correct basis of determination, the court insisted, is that of "*European* descent."[24] Syrians, it concluded, because they are "certainly Asiatic," clearly are not.[25]

Syrians objected, claiming humiliation on the at-best awkward grounds that in being denied their claim to whiteness, they were relegated to the inferiority of a "colored race." The District Court reconfirmed its earlier finding that Syrians are not racially European, adding also the excludability of Parsees and Persians, Hindoo and Malay. It nevertheless encouraged the applicants to pursue that matter to the Supreme Court to "[settle] . . . this most vexed and difficult question."[26] In 1915, the U.S. Appeals Court obliged, overturning the District Court rulings. The Appeals Court pointed out that "Syrians, Armenians and Parsees," many of whom had already been naturalized, had been considered and treated self-consciously by U.S. immigration law over the previous fifty years as white.[27]

We find in the complex of these examples, then, the tensions over racial definition within and between state agencies. The Justice Department, and indeed in some cases the Congress, occasionally is at odds with the judiciary over the scope of whiteness and even at times over its fact. These cases reveal a struggle, one internalized within the courts, over the face of America, over the boundaries of belonging and the homogeneity of the national constitution, of who could claim a home and claim to be at home. They highlight the ambiguities and ambivalences over the definition of whiteness cracking at the smoothed surface of national commitment, just as racial belonging and excludability were taken as givens of national order. Thus, the renegotiation of whiteness re-creates no straightforward homogeneity but a troubled hierarchy of internally differentiated and differentially privileged "white races" (cf. Barrett and Roediger 1997; Jacobson 1998). But these cases reveal also, contrary to Anthony Marx, that even though racial boundaries in the United States were most clearly articulated in the dualism of black and white, racial rule in America from the mid-nineteenth century on was never simply binary.

AMBIGUOUS BOUNDARIES

If the redefinition of whiteness in the wake of abolition and (im)migratory movements was contested, the reconceiving of blackness was contested and complex also. The one-drop rule furnished perhaps the most extreme administrative fix for racial definition, a sort of bureaucratic plastic surgery in the face of these increasingly evident social cracks that came to mark the United States following the Civil War and the segregationist attack on Reconstruction. Neil Gotanda reveals that the principle of hypodescent consists of two related decision rules, one of "recognition" and the other of "descent." The former insists that a person will be black if his or her black or African ancestry is visible. The latter claims that a person will be black if known to have a trace of black or African ancestry (Gotanda 1995, 258). Clearly, the rule of descent is designed to plug the hole thought to be left by the rule of recognition.

Now if white supremacy could no longer safely be assumed as a given of nature, it had to be reset in place by the state, reified in the edifice of social structure, and the one-drop rule was taken as the cement. Social order was to be resettled by administrative fiat, homogeneity reestablished by state imposition, white supremacy re-created by decree. Just as the onslaught of lynching at the time might properly be read in part as "the denial of the black man's newly articulated right to citizenship and, with it, the various privileges of patriarchal power" (Wiegman 1995, 83, 90), so the one-drop rule would provide segregationism with its principle of administrative operationality. "Separate but equal" was to be reduced to rote application. At the very moment the racial state, in the United States as elsewhere, seemed in more or less unsalvageable crisis, it was able to reinvent itself through definitional (re-)assertion. The slave state is dead; long live its racial legacy.

Or so the story has gone (for a clear example of this prevailing position, see Hickman 1997). Even at its height, at its most authoritatively insistent, ambivalence marks "one-drop" statability. Ambivalence, in this scheme of things, one might say is that space between arrogance and self-doubt, between power's self-denial and its immobility, between the celebrated assertion of privilege and the sheer despair over power's conceits. If Louisiana was at the center of white assertibility, segregationism, and hypodescent, racial definition, design, and order(ing) were in question there almost as much as in sites less amenable to the extremes of the racial state. *Plessy v. Ferguson,* after all, initiated in 1892 in the Louisiana courts as a challenge to the 1890 state law restricting "colored races" to separate railway cars from "white races." Homer Plessy, a man classified in the 1890 U.S. census as "octoroon" but as "negro" in the 1900 census, was arrested for insisting on sitting in a first-class car reserved for whites. If the one-drop rule can be said to have a place of baptism, Louisiana is a pretty strong candidate for its annunciation. But this nominating site of segregation is also a state of considerable racial ambivalence, revealed not least by the ambiguities in its legal administration of racial rule.

Thus, in 1908 the State of Louisiana had enacted an edict insisting "that concubinage between a person of the Caucasian or white race and a person of the negro or black race is . . . a felony" punishable by imprisonment not less than one month and not more than a year "with or without hard labor." Curiously, while cross-racial marriage had been outlawed by the state in 1894, cohabitation between white and black, "including even the pure-blooded negro," was "not forbidden except in concubinage." "Proximity to negroes" was considered otherwise "unavoidable" in the public spaces of railway cars, whereas cross-racial cohabitation was a matter of private and so voluntary choice.

Octave Treadaway, a man characterized as "octoroon," and a white woman who revealingly remains anonymous were arrested for engaging in "concubinage." The lower courts acquitted them on grounds that the law did not apply explicitly to an octoroon person, and the district attorney's office appealed to the Louisiana Supreme Court.[28] The sole question addressed by the Supreme Court was "whether an octoroon is a person of the negro or black race within the meaning of the statute."

The court acknowledged that the "science of ethnology" at the time deemed a person "Caucasian or negro in the same proportion in which the two strains of blood are mixed in his veins." "Octoroon" accordingly would not count among "negro." The rule of hypodescent admittedly, thus, was not a scientific but a popular one, and the court revealed via a comprehensive survey of dictionary and nationwide popular and legal usage the identification of "colored," and so "octoroon," with "negro." This said, the court admitted that the concubinage act, when originally presented to the Louisiana State Legislature, had included a clause, explicitly struck by the legislature as an outcome of its deliberations, defining "a person who is as much as one thirty-second part negro shall be . . . a person of the negro race." The court concluded as a consequence that the legislature intended thus to exclude "mulattoes" and "quadroons" from the scope of the concubinage act, no doubt because it might just apply to some of its own members or their relatives. The defendants' acquittal was upheld, and, as Treadaway's name ironically suggests, he walked away free for another day at least where less lucky "transgressors" of racial morality at the time had paid with their lives.

The State of Louisiana v. Treadaway et al. reveals not simply that the principle of hypodescent was hypocritical but that at most it was unevenly assumed and applied and at least in contest with more ambivalent competing assumptions and applications concerning everyday racial interactions. This complexity in state racial conception and circulation was hardly restricted to Louisiana. Virginia, like states throughout the South, outlawed miscegenation, nevertheless legally allowing marriage "between a white man and a woman who is of less than one-fourth Negro blood though it be a drop less."

A comprehensive survey of state definitions of race throughout the United States in 1909 reveals the checkered assumption and implementation of the one-drop rule even in state regimes supposedly most driven by its logic. Thus,

> Alabama, Kentucky, Maryland, Mississippi, North Carolina, Tennessee and Texas define one as a person of color who is descended from a Negro to the third generation inclusive, though one ancestor in each generation may have been white. Florida, Georgia, Indiana, Minnesota, Missouri and South Carolina declare that one is a person of color who has as much as one-eighth Negro blood; Nebraska and Oregon say that one must have as much as one-fourth Negro blood in order to be classed with that race. Virginia and Michigan apparently draw the line similarly.[29]

Shortly after this, Alabama nevertheless ruled that a person "descended on the part of the father or mother from negro ancestors, without reference to or limit of time or generations removed" would be Negro (Wallenstein 1994, 407). "Colored" of course was often, but not exclusively, used to exclude those of mixed racial descent from claiming whiteness (for a survey of legislation nationwide to this effect, see *State v. Treadaway et al.* [1910], 15 ff.).

The application of hypodescent, as much socially as legally, however, is better understood as a pragmatic application of racial regulation than as an absolute requirement of racial rule. The supremacy of whiteness, viciously presumptive as it no doubt was for many, was not without its contradictions and contestations, its ruptures and restrictions, its self-doubts and slippages, its contrary desires and choices, responses and resistances. These fault lines required the imposition of the state to mediate and manage, minimize and mask, even their most minute manifestations.

Hickman herself (1997, 1227–28) cites a series of cases from 1885 to 1911 that bears out the dubitability of generalizing the one-drop rule or taking it too literally. In 1885, Isaac Jones successfully appealed his conviction and almost three-year sentence for feloniously marrying a white woman on the grounds that he was less than "one quarter black" as required by the Virginia statute. The court explicitly declared Jones a "mulatto of brown skin" and his mother "a yellow woman" while admitting that his "blood quantum" amounted to less than that statutorily necessitated.[30] In North Carolina, a white man in 1910 tried to annul his marriage because his wife "was and is of negro descent within the third generation," thereby avoiding his spousal and child maintenance responsibilities. The court ruled that the husband was unable to prove his wife was at least "one-eighth negro," as statutorily required, because he could not establish without doubt that her great grandfather "was a real negro of unmixed blood."[31] The following year, again in Virginia, two children were initially removed from a white mother on grounds that their stepfather was part Negro. The man had married his white wife after the children's father had died, leaving the family destitute, and the defendant had cared well for his new family. The children were returned after her new husband's mother insisted that she was only one-eighth black and his father had been white, making the man at issue one-sixteenth black, too little for the law even if more than sufficient for the one-drop rule.[32]

Thus, as the rights and privileges of citizenship were revised in the face of a perceived crisis of national identity and identification, not all would be able to qualify. Some "self-evidently" were not white, some clearly failed to qualify racially under the various naturalization laws and their amendments and found themselves forced into pained choices, many were deemed simply "racially unacceptable," and even when recognized as white some were positioned as less so than others. There were obviously tensions between state agencies—the immigration service, on the one hand, running up against the judiciary on a range of cases, and lower courts in contrast with higher jurisdictions. One jurisdiction might be at odds judicially with another. Thus, racial covenants might not be implemented in Manhattan, while in Los Angeles in 1944 there were neighborhoods that legally "prohibited occupancy by any 'persons other than Caucasians'" (Hickman 1997, 1167).[33] Legal realism is intimately wedded to racial realism (cf. Bell 1995). In the end, the power of judicial (re)definition (in the hand of the upper courts especially) can be seen in the business of re-creating and regulating the contours of whiteness, of continuing to massage the boundaries of national belonging and the definition of citizenship.

The reinvention of whiteness bridging the close of the nineteenth century and the opening of the twentieth accordingly was not simply about the undertaking to maintain "a bulwark against undesirable Others without" and the "minimizing [of] perceived 'difference' among the varied peoples and races within," as Jacobson (1998, 233) would have it. This imputation so obviously blurs the sordidly subtle complexities of segregationism, the contradictions within the rule of hypodescent, and the checkered derogation assigned to racial distinction, as well as the ambiguous racially driven responses to immigration as to warrant no further comment. The sociolegal refashioning of whiteness on which I have dwelled at length here was a more or less complex set of responses to the perceived threats of growing heterogeneity within that flowed from imperial and international engagement and by the consequent challenges to the presumed supremacy of whites—in numbers and power, abilities and political domination, opportunities and access. It was, in short, nothing more nor less than a transforming pragmatics of rule through and by race. At the same time, it must be recognized that whiteness refers to a structural condition and, as Roediger (1999) notes, is in no way meant to fix absolutely and disrespectfully in privileged and racist place the subject positions and experiences of every particular person classed as white.

The possessive investment in whiteness (Lipsitz 1998) was not only state created and sustained in the face of transforming social conditions; the contours of whiteness itself were refashioned and reshaped sociolegally in the face of new challenges and charges, both global and local in cause and condition. The more contemporary mode of racial rule in the name of color blindness assumes its force by leaving almost altogether untouched the material conditions and distinctions structurally sewn through formalized segregationism into a social order like the United States. But this is a broader argument that I must leave to another occasion.

Notes

This is a considerably shortened version of chapter 6 of my book *The Racial State* (Oxford: Basil Blackwell, 2001). I am grateful to Kim Furumoto for her fine legal research in identifying key sources informing the argument in this chapter.

1. The pragmatics of segregationism are not inconsistent with assimilationism. Thus, French colonial policy could accommodate assimilation of native elites—precisely by rendering them "less native"—while segregating the bulk of the colonized population.

2. *Plessy v. Ferguson* 163 U.S. 537, 543, 16 S. Ct. 1138.

3. *Plessy v. Ferguson* 163 U.S. 537, 543, 16 S. Ct. 1142, 1143.

4. *Plessy v. Ferguson* 163 U.S. 537, 543, 16 S. Ct. 1142.

5. Consider the fascinating work on English panics, spanning at least the past century, regarding continental invasion in considering construction of the Channel tunnel (Pick 1994; Darian-Smith 1999).

6. See, for instance, the essays and reviews written between 1910 and 1930 and collected in Boas (1940).

7. As all generalizations go, this one has exceptions, as much in the differences between those bearing it out as in those exceptions proving the rule. Regarding the former, contrast Robert Park's (1950) empiricist sociology with John Dollard's (1988) Freudian social psychology. For the extent of the material in the social psychology of intelligence, attitudes, and prejudice from the 1920s on, see especially the bibliography in Richards (1997) as well as the analysis at pages 65 to 159. Notable critics who theorize racism as systemic and sustained, "naturalized" and "normalized" conditions of modern political economies—like W. E. B. du Bois and Oliver Cromwell Cox and even the more liberal centrist Gunnar Myrdal—are anomalies nevertheless proving the rule of the prevailing shift to an urban focus.

8. *Dred Scott v. Sanford* 60, 407; 1857 U.S.

9. This is not to deny that the renegotiation of whiteness in Britain intensifies after 1945, with the falling apart of classic colonial conditions. The crack in British colonial self-confidence, however, comes almost a century earlier with the Indian Rebellion in 1857, a crack that becomes a gorge in the wake of the Anglo-Boer War at century's turn. It took two world wars and a global economic depression to shatter that self-confidence completely.

10. *In re Sadar Bhagwab Singh* 246 F. 498, 499; 1917 U.S. Dist. As Barrett and Roediger (1997, 2) point out, this concern with the threat to homogeneity was not restricted to the courts. Unions like the AFL defended the admission of immigrant labor from northern and central Europe over "the scum" from the "least civilized countries of Europe" precisely because of the supposed implications for urban conditions.

11. *In re Cruz* 23 F. Supp. 774; 1938 U.S. Dist.

12. *Ex parte Dow* 211 F. 489; 1914 U.S. Dist.

13. *In re Saito* 62 F. 126; 1894 U.S. App.

14. See petition of Easurk Amsen Charr to the Missouri District Court 273 F. 207; 1921 U.S. Dist.

15. *In re Sadar Bhagwab Singh* 246 F. 499; 1917 U.S. Dist.

16. Reaffirmed in 1922 by the Supreme Court in *Takao Ozawa* 260 U.S. 178; 43 S. Ct. 65; 1922 U.S.

17. *In re Mohan Singh* 257 F. 213; 1919 U.S. Dist.

18. *United States v. Bhagat Singh Thind* 261 U.S. 204; 43 S. Ct. 338; 1923 U.S.

19. Or, indeed in, Filipinos or "Porto Ricans" who provided military service to the United States in times of war and were honorably discharged could be eligible for naturalization within a strict statute of limitations. *Petition of Easurk Emsen Charr* 273 F. 209; 1921 U.S. Dist.

20. *In re Halladjian et al.* 174 F. 83; 1909 Cir. Ct.; Franz Boas, among a litany of prominent anthropologists, gave supporting evidence in behalf of the successful petition of an Armenian woman whom the U.S. government was seeking to denaturalize after eleven years. *United States v. Cartozian* 6 F. 2d 919; 1925 U.S. Dist.

21. *United States v. Balsara* 180 F. 694; 1910 U.S. App.

22. *In re Halladjian et al.* 174 F. 834 Cir. Ct. D.; 1909 Massachusetts; *In re Ellis* 179 F. 1002; 1910 U.S. Dist., D. Oregon.

23. *Ex parte Shahid* 205 F. 812; 1913 U.S. Dist.

24. *Ex parte Dow* 211 F. 489; 1914 U.S. Dist.
25. *In re Dow* 213 F. 362; 1914 U.S. Dist.
26. *In re Dow* 213 F. 366, 367; 1914 U.S. Dist.
27. *Dow v. United States et. al.* 226 F. 145; 1915 U.S. App.
28. *State v. Treadaway et al.* 126 La. 300; 52 So. 500; 1910 La. The woman arrested with Octave Treadaway is referred to anonymously throughout, where referenced at all, as "et al." or "another."
29. Cited in *In re Cruz* 23 F. Supp. 774; 1938 U.S. Dist.
30. *Jones v. Commonwealth* 80 Va. 18 (1885).
31. *Ferrall v. Ferrall* 69 S.S. 60 N.C. (1910).
32. *Moon v. Children's Home Society* 72 S.E. 707 Va. (1911).
33. *Stone v. Jones* 152 P. 2d 19 (Cal. Ct. App. 1944).

References

Allen, Theodore. 1994. *The Invention of the White Race: Racial Oppression and Social Control.* London: Verso.

Balibar, Etienne. 1990. "Paradoxes of Universality." In D. T. Goldberg, ed., *Anatomy of Racism* (283–94). Minneapolis: University of Minnesota Press.

Barrett, James, and David Roediger. 1997. "Inbetween Peoples: Race, Nationality and the 'New Immigrant' Working Class." *Journal of American Ethnic History* (spring): 3–44.

Bell, Derrick. 1995. "Racial Realism." In Kimberle Crenshaw et al., eds., *Critical Race Theory: The Key Writings That Formed the Movement* (302–12). New York: The New Press.

Boas, Franz. 1940. *Race, Language and Culture.* New York: The Free Press.

Bonnett, Alastair. 1998. "How the British Working Class Became White: The Symbolic (Re)formation of Racialized Capitalism." *Journal of Historical Sociology* 11, no. 3 (September): 316–40.

Crenshaw, Kimberle. 1995. "Race, Reform and Retrenchment: Transformation and Legitimation in Antidiscrimination Law." In Kimberle Crenshaw et al., eds., *Critical Race Theory: The Key Writings That Formed the Movement* (103–22). New York: The New Press.

Darian-Smith, Eve. 1999. *Bridging Divides: The Channel Tunnel and English Legal Identity in the New Europe.* Berkeley and Los Angeles: University of California Press.

Dollard, John [1937] 1988. *Caste and Class in a Southern Town.* Reprint, Madison: University of Wisconsin Press.

Dummett, Ann, and Andrew Nicol. 1990. *Subjects, Citizens, Aliens and Others: Nationality and Immigrant Law.* London: Weidenfeld and Nicolson.

Dworkin, Ronald. 1988. *Law's Empire.* Cambridge, Mass.: Harvard University Press.

Goldberg, David Theo. 1993. *Racist Culture: Philosophy and the Politics of Meaning.* Oxford: Basil Blackwell.

———. 1997. *Racial Subjects: Writing on Race in America.* New York: Routledge.

———. 2000. "Liberalism's Limits: Carlyle and Mill on 'The Negro Question.'" *Nineteenth Century Contexts* 22, no. 2: 203–16.

Gotanda, Neil. 1995. "A Critique of 'Our Constitution Is Colorblind.'" In Kimberle Crenshaw et al., eds., *Critical Race Theory: The Key Writings That Formed the Movement* (257–75). New York: The New Press.

Haggard, Rider. 1902. *Rural England.* London: Longmans, Green and Co.

Haney-Lopez, Ian. 1996. *White by Law: The Legal Construction of Race.* New York: New York University Press.

Harris, Cheryl. 1995. "Whiteness as Property." In Kimberle Crenshaw et al., eds., *Critical Race Theory: The Key Writings That Formed the Movement* (276–90). New York: The New Press.

Hegel, George Wilhelm Friedrich. 1821. *The Philosophy of Right.* Oxford: Clarendon Press.

Hickman, Christine. 1997. "The Devil and the One Drop Rule: Racial Categories, African Americans, and the U.S. Census." *Michigan Law Review* 95 (March): 1161–1265.

Ignatiev, Noel. 1995. *How the Irish Became White: Irish-Americans and African-Americans in Nineteenth Century Philadelphia.* New York: Verso.

Jacobson, Mathew Frye. 1998. *Witness of a Different Color: European Immigrants and the Alchemy of Race.* Cambridge, Mass.: Harvard University Press.

Lipsitz, George. 1998. *The Possessive Investment in Whiteness: How White People Profit from Identity Politics.* Philadelphia: Temple University Press.

Park, Robert. 1950. *Race and Culture.* Glencoe, Ill.: The Free Press.

Pick, Daniel. 1994. "Pro Patria: Blocking the Tunnel." *Ecumene* 1: 77–94.

Richards, Graham. 1997. *Race, Racism and Psychology: Towards a Reflexive History.* London: Routledge.

Roediger, David. 1991. *The Wages of Whiteness: Race and the Making of the American Working Class.* New York: Verso.

———. 1999. *The Wages of Whiteness: Race and the Making of the American Working Class.* Rev. ed. New York: Verso.

Sacks, Karen Brodkin. 1995. "How Did Jews Become White Folks?" In Roger Sanjek and Steven Gregory, eds., *Race.* New Brunswick, N.J.: Rutgers University Press.

Saxton, Alexander. 1992. *The Rise and Fall of the White Republic.* New York: Verso.

Stephenson, Gilbert Thomas. 1909/10. "Race Distinctions in American Law." *American Law Review* 43: 29–905.

Stoler, Ann Laura. 1997. "Racial Histories and Their Regimes of Truth." In D. Davis, ed., *Political Power and Social Theory,* Vol. II (183–206). Ann Arbor, Mich.: JAI Press.

Taussig, Michael. 1997. *The Magic of the State.* New York: Routledge.

Voegelin, Eric [1933] 1998. *The History of the Race Idea, Collected Works, Vol. 3.* Translated by Ruth Hein. Reprint, Baton Rouge: Louisiana State University Press.

Wallenstein, Peter. 1994. "Race, Marriage, and the Law of Freedom: Alabama and Virginia, 1860s–1960s." *Chicago-Kent Law Review* 70: 370–71.

Wiegman, Robyn. 1995. *American Anatomies: Theorizing Race and Gender.* Durham, N.C.: Duke University Press.

Part III

Identities

9

Ethnicity, Identities, and the Basis of Support for Authorities

Yuen J. Huo and Tom R. Tyler

Conflict is a natural and inevitable consequence of social relations. By securing compliance with decisions they make and with community policies and regulations they enact, authorities play a key role in managing intragroup conflicts. As U.S. society becomes more diverse, legal authorities, among others, must govern in an era marked by sharp conflicts in interests and values. Increasingly, judges, police officers, managers, politicians, and other authorities will have to make decisions and enact policies with which all citizens will not agree. To what extent will authorities be able to maintain their legitimacy and secure voluntary compliance in an era of diversity?

Procedural justice is one mechanism whereby conflict generated by competing values and interests might be ameliorated (see Tyler and Lind 1992; Tyler 1994; Tyler, Smith, and Huo 1996). When people perceive that authorities make decisions fairly, they are more willing to comply with them. Voluntary, as opposed to coerced, acceptance allows authorities to make difficult judgments without losing the support of those who either disagree with or do not benefit from their decisions. The issue we address in this chapter is whether procedural justice is a viable strategy for managing conflicts in an era of ethnic diversity. We draw on empirical studies to examine how ethnic group membership and ethnic identity may influence citizens' reactions to authorities. Does ethnic identity or ethnic group affiliation shift citizens' concerns away from procedural fairness, thereby undermining its ability to bridge differences?

Diversity, Procedural Fairness, and Authority Relations

Demographic trends indicate that the United States is reaching an unprecedented level of diversity. Estimates suggest that 45 percent of all additions to the American workforce will be nonwhite, with 50 percent coming from Asian and Latin American countries (Cox 1993). In California, one of the nation's most populous and ethnically diverse states, projections indicate that by 2020 no ethnic group will constitute a majority of the population (California Department of Finance 1993). Accompanying these demographic changes, public opinion has shifted, as the populace considers the extent to which such diversity should be accommodated. Increasingly, both new immigrants and historically disadvantaged groups are rejecting assimilation, questioning the degree to which minority groups should accept and adopt mainstream societal values, and calling instead for a mosaic or multicultural society where people retain strong loyalty to their ethnic group. Political organizations and community-based groups have made efforts to encourage the adoption of multicultural policies, such as bilingual education, while demands for social science and humanities courses recognizing the contributions of ethnic minorities have increased. These proposals take on special significance given that the educational system has historically served as a primary means for assimilating new immigrants into American society and culture. Based on these changes and trends, studies of authority relations would do well to incorporate analyses of ethnicity. Our research is concerned with how ethnic group membership and ethnic identities affect people's judgments about their treatment by authorities and their acceptance of such authorities.

As studies of authority relations suggest, leaders play a crucial role in groups by effectively managing internal conflicts and coordinating the efforts of individuals and subgroups (Thibaut and Faucheux 1965; Messick et al. 1983; Yamagishi 1986, 1988; Rutte, Wilke, and Messick 1987; Sato 1987; Wit 1989; Samuelson 1991). Decisions made by authorities often significantly affect the lives of others. Group members may not always agree with or personally benefit from such decisions. If people's willingness to voluntarily comply with an authority's directives depends on whether they agree with or benefit from such decisions, then authorities' ability to bridge differences, manage internal conflicts, and coordinate efforts may be seriously limited. However, as past research suggests, the key antecedent of voluntary acceptance of authorities and their decisions is not instrumental judgments of gain and loss but, rather, relational judgments about the extent to which authorities have treated individuals fairly (see Lind and Tyler 1988; Tyler 1990; Tyler and Lind 1992; Tyler et al. 1997). In a variety of contexts, people appear to use procedural fairness as a guide when deciding whether to accept decisions made by organizational, legal, and political authorities. One implication of this research is that encouraging reliance on procedural information might empower authorities to make decisions for the good of the group without losing the support of those who do not agree with those decisions.

The Relational Model of Authority

In an effort to explain the psychological processes underlying the observed procedural fairness model, Tyler and Lind (1992) developed a relational model of authority. According to the relational model, three types of concerns are closely linked to judgments about procedural fairness judgments: neutrality (authorities are viewed as unbiased, as acting on the basis of facts rather than prejudices), trust in benevolence (authorities consider one's needs and point of view), and status recognition (authorities recognize group members' rights and treat them with dignity and respect). When such concerns are satisfied, authorities' decisions are viewed as fair, and their policies tend to be accepted, even when the authority makes decisions with which individuals disagree or that do not benefit them. Conversely, when such concerns are not satisfied, authorities are viewed as unfair, and their decisions and policies are often not accepted.

From the perspective of the relational model, individuals care about being treated fairly by group authorities because such treatment communicates information about one's status in the group. Fair treatment suggests that one is a respected and valued member of the group. In contrast, unfair treatment communicates a message that one is unimportant or marginal. Information about one's status in the group is important because such social identity information affects the self-concept (Tajfel and Turner 1986). Recent studies suggest that people's perceptions of fair/unfair treatment affect their sense of self, including their level of self-esteem and feelings of being respected by the group (Koper et al. 1993; Smith et al. 1998).

The relational model's explanation of procedural fairness effects departs from the traditional "control model," developed from earlier research on legal disputes. Thibaut and Walker (1975) developed a control model, arguing that concerns about the fairness of decision-making procedures stem from instrumental concerns about the outcome of authorities' decisions. In legal disputes, when those involved approach a third party for help in developing a resolution, control ultimately rests in the hands of the authority. The only control over the outcome the disputants may have is the presentation of evidence. Procedures affording "voice" or opportunities to explain one's case are considered fairer than those that do not. Both the relational model and the control model link voluntary acceptance of authorities and their decisions and policies to perceptions of procedural fairness. However, they depart in their explanation as to why people are motivated to care about procedural fairness: The control model suggests an instrumental motive, while the relational model posits the importance of social identity-based motives.

Empirical tests of the relational model of authority support the hypothesis that judgments about neutrality, trust in benevolence, and status recognition are linked to judgments about procedural fairness. Such relational judgments are also linked to general evaluations of authorities and to voluntary acceptance of their decisions or the policies they adopt. However, much of this research has overlooked the moderating effects potentially introduced by diversity. Two factors may alter the basic processes of the relational model as documented in past research: (1) social categorization: Are the basic processes altered when interactions cross ethnic group boundaries; and (2) social identities: How does community identity and ethnic identity affect the basic processes?

Social Categorization

Perceptions of difference brought about by the introduction of a salient social attribute such as ethnicity shape the resulting social dynamics in fundamental ways. For example, studies based on social identity theory show that the assignment of individuals to groups based on arbitrary distinctions brings about important changes in attitudes (for a summary of relevant research, see Taylor and Moghaddam 1994). People are more likely to attribute positive traits to their in-group than to their out-group. They are also more likely to develop stereotypes of out-group members' behaviors and traits. Such research illustrates the undesirable consequences of social divisions.

The relational model of authority draws some similar conclusions about the potential negative effects resulting from cross-group interactions. In essence, the relational model is a theory of intragroup processes, one describing the social dynamics occurring within a group or a social structure. When group members evaluate their experiences vis-à-vis authorities who are empowered by the group, they are motivated to use the opportunity to assess their status in that group. Because authorities may be important representatives of the group and reflect the group's opinion, their views may carry particular weight.

Relational concerns about neutrality, trust in the benevolence of authority, and treatment with dignity and respect convey important status information. When authorities act in a manner consistent with these relational criteria, the individual feels valued as a group member. In comparison, when authorities act inconsistently in regard to relational criteria, the individual feels rejected and marginalized. Perceptions of fair treatment carry weight because they communicate important information about how one is regarded by a group to which one belongs and with which one affiliates.

Based on the previous analysis, the social categorization hypothesis of the relational model suggests that the basis of reactions to authorities differs, depending on whether the individual belongs to and cares about the group empowering the authority in question. When the individual is dealing with an in-group authority, the hypothesized relational processes are at work. Because an out-group authority by definition does not represent the views of a group that an individual cares about, their directives may embody less social identity information of the sort people seek within group interactions.

Empirical Test of the Social Categorization Hypothesis

We tested the hypothesis that objective group membership affects the basis of reactions to conflicts in two studies of employees who approached their supervisor for help in resolving a problem. The first was a study of Japanese and Western teachers who were part of a teaching program in Japan, and the second was a study of employees at a multiethnic public sector work organization in the United States. In each study, respondents were asked to rate how fairly they were treated and whether the supervisor made a decision beneficial to them. They were also asked to indicate how willing they were to accept and go along with the supervisor's decision.

Analysis was conducted to examine whether the basis of decision acceptance differed when the employee and the supervisor shared common group membership. In the Japan study, interactions were coded as occurring within group when they took place between two Japanese or two Westerners (e.g., Americans and Canadians). Interactions were coded as occurring across groups when they involved a Japanese and a Westerner. In the U.S. study, interactions were coded as occurring within group when they involved two individuals from the same ethnic background (e.g., two Asian Americans). Interactions were recorded as across groups when two people from differing ethnic backgrounds were involved (e.g., an Asian American and a European American).

The analysis produced consistent findings across the two studies, as illustrated in figures 1 and 2. Individuals focused more on how fair the process was when the supervisor was from the same cultural or ethnic group than when the supervisor was from a different cultural or ethnic group. In contrast, individuals focused less on the instrumental aspects of the decision when the supervisor was from the same group than when the supervisor was from a different group.

These two studies demonstrate the importance of the group context of interaction. Authorities benefit the most from a procedural fairness focus when they are perceived as sharing a common group membership. Reliance on procedural information appears to diminish when interactions occur across group boundaries. In interactions with out-group

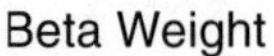

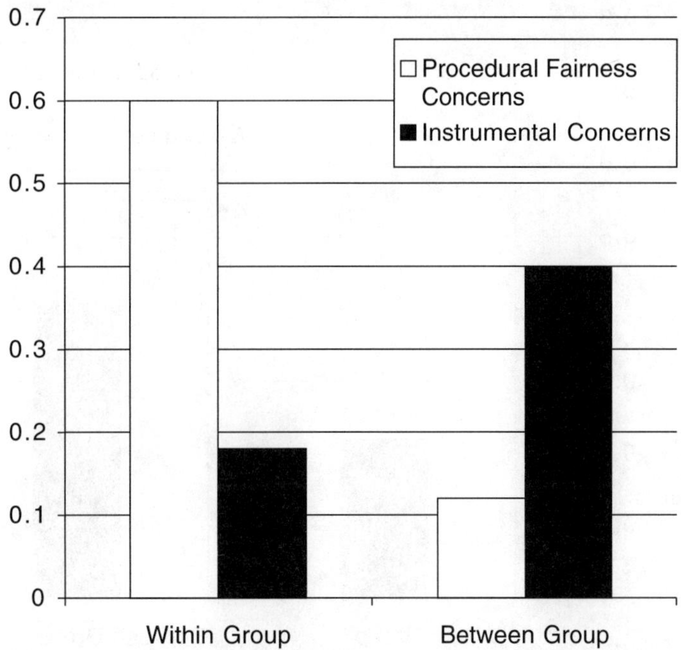

FIGURE 1. *Predictors of decision acceptance in Japanese/Western teacher study. Note: The bars represent standardized regression coefficients. Two separate regressions were run—one for within-group interactions (e.g., interaction between two Western teachers or between two Japanese teachers) and one for between-group interactions (e.g., interaction between a Western teacher and a Japanese teacher). In each case, procedural concerns and instrumental concerns were entered into the regression as main effects to predict variance in self-reported acceptance of decisions made by the authority in charge.*

authorities, the link between procedural fairness concerns and decision acceptance is weakened. In an ethnically diverse society, a procedural fairness focus seems to have limited utility. In cross-cultural, cross-ethnic interactions, a procedural focus may be a less viable strategy for bridging differences.

Implications of Social Categorization Studies

The results of the two studies paint a rather dismal picture for the peaceful resolution of conflict in a society where ethnic group membership has taken on an increasingly important role in social life and in politics. Support for controversial policies in the United States, such as affirmative action, welfare reform, immigration restrictions, and bilingual education, is clearly divided along ethnic and racial lines. Conflicts in interests and values may not be easily resolved because the ability of authorities to make decisions and enact policies with which all people comply is diminished when they deal with members of

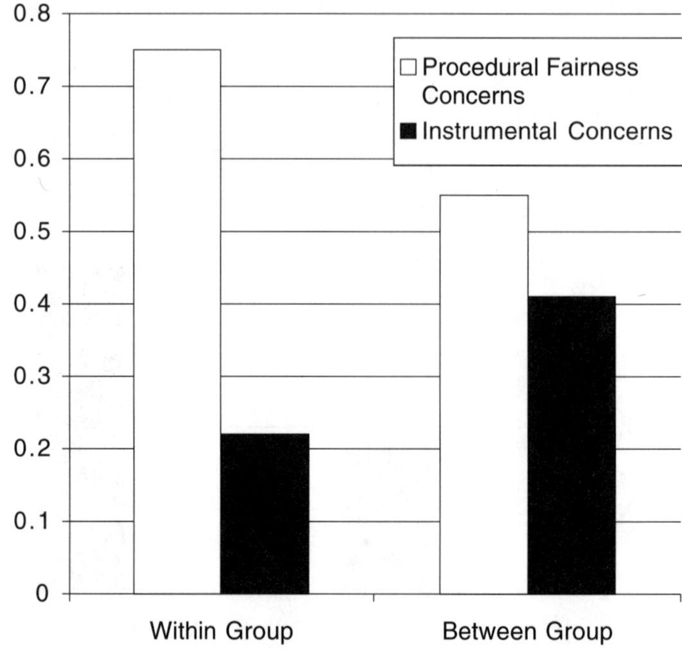

FIGURE 2. *Predictors of decision acceptance in U.S. employee–supervisor study. Note: The bars represent standardized regression coefficients. Two separate regressions were run—one for within-group interactions (e.g., interaction between a Latino supervisor and a white employee) and one for between-group interactions (e.g., interaction between an African American supervisor and an African American employee). In each case, procedural concerns and instrumental concerns were entered into the regression as main effects to predict variance in self-reported acceptance of decisions made by the supervisor.*

different ethnic groups. Is there a mechanism whereby authorities can maintain their ability to elicit compliance and hence effectively manage conflicts in environments where ethnicity represents a source of social divisions?

Social Identities

How can authorities make decisions that will be acceptable to members of different ethnic groups? What we have demonstrated thus far is that objective group membership may be viewed as a social boundary such that individuals with different ethnic affiliations interpret their interactions in intergroup terms. However, each individual is a member of many social groups (Turner et al. 1987). If a common group membership is made salient, then members of different ethnic groups may view their interactions as occurring between members of the same overarching category. For example, within the United States, ethnic groups may be viewed as subgroups nested within the larger group, Americans. "American" is a superordinate group inclusive of various ethnic subgroups. If members of different ethnic groups came to perceive themselves as part of the larger group, America, then they may perceive each other as part of the same group rather than as out-group members. Encouraging identification with a superordinate group may be a useful strategy to reframe cross-ethnic interactions as interactions occurring among members of the same superordinate category.

Empirical Test of the Identity Hypothesis

We tested whether superordinate identification actually facilitates reliance on procedural fairness information in a field study of employees at a multiethnic work organization (Huo et al. 1996). In this study, we isolated our analysis to reports about interactions in which the employee and supervisor were members of *different* ethnic groups. We asked employees to rate their experience on a variety of dimensions, and we also asked them to rate the extent to which they identified with the organization (superordinate identity) and with their ethnic group (subgroup identity). Based on the employees' responses to the identification items, three categories of respondents were created: (1) assimilators (high organization identification and low ethnic identification), (2) biculturalists (high organization identification and high ethnic identification), and (3) separatists (low organization identification and high ethnic identification). We analyzed each of these three categories to explore the factors associated with willingness to accept and go along with decisions made by the work supervisor.

The results of this analysis are shown in figure 3. Among assimilators and biculturalists (individuals who are highly identified with the work organization), evaluations of procedural fairness were more strongly related to decision acceptance than were evaluations of the extent to which self-interest was served. In contrast, among separatists, individuals who were *not* strongly identified with the organization but were instead identified with their ethnic group, evaluations of the nature of the decision (favorable or unfavorable) were more strongly related to decision acceptance than were evaluations of the process.

What these findings suggest is that identification with a superordinate group reframes an interaction between members of different ethnic groups as one occurring within a single category. Identification with the superordinate category (i.e., work organization) emerges as the most important factor. Regardless of the extent to which individuals identified with their ethnic group, as long as they identified with the organization, they focused on the relational information conveyed by the process through which decisions are made.

Implications of Identity Studies

Critics of the multicultural movement in the United States argue that policies that emphasize ethnic affiliations will lead to escalation of conflicts and potential societal fragmentation (Schlesinger 1992). This argument assumes a linkage between strong ethnic identification and lack of identification with the larger society. According to our findings,

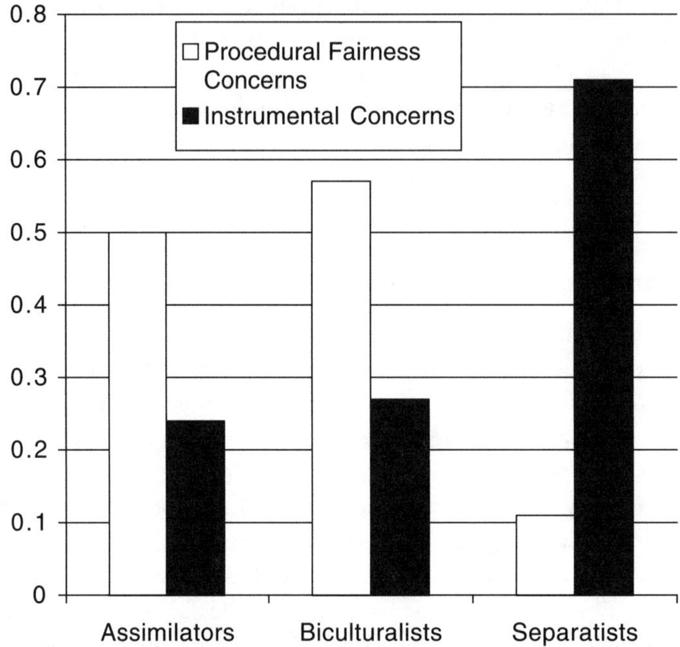

FIGURE 3. *Predictors of decision acceptance for assimilators, biculturalists, and separatists (from Huo et al. 1996). Note: Only cross-ethnic interactions were included in the analysis. The bars represent standardized regression coefficients. Three separate regressions were run—one for assimilators, a second for biculturalists, and a third for separatists. In each case, procedural concerns and instrumental concerns were entered into the regression as main effects to predict variance in self-reported acceptance of decisions made by the authority in charge.*

people may simultaneously identify with and form attachments to the dominant society and their ethnic group. Increasing interest in the fairness of the process and decreasing interest in the favorability of outcomes does not require people to devalue their ethnic group membership. Authorities' ability to resolve cross-ethnic conflicts effectively might be enhanced if those who are governed can be persuaded to care about the group empowering authorities and to reply on process information to form evaluations of their experience.

The results of our study offer optimistic evidence for the viability of diverse communities. If people are self-interested and outcome oriented in their dealings with authorities, then competition for scarce resources and differences in goals, values, and beliefs will lead to irreconcilable conflicts. However, the findings we described show how identification with a superordinate group, especially one empowering authorities, may redirect people's focus away from outcomes to relational, process-oriented concerns. Such a shift allows authorities to worry less about providing desired outcomes to group members and to concentrate more on maintaining social cohesion. If people are treated fairly, if they are accorded dignity, respect, and consideration by honest, unbiased authorities, they can overlook minor setbacks and remain committed to the larger group.

Summary

Our empirical studies were based on observations of the relationship between organizational authorities and their subordinates. However, the problem we have described applies to authorities in a variety of contexts. Both political and legal authorities are naturally concerned with securing compliance with their decisions as well as acceptance of the rules and policies they enact. However, securing voluntary acceptance is a persistent problem for these authorities. In the legal context, this problem is apparent across a wide variety of issues, including, for example, the difficulties of obtaining compliance with child support orders or enforcing drug laws. The Rodney King incident and the events following it, as well as long-standing problems between legal authorities and disadvantaged groups, illustrate the special problems arising when authority structures extend across ethnic boundaries.

We noted that a procedural justice strategy is potentially useful in helping authorities to bridge competing interests and differences in values. When people feel that they have been treated fairly by authorities, they are likely to go along with the decisions authorities make, even if the outcomes are not favorable to them. We argued that this focus on the process and the social information it provides is useful because it enables authorities to make decisions and enact policies for the greater good without losing support of individuals who do not directly benefit from their actions.

We explored situations in which the effectiveness of a procedural fairness strategy may be diminished in an ethnically diverse society using data from several empirical studies we have conducted. Individuals tend to view authorities from other ethnic groups as "outsiders" and to evaluate them in a more self-interested way than when authorities are from the same ethnic group. It appears that a procedural fairness strategy is less effective in cross-ethnic interactions. Further analyses suggest that what matters is not objective group membership per se but, rather, an individual's feelings of common group membership. Individuals who indicate strong identification with a superordinate group that encompasses ethnic subgroups continue to focus on the process even when evaluating an authority from a different ethnic group. In contrast, those individuals who do not identify with the overarching group tend to evaluate their experience in terms of material gains and related self-interested concerns. Interestingly, the findings suggest that using superordinate identity to facilitate reliance on process issues does not require relinquishing important attachments to ethnic group membership.

The relational model of authority on which we base our analysis is at its core an identity-based theory of social relations. It assumes that our conception of self is intertwined with our social identities. People care about how fairly they are treated by important group representatives because of the status information that such treatment conveys. To understand authority relations requires attention to the complex ways in which identity influences people's reactions to authorities. Moreover, the incorporation of identity issues into studies of authority relations may provide important insights into how democratic authorities might effectively coordinate efforts within groups and successfully manage internal disagreements in an era in which values and interests frequently clash.

References

California Department of Finance. 1993, May. *Projected Total Population of California Counties: 1990 to 2040.* Report 93-P-3. Sacramento: California Department of Finance.

Cox, T. J. 1993. *Cultural Diversity in Organizations.* San Francisco: Berrett-Koehler Publishers.

Huo, Y. J., H. J. Smith, T. R. Tyler, and E. A. Lind. 1996. "Superordinate Identification, Subgroup Identification, and Justice Concerns: Is Separatism the Problem; Is Assimilation the Answer?" *Psychological Science* 7: 40–45.

Koper, G., D. Van Knippenberg, F. Bouhuijs, R. Vermunt, and H. Wilke. 1993. "Procedural Fairness and Self-Esteem." *European Journal of Social Psychology* 23: 313–25.

Lind, E. A., and T. R. Tyler. 1988. *The Social Psychology of Procedural Justice.* New York: Plenum Press.

Messick, D. M., H. Wilke, M. B. Brewer, R. M. Kramer, P. E. Zemke, and L. Lui. 1983. "Individual Adaptations and Structural Change as Solutions to Social Dilemmas." *Journal of Personality and Social Psychology* 44: 294–309.

Rutte, C. G., H. Wilke, and D. M. Messick. 1987. "Scarcity or Abundance Caused by People or the Environment as Determinants of Behavior in the Resource Dilemma." *Journal of Experimental Social Psychology* 23: 208–14.

Samuelson, C. D. 1991. "Perceived Task Difficulty, Causal Attributions, and Preferences for Structural Change in Resource Dilemmas." *Personality and Social Psychology Bulletin* 17: 181–87.

Sato, K. 1987. "Distribution of the Cost of Maintaining Common Resources." *Journal of Experimental Social Psychology* 23: 19–31.

Schlesinger, A. M., Jr. 1992. *The Disuniting of America: Reflections on a Multicultural Society.* New York: W. W. Norton.

Smith, H. J., T. R. Tyler, Y. J. Huo, D. Ortiz, and E. A. Lind. 1998. "The Self-Relevant Implications of the Group-Value Model: Group Membership, Self-Worth, and Treatment Quality." *Journal of Experimental Social Psychology* 34: 470–93.

Tajfel, H., and J. C. Turner. 1986. "The Social Identity Theory of Intergroup Behavior." In S. Worchel and W. G. Austin, eds., *Psychology of Intergroup Relations* (7–24). Chicago: Nelson-Hall.

Taylor, D. M., and F. M. Moghaddam. 1994. *Theories of Inter-Group Relations: International Social Psychological Perspectives.* Westport, Conn.: Praeger.

Thibaut, J., and C. Faucheux. 1965. "The Development of Contractual Norms in a Bargaining Situation under Two Types of Stress." *Journal of Experimental Social Psychology* 1: 89–102.

Thibaut, J., and L. Walker. 1975. *Procedural Justice: A Psychological Analysis.* Hillsdale, N.J.: Erlbaum.

Turner, J. C., M. A. Hogg, P. J. Oakes, S. Reicher, and M. S. Wetherell. 1987. *Rediscovering the Social Group: A Self-Categorization Theory.* Oxford: Basil Blackwell.

Tyler, T. R. 1990. *Why People Obey the Law: Procedural Justice, Legitimacy and Compliance.* New Haven, Conn.: Yale University Press.

———. 1994. "Governing amid Diversity: The Effect of Fair Decisionmaking Procedures on the Legitimacy of Government." *Law and Society Review* 28: 809–31.

Tyler, T. R., R. J. Boeckmann, H. J. Smith, and Y. J. Huo. 1997. *Social Justice in a Diverse Society.* Boulder, Colo.: Westview Press.

Tyler, T. R., and E. A. Lind. 1992. "A Relational Model of Authority in Groups." In M. Zanna, ed., *Advances in Experimental Social Psychology,* vol. 25 (115–91). New York: Academic.

Tyler, T. R., H. J. Smith, and Y. J. Huo. 1996. "Member Diversity and Leadership Effectiveness: Procedural Justice, Social Identity, and Group Dynamics." *Advances in Group Processes* 13: 33–66.

Wit, A. P. 1989. "Group Efficiency and Fairness in Social Dilemmas: An Experimental Gaming Approach." Doctoral diss., University of Groningen, The Netherlands.

Yamagishi, T. 1986. "The Provision of a Sanctioning System as a Public Good." *Journal of Personality and Social Psychology* 51: 110–16.

———. 1988. "Seriousness of Social Dilemmas and the Provision of a Sanctioning System." *Social Psychology Quarterly* 51: 32–42.

10

Cop Identity and the Communicative Aspects of Policing

Trish Oberweis and Michael Musheno

We examine cops' identities, drawing attention to the communicative aspects of policing. Bringing identity to the forefront fractures any singular representation of cops while suggesting that they are highly adept at classifying and categorizing their colleagues and the people they encounter on the streets. An identity framework moves beyond the familiar process of categorization in which cops, as a unified force, mark whole groups of people as "other" or as internal enemies to be feared (e.g., urban youth gang members, rogue cops) and invoke their coercive powers to remove them from society.

We provide evidence of more subtle processes of communication at work in which police officers draw on the complex web of identity categories operative in modern America (e.g., race, class, gender, sexual preference) and act as agents invoking the particularity of those they encounter. These invocations are tied to their own particular identities, aspects of which are activated depending on the context at hand. In these instances, citizens are drawn to the administrative apparatus of the state affirmatively because cops bond with subjects as being like them and worthy of their support, sometimes even if they have violated the law.

While these communicative processes have been suggested as operative in the abstract, this chapter provides empirical observations of cops affirming peoples' citizenship in particularized ways and, in doing so, sometimes cutting people breaks by not exercising their coercive powers. Consistent with the ideas that have guided our inquiry, we show that, while appearing to be the warm, friendly face of policing, these communicative processes and the exceptionalism they produce are better understood as crucial to the constitution of state-centered subjects, including citizens who are simultaneously cops.

Foucault (1988) claims that from the eighteenth century on, police practices and "policing" have been integral to "giv[ing] a concrete form . . . [to] political rationality and to this new kind of relationship between the social entity and the individual" (153). Policing, in Foucault's formulation, is the full range of state administrative activities and is treated as a curiously "positive" aspect of governance.[1] As Foucault puts it, "Life is the work of the police"; they ensure the "things that we need . . . that people survive, that people live, and that people do even better than just survive and live" (157). With this mode of policing, the police thus deal with citizens not merely as juridical subjects but as "working, trading, living beings" (156). Invoking the particularity of others, or recognizing a person's uniqueness, may be a key to the modern regime of policing, a regime that requires more than coercion to secure citizens' allegiances.

Drawing on stories provided to us by police officers, we suggest that cops simultaneously constitute and refashion their identities and those with whom they engage by distinguishing themselves from and also connecting or bonding with others. Our analysis suggests that cops weave together several identity categories (e.g., gender, sexual orientation) and constitute state-centered citizens through the dynamics of "binding and dividing." Police officers do engage in raw forms of division, marking some as Others to be feared, and "put themselves forward as the protectors of 'what is in us more than ourselves,' that is, that which makes us part of the nation" (Salecl 1994).

However, cop identity is not monolithic, as officers have more than merely professional identities. Partly because of the many ways they identify themselves, cops often connect with people as unique individuals and sometimes defy the simple coercive politics of stereotyping whole groups as unworthy. Here, they bond with people whose categorical identities (e.g., illegal alien, drug addict) put them at the margins of society. Woven into these performances of policing is the constitution of particular individuals with certain virtues (e.g., hard working) who deserve exceptions to the exercise of coercion or are deserving of the services of the state. Classifying some whose categorical identities put them at the margins as worthy individuals needing state administrative services or deserving breaks preserves the ranks of society. Simultaneously, exceptionalism creates the illusion that individual virtue, coupled with timely state administrative beneficence, enables movement from the margin to the center of society.

Conceptualizing Identity

Following Chantal Mouffe, we suggest that identity is defined relationally. She writes, "The social agent is constituted by an ensemble of 'subject positions' that can never be totally fixed in a closed system of differences. . . . The 'identity' of such a multiple and contradictory subject is therefore always contingent and precarious, temporarily fixed at the intersection of those subject positions and dependent on specific forms of identification" (Mouffe 1995, 33). Thus, we are never only women or men, only a member of a race or nation or profession. These forms of identification[2] intersect, mutually defining the way each subject position becomes part of a nonfixed whole at any particular moment. The ways in which a woman, for example, takes up her femaleness depends on her racial, national, and/or professional positionings and so on and vice versa. Multiple subject positions that combine to create an identity thus do not coexist but interexist. They are not separate entities but rather determine each other in a constant process of formation and transformation.

Our conception of identity insists on this basic dynamism. Identities are interactive. Within the same individual, a particular subject position, in our case a police officer, might be taken up one way by one officer and a different way by another officer, depending on what other subject positions are interacting with the occupational subject position. It may even be—and often is—taken up differently by the same officer at different times. Across individuals, we see the importance of context. The combination of localized social relations, events, and territory make some particular identities more directly germane and others relevant only indirectly.

Contemporary feminist, queer, and antiracist theory focuses on the ways that identity excludes. (See also Butler 1990; Halley 1993; Hall 1996). Descending from a Derridean logic of differánce, these theorists tend to focus largely on who might be excluded from an invocation of a "we," identified as some identity group. In other words, identity tends to be seen as something that divides people across (perhaps arbitrary) attributes. Judith Butler, speaking about the subject of feminism, describes the problem: "The minute that the category of women gets invoked as *describing* the constituency for which feminism speaks, an internal debate invariably begins over what the descriptive content of that term will be. . . . Identity categories are never merely descriptive, but always normative, and as such, exclusionary" (Butler 1992, 15–16). Thus, the terrain of identity is itself not neutral but political. Lines are drawn between "us" and "them," and sides must be taken. In this sense, identity divides people from one another by its inherent inclusions and exclusions.

However, identity is not only about division. Cornel West suggests that "in talking about identity, we have to begin to look at the various ways in which human beings have constructed their desire for recognition, association and protection over time and in space, always in circumstances not of their own choosing" (West 1995, 16). For West, identity facilitates social coherence. "Identity is about binding," he argues, "and it means, on the one hand, that you can be bound. . . . But it also means that you can be held together" (16). Thus, identity is not only a means of classification but a source of connection as well. We pay attention to the ebb and flow of both identity division and connection in the context of the everyday life of policing. Focusing on cops, we are able to explore the connotations of binding and dividing as microprocesses at work in the construction of state subjects or citizens. Our focus includes both citizens and agents as political subjects and conceives of each such that "state agent" and "citizen" are not mutually exclusive labels.

Because of the many ways they may define themselves (e.g., in terms of race, class, gender, sexual preference, and so on), cops sometimes recognize citizens as being like themselves. As officers go about the everyday business of law enforcement, aspects of their own identity are evoked and become salient as human actors respond to the context at hand. Defying the coercive politics of stereotyping, officers may bond with citizens such as illegal aliens or drug addicts, who are often viewed as occupying marginal space.

Mode of Inquiry

To inquire about citizen making, we follow the suggestions of Shearing and Ericson (1991) by "examining police stories as stories" (489). In viewing cops' stories from the perspective of identity, we suggest that what officers think ought to be done and what they do in particular situations depends, in part, on who is involved.[3] Although these processes of identity have been suggested as operative in the abstract, we offer empirical observations of the ebb and flow of identity formation.

Compared to other U.S. citizens, cops, by virtue of their profession, find themselves in a relatively unique, although certainly not unified, position compared to other American citizens. As agents of the state with coercive powers, police officers possess broad-ranging authority, which enables them to mark, figuratively and often literally, some citizens as dangerous or undesirable. Yet officers also draw on other subject positions that may connect them to fellow officers or those whom they are called on to police. In the following, we explore processes of division and connection in the context of the everyday life of police practice, exploring how both contribute to the constitution of state subjects and citizens.

We spent six months in the field with the officers from two squads in a police department in a metropolis of the western United States, riding in patrol cars, attending briefings, interviewing them, and generally hanging out. After getting to know them and letting them get to know us, we selected a subset of ten officers from the squads, selected not only for their willingness to talk to us and their verbal animation but also partially with the goal of diversifying storytellers in terms of rank, age, sexual preference, and so on. Still, the majority were predictably white, male, street-level officers whom we presumed to be heterosexual. As we talked with the officers, other factors began to emerge as important sources of identity, such as religion, marital status, parenthood, and even (usually the lack of) membership in the department's special assignment teams.

Officers were asked to tell us work-related stories[4] about their interactions with people on the street and in the hallways of their department. Transcripts of these storytelling sessions, worked into narratives, were returned to officers, who added or subtracted information as they wished. Identities of characters were probed where necessary. The result was twenty stories, some about identity in the context of internal departmental affairs, some about interactions on the street, and others about the interaction between the two.

In the remainder of this chapter, we use the following questions to frame our interpretation of the stories, relying on a framework of identity.[5] Does identity appear as a salient dimension in the stories, and, if so, how does the activation of particular subject positions enable connection, and how does it foster exclusion or division? How does identity operate in the daily work of police officers? How do they negotiate their own and others' identities in the stories that they have chosen to tell? What are the implications of these processes for making political subjects? To address these questions, we examined the stories first for their descriptions of cops enacting their occupational identities in various ways that bind them to the community of police officers and other uniformed state agents. We also explore how aspects of identity that mediate occupational identification create moments of division between officers. Some stories included descriptions of events or themes that reflected a simultaneous binding and dividing of officers. Later in the chapter, we explore the ways that identities allow moments of both connection and division between cops and citizens.

The Binding of Officers as Officers

Many of our stories reflected a great deal of solidarity among officers, and officers made decisions to protect that unity:

> *It looked like a plain suicide, which is really all that it was. Tragic suicide, but really nothing more complicated than that. They had to go through his property and other things, his dresser and things of that effect, to look for any suicide notes or anything that may have foretold what was to happen. As he was doing this, in a pair of the fireman's socks, he found a small vial of cocaine, and instead of turning it over to the wife or letting the family know about it or anything to that effect, he just got ahold of the prosecutor, and they decided just to get rid of it and be done with it and throw it away, which is exactly what happened. And here was a case where you really could have turned that thing into a big mess.*[6]

The family was never informed of the drug find, and because of the "fraternity" of uniformed emergency workers, the deceased fireman's identity as one of the "good guys" was never challenged. The story of the fireman's suicide and the vial of cocaine marks the territory of exceptionalism in which officers withhold their coercive powers to serve their individualized notions of "justice." In this instance, the officer demonstrates police compassion by referencing concern for "wife" and "family" coping with "tragic" suicide. In making an exception, the officer mutes the routine of police intrusiveness into the lives of the friends and lovers of criminal suspects, thus softening the state's coercive capacities while re/enforcing dominant notions of those whose professional identity resonates with his own.

Through this power of determination, cops create a gulf between themselves and other citizens. Some officers were extremely committed to their professional identities, acting in ways that clearly elevated police status over other identifications. In one story, an officer had to break a love bond literally in order to preserve his identity as an officer. The officer and his dog made up the canine unit on call for the department when an armed individual took refuge in a stranger's home, resulting in a volatile situation with potential hostages:

> *Lt. Grangier asked our team leader, Gould, what he wanted to do next, and he said that he wanted to send our canine in to check the door entry to see if the suspect was still alive. . . . At that point I had a real, kind of sick, feeling in my stomach because I knew if the suspect was alive that he was going to kill my dog. I thought about it, and my first thought was I'm not going to send him in a situation like this; I decided to go ahead and send him in because this was a crisis situation. You could be fired at the scene if you refuse a direct order according to the general orders of operations that were written at that time. So, I sent my canine in, and it was kind of a strange one because I had already done over 300 searches with him, building searches with him, and every time I sent him in, I followed right in after him. . . . The dog went in about thirty seconds then I heard a gunshot and a yelp, and I recalled the dog two or three times, and he came back to me. . . . The dog died about a half hour later or so at the vet's. The bullet just bounced around and hit a lot of the main organs, and there was nothing they could do. . . . I don't know, sometimes I wonder about the decision and if it was the right one or not. . . . I did not know how much of an impact it would have until it was my dog, how important this dog was to me, how close we really were, how much of a friendship I had with the dog.*

The performance of his cop identity bound this officer to his fellow officer, lieutenant, and orders in such a way that his allegiance to them was maintained throughout the crisis, despite the huge cost. Acting another way could have cost him his identity as a cop. The story illustrates the power of occupational identity and the partial coercion involved in evoking actions that are compatible with cop identity. At the same time, however, the story reveals that this coercion is internalized as normal. Indeed, the officer acknowledges his own agency in the events and takes responsibility for the decision to send in his dog. Thus, the state is not made to appear as a unilateral force of domination but rather as a legitimate authority to be voluntarily obliged.[7]

Another officer committed herself even more deeply to her identity as a police officer when she shot and killed an assailant. Her thoughts at the time of the incident are revealing about how her actions are tied to her identity:

> *I'm being honest with you here. I was thinking, "Hey, shit. Frankly, I don't want to be here," and for a fleeting moment I just wanted to get the hell out of there. I remember thinking, "There's something wrong with this guy. I want to get the hell out of here." He's coming at us with this weird sort of gait and these black eyes, and there's something wrong with him. He's not listening to us. Let's get the hell out of here, but I knew I couldn't. So, for a fleeting moment we kind of retreat. I realized that, you know, you can't really run away. This is your job. You're going to have to handle it, but I would rather not have been there. Unfortunately that is my job, and I remember having to tell myself, "Susan, this is your job. You have to handle this."*

Thus, despite whatever other identities might have been salient, Susan defined the situation in terms of her occupational identity and eventually invoked the ultimate power of the state, killing the assailant and clearly committing herself to her cop identity, her job, her duty, and her performance of self.

Officers identify with one another as officers, as is evident from the previous examples. However, the cop identity is far from homogeneous. Other identifications combine with occupational identity, dividing officers from one another and binding them in other social affiliations. Even the way that different people took up the identity of "officer" reveals the simultaneity of binding and division. Although the following two officers react differently, both must explicitly manage the social isolation and coercive powers that accompany one's identification with policing. One officer told us during a ride-along,

> When I'm off duty at home, I . . . When we go out to restaurants, I never sit where they put the menu, I always have to sit in certain spots. I have to have a good view of the door, the front door. My back has to be to a corner. It's just a type of . . . it's a lifestyle. And that's what I am is a police officer, and I see people off duty that I've arrested before. A lot of times they don't recognize me without my uniform, but I carry a gun everywhere I go.

He seems unable to abandon, even temporarily, his occupational identity. A second officer relates to her cop identity differently. In field notes after a ride-along with her, one of us wrote,

> She indicated that while going to the university, she found herself deceiving fellow students about her being a police officer. And, even now, while pursuing a Masters Degree, she conceals her identity as a cop. She said that being a cop "tags your identity" in the minds of others. People either really like that you are a cop and want to talk about it, or they instantly distance themselves.

Both officers addressed the issue of how they handled themselves while off duty, but each took a different approach, one being consumed by his cop identity and the other explicitly and intentionally putting it aside when she leaves work.

We locate "officer" as one among many mutually defining subject positions occupied by an "individual." To assume an identity as a police officer is not the same as identifying solely as a cop, nor does it mean that one merely relates to or identifies with other agents of the state. Occupational solidarity does not necessarily denote homogeneity. To "identify as" is not to become "identical to." Instead, we found differences among officers as they are associated with and/or affirm other identity categories.

The Dividing of an Occupation: Other Binds Divide

Like other studies (e.g., Reuss-Ianni 1983), we found some division between street-level officers and the command staff. The timing of our fieldwork was such that we had the opportunity to observe the creation of an association of officers that linked itself to other police and firefighters' unions in the metropolitan area. A very involved officer told us about the union in one of his stories:

> *I guess it started somewhere around '94–'95. A gentleman was hired to do a reclassification study on the police department. . . . Well, as a result of this study, commanders got a raise, lieutenants got a raise and sergeants got a raise. The officers were not given a raise. . . . That, in addition to other problems we were having, caused the officers to say, "Let's get together and discuss what's going on." This time the atmosphere was a lot different. A lot of the officers didn't feel intimidated. There was a lot more things to discuss, and so we held a meeting, and about sixty officers showed up . . .*
>
> *That experience was discussed with the officers at our meeting, and the general feeling was that we need to start a union. We talked to a lot of officers, and we could see that the support was there. We had another meeting, and we decided that yes, we are going to form an association, and we started collecting names of officers who were interested in joining. We collected over a hundred names. Pretty close to a hundred and thirty.*

There was a general division among officers across rank lines in the sense that officers were forming a union that excluded, and perhaps would even be somewhat antagonistic to, command staff. Street-level officers began to identify themselves as different cops from the management team and acted to create an association that excluded cops identified as different from street-level workers.

Other identifications divided officers from one another and bound some to identities that were not occupationally specific. One female officer, for example, told us a story about gender and work:

> *This is definitely an organization where you can pursue opportunities that are available to you, but . . . when I pursued those opportunities, they haven't always been accepted with open arms. And sometimes it would seem that's because I'm a woman. There's been openings that I haven't applied for but that I know other female officers have applied for, for example, within the narcotics division, that they simply won't allow a woman into. Actually, I think a woman could do a fine job as a decoy in a lot of those cases. There's been one person who is a peer of mine, and our careers have pretty much paralleled. We did go for a couple of the same opportunities, whereas maybe he was chosen and I wasn't. I'm not meaning to sound bitter, but after three or four of those kinds of incidents, you've got to kind of wonder what's going on.*

For her, femaleness divided her from other officers, making her a particular kind of officer, able to be differentiated from other officers. She indicated a very high identification with women outside the department as well. She told us in her initial interview, "I tend to . . . gravitate more towards women. I personally like upwardly mobile women. The climbers, the shakers, the movers."

This officer told one of us an anecdote while on a ride-along about how being a female gave her an advantage in some circumstances, helping her identify with and connect to the citizens of her community as a woman more than as an officer. She explained what happened on a domestic violence call where the woman involved was extremely upset but apparently not seriously physically injured. The goal was to get the victim to an inpatient psychiatric treatment facility:

> It's just kind of a matter of who you latch onto first at the scene. And John latched onto the victim, and the other L unit was with somebody else, and I ended up with somebody else. So I never saw the victim. Well, John came out of the room and said she's not going to go to Mercyville voluntarily, you know, so now we have to try to get an emergency medical admission and what have you and I said to him, "Well, John, do you mind if I go in and talk to her?" I didn't want to step on his toes or anything like that. And I think it was simply because I was a woman. I stepped in there, and she instantly related to me, and within two minutes I said to her, "Do you want to go to Mercyville?" and she agreed.

Here, the process of identification binds and divides in complex and fluid ways. The officer was connected to other officers as she arrived at the scene, as demonstrated by her knowledge and willingness to address the situation in "police style"; that is, each officer "latched onto" somebody at the scene and worked as a team to gather information. Even as her gender identity offered a means of connecting with the victim, distance was created between the female officer and her partners.[8]

Race, too, was important to the fabric of identity that divided some officers from others, both on the street and at the station. The matter of race inside the department was addressed very explicitly by one African American officer who wanted the department to become more conscious of racism. Recalling his own experience when he joined the department sixteen years ago, he described the following exchange between himself and another officer:

> *We went to a baseball game, our squad did. . . . And that same officer that I felt had been prejudiced was there. . . . So at the baseball game, it was very apparent he had been drinking a lot. He was becoming very belligerent and loud. After the game, we were walking down the walkway to the parking lot, and he was behind me, and there was another officer from my squad walking side by side with me with his wife. Well, the officer walking behind me, he all of the sudden puts his arm on my right shoulder, and he says to me, "How much money do you have, nigger?" I was shocked, and I turned around to see who it was, and it was this other officer. I pulled my shoulder away from him, and I just kept walking to my car.*

He recognized his difference from the rest of the department: "*I was one of two black officers working in the Glenville Police Department.*" In the rest of the story, he described how he has tried, with little success, to lead his department to hiring a more racially diverse group of officers:

> *I continue to ask, "Why has it taken so long to hire minorities?" . . . After I was hired, ten years later, a third black officer was hired. In those ten years, I continued to ask, "What is the problem? Why can't you find minorities?" The answer was, "We can't find any qualified." I myself was asked to be a recruiter. So I went to a recruitment class the department held and was told that they would send me to college fraternities and various African American associations as a recruiter for the police department. Well, I waited and waited, and pretty close to a year went by and there was nothing.*

Again from this story the theme emerges that identity divides some people from others. This officer's racial affiliation separated him from his fellow officers but bound him to other minority officers, even if they were not African American in particular. Interestingly, there seemed to be an antagonism rather than a connection between the officers of racial minorities (male and female) and white lesbian officers, a point we take up next.

A mainstream view among officers seems to be that recruitment into the ranks is highly selective and determined entirely on the basis of *merit.* The relatively small number of African American and Hispanic police officers in the ranks is believed to be due to a process that judges all applicants *blindly* and *objectively.* Many officers believe that minorities who apply tend to be less qualified than the pool of Anglo applicants. Some hold the view that the department fails to recruit the most qualified minorities. Others take the position that the *ratio* of minorities to the citizenry is roughly equivalent, indicating a difference in perspective as to whether the department should make more of an effort to find *qualified* minorities.

Some of these white male and female officers hold the view that the process of selecting officers is based on individual merit; however, they view the selection process for special assignments units (e.g., narcotics) differently. They take the contradictory position that special assignments are distributed *subjectively,* despite similar testing and oral board procedures. According to a number of them, special assignments are controlled by a "good old boy" network of senior white males with rank. A small number of officers, mostly white males who are part of the senior officer network, routinely circulate across assignments. Describing her struggle to move up in the departmental ranks, one female officer told a story about sexist promotional habits:

> *It does seem that as a woman I have to work a little bit harder to prove myself as far as moving up the ladder around here. . . . Again, in another incident [my peer] was recently promoted. What happened was that there were opportunities, and a letter of interest was put out, and if anybody wanted to apply for the position, they could do so. Several people did. But this particular officer, I feel, was kind of hand chosen before that process even got done.*

In another instance, Officer Bolt, who is young, white, and male, reveals that he, too, felt victimized by a "good old boys" network. He told us during an interview that a lot of the competition for promotion is determined by the good old boys. He went to great extremes, even spending a good deal of his off-duty time making himself the most qualified candidate for a promotion, but the job was given to someone Officer Bolt believed to be less deserving:

He didn't want it as much as me, and that was obvious because of the preparation that he did and that he didn't do. I had a real problem with that, and that gave me a real bad outlook on the department. You know, it's not what you know, it's who you know. It goes beyond the testing policy.

For these newer-to-the-ranks white males and for the female officers hired in the last decade, the hiring process that includes them and excludes most minorities is fair, or based on objective standards, while the process for determining special assignments is unfair, based on subjective judgments of an identity group marked by whiteness, generational difference, and strong occupational bonds.

Male minority officers see the preferences within special assignments as reflective of a larger system of racial discrimination that includes the way the department recruits citizens into the ranks. They view white lesbian officers with suspicion and distance themselves from them because of their judgments about preferential recruitment. Some minority officers define the situation in terms of competition and believe that special efforts have been made to recruit lesbians into the department at the expense of the recruitment of minorities. These officers point to the relatively large investment the department makes in Gay Pride events, by donating time and setting up a recruitment booth that actually generates good contacts, and they compare that investment to efforts to recruit minority officers. Despite a dire need for Spanish-speaking, bicultural officers and the very low number of African Americans on the force, several officers noted that "alternative" recruitment efforts were directed more toward gays and lesbians and less toward people of color. One African American officer actively joined in the recruiting process, hoping to rectify the problem. The following narrative excerpt reflects a certain cynicism and frustration:

As far as the recruitment at the university career day, I felt that was a waste because they have our booth next to top law enforcement agencies, like FBI or Big City Police Department, and then you have other companies not in law enforcement nearby, like the big engineering companies. And the whole time I was there maybe five minorities stopped by, just to pick up a brochure to look at. I never once got to address the African American groups and fraternities on campus. . . . I think I did it about three times, and each time I did it, I came away with the feeling that this is a waste. The recruitment is not being done right.

Inclusions and Exclusions on the Streets and in the Hallways

Not only did racial identity divide officers within the ranks, but race seemed to matter on the street as well. The following stories reveal the particularized classifications embedded in cop decision making and how these identifications affirm the citizenship of some while simultaneously excluding others from membership. In a case involving a working-class Hispanic man who confessed to dealing marijuana, officers disagreed about how to proceed. Two of the man's marijuana affiliates came to his house to rob and kill him. Because he was larger than his assailant, Francisco was able to grab the assailant's gun and fire shots at them. The Hispanic officer[9] telling us the story felt that "*Francisco had been through enough. Francisco had been traumatized, upset, fearful for his life, and he was just defending himself. Period.*" He had every right to shoot. He wanted no charges to be brought against Francisco regarding either his drug violations or his unsafe firing of a gun.

The marijuana business is dismissed as a class problem, the officer assuming that Francisco was selling pot to "make ends meet." Perhaps the male requirement to provide for one's family may also have been integral to the officer's recognizing an aspect of himself in Francisco:

> *He had a wife and a baby and wasn't able to make ends meet. So he started dealing small amounts of marijuana. . . . Francisco was just doing the best he could. These were terrible burdens he had on his back, for a twenty-eight-year-old guy. He also had his little sister living with him. She was still in high school. I'm not sure where the parents were, but he was raising his little sister. He had a little brother living with him, and his brother was in high school. He had a little family situation set up there, and he was trying to make ends meet. I've seen people that have worked hard during their lifetimes, like Francisco had.*

The supervisors did not share the officer's desire to not file charges on Francisco. The officer himself points to the intersection of race, ethnicity, and class in narrating the discrepancy of opinion: "*The supervisors were adamant that Francisco be arrested. I didn't care for that idea. I think to them, Francisco was seen as a semi-literate Hispanic. These were white supervisors making the decision.*" The officer identifies with Francisco as a hard-working Chicano trying to make ends meet. At the same time, he distances himself from his fellow officers, suggesting the permeability and tenuousness of his professional identity. On the street, the salience of other subject positions surfaces as paramount. Identification with the "Other" becomes a crucial factor in the officer's definition of self, even as such identification, and the exceptionalism it engenders, binds Francisco to the officer as an agent of the state.

The story of Francisco is, in part, about police exceptionalism in which coercive powers are withheld to benefit a citizen occupying marginal cultural space. The officer's *bonding* with Francisco is sufficiently entangled that he risks severe consequences for overlooking charges that superiors expected him to file. On the face of it, he seems to act contrary to his self-interest. But this is also a story about the construction of a political subject, Francisco, who receives his *just deserts* because he exhibits a work ethic and family commitment that enfolds him—along with the officer as subject—into the mainstream fabric of sociocultural (hard-working immigrant) and normative orderings (just deserts). The benevolence of the cops is foregrounded by the officer as state agent, and yet his categorization of those who tried to rob and kill Francisco as "criminal" marks them as particularly requiring coercive police action. The officer describes "Steve," one of the "bad guys," in the following manner:

> *Steve . . . deserves trouble. He had been involved in other shootings. Steve had told another homicide detective before that he was untouchable because his family was judicial. [In a different incident] he pulled up to a stop sign and ran it and saw some people from another car with a gun. They started shooting at him with high-capacity 9 millimeters. Steve seemed to have*

nine lives. One went across him and hit his girlfriend in the face, and eventually she wound up with paralysis and nerve damage. His brother was hit twice in the back of the head in the back seat. . . . You'd think that he'd go to the hospital. Not Steve. Steve drives down the street, parks the vehicle, and goes to a safe place and starts changing tires. He's got two bleeding people in his car, and he's changing tires.

The following excerpts from one lieutenant's story highlight the importance of identity in defining an individual as criminal:

We have an officer who had a domestic violence situation. I don't want to go into what it was about, but they were having domestic problems. . . . They were in the process of getting a divorce, and things were not going well. There was a very young child involved in it. He [the officer] was just losing it. He made a series of phone calls. Not a good idea, granted. She, of course, filed a police report in Jefferson City. He winds up being charged [and convicted] with making harassing phone calls. Well, she gets linked up with, of all people, an ex-convict, which is not like his thing to decide, but that's who's raising his son now. And his son is still involved, and they're still trying to write the visitation issues. And he starts yelling at her . . . and the next thing you know they're in a big argument in which our officer is probably the aggressor. There's no physical contact or anything, it's just loud. So, they wanted to file a complaint. Now he's convicted again. What do we do with this guy? Two convictions now. Two convictions on a police officer. Is this about his ability to be a police officer, or is this about his broken heart? Wait a minute, let's just put this in the proper perspective. I'm saying this is not a professional issue. It's a personal issue. How is he a police officer when he's convicted of these things? When he comes here, he's a police officer. Well, if we can say about a month after this thing is dealt with that he winds up at a call where he saves somebody's life, then we save face, too. Interesting, eh?

What is compelling about this story is that two men—the divorcing officer and the woman's new boyfriend, both convicted of lawbreaking—are identified quite differently by this lieutenant. One is an "ex-convict" who is a source of frustration, in part, because his status as a convicted criminal throws into question his ability to raise a child. In contrast, the *officer's* convictions are the result of a "broken heart," a "personal" rather than "professional" problem. The ex-husband's indignation at having an "ex-convict" raise his son is legitimated by the lieutenant's telling of the story. In this way, the officer's identity as a cop protected him from the social stigma that accompanies being identified by the cops as a criminal. He remains an agent of the state while his subject position is constituted as a troubled worker in *need* of help. State administrative apparatuses, as manifested in the story by the lieutenant, are presented as caring for one of its workers while, at the same time, the territory of coercive engagement is marked in the referencing of another individual as an "ex-con," as the opposite of the deserving cop.

As a final example of the simultaneity of binding and dividing, we turn to the large group of lesbians who work in the Glenville Police Department. Because her partner required surgery and aftercare, a lesbian officer, whom we will call Ann, approached her lieutenant who is also lesbian and requested a family emergency leave day, a paid day reserved for "family" emergencies. The lieutenant recounted the incident, opening with Ann's position:

> *"I think the right thing for us to do is that I should be afforded the same opportunities toward emergency leave for a family situation as others in this agency are allowed to do . . ." [Ann] reminded me by way of example. A sergeant had just recently married, maybe four or five years ago. She said, "Here we have a sergeant who's been married four or five years, and he recently took family emergency leave for something. Who knows what it is. Well, I'm here to tell you that me and my partner have been together for over nine years, so I have been involved in a domestic relationship for longer than even this guy, and he gets the pay benefits. Why shouldn't I?" I said, "You're right. You're absolutely right."*

Ann argued her case successfully and got the paid day by defining her family situation as similar to another individual officer who is a member of a straight family. The lieutenant accepted this definition. Thus, like the male officer in the department, her subordinate was entitled to the benefit. At its core, Ann's argument uses the logic that she, as an officer, should be entitled to the same city benefits that other officers—and one in particular—received, binding her to other officers as a whole and one male officer specifically, for the political end of getting benefits. At the same time, however, making explicit that she is homosexual simultaneously divides her from the exemplified officer as well as from other officers, producing a binary between heterosexual and gay and lesbian officers.

Conclusion

Our analysis suggests that cops' identities as cops are strong even as officers find different ways to manage their occupational identities. Several of the narratives suggest that occupational identity defines, indeed trumps, other reactions. For example, one of the officers told a story about his inability to abandon, even temporarily, his occupational identity. Even when off duty and at a restaurant with his spouse, he would always sit so as to have a good view of the front door. A female officer's story of killing an assailant is deeply interwoven with her marking this event as the point of realization about the salience of her cop identity. Other stories reveal the strength of the bonds among officers, including a strong tendency of cops to withhold their coercive powers when dealing with other citizen-cops, as revealed in the story about the police officer who was "the aggressor" in a series of family violence incidents.

Nevertheless, different officers live their occupational identities differently. For example, contrast the way of the cop who always positions himself to see the front door in a restaurant with the cop who conceals her identity as a police officer while attending a university. Viewing officers' decision making through the lens of identity suggests that cops inhabit a variety of subject positions, some of which undermine and destabilize their professional identity while others reinforce it. On the one hand, this dynamism stems from the diversification and transformation of a formerly white, male, mostly working-class profession. Heterogeneity disrupts the domain of officer discretion, increasing the potential for conflict and opening up the possibility for different types of affiliations and identifications. To view police culture as cohesive obscures the diversity of practices, homogenizes identity, and reifies culture. On the other hand, cops' unique relationship to the state and citizenry plays a crucial role in the constitution of their identity and identifications. Officers' beneficence and exceptionalism may reinforce rather than fracture dominant identity tropes, such as "white middle-class lesbianism," and bolster norms central to the liberal state, such as "individual just deserts." Cops reposition themselves as agents of the state apparatus, relying on a range of subject positions and thus counteracting any simple categorical definition of police culture or behavior. In so doing, they may, ironically, reinforce the legitimacy of policing. The more greatly varied range of subject positions on which police officers routinely draw endorses and serves a more greatly varied range of citizenry who legitimate the state and its police even as they are legitimated and constituted as state subjects.

Cops are part of an organizational culture, but "different individuals . . . possess different amounts and types of cultural resources" (Herbert 1998, 346). Our identity framework embraces the sociology of culture that treats culture as particular, fractured, and contingent (Garfinkel 1967; Swindler 1986; Gamson 1992; Sewell 1992). It builds on those works specific to police culture that depict cop decision making as "both guided and improvisational" (Shearing and Ericson 1991, 500; see also Van Maanen 1978; Manning 1989) and that recognize that "while coherence is at times obvious in the police world . . . conflict is also always present" (Herbert 1997, 146).[10]

Among those embracing this view of policing, Steve Herbert (1997) shows that police officers employ a web of "normative orders," each representing "a set of rules and practices centered on a primary value" (4). He uncovers six normative orderings at work—law, bureaucratic control, adventure/machismo, safety, competence, and morality—and argues that conflicts arise among officers over which set of rules and practices should be used in what street contexts (Herbert 1998, 361–64). Herbert's framework, grounded in space and territoriality, is illuminating, but it gives limited insight into how cops manage their conflicts over norms and the contexts that seem to invite police officers to use one normative order over another—"Just which order, or combination of orders, will capture a particular officer's allegiance at any given time eludes prediction" (Herbert 1997, 171).

Our work suggests that the invocation of norms is strongly bundled with processes of identification. How cops identify with one another and the people they encounter on the streets is wrapped up or ontologically interwoven with the norms they invoke. At times, cops rely on crude categorizations, denying the uniqueness of individuals and enfolding them into social categories already marked for exclusion and the invocation of coercion (e.g., homeless vs. home owner, illegal alien vs. citizen). Indeed, some report that cops have become more skilled in constructing these categories through the invocation of a discourse of war and in using paramilitary strategies to enforce the boundaries that they themselves have been active agents in constructing (see Fishman 1978; Zatz 1987; Ericson 1991; Welch, Fenwick, and Roberts 1998).

Our research suggests a more complex relationship between cops and citizens that the existing literature intimates (see Manning 1977; Crank 1998). Professional identity is divided rather than a unitary construct; accordingly, the complexity of identification sometimes generates connections across this division. Rather than a rigid us/them dichotomy, one inherently dividing citizens from officers, we found that a variety of subject positions, including gender, race, and class, may distance officers from one another as well as connecting officers and citizens. Through the dynamics of connection and identification, officers sometimes withhold their coercive powers, defining themselves in relation to citizens with equally complex identity structures. While it may be impossible to predict an officer's allegiances since they are context specific, we can understand how such affiliations impact the lives and shape the identities of the individuals involved.

In the late twentieth century, police officers' identification with citizens may be crucial to stabilizing their own identity as both citizens and agents of the state. Our observations highlight a constitutive dynamic, as diversification of the rank and file couples with the fragile, multiple, and context-specific activation of people's identities. On the basis of our observations, we suggest that attending to the particularities of individuals may be crucial to staving off group conflict and providing some semblance of cohesiveness among cops.

Generally, police officers are cautious when they make judgments about citizens' representations of their own culpability, even as they are influenced by their verbal presentation of self and physical appearance. A citizen's performance of self in combination with an officer's may generate identifications that defy the logic of binary opposites. For instance, interpretations of the actions taken by Francisco (the sympathetic, pot-dealing character) were mitigated by identity (dis)connections. Police officers' actions may also set them apart from others, revealing that police are, indeed, adept at classifications and the deployment and reinforcement of political rationality. Francisco's assailants are constructed as citizens gone awry, as violent, dangerous criminals. Accordingly, the full force of police coercion is applied. It is important to place these moments of connection and division in context. Police officers enforce these binaries routinely, and they also actively undermine them, reconstructing them anew. They police identities and, in so doing, engage in the technology of state formation and legitimation. Privileging the particularities of some citizens while simultaneously revealing the particularities of their own identities may enable cops to generate necessary support from the diversity of middle-class communities occupying contemporary urban space who are crucial materially and culturally to the sustenance of municipal police administration.

Notes

The original version of this chapter appeared in *Law and Social Inquiry* (vol. 24, no. 4 [fall 1999]). Copyright 1999 American Bar Foundation. The research related to this chapter was supported by a National Science Foundation Grant, Law and Social Sciences Program, grant number SBR-9511169.

1. In tracing the genealogy of police and policing in France and Germany, Foucault (1988) shows that the term "police" from the sixteenth century on referred to the entire state administrative apparatus and "policing" to the full range of state administrative activities (154–55). While the naming of agencies of the state has become more specified and the numbers of state agencies have proliferated from the eighteenth century on in the West, we take the long view that policing remains the task of all state agencies or, in Foucault's words, "what the police are concerned with is [people's] coexistence in a territory, their relationships to property, what they produce, what is exchanged in the market, and so on" (155). We focus on the activities of officers in a contemporary police agency while anticipating that they, like their counterparts in other state agencies (e.g., welfare offices), are attendant to the full range of tasks outlined by Foucault in his essay "The Political Technology of Individuals." Currently, in collaboration with others, we are conducting parallel research in other state agencies, including a public school and two agencies that deal with vocational rehabilitation.

2. Identification takes place in at least two directions: We identify ourselves and act ac-

cordingly, and we are also identified by others according to how we act/appear. The act of identification in either direction can be more or less rigid. (This is particularly clear in the example of defining "homosexuality"; see Halley 1993.) Subjects can identify themselves and others more or less according to stereotyped images that flatten identities and make rigid what is permeable. In this sense, rigid identifiers are not unlike stereotypes.

3. The work of Shearing and Ericson has been important in challenging the prevailing views that police officers' decision making is structured by an externalized body of rules and/or that some fixed "police culture" produces "informal" rules that the officers then follow. Rather, they see the police as "active participants in the construction of action" and view police culture as "gambits and strategies" rather than some organic whole. Building on Shearing and Ericson, we think that the multiplicity and fluidity of identities provides insight into how police construct action and constitute cultures of policing. We elaborate on this view and relate it to the police literature in this chapter's conclusion.

4. Throughout this chapter, the actual words of officers appear in two formats. Excerpts from interviews, where an officer is simply answering a question or making an observation, are set in roman type. Excerpts from stories, however, appear in italics to mark that they were somewhat more crafted both by us as we moved the words from a spoken to a written format and also by officers who were given an opportunity to read and revise the stories they had told.

5. Our intention is not to be reductionist. While our focus is on describing how identity shapes action, certainly we recognize that the actions in the stories are not purely identity driven. For example, Steve Herbert (1997, 1998) shows how territory and space define the action norms that police officers invoke when working the streets. Situational factors of all kinds have a hand in the outcomes.

6. Italics indicate excerpts from the stories.

7. For theoretical support, compare Althusser (1991).

8. This is not to suggest that being a cop can be completely separated from being female or vice versa, merely that various qualities of membership are highlighted in varying intensities.

9. The Hispanic officer defined himself as "working class" in conversations with us and in interview sessions with him. In fact, several of the officers in the two squads asserted a working-class identity, to our surprise. They chose the territory of their squads in part because it is inhabited by other "working Joes." They referenced other space as alien to their self-identity—affluent neighborhoods full of professionals, doctors, lawyers, and scientists—and viewed many calls from such areas as "petty."

10. Shearing and Ericson critique the scholarship on police officer decision making that presumes action follows rules, even those who have posited the importance of local rules devised at the organizational level and modified by what is often referenced as the "police subculture" (see Manning 1977, 1989). Scholars have long recognized that there is a "culture" of policing but are divided over what "culture" means in this context (for an overview, see Crank 1998) and vague as to how culture shapes cops' decision making. Even when scholars have observed the centrality of officers' stories to the "craft" of policing (see Bayley and Bittner 1984), there is a great reluctance to privilege the power of this form of communication as constitutive of the practical reasoning of cops or local culture, in part because police scholars themselves embrace the importance of rule-driven decision making to liberal democracy. The significance of stories to understanding normativity and action is well recognized today in sociolegal studies (e.g., Conley and O'Barr 1998; Ewick and Silbey 1998) and in policy inquiry (e.g., Schram and Neisser 1997). We embrace these writings as well as the early groundbreaking work of Shearing and Ericson that is specific to policing and suggest that cops' stories reveal the importance of identity and identification to their practical reasoning. While others have invoked

the importance of "social" identities to understanding policing (see Crank 1998, 5), only a very few have taken up identities (see, e.g., the classic study of "the asshole" by Van Maanan 1978), particularly reflective of current thinking about the meaning of identity and how identities are acted out in the everyday.

References

Althusser, Louis. 1991. "Ideology and State Ideological Apparatuses (Notes toward an Investigation)." In Ben Brewster, trans., *Lenin and Philosophy, and Other Essays,* 121–73. London: New Left Books.

Bayley, David, and Egon Bittner. 1984. "Learning the Skills of Policing." *Law and Contemporary Problems* 47: 35–59.

Butler, Judith. 1990. *Gender Trouble: Feminism and the Subversion of Identity.* New York: Routledge.

———. 1992. "Contingent Foundations: Feminism and the Question of Postmodernism." In Judith Butler and Joan W. Scott, eds., *Feminists Theorize the Political* (3–21). New York: Routledge.

Conley, John, and William O'Barr. 1998. *Just Words: Law, Language, and Power (Language and Legal Discourse).* Chicago: University of Chicago Press.

Crank, John P. 1998. *Understanding Police Culture.* Cincinnati: Anderson Publishing.

Ericson, Richard. 1991. *Representing Order: Crime, Law and Justice in the News Media.* Toronto: University of Toronto Press.

Ewick, Patricia, and Susan Silbey. 1998. *The Common Place of Law: Stories from Everyday Life.* Chicago: University of Chicago Press.

Fishman, Mark. 1978. "Crime Waves as Ideology." *Social Problems* 25: 531–43.

Foucault, Michel. 1988. "The Political Technology of Individuals." In Luther H. Martin, Huck Gutman, and Patrick H. Hutton, eds., *Technologies of the Self* (145–62). Amherst: University of Massachusetts Press.

Gamson, William. 1992. *Talking Politics.* New York: Cambridge University Press.

Garfinkel, Harold. 1967. *Studies in Ethnomethodology.* Englewood Cliffs, N.J.: Prentice Hall.

Hall, Stuart. 1996. "Introduction: Who Needs Identity?" In Stuart Hall and Paul du Gay, eds., *Questions of Cultural Identity* (1–17). London: Sage Press.

Halley, Janet M. 1993. "The Construction of Heterosexuality." In Michael Warner, ed., *Fear of a Queer Planet* (82–104). Minneapolis: University of Minnesota Press.

Herbert, Steve. 1997. *Policing Space: Territoriality and the Los Angeles Police Department.* Minneapolis: University of Minnesota Press.

———. 1998. "Police Subculture Reconsidered." *Criminology* 36: 343–69.

Manning, Peter. 1977. *Police Work.* Cambridge, Mass.: MIT Press.

———. 1989. "Occupational Culture." In William Bailey, ed., *The Encyclopedia of Police Science.* New York: Garland.

Mouffe, Chantal. 1995. "Democratic Politics and the Question of Identity." In John Rajchman, ed., *The Identity in Question* (33–46). New York: Routledge.

Reuss-Ianni, Elizabeth. 1983. *Two Cultures of Policing: Street Cops and Management Cops.* New Brunswick, N.J.: Transaction Books.

Salecl, Renata. 1994. "The Crisis of Identity and the Struggle for New Hegemony in the Former Yugoslavia." In Ernesto Laclau, ed., *The Making of Political Identity* (205–32). London: Verso.

Schram, Sanford, and Phillip Neisser. 1997. "Introduction to Tales of the State." In *Tales of the*

State: Narrative in Contemporary U.S. Politics and Public Policy (1–14). Oxford: Rowman & Littlefield Publishers.

Sewell, William. 1992. "A Theory of Structure: Duality, Agency and Transformation." *American Journal of Sociology* 98: 1–29.

Shearing, Clifford D., and Richard V. Ericson. 1991. "Culture as Figurative Action." *British Journal of Sociology* 42: 481–506.

Swindler, Ann. 1986. "Culture in Action: Symbols and Strategies." *American Sociological Review* 51: 273–86.

Van Maanen, John. 1978. "The Asshole." In John Van Maanen and Peter Manning, eds., *Policing: A View from the Street* (221–38). Santa Monica, Calif.: Goodyear Publishing.

Welch, Michael, Melissa Fenwick, and Merideth Roberts. 1998. "State Managers, Intellectuals and the Media: A Context Analysis of Ideology in Experts' Quotes in Feature Newspaper Articles on Crime." *Justice Quarterly* 15: 219–42.

West, Cornel. 1995. "A Matter of Life and Death." In John Rajchman, ed., *The Identity in Question* (33–46). New York: Routledge.

Zatz, Marjorie. 1987. "Chicano Youth Gangs and Crime: The Creation of a Moral Panic." *Contemporary Crises* 2: 129–58.

11

Nuancing Anti-Essentialism

A CRITICAL GENEALOGY OF PHILIPPINE EXPERIMENTS IN NATIONAL IDENTITY FORMATION

S. Lily Mendoza

The effect of a theoretical encounter between . . . cultural politics and the discourses of a Eurocentric, largely white, critical cultural theory . . . is always an extremely difficult, if not dangerous, encounter . . .

. . . Once you abandon essential categories, there is no place to go apart from the politics of criticism and to enter the politics of criticism in [any] culture is to grow up, to leave the age of critical innocence.

—HALL 1996C, 443, 448

An early edition of *Reinventing the Filipino Sense of Being and Becoming* (Azurin 1993) opens one of its essays with a curious illustration. A ruthless tyrant (identified allegorically as "*Ignorancia*") brandishes a whip of multiple cords and is shown lashing a throng of people into disciplinary submission (214). Inscribed on each of the whip's cords are the words "Fakelore," "Nativism," "Postmodernism," and "Op. cit., Loc. cit." (the last one, I surmise, referring to the penchant in the Philippine academy for constantly referencing foreign authorities as a legitimating practice). Unlabeled on his tyrant's whip but similarly identified in the text as serving a needless mystifying purpose is "post-colonialism," one of many discourses imported wholesale from their Euro-American origins by returning Filipino scholars (or those simply up to date in that part of the world).

Humorous if crude (the 1995 edition no longer carries it), the illustration places center stage the author's concern for how certain discourses that are meant to serve a sense-making function in the form of historical analyses of cultural texts in fact may be experienced as oppressive by a people struggling for ways to constitute themselves into active, choosing subjects. This is especially so when discourses ordering such texts and their reading are based on dubious assumptions and contextually ill-fitting frameworks of analysis. Azurin warns that we would do well to be wary of them.

I begin with this reference not to rehash the reductionist debates on the virtues of "indigenous" compared to "foreign" theorizing, as they have sometimes been framed. This Azurin himself avoids, even as he spares no one in his critique, including those whose perspectives come from within (the nation),[1] when in his estimation these fail to use adequate historical analysis. Rather, what I am interested in is a more complex issue, one that has to do with the link between cultural politics and intellectual practice. I am concerned here with theorizing across contexts[2] and what that entails in terms of articulating theory originating in one context to another in ways that can productively inform instead of coming across as one more alien(ating) disciplinary imposition onto subjects unable to perceive its relevance and usefulness to their particular situation. Conversely, I am interested in encouraging a way of reading cultural politics that precludes a prejudging or forcible fitting of phenomena into preexisting theoretical frameworks, one that allows instead for cultural politics to contribute to the refinement or enlargement of the scope and usefulness of the latter (theory). In other words, I want to find ways of making theory and context speak to, and mutually inform, each other.

Coming out of the Philippine academy, traditionally at the short—that is, receiving—end of the theoretical exchange relation with the West, I have much to say about the primacy of context. Context matters not only for the sake of sharpening theoretical insight but also in recognizing at once the limits and contingency of theory as well as the widest range of possibilities for its application. Power, then, is an implicit theme in this discussion. In asserting and insisting on contextual sensitivity as a requisite for more adequate theorizing, I want to prevent precisely the making invisible of that theoretical contingency, to preclude the unwitting hegemonization of any one discourse (no matter how potentially liberating within its originary context) into a new theoretic universal without taking care to define, or, at least, to be aware at all times of, the contextual limits and requirements of its applicability elsewhere. For how many times has the uncritical, un-self-reflexive stance of some rabid advocates of certain theoretical positions served unwittingly to blunt the cutting-edge potential of many a radical critique by their (often unintended) sweeping, unqualified claims and posturing?

I am thinking in particular of the radical insights of deconstructive theory and how these can be articulated in ways that can transform the politics of social movements working for change in a variety of contexts. This is important to address in view of my suspicion that those who would most benefit in their struggle from such a theoretical perspective tend also to feel the most threatened by it.[3] They thereby miss out on its potential contribution in their rejection of its premises. Given my own stake in this dialogue,[4] I am particularly curious to find out, for instance, how a movement for decolonization (e.g., the indigenization movement in the Philippine academy) that has traditionally operated on essentialist politics can be framed or understood differently. Can one employ in this context the perspective of radical anti-essentialism without having the movement lose its motive power or, worse, have its gains in the realm of cultural practice and politics completely reversed or unraveled by the deconstructive critique? Can an anti-essentialist framework go beyond deconstruction and speak to the reconstitution of (national) identities that can compel unity among a historically fractured, marginalized, multiethnic people? Can it move them toward a vision of a common future without erasure of difference or reinscription of hierarchy? On the other hand, is there anything in a properly contextualized reading of the cultural practices and politics of specific social movements that can nuance the articulation of anti-essentialism as a theoretical framework? And to do it so as to increase its likelihood of being effective in contributing to the emancipatory goal(s) of these movements? Considering that no idea, no matter how radical, can be expected to make a significant impact without its successful articulation to popular culture, how must radical anti-essentialism be reframed or articulated differently so as to make its complex philosophical perspective more accessible to the popular imagination?

I propose that a lot of the quarrel between the practical politics of social movements on the one hand and the discourse of anti-essentialism on the other can be mitigated by two factors: by context-sensitive translation and receptor-oriented rearticulation and re-reading of both sides' positions and perspectives. I hope here to use insights from linguistic translation theory and cross-cultural communication to clear space for a more productive dialogue between these two "texts." For a specific context for discussion, the indigenization movement in the Philippine academy with its anti-colonialist agenda will be used as a primary reference point for engaging the discourse on anti-essentialism.

Minimizing the Static through Dynamic Equivalence Translation

There is a way of speaking theoretically that unwittingly essentializes. In trite cross-cultural communication parlance, this is what happens when the receptor context is neglected or ignored and articulation fails to recast the "message" (theory) from its "original" encoding in the source "language" (or epistemic context) into that of the target receptor. This failure produces nothing more than a direct formalistic or literal transfer of concepts from one signifying system to another without adequately preserving meaning in translation. The same phenomenon may occur in the reading or decoding of a text articulated in one language (or signifying system) and read or interpreted by someone coming from another linguistic, cultural, or historical milieu or context. When the reader attends only to the individual surface codes[5] without awareness of the complex system of signification to which they belong and that alone provides clues as to their adequate interpretation, the resulting interpretation can become narrowly ethnocentric. Here, the reader extracts those surface codes from their source context and interprets them using her own frame of reference as an all-around universal(izing) grid against which all else is judged or interpreted.

Within (linguistic) translation theory, this approach to transcultural[6] communication is known as the "formal correspondence" model (cf. discussion in Nida and Taber 1969). Now largely discredited as severely inadequate, it is premised on nineteenth-century nominalist views of the nature of languages originating in Platonic and Aristotelian philosophy that see different linguistic systems merely as alternative codes made up of different sets of labels but expressive of the same unchanging reality (Steinfatt 1989). Thus, all that is required in translation is finding the surface-level linguistic forms or literal codes in the target language that *form*alistically correspond to (and therefore easily, even immediately, are taken to be "accurate" translations of) those used in the source language.

This rather unproblematic view of what it takes to engage diverse contexts in the communication of ideas or concepts may be found in all kinds of (signifying) systems that utilize a mechanistic and static approach to translation. One example is the objectivist framing in legal systems of abstract notions of justice and fairness where a uniform rendering of the law, regardless of the differing situational variables in specific cases, is taken to be the only "proper" interpretation of what it means to be "impartial" and "egalitarian."[7] Within certain academic disciplines (e.g., communication), the same tendency toward static formalism can be noted in the behaviorist orientation of early social scientific theorizing. Here, notions of (communicative) competence and effectiveness tend to get reduced to a set of codified rules and norms based on an assumed common universal human nature. (Incidentally, this has the summary effect of largely removing all that is human from human communication, save for its most machine-like or habit-conditioned aspects.) More generally, one finds the same logic operating in the representational view of "Truth" and "Reality" in traditional social science—one that presupposes the givenness and transparency of social phenomena without the necessary mediation of the social construction process in its explication and comprehension. Research findings become simply "statements of fact," pure descriptions of the "nature" of things as such, regardless of the viewer and without taking into consideration the background set of constitutive conditions and practices, which is what lends the social its natural(ized) appearance in the first place (cf. Bourdieu's [1977] notion of "habitus" and Gramsci's [1971] concept of "hegemony").

Closer to home, within cross-cultural theorizing, an example of this reductive mode of transculturation is the swiftness with which all dispositions to indigenization, regardless of context and historical specificities, tend to get easily dismissed or dubbed as nothing more than "a reinscription of binary oppositions (between the colonial and the indigenous)," "the romanticism of the 'vernacular' and 'nativist' turn," or simply "dangerous essentialist moves that can only lead to exclusionary politics." This reading is based mainly on dominant understandings of the term "indigenization" within the U.S. discourse on identities. Here, owing to the differing historical and political specificities obtaining in this context, the term "indigenization" tends to carry other connotations and political baggage not necessarily inherent in its use in those other contexts where its invocation happens to turn on a range of contrasting strategic political goals and purposes. Such dismissive hermeneutical tendencies[8] (and this I have experienced firsthand on many different occasions in my sojourn here in the U.S. academy) have the effect of immediately stopping conversation. It is like being clobbered on the head at the first sign of what is considered "theoretical incorrectness" by whoever is the more powerfully positioned reader even before one is fully understood. This automatic ascribing of the same meanings to the same label, concept, or terminology (regardless of its differing functions, connotations, and implications in alternative contexts) renders static and fixes theoretic formulations (including, as will be shown later, the discourse on radical anti-essentialism), turning them into essentialized (and essentializing) universal propositions that then get slapped onto all kinds of phenomena regardless. Here we have perhaps another form of canonizing move to police all theoretical deviations and thus bring them into line.

An alternative to this static conception of the translation process is the "dynamic equivalence" model (cf. Nida and Taber 1969). Paving the way for this new conception of what is involved in translation is the advent in linguistic science (consistent with Saussurean semiotics) of the Sapir-Whorf linguistic relativity hypothesis.[9] Here linguistic codes are not merely expressive, but *actually constitutive,* of conceptual understandings and meanings in different cultures. As such, they are not mechanically or unproblematically interchangeable between languages given that

> people of different cultures, speaking different languages, are not simply attaching different linguistic labels to elements of the same real world but are actually operating in terms of *different* [linguistic] *realities.* (Kraft 1979, 288)

To translate (or even to read) across contexts or cultures, then, requires the mediation of context-sensitive analysis and understanding of both the source's and the receptor's epistemic contexts in order to establish roughly equivalent meanings for individual codes. In other words, one is no longer just searching for the corresponding code in the other language expressive of the same concept in the source language (since no such exact correspondence exists between languages) but rather

> doing whatever must be done (including a certain amount of explanatory paraphrase . . .) in order to [rearticulate] the message originally phrased in the words and idioms of the source language . . . in the *functionally equivalent* words and idioms of the receptor language. (Kraft 1979, 272; italics added)

Within this new conception of languages, the traditional distinction between a "paraphrase" and a strict "translation" disappears, with the former (which, by definition, requires precisely an *alteration of the forms* in order to convey a functionally equivalent "message" within the logic of the target receptor language) now becoming the norm in linguistic translation. As Kraft (1979) makes clear in this regard, "Whatever of paraphrase must (because of the requirements of the target language and culture) be included in the translation to make it equivalently intelligible and impactful is legitimately to be called 'translation' . . . [and] should not be dismissed as 'mere paraphrase' . . . or italicized as if it were optional matter inserted at the whim of the translator" (272).

What implications can be drawn from these insights in linguistic theory for the translation of theory or the process of theorizing across contexts? Some caveats are called for. One is the need to take cognizance of the fact that individual codes[10] come in systems and take on meaning only within the signifying system to which they belong. Extracting them therefore from their source contexts and reading or assessing them from the standpoint of a generalized criterion or a framework imbues them with other meanings or connotations that may not have been intended in their originary context, for instance, concluding that the ethnic cleansing occurring in Bosnia is, theoretically speaking, of a piece with the decolonization movement, say, in the Philippines since both operate on the same assertion or valuing of (essential) ethnic indigeneity. Notice that there is in this kind of indiscriminate conflation of the two phenomena made, ironically, on the basis of an essentializing application of the discourse of anti-essentialism, a presumption or expectation of an identical end result of their political momentum—the senseless violence of a fratricidal war.[11] What is missing in this essentializing analysis is a "radical historicization" (or in communication/translation parlance, "radical contextualization") of each phenomenon (Hall 1996b, 4) so that each is first understood on its own terms prior to cross-contextual comparison. This alone is what allows for a more dynamic (processual) and less deterministic theoretical linking of the two nationalizing imperatives. Furthermore, using the framework of dynamic equivalence transculturation, we may want to ask, What conditions could be fueling the two movements and are accounting for the rabid invocation of essentialist self-definitions in each particular context? As Hall (1996b) proposes, a more productive question to ask in this regard might be, "[I]n relation to what set of problems [by way of assessing the function served by the invocation of identity politics within each historicized context] does the *irreducibility* of the concept, identity, emerge?" (2). In other words, what does the invoking of essential identities do for the respective movements, and how does it articulate to the movements' emancipatory agenda? Is there a way that the same end or agenda could be served just as well (or even better) using non-essentialist ways of constituting identities? If so, how does one work for the replacement of one form of politics with another without being perceived to undermine the whole movement's agenda, which, theoretically, appears to rest on an essentialist view of identities?

In the section that follows, I tease out potential answers to these questions in relation to the specific case of the indigenization movement in the Philippine academy.

The Indigenization Movement in the Philippine Academy: An Overview[12]

The indigenization movement in the Philippine academy appears to have developed from different sectors of the intelligentsia enthused by a nationalist[13] imperative. Its roots are traceable to a long tradition of resistance movements, first, against centuries of Spanish and, subsequently, of American colonial domination of the Philippines. Despite this long nationalist tradition and the country's observance of its centennial in 1998 (the Philippine Republic being hailed as the first independent republic to be founded in Asia[14]), a systematic undoing of more than four centuries of the colonial legacy[15] of epistemic violence does not appear until the later 1970s. Since colonial domination was secured most effectively through installing a colonial system of education,[16] the academy became the logical site for contestation and critical intervention by Filipino nationalist intellectuals.

The project to undo colonization began mainly as a contest over historical representation and interpretation. From the late 1950s to the 1970s, Filipino nationalist scholars saw it as their primary task to rectify what they considered to be gross and systematic distortions in the colonial historical narratives meant to secure the colonial order. Examples include the denial that there ever was a strong and sustained anti-colonial revolutionary tradition among Filipinos and the consequent dismissal of the now well-documented widespread popular uprisings throughout the colonial era as nothing more than sporadic outbreaks or aberrations in what were otherwise "peaceful civilizing missions" by Spain and America. Such revolutionary uprisings were alternately depicted as the demented riotings of weak-minded individuals cracking up under the strain and stress of culture change, the greedy opportunism of ordinary "bandits" and "criminals," or else the misguided zeal of uneducated, ignorant, and irrational "troublemakers" who knew nothing of the civilized rule of law. In addition, assimilationist and reform-minded members of the elite class were hailed as the "true Filipino heroes" along with the promotion of the image of Americans as "benevolent saviors," "benefactors," and "allies." These, among many other, glaring factual distortions and deliberate misrepresentations were to remain firmly lodged in the Filipino popular imagination for years to come.

Historiography played a significant part in initially uncovering the exercise of surveillance identified as the true motive behind the brand of knowledge production under colonial conquest. The blatantly racist/colonialist discourse formed the implicit epistemological base of the academic disciplines introduced in the Philippine educational system during the colonial era. The goal of such discourse was to secure compliance, loyalty, and the willing self-subjection of a people via the internalization of their ascribed helplessness, ignorance, immaturity, and sheer lack of humanity. This was enabled by the degraded (and degrading) colonial narrative representations.[17] By the early 1970s, the impetus that thus started within the discipline of history found similar echo in psychology with the significant pioneering work of Enriquez (1975, 1977, 1978, 1992). Enriquez (1992) first developed "liberation psychology" as a way of doing psychology differently from the West. His goal in this regard was not merely to counter the effects of the degrading colonial representations on the Filipino psyche but to constitute a more adequate framework for understanding Filipino "indigenous" culture. Within this framework, Enriquez (1992) distinguishes between two approaches to indigenization: "indigenization from without" and "indigenization from within" (101). Enriquez defines the former as having a starting point in the exogenous (colonial) culture. The West, in this case, serves as the source of theoretic constructs with the indigenous (Filipino) culture as the target recipient of culture flow. Its main method or strategy is "content indigenization[,] test modification and translation of imported materials" (85). This was the starting point of nationalist Filipino psychologists in their initial attempts to indigenize Philippine psychology. However, despite efforts to deepen theoretical understanding of the inner dynamics of the indigenous culture, this model failed to dislodge the implicitly racist cultural assumptions and biases of Western psychology's analytic constructs.

Indigenization from within, by contrast, uses the indigenous culture as, at once, the starting point, source, and basis of concepts, methods, and theories. The goal is not merely to build on exogenous constructs and indigenize their use and application. It is to develop its own analytical tools, instruments, and conceptual frameworks using the indigenous culture as the main reference point. The resulting framework is a potent formulation that called into question the universalist assumptions of Western experimental psychology as the only legitimate "science." Called *Sikolohiyang Pilipino* (Filipino Psychology), it formed a distinctive critique of the negative framing and representation of the so-called essential Filipino personality. Filipino Psychology rejects the degrading images inscribed in the colonial narratives as little more than the ethnocentric shadow projections of Western colonial scholarship.

In anthropology, a rethinking of disciplinary perspectives began with the works of Jocano (1965, 1975) reacting to studies done by American anthropologists Beyer and Fox (cf. Bennagen 1990). Jocano (1975), along with Filipino anthropologists Salazar (1974–75) and Bennagen (1977), among others, challenged what were deemed to be the unimaginative explanations of Filipino origins based on "wave migration" and "diffusionist" theories. These theories tended to trace everything found in the Philippines, including the early inhabitants and their material and symbolic culture, as deriving from or as having been adapted from the outside (neighboring continents). From this unidirectional tracing of influence came the unstated implication that everything Filipino is, hence, "borrowed," "unoriginal," and always derived from elsewhere. Such portrayal of Philippine prehistoric culture and civilization was seen as one more baseless interpretation that needed countering, all the more so because presented in old textbooks as fact, with the slide from theory to fact obscured by the lack of alternative interpretations up to that point.

A further contribution in this regard is the firsthand research work of humanities scholar De Leon (1981, 1990). De Leon explores the surviving indigenous art forms of the various ethnic communities nationwide. Belying allegations of "cultural lack" and "deficiency" among precolonial Filipinos prior to contact with the purportedly "superior" cultures of the West, he documented a vast array of rich, diverse, and unique Philippine precolonial art forms. These, he argued, persisted through time against the onslaught of colonization and westernization. Using art as a projective tool, he combined rigorous cultural analysis of Philippine traditional arts with insights from *Sikolohiyang Pilipino* to establish an alternative "image of the Filipino in the arts."[18] This alternative portrayal of Filipinos through their indigenous cultural productions challenged the colonial stereotypes of Filipino natives as "barbaric," "uncivilized," and "culturally deficient" prior to the coming of the West.

In political science, Constantino's nationalist writings (1975a, 1975b, 1977) delivered the most scathing denunciation of the systematic process by which the colonial stereotypes and representations of Filipinos, their culture, and their history were naturalized in the popular imagination through the instrumentality of a colonial educational system. His seminal essay, "The Miseducation of the Filipino" (1977), in particular, criticized continuing neocolonial conditions in the Philippines long after the formal ending of American rule in the country. In unmasking the vested interests that have fueled the maintenance of a dependent Philippine economy through educational policies that catered more to foreign than to Filipino interests, he helped end, once and for all, the innocent view of education and knowledge production as neutral enterprises. This is a realization that further underscored the strategic need to recapture agency in determining the kind of education essential for Filipinos to win the struggle for independence, particularly in the ideological arena.

In all these efforts, the challenge had to do not only with the need to change the subject content of the disciplines from foreign to Philippine material ("indigenization from without") but, more critically, with the conceptual tools of analysis ("indigenization from within"). Autonomously conducted at first within each academic discipline, the search for new concepts, categories, instruments, and theoretical frameworks "better suited" to Philippine cultural and social realities inevitably progressed into an intensely interdisciplinary endeavor. Scholars became aware of one another's works and of an emerging consensus (more amazing because arrived at semi-independently) on an indigenous (versus colonial) framework across the disciplines.

It is clear from this much-abbreviated historical account that the indigenization movement in the Philippine academy received most of its initial impetus from the need to reject Western impositions on Philippine scholarship that had sought to squeeze Philippine realities into a certain mold using a colonial framework of analysis. Indeed, within this (colonial) framework, there was no way for Filipinos to speak (among themselves or with one another) or to make sense of their everyday experiences without the constant intrusion and self-disparagement from an internalized dominant Other's point of view inscribed in the very instruments of learning. This was deemed the most serious and detrimental consequence of a colonial education. As Covar (1991) laments in this regard,

> We were made to hope that western education was going to liberate our minds and elevate our quality of life, but the opposite happened—we became captive to western ways of thinking and system of economy. Our thinking, culture and society became virtually westernized, when we were, in fact, Asians. The categories we used to make sense of our world were not ours; they were borrowed and offered by the academic disciplines. We became mesmerized and awed by the claim and promise of universalism. We disparaged and

> marginalized our own indigenous view as "ethnic," "parochial," and "provincial." Who will not be appalled at such insult? (40; as translated from the Filipino original)

Indigenization, then, as it originated, appears to be mainly a decolonizing move. As such, it turns on the *functional need* to separate out what were considered the repressive impositions from without versus those deemed to be relatively more spontaneous, self-directed, autonomous ways of being (Filipino). As one proponent of *Sikolohiyang Pilipino,* Pe-Pua (1991), acknowledges, the term "indigenization" itself is a misnomer: "How can you indigenize something which is already indigenous?" (154). But for lack of a better word, and in view of the movement's original emphasis on decolonization, the term came to represent what the nationalist struggle for self-determination stood for in the Philippine academy.

Strategies in National Identity Formation within the Dynamics of Indigenization: Phases, Shifts, and Contemporary Developments

Evident in the language of the indigenization movement is a seemingly unproblematic assumption of an "essential" (i.e., indigenous), precolonial, unitary Filipino "self." This "self" was believed to have been submerged, repressed, and marginalized in colonization. Decolonization must "recover" and "restore" that self through the process of indigenization (understood on this reading more as a sort of "uncovering"). The anti-essentialist response to such a conception would argue that one cannot ever return to a mythical "pristine" self, nor can one base a national unification strategy on such illusory cohesiveness, achieved or purchased at the cost of denying what is in fact the constituents' multiethnic heterogeneity. Such a strategy furthermore can devolve into exclusionary politics marginalizing or denying recognition to those who do not fit the profile of the "authentic" Filipino (as defined by those constructing the discourse). These criticisms are not wholly unjustified, given the observed effects of essentialist politics in other contexts, particularly in state-sponsored nationalisms where one form of imposition (colonial) is merely replaced with another (state domination). I suggest, however, that we read the essentialist invocations of a unitary "Filipino" self in the Philippine indigenization movement within a more transformational (in contrast with a fixed or determinate) framework. This way, we (re-)interpret specific forms of identity articulations not in static or foundationalist terms but as likely coinciding with perceived strategic political demands at differing phases or stages of the struggle for decolonization and nationhood. The following section outlines the phases of definition that the Filipino "national" identity has undergone within the indigenization movement. In so doing, I do not mean to imply a simplistic unilineal process, for, to this day, one can find in the current literature the simultaneous articulation of different models of identity definitions. Rather, the sequential narrative is meant simply to trace the logic of the process (of identity constitution) as shown by the range of models that predominated at various stages of the indigenization movement.

From the initial works of foreign scholars training their Western colonial disciplinary lenses on what they presumed to be the "indigenous" culture of Filipinos, Filipino "identity" was constructed in terms of a constellation of traits. These traits revolved around certain surface values that had mostly to do with preserving "face," or what has been labeled the SIR syndrome (that is, the penchant for "smooth interpersonal relationships"). Identified as its concomitant trilogy of values are *utang na loob* (roughly, debt of gratitude), *pakikisama* (getting along), and *hiya* (shame). Accompanying this trilogy of values is a set of loose negative trait attributions: the habit of *mañana* (chronic procrastination), *ningas cogon* (good starters, poor finishers, like the short blaze of cogon grass), *bahala na* (fatalism), and *talangka* mentality ("crab mentality," i.e., the tendency to pull down those who strive to be better). For decades, such identity constructs were generally accepted and used in textbooks to teach Filipinos about themselves.

A second phase in Filipino identity formation sought to reinterpret the same constellation of values, but from a more affirming trajectory. Thus, *bahala na* (fatalism) was reinterpreted as "determination and risk-taking," "a way of pumping courage into [one's] system so that [one does] not buckle down" in the face of formidable obstacles (Pe-Pua 1991). *Talangka,* or crab mentality, became a call for community members to acknowledge indebtedness to others and to work for the good of the entire community and not just for themselves (cf. Jocano 1965). While such reinterpretations may have improved the Filipino self-image, the laundry list of traits remained largely untouched, with the positive reinterpretations being mainly reactive (like some kind of reverse stereotyping), leaving the old defining colonial framework intact.

A third phase of the process of identity definition emerged with the total rejection of the colonial framework and its replacement with an entirely new paradigm, emanating mainly from *Sikolohiyang Pilipino.* Instead of seeking positive ways to reinterpret the colonial framework, this phase argued that it was necessary to critique the very premises and assumptions of a universalist, transcultural social science. Though framed within psychology, inputs came from all quarters in the academy, as scholars from the various disciplines independently and then collaboratively discovered surprising parallels in their findings. Here, the impetus has been to challenge the dominant paradigm with alternative evidence from various sources (historical, ethnographic, ethnolinguistic, folkloristic, and so on). Such firsthand research on the diverse Filipino indigenous communities, conducted in a range of academic disciplines (particularly anthropology, linguistics, humanities, psychology, and history), has contributed to the emergence of a different concept, *kapwa* (roughly, shared identity) as constituting the core of the Philippine value system (Enriquez 1992). In contrast to previous models that stressed the maintenance of surface harmony, this core value of *kapwa,* once adopted, generated a set of associated social values totally different from those culled from a putatively mistaken locating of the pivotal value on the surface instead of in the "deep structure" of the culture. These associated values were identified as *karangalan* (dignity), *katarungan* (justice), and *kalayaan* (freedom). Together, they formed the constitutive elements of "the" Filipino identity in *Sikolohiyang Pilipino.*

At this phase of indigenous theorizing, a growing consciousness of the political and historical dynamics involved in the very process of identity construction also began to emerge. This amounted to an awareness that identity is not a fixed datum but undergoes shifts and changes in response to external demands in the environment, although still retaining a "core." Maggay's (1993) contribution in this regard is in highlighting the need for historical mediation in the practice of "reading" culture. Her suggested framework distinguishes between "core values" (the *Sikolohiyang Pilipino* framework of *kapwa*) on the one hand and what she considered mainly as "survival values" developed as coping strategies in the face of colonial oppression and marginalization on the other (cf. also Mendoza 1997). Though still premised on the presumed existence of "inherent" cultural characteristics (e.g., in terms of worldview, time orientation, and other cultural dimensions suggested by traditional cultural anthropology), Maggay's framework provided a way of looking at the seeming contradictions, fissures, and fractures in Filipino culture and personality (found to be most evident in the urban communities more heavily exposed to the Western influences of modern industrial living) without naturalizing them. This framework was seen to be more imaginative than the mere drawing up of a laundry list of negative and positive traits. The latter was rejected in that it tended to fix what it took to be "the" inherent Filipino character and personality into nothing more than a distorted image. Unfortunately, despite the latter's debunking as a positivist, reductionist model, it remains influential in the minds of many, with unwitting adherents even among well-meaning reformists in the Philippine bureaucracy (cf. Philippine Senate Committee on Education, Arts and Culture and the Committee on Social Justice, Welfare and Development 1994). Rimonte (1997) warns that a historically unmediated approach to understanding "the" Filipino "character"

> endorses the essentialist myths that their problems are entirely due to who they are: that history has little to do with them and the problems they confront; that the only way for them to solve their problems is to change themselves; that if they have not changed themselves yet, it is because they are too lazy or too cheerful or too ignorant or too feckless or too sinful, having strayed from the prescribed . . . path of righteousness. (59)

This historicized framework is a significant move away from the more received (and essentialist) view of the earlier models. For one, it stresses the role played by the abnormality of the colonial condition in producing the cultural "distortions." In the past, such distortions tended to be blamed entirely on an inherent "flaw" in "the" Filipino "character" (cf. Fallow's [1987] notorious article on the alleged "damaged culture" of Filipinos). By contrast, where they occur at all and are not simply projections of a view rationalizing domination, these "distortions" can now be interpreted more adequately as symptomatic of a pathology borne of marginalization, denigration, and the prevention of a people from assuming their own processes of self-direction and self-formation.[19]

From essential(ized) forms of identity definitions premised on an underlying unity beneath the plurality of ethnicities in the archipelago, there appears to be, in the discourse on identities within indigenization, a steady movement toward increasingly complex ways of construing identity definitions. In fact, over the last two decades, the indigenization movement formally declared a "concerted, deliberate effort to establish a new order of life" of which "colonization is merely a temporary detraction" (Covar, in Azurin 1993, xii). This new trajectory oriented the movement less toward reacting to the past (decolonization) and more toward constituting a national discourse on civilization. The goal, this time, is to bring together in a lively spirit of democratic participation in the political process the majority of the Filipino masses and not just the intelligentsia. To this end, a theoretically innovative communication-based framework emerged from the field of Philippine historiography.

Termed *Pantayong Pananaw,* this new theoretical perspective refers to the speaking context within which scholars in the movement seek to forge this "national" discourse on civilization. Developed by historian Salazar (1991), the term *pantayo* comes from the root word *tayo,* one of the pronouns marking the first-person plural "we" and the prefix *pan-*, roughly the equivalent of the preposition "for." With *Pananaw* translating to "perspective," *Pantayong Pananaw* can be roughly (awkwardly) phrased in English as "A For-Us Perspective." Taking the various pronoun referents and their equivalent terms in the Filipino languages and dialects, namely, *kayo* (you-plural), *kami* (we-speaking to others), *sila* (they), and *tayo* (we-speaking among ourselves),[20] Salazar chooses the last pronoun referent *tayo* as his basis for building a theoretical perspective. He explains his choice by referring to the taken-for-granted speaking contexts of the various pronoun categories. The two contending possibilities among the four pronoun referents are *kami* (we-speaking to others) and *tayo* (we-speaking among ourselves). Salazar chooses the latter because *kami,* he reasons, implies a context where one is discoursing with an "other." Within this discursive context, one must constantly take the other's context and perspective into consideration in any communicative agenda. Such is the case in (de-)colonization in that the self is constantly aware of an outsider's presence. This is an outsider who, far from friendly and sympathetic, happens to be the self's very own demon-tormentor.[21] This outside entity is seen at once as the cause of one's identity distortion and crisis and yet one still powerful enough (whether in actuality or through habitual psychic conditioning) to harm if not somehow catered to. As long as this outsider is included in the conversation, he or she remains an influential determinant of the tone, direction, content, and rules to be set in conducting the discourse. Likewise, the constraint placed on the speakers by a context where the "other" or "others" are constantly included even just as overhearers, in Salazar's view, ensures that the discourse on nationhood by Filipinos will remain unproductive and trapped in a reactive mode, unable to move forward or to create new initiatives.

What Salazar (1991) proposes by *Pantayong Pananaw,* if only figuratively speaking, is a "closed circuit" of interaction where discourse is to be carried on only by and among Filipinos without the inclusion (constant intrusion or meddling) of outside participants or dominant perspectives inimical to Filipino interests. That way, he argues, Filipinos can discourse and communicate freely—in their own terms, in their own language, using their own thought patterns and manner of relating, and, most important, with their own interests (as Filipinos) kept in mind first and foremost. While this call for a closed circuit of interaction appears retrogressive in comparison to the outward-looking thrust of, say, the newly democratizing countries of Eastern Europe, proponents of *Pantayong Pananaw* see the move as a much-needed first-time marking of boundaries, if only ideologically, by a people whose former all-inclusiveness (borne not so much of generosity as of a distorted prioritizing of others' interests above one's own in a kind of reverse ethnocentrism) served to work only to its own detriment. Traditionally, for instance, what was considered "*the*" Filipino "nation" is one constructed by a national elite under the banner of "official nationalism." This elite is one whose sentiments, loyalties, worldview orientation, and interests were tied more to the imported ideology of its former (colonial) master than those of the Filipino people. Under its leadership, the country is deemed to have succeeded only in being steered along the same beaten path to neocolonialism and dependency, unable to chart its own course. Stuck in a purely reactionary mode, it is indicted as being locked in global discourses without an agenda of its own to place on the table. Only by instituting such a closed circuit of interaction does Salazar envision the possibility of a "truly" Filipino consensus emerging, participated in widely by formerly excluded voices from the diverse Philippine cultural communities. In what follows, I outline the constitutive elements of Salazar's (1991) framework for the *Pantayong Pananaw.*

Historically, Salazar (1991) argues, there was not, prior to the coming of Spain, one unified *Pantayong Pananaw* among the estimated 126 (some say 80) ethnolinguistic groups in the Philippine archipelago. He traces the constitution of the Philippines into a national political entity to the efforts of the elites in the Christianized areas to attain reforms and eventual independence toward the end of the Spanish colonial regime. These elites he refers to as "the acculturated group," or the *ladino* class (51). By his account, these *ladinos* had very complex and convoluted transactions and acculturative collaborations with the Spanish colonizers: Not only were they responsible for helping the Spaniards insert their culture into the lives of Filipinos by indigenizing it and translating Spanish works into Tagalog (one of the Philippine languages), they were also instrumental in the hispanization of Filipino culture by promoting the learning of Spanish. Because of their privileged status as culture brokers knowing both Spanish and Tagalog, they prospered during the Spanish regime. Eventually they also emerged as the elite during the American occupation. Included in these ranks, in Salazar's estimation, are the Filipino propagandists who, in the latter part of the Spanish period, became exposed to liberal and progressive ideas in Europe and launched a movement (the Propaganda Movement) for reform against Spanish abuses and oppression. Although an expression of resistance, Salazar regards the Propaganda Movement as still portraying primarily a *pangkami* (we-speaking to others) form of discourse. This is because the Filipino propagandists wrote mostly in Spanish, directed their writing toward the Spaniards, and used mostly concepts and ideas they learned from the liberal traditions of Europe, which the Spaniards understood as well.

Since the American period, the elite have continued to derive from the ranks of *ladino*-descent and the European-educated propagandists, with the addition today of Fulbright scholars and other intellectuals sponsored by American foundations, Japan, and other foreign countries. Salazar contends that because such scholars and intellectuals continue to discourse in English and use alien constructs in their study of Philippine society adopted mostly from their graduate studies abroad, their scholarly practice serves to marginalize Filipino culture in their own eyes, that is, even when they desire to work for national liberation. Whether from the ideological left or right, Salazar finds that the discourse of these individuals (labeled "National Culture from Propaganda" in the framework) remains largely unrelated to the larger discourses of the majority of Filipino masses. One reason offered is that the latter's primary medium of communication is in the languages and dialects of their respective ethnic communities governed by totally different modes of thinking, conceptualizing, categorizing, and speaking about their lived reality.

Herein, then, lies what proponents of *Pantayong Pananaw* hold responsible for the phenomenon they refer to in the framework as "The Great Cultural Divide." Maggay (1994) offers a representative expression:

> Perhaps the greatest single source of anomie in this country, there exists in the Philippines an invisible yet impermeable dividing line between those who are able to function within the borrowed ethos of power structures transplanted from without and those who have re-

> mained within the functional and meaning system of the indigenous culture. Termed by academics as the "great cultural divide," this sharp disjunction in sensibility has on top a thin layer of culture brokers known as the "ladino" class, often co-identical with the economic and political elite but also including middle class intellectuals and technocrats sufficiently educated and domesticated into the formal systems of power introduced into the country by its colonial past. The vast bottom half consists of that supposedly silent and inert mass whose universe of discourse is limited to the indigenous languages and whose subterranean consciousness has remained impervious to colonial influence. Thus is a situation where the grammar of power is conducted within the terms and the structures of a language alien to the people's ways of thinking and feeling, rendering centers of power not only inaccessible but profoundly uninteresting, a political sideshow that interfaces only tangentially with what to the poor is the more serious business of survival. (3)

Salazar admits that, at the moment, even while the Filipino ethnic communities may be said to have their own respective *pantayong pananaw,* there is still not one *Pantayong Pananaw* discourse to unify all Filipinos. But because he believes in the strength, vibrancy, and close interrelatedness of the cultures of these indigenous communities, his vision is that Filipinos can eventually move in this direction.

What is the methodology of *Pantayong Pananaw*? Utilizing the insights from *Sikolohiyang Pilipino* and the newly emerging discipline of *Pilipinolohiya*[22] (Philippine studies), *Pantayong Pananaw* seeks the possibility of "calibrating ethnicity progressively into nationhood" (Azurin 1993, 12). And here is where the essentialist-leaning reckoning of Filipino identity dominant in the early phases of the indigenization movement gives way to a more dynamic non-essentialist, nonreactive strategy for (re-)constituting Filipino national identity, one that does not gloss over the plurality of ethnic identifications across the archipelago. As far as locating the constitutive elements of a shared national identity is concerned, *Pantayong Pananaw* points to several directions. One is to advocate a synthesis or crystallization of a consensus from below (in contrast to a state-imposed "National Culture" from above), that is, from the multiple discourses of the Philippine ethnolinguistic communities to a shared discourse in which the masses of Filipinos can, and will want to, participate freely. For this, the adoption of Filipino[23] as the de facto national language, though not uncontested, is deemed an important strategic move.

From Azurin's (1993) refinement of the framework, another guideline is to adopt a view of ethnicity that does not contradict but rather complements nationhood. As long as there is no infraction on other groups' right to exist through exploitative acts and repressive impositions, ethnically manipulated aggression need not be feared. Additionally, rather than seeing ethnic distinctions and dichotomies as always and forever permanent, they may be viewed more productively as "shifting, [at times] superficial, and situational," that is, the result of certain expediencies (Azurin 1993, 53, citing Padilla). An even more fruitful approach from a historical perspective, Azurin suggests, is to trace and underscore in the constitution of a national identity the precolonial interethnic linkings through trade and migratory contacts between and among the different highland, midland, and lowland tribal settlements that have been preserved amazingly in such native institutions as the peace pact (*Bodong* or *Beddeng*)—a native practice still observed in many places to this day.

This notion of there being a basis for the conception of what Azurin (1993) calls "intersecting ethnicities" or "correlative cultures" located not necessarily in a correspondence of cultural traits and characteristics but in the historically continuous and continuing interethnic transactions that have created bonds of commonality and identification between and among the various communities is what finally shifts the discourse on Filipino identity from essentialist to more anti-essentialist perspectives. Along with the project of rewriting Philippine history to highlight the concerted and sustained struggle of an entire people who rose in concert during the 1896 Philippine revolution to wrench its destiny out of the hands of the colonizers and, more recently, from the clutches of a home-grown native despot (in the 1986 People Power Revolution), this focus on shared national experiences and common identification with the aspirations for freedom, justice, and unity can now form the alternative bases for a national consensus.

Conclusion

I began this chapter with the problematic of what it means to theorize across social contexts in a nonhegemonic fashion. In particular, my goal had been to find ways to make critical theory and cultural politics (often perceived to be contradictory in their form of politics) productively speak to, and mutually inform, each other. One way I saw this possible is through utilizing dynamic equivalence (inter-)translation where both discourses undergo simultaneous nuancing and are given adequate interpretation through rigorous contextualization (or historicization). In this study, I focused specifically on the Eurocentric discourse on anti-essentialism and the perceived "threat" posed by its critique of identity politics for the theoretical end of the dialogue. For the other, I chose the experiments in national identity formation within the indigenization movement in the Philippine academy as a specific expression of practical cultural politics. In drawing insights from the foregoing discussion on what might constitute a nonhegemonic, mutually productive dialogue between such theoretical texts and the diverse (con-)texts of practical cultural politics, I focus mainly on the communicative dimension of the engagement. Following are a number of insights that come to mind.

On the part of critical scholars wishing to speak to the cultural politics of a given social context, there is a need, first of all, to guard against effecting a discursive closure by quickly dismissing as "theoretically naive," "nativistic," or "illusory" what *form*alistically appears to be mostly essentialist articulations of the cultural politics obtaining in a given context. A way toward a more fruitful dialogue is not to stop at the surface rhetoric of a movement but to go on further to historicize these essentialist invocations and identify the function they serve. After all, it could very well be, as Hall (1996b) argues, that such invocations are

> about questions of using the resources of history, language and culture in the process of becoming rather than being: not "who we are" or "where we came from," so much as what we might become, how we have been represented and how that bears on how we might represent ourselves. (4)

As shown in the indigenization narrative in Philippine scholarship, essentialist claims undergirding a unitary constitution of a national identity often arise out of a need to counter degrading and inferiorizing colonial representations by constituting new (empowering) ones through the power of self-naming and self-definition (Rimonte 1977).

Second, in cross-cultural communication directed mainly toward social change and transformation, a point can be made about the sufferance of a particular form of cultural expression or practice, no matter how seemingly inadequate, until such time that what is called a *functional equivalent* (Kraft 1979) can be effectively developed (or agitated for) to replace the old. This principle derives from the notion that not until a people is able to perceive the proferred alternative or functional "substitute" as having greater efficacy in meeting its felt needs at any given moment does it "ripen" enough to a point where it is ready or open even to consider the innovation or change (particularly of the type involving drastic shifts in paradigm). In the case of the Philippine indigenization movement, for example, only when new historical conditions had made clear the limits of essentialist formulations having exhausted their pragmatic usefulness did the movement find it imperative to search for other forms of political struggle.

Speaking of the need for "functional substitutes," however, this is where, I must say, the particular burden (or terror) of the deconstructive critique lies, in that the "essence" of radical anti-essentialism consists precisely in that refusal to supplant concepts found to be inadequate with "positive," "truer" knowledge, what Hall (1996b) refers to as putting such concepts, as it were, "under erasure" (1). In other words, anti-essentialism holds no promise to provide "true" identity formulations in place of those seen as patently "false" ones. At the same time (again, consistent with the dynamic equivalence model of translation discussed earlier), it is possible, on another level, to "supplant," say, the essentialist politics of the decolonizing phase of a movement for national solidarity with more non-essentialist approaches without sacrificing the same goal (of unity in difference). This is so since a "functional equivalent" need not take the same form as its predecessor but, after the model of the paraphrase, may precisely require changing the form of the "substitute" term. This supplanting is possible as long as the conditions necessary for effecting such ends are adequately provided. In the case of the Philippines, the logic of indigenization provided that for as long as it was in the reactive phase of decolonization, proponents had found it necessary to rely heavily on essential(ized) assertions of a unitary Filipino identity if only to present a united front against a seemingly monolithic threat to the national community's survival (colonialism). But as soon as that objective was deemed to have been sufficiently (though never completely) secured, the struggle then could move toward a new phase where the search for identity now takes place separate from the context of a dominant Other (the phase of *Pantayong Pananaw*). By this time, too, other non-essentialist bases for national unity (for instance, shared historical experiences, intersecting ethnicities, cross-national interactions, and so on) would have become possible (not, I suspect, without the help of prior, more essentialist forms of nationalism). It follows that these new forms of cultural politics are now (not before) ready to serve as viable "functional equivalents" with radically differing *form*al characteristics but serving a roughly similar purpose: in the Philippine case, the securing of national consensus. This is not to take the "national" in itself as unproblematic but, rather, as one needing interrogation almost immediately, as soon as constituted or, better yet, along the way, in the very process of its constitution. But its apparent privileging here must be seen only instrumentally, as a vehicle for the push toward collective self-determination in the aftermath of colonization.

A word must be said, however, about the radically differing "methods" of anti-essentialist in contrast to essentialist politics. Whereas essentialist politics sees the fixing and stabilizing of boundaries and the homogenizing of identities as desirable and attainable ends and bases for solidarity, anti-essentialist politics, on the contrary, locates the constituent elements of solidarity precisely in *engaging* rather than suppressing difference and in making permanent the condition of critique (Hall 1996c). Often perceived as a threat by those coming to the discourse from a marginalized position,[24] such politics of difference and permanent contestation is what, in fact, enlarges the space of freedom and democratic participation for all players. The critique of anti-essentialism does this by giving no one any guarantees or privileges. In its unrelenting critique of all claims to consensus, no one is exempt from scrutiny—not even a purported "consensus" from below (that is, not even *Pantayong Pananaw,* should it ever succeed in attaining hegemony). But it is precisely in this absence of guarantees where there can be a free play and contestation of forces and agencies and where participants can engage in productive and creative experimentation in the forging of different modes of communal solidarity.

This is where I feel that theorizing in the Philippine indigenization movement, for its part, can benefit from the critical perspectives that anti-essentialism has to offer. It may benefit from the latter's capacity to sharpen the movement's awareness of the power politics involved in the very process of consensus formation, in keeping ever present the questions as to who or which group (or groups) is (are) calling the shots in the emerging dominant discourse, whose rules for the conduct and direction of the dialogue are followed, and whether there is increasing space in which heterogeneous voices can participate and be heard. Indeed, even in the very process of working for the successful hegemonizing of a *Pantayong Pananaw,* contestation, rather than complacency, should be the norm in its construction. Ellul's (1981) caveat is instructive in this regard. Speaking of the "positivity of negativity" with reference to the operation of the principle of the dialectic, he makes a categorical endorsement of the value of opposition in any transformative endeavor:

> This [negative prong of the dialectic] is essential, for if the positive remains alone, it remains unchanged: stable and inert. A positive—for example, an uncontested society, a force without counterforce, a [person] without dialogue, an unchallenged teacher, a church with no heretics, a single party with no rivals—will be shut up in the indefinite repetition of its own image. It will live in satisfaction at what was produced once, and will see no reason to change. . . . We thus have sclerosis, paralysis, a redundant monologue of self-satisfaction and self-reproduction . . . the situation one encounters in every totalitarian society. (295)

Although no longer the main emphasis of the movement, the continuing vigilance against the reinscription of a colonial consciousness has kept some members of the indigenization movement wary, if not altogether indifferent, to outside or foreign discourses, all the more so when these are mouthed by those who find no need to bother with issues of relevance and translation. I suggest that for there to be a mutuality of dialogue (or, at least, the possibility of movement toward equalizing power) between the academy and those engaged in popular struggles and between the West and its Others, there needs to be a willingness to engage in the hard work of intertranslation. For this, a casting away of all pretensions to a monopoly of critical understanding is needed, as is a sober(ing) acknowledgment of the partiality and contingency of all perceptions, much more so when these emanate from positions of privilege and power.[25] This is certainly a tall order, especially for those of us who, Hall (1996a) warns, have come to speak with "theoretical fluency" (274).

Finally, in the way that I had done it here, I would like to suggest that translation, as "the most intimate act of reading" (Spivak 1992, 181), is more than simply a slavish (formally correspondent) imitation of the "original." Effective translation, in this view, is ultimately transformative in that it has capacity to sense the incipient aim of the "original" and to render it articulate. Yet it does so without undue valorization or entertaining the illusion of having finally captured its entire range of meaning or possibilities for interpretation. In giving the Philippine indigenization movement a more dynamic reading than what it is likely to get from other quarters not intimately acquainted with its spirit and inner dynamics, this is what I had sought to do, sharpened in my own understanding by my having learned a different language—the language of deconstructionism and anti-essentialist politics.

In the same vein, I assign to theorizing the same task that I give to translation: that of not merely fulfilling a mimetic or representational function but of being able, in the long run, to influence the direction of change one is committed to effecting in the world of the everyday. This I envision possible through the power, through theorizing, to imagine, in Spivak's (1990) words, other ways of "worlding the world."[26] In my (re)narrativizing of the Philippine indigenization movement with the anti-essentialist critique in mind, I had taken liberties to envision the kind of cultural politics one senses the movement moving toward but has yet to attain fully. I offer it as a way of reading and theorizing that might be mutually enabling of cultural politics and theory alike through a venturesome application of the principles of dynamic equivalence intertranslation.

Notes

1. For example, those espoused even by such revered icons as national hero Jose Rizal or well-known Filipino literary writer who publishes in English, Carlos Bulosan, author of *America Is in the Heart* (1946), among others.

2. See Hall's reference to "translation," "re-articulation," "transcoding," and "transculturation" (in Chen 1996, 393). These are terms he uses with the qualification that by no means does he imply an original copy. I will be using "translation" in this same sense.

3. Retorts similar to Hartsock's (1987) are not all that uncommon: "Somehow it seems highly suspicious that it is at this moment in history, when so many groups are engaged in [reclaiming their past and remaking their future in their own terms], . . . that doubt arises in the academy about the nature of the "subject," about the possibilities for a general theory which can describe the world, about historical "progress." Why is it, exactly at the moment when so many of us who have been silenced begin to demand the right to name ourselves, to act as subjects rather than objects of history, that just then the concept of subjecthood becomes "problematic"? Just when we are forming our own theories about the world, uncertainty emerges about whether the world can be adequately theorized?" (196)

4. As a Filipino scholar doing graduate work (in critical intercultural communication) in America.

5. Which may vary in nature, depending on the kind of "text" (e.g., linguistic, cultural, institutional, and so on).

6. The communication/transfer/translation of a whole, or aspects of a whole, culture (or episteme) to another.

7. Similar to the simplistic reasoning of those opposed to, say, the policy of affirmative action that invokes mechanical interpretations of "equal opportunity" as demanding "merit"-based evaluation as the sole legitimate criteria for hiring. Here, "merit" is defined in terms of fixed "objective" standards of "achievement" and "performance" that should apply across the board. Categories of race, color, gender, and so on are deemed irrelevant to the issue of what is "just" and "fair."

8. Dismissive because having the knee-jerk reaction of quickly evaluating and judging the forms (of such a project) from within one's own framework instead of on their own terms first.

9. For a more extensive discussion, see Sapir (1929) and Whorf (1940, 1956).

10. Taken in the larger sense of elements/parts/aspects of any signifying system, "social text," or episteme.

11. A criticism actually leveled against me in my presentation of the decolonizing thrust of the Philippine indigenization project in one Cultural Studies discussion session.

12. Because of space limitations, this overview is necessarily sketchy and far from comprehensive. It may not include important contributions coming from those in the provincial universities and research centers in the country likewise notable for their many initiatives in the concerted effort toward indigenization.

13. An important distinction might be made here concerning the ideological differences between insurgent and dominant forms of nationalism.

14. Formally inaugurated on June 12, 1898, on the defeat of the Spanish forces by the Philippine revolutionaries, the fledgling republic suffered a major setback when Spain, refusing the humiliation of conceding defeat at the hands of the native "Indios," decided instead to strike a deal with the invading American forces. Spain accordingly ceded the Philippines to the latter for a token price of $20,000,000 in the now infamous 1898 Treaty of Paris after staging a mock battle (cf. Constantino 1975b; Agoncillo and Guerrero 1977).

15. Three hundred and fifty years under Spain and more than half a century under America with a three-year Japanese interlude between 1942 and 1945.

16. An alarming trend documented in a study by Canieso-Doronila (1989) is that "as students progress through the grades, their preference for their own nationality decreases" (72).

17. See Lynch (1990) for a discussion of the systematic disenfranchisement of all the indigenous peoples of the Philippines during the Spanish regime through their effective representation as *indio* and their consequent denial of legal status and legal rights before the colonial state law. Lynch likewise shows how the same policy continued not so much in formal terms of the law during the American colonial regime but in much more subtle and dissimulated forms than the Spanish.

18. A graduate course he designed and incorporated into the Humanities Program at the University of the Philippines, Diliman, Quezon City. I audited the course in 1982, and I mark the radical transformation of consciousness I underwent as a result, as a new and decisive turn in my decolonization process.

19. See Fanon's (1965) eloquent depiction of the effects of colonialism: "Colonialism is not satisfied merely with holding a people in its grip and emptying the native's brain of all form and content. By a kind of perverted logic, it turns to the past of the people, and distorts, disfigures and destroys it" (210).

20. The Filipino pronouns *tayo* and *kami* are the equivalent in linguistics of the terms "we-inclusive" and "we-exclusive," respectively.

21. Rimonte (1997) notes, "The other is the colonizer, representative of everything one re-

gards as superior and therefore longs for" (42). She quotes W. E. B. DuBois on the phenomenon of the internalized other: "'It is a peculiar sensation, this double consciousness, this sense of always looking at one's self through the eyes of others, of measuring one's soul by the tape of a world that looks on in amused contempt and pity. One ever feels this twoness . . . two souls, two thoughts, two unreconciled strivings, two warring ideals in one dark body whose dogged strength alone keeps it from being torn asunder'" (42).

22. Another intellectual tradition arising from the indigenization movement along with *Sikolohiyang Pilipino* and *Pantayong Pananaw.*

23. The Filipino language is based on one of the regional languages, Tagalog, but is deemed evolving currently into a widely used medium of communication that incorporates elements from the other ethnic languages.

24. See West's (1995) distinction concerning the very different political status between what he calls "identity from above" and "identity from below" (17–18).

25. Spivak's (1992) caution is instructive in this regard, as she notes, "You cannot translate from a position of monolinguist superiority" (193).

26. See also Deetz (1992) on the role of theory.

References

Agoncillo, T. A., and M. C. Guerrero. 1977. *History of the Filipino People.* 5th ed. Quezon City: R. P. Garcia Publishing.

Azurin, A. M. 1993. *Reinventing the Filipino Sense of Being and Becoming.* Quezon City: CSSP Publications and University of the Philippines Press.

Bennagen, P. L. 1977. "Mirror, Mirror on the Wall, Are We Human After All? (Towards a Humanist Anthropology)." In A. G. Carlos and A. R. Magno, eds., *The Social Responsibilities of the Social Scientist as an Intellectual* (42–50). Quezon City: University of the Philippines Press.

———. 1990. "The Indigenization and Asianization of Anthropology." In V. G. Enriquez, ed., *Indigenous Psychology: A Book of Readings* (1–30). Quezon City: Akademya ng Kultura at Sikolohiyang Pilipino.

Bourdieu, P. 1977. *Outline of a Theory of Practice.* Translated by R. Nice. Cambridge: Cambridge University Press.

Bulosan, C. 1946. *America Is in the Heart: A Personal History.* New York: Harcourt, Brace.

Canieso-Doronila, M. L. 1989. *The Limits of Educational Change: National Identity Formation in a Philippine Public Elementary School.* Quezon City: University of the Philippines Press.

Chen, K. S. 1996. "Cultural Studies and the Politics of Internationalization: An Interview with Stuart Hall." In D. Morley and K-S. Chen, eds., *Stuart Hall: Critical Dialogues in Cultural Studies* (392–408). London: Routledge.

Constantino, R. 1975a. *A History of the Philippines: From the Spanish Colonization to the Second World War.* New York: Monthly Review Press.

———. 1975b. *The Philippines: A Past Revisited.* Quezon City: Tala Publishing Services.

———. 1977. "The Miseducation of the Filipino." In C. N. Lumbera and T. Gimenez-Maceda, eds., *Rediscovery: Essays in Philippine Life and Culture* (125–45). Quezon City: National Book Store.

Covar, P. R. 1991. "Pilipinolohiya." In V. V. Bautista and R. Pe-Pua, eds., *Pilipinolohiya: Kasaysayan, Pilosopiya at Pananaliksik* [Philipinology: History, philosophy and research] (37–45). Manila: Kalikasan Press.

Deetz, S. T. 1992. *Democracy in an Age of Corporate Colonization: Developments in Communication and the Politics of Everyday Life.* Albany: State University of New York Press.

De Leon, F. M., Jr. 1981. "Towards a People's Art." *Lipunan* 3: 1–15.
———. 1990. "The Roots of a People's Art in Indigenous Psychology." In V. G. Enriquez, ed., *Indigenous Psychology: A Book of Readings* (311–27). Quezon City: Akademya ng Kultura at Sikolohiyang Pilipino.
Ellul, J. 1981. "Epilogue: On Dialectic." In G. C. Christians and J. M. Van Hook, eds., *Jacques Ellul: Interpretive Essays* (291–308). Urbana: University of Illinois Press.
Enriquez, V. G. 1975. "Mga Batayan ng Sikolohiyang Pilipino sa Kultura at Kasaysayan" [Cultural and historical foundations of Filipino psychology]. In V. G. Enriquez, ed., *Sikolohiyang Pilipino: Batayan sa kasaysayan, perspektibo, mga konsepto at bibliograpiya* [Filipino psychology: Historical foundations, perspectives, concepts and bibliography] (1–20). Quezon City: University of the Philippines Press.
———. 1977. "Filipino Psychology in the Third World." *Philippine Journal of Psychology* 10, no. 1: 3–18.
———. 1978. "*Kapwa,* a Core Concept in Filipino Social Psychology." *Philippine Social Science and Humanities Review [Rebyu ng Agham at Humanidades ng Pilipinas]* 42: 91–94.
———. 1992. *From Colonial to Liberation Psychology.* Quezon City: University of the Philippines Press.
Fallows, J. 1987. "A Damaged Culture: A New Philippines?" *Atlantic Monthly,* November, 49–54, 56–58.
Fanon, F. 1965. *The Wretched of the Earth.* New York: Grove.
Feliciano, G. D. 1965. "Limits of Western Social Research Methods in Rural Philippines: The Need for Innovation." *Lipunan* 1: 114–28.
Gramsci, A. 1971. *Selections from the Prison Notebooks.* Edited and translated by Q. Hoare and G. N. Smith. New York: International Publishers.
Hall, S. 1996a. "Cultural Studies and Its Theoretical Legacies." In D. Morley and K-S. Chen, eds., *Stuart Hall: Critical Dialogues in Cultural Studies* (262–75). London: Routledge.
———. 1996b. "Introduction: Who Needs 'Identity'?" In S. Hall and P. Du Gay, eds., *Questions of Cultural Identity* (1–17). London: Sage.
———. 1996c. "New Ethnicities." In D. Morley and K-S. Chen, eds., *Stuart Hall: Critical Dialogues in Cultural Studies* (441–49). London: Routledge.
Hartsock, N. 1987. "Rethinking Modernism: Minority vs. Minority Theories." *Cultural Critique* 7: 187–206.
Jocano, F. L. 1965. "Rethinking Filipino Cultural Heritage." *Lipunan* 1, no. 1: 53–72.
———. 1975. *Philippine Pre-History.* Quezon City: Philippine Center for Advanced Studies.
Kraft, C. 1979. *Christianity in Culture: A Study in Dynamic Biblical Theologizing in Cross-Cultural Perspective.* Maryknoll, N.Y.: Orbis Books.
Maggay, M. P. 1993. *Pagbabalik-loob: A Second Look at the Moral Recovery Program.* Quezon City: Akademya ng Kultura at Sikolohiyang Pilipino.
———. 1994. "Philippine Country Paper: Issue Paper on Social Integration." World Summit on Social Development. Unpublished draft manuscript.
Mendoza, S. L. 1997. "Decolonization and Cultural Hermeneutics: Fleshing Out Some of the Power Issues in Intercultural Communication." Paper presented at the annual meeting of the Western States Communication Association, Monterey, California, February.
Nida, E., and C. R. Taber. 1969. *The Theory and Practice of Translation.* Leiden: Brill.
Owen, Lynch O. 1990. "Indigenous Social Formations and the Philippine State." In D. Flaminiano and D. Goertzen, eds., *Critical Decade: Prospects for Democracy in the Philippines in the 1990s* (144–51). Berkeley, Calif.: Philippine Resource Center.
Pe-Pua, R. 1991. "UP Pioneers in Indigenous Filipino Psychology." In B. A. Aquino, ed., *The*

University Experience: Essays on the 82nd Anniversary of the University of the Philippines (152–64). Quezon City: University of the Philippines Press.

Philippine Senate Committee on Education, Arts and Culture and the Committee on Social Justice, Welfare and Development. 1994. *Moral Recovery Program* (commissioned study sponsored by Senator Leticia Ramos-Shahani).

Rimonte, Nilda. 1997. "Colonialism's Legacy: The Inferiorizing of the Filipino." In M. P. P. Root, ed., *Filipino Americans: Transformation and Identity* (39–61). Thousand Oaks, Calif.: Sage.

Salazar, Z. 1974–75. "Ang Pagpapasakasaysayang Pilipino ng Nakaraang pre-Spaniko" [The Philippine historicization of the pre-Hispanic past]. Unpublished manuscript.

———. 1991. "Ang Pantayong Pananaw bilang Diskursong Pangkabihasnan." In V. V. Bautista and R. Pe-Pua, eds., *Pilipinolohiya: Kasaysayan, Pilosopiya at Pananaliksik* [Philipinology: History, philosophy and research] (37–45). Manila: Kalikasan Press.

Sapir, E. 1929. "The Status of Linguistics as a Science." *Language* 5: 207–14.

Spivak, G. C. 1990. *The Post-Colonial Critic: Interviews, Strategies, Dialogues.* Edited by S. Harasym. New York: Routledge.

———. 1992. "The Politics of Translation." In M. Barrett and A. Phillips, eds., *Destabilizing Theory* (177–200). Cambridge: Polity Press.

Steinfatt, T. M. 1989. "Linguistic Relativity: Toward a Broader View." In S. Ting-Toomey and F. Korzenny, eds., *Language, Communication, and Culture: Current Directions* (35–75). Newbury Park, Calif.: Sage.

West, C. 1995. "A Matter of Life and Death." In J. Rajchman, ed., *The Identity in Question* (15–19). New York: Routledge.

Whorf, B. L. 1940. "Science and Linguistics." *Technological Review* 42: 229–41, 247–48.

———. 1956. *Language, Thought, and Reality: Selected Writings.* Edited by J. B. Carroll. Cambridge, Mass.: Technology Press of the Massachusetts Institute of Technology.

12

Slippery Identity and the (Micro-)Politics of Direct Address

Deborah Henderson

The postmodernist contends, in a way that overtly presents the contention as a contestable supposition, that we live in a time when a variety of factors press thought into relatively confined and closed fields of discourse. The persistent drive to personal and collective identity, the way in which a common code of discourse tends to condense and normalize difference, the way in which the onotheological tradition is encoded in the grammar and terms of the language, the intensification of interdependence and the demands of coordination in the late-modern world—all of these elements coalesce to promote closure in discourse, a closure not in which one theory gains hegemony, but in which complementary theories compete with each other in ways that tend to conceal affinities and complementarities between them. The political task, in a time of closure and danger, is to try to open up what is enclosed, to try to think thoughts that stretch and extend fixed patterns of insistence.

—WILLIAM CONNOLLY (1991, 59)

Underneath this cultural system lurks the postmodern individual. He or she is the sine qua non of the system. Neither a myth nor an illusion, the individual struggles with the language systems that are presented by the larger culture. He or she fights for personal meaning, carves out social relationships, builds moral careers through work and family, accumulates and loses wealth and property, lives and dies and feels emotion. This individual confronts the hyperreality of the postmodern period: Sometime she does it with grace, sometimes she is duped—at other times she takes it for granted. What is assured, however, is that as she lives her life she leaves a mark upon it, and that mark cannot be solely or entirely given by the larger culture and its fabricated structures of social experience.

—NORMAN K. DENZIN (1992, 298)

The problem has never been our political logic, but the way we enact it. We can imagine a perfect society but can't maintain a decent relationship.

—MICHAEL FRANTI (1991)

■ ■ ■ ■

Politically charged identities often are deployed in everyday life to rearticulate and inculcate the oppressiveness of identity itself, and perhaps for a good reason. The tension between freedom and social control is played out as subjects inhabit identities shaped by the mundane routines and interactions of everyday life. I focus here on exploring the ways in which the political is implicated in the process of interpersonal interaction, and vice versa.[1]

With my theoretical roots embedded in symbolic interactionism, I move my thinking to an almost mythical space where interactionists and poststructural political theorists engage each other. Bringing together poststructuralist political theory and symbolic interactionism (i.e., acknowledging interaction as a political site and political sites as sites of symbolic interaction) is my effort, borrowing from the opening quote by Connolly, to open up what is enclosed and to try to think in ways that stretch and extend fixed patterns of insistence. In other words, I point to the "affinities and complementarities" between and among interactionist and poststructuralist political perspectives and suggest ways that each may inform the other—a project inspired by the calls of Fred Davis (1992) and Norm Denzin (1992) to rethink the "symbolic" in symbolic interactionism.

Poststructuralist attention to the interiority of the subject via Lacanian psychoanalytic theory certainly speaks to the question of "why" actors do what they do when they encounter others. Symbolic interactionism, however, taking a certain pragmatic and rather behaviorist slant toward social analysis, speaks to the question of what actors do and "how" they accomplish anything in interaction with each other at all. Both perspectives rest on very similar philosophical assumptions of agency and subjectivity. Each considers slightly different yet fundamentally interconnected aspects of social action that, when read together, may offer a look at how political subjects enable and limit social transformations and resignifications in everyday life.

Identity, its uses and effects, rests on processes of reciprocity and negotiations of meaning that occur among social interactants. Consider a world of theoretically rich practice that so easily goes unremarked, most evidently in the micropolitics of identity in classroom interactions, even classrooms where poststructuralist theory destabilizes understandings of subjectivity, identity, and justice.

Identifying the Subject

"Who am I?" Answering this question helps me and others make sense of my life as it takes shape over time through social interaction. Who I am defines me in relation to others. It ostensibly tells me (and others) if I have any legal rights that I can invoke or need to protect, if I can speak in certain situations or if I should remain silent, and if I can claim full membership privileges in certain groups or if I should defer to the privileges of others. Who I am, presumably, tells me (and others) who I can refer to as "us" and who I can refer to as "them" (or, more ominously, "those people"). Once I (and others) know who I am, I (we) supposedly know if I am to be believed and accepted, who my friends are, who my enemies are, and where I can boldly go and when or if I can or should go there on my own, by my "self."

However, I do not decide or determine who I am. Since the day I was born, I am a subject of and thus subjected to state, cultural, social, national, and interpersonal regulation. My birth certificate constituted me on that day, the day I more or less literally "came out" to the world with a categorical identity. Unable to speak for my "self" at birth (having no language and having no self), I was "othered" by the state. Discourses articulated me into existence: I was identified as an autonomous individual, gendered, heterosexualized (by default), racialized (whitened by default), legalized, nationalized, named, dated, placed, and linked to social history through my "biological" lineage. I was unique just like everyone else. Such acts of identification served, paradoxically, to constitute my subjectivity. How does this happen, and why?

STRUCTURES THAT ACT

According to Louis Althusser (1991), the rules regulating me are articulated and activated through particular social institutions—what he calls "Ideological State Apparatuses" (ISAs). I am "interpellated" or "hailed" into existence by my family, church, and school; I am constituted by them just as they keep me "in control" and "in my place" throughout the course of my life. Institutions teach me what my identity is and what it means, what behavior is expected of me, and how I might manage my social relations. In other words, ideological discourses teach me "my place," who I "am," and how I should interact. I am identifiably different from others who may be just like me. I am taught, and learn, to recognize the boundaries separating me from those who are not me. And I am encouraged to maintain that boundary by learning to take for granted the ideological assumptions that appear to stabilize the social world—for example, I will go to school and "learn my lessons," graduate, enter the workforce, work diligently and reliably, get married, have children, fear and love God, pay taxes, obey civic laws, honor tradition, celebrate certain holidays, defer to authority, have regular check-ups, respect property, mind my own business, defend my country, "be all I can be," desire the latest everything, and so on. These assumptions supposedly render the world, in that romantically longed-for way, predictable.

Suppose I question these assumptions. Suppose this taken-for-granted stability begins to terrify me. Suppose the order I desire seems too restrictive, small, boring, blasé, oppressive, or privileged. How do I resist subjugation without sacrificing coherence and predictability? How do I create social change?

From the moment I was able to speak and act, have I been able to say or do anything that transgresses the boundaries or destabilizes the identifications and assumptions institutionally established by the ISAs? And, speaking of "I," is there a real self, a free-thinking self, outside the fashioned subject "hailed" into subjection by the ISAs? (Althusser suggests there is not.) Must "I" remain both a subject of and subjected to ideology, social norms, and conventions, bound by habit and discursive technologies? Can these master's tools, as in Audrey Lorde's famous question, ever dismantle or perhaps just unsettle the master's house?

Recently, political theorists have begun to consider the question of subjection and subjectivity from a poststructuralist perspective. Fracturing the transcendental subject and moving the site of political conflict into the social arena locates political theory in the midst of social interaction in everyday life. How, then, are the processes of social interaction implicated in constituting and subjugating social subjects?

The Subject of Interaction

Attempts to theorize and abstract discursively constituted, or ideologically articulated, political subjects[2] seem to run into trouble when people actually engage in the everyday practice of interacting with others. In practice, we find ourselves (re-)enacting the modern liberal subject. As discussed in more detail in this chapter, we "hail" ourselves into existence, for example, in the act of calling for and offering introductions. We are, cleverly, discursively constituted subjects, but ones who have been constituted by and through the Kantian discourse of individuality—the hard-wired individual who thinks and doubts and who, therefore, exists.

Theoretically, the sense-making subject at the center of symbolic interactionism learns to think, develops (and continues to develop) a consciousness, only through language. The subject of interactionism is a discursively constituted, multifaceted, work-in-progress collection of "selves" made possible only in interaction with others. In practice, however, the Kantian version of the subject is usually the one we haul into the interaction process when we encounter someone else. During the business of interacting, it seems, we tend to think of ourselves and (some/most) others as instrumental and autonomous "agents" who use language to express inner selves, who reify some "core" identity, placing our own and an other's "doer" behind the deeds done, and who judge authenticity, authority, and credibility on the basis of "truth." This is the subject, for example, of dramaturgical analysis—the actor who acts and who acts toward others with the Hegelian desire to be recognized as a free agent. Goffman's (1959) presentation of self in everyday life is, indeed, the actor's presentation of someone who appears to be the perfect image of Kant's transcendental subject, regardless of how he or she has been theorized. A competing discourse, I think, has not been fully realized in practice, and so we continue to interact, most of the time, using a version of the subject that perpetuates and exacerbates, on the micropolitical level, everything we aim to critique and unsettle through macropolitical social theorizing.

That poststructuralists and others have theorized the subject as discursively constituted has little bearing on how interactants act toward each other as they actually interact with each other—and that they do interact seems to beg the question: What would a fundamentally interaction-oriented version of discursively constituted and politically invested subjectivity look like in practice? This question points to a gap both in poststructuralist theories of subjectivity and political address and in social psychological theories of symbolic interaction. A closer look at an actual interaction may illustrate some of the difficulties theories of politics and interaction face.

The Justice and Identity Seminar

Depending on the course, the classroom is an interesting site for observing identity because many of the class members meet each other for the first time and interact only in the context of the course. Prior to my introduction to the others in the "Justice and Identity" seminar, I was familiar with only two other students and had a passing acquaintance with two of the three professors. In large part, I constructed my knowledge of the other participants based on their presentations of self (appearance, manner, and setting), the statements they made about who they were, and how they used their identity to ground their authority to speak about issues relevant to the course material. During the sixteen weeks of the seminar, we invoked our identities many times (often tacitly) to engage each other directly or in the third person.

If I had a transcript of our "Justice and Identity" seminar, I could draw on it to describe our interactions. I might comment on how we, the participants, identified ourselves during the course of the seminar. Some self-descriptions I recall are "sociology student," "attorney," "undergraduate," "department chair," "Hawaiian," "anarchist," "lesbian," "faculty-student," "communications student," "eastern European," "legal scholar," "interactionist," "activist-scholar," and "musician-freak." (There were also a few participants who were rendered mysterious or forgettable either by their silence or by my obliviousness. And there was a man in a motorized wheelchair who, perhaps without invoking an identity based on disability at all, may have been marked, by our imputations, by his appearance in the wheelchair.) A transcript also would make it possible to examine how we inhabited and constructed our identities: what was said by whom and to whom, under what circumstances, and what words, gestures, and tone of voice were used. A transcript might suggest how others responded (or did not respond) to what was said and how those dynamics shifted over the course of sixteen weeks. In other words, if I had a transcript, I could trace our identity claims and enactments and interpret the consequences they invoked. I might explore at what points in the interaction participants were silenced (by others or by themselves), at which junctures they were empowered to speak, how they gained or lost authority and credibility and how that was managed, and how and when a core identity was either directly invoked or tacitly imputed. If I had a transcript or, even better, an audiovisual recording of the classroom interactions, I could use various methods of analysis to offer "evidence" of the role that identity (micro)-politics played in the interactions. Arguably I could reconstruct what we apparently did to each other and to ourselves in interaction and how we enacted and embodied discourses and conventions that demanded, denied, enabled, constrained, ignored, rejected, and subjected each others' identities.

However, since I attended the seminar as a student rather than as a researcher, I made no record of the seminar's group dynamics for ethnomethodological analysis. All I have, and all we ever have left over from our usual everyday interactions most of the time, is a somewhat faulty and one-sided memory of the experience. The impression the seminar left on me has influenced, and continues to influence, the ways in which I make sense of the class. The rest, I guess, I have forgotten—or I just cannot remember until something jogs my memory.

The classroom setting involves its own peculiar set of dynamics, as well as the usual reciprocal dynamic of sense making, as it occurs in interactions. In the classroom, as in other settings, the interactants govern themselves by invoking or tacitly enacting a set of rules, rules constituting a particular form that orders the interaction and renders it intelligible, in this case, as a "classroom" (i.e., taken-for-granted rules or norms governing deference and demeanor among students and faculty). The forms change, as Simmel has shown (Levine 1971), but the process of social reciprocity in each form remains constant, allowing the interactants to adapt the various forms to new situations and adapt to the constraints the forms require for a new situation's intelligibility.

In the case of the "Justice and Identity" seminar, we "tacitly agreed to agree" (Garfinkel 1967) that "university classroom" provided the form, and we seemed to proceed *as if* the rules of the classroom were exactly the same for all of us, exactly understood in the same way by all of us, held the same meaning for all of us, and were limiting our behavior in the same way. But I would argue that in the classroom we negotiated conflicts over meaning with each other, specifically regarding identities, and that those conflicts were somewhat contained but not eliminated or fully determined by the institutional form ostensibly governing the interaction.

The Process of Interaction

From an interactionist perspective, interaction appears as a constant process of trying to make sense of what seems to be going on around us. We may invoke certain discourses like medicine, psychology, religion, or various social theories to help make sense out of social phenomena. We may also call on a plethora of social forms, such as the greeting, sociability, conflict, domination, education, and so on, to help structure various portions of our interactions (Levine 1971). One of the most familiar yet perhaps the most politically charged of these forms is the introduction. Symbolic interactionism offers a useful analysis of how introductions work.

At least in practice, the project of introductions assumes a "core self" that hangs together long enough to be known. Caught up in the immediacy of interacting, we sometimes try to (re)present, skip to, this transcendental self and ignore the possibility of a self in the process of continuous becoming. An introduction functions like a shortcut. To an extent, once introduced, others act as if they now know who we are. Typically, when the other represents him/herself, we tend to view such presentations of self as accurate and true, and we assume the coherence of the subject. On the basis of introductions, we assume that we can predict how others will behave: what they like, what they want from us, what they expect from us, what they understand, what they agree with, what offends them, and so on. An introduction to a person with a supposedly fixed identity provides a map of the other's behavior, and it also provides a map of the interaction: given who I think I am and given who I think you are, I now think I know how to make certain predictions about the interaction itself[3] and the relationship between us (the interactants). A more fundamentally flawed and philosophically problematic notion is hard to imagine, yet it is only by using this flawed conception that we are able to manage interactions with each other at all (Goffman 1959; Mead 1962).

The saving grace of many interactions may be that our introductions often serve as smoke screens, diverting the gaze of the other from certain aspects of our supposed selves and, instead, focusing it on other aspects that we believe are more relevant or advantageous to us in the interaction. For example, people of color who pass for white in a racist culture necessarily hide an invisible, albeit politically charged, racialized identity in their introductory statements. Conversely, the coming-out moment(s) of those who claim a gay or lesbian identity intentionally expose(s) a more or less invisible, albeit politically charged, sexualized identity. For others, however, the attempt to hide certain privileged identities related to wealth, education, professional status, sexual orientation, and so on may be useful in certain situations. (Such attempts to conceal identity also may be moot since failing to come out as heterosexual, for example, simply suggests one's taken-for-granted heterosexuality.) Regardless of our intentions, these secret(s), those parts of our experiences we prefer to keep hidden from view for whatever reason, always situate us in the midst of a potential minefield of judgments.

In a world that many of us like to think of as orderly and fair, we sometimes do very nasty things to each other and to ourselves in interaction: We categorize, evaluate, and nail each other to a fixed identity. Fixing another's identity can limit or expand the range of possibilities we allow in our expectations for their behavior. The injury of stereotyping and its concomitant role in discrimination and prejudice indicates the dangerous potential of introducing ourselves to others. It is not always wise to be "honest" when introducing ourselves, for the complexities of our identities may make us too vulnerable to their judgments.[4] We always risk opening ourselves to ridicule, persecution, or being dismissed as too tedious. Everything we say, or do not say, can work against us in interaction. Still, we often produce an introductory statement when asked to do so, perpetuating the violence of categorization and the myth of the transcendental subject, even though we know ourselves as multidimensional. We produce a neat introduction in an attempt to control how others define us (Goffman 1959; Stone 1975). Seen in this way, performing our identity becomes a reciprocal endeavor in which we try to hide all the contradictory stuff about our selves or what we anticipate to be unsavory or secret while we manage to appear coherent, consistent, and, most important, identifiable and socially acceptable to another actor.

*Inter*action, by its very nature, is problematic because relatively few aspects of interaction can be individually controlled. Not everything goes as expected. In the process of interacting, power is created and then slips in, out, and between the interactants, perhaps creating effects we wish to avoid. However ambiguous, unpredictable, and uncontrollable interactions may be, many of us still muddle through by believing that we have some control over most aspects of our lives. And because we believe we have control, we tend to overlook the enormous amount of knowledge, skill, trust, and luck our everyday interactions require of us, and we overlook the precariousness of our ability to accomplish our goals.

The presumably simple act of introduction is embedded in a complex system of identity (micro)-politics, consisting of, among other things, presentations, interpretations, expectations, reciprocity, negotiations, power, and privilege. Here the conceptualization of identity is not about the individual *qua* individual; rather, it is about the reciprocal process of *inter*acting. This point is crucial. By focusing on reciprocity rather than individual acts, identities begin to appear as something we must continually construct as an ongoing achievement.

Identity and Poststructuralism

Interactionists, however, do not have a corner on the conceptualization of identity as an ongoing performative achievement. Judith Butler (1995) has argued, like the interactionists, that identities (specifically gendered identities) are constituted in performances, in the "doing" of identities, rather than preexisting or essential. Additionally, she points to how linguistic conventions, or codes, are central to the constitution of identities:

> A performative act is one which brings into being or enacts that which it names, and so marks the constitutive or productive power of discourse. To the extent that a performative appears to "express" a prior intention, a doer *behind* the deed, that prior agency is only legible as the *effect* of that utterance. For a performative to work, it must draw upon and recite a set of linguistic conventions which have traditionally worked to bind or engage

> certain kinds of effects. The force or effectivity of a performative will be derived from its capacity to draw on and reencode the historicity of those conventions in a present act. (134)

Butler's arguments share some strikingly similar dispositions with symbolic interaction theory and, more specifically, with certain aspects of ethnomethodology.[5] Butler, like interactionists and ethnomethodologists, recognizes that identity is produced by enacting the rules or conventions constraining individual behavior. However, Butler goes on to say,

> Benhabib chooses not to consider what meaning of performativity is at work, and proceeds to reduce "performative constitution" to a behaviorist model in which the term "expressions" are said to construct or fashion a social self (Goffman appears to be the model for such theory). The notion of performativity that I use, however, is one that runs directly counter to the one that Benhabib describes as "we are no more than the sum total of the gendered expressions we perform." (134)

Butler attempts to separate herself from interactionism by referencing Goffman, whom, I believe, she misreads. Although dramaturgy is a derivative of symbolic interactionism, it is specifically an analytical tool for the empirical study of interaction. Brissett and Edgley (1975) cogently describe the dramaturgical perspective:

> The fusion of individual and society and the insistence that human activity be examined within the framework of interaction is buttressed by an epistemological stance that impugns any form of classic determinism. The concern is to describe the process of human behaving—an analysis of the possible consequences of ongoing activity—does not lead to a search for the antecedents of this activity and does not involve explaining the causal relations between individual characteristics and elements of the culture or society. (4)

Goffman's use of "performance" does, indeed, suggest that identity is constructed around "expressions" given and given off by the actor, but his purposes are not to establish the interior of the actor but rather to explore the interaction process in which only perceivable expressions are accessible to the other interactant. Hence, what he offers is a systematized method for studying *how* identity performances operate within interaction. To find the theoretical underpinnings of Goffman's analytical work, one must refer to G. H. Mead's philosophical development of mind, self, and society from his social behaviorist perspective.[6]

Butler's poststructuralism and Mead's particular social psychology are strikingly similar in terms of both the centrality of language and the location of agency in a discursively constituted subject. Much of Mead's project, delineated in *Mind, Self, and Society* (1934), is oriented toward exploring how language and interaction socially constitute the "individual" or actor—a work in progress who repeats and enacts social conventions and linguistic codes as he/she engages in symbolic interaction. Ralph Turner (1975) develops the notion of "role-making" from Mead's preliminary work on the socially constituted self (role-taking). Anticipating poststructuralist theories of subjectivity, Turner argues that roles are nothing more substantial than idealized sets of behaviors we come to expect and to which we hold each other accountable in various situations over time. Individuals become socially intelligible subjects through situationally contingent enactments of those idealized roles (or subject positions) vis-à-vis reciprocating others.

Butler's work on subjectivity and agency, particularly in *The Psychic Life of Power* (1997b), clarifies Mead's fuzzy distinction between the "I" and the "me," a distinction in which he tried to articulate the location of agency in the actions of discursively constituted actors. However, he left his work in this area unclear, as many theorists after him have demonstrated.[7]

Butler's explorations into the interiority of the subject, on the other hand, somewhat clarify but extend beyond the scope of Mead's work in an attempt to explain "why" actors do what they do. Mead's behaviorism pointed his attention toward the "how" of symbolic interaction and shaped his thinking around explaining what makes interaction possible and how it works. Although much of his work skirts the edges of Freud's concepts of the id, ego, and superego (Melzer 1972), he was concerned with the workings of interactions more than he was with the workings of the human consciousness as such. As Melzer suggests, the best way to understand Mead is to invert the usual order (mind/self/society) and to see his thought as proceeding society/self/mind. For Mead, the self *is* clearly generated in the organism through society (see, e.g., his discussions of play and games in childhood socialization) and then becomes evidence for the existence of mindedness. Importantly, then, what the self is is the reaction of others and the expression of what it takes to behave in ways that they find appropriate.[8] Butler's work more fully explores the components of the socially constituted mind and offers a more complex look inside.

However, by separating herself from interactionism, Butler has no theoretical model for incorporating an interacting, reciprocating other into her analysis of subjectivity. Much of her work seems to assume a solitary subject constituted in/by discourse as if discourses were reified and transcendental themselves and somehow existing "out there."

> When the subject is said to be constituted, that means simply that the subject is a consequence of certain rule-governed discourses that govern the intelligible invocation of identity. The subject is not *determined* by the rules through which it is generated because signification *is not a founding act, but rather a regulated process of repetition* that both conceals itself and enforces its rules precisely through the production of substantializing effects. In a sense, all signification takes place within the orbit of the compulsion to repeat; "agency," then, is to be located within the possibility of a variation on that repetition. (Butler 1990, 145)

A subject stumbles into the quagmire of discourse, or stumbles into fixed conventions and rules that exist without their being invoked, interpreted, and enforced by someone. Her attempts to include others in the constitution of the subject acknowledge the "caller" or the "interpellator" as initiating subjection, but she never quite seems to involve them in the complexity of interaction as reciprocating, rationalizing actors in the scene (see Butler 1997a, 1–41). Repetition, for Butler, is the result of a psychological "compulsion" to repeat. By sidestepping the subject's reciprocal interaction with others, "compulsion" appears to have no social context. Without a link between the ongoing social exterior that includes others and the psychological interior, we lose the accountability of the society that has subjugated us—an aspect of subjectivity that Turner's process of "role-making" and, more generally, ethnomethodology address. Butler is perched on a very significant precipice, I think: taking theories of language, discourse, psychoanalysis, and subjectivity to an exciting height and needing only the addition of *inter*action to achieve a truly compelling *social* insight. Certainly I am not suggesting that symbolic interactionism has all the answers. But I do think that without attention to human sociality, for which symbolic interaction offers a compelling body of research and thinking, poststructuralism, perhaps unnecessarily, loses some of its intuitive appeal.

Interactionists and ethnomethodologists argue that there are interacting and reciprocating others behind the compulsion and the signifying. Discourses and structures do not "act"; people are not compelled to act by institutions in the abstract. What is necessary, what is lurking behind the compulsion and the enforcement of regulations, what is doing Althusser's interpellating, in other words, are other people—who invoke socially constructed and conventionalized rules as they interact through language while simultaneously constructing and conventionalizing them.

Both Butler and symbolic interactionists would agree that rules and conventions precede the actor and that identity is a matter of continually acting within the boundaries of such rules and then successfully repeating the performances over and over again. For the interactionists, however, performances are given before others. The performances we give are those we think others expect, those we imagine as intelligible to others. I will come back to this point in a later section. Butler provides a psychological component to identity performance, but I suggest that she is guilty of a kind of reductionism as long as she ignores the role that other people enact in the ongoing development of our psychological states.

Although rules, discourses, and conventions may precede the actor, meaning is not fixed but negotiated within the context of the interaction and based on others' responses (see Brissett and Edgley 1975). Symbolic interactionism offers a radically indeterminate picture of interaction that both mirrors Butler's philosophical grounding (up to a point) and could provide that piece of social psychology to enrich the analyses she has developed. Performances take place before an audience, and the meaning of the actor's identities, the situation, and the discourses that constitute conventions and rules are all contestable within the boundaries of the interaction. To analyze such a process, as I have already discussed, some attention must be directed to the interaction, not only to the individual. To anticipate responses, interpret observable data, and impute motives is a social process. In this regard, interactions become sites where subjects struggle for control over meanings. This radical indeterminacy is the intersection of discourses; it marks interaction as the site where performances enable agency.

According to symbolic interaction theory, an interactant's psyche is ultimately inaccessible to other interactants. Psychological drives and compulsions are pragmatically inaccessible to the actor him/herself, typically constructed after the fact (Scott and Lyman 1975), and therefore irrelevant to the unfolding interaction (the social behaviorist's philosophical debt to American pragmatism). Such a perspective reorients analyses of the signifying power of language by shifting its gaze to the signifying power of actor(s) who invoke certain utterances in meaningful ways, utterances that, in turn, must be interpreted and negotiated by other meaning-giving actors (Mead 1962). Language, then, is not irrelevant in symbolic interactionism simply because meaning is contestable. Here, in fact, is to be found the point of entry for poststructural insights.

Butler's work shifts the question of "agency" away from the need for a foundational active agent, reformulating agency as a "question of how signification and resignification work" (Butler 1990, 144). Agency, claims Butler, "is to be located within the *possibility* of a variation on that repetition" (145). According to her,

> If the rules governing signification not only restrict, but enable the assertion of alternative domains of cultural intelligibility, i.e., new possibilities for gender [for example] that contest the rigid codes of hierarchical binarisms, then it is only within the practices of repetitive signifying that a subversion of identity becomes possible. (145)

Recent political theory, then, has found poststructural theory, like Butler's work on gendered identities, useful in addressing the identity crisis in political movements. New political theory reformulated the "subject of rights" from "liberalism's autonomous, rational, individual" into a social subject whose subjectivity is "socially located, temporally specific and potentially riven within a series of other relational difference" (McClure 1992, 122) and the diffusion of what can be called "political sites" across the surface of the social itself (123). These shifts in political theory suggest an opening for the unique insights of symbolic interactionism and, perhaps, a much needed critique of its self-touted apolitical "interest" in how interaction works.

Most symbolic interactionists continue to consider the "political" as something *outside* the process of interaction. Many interactionists *imply* a self-motivated, more or less instrumental, agent when they refer to their "actor." To the extent that the self is an Enlightenment version in Mead, it is the product of others treating it in that way as evidence of the tenancy of the organism by an Enlightenment subject who can display a mastery of body, behavior, and environment orientation acceptable to them.[9] The slippage between what the actor does (the dramaturgical actor) and what the actor is (Mead's socially constituted, work-in-progress subject) often defies detection in theoretical and empirical work within interactionism. Such an agent is assumed to possess the qualities of the able-bodied, white, heterosexual, male (i.e., rational, neutral, and objective), despite Mead's claim that such a transcendental subject is impossible. Presumably because we all must negotiate language's inherent ambiguities, such an agent appears to interact on the infamous sociopolitical "level playing field." Language's ambiguity, then, provides the actor a certain degree of freedom, including freedom from overdetermination by language, discourses, institutions, others, and so on. With meanings and discourses in competition for the attention of the sense-making actor, he or she, though never outside their constitutive power, finds the constraints of language and discourse unavoidably ambiguous (Davis 1992). Only through "interaction with one's fellows" (Mead 1962; Blumer 1969) can actors arrive at some degree of shared meaning, and it is in interaction with others that actors feel and then enact the effects of social inequality.

Political discourses and political ideologies may (or may not) influence the "self-talk" of interacting subjects. Thus, an actor who begins to think of him/herself, act, and react as if interaction itself takes place on a decidedly unlevel playing field experiences interaction as a site of the political. This collision of power with indeterminacy introduces political conflict into the process of interaction and makes the exploration of actors' interiority a useful analytic undertaking.

Butler overlooks the interactional processes wherein discourses are animated through performances and those performances are perceived, interpreted, sanctioned, ignored, invoked, or imputed by others over time. Interactions are the sites of contestation. They provide the stage, the audience, the subtext, and the reason for the iterative, potentially subversive act of performativity. Interactions are where power and resistance occur. By definition, in order for a performance to be a performance, it must have an audience (even if the audience is one's reflective self). In order for a subversive act to be labeled as such, it must respond to someone else's enactment of oppression, and it must be perceived and defined by someone as subversive. The text of identity must have a reader, but, once the reader enters the analytic picture, complicating and confounding interpretations of what is being read (i.e., the "self") enter as well.

THE POSSIBILITY OF POSTSTRUCTURAL POLITICAL ACTIVISM

Instrumental political social activism, as Kirstie McClure (1992) suggests, is a notion that presupposes the modern liberal subject of rights who makes claims as juridical demands on the state. In response to postmodern pluralism's discursively constituted and multiply situated subject, political subversion, or boundary transgression, or instrumental social activism appears to have lost its unitary, transcendental "agent." How, then, can the poststructuralist subject ever unsettle the "master's house"?

Butler (1995) locates agency in the "doer" who is produced by the uncertain working of discourse:

> If the subject is a reworking of the very discursive processes by which it is worked, then "agency" is to be found in the possibilities of resignification opened up by discourse. In this sense, discourse is the horizon of agency, but also, performativity is to be rethought as resignification. There is no "bidding farewell" to the doer, but only to the placement of that doer "beyond" or "behind" the deed. For the deed will be itself and the legacy of conventions which it re-engages, but also the future possibilities that it opens up; the "doer" will be the uncertain working of the discursive possibilities by which it itself is worked. . . . In this sense, the "doer" will be produced as the effect of the "deed," but it will also constitute the dynamic hiatus by which further performative effects are achieved. (135)

Political subversion is a possibility because constitutive discourses converge and compete and necessitate repetition. Repetition, then, enables variation. Butler (1990) states that "variation generates a variety of incoherent configurations that in their multiplicity exceed and defy the injunction by which they are generated" (145). She teases out the possibility of agency for the discursively constituted subject, an undertaking that, as I already suggested, Mead never successfully completed.

Adding the interacting other into the analytical frame, enactments of repetitive identity performances appear reciprocal. For interactionists, iterability cannot be sustained, in part because it occurs in a negotiated and reciprocal interchange between the interactants. Repetition does produce failures. Variations in the repetition of successful past performances (performances that have achieved the desired response from one's audience) occur simply because interactants repeat them in a range of situations before numerous interactants over time; others get used to the variations and so adjust their expectations. Individuals are bombarded by constituting discourses such as demands *by others* to occupy a variety of subject positions at once (similar to what sociologists would call "role strain" or "role conflict"), or to perform them in differently "appropriate" ways by differently interpreting others, or to perform them in new situations. Such variations in audience, setting, and situations necessarily produce a plethora of variation in the iteration of complex performances, thus, as Butler argues, enabling new possibilities for resignification.

Others desire and so demand repetitions of us, and we of them, for the sake of stability (e.g., so that "we appear to be ourselves today"). We reenact our identities, reaffirming our own subjection, over and over again in interaction with reciprocating others as a way of imposing consistency, stability, and some degree of predictability onto our otherwise chaotic worlds. Social order, then, is a condition of our "subjecthood." We compel each other to maintain it, we "police" each other (Garfinkel 1967), we make each other into intelligible subjects (Turner 1975).

THE POLITICS OF "DIRECT ADDRESS"

Moving away from social change strategies that reinscribe the modern liberal subject who addresses grievances to the political or legal system, McClure (1992) suggests that seemingly stable political identities can be destabilized through tactics enacted in our everyday lives, tactics she refers to as a politics of "direct address." Drawing on McClure, Lisa Bower (1994) claims that such a politics can be a useful tactic, particularly when engaging law, to destabilize identity in everyday encounters because it causes us to "question in the most profound way the assumptions we make about the meaning(s) of others' (as well as our own) identities" (1011).

The "direct address" tactics of the political activist group, Queer Nation, provides an empirical example of how the need to repeat our enactments of identity might be strategically deployed. In response to the U.S. Supreme Court's decision in *Bowers v. Hardwick* (1986), Queer Nation instituted a number of subversive political tactics through a "kind of guerilla warfare that names all concrete and abstract spaces of social communication as places where 'the people' live. . . . Its tactics are to cross borders, to occupy spaces, and to mime the privileges of normality" (Berlant and Freeman 1993, 196). One example of Queer Nation's tactics of "direct address" targeted shopping malls—an assumed (heterosexual) "family environment":

> In dressing up and stepping out queer, the network uses the bodies of its members as billboards to create what Mary Ann Doane calls "the desire to desire." As queer shoppers stare back, kiss, and pose, they disrupt the antiseptic asexual surface of the malls, exposing them as sites of any number of explicitly sexualized exchanges—cruising, people watching, window-shopping, trying on outfits, purchasing of commodities, and having anonymous sex. (211)

The impact of this tactic is the creation of "desire," marketing queerness, like the latest fashion, as a desirable commodity to shoppers who do not already desire it. Shifts in what we consciously or unconsciously desire potentially creates a shift in the ways we align ourselves with others—how we identify others and how we identify with them. According to Bower (1994),

> Cultural and social transformation is best understood from a perspective of shifting affiliations and identifications. Transformation occurs not merely by exposing differences and arguing for their inclusion under the guise of liberal tolerance; rather, change occurs when the affiliations of "ordinary people" are reconstituted. (1030)

Citing Douglas Crimp, Bower says that "identities are constituted in relation to each other, but they are also constituted through political identifications which constantly reconfigure those identities" (1030).

Both McClure and Bower acknowledge the interactional nature of direct address. Queer Nation offers an empirical description of how the tactic was deployed in interaction. But the discussions of "direct address," like Butler's discussions of identity subversion, do not extend analyses to the interaction processes among the actors, activists, and their audiences, who are directly and reciprocally involved. The micropolitical realm of the social, the process of interaction, is not really their focus, just as it never really was Butler's, even though, I would argue, it is implicit in the very notion of "direct" address.

These thinkers do insinuate, more or less directly, that variations in performances can reorient the expectations—and desires—of those who are reciprocally engaged in interaction. Recognition of the interactional nature of subject formation and transformation suggests that "direct address" targets political agency as a tenuous characteristic, or potential, of the interacting subject.

I suggest that everyday interpersonal interactions themselves entail tactics that are always already a form of "direct address," albeit a form that truly is dispersed throughout the social body. A closer look at the micropolitics of interaction suggests how and under what circumstances "direct address" does its political work.

Interaction and the (Micro)-Politics of "Direct Address"

In *inter*action, two people (at minimum) engage in an ongoing process of constituting each "other" through the invocation and enactment of various discourses that, in turn, constitute their "selves." Sites of political contestation over meaning become scattered throughout the minutiae of the interaction process. The power to define is reciprocal and, as Foucault (1978) has argued, the opportunities for resistance are everywhere at all times.

AMBIGUITY AND STRUCTURE

In everyday life, ambiguity in the form of an other's interpretation not matching the self's intentions is rampant. Our interactions with others, while often relatively unproblematic, just as often include misinterpretations, mistaken identity, misidentifications, misattribution of motive, mistaken assumptions, and misrepresentation, not to mention self-silencing, boorishness, hurt feelings, incomprehension, rudeness, insincerity, and the like (Davis 1992, 274). Slippages in meaning, which are features of any interaction, unsettle the interaction itself. They are the products of interaction between interpreting individuals in interaction. There are no underlying meanings or "truths" appearing, somehow, to transcend the process of interaction. In the absence of objective meaning (Derrida 1982), social life unfolds as a process of continual negotiation where meaning can be inferred only from the response others make to our actions[10]—a response based on how performances square with our expectations for them.

An expanded view of interaction might illuminate these moments of meaning, many of which may occur simultaneously: my concept of myself and the situation (vis-à-vis you), yours (vis-à-vis me), my interpretation of the situation (vis-à-vis you), yours (vis-à-vis me), my statement of identity (vis-à-vis you), yours (vis-à-vis me), my interpretation of your statement of identity (vis-à-vis you), yours (vis-à-vis me), my performance of my concept of my self and stated identity (vis-à-vis you, i.e., what I "do"), yours (vis-à-vis me, i.e., what you "do"), my interpretation of your performance (what I impute to you) and evaluation of that performance given my expectations from your statement of identity (vis-à-vis you), yours (vis-à-vis me), my actions and reactions to you (vis-à-vis you), yours (vis-à-vis me), my interpretation of your reactions to my actions and reactions (vis-à-vis you), yours (vis-à-vis me), my reinterpretation of the situation (vis-à-vis you), yours (vis-à-vis me), my reinterpretation of my self (vis-à-vis you), yours (vis-à-vis me), my reinterpretation of you (vis-à-vis you), yours (vis-à-vis me), and so on.

Interaction appears as an ongoing process fueled by the negotiation of meaning based on perceptible responses that meet or fail to meet our expectations in some way; and, as we interact with others, it is clear that this is all we have to go on. In this sense, interactants are neither rational nor irrational—they are rationalizing (Brissett and Edgley 1975).

In interaction, nothing is stable (Levine 1971). Stability, or rather the pretense of stability, must be imposed—and indeed, one must impose it. We cannot get into the head of the person who is interacting with us, and we certainly cannot look to language to infuse both parties with "shared meaning." We simply are not telepathic. Even if we were telepathic, we still might find only the constant deployment of more discourses anyway, more language at the mercy of yet more interpretation (Becker 1975a).

Thus, in order to render intelligible such radical ambiguity, actors try to make interactions orderly (Becker 1975b; Berger 1975). Expectations do just that. Who I say I am (indicting the speaking subject) implies my experience in the world. Others expect me to be who I say I am; they expect me to perform within their limited and limiting expectations of my identity (Brissett and Edgley 1975), or else they may not believe me to be who I say I am.

In everyday interactions, despite our intentions, we continue to impute our own identities and characteristics and those of others based on expectations that trap us in a signifying field and reinscribe relations of power and privilege. Consequently, we continue ignoring the power we deploy in micropolitical practices of identification—that is, until we are challenged. A politics of "direct address" may be useful because its political work takes place in the social enactments of identities and intentionally challenges expectations of others' and our own behavior in certain settings.

To illustrate how expectations about interaction impose order and still remain radically indeterminate and unstable, I return to the "Justice and Identity" seminar. Some of the dynamics of "direct address" in everyday interactions may emerge if we can see how identity is problematized by others' interpretations and expectations.

THE (MICRO)-POLITICS OF IDENTITY: THE "JUSTICE AND IDENTITY" SEMINAR REVISITED

On the first night of the "Justice and Identity" seminar, one of the instructors asked the seminar's participants to present a brief introductory statement. The professors called on us to claim an identity, making salient our uniqueness, peculiarities, differences, and, conversely, our affinities, allegiances, and memberships. We hailed each other into existence. Although we arguably considered the reactions of others before speaking, I do not know whether or not we spoke with a sense of the injustice we might do to ourselves or to each other. Did we recognize the problem of claiming a coherent self? Did we have a clear sense of the limitations inherent in the labels or categories we could choose—and did choose—to apply to our "self"? Were we aware of the specific discourses our identity labels invoked? Did we have a sense that the experiences that constituted our biographies themselves have been constituted in and defined by discourse? Did we have a sense that the discourses we were invoking to establish our individuality also were invoking an image of us that would be interpreted by the others and generate expectations for our behavior? Did we have a sense that our own constructions were taking discursive shape as the initial interaction unfolded? Did we realize that we were responsible for policing the boundaries between "acceptable" and "unacceptable" behavior as we responded or did not respond to each other's performances?

In struggling to "face" a new group of strangers and to take on theoretical issues of identity and justice, I know that I, for one, focused my energies on attending to my self in relation to others: how I was constructing myself as an acceptable member of the class and how I was dutifully and respectfully accepting the constructions of themselves the others were introducing. I certainly did not want to draw attention to my self by disrupting the intelligibility and flow of the classroom form. I was aware of trying to escape certain categorizations by others, but I am not sure I was fully aware of questioning my role in categorizing them.

According to one of the professors, the point of the introduction "exercise" was to place all the expectations of introduction in question. Could it be that the ambivalence many felt about the exercise indicated that some had just this constitutiveness in mind? One of the instructors, last to introduce, precisely said, "I am [name], and I find fascinating the unremarked identity of the [American Indian] art work on the wall surrounding us"—a tactic the instructor suggests called the very nature of introductions into question.

But were introductions called into question with the instructor's statement? Did the comment do what the speaker intended it to do? Did we "get" the point? Was there only one point to get? Similarly, when I changed my name tag to read "Call me Ishmael" at a "Law and Society" conference, did I call the credentializing function of identity claims into question? Were we both, myself and the instructor, kept in control by others' nonresponse to our tactics? Did the unintelligibility of our tactics call our own identities into question? If so, did it expand or delimit the interpretation others made of us? The interactants may have interpreted our tactics in various ways, each with differing consequences in the interaction. My part in the seminar as a reciprocating, interpreting, and rationalizing participant in the classroom, for instance, provides a look at how en-actions often have unintended consequences and, perhaps, transformative resignifications.

Flying in the face of one of the most taken-for-granted assumptions in a graduate seminar, one of the students announced her undergraduate status. As a subject position, "undergraduate" carries very little credibility in terms of establishing the performer as an authoritative knower. Since it is an invisible identity (one could not tell by looking), why did this student "come out" to us the first night of the class? What did her claim to be an undergraduate accomplish? I would argue that it did accomplish something. However, stating with any certainty what that something was and how and whether or not that something held for everyone in the room, over time, is impossible. Of the many identifications made by the students in the seminar, the "undergraduate" comes to mind as I think back on the seminar because her disclosure invoked my own discomfort of inhabiting that particular subject position, under similar circumstances, eight years earlier.

During the course of the seminar, this "undergraduate" gave a very atypical performance, upsetting what some of us might have expected would follow. Her performance as a bright, articulate, informed student familiar with the theoretical complexity of the course material might have established her credibility as a knowledgeable scholar in that room full of graduate students. But whether it did or not is unclear. While I was busy constructing my own modern liberal subject to introduce to the class, I was trying also to figure out just who this undergraduate really was. The logic of Goffman's impression management suggests that the undergraduate declared and performed her identity so as to reorient our taken-for-granted assumptions about her. Her atypical behavior may have sent a destabilizing message: I inhabit an undergraduate subject position, but I am not what you expect.

Did her performance successfully constitute her as someone with the authority to speak despite the discrediting status her identity claim betrayed? She might have convinced the rest of us (or some of us) to judge her on the basis of her unusual performance of "undergraduate student" rather than on a performance we were expecting. But things could have and (for all I know) might have gone a different way.

Once upon a time, as a nontraditional undergraduate, I disclosed my status in a graduate seminar, too. What was I thinking? I followed my statement with an enactment of shyness that was part embarrassment for being too old for the position, like a fifteen-year-old sixth grader. I disclosed my position, a preemptive strike, because I was afraid I would not be able to rise to the intellectual level of the other "graduate students" and I wanted the others to make allowances for me. And I disclosed my position because I had heard the others introduce themselves, and chances were looking pretty good that I was as smart as they were (and me only an undergraduate). I considered my past experiences and my rationalizations as I tried to make sense of the undergraduate in the "Justice and Identity" seminar.

Why did she invoke her undergraduate status? She appeared older than the stereotypical undergraduate; she was "passing" successfully. Perhaps the specter of "justice and identity" made passing more salient than usual. Perhaps she feared her "real" identity might be exposed by several class members who were "on to her," who knew the "truth" about her. She risked being defined as dishonest should she have been exposed as an imposter, pretending to be something others knew she was not. Coming clean, her preemptive strike, may have been the moral high road in this context. Honesty just might have been the best policy because *honesty* could and often does establish credibility. I could empathize with this position.

But if a person imagines that his/her unexpected performance will be favorably received by others or pragmatically useful, why not just "come out"? It could be that transcending a stigmatized real identity gains one more political purchase in interaction than the conventional performance of an identity others expect one to give. A more favorable response is elicited from others if one transcends anticipated limitations. After all, one of the discourses constituting "Americans" as "free individuals" is the legacy of Horatio Alger and our morally noble attitude about the "determination of the human spirit." This particular undergraduate rose above the intellectual limitations of undergraduate experience. I should be ashamed of the expectations I had for "undergraduate." After all, I had to struggle, too, to rise above others' assumptions about me, the thirty-seven-year-old undergraduate.

Perhaps some of us did make sense of her by drawing on the discourse of "success through hard work." She was the undergraduate who rose above those whose lack of effort tends to discredit many undergraduates, who escaped the seduction of the university "party culture," and who, through hard work and perseverance, elevated herself to a higher intellectual level—a woman who, perhaps, survived and overcame patriarchal oppression to develop a sophisticated intellect and get herself to college despite obstacles. In many ways, she represented the undergraduate as heroine. I, as a feminist, should be proud of her.

After "coming clean" about her "real" identity, class members still might have defined her as pretentious, as someone who was trying to act like something she experientially was not (a graduate student), someone who was trying deliberately to pull off a performance she was not authorized to play. Once her audience knew that she was an undergraduate, every move she made might have brought her identity under closer scrutiny as we weighed her "real" identity, the one we imputed to her, against her obviously contrived performance (the one she was enacting). We might have construed all her actions as proof that she was an arrogant graduate student *wannabe* (cf. Becker 1963; Scheff 1966; Lofland 1969). There might have been no escaping the limits of the undergraduate identity. Perhaps this is what my fellow students thought about me in 1990 when I was the undergraduate in their seminar.

To deploy her confession strategically, supposing that is what she did, suggests that identity claims, because they are also subject positions, operate in the realm of the semiotic within the larger signifying field superceding specific interaction (Butler 1997a). Perhaps she was trying intentionally to challenge our assumptions and expectations of an undergraduate performance in a graduate seminar. Maybe she was trying to unsettle identity. That notion never occurred to me.

Actors cannot fully anticipate which discourses interactants will invoke to define situations[11] or how those discourses, once invoked, may be used (Thomas and Thomas 1928). The undergraduate may have had some control over her introduction, over her attempts at impression management (Goffman 1959), but still she was trying to construct her self in interaction with others who made imputations and interpretations beyond her control. She could not have anticipated the convolutions my thinking went through as I tried to make sense of her. In the end, I made sense of her based on my own experiences: She was an undergraduate in a graduate seminar and should have enacted a deferential demeanor. I expected her to act like I would act if I were in her place, like I acted when I *was* in her place—but she did not.

Either our expectations of others' actions hold up, are supported by their performances, or they do not. If they do not hold up, it is possible that one may outperform an identity (escape the limits) with favorable results (Turner 1975). Or one may fail to perform it adequately enough. Or one may end up in a less flattering defining frame—"pretentious graduate student wannabe" instead of "undergraduate." Or one's audience may reexamine assumptions about the labels and categories they use; for example, maybe "undergraduates" are not as intellectually limited as we thought. Maybe strangers, like an undergraduate among graduate students, should not be expected to defer.

The undergraduate did not act like me. She was not shy. She was not quiet. She was not deferential. This was all I knew about her. She simply did not meet my expectations. She did not fit into my ordering of the world, so I made her fit (Garfinkel 1969). Rather than shifting my assumptions, exploding the category "undergraduate" (like I should have done as a feminist, a nontraditional student myself, a Christian perhaps, or a poststructuralist), I reinterpreted her. I developed a "quasi-theory" that satisfactorily explained her and let me, after all, contain her in my defining frame. She did not unsettle my assumptions; rather, I used them against her, unfortunately, to discredit her. Consequently, I never spoke to her. What is more important, however, is that I never engaged with her comments when she spoke in class and so never allowed her contributions to influence my thinking. Had I been the only one in the class or the professor (some "significant" other), I might have silenced her with my nonresponse, suppressing her voice, her standpoints, and her experiences.

The part that I and others might have played in responding to her arguably transgressive performance must not be overlooked. Why she acted in a particular way—all her motives, all her rationalizing—is something I could only imagine; her psyche was inaccessible to me. Whether she altered her *intended* performance based on her audience's response is moot; I simply cannot know. But what I do know is that we enacted social control, either with our silence or with our direct engagement with her, in response to her performance.

The key to this example and, I would suggest, any other interaction is that we are not just abstractly constituted by discourse or that we constitute discourses with fixed and unitary meaning but that the process of identification is interactional and reciprocal. We impute identities to others and struggle within the confines of our/their assumptions. The process is both complicitous with and resistant to supposedly taken-for-granted social conventions because we are stuck in an ongoing negotiation of meaning with someone else. Destabilizing an identity potentially makes its politicized nature salient and exposes the identification/introduction process as a site where we struggle to categorize our interlocutors so as to contain them within our assumptions and expectations. But our/others' performances are co-created and coterminous with our/others' expectations of those performances. Both the actor and the audience are implicated in the identification process.

THE "SLIPPERY" IDENTITY

When the spotlight of "Truth" finally found me in the seminar, I had already prepared my self for introduction. Introductory statements, as I have argued, are all about "coming out"—coming out and, perhaps, *coming clean,* owning up to identities that are supposedly "written on the body" and intransigently grounded in experience. In that initial moment, we decide who we think we are, a decision usually steeped, as I have already suggested, in hegemonic conceptions of autonomous individuality and hounded at every step by the dogs of "Truth." In moments of introduction, we force ourselves swiftly to sum up the situation and decide how much of the "truth" of our fictitious coherent self we are willing to risk disclosing before this particular audience. After all, this bit of impression management is the basis on which we not only define others but judge them as well.

In the first moments of the "Justice and Identity" seminar, I "came out" as someone who has, to quote myself, "no morals, no integrity, and no clear understanding of the word 'justice.'" Sitting there in the public confessional hearing myself talk, I worried about how the eighteen or so other members of the class would interpret my statement. Did it make me seem like a clever, witty adult whose aim was not to be pigeonholed, whose goal was to destabilize the foundation on which the inclusions and exclusions of identity politics are based? Or did it make me seem like an asshole stranger from the Sociology Department who has no social skills? The audience decides.

Constructing an introductory statement, or identifying my self, is, for me, a painful and, in the end, disappointing experience, in part because identity statements are contingent on others' interpretation. What we say, and the coordination of our introductory statements with our presentations of self, is not totally within our control. I am never sure about who I "really" am or who I can get away with *saying* I am, despite the seemingly definitive proclamations of my birth certificate. And I am never sure who I want to "risk" saying I am. Worse, I am never sure that, once I "come out" as someone, the authenticity police (other interactants) will not bust me for the failure of my performance to live up to others' expectations based on my claims. I really *do* have no integrity, no objective core self to provide my identity with some structural character. Beyond the interactionism discourse that helps me continually (re)present the interactionist rap, I obviously have no moral ground other than hypocrisy. I usually go ahead and struggle anyway to come up with something I can say or do in a few seconds that effectively will give the impression of cohesion and integrity to that fragmented work in progress, my discursively constituted self. I do this despite my theoretical bent and my skepticism toward truth claims. I will try, with the best of 'em, to manipulate the impression I make, regardless of (or perhaps because of) its potential political effects. Alas, despite my theoretical, political rationalizing, when pressed, I still shamelessly try to pretend that I am an autonomous transcendental subject whose self is outside the discourses constituting me. And in the spirit of good old American pragmatism, it works—some of the time. After all, the uncertainty of identity is the point: a recognition of both the limitations *and* the enabling power of ambiguity and instability.

But all the elements of identity construction come into play, as I have argued, through the embodied, interpreting actor. As Simmel might argue, nothing happens until people start to talk and use meaningful gestures. The interpreting actor puts language into circulation and negotiates with others to give it meaning. People exist in signifying fields that articulate but can never predictively determine how our social relations cohesively hang together (Hall 1979). Those fields are maintained by interaction. Any cohesive structure we may believe orders our social relations is a chimera that "we" continuously maintain by imposing our expectations of appropriate behavior on others and seeing those expectations either met or challenged.

Our identities *mean* something, based not only on the identities we claim but also on how those identities, as well as those that are imputed to us, figure in the signifying field of social relations that we discursively articulate together (McClintock 1995). Embodied actors make discourses live and breathe, so to speak, and give them constitutive power by invoking them. Interacting human subjects, just by "doing," activate, circulate, privilege, and interpret certain discourses in the process of acting and constructing interpretations of the world around them. Discourses, deployed in interactional performances, constitute actors, and through those discourses we impose the violence of categorization on each other through our expectations and assumptions and, thereby, constitute our selves as individuals. They do this not because they are outside of language but because they are constituted in language's excesses.

To see interaction as always already political, in that meaning is always up for grabs, is to see people drawing on a variety of overlapping discourses in order to make sense of social life and circulating them with various degrees of authority. We may critique political identities in the macropolitical realm, but without a turn to interaction we often overlook the way we uncritically employ an insidious form of identity politics, of limiting and enabling, of inclusion and exclusion, in the *micro*political realm.

Introductions, for example, are always already a politics of "direct address" of sorts, even though we may not recognize it as we struggle to control identity. Refusing the confinement of categorization, resisting identity arrest, has the potential to disrupt the fundamental taken-for-granted assumptions and expectations through which power operates (West and Zimmerman 1987; West and Fenstermaker 1993). But we are doomed only to potential disruption because interaction is a messy and complex process. "Direct address" may be the wisest strategy for social change precisely because it targets social structure at its source: others' expectations in reciprocal interactions. But, though it does not guarantee social transformation, it is a tactic that operates at the potential source of human agency.

Concluding Remarks: "Slippery" Identity and "Direct Address"

McClure (1992) argues that "post-modern pluralism opens the possibility of a quotidian politics—a politics which extends the terrains of political contestation to the everyday enactment of social practices and the routine reiteration of cultural representations" (123). Such a move toward everyday social practices locates politics in interaction—in the intellectual and empirical terrain of symbolic interactionism. Further, problematizing subjectivity and the signifying fields within which interpreting actors attempt to define situations and negotiate the excesses and overflows of meaning may strengthen Mead's symbolic interactionism and speak to the calls of Davis (1992) and Denzin (1992) to rethink the "symbolic" in symbolic interactionism.

Both symbolic interactionism and poststructuralist political theories, though they narrow their focus differently, rest on very similar philosophical assumptions. Butler's work on agency and performativity extends and clarifies a distinction that Mead tried to make between the fleeting "I" of potential agency and the ongoing construction of the subjugated "me." However, Butler's dismissal of "Goffman" and "those behaviorist approaches to performativity" (Butler 1995, 134) rests on a misreading of dramaturgy and closes a potentially useful dialogue between her theoretical insights and Goffman's unique method of empirical observation. Such a misreading tends to set up interactionism, by association, as a straw man that she and others can then dismiss.

Mead's use of the term "individual" can be confusing. However, the "actor" at the center of his symbolic interactionism is taken for granted to be a socially constituted subject. Butler and others explore the regulating conventions of language and discourse as they operate to constitute subjectivity in the interior of the social actor. Mead emphasizes social symbolic interaction, or how actors use language and discourse in everyday interaction to constrain and constitute social subjects in a reciprocal relationship with others. Developing a way to read the two perspectives together may offer insights into the problematic nature of sociopolitical activism.

While introducing ourselves may appear to be a means of self-definition, the process is much more complex and politically charged because of the interpreting other to whom we orient our introductions. In a micropolitical maneuver, we invoke as well as impute identity in our interactions, and those invocations and imputations have consequences in ongoing activity. In our interactions with others, we maintain or unsettle established social order; we constitute and resignify social identities and identifications.

Sociopolitical life *is* the process of interaction, and so transformative tactics, like a politics of "direct address," must begin at a very concrete level with the question, How far are we willing to go to unsettle other people's expectations and assumptions about appropriate identity performances, to interrupt convention in order maybe to alter their defining frames? And further, how far are we willing to go to alter our own expectations and assumptions? In the interest of unsettling the "master's house," what if we do recognize the impossibility of a core self as we interact with others? What if we resist invoking or imputing a fixed identity at all? How much are we willing to risk in order to resist being identified by others and identifying others in ways that constitute and reinscribe power relations—if we are so inclined?

Given the nature of stigmatizing identities, to what extent are many people even able to come out as someone whose identity is more or less "slippery"? And further, how might slipperiness itself become a privileged position? In everyday interactions, many people are faced with managing socially stigmatized perceptible identities vis-à-vis others (i.e., not white, not male, not Anglo featured, not able-bodied, not old enough or young enough, and so on) in order to be taken as, or responded to, as if they are privileged and treated with respect, civility, or courtesy. Attempting to perform within the existing limits of others' expectations maintains the status quo while buttressing the exclusions and inclusions that define acceptable behavior. Interactions, then, unfold in the nexus of power and knowledge, in the reciprocal process of maintaining order and intelligibility.

But for those who can question interpellation, who can resist turning around to answer to their own subjugation, the political question becomes, Am I willing to come out as a slippery character? Am I willing to destabilize my own taken-for-granted (and possibly socially acceptable) identities? Am I willing to do my part to resist identity arrest; to refuse to provide information for others that makes them comfortable with my, perhaps, socially acceptable identities; and to refuse to provide information that allows others to assume that the world is as they expect it to be? Am I willing to stop demanding this from others?

Just how do we juggle sharing a destabilized self with the power that privileges the credible speaking subject, those with the power and privilege to speak and to identify the world in relation to them? How do we learn to speak from a destabilized position, keeping in mind that to claim any position reinstitutes expectations and identifications that a politics of direct address aims to destabilize? An authentic identity implies that we occupy a position that is always already contingent on some center/margin binary, and making an identity claim means that we must invoke this system of signification. "Speaking up" forever traps us in the signifying system of language. Speaking up for our selves, ironically, binds and gags us in language's binary opposition of inclusion/exclusion. But we cannot remain silent against the politics of interaction, as I have stated already, lest we become complicit with the status quo and concede that transgression is not possible (except by accident).

Is it possible to speak from an unstable position or claim an unstable identity? How do we reconceptualize this technology of identity in such a way that it still facilitates interaction but explodes the assumptions and expectations that make interaction painful and politically oppressive?

I would argue that destabilizing one's identity does not really threaten the interaction process, necessarily. As in the example of the undergraduate, it does not render interaction impossible. But destabilizing one's identity fundamentally challenges the expectations and assumptions on which social judgments are made culturally intelligible. It sets on slippery ground both the invocation and the imputation of stable identities. It problematizes expectations, but it does not eliminate them.

Destabilizing identity requires the disclosure not of what or who we are but of our failures, however intentional, in performing those taken-for-granted identities that have been imputed to us or are expected from us—the contradictions and excesses that destabilize a unitary and conventional classification. But seen as a process of interaction, proactive social change is not just about presenting a "slippery identity" in order to destabilize others' expectations or reconstitute or realign their affiliations. But also, in the (micro-)politics of identity, we need consciously to destabilize our own expectations of others.

Future work might look at the notion of a "slippery identity" and its effects within interaction. What, we might begin to ask, is the impact of a "slippery" identity on social interaction; what is gained and what is lost? And what are the implications for social order and social change once the political subject truly is destabilized, not abstractly, but in the concrete processes of symbolic interaction with others?

Notes

1. I have chosen to focus here on the actor in interaction. This is not to ignore the material consequences of patterns and practices of injustice. It is, however, an effort to contribute to thinking about the relationship between meaning-making and agency, resistance, and power.

2. Foucault argued, at least in his later work (1988), that the human "subject" is not as overdetermined as it might seem from within Althusser's prison-house of State Ideological Apparatuses: "We are thinking beings, and we do . . . things not only on the ground of universal rules of behavior but also on the specific ground of a historical rationality" (148)—we take into consideration the past and the possibility of future consequences when we act. Because Foucault sees power dispersed throughout the body social in forms that are generative as well as repressive and deployed by people ostensibly in interactions with each other, he argues that the possibility for resistance must necessarily be equally dispersed throughout the body social as well (Foucault 1978). It is precisely at the intersections of competing discourses that one finds sites of resistance—sites of political contestation—waged by "rational," thinking beings, beings who are caught between conflicting interpretations of reality, drawing on past experiences, and trying to figure out how to behave and what to do in the present situation by considering future consequences of their potential actions.

3. As far back as 1902, Simmel (Levine 1971) articulated a method of social analysis that begins with the notion of social forms, similar to the Platonic notion of forms, applied not to things but to social interaction. These social forms serve as frameworks that we use to make sense of and give order to what we perceive to be going on in the social world around us. The identification of the proper form for use within a given situation, then, begins with that swift assessment of who is involved in the interaction and under what circumstances the interaction is occurring.

4. Simmel (Levine 1971) was among the first sociologists to conceptualize the self as contingent on the other pointing to the risk to the construction of the self, in particular, and to interaction, in general, that this contingency engenders. Ernest Becker (1975b) argued that, in order to protect our fragile self-concept and to facilitate interaction, we risk a certain amount of self-exposure to the other and trust that the other will respect our gesture by responding in kind. Garfinkel (1972) argued that when we engage in interaction with each other, we tacitly "agree to agree" that certain rules exist and that we should follow them. In this sense, interaction is built on a tacit contract struck between self and other, between risk and trust, and unfolds within the confines of the strict policing of convention. The limitations of convention and repetition, in conjunction with the absence of objective meaning, enable agency by rendering interaction as sites of unavoidable ambiguity and, thus, political contestation.

5. For an ethnomethodological analysis of gender as the nexus of cultural assumptions and discourses and sets of performative acts that take place in interaction with others, see, for example, West and Zimmerman (1987) and West and Fenstermaker (1993).

6. For an excellent overview of Mead's social psychology, see Melzer (1972).

7. See, for example, Kolb (1944).

8. I would like to thank Robert Dingwall for his guidance in this area.

9. Again, I would like to thank Robert Dingwall for his guidance in this area.

10. Mead's (1962) philosophy begins from a social behaviorist orientation positing the impossibility of getting into the heads of humans and knowing absolutely what goes on in there. For Mead, when we engage in interaction with others, all we can ever know about what the other is thinking are the inferences we make based on what we perceive about their behavior. This does not preclude the work of cognitive psychologists; it renders their work relevant to interacting actors only insofar as they draw on psychological discourses to attribute motive to others in the process of making sense of what is going on in the interaction.

11. This notion, one of the most important tenets of symbolic interaction, is based on W. I. Thomas's famous axiom: "If a man defines a situation as *real,* it will be *real* in its consequences" (Thomas and Thomas 1928; italics added).

References

Althusser, Louis. 1991. "Ideology and Ideological State Apparatuses (Notes Toward an Investigation)." In Ben Brewster, trans., *Lenin and Philosophy, and Other Essays* (121–73). London: New Left Books.

Becker, Ernest. 1975a. "The Self as Locus of Linguistic Causality." In Dennis Brissett and Charles Edgley, eds., *Life as Theater: A Dramaturgical Sourcebook* (58–67). Chicago: Aldine Publishing.

———. 1975b. "Socialization, Command of Performance, and Mental Illness." In Dennis Brissett and Charles Edgley, eds., *Life as Theater: A Dramaturgical Sourcebook* (292–301). Chicago: Aldine Publishing.

Becker, Howard S. 1963. *Outsiders: Studies in the Sociology of Deviance.* New York: The Free Press.

Berger, Peter. 1975. "Religion and World Construction." In Dennis Brissett and Charles Edgley, eds., *Life as Theater: A Dramaturgical Sourcebook* (234–42). Chicago: Aldine Publishing.

Berlant, Lauren, and Elizabeth Freeman. 1993. "Queer Nationality." In Michael Warner, ed., *Fear of a Queer Planet: Queer Politics and Social Theory* (193–229). Minneapolis: University of Minnesota Press.

Blumer, Herbert. 1969. *Symbolic Interactionism: Perspective and Method.* Berkeley and Los Angeles: University of California Press.

Bower, Lisa. 1994. "Queer Acts and the Politics of 'Direct Address': Rethinking Law, Culture, and Community." *Law and Society Review* 28, no. 5: 1009–33.

Brissett, Dennis, and Charles Edgley, eds. 1975. *Life as Theater: A Dramaturgical Sourcebook.* Chicago: Aldine Publishing.

Butler, Judith. 1990. *Gender Trouble: Feminism and the Subversion of Identity.* New York: Routledge.

———. 1995. "For a Careful Reading." In Seyla Benhabib, Judith Butler, Drucilla Cornell, and Nancy Fraser, eds., *Feminist Contentions: A Philosophical Exchange* (127–43). New York: Routledge.

———. 1997a. *Excitable Speech: A Politics of the Performative.* New York: Routledge.

———. 1997b. *The Psychic Life of Power: Theories in Subjection.* Stanford, Calif.: Stanford University Press.

Connolly, William. 1991. *Identity/Difference: Democratic Negotiations of Political Paradox.* Ithaca, N.Y.: Cornell University Press.

Davis, Fred. 1992. "On the 'Symbolic' in Symbolic Interaction." In John Johnson, Harvey A. Farberman, and Gary A. Fine, eds., *The Cutting Edge: Advanced Interactionist Theory* (267–82). Greenwich, Conn.: JAI Press.

Denzin, Norman K. 1992. "On Semiotics and Symbolic Interactionism." In John Johnson, Harvey A. Farberman, and Gary A. Fine, eds., *The Cutting Edge: Advanced Interactionist Theory* (267–302). Greenwich, Conn.: JAI Press.

Derrida, Jacques. 1982. "Differance." In Alan Bass, trans., *Margins of Philosophy* (3–27). Chicago: University of Chicago Press.

Foucault, Michel. 1978. *The History of Sexuality: Volume 1.* New York: Random House.

———. 1988. "The Political Technology of Individuals." In *Technologies of the Self* (145–62). Amherst: University of Massachusetts Press.

Franti, Michael. 1991. "Hypocrisy Is the Greatest Luxury." The Disposable Heroes of Hiphoprisy. Beat Nigs Music (ASCAP). New York: 4th & B'way, A Division of Island Records.

Garfinkel, Harold. 1967. *Studies in Ethnomethodology.* Englewood Cliffs, N.J.: Prentice Hall.

Goffman, Erving. 1959. *The Presentation of Self in Everyday Life.* Garden City, N.Y.: Doubleday.

Hall, Stuart. 1979. "Race, Articulation and Societies Structured in Dominance." In *Sociological Theories: Race and Colonialism* (305–45). Paris: UNESCO.

Kolb, William L. 1944. "A Critical Evaluation of Mead's 'I' and 'Me' Concepts." *Social Forces* 22 (March): 291–96.

Levine, Donald, ed. 1971. *Georg Simmel: On Individuality and Social Forms.* Chicago: University of Chicago Press.

Lofland, John. 1969. *Deviance and Identity.* Englewood Cliffs, N.J.: Prentice Hall.

McClintock, Anne. 1995. *Imperial Leather: Race, Gender and Sexuality in the Colonial Contest.* New York: Routledge.

McClure, Kirstie. 1992. "On the Subject of Rights: Pluralism, Plurality and Political Identity." In Chantal Mouffe, ed., *Dimensions of Radical Democracy: Pluralism, Citizenship, Community* (108–27). London: Verso.

Mead, George H. 1962. *Mind, Self, and Society: From the Standpoint of a Social Behaviorist.* Chicago: University of Chicago Press.

Melzer, Bernard M. 1972. "Mead's Social Psychology." In Jerome G. Manis and Bernard N. Melzer, eds., *Symbolic Interaction: A Reader in Social Psychology,* 2nd ed. (4–22). Boston: Allyn and Bacon.

Scheff, Thomas J. 1966. *Being Mentally Ill.* Chicago: Aldine Publishing.

Scott, Marvin B., and Stanford Lyman. 1975. "Accounts." In Dennis Brissett and Charles Edgley, eds., *Life as Theater: A Dramaturgical Sourcebook* (171–91). Chicago: Aldine Publishing.

Stone, Gregory P. 1975. "Appearance and the Self." In Dennis Brissett and Charles Edgley, eds., *Life as Theater: A Dramaturgical Sourcebook* (78–90). Chicago: Aldine Publishing.

Thomas, W. I., and D. A. Thomas. 1928. *The Child in America: Behavior Problems and Programs.* New York: Alfred A. Knopf.

Turner, Ralph H. 1975. "Role-Taking: Process versus Conformity." In Dennis Brissett and Charles Edgley, eds., *Life as Theater: A Dramaturgical Sourcebook* (109–22). Chicago: Aldine Publishing.

West, Candace, and Sarah Fenstermaker. 1993. "Power, Inequality, and the Accomplishment of Gender." In Paula England, ed., *Theory on Gender/Feminism on Theory* (151–74). New York: Aldine de Gruyter.

West, Candace, and Don H. Zimmerman. 1987. "Doing Gender." *Gender and Society* 1, no. 2: 125–51.

Part IV

Sexualities

13

The Globalization of Sexual Identities

UNIVERSALITY, TRADITION, AND THE (POST)COLONIAL ENCOUNTER

Carl F. Stychin

This chapter explores what happens to sexual identity categories when they are appropriated outside the Western political context in which they were first deployed. It is now commonplace to speak of the construction of "heterosexuality" and "homosexuality" as the product of medical and legal discourse in the nineteenth century in the West. Subsequently, the identity homosexual was redeployed in positive and self-affirming terms, and the identities lesbian, gay, and bisexual were taken up within a politics of identity in North America and Western Europe beginning in the 1960s. In an era of rapid communications, increased mobility, diasporic communities, and the hegemony of American culture, the globalization of originally Western identity categories is an ongoing phenomenon. The argument, which draws largely on the experience in the southern African region in recent years, is that as sexual identity politics are manifested in different geopolitical arenas, those identity categories are not simply reproduced. Rather, they are articulated in new ways, engaging with and responding to local cultural conditions. Mobilization around sexual identity categories is frequently met by state and popular censure based on the claim that "homosexuality" is a Western, colonial importation foreign to an indigenous, essentially heterosexual culture. This "cultural nationalist" position is often expressed through the language of postcolonial nationalism in which same-sex eroticism is viewed negatively as the constitutive other of national identity.

The relationship between the appropriation and condemnation of identities based on same-sex sexualities is not one-dimensional, however. The appropriation of sexual identity categories in positive terms, what might be described as a "postcolonial gay" position, is frequently bound up with an appeal to the universality of rights discourse, increasingly expressed in the language of international human rights. In contrast, the cultural nationalist position is framed in the language of local traditions, especially the belief in a precolonial cultural tradition in which same-sex sexual acts and/or identities had not yet been imported through the colonial encounter. Demands for homosexual rights are constructed as illegitimate because of their essential foreignness to national traditions and culture. In this form, gay rights are constituted as a modern-day continuation of a colonial past, which undermines a previously colonized people's right to self-determination. Homosexuality and calls for rights by self-described lesbians and gays, emanating both from within and outside the nation, are thereby antithetical to a postcolonial national imaginary.

The relationship between rights, culture, and tradition is more complex than that expressed by cultural nationalists. The postcolonial gay position is not grounded solely in the language of universalism and rights. Postcolonial gays locate same-sex sexuality within a national tradition as well, existing alongside opposite gender sexual preference in precolonial, pluralistic societies prior to European missionaries' and colonial administrators' condemnation. The two positions interpret the history of colonialism and the authenticity of tradition, as well as colonialism's relationship to sexuality, differently. Both embrace, in competing ways, "national identity" and "universal rights," yet each fails to recognize how the opposing position is intimately related to and constitutive of its own argument. That is, both positions prioritize the sexual in the construction of individual and national identity, and each position is constituted through an antagonistic relationship with the other.

This chapter explores the constitution of the cultural nationalist and postcolonial gay positions, drawing on recent political developments in South Africa and Zimbabwe. In this region, tensions between competing appeals to tradition are continuous with the colonial relationship and readily apparent in popular and legal discourse. The friction between the cultural nationalist and postcolonial gay positions reproduces ideological disagreements between cultural nationalism and liberal universalism that have long been present in this region. However, architects of the new constitutional order in South Africa innovatively manage the interpretive differences between these positions, as well as others, by selectively appropriating both the language of universal rights and tradition.

Colonialism's Sexual Legacy

Both the postcolonial gay and the cultural nationalist positions recognize a historical and ongoing relationship between sexual acts and identities and national identity. The difference between the positions rests in their interpretation of "authentic," historically "original" (and therefore legitimate) sexual practices and precolonial societies' prohibitions. While some postcolonial theorists (see, e.g., Darian-Smith and Fitzpatrick 1996) have criticized the search for an authentic identity or culture, insisting on the interrogation of identity from the perspective of economic, political, and historical factors, both cultural nationalists and postcolonial gays scan the past, searching for the "truth" about sexual relations in the present. In analyzing sexual identities, both postcolonial gays and cultural nationalists are correct to emphasize the importance of the colonial encounter. Metaphors of gender and sexuality were crucial to colonialism and imperialism (Mosse 1985), and those metaphors still resonate today not only in the political space of the colonized but in that of colonizer as well.

The "south" was feminized and sexualized, and this is closely related to the emergence of a homosexual identity in the West. As sodomy was disconnected discursively from other nonprocreative sexual acts and viewed as an act that only some might commit, it became the basis of a (homo)sexual identity. Sodomy was increasingly viewed as a sign of difference, but not solely in sexual terms. Sodomy was also a central site for the construction of racialized otherness. In the period of European exploration and colonization (particularly in the eighteenth and nineteenth centuries), same-sex activity was represented as endemic among national others, with sexuality becoming a metaphor of cultural difference (Bleys

1996, 17–62). The colonial encounter required a close connection between femininity and sexual passivity that was integral to the construction of European (and American) national subjects as manly. In other moments, sexual aggressiveness and barbarity were associated with racial difference. Sex role confusion and sexual excess were ascribed to those most clearly defined as outside the (Western) nation. So, too, the homosexual, a historically and culturally specific construct, symbolized the confusion of the sexes and a sexual excess that was foreign, yet also critical, to European national self-constitution (Mosse 1985; Bleys 1996).

Gender stereotyping was one of the keys to European consolidation. Women were controlled by prescribing fixed gender roles deemed essential to the flourishing of the European nation. White, Christian women were configured as the "embodiments of respectability" (Mosse 1985, 97). By valorizing motherhood and the "cult of domesticity" (McClintock 1995, 209), white "woman" became a symbol of innocence and chastity (see also Stoler 1995). The depiction of racial hierarchy in naturalized and familial terms—of colonizers as fathers and the colonized as children—was dependent on "the prior naturalizing of the social subordination of women and children within the domestic sphere" (McClintock 1995, 358). These gender constructions still resonate in postcolonial conditions, and they are resisted in postcolonial struggles in an array of different national and regional contexts.

The construction of gender and sexual identities "cannot be understood apart from their position in relation to local and global political processes" (Murray 1996, 251). This thesis has been developed by Jacqui Alexander (1991, 1994) in her analysis of sexuality and nationalism in the postcolonial state. Linking the impact of globalization to race, gender, sexuality, and nationhood in Trinidad and Tobago and the Bahamas, Alexander explores the criminalization of nonprocreative sexual activity, particularly lesbian sexuality. Heterosexuality has been nationalized, and some sexualities are constituted as perils to the state, in response to challenges to the legitimacy of the nation-state resulting from economic globalization (1994, 7). Lesbianism and gay male sexuality become threats to national identity.

The sexualization of the postcolonial state is complicated by the role of "a political economy of desire in tourism that relies upon the sexualization and commodification of women's bodies" (Alexander 1994, 6). The sexualization of black bodies to buttress white tourism does not imperil the nation through a neocolonial fetishizing of race. The combination of events that signal globalization (e.g., capital flows, large-scale north-to-south tourism, and the separation of production and consumption across continents) is interpreted as central to national vitality and virility (11).

The heterosexualization of national identity underscores how postcolonial deployments of nationalism may reinforce domination and inferiorization along new dimensions in response to economic change, the growth of a global economy, and so on. One example of this is the discourse of colonial contamination, wherein homosexuality is attributed to the white colonizer, and homosexual relations were used to exploit the colonized sexually. According to Alexander, the postcolonial project of nation building has required a "Black nationalist masculinity" as a sign that it was "ready" to govern through the replication (and reification) of Western nationalist norms of "respectability" (13). Homosexuality thus is crucial to the identity of the nation state and the masculine subject (Murray 1996, 252).

The Sexual Identities "Crisis" in Southern Africa

Similar dynamics around sexuality and nation are readily apparent in southern Africa. In 1995, a major news story in the region concerned the Zimbabwean International Book Fair. The theme of the 1995 Fair was "human rights," with Gays and Lesbians of Zimbabwe (GALZ) included. On the eve of the opening, a letter from the state director of information advised the Book Fair trustees that the government strongly objected to the presence of GALZ. Claiming that they had been placed in an impossible position, the trustees cancelled GALZ's registration. A storm of protest ensued, much of it emanating from South Africa. At the Book Fair's opening, President Robert Mugabe stated that he found it "extremely outrageous and repugnant that such immoral and repulsive organisations like those homosexuals . . . should have any advocates in our midst" (Wetherell 1995, 15). Previously, Mugabe had equated homosexuality with immorality, condemning it as an abhorrent Western import (Dunton and Palmberg 1996, 8; Phillips 1997).

The Zimbabwean International Book Fair episode might be dismissed as an isolated outburst from a virulently homophobic national leader, and there are plenty of those throughout all parts of the world. It might also be interpreted as Mugabe's attempt to reassert political leadership in the region in the face of Zimbabwe's declining international role subsequent to Nelson Mandela's election as president of South Africa. Homosexuality is deployed to consolidate the declining power of a nation-state facing a loss of regional political influence and the severe economic dislocation all too common in contemporary African states. In this respect, developments in southern Africa mirror Alexander's (1991, 1994) claims concerning the impact of economic globalization on Trinidad and Tobago and the Bahamas. On another level, the episode exemplifies a particular use of the term "homosexuality," one linking it to the degeneration of an indigenous African (hetero)sexuality brought about by colonialism, capitalism, and the sexual exploitation of Africans by white men. Attacks on so-called perverts thereby serve to reproduce tensions around ongoing racially based economic inequalities in Zimbabwe (Phillips 1997, 482–83). The discourse of black nationalism aims to resist a history of exploitation, subsequently demanding the physical expulsion of homosexuality from the public sphere. The expulsion of GALZ from the Book Fair is metaphorically equated with the erasure of the white colonizer and, with him, his degenerate influence on a mythologized, precolonial African sexuality. Such condemnations of sexual perversion are made in the name of an Afrocentric and Zimbabwean national tradition.

As evidenced in Zimbabwe, the postcolonial appropriation of Western norms of heterosexual respectability and order can be understood as a means of consolidating a national identity under conditions of globalization and also as an attempt to resist the ways in which non-Western nation-states are constructed in gendered and sexualized terms in the West (Cooper 1995, 72). For example, postcolonial African states are seen as sites of disorder and irrationality. The relationship between Western states, by contrast, displays a homosociality, with the sovereign Western nation-state "represent[ing] the fantasy of a certain kind of heterosexual masculinity . . . impermeable, bounded, separate and Other to the chaotic world that surrounds it" (Orford 1996, 63).

The fear of the other in the West is compounded by the effects of globalization: national borders are perceived as more porous and boundaries less rigid, and diasporic communities threaten to infiltrate and rupture the "coherence of the masculine state's corporate identity" (Cooper 1995, 72). The postcolonial state's appropriation of heterosexuality and masculinity as culturally monolithic signifiers is, ironically, a resistance to their construction as the unruly, disordered, passive other.

Reliance on the language of tradition and cultural authenticity, in which heterosexuality is employed as the sexual essence of the postcolonial state, is contradictory and paradoxical. The construction of the colonial subject as tied to custom and tradition made that subject unsuited to the exercise of rights of "universal" citizenship. On the one hand, universal citizenship had to recognize the commensurability of colonizer and colonized (Fitzpatrick 1995). On the other, the construction of "new-found beings" (97) as the savage other made them necessarily incommensurable, located outside modernity's universals, enslaved to the particularity of their "traditions," and in need of the sexual discipline of the civilizing mission (105).

Within contemporary "liberal" Western discourses, the portrayal of "traditional" sexual cultures may well have shifted within the colonial imagination from immoderate and savage to "heterosexual and gender conservatism" (Povinelli 1996, 82). "Traditional" culture is romanticized as pure and founded on stable heterosexual families, which were then damaged in the colonial encounter. Exposure to the European imperial project contaminated that culture and irreparably damaged those traditional family structures. Among some gay activists and academic commentators alike, there is an equally romantic construction of traditional cultures in the Western imaginary: Sexuality "there" embraces both same- and opposite-sex sexual acts freely and interchangeably, without the presence of a categorical Western discourse of sexual identities. In both of these moments, the past is invented and frozen in a pure, uncontaminated, and unreal form as a means of managing the present. While interpretations of tradition may alter, the orientalist urge to exoticize and romanticize remains. This is true of both cultural nationalists and some postcolonial gays.

The combined legacy of colonialism and apartheid has had an overwhelming centrality in the construction of identities in the South African region, and identities today bear the scars of that history. In the nineteenth century, Methodist missionaries sought to reform and "civilize" Tswana conjugal relations so as to regulate their sexuality and inculcate a legalistic view of selfhood, one encompassing a Western model of property rights (Comaroff 1995, 206). But colonialism employed a contradictory discourse about group sovereignty: Europeans fashioned an ethnology of southern Africa that ascribed a series of primordial ethnic identities to Africans, forming the infrastructure on which colonial rule and later apartheid were built. Claims grounded in the language of rights and equality could be met with the following response: The "native" was unsuited for rights because he was "naturally" antimodern and ineluctably attached to the traditions of his ancestors (225). Group sovereignty and identity, grounded in tradition, were used to dispossess and disenfranchise South Africans.

The constitution of South African tradition and ethnic identities was a product of this colonial encounter and depended on "an entire ethnology, [which divided South Africans] into 'tribes' and ascrib[ed] to them a primordial identity based on common ancestors and origins, language and lore, culture and customs, sentiments and interests" (Comaroff and

Comaroff 1992, 214). In the domain of sexuality, that tradition constructed gender roles, domestic arrangements, and relationships to private property as immoderate, undomesticated, and improper.

This colonial construction of Africans' sexual excess and inappropriateness is repudiated and replicated in the events surrounding the well-known 1991 trial of Winnie Mandela for kidnapping, assault, and intent to do grievous bodily harm, in which a supporter carried a placard outside the courthouse that read, "Homosex is not in black culture" (Holmes 1995, 1997). Importantly, Mandela's defense relied on the logic of colonial contamination, which sought to counter the trope of sexual excess by appropriating a mythologized, precolonial African family, untainted by the colonial importation of homosexuality that ostensibly caused its degeneration. Western norms of "respectability" are attributed to precolonial African societies, and homosexuality is a symptom of exploitation by white masculinist colonialism.

Mandela's defense argued that she was attempting to save young black men from the alleged homosexual advances of a white Methodist minister. As Rachel Holmes (1995, 289) argues, this colonial discourse configures white homosexual men as politically suspect. Moreover, not only are homosexual practices a product of colonial exploitation, but Africans also are infantilized, viewed as malleable children, despite the history of political activism among South Africa's township youth. This renders the alleged "victims" devoid of political agency, with Mandela constructed as the "mother" of her nation, fighting to save her children, which reproduces the colonial imaginary historical role of gender in nation building (292). The violence and, perhaps more important, the alleged sexual infidelities and financial corruption associated with Winnie Mandela (the truth of which is largely irrelevant) serve to reproduce colonialism's discursive construction of the African woman as excessive, unruly, disordered, and maternally deficient. The description of Winnie Mandela as mother of the nation has an ironic inflection, as it symbolizes the perceived disorder, violence, and corruption that colonial discourses claimed inevitably followed national independence.

Both the Book Fair incident and the Mandela trial exemplify a central tension between the appropriation and the condemnation of same-sex sexualities and thus a tension between postcolonial gay and cultural nationalist positions. In South Africa, the Mandela trial was a key moment in the crystallization of a national, antiapartheid lesbian and gay movement (Holmes 1997, 177) that has relied on the language of rights and the authenticity of same-sex sexual acts within African cultural traditions. The ongoing campaign against homosexuals (and others) by the Mugabe government has had similar consequences in that it has served to consolidate an emerging lesbian and gay movement in Zimbabwe in which political demands are voiced in the language of individual rights and in terms of the connections among and between Africanism, postcolonialism, and same-sex eroticism. Lesbian and gay identities increasingly are being taken up by black Zimbabweans and South Africans of all races in the public sphere (Dunton and Palmberg 1996). A history, whether mythological or "real," of same-sex sexual acts in African traditional societies thereby is used by some southern Africans to constitute sexual identities. In this way, activists replicate their opponents' discursive strategy: Both draw on a claimed "authentic" identity, one grounded in tradition and ancestry. Cultural nationalists claim that heterosexuality was the only form of sexuality known to precolonial African societies and therefore is the only authentic and legitimate set of sexual practices today. Postcolonial gays argue that a diversity of sexual practices were known, all of which consequently should be validated today as properly "African."

Both cultural nationalists and postcolonial gays also trace the impact of capitalism on the displacement of African men. Focusing particularly, although not exclusively, on the late nineteenth-century development of the gold mining industry in South Africa, cultural nationalists argue that the industry demanded the mass dislocation of African men who were forced to live in single-sex hostels miles away from their families. This displacement underscores how thoroughly colonialism, apartheid, and capitalism are implicated in damaging the African family and in economically exploiting black labor. One aspect of the industry was the presence of "situational homosexuality" in the mining hostels (Moodie, Ndatshe, and Sibuye 1988, 230–36; Harries 1990). This phenomenon was thoroughly documented by colonial administrators and was well known within African communities. It has often been interpreted exclusively in terms of economic exploitation: Homosexuality was produced by the conjunction of capitalism and colonialism, which "perverted" the miners by creating a prison environment.

Cultural nationalists' reductivist and historically narrow reading of same-sex sexual acts in the mines is problematic in that it "serves as an historical apology for male homosexuality in institutions with a preponderance of African men" (Achmat 1993, 104). Zackie Achmat posits that while same-sex practices did occur in precolonial societies (as did prohibitions), colonialism and capitalism "helped establish a new constellation of power relations" that separated the bodies and desires of African men from purely reproductive functions (105). As Pierre de Vos (1996) reiterates, "The central role of missionaries in the process of colonial conquest, the rise of the colonial state as the new sovereign power on the subcontinent, and the interests of the mining houses sometimes contested but mostly colluded in the formation of institutions to regulate the distribution of discipline on the bodies of all its subjects" (274). Cultural nationalists and, to some extent, postcolonial gays thus overlook the effects of colonialist and capitalist power in managing the sexualities of all its subjects.

These examples suggest why the cultural nationalist position offers an insufficient account of the role of same-sex practices and identities in southern Africa. The argument that homosexuality is "un-African" does nevertheless have a ring of truth in that a Eurocentric analysis of sexuality has tended to view same-sex practices in other cultures through the prism of Euro-American sexual identity categories. In a number of cultural locations, same-sex practices occurred without the ascription of a discrete identity, be it "sodomite," "homosexual," or anything else (see generally Herdt 1997; Murray and Roscoe 1998). Thus, Western categorical discourses of sexuality clearly do not apply universally. Cultural nationalists, however, mistakenly think they do and thus are caught in the logic of colonialism without realizing it. The imposition of a colonial system does not necessarily introduce the colonized to same-sex practices. Rather, colonial discourse names and forbids practices that may have been accepted in some cultural contexts (and forbidden or ignored in others) while, at the same time, frequently exploiting the colonized sexually. One of the exploitative effects of colonialism was to construct the "native" as sexually depraved.

Responding to this legacy, some South Africans have drawn on the colonial construction of sexuality and have sought to redeploy the signifier "African," resisting discourses of antihomosexual Africanism, through the postcolonial gay position (Gevisser 1995, 72–73). African homophobia thereby is read as an appropriation of a colonial discourse. By contrast, opponents claim that South African lesbians and gays have imported their ideas (and identities) from the lesbian and gay movements in Europe and North America (a cultural nationalist argument). In this process, Africans have been coopted so as to put a black face on an essentially white, Eurocentric movement.

Cultural nationalism thus is problematic in that it denies the agency of Africans who have appropriated and, perhaps through discourses of Afrocentrism, reworked the identities "lesbian," "gay," or "bisexual." It serves "to misrepresent Africa as statically monocultural, to ignore the richness of differing cultural constructions of desire, and . . . simply replicates much of the colonial discourse on African sexuality" (Phillips 1997, 474).

Postcolonial gays as well must be wary of framing homosexuality as a universal category of identity without recognizing its historical and cultural specificity. Thus, "just as the notion of a singular 'African' culture dangerously misrepresents the wide variety of a multiplicity of African cultures, so it is misguided to assume that the same behaviour will be construed as 'sexual' within different locales" (Phillips, 1997, 474). Such universalizing interventions can act as a form of neocolonialism, ignoring the great cultural diversity within Africa, which is shaped inevitably by the colonial experience and capitalist exploitation (see Murray and Roscoe 1998).

As lesbian and gay social movements develop within South Africa, their relationship to national identity formation continues to unfold. The dismantling of official apartheid has created space for a previously unthinkable range of sexual expression including, but not exclusively, gay and lesbian organizing. The election of the Government of National Unity in 1994 and the beginning of a new constitutional order inaugurated a public debate about the content of the Republic of South Africa's final Constitution. Lesbians, gays, and bisexuals participated actively in that conversation through a carefully managed and orchestrated campaign to ensure the inclusion of sexual orientation in the equality provisions of the Constitutional Bill of Rights (see generally Stychin 1996). Debates about the meanings of homosexuality produced by the Winnie Mandela trial energized the mobilization of gay activists. A "grassroots" campaign was eschewed in favor of a high-level lobbying approach aimed at members of Parliament, organized by the National Coalition for Gay and Lesbian Equality. On October 10, 1995, the Constitutional Committee of the Constitutional Assembly accepted the explicit inclusion of sexual orientation in the equality provisions of the Bill of Rights, thereby ensuring its place in the final Constitution.[1] Self-identified lesbians, gays, and bisexuals read the explicit inclusion of "sexual orientation" as a prohibited category of discrimination as a legitimation of their sexual identities. They became another "color" in the rainbow nation, a metaphor often used to describe emergent South African national identity.

Traditions and Futures

A discourse of liberal pluralism and universal rights, which informed many of the debates about the South African Constitution, was central to arguments for the inclusion of sexual orientation in the equality provisions of the Bill of Rights. Pluralism, heterogeneity, and rights, in this and other contexts, were deployed as the basis on which to construct contemporary South African national identity, whose recent history can be traced back to the Freedom Charter, which was drafted as a statement of political demands by the African National Congress in 1955 (see Stychin 1998, 55–60). According to the Freedom Charter, South Africa belongs to all who live in it, black and white, and no government can justly claim authority unless it is based on the will of all the people (Thompson 1995, 208). Nonracialism, as opposed to Africanist cultural nationalism, was the dominant, although not exclusive, discourse opposing apartheid. The Freedom Charter embraces heterogeneity and plurality rather than the singularity usually associated with nationalist manifestos (Norval 1995, 41–43). While a diversity of voices resisting apartheid made up this umbrella coalition, its rhetoric rested on universals, such as freedom and equality for all on the basis of personhood. The logic of apartheid was confronted by an opposing logic, one grounded in universal rights. The particularism of apartheid, its contingency and its perversion of equality and freedom, was thus revealed. In contrast, a cultural nationalist, "pan-Africanist" standpoint assumed a secondary position within liberation discourses and is now associated particularly with the Inkatha Freedom Party (Norval 1995).

Today, cultural nationalism and liberal universalism remain the two central trajectories around which competing visions of national identity in South Africa are articulated. Struggles around the inclusion of sexual orientation in the constitutional settlement serve as a microcosm for this broader context because they have been articulated primarily through the language of liberal universalism. In this way, the postcolonial gay position is channeled into liberal rights discourse, in large measure because of the central role of legal struggle in the lesbian and gay political agenda in South Africa today (see Stychin 1996).

The equality provisions of the Bill of Rights are a continuation of the African National Congress' (ANC's) tradition of nonracial liberal rights discourse grounded in equality and universal citizenship. They reproduce the ANC's "commitment to a classically European form of nationalism" and to modernity itself (Comaroff 1995, 233). Historically, that standpoint resisted the construction of Africans within colonial discourse as ineluctably tied to tradition, customary law, and the "premodern" world and therefore as unsuited to the holding of "universal" rights (231). Official ANC support for lesbians and gays is articulated within this same discourse. Opposition (even within the ANC), by contrast, has been grounded in a cultural nationalism that reproduces the colonial construction of the African subject as essentially tied to a sexually "pure," precolonial, heterosexual cultural tradition.

When some South Africans responded to the Zimbabwean International Book Fair controversy with protests and stinging condemnation, they reproduced these tensions on an international stage: The South African nation-state symbolized the triumph of liberal tolerance, pluralism, and universal citizenship, while the Zimbabwean government was seen by some as unable and unwilling to transcend the premodern, "'traditional' structures of power" (Phillips 1997, 481). Those structures themselves had been constructed and manipulated historically in the service of colonialism and racialism. By contrast, Zimbabwean government (cultural nationalist) supporters could inaccurately construct South African pro-gay protests as generated by white South African (and other foreign) lesbians and gays as yet another example of the colonial contamination of Zimbabwean culture.

The new South African constitutional order does not simply reflect the triumph of liberal rights over local tradition, however, which would suggest some kind of resolution to a dialectical relationship. Rather, the emerging order attempts to manage these competing conceptions of nationhood as grounded in either traditional culture or universal citizenship. On a broader scale, constitutional discourse reproduces the same contested terrain—the role and meaning of tradition—on which claims for sexual identity rights were made. On the one hand, the South African legal system is now strongly influenced by an international order in which legitimacy has been tied to a constitutional culture founded on a discourse of universal, liberal rights (Klug 1996, 25–29). The influence of comparative and international law in constitution drafting and judicial interpretation underscores this point.[2] This is the discourse through which claims for lesbian and gay rights have been predominantly made. On the other hand, constitutional law is explicitly grounded in an Afrocentric "tradition," which members of the Constitutional Court have drawn on in ruling that capital punishment is contrary to the Bill of Rights, for example.[3] This constitutional accommodation of universality and tradition reproduces the dichotomy that was present within South African liberation ideology as well as in current constructions of sexuality.

Tradition, however, can never be "discovered" in a pure, precolonial form, as is apparent in the way in which sexuality has been constructed, and this point is widely recognized by South African lawyers. While constitutional law recognizes the validity of traditional, local authorities and legal orders, indigenous law is also understood as a product of the colonial encounter. Once manipulated in the service of colonialism and apartheid, many South Africans embrace the universalism of equality rights (particularly around gender), which, they argue, should not be "trumped" by "traditional" values (Mokgoro 1996, 60). The uniqueness of South African constitutional identity may be the way in which constitutional rights discourse, drawn from international law and comparative jurisprudence, interacts with the ongoing construction of explicitly Afrocentric legal concepts, such as *ubuntu,* that are attributed to traditional, precolonial societies (see note 3). A legal hybridity thus may be produced by the incorporation of both universalist and traditionalist approaches, as a result of which the tension between them can never finally be resolved. The limitations of each position always remain open to challenge through the opposing discourse. The embracing of both the universal and the traditional within the constitutional order represents a commitment to a politics of transformation in which two competing trajectories are explicitly recognized as constitutive of national identity itself.

Concluding Thoughts

This chapter has focused on the ways in which the colonial encounter in southern Africa is deployed in the construction of sexual and national identities today, both by cultural nationalists and by postcolonial gays. Advocates of both positions problematically cling to the belief that the legitimacy and authenticity of sexual acts and identities in the present depends on their place in the distant past. The argument of this chapter has been that such appeals to tradition provide at best a partial but often incomplete story and at worst a misreading of history in the service of current political struggles.

In South Africa, the debates about sexuality have been complicated by the centrality of legal discourse in the public sphere, which has largely been grounded in a liberal, universalist belief in the transformative power of rights, a position that itself has had a central historical role in antiapartheid struggles. That discourse was appropriated successfully by gay and lesbian political actors in a successful campaign to gain constitutional recognition in the Bill of Rights. The campaign relied heavily on the language of international human rights and comparative constitutional rights, both of which are explicitly recognized as aids to the interpretation of the South African Constitution.

This appeal to liberal rights is itself problematic and limiting in that it can reproduce a Western hegemony masked by the language of universalism. Thus, for lesbians and gays, it has meant that their claims were articulated largely through the language of universal human rights, which tended to eliminate discussion of the specificities of the colonial encounter in this region. Postcolonial discourse thus was left open to misinterpretation by cultural nationalists, to which lesbians and gays were then forced to respond, often through debates about the sexual practices of ancestors. Law thus played a role both in empowering social movement actors and in shaping and perhaps constraining the way in which demands have been framed.

But legal discourse is also itself shaped by an implicit recognition that neither liberal universalism nor cultural traditions are unproblematic. Both have resonances in the history of the colonial encounter, and both have served as discourses of resistance to colonialism and apartheid, in different ways and with varying degrees of success. Neither of these trajectories thus can be "transcended." Rather, both remain important sources in the construction of a new national identity for South Africa that acknowledges the gross injustices of the past (for which reparations are necessary) but in which identities are not validated or legitimized solely through claims about the meaning of traditional culture.

Notes

Funding for research in South Africa, on which this chapter depended, was provided by the British Academy and is gratefully acknowledged. Thanks to Davina Cooper, Daniel Monk, Peter Fitzpatrick, and the editors for their invaluable comments on previous drafts, and thanks to the participants of the "Justice and Identities" seminar, Arizona State University, for their many insights. Special thanks to Lisa Bower for her many suggestions on earlier drafts.

1. The relevant equality provision (sec. 9 [3]) of the final Constitution of the Republic of South Africa declares, "[T]he state may not unfairly discriminate directly or indirectly against anyone on one or more grounds, including race, gender, sex, pregnancy, marital status, ethnic or social origins, colour, sexual orientation, age, disability, religion, conscience, belief, culture, language, and birth."

2. Section 39 (1) of the final Constitution reads, "When interpreting the Bill of Rights, a court, tribunal or forum—(a) must promote the values that underlie an open and democratic society based on human dignity, equality and freedom; (b) must consider international law; and (c) may consider foreign law."

3. The Afrocentric concept of *ubuntu* is central to this construction of tradition and has been used by the judiciary as a tenet of constitutional interpretation. See especially the judgment of Justice Mokgoro in *S. v. Makwanyane and Another* (1995), where the Constitutional Court of South Africa found the practice of capital punishment contrary to the Bill of Rights: "[W]hile it envelops the key values of group solidarity, compassion, respect, human dignity, conformity to basic norms and collective unity, in its fundamental sense it denotes humanity and morality. Its spirit emphasises respect for human dignity, marking a shift from confrontation to conciliation" (772).

References

Achmat, Zackie. 1993. "'Apostles of Civilised Vice': 'Immoral Practices' and 'Unnatural Vice' in South African Prisons and Compounds, 1890–1920." *Social Dynamics* 19, no. 2: 92–110.

Alexander, M. Jacqui. 1991. "Redrafting Morality: The Postcolonial State and the Sexual Offences Bill of Trinidad and Tobago and the Bahamas." In Chandra Talpede Mohanty, Ann Russo, and Lourdes Torres, eds., *Third World Women and the Politics of Feminism* (131–52). Bloomington: Indiana University Press.

———. 1994. "Not Just (Any)Body Can Be a Citizen: The Politics of Law, Sexuality and Postcoloniality in Trinidad and Tobago and the Bahamas." *Feminist Review* 48 (autumn): 5–23.

Bleys, Rudi C. 1996. *The Geography of Perversion.* London: Cassell.

Comaroff, John. 1995. "The Discourse of Rights in Colonial South Africa: Subjectivity, Sovereignty, Modernity." In Austin Sarat and Thomas R. Kearns, eds., *Identities, Politics, and Rights* (193–236). Ann Arbor: University of Michigan Press.

Comaroff, John, and Jean Comaroff. 1992. *Ethnography and the Historical Imagination.* Boulder, Colo.: Westview Press.

Cooper, Davina. 1995. *Power in Struggle.* New York: New York University Press.

Darian-Smith, Eve, and Peter Fitzpatrick, eds. 1996. "Special Issue: Law and Postcolonialism." *Social and Legal Studies* 5, no. 3: 291–434.

De Vos, Pierre. 1996. "On the Legal Construction of Gay and Lesbian Identity and South Africa's Transitional Constitution." *South African Journal on Human Rights* 12, no. 2: 265–90.

Dunton, Chris, and Mai Palmberg. 1996. *Human Rights and Homosexuality in Southern Africa.* Uppsala: Nordiska Afrikainstitutet.

Fitzpatrick, Peter. 1995. "Passion Out of Place: Law, Incommensurability and Resistance." *Law and Critique* 6, no. 1: 95–112.

Gevisser, Mark. 1995. "A Different Fight for Freedom: A History of South African Lesbian and Gay Organisations from the 1950s to the 1990s." In Mark Gevisser and Edwin Cameron, eds., *Defiant Desire: Gay and Lesbian Lives in South Africa* (14–86). New York: Routledge.

Harries, Patrick. 1990. "Symbols and Sexuality: Culture and Identity on the Early Witwatersrand Gold Mines." *Gender and History* 2, no. 3: 318–36.

Herdt, Gilbert. 1997. *Same Sex, Different Cultures: Gays and Lesbians Across Cultures.* Boulder, Colo.: Westview Press.

Holmes, Rachel. 1995. "'White Rapists Made Coloureds (and Homosexuals)': The Winnie Mandela Trial and the Politics of Race and Sexuality." In Mark Gevisser and Edwin Cameron, eds., *Defiant Desire: Gay and Lesbian Lives in South Africa* (284–94). New York: Routledge.

———. 1997. "Queer Comrades: Winnie Mandela and the Moffies." *Social Text* 15, no. 3/4: 161–80.

Klug, Heinz. 1996. "Participating in the Design: Constitution-Making in South Africa." *Review of Constitutional Studies* 3, no. 1: 18–59.

McClintock, Anne. 1995. *Imperial Leather: Race, Gender and Sexuality in the Colonial Contest.* London: Routledge.

Mokgoro, Yvonne. 1996. "Traditional Authority and Democracy in the Interim South African Constitution." *Review of Constitutional Studies* 3, no. 1: 60–75.

Moodie, T. Dunbar, with Vivienne Ndatshe and British Sibuyi. 1988. "Migrancy and Male Sexuality on the South African Gold Mines." *Journal of Southern African Studies* 14, no. 2: 228–56.

Mosse, George L. 1985. *Nationalism and Sexuality.* New York: Howard Fertig.

Murray, David A. B. 1996. "Homosexuality, Society, and the State: An Ethnography of Sublime Resistance in Martinique." *Identities* 2, no. 3: 249–72.

Murray, Stephen O., and Will Roscoe. 1998. *Boy-Wives and Female Husbands: Stories of African Homosexualities.* New York: St. Martin's Press.

Norval, Aletta J. 1995. "Decolonization, Demonization and Difference: The Difficult Constitution of a Nation." *Philosophy and Social Criticism* 21, no. 3: 31–51.

Orford, Anne. 1996. "The Uses of Sovereignty in the New Imperial Order." *Australian Feminist Law Journal* 6: 63–86.

Phillips, Oliver. 1997. "Zimbabwean Law and the Production of a White Man's Disease." *Social and Legal Studies* 6, no. 4: 471–91.

Povinelli, Elizabeth A. 1996. "Of Pleasure and Property: Sexuality and Sovereignty in Aboriginal Australia." In Pheng Cheah, David Fraser, and Judith Grbich, eds., *Thinking through the Body of the Law* (80–101). Sydney: Allen and Unwin.

Stoler, Ann. 1995. *Race and the Education of Desire.* Durham, N.C.: Duke University Press.

Stychin, Carl F. 1996. "Constituting Sexuality: The Struggle for Sexual Orientation in the South African Bill of Rights." *Journal of Law and Society* 23, no. 4: 455–83.

———. 1998. *A Nation by Rights: National Cultures, Sexual Identity Politics, and the Discourse of Rights.* Philadelphia: Temple University Press.

S. v. Makwanyane and Another. 1995. In Butterworth's *Constitutional Law Reports* 6: 665–792.

Thompson, Leonard. 1995. *A History of South Africa.* Rev. ed. New Haven, Conn.: Yale University Press.

Wetherell, Ian. 1995. "Mugabe Cracks Down on Gay Rights." *Mail and Guardian,* August 4, 15.

14

Walking the Straight and Narrow

PERFORMATIVE SEXUALITY AND THE FIRST AMENDMENT AFTER *HURLEY*

Christine A. Yalda

Parades are public dramas of social relations, and in them performers define who can be a social actor and what subjects and ideas are available for communication and consideration.

—SUSAN G. DAVIS (1986)

Nowadays, the First Amendment is the First Refuge of Scoundrels.

—STANLEY FISH (1994)

In *John J. Hurley et al. v. Irish-American Gay, Lesbian and Bisexual Group of Boston* (1995), the U.S. Supreme Court ruled that a group of openly gay Irish-Americans (and their supporters) could not participate in Boston's annual St. Patrick's–Evacuation Day parade. The Irish-American Gay, Lesbian and Bisexual Group of Boston (GLIB) wished to march in the parade to celebrate, among other things, pride in being Irish *and* gay. The parade organizers, a group of veterans from the Boston area (Veterans' Council), did not want GLIB to march. The Council maintained that it did not want to exclude the gay group as such but rather the pro-gay message. The Supreme Court accepted the Council's argument, ostensibly on First Amendment grounds.[1] The Court held that the parade, despite its 10,000 participants and 750,000 spectators on the public streets of Boston, was a private speech act. As a result, the Veterans' Council legally controlled the messages of the parade participants and could not be forced to include GLIB's Irish gay message.

Although resting within established First Amendment law, this holding suggests much broader implications when read through a critical lens. In *Hurley,* the Court transformed a public celebration into a private affair, redefined ambiguous parties as exclusively heterosexual or homosexual subjects, and drew clear boundaries between them to exclude openly gay Irish-Americans from meaningful participation in the parade *as* Irish gays. How did this happen? How did the First Amendment serve to define the parties' sexual and ethnic identities in relation to the parade? How did First Amendment law help or harm GLIB's attempts to represent its members as Irish-American as well as gay? What does this decision imply for future gay participation in American social life?[2]

This chapter takes up these questions. The first section provides some necessary background. It traces the development of the act-identity separation strategy used by gay rights advocates in the United States to overcome the limits of Supreme Court doctrine and "queer" activists' responses to the construction of sexuality implicit in that separation strategy. This brief detour provides a context for considering how the parties and the Court deploy and resist these various strategies in *Hurley.*

The second section focuses on how the *Hurley* Court and the parties used and interpreted symbolic expressions to represent sexual identities. The Court constituted the parties as private speaking subjects before the law, defining the Veterans' Council as an expressive association (and the parade as its protected speech) rather than a mere coordinator of multiple speech acts. To create the Council as a private stable heterosexual speaking subject with First Amendment rights, the Court equated the heterosexual veterans with their speech act, the parade. Ironically, the Court's conflation of heterosexual (speech) act and identity reflects queer notions of identity and serves to coopt queer strategies.

The next section reveals how, in similar fashion, the Court effectively embraced a gay rights separation strategy to silence gays. The Court rejected GLIB's claims that public self-identification is a critical component of gay identity. By separating the homosexual (speech) act of self-identification from homosexual identity, the Court was able to exclude openly gay participants while claiming only to exclude their message. This rejection and exclusion reveals the politics of visibility and the "privilege of unknowing" (Sedgwick 1990) as two opposing strands of discursive politics.

The last section addresses the implications of the *Hurley* decision for queer identity and politics. The *Hurley* Court bound and erased transgressive identities by "fixing" geographic, sexual, and discursive space. In effect, the Court appropriated traditional gay rights strategies to "normalize" the sexual binary, narrowing future political possibilities for transgressive sexuality, for a sexuality that strays too far from heteronormative notions of the "good" homosexual. Thus, *Hurley* reveals the limits of the First Amendment for contesting hegemonic ideas about sexuality. *Hurley* also might be read as sanctioning the rapidly increasing exclusion of identifiable gays, lesbians, and bisexuals from most religious, social, and civic organizations. Even so, many gay and lesbian activists and scholars were not particularly troubled by the *Hurley* Court's holding. They justified the decision with a repeated refrain: "At least we won't have to allow the 'religious right' to march in the gay pride parades." However, there may be strategic value in embracing a politics that includes such contradictory groups. At the least, a radical politics of inclusion may trouble the oppressive politics of exclusion grounding the First Amendment.

The (Un)Making of Sexual Identities

For decades, the homosexual body, as well as the "sign" of homosexuality, has served as a site of conflict. In the face of psychiatric and religious discourses of perversion, political efforts at normalization (Seidman 1994), the visions and challenges of "community" (Phelan 1994; Seidman 1994), the stigma of AIDS as a "gay disease," and, most recently, *Ellen*'s mass mediation of lesbianism on U.S. television, one can still ask, What is homosexuality? What does it mean to *act* like a homosexual? What does it mean to *identify* as a homosexual? What does it mean to be *identified* as a homosexual?

Answers to these questions rest on assumptions that frequently have been translated into strategies. For example, gay civil rights activists often have emphasized public education and an assimilationist agenda to convince middle America that "we are the same as you." Others—butches, femmes, dykes, faggots, queens, queers—have accepted or claimed the mark of difference as a sign of resistance. At least until 1986, gay and lesbian litigators argued that the Fourteenth Amendment protected a fundamental homosexual right to privacy, effectively erasing sexual difference by espousing equality for all.

In 1986, however, the Supreme Court decision in *Bowers v. Hardwick* left gay and lesbian activists, attorneys, and scholars clambering for an identity foothold on the rocky pinnacle of constitutional law. Hardwick was charged with criminal sodomy after a police officer entered his home and found him having sex with another man. Hardwick claimed that the charge violated his constitutional right to privacy. The Court, however, rejected this argument. Homosexual acts, pronounced the Court, were immoral and therefore illegal, even in the privacy of the home. For the *Hardwick* majority, homosexuals, *as a class,* were those persons who engaged in homosexual acts. Homosexual identity was coterminous with a sodomitical act; homosexual acts equaled homosexual identity. For the *Hardwick* Court, one *is* what one *does.*

Although gay and lesbian activists and litigators had been struggling with the act-identity distinction for nearly a decade (see Cain 1993), *Hardwick* forced activists and litigators to adopt the strategy of separating homosexual act from homosexual identity per se. Based on this separation strategy, then, one arguably could "be" a homosexual without engaging in homosexual activity. Though a pragmatic choice at the time, this separation strategy proved increasingly problematic for gay rights efforts in the United States.

By the late 1980s, "queers" began rejecting the essentialized notions of the hetero/homo binary as well as the inclusionary goals of the gay rights movement that had dominated sexual discourse (Gamson 1995). Like the radical gay men and lesbians preceding them,[3] queers focused on public acts and the visibly gay transformation of public space; queers acted up and acted out the transgressive performance of sexual identity, rearticulating public spaces through the actions of their everyday lives (Berlant and Freeman 1993).

Queer politics and its academic explication, queer theory, embraced fluid notions of subjectivity and sexual identity and reconceptualized notions of community and political alliance (Stychin 1995, 141). Queer theory revealed how laws, policies, and social customs frame the local experience of the (sexualized) body (Berlant and Freeman 1993, 195). Identity thus becomes unmoored; it becomes a site of politics, fluid and fragile, contingent and situated, where subjects can fashion and claim new identities and resist those imposed by the hegemonic order (Gamson 1995; Stychin 1995). Queerness thus focused explicitly on "doing," not being, as a basis for articulating sexual and political identity (Stychin 1996, 6).

The use of transgressive self-expression as a means of claiming an identity to transform public space, an underlying strategy of queer politics, arguably grounds GLIB's claims in *Hurley.* It did not survive constitutional challenge in this case. Nearly ten years after *Hardwick,* the Supreme Court again proclaimed the constitutional significance of homosexuality, unanimously excluding Irish-American gays from meaningful participation as gays in Boston's annual St. Patrick's–Evacuation Day parade. As defined by the Court, the issue was "whether Massachusetts may require private citizens who organize a parade to include among the marchers a group imparting a message the organizers do not wish to convey" (515 U.S. at 559). Although the decision arguably rests on established principles of First Amendment law, a critical reading of the Court's decision reveals how it rests on and reinscribes established heteronormative assumptions as well.

The Judicial Constitution of Heterosexual Performative Identity

THE FACTS OF THE MATTER

March 17 is a day of great significance in South Boston. Since 1737, some people in Boston have celebrated St. Patrick's Day. Since 1776, Bostonians have celebrated March 17 as Evacuation Day, marking General Washington's initial military victory over the British and the Royalists' departure from South Boston. The General Court of Massachusetts officially recognized Evacuation Day in 1938.

Until 1947, the City of Boston sponsored an annual St. Patrick's/-Evacuation Day celebration. That year, Boston's mayor granted the authority to organize and conduct the annual parade to the South Boston Allied War Veteran's Council, a private unincorporated association of individuals who represent various veterans organizations throughout Boston. For nearly 50 years, the Council has organized the annual St. Patrick's–Evacuation Day parade in South Boston and, until 1992, did so under the city's seal and with direct city funding (515 U.S. at 561). According to the record, the parade has included up to 20,000 participants and drawn up to 1,000,000 watchers in years past (560–61).

In 1992, GLIB, a social organization of "gay, lesbian, and bisexual descendants of Irish immigrants . . . [and their] supporters" applied to march in the parade (561). GLIB's stated purposes were

> to express its members' pride in their dual identities as Irish or Irish-American persons who are also homosexual or bisexual, to demonstrate to the Irish-American community and to the gay, lesbian and bisexual community diversity within those respective communities, and to show support for the Irish-American homosexual and bisexual men and women in New York City who were seeking to participate in that city's St. Patrick's Day Parade. (418 Mass. 241–42)

The Council denied the application, citing "safety reasons and insufficient information about the social club" (242). GLIB challenged the decision and won. Under the protection of court order, GLIB "march[ed] 'uneventfully' among that year's 10,000 participants and 750,000 spectators" (515 U.S. at 561).

In 1993, GLIB again applied to march, and again the Council refused permission. This time, the Council claimed that the "decision to exclude groups with sexual themes merely formalized that the parade expresses traditional religious and social values" (418 Mass. 242).[4] In response, GLIB filed suit in state court. GLIB argued that the parade, which had occurred on the public streets of South Boston for forty-seven years with the city's permission, was a public event. The Council's exclusionary decision violated GLIB's rights under the state public accommodation law, which prohibited discrimination based on sexual orientation.[5] The Council responded that the parade was a private event and charged that GLIB's court-ordered participation violated the Council's First Amendment rights.

In the past, the Council had excluded few groups from participating in the parade. According to the trial record, only ROAR (an antibusing organization), NORAID (an organization supporting efforts in Northern Ireland), and the Ku Klux Klan (in 1993) had been denied. The trial court found that the Council lacked formal selection criteria, generally allowing everyone to march without examining the applicants' specific messages or views. The Court also found that the parade had no particular expressive purpose and was an open public event subject to the state public antidiscrimination law (515 U.S. at 563). The trial court ordered the Council to include GLIB "on the same terms and conditions as other participants" (563). In 1994, the Council canceled the parade rather than comply with this order.

The Council appealed this decision to the Massachusetts Supreme Judicial Court, claiming that the parade was an event, not a "place" with a fixed physical location, and therefore was not subject to the public antidiscrimination law (418 Mass. 248, n. 14). The Supreme Judicial Court affirmed the trial court's decision, holding, among other things, that every parade is not per se speech protected by the First Amendment (249–50). Rather, in order to gain First Amendment protection, the Council would need to establish that the parade had an expressive purpose. It had not done so. The Council requested U.S. Supreme Court review of the Supreme Judicial Court's decision and, in 1995, held the parade with the *specific expressive purpose of protesting the Supreme Judicial Court's decision,* thus arguably bringing the parade within First Amendment protection. Ironically, the state court decisions gave more protection to the Council's purposive homophobic speech than they did to its ambiguous claim of silence.

Before the Supreme Court, the Council argued that it is a private organization not bound by the state's public antidiscrimination law. It further argued that it is an expressive association formed specifically to put on the parade, its principal expressive activity. The Council identified itself as the speaker and the parade as its speech, with its message expressed by those whom the parade organizers allow to participate. The Council further argued that the parade was intended to communicate traditional family values and that including GLIB's message (the message, not gays, lesbians, or bisexuals per se) would force the Council to speak contrary to this intent. The Council asserted its "right to remain silent" on the issue of homosexuality.

In response, GLIB claimed that the Council merely administers the parade, a public civic event without an expressive purpose per se belonging to the people of Boston. Participating organizations may be speaking, but the parade itself is not speech. GLIB also claimed that the Council excluded GLIB *as* gays, lesbians, and bisexuals and that *self-identification is a necessary part of public participation based on sexual orientation since gays, lesbians and bisexuals are not readily identifiable.*[6] GLIB maintained that failure to protect this self-expression would undermine the intent of the public accommodation law. Finally, GLIB argued that the Council's First Amendment claims were pretextual, raised after the fact to hide its discriminatory conduct. Thus, the stated issues before the Supreme Court were (1) whether the parade was a public event subject to the Massachusetts public antidiscrimination law, (2) whether the parade was in and of itself speech protected by the First Amendment, and (3) whether the Council was an expressive association formed for the purposes of conducting the parade and legally able to exclude GLIB from participation. These issues implicitly ask whether and to what extent transgressive (sexual) identities may be deployed in public and private spaces and to what extent "normal" identities might be resignified as transgressive.

The Supreme Court ruled in favor of the Council. The Court found that the parade is a private event. It explicitly held, for the first time, that a parade, even a private parade, is speech protected by the First Amendment. Finally, it held that the Council's selection of parade participants was entitled to First Amendment protection (515 U.S. at 566). The compelled inclusion of GLIB's message violated the Council's First Amendment rights.

THE PARADE AS A SPECTACLE OF HETEROSEXUAL PERFORMATIVE IDENTITY

The Supreme Court heavily relied on the Council's construction of its position as a private subject existing before the law: a self-determining subject who acts from and to protect its self-interest. The Court constituted both the Council and GLIB as expressive associations—private speaking subjects organized for the purposes of communicating a particular message—and proceeded to weigh their competing First Amendment claims. However, the Court failed to recognize its own role in constructing both the speakers and the messages they conveyed.

The Court read the word "parade" to mean "marchers who are making some sort of collective point, not just to each other but to bystanders along the way" (568). It viewed parades as a form of protected expression, "not just motion." This protection encompassed not only the parade's banners and songs but its symbolic expression as well (569).[7] The Court held that the First Amendment protected the Council's selection of parade participants, the combination of "multifarious voices," and the selection of each message (569).

Next, the Court recognized GLIB as an expressive association, finding its "participation as a unit in the parade was equally expressive . . . [and that] GLIB understandably seeks to communicate its ideas as part of the existing parade, rather than staging one of its own" (570). However, the Court found that "petitioners disclaim any intent to exclude homosexuals as such, and no individual member of GLIB claims to have been excluded from parading as a member of any group that the Council has approved to march" (572). Thus, the Court defined the disagreement not in terms of exclusion based on sexual orientation but rather on whether GLIB should be admitted to march in the parade "carrying its own banner" (572). Relying on a long line of First Amendment cases protecting a private speaker from carrying a forced message, the Court held that the Council was free to exclude GLIB's message (573).

In order to accomplish this end, the Court refused to consider the expressive intentions of the parade's 10,000 participants. Instead, the Court treated the Council's relatively loose selection procedures *as if* they reflected evaluative criteria of inclusion and exclusion and assigned normative motives based on the apparent message of the parade and the Council's post hoc justifications. The Court read the parade as the Council's intentional expression, treating the plurality of voices as components of an overarching message. Avoiding both the harmony and the dissonance of multiple voices, the Court reduced the parade's speech to a single note, one supposedly sung by the Council alone. The parade was speech. The Council's speech act, the parade, was protected under the First Amendment. The Court legally could not put words in the Council's mouth, could not compel the Council to deliver GLIB's message against the Council's will (575).

The Court apparently assumes the "natural" existence of the Council and GLIB prior to the litigation and purports only to weigh their respective First Amendment claims. However, a closer look troubles this notion of the Council as a transcendental speaking subject (Peller 1985).[8] The Council claims, and the Court finds, that the Council is an expressive association organized specifically to speak through the parade. In other words, the Court's decision implicitly identifies the Council's sole purpose, and the sole basis of its identity, as speech. The parade is a discursive act, a pure speech act that constitutes the identity of the Council. In effect, the Council does not exist prior to or separate from the parade. *The Council is what it says, which is also what it does.* In this way, the Court constructs the parade as a private (heterosexual) speech act. Through its exclusion of the homosexual message, the parade may be read as a spectacle of heterosexual performative identity.

The Judicial Erasure of the Homosexual Subject

COMING OUT AS A PERFORMATIVE SPEECH ACT

Although the *Hurley* Court conflates heterosexual act and identity to constitute the Council, it separates homosexual act and identity to exclude GLIB from the parade. This separation of homosexual act and identity reveals and perpetuates existing heteronormative attitudes toward homosexuality, silencing and erasing the open expression of homosexuality while claiming an unbiased position regarding homosexuality per se. Similar to white liberal notions of the "color-blind" society, this dangerous assimilationist stance hides what Sedgwick (1990) has called the "epistemological privilege of unknowing" (8).

As noted previously, a queer politics of visibility resists assimilation by (re)constituting public and private spaces for multiply sexed subjects. Critical to this politics of visibility is the performative speech act of "coming out," an act that not only discloses but also constitutes identity (Creet 1995). "Coming out" becomes a critical marker of homosexuality, the lens through which inherently contingent and ambiguous same-sex acts may be read as "homosexual." By coming out, the homosexual subject reveals the ambiguity of sexuality and claims for him-/herself the power of self-definition (Stychin 1995).[9] *Hurley* seemingly narrows the visible public expressions necessary to maintain this politics of identification, thus blocking queer possibilities to transform public space through transgressive acts.

Judicial Protection of Presumptive Heterosexuality

Separating homosexual acts and identities may generate politically useful ambiguous and contingent sexualities (Stychin 1996) as well as offer the opportunity for coalition building (Halley 1994; Mezey 1995). The strategy remains problematic, however. In *Hurley,* the veterans moved to separate identity from conduct, arguing that they were not excluding homosexuals per se, simply the homosexual message. The veterans claimed their willingness to separate out GLIB's message from the sexual orientation of its members. If GLIB wanted to march without carrying a banner identifying the group as pro-gay, it could do so. The Supreme Court embraced this separation strategy, finding no discriminatory exclusion based on sexual orientation. Instead, the Court held that the Council could legally refuse to include GLIB's message. However, as GLIB argued, its homosexual message was critical to its identity. The Court's tactical separation of homosexual identity from this crucial speech act preserved the parade as heterosexual social space.

This legal deterrence of homosexual expression forces gays back into the closet, suggesting the mutability of "public" homosexuality and the law's power to define future "private" space in an exclusionary manner (Halley 1994). Presumably, those with a homosexual identity would be allowed to participate in the parade as long as they did not "act gay" or otherwise identify their (deviant) sexuality. Indeed, the decision implicitly recognizes that homosexuals may well be marching as members of other groups. While this arguably leads to opportunities to "infiltrate" the parade, one can only wonder at the acceptable limits of self-expression under these circumstances. Does the decision, in effect, require homosexuals to remain invisible even absent a pro-gay message?

What would the Council have permitted had GLIB agreed to its terms? What is the "sign" of homosexuality? What would constitute appropriate homosexual performance? Certainly, men in dresses would not be allowed to march. But what about men in kilts? Women in pants and boots or neckties? What about women holding hands? Men holding hands? Women or men wearing lavender shirts? Women with crew cuts? Men in wigs? Men with an earring? With two? Clearly, the "authentic" performance of sexuality and gender rapidly conflate as one struggles to find the boundaries of the straight and narrow. One can only wonder how *much* queerness it would take to contaminate the whole.

In addition, what are the implications of separating group identity from speech act under the Court's analysis? Suppose, for example, a group calling itself the "South Boston New Neighborhood Association" marched in the parade in support of all newcomers to South Boston, carrying a sign stating "WE LOVE SOUTH BOSTON"? What if the sign was lavender? What if the group was comprised entirely of same-sex couples holding hands, or men in dresses, or women on motorcycles? Even without an explicit pro-gay message or agenda, would the Council read the marchers as gay or pro-gay and therefore exclude them?

Indeed, what *is* queerness without its explicit articulation? As Janet Halley (1994) has noted, "The public status 'heterosexual' is an unmarked signifier, the category to which everyone is assumed to belong. Something has to *happen* to mark an individual with the identity 'homosexual'" (168). By erasing the homosexual subject, the *Hurley* Court can freely construct heterosexuality as the default category, defined by the remaining traces of what it is not, that is, not homosexual. The Council might argue that it has organized the parade for forty-seven years and that the parade is about "traditional religious and social values," a position that the Council did not articulate explicitly before this litigation. With queers under erasure, the First Amendment then serves as a vehicle for the Council's implicitly heterosexual message. The veterans' claim that the parade represents "traditional social and religious values" can be read as code words for saying that the parade celebrates straight Catholic procreative sex.

Nevertheless, the Council could maintain its message and its group coherence only through coercion, by silencing GLIB and asserting its privileged (heterosexual) power "to define heterosexual and homosexual classes, to know the truth about their inhabitants, to label indelibly, and to expel unilaterally" (Halley 1993, 88–89). It could maintain clear-cut boundaries and internal coherence only if GLIB and other Irish supporters remain silent. By excluding GLIB, the veterans gained what GLIB had lost, "the epistemological authority to know and to designate what [and who] a homosexual is" (88). Those with definitional power decide not only whom to exclude but also whom to include. Even those who have passed the initial threshold of acceptability suffer a tenuous membership, subject to exclusion if their later messages (or identifications) seem suspect. *Hurley* reminds us once again of the instability of group identifications and associational rights under the First Amendment, identifications and rights that are subject to majoritarian interests, to whomever happens to control the definitional moment.

Exclusion from the parade does not absolutely silence gays and lesbians. Arguably, gays and lesbians could challenge the parade from the sidelines, as spectators reinterpreting the parade's message. This presents a qualitatively different experience, however. Rather than parading with one's neighbors before a crowd of hundreds of thousands, proceeding through the space of the city as part of the (re)presentation of community life, sidelined gays would be fixed in geographic and discursive space. Their immediate audience, in effect, would be the participants in the parade. Their message, rather than being incorporated into the parade to transform the whole, would stand in stark contrast to the parade's hegemonic heterosexual themes. Perhaps this would be effective in terms of gaining mediated attention, but it does not necessarily further those efforts to gain recognition and legitimation from one's fellow citizens. From the sidelines, gays and lesbians remain "abnormal member(s) of an immutable sexual minority who deserve tolerance and protection" (Herman 1993, 37) but not equal treatment.

Similarly, gays and lesbians might encourage other parade participants to show their solidarity by carrying signs, rainbow flags, and so on. However, *Hurley* would allow the Council to exclude these pro-gay messages as well, even if carried by non-gay supporters. Whether or not non-gay supporters would be strong enough to insist they be allowed to carry pro-gay messages or would withdraw from the parade in protest under these circumstances is unclear. In either case, the parade would remain a presumptively heterosexual space.

THE TOTALIZING TATTOO OF HOMOSEXUALITY

Finally, it is critical to note that the facts presented to the Court do not indicate the specific sexual identification of GLIB's participants. Members were "gays, lesbians, bisexuals . . . *and their supporters.*" GLIB's strategy troubles the established hetero-/homosexual binary not only by including bisexuals but also by leaving sexual identifications ambiguous. The Court, however, discursively reestablishes the sexual binary and grants the Council the power and privilege to treat GLIB as a *homosexual organization,* erasing GLIB's pro-gay message from the parade.[10]

To accomplish this, the Court constructed GLIB's subjectivity as singularly homosexual. GLIB wanted to march identifying as *Irish* gays, lesbians, and bisexuals (and their supporters). The Court did not allow the communication of that message but rather treated sexual orientation and ethnicity as two discrete categories. While Eaton (1995) suggests that "homosexuality has been legally coded as white" (112), *Hurley* suggests that homosexuality is a totalizing tattoo. The Irish gays could be publicly Irish or privately gay but not publicly both.[11] The decision perpetuates the fragmenting effects of liberal identity politics, discursively reifying identity (see Eaton 1995). Possibilities for coalition formation and the recognition of nonunitary subjectivities are simultaneously undermined and sanctioned by the law. *Hurley* upholds freedom of speech as it represses it, undermining the struggle to speak multiple "truths," that is, that someone can be both Irish and queer.

First Amendment Implications for Performative Identity
WALKING THE STRAIGHT AND NARROW

In the public sphere, gay and lesbian efforts to separate homosexual acts and identities have had mixed success. Under First Amendment analysis, the courts carefully have distinguished political speech regarding sexual orientation from criminal homosexual conduct (Halley 1994). They also have protected homosexuals from the "legal coercion of expression about sexual identity," from being forced out of the closet (Halley 1994, 184). In many ways, the Supreme Court's separation of act and identity in *Hurley* reflects a victory for gay rights litigators who argued this strategy in the lower courts. The decision may buttress arguments that homosexuals have a Fourteenth Amendment right to participate equally in the political process and in the public discourse critical to that process without being inhibited by state prohibitions on sexual conduct (see Halley 1994; Currah 1995). After *Hurley,* one might wonder at this (re)turn to the state for legitimation and recognition, for the mark of acceptable citizenship (see Bower 1997). Just how "queer" may one be? To what extent must one "straighten up" as a condition of entry into full social, civic participation?

The ultimate instrumental success of the act-identity separation strategy remains unclear. Under the Fourteenth Amendment's equal protection clause of the U.S. Constitution, the courts have not protected the speech act of "coming out." In *Rowland v. Mad River Local School District* (1985), the appeals court found that "coming out" justified the bisexual teacher's dismissal. Justice Brennan carefully dissented from the Supreme Court's refusal to review *Rowland,* noting, "Petitioner's First Amendment and equal protection claims may be seen to converge, because it is realistically impossible to separate her spoken statements from her status" (Rowland, J. Brennan at 1016, n. 11). After *Hurley,* status and spoken statement *can* be separated, even under the First Amendment. Whether this offers more or less protection for public disclosure remains to be seen.

Hurley apparently has had little effect in the military context. The current Department of Defense policy on homosexuality ("Don't Ask, Don't Tell") equates "coming out" with homosexual conduct. The courts generally have upheld these regulations, arguing that identifying oneself as a homosexual is grounds for discharge. In *Selland v. Perry* (1995), Judge Young specifically considered this issue in light of *Hurley.* The government claimed that its action was based not on Selland's identification as gay but on the propensity for homosexual acts that such identification reveals. Judge Young found that the military's interests outweighed Selland's First Amendment rights: "[T]he Policy will probably inhibit members from expressing their homosexuality . . . [however] the Policy is designed to prevent homosexual acts and any incidental burden on speech resulting from its application does not violate the First Amendment" (264).

The *Hurley* decision may limit identifiable homosexual participation in the private sphere. Since the Court's decision, at least one lawsuit has been filed, by the College Republicans in Colorado, who claim a right under *Hurley* to exclude homosexuals from their organization. The First Amendment allows state interference with the freedom of expressive association only when the expressive purpose of the association is incidental (*Roberts v. Jaycees* 1984; *New York Club Association v. New York* 1988).[12] As the *Hurley* Court notes, "GLIB could nonetheless be refused admission as an expressive contingent with its own message just as readily as a private club could exclude an applicant whose manifest views were at odds with a position taken by the club's existing members" (63 U.S.L.W. 4632). One can imagine that many associations soon will find the expression of "traditional values" a critical reason for their existence. In short, any civic or religious organization might claim the expression and maintenance of heterosexual culture, thereby excluding homosexuals under the guise of policing homosexual expression.

Hurley may have other potential effects. The case suggests the destabilizing power of queer politics and the constraining force of formal legal discourse. In an essentially antiessentialist way, *Hurley* is about performative identity and how differences are marked as transgressive. Faced with the parade as a potential site for the public performances of transgressive identities and its inability to control each and every act(or), the Supreme Court constructed geographic, sexual, and discursive space to "fix" boundaries and erase differences. Caught in a potential din of contradictions, the Court carved out a singular, albeit symbolic, expression and thereby silenced the irreducible voices. The parade became a site of legal (re)signification, a space of simultaneous, though presumably homogeneous, performances where everyone but gays, lesbians, bisexuals, and their supporters could be Irish for a day.

Hurley constricts the available space in which to constitute and contest the hegemonic meanings attached to sexual identifications. The decision closes off First Amendment rights for some by privatizing miles of public streets in Boston and rendering a public celebration a private party subject to the will of a few. Parades are usually linear displays of social order, a public enactment of community and community boundaries. Parades also are a potential metaphor for the pluralism and unity of community, revealing identity as a constructive collective heterogeneous activity. As more venues where the public can gather and display itself are privately or corporately owned, what does it mean to participate publicly in community? The *Hurley* Court further narrows the boundaries of legally sanctioned public display.

Hurley suggests that gays, lesbians, bisexuals, and queers must draw on material and rhetorical gaps to fashion a (transgressive) politics of identification. If *Hurley* permits the exclusion of identifiable gay and lesbians from "private" civic spectacles and private associations, vis-à-vis the exclusion of their messages, what arenas remain for political action? What are the possibilities for resignifying the meaning of key cultural signs and symbols and transforming their meaning so as to give voice to those who have been excluded (Coombe 1993)? What means still exist for those who have been excluded and silenced to seek recognition and legitimation from their fellow citizens (Bower 1994)? Other than a gay pride parade or agitating as unhappy bystanders, *Hurley* threatens to disable traditional gay rights strategies and a "politics of direct address"[13] as well, leaving little more discursive space than a public access cable television station, a public service announcement at 4:35 A.M. on a Tuesday morning, or a ten-foot cordoned square of concrete at the Super Bowl. *Hurley* reflects a trend toward the forced mass mediation of queer messages. While multiplying sites for public exposure, it is unclear whether such publicity, subject as it is to appropriation and commodification, enhances or limits the possibilities of identification among and between various social actors. The commercial appropriation of homosexual images and transgressive practices opens up discursive spaces while simultaneously commodifying the transgressor's message.

Making a Spectacle

We may read in *Hurley* the logic of the law, its indeterminacy and its legitimating function. Law appropriates and withholds meaning and legitimacy as it sees fit through its power to construct boundaries. *Hurley* reveals the performativity of the law as well, how the law resignifies transgression and contains a politics of identification. This concluding section will move away from the First Amendment per se to consider the implications of a politics of inclusion for traditional gay rights and queer politics. What might happen if any and all interested groups and individuals were allowed to march in a hypothetical gay pride parade? What happens if the multiplicity of participating and perhaps contradictory voices is not reduced to a single subjectivity? Several key questions are raised: What is "gay"? What is "pride"? What is "community"? Well-rehearsed questions from the realm of discursive politics also surface: Who speaks with an "authentic" voice? What is their message? Who reads or hears such voices? How do they interpret the messages' meanings? Finally, how is meaning produced and contested?

These questions become more concrete if one considers specific examples.[14] For example, three weeks after the *Hurley* decision, the organizers of the gay pride parade in San Diego used *Hurley* to obtain dismissal of an action by NORMAL, a conservative religious organization suing for permission to march in the parade (American Civil Liberties Union 1995). Suppose NORMAL had been permitted to participate. Would "straight" floats or groups rigidly defined as heterosexual erase homosexuality in all its glorious plurality? Would "straight" groups be read within the context of a (presumably) "normal" heterosexuality? I suggest that NORMAL's presence could have served as an interruption, a rhetorical contradiction, signifying the relative powerlessness and isolation of gays, lesbians, bisexuals, and queers and the hatred that they experience from others. One might have included a group marching somewhere in line carrying signs reading, "I'm gay (lesbian, bisexual, queer) and normal, too!" By including the "normal" message and resignifying it, one might incorporate and transform the communicative intent.

How might the inclusion of self-identified gay, lesbian, bisexual, or queer individuals or groups that transgress the "acceptable" limits of (traditional) gay and lesbian community be addressed? The question itself reveals the hegemony of the politics of exclusion, the assumption that community is based on the right to exclude people who are not like "us" or whom "we" do not like. In the gay and lesbian community, the question reflects a reinscription of "normal" or "natural" sexuality, the boundaries of acceptable same-sex behavior.[15] In Seattle, efforts by local members of NAMBLA (North American Man/Boy Love Association) to participate in the 1996 gay pride march had some organizers threatening to turn the march into a parade, thus legally allowing organizers to exclude NAMBLA (Freedom Day Committee 1996). Many national and local gay rights organizations have excluded NAMBLA from participating in organizational events. Moral and therapeutic discourses prevail, with opponents characterizing NAMBLA members as "sick" and NAMBLA's self-identified "boy-lovers" characterizing mainstream gays as uninformed and reactionary. The debate reveals the constant return to tropes of "normal" and "natural" "human" behavior that are deployed to exclude "undesirable" social actors. Yet community moral standards are arbitrary and often oppressively majoritarian. Those who hold the rhetorical power to define hold within their control the political power to exclude as well.

To fashion a viable politics of identification may require a radical politics of inclusion and necessitate careful attention to the exclusions supported by the Court's reading of First Amendment cases such as *Hurley.* A politics of inclusion is not equivalent to mere liberal tolerance or assimilation, however (see Goldberg 1998). Rather, the task is to include, challenge, and resignify "undesirable" messages. Social activists and organizers might publicly circulate messages disclaiming and opposing the rhetoric of groups that currently or historically have oppressed and excluded others. This politics of absolute inclusion and counterexpression contemplates nonviolent expression. However, opening up spaces as forums for groups or individuals with diametrically opposed views or ideologies might provoke violence, leaving event organizers liable for potential injuries and inviting public disapproval and state surveillance. All participants must recognize and assume the risks arising from their participation.

Perhaps gays and lesbians might not want to march with right-wing Christians or gay fascists in a gay pride parade. However, an inclusionary strategy opens up space for counterhegemonic messages: The political power of gay participation in a St. Patrick's Day parade far outweighs the threat of reactionary groups' involvement in a gay pride parade. Despite feelings of anger, uncertainty, and fear that conservative participation might invoke in the gay community, including such contradictory groups may serve to strengthen and refine gays' resistance to messages already permeating and, in significant ways, grounding American culture. Including gays necessarily will open up new audiences and associations, allowing citizens to hear and interpret previously silenced or subordinated messages. Exclusion as law, practice, or politics may serve to keep gay pride parades gay. However, exclusion as law, practice, or politics ultimately justifies keeping gays out of critical arenas of everyday life.

Conclusion

The Supreme Court's decision in *Hurley* reveals the inherent instability of notions of homosexual acts, identities, conduct, and speech. The Court sometimes conflates these terms or separates them when convenient. In *Hurley,* the Court forced ambiguous social identities into fixed categories, effectively erasing their message from a public, "private" event. Reading *Hardwick* and *Hurley* together suggests an ironic result. The queer's private home is "public" for purposes of law enforcement, while the heterosexual's "private" parade, though certainly a public spectacle, is not.

The decision raises further questions about community and association. Boundaries between various social actors appear much more permeable than we might be led to believe. Any attempt to define affiliation must recognize that identity and self-identification are discursive, performative, and relational, based on how we present ourselves to each other, how others perceive us, how we choose to draw the lines that define us as individuals and groups, and who gets included and excluded by our definitions. This recognizes the law as a site for discursive politics, that is, for contesting identity and meaning, how these various lines are to be drawn. Thus, the St. Patrick's Day parade is a location where cultural signs and symbols are constituted and (re)articulated, a place where transgressive identifications might be made.

However, queer politics, which is in large part a politics of "acting up" in public arenas, may be limited by the *Hurley* holding. Homosexuality may become, if not an empty signifier, then a muted one, effectively under erasure in all but the most public or the most intimate of circumstances. One may claim the First Amendment right to be out in "public" and face the consequences. Or one can be silently straight by default. The limits of acceptable difference remain unclear.

Hurley demands a reconsideration of the limits of First Amendment protection and the role of state intervention. The decision might be read as sanctioning the increased exclusion of identifiable gays, lesbians, and bisexuals from most religious, social, and civic organizations. *Hurley* "normalizes" sexual binaries while narrowing future political possibilities for transgressive sexualities. It reveals that the act/identity distinction remains a troubling strategy at best: a means of destabilizing sexual categories and creating new political opportunities for collective action but also a discursive tool for antihomosexual forces. A politics of inclusion, however, that explodes First Amendment exclusions may serve to revitalize meaningful political space.

Notes

I would like to thank Lisa C. Bower, David T. Goldberg, Michael Musheno, and Deb Henderson for their critical commentary on previous drafts of this chapter.

1. The First Amendment is the first provision of the Bill of Rights in the U.S. Constitution. Among other things, it prohibits Congress from making any law that inhibits freedom of speech and freedom of association. Traditional liberal ideology views the First Amendment as "a marketplace of ideas," where "free speech" (unrestricted discourse) is the protected right of all citizens. No judgment is made about the particular content of the ideas, as long as they do not violate certain judicially imposed limits—for example, constitutionally protected speech cannot be conspiratorial, inciting, fraudulent, obscene, or defamatory (Matsuda 1993). The U.S. Supreme Court has characterized this freedom of expression as one of the most fundamental rights protected by the Constitution, ostensibly a guarantee of freedom from government coercion (see, e.g., *R.A.V. v. City of St. Paul* [1992]). Even speech that might be deemed repressive and therefore morally wrong (e.g., sexist, racist, or homophobic speech) must be tolerated to maintain the basic liberal commitment to freedom (and free expression). According to this traditional view, such antidemocratic speech can be opposed only by countering speech, not by silencing the undesirable message, thus leaving citizens free to choose among competing ideas.

This liberal conception rests on certain theoretical assumptions. First, parties are treated as transcendental speaking subjects before the law (Peller 1985). That is, the Court assumes the "natural" existence of the parties prior to the litigation and purports only to weigh their respective First Amendment claims, when actually the Court constructs this subject. Second, the conception rests on relatively discrete distinctions between public and private space. In public space, regulation of speech will be permitted; in private space, little regulation is allowed. Third, each citizen is presumed capable of self-expression—free speech serves to promote values of individualism and constitutional democracy, including, for example, individual self-fulfillment, truth, participation in decision making, and social equilibrium (see Delgado 1993).

Finally, traditional First Amendment doctrine distinguishes between speech and conduct. While the Constitution protects written or spoken words (with the previously noted exceptions), it also protects certain symbolic acts, such as saluting or refusing to salute the flag, wearing an armband to protest the war (*Tinker v. Des Moines*), and even marching with Nazi regalia (*National Socialist Party v. Skokie*).

Some commentators, however, have recognized the First Amendment as a social and cultural effect and as a site of cultural struggle where cultural norms, attitudes, and values are legitimated (see Fish 1994). First Amendment decisions are based not on established principles but on particular constructions that protect favored speech and regulate disfavored speech. Arguably, then, the First Amendment does not simply protect speech but serves as a vehicle for creating meaning and as a site for political contest.

2. Implicit in these questions, and in this chapter, are several assumptions: Law is a potential site of transgression, gay-rights-cause lawyers have incorporated queer theory into their litigation strategies, legal discourse constrains attempts to "queer" the articulation of the law, transgressive identities reveal the indeterminacy of the law and its limitations as vehicle for liberation, and gay-rights-cause litigation is always already transgressive because law acts to define and maintain the heteronormative center.

3. As noted previously, publicly marking one's difference as a form of resistance pre-dates queer politics. As Nestle (1992) argues, butch-femme identities have troubled binary notions of gender and sexuality for decades, providing a rich and complex history of "queer" women.

4. During the four-day trial, Hurley gave several different reasons for excluding GLIB from the parade. The trial court concluded that Hurley's equivocation reflected the pretextual nature of the Council's reasons. The court also found that although the Council formally voted on participant applications, the actual decisions were made by Hurley (418 Mass. at 244, n. 11). However, Yackle (1993) has discussed certain direct actions taken by ACT UP and Queer Nation in South Boston that indicate that the Council's fears might have been well founded. Barbra Kay, one of the organizing members of GLIB, admitted that she was a member of ACT UP. Although she could speak for herself, she could not guarantee that other GLIB members would not "act up" during the parade.

5. Under Massachusetts state law, it is illegal to discriminate on the basis of sexual orientation in any public place, activity, or event. Massachusetts General Law (sec. 272:98) prohibits such discrimination "in the admission to or treatment in any place of public accommodation, resort or amusement." Section 272:92A defines "[a] place of public accommodation, resort or amusement" as "including any place which is open to and accepts or solicits the patronage of the general public and, without limiting the generality of this definition, whether or not it be . . . (6) a boardwalk or other public highway (or) . . . (8) a place of public amusement, recreation, sport, exercise or entertainment."

6. In part, GLIB's claim reflects how the meaning of the term homosexual "acts" has expanded beyond a code word for "sex" to encompass the speech act of sexual self-identification and the acts of daily life through which one expresses one's sexuality. As discussed in the following, I suggest that *Hurley,* in part, reflects this slippage between act and identity, the speech act serving as a marker of and proxy for sexual identification.

7. The Court reviewed those cases recognizing First Amendment protection afforded to the communicative value of symbolism, including *West Virginia Board of Education v. Barnette* (1943) (refusal to salute the flag), *Tinker v. Des Moines Independent Community School District* (1969) (wearing an armband to protest a war), *Stromberg v. California* (1931) (displaying a red flag), and *National Socialist Party of America v. Skokie* (1977) ("marching, walking or parading" in uniforms displaying the swastika).

8. Gary Peller's autonomous self-defined transcendental subject exists prior to and separate from the public sphere: "Social relations are imagined to take place outside the context of public power, in a private realm in which the individual is self-present. In this private realm, the individual is at liberty to pursue private ends, no matter how arbitrary, so long as others are not harmed. This conjuncture of freedom and privacy is contrasted with the 'public' sphere, which connotes the absence of self-presence, where we are not free to simply 'be ourselves,' but must conform to external demands. The public realm is thus to a certain extent 'coercive,' regulated by 'others.'" (1985: 1195)

9. Of course, heterosexuality is performed as well, and performing heterosexuality badly has been a continual source of discredit and amusement as well as a means of destabilizing the heterosexual / homosexual binary. While coming out may be a necessary marker of homosexuality, it may not be sufficient. Any claim to, and performance of, sexuality remains subject to interpretations and judgments about the authenticity of that performance.

10. Subsequent to *Hurley,* it is likely that any group espousing a pro-gay message could be excluded from the parade, even if comprised solely of self-identified heterosexual supporters. In *Hurley,* this reductionism served effectively to maintain heterosexuality as the homogeneous center of the parade and the parade as a unitary heterosexual speech act.

11. Though the veterans sought to present Irish culture itself as unmarked, GLIB's exclusion seems to mark the boundaries of Irish culture as well. Furthermore, who is to say that within the group of Irish who are marching, the same statement of Irish authenticity is being made.

12. For a thorough discussion of the First Amendment and the right to join associations, see Soifer (1995).

13. In a "politics of direct address," rights claims are made by citizens to each other through the actions and experiences of their everyday lives (McClure 1992; Bower 1994). Possibilities for political change are diffused through cultural and social space (McClure 1992, 123). Unlike a "politics of official recognition" requiring (legal) claims made to the state based on similar identities, a "politics of direct address" embraces the complexity and contingency of identity, recognizes the difference of others, and anticipates alliances made across those ever-shifting differences (Bower 1994, 1997). Through a "politics of direct address," "[legal and social] change occurs when the affiliations [the political identifications] of 'ordinary people' are reconstituted" (Bower 1997, 283).

14. One commentator asked whether an inclusive politics would justify allowing "gay Nazis" to march in a gay pride parade. While this certainly would make the point that "we are everywhere," this hypothetical bugbear reveals the limits of a politics focused solely on shared definable sexual identity. It reveals, as well, the intersection of this discussion with efforts to constrain hate speech, an intersection beyond the scope of this chapter but in need of further discussion. Asking about the religious right on the one hand and about NAMBLA (North American Man / Boy Love Association) on the other frames the issue of exclusion more realistically. Each of these groups has been sanctioned in the past by "mainstream" gay rights organizations.

15. It may be that the meaning of "normal" in terms of gay pride parades is always already transgressive. For example, during Toronto's 1997 gay pride parade, a group of gay naturists paraded nude except for shoes and socks, raising cries of "indecency" from conservative voices. According to Simm (1997), authorities declined to prosecute the naturists. Under Canadian law, the question is whether one is "so clad as to offend against public decency." Authorities determined that context must be considered—the standards of decency are broader for gay pride (transgressive performances of sexuality) than, for example, the Santa Claus parade. This ex-

ample reveals how the law itself performs, shifting its limits and expectations, in relation to the identity performances involved.

References

American Civil Liberties Union. 1995. "Anti-Gay Group Drops Lawsuit to March in San Diego Pride Parade." Press release, personal records.

Berlant, Lauren, and Elizabeth Freeman. 1993. "Queer Nationality." In M. Warner, ed., *Fear of a Queer Planet* (193–229). Minneapolis: University of Minnesota Press.

Bower, Lisa C. 1994. "Queer Acts and the Politics of 'Direct Address': Rethinking Law, Culture, and Community." *Law and Society Review* 28: 1009–33.

———. 1997. "Queer Problems/Straight Solutions: The Limits of a Politics of "Official Recognition." In S. Phelan, ed., *Playing with Fire: Queer Politics, Queer Theories* (267–91). New York: Routledge.

Cain, Patricia A. 1993. "Litigating for Lesbian and Gay Rights: A Legal History." *Virginia Law Review* 79, no. 9: 1551–1641.

Coombe, Rosemary. 1993. "Tactics of Appropriation and the Politics of Recognition in Late Modern Democracies." *Political Theory* 21: 411–33.

Creet, Julia. 1995. "Anxieties of Identity-Coming Out and Coming Undone." In M. Dorenkamp and R. Henke, eds., *Negotiating Lesbian and Gay Subjects* (179–99). New York: Routledge.

Currah, Paisley. 1995. "Queers, Identity Politics, and *Evans v. Romer.*" Paper presented at the annual meeting of the Western Political Science Association, Portland, Oregon, March.

Davis, Susan G. 1986. *Parades and Power: Street Theater in Nineteenth-century Philadelphia.* Philadelphia: Temple University Press.

Delgado, Richard. 1993. "Words That Wound: A Tort Action for Racial Insults, Epithets, and Name Calling." In M. Matsuda, C. Lawrence III, R. Delgado, and K. Crenshaw, eds., *Words That Wound: Critical Race Theory, Speech and the First Amendment* (89–110). Boulder, Colo.: Westview Press.

Eaton, Mary. 1995. "Homosexual Unmodified: Speculations on Law's Discourse, Race, and the Construction of Sexual Identity." In D. Herman and C. Stychin, eds., *Legal Inversions: Lesbians, Gay Men, and the Politics of Law* (46–73). Philadelphia: Temple University Press.

Fish, Stanley. 1994. *There's No Such Thing as Free Speech, and It's a Good Thing Too.* New York: Oxford University Press.

Freedom Day Committee. 1996. "NAMBLA." www.webworqs.com/users/blackhawke/FDC/fdc.html.

Gamson, Joshua. 1995. "Must Identity Movements Self-Destruct? A Queer Dilemma." *Social Problems* 42: 390–407.

Goldberg, David Theo. 1998. "Die Macht der Toleranz" (revised, in German, "The Power of Tolerance"). *Das Argument* (Berlin) Special Issue: Grunzen (Borders) 224 (spring): 11–27. (English version on file with the author)

Halley, Janet E. 1993. "The Construction of Heterosexuality." In M. Warner, ed., *Fear of a Queer Planet: Queer Politics and Social Theory* (82–102). Minneapolis: University of Minnesota Press.

———. 1994. "The Politics of the Closet: Towards Equal Protection for Gay, Lesbian and Bisexual Identity." In J. Goldberg, ed., *Reclaiming Sodom* (145–204). New York: Routledge.

Herman, Didi. 1993. "Beyond the Rights Debate." *Social and Legal Studies* 2: 25–43.

Matsuda, Mari J. 1993. "Public Response to Racist Speech: Considering the Victim's Story." In M. Matsuda, C. Lawrence III, R. Delgado, and K. Crenshaw, eds., *Words That Wound:*

Critical Race Theory, Speech and the First Amendment (17–51). Boulder, Colo.: Westview Press.

McClure, Kirstie. 1992. "On the Subject of Rights: Pluralism, Plurality and Political Identity." In C. Mouffe, ed., *Dimensions of Radical Democracy* (108–27). London: Verso.

Mezey, Naomi. 1995. "Dismantling the Wall: Bisexuality and the Possibilities of Sexual Identity Classification Based on Acts." *Berkeley Women's Law Journal* 10: 98–133.

Nestle, Joan. 1992. "Flamboyance and Fortitude: An Introduction." In J. Nestle, ed., *The Persistent Desire: A Femme-Butch Reader* (13–20). Boston: Alyson Publications.

Peller, Gary. 1985. "The Metaphysics of American Law." *California Law Review* 73: 1151–290.

Phelan, Shane. 1994. *Getting Specific: Postmodern Lesbian Politics.* Minneapolis: University of Minnesota Press.

Sedgwick, Eve Kosofsky. 1990. *Epistemology of the Closet.* Berkeley and Los Angeles: University of California Press.

Seidman, Steven. 1994. "Symposium: Queer Theory/Sociology: A Dialogue." *Sociological Theory* 12: 166–77.

Simm, Peter. 1997. "Letter of the Day Column." *Toronto Sun,* July 22, 11.

Soifer, Avraim. 1995. *Law and the Company We Keep.* Cambridge, Mass.: Harvard University Press.

Stychin, Carl. 1995. *Law's Desire.* London: Routledge.

———. 1996. "To Take Him 'At His Word': Theorizing Law, Sexuality and the U.S. Military Exclusion Policy." *Social and Legal Studies* 5: 179–200.

Yackle, Larry W. 1993. "Parading Ourselves: Freedom of Speech at the Feast of St. Patrick." *Boston University Law Review* 73, no. 5: 791–871.

CASES

Bowers v. Hardwick, 478 U.S. 186 (1986).

John J. Hurley et al. v. Irish American Gay, Lesbian and Bisexual Group of Boston, 515 U.S. 557 (1995).

Irish-American Gay, Lesbian and Bisexual Group of Boston. City of Boston, 418 Mass. 238 (1994).

National Socialist Party of America v. Skokie, 432 U.S. 43 (1977).

New York State Club Association, Inc. v. City of New York, 487 U.S. 1 (1988).

R.A.V. v. City of St. Paul, 505 U.S. 377 (1992).

Roberts v. United States Jaycees, 468 U.S. 609 (1984).

Rowland v. Mad River Local School District, 730 F.2d 444 (6th Cir. 1984), cert. denied, 470 U.S. 1009 (1985).

Selland v. Perry, 905 F. Supp. 260 (1995).

Stromberg v. California, 283 U.S. 359 (1931).

Tinker v. Des Moines Independent Community School District, 393 U.S. 503 (1969).

West Virginia Board of Education v. Barnette, 319 U.S. 624 (1943).

15

Governing Sexuality

THE SUPREME COURT'S SHIFT TO CONTAINMENT

Paul A. Passavant

During the 1950s and 1960s, the U.S. Supreme Court tried, with little success, to define obscenity. In *Miller v. California* (1973), the Court produced its last major attempt to distinguish free speech from obscenity. Since then, obscenity decisions by the Court have "diminished dramatically" (Gunther and Sullivan 1997, 1142). The Supreme Court continues, however, to struggle with controversies over sexual expression.

After the *Miller* decision, the Court changed its approach toward the regulation of sexual expression. When cases involving sexual expression were addressed against the background of obscenity, legal discourse was organized around positivist assumptions regarding legality on the one hand and the nature of society on the other. This formalist model, premised on law's ability to create clear rules distinguishing speech from obscenity and to discern community norms, was poorly suited to governing a complex disciplinary society in which value and differences are more modulated and economically produced (Foucault 1977). Indeed, such a juridical model is a technique mismatched to the goal of disciplining individuals and normalizing the population. As the contradictions within the formalist model became unworkable, a different approach, one more consistent with a model of "social law," emerged to address sexual expression (Ewald 1986, 1987). More in line with Michel Foucault's conception of "governmentality," the Supreme Court has since sought to *contain* the ill effects of indecent sexual expression on the American people rather than merely censoring such expression.

Mainstream legal and sociopolitical theories oscillate between law and society as they seek a foundation for their analyses and prescriptions (Horwitz 1992). Considering the Court's repeated attempts to justify its obscenity decisions, I suggest that neither law nor society offers a ground sufficiently stable for the Court to build its obscenity jurisprudence. Law cannot measure up to the hopes of legal formalism. Law is not a self-contained practice underwritten by unifying principles adequate for the governance of that entirely separate entity, society. Rather, law is incomplete and relies on a cultural supplement in order to define and justify legal tests distinguishing speech from obscenity.[1]

Yet law's necessary reliance on a cultural supplement does not mean that a mere shift of emphasis from law to society can provide any more certainty in the quest for a foundation that will legitimize the censorship of obscenity. If one seeks to derive principles of governance from society, then there must be an underlying social identity that is unified at one point. Should social space be understood to exist without an obvious core identity, as decentered and overlapping relations of connection and difference, then no single, coherent set of governing principles can be derived from the social. Instead, disagreement over what constitutes the center will lead to disagreement in the area of policy as partisans seek to preserve different "centers" and core values. American identity will then be understood as having been called into being through the decision to represent "it" as one thing rather than another. Because American identity does not preexist the varied and interested attempts to represent it, American identity—and the same goes for other forms of social identity that might be called upon to replace American identity—will not be able to provide a sufficiently stable and cohesive ground to anchor obscenity decisions.

Judgments that obscenity presents a problem to the national community rest on the discursive connections between "Americanness" and "Western civilization." As part of the civilized West, the American people celebrate their self-governing capacity. In the area of sexuality, this is suggested by the way that Americans govern their sexual expression according to norms of decency. In the area of social governance, U.S. citizens' cultural heritage derives from their connections to the civilized West, as manifested by their capacity to be governed by the rule of law. These two dimensions of American identity, however, produce a paradox. The embrace of decency and respect for the rule of law conflict when the Court attempts to censor obscenity.

If decency distinguishes U.S. society from less civilized societies, then a category of obscenity enables American self-preservation. Yet the legal test to determine whether a given work is obscene requires a finding of "prurience," meaning that the materials in question incite uncontrollable desires on the part of the viewer. When U.S. Supreme Court justices review sexual materials to determine whether they are obscene, they are forced to admit to personal temptation if they find the materials "prurient." A finding of obscenity is not based on legal impartiality but on an admission that one has been seduced by the materials in question. Such a confession destabilizes the veneer of civilized self-governance attendant to the image of an "unbiased" rule of law. Obscenity cases and the paradoxical contradiction these cases force to the surface create a legitimation crisis for the Supreme Court, one remarked on by both members of the Court and outside observers. The iconicity of Justice Stewart's comment on pornography, that although he could not define it, he could still say "I know it when I see it," reinforces popular perceptions about the Supreme Court justices: Legal decisions in this area are based on personal bias instead of the rule of law (*Jacobellis v. Ohio* [1964], 197).

What has superseded the Supreme Court's preoccupation with obscenity? Attempts to enunciate an absolute rule distinguishing free speech from obscenity, a division required for the rule of law and good of the community, have floundered. Since the 1970s, the Court has encouraged governments to manage indecent sexual expression so as to contain its effects. Distinguishable from the logic of censorship, a feature of legal positivism, this policy of containment has no legal test defining speech and regulable indecencies. Nor does it suppose that all American society can be defined by one sociosexual principle. This model of containment moves away from positivism in the legal and social spheres and embraces uncertainty on a number of different levels: What is indecent speech that can be regulated? Does indecent speech cause crime and urban decline? Is there an essential American identity that authorizes particular sexual policies? Although the threshold for national concerns with indecency has been lowered, the strategy of containment concedes the existence of alternative sexual practices even as it seeks to quarantine their effects and cultivate national sexual decency. These sociolegal tendencies, more sensitive to the governance of a differentiated social body, are in line with Foucault's discussions of governmentality and François Ewald's conception of social law.

In sum, the containment model differs from the censorship model because it has not sought, thus far, to enunciate an abstract legal test for decency that can be applied regardless of context. Nor has the containment model sought to enforce one sexual norm *directly* on the entire U.S. population. Instead, while we see social norms inhabiting legal judgments, the containment model concedes the existence of spaces in which deviant and incommensurate sexual practices eke out a shunned and burdened existence. In this way, the population is encouraged to act in conformity with legally valorized norms *indirectly.* Indecent sexual expression is not directly censored, though it is discouraged. These indirect means of discouragement may include time-of-day requirements for indecent broadcasts, spatial zoning regulations, the denial of a liquor license for one's business, or a lack of financial support for one's art.

Formalism's Failure

A liberal legal approach to the problem of obscenity depends on law's ability to distinguish constitutionally protected speech from obscenity. The Supreme Court preoccupied itself with this task between 1957 *(Roth v. United States),* when it made its first attempt to define obscenity, and 1973 *(Miller v. California),* when it made its most recent attempt. For almost two decades, the Supreme Court was guided by a model of legal power with juridical tendencies, one poorly suited to protecting the welfare of the American people from the social problem of obscenity (Foucault 1977, 183; 1978, 144). A disciplinary concern with normality and deviance, however, is a more efficient means of achieving the latter goal.

In *Miller v. California* (1973), Chief Justice Burger outlines the current legal definition of obscenity. The legal test asks three questions: (1) Would the average person, applying contemporary *community* standards, find that the work as a whole appeals to the *prurient interest*? (2) Would the average person, applying contemporary community standards, find that the work as a whole describes sexual conduct in a *patently offensive way*? (3) Does the work lack serious *value?* The definition of community that informs the first two parts of the test was understood to be national during the 1960s but is described as local in *Miller.*

Burger defends obscenity's exclusion from First Amendment protection by arguing that its regulation does not compromise the goals of free speech or the capacity for individual rational self-determination. As he argues in another obscenity case decided the same day, regulating obscenity is distinct from a "control of reason and the intellect" (*Paris Adult Theatre I v. Slaton* [1973], 67). Burger cites John Finnis's (1967) essay "Reason and Passion" to demonstrate why censoring obscenity is consistent with the value of free speech and to justify his reading of the First Amendment.

According to Finnis (1967), the Supreme Court's treatment of free speech reflects a reason: passion dualism. Finnis argues that obscenity is without value because "it pertains, not to the realm of ideas [or] reason," but to the realm of "passion, desires, cravings and titillation." Obscenity is outside the First Amendment's protection because appeals to passion "are not the concern of the first amendment" (227). Nevertheless, Finnis recognizes that art disrupts his neat reason-passion dualism. Artistic value does not derive from pure reason because it symbolizes human feeling and gives insight into human emotions (232–33). Moreover, sexual matters are not off limits to art. Therefore, Finnis must find some way to distinguish between art and pornography in an objective way. For this, he turns to the concept of distance.

Finnis associates "distance" with an ability to maintain rational control rather than becoming emotionally overcome (240). For Finnis, pornographers violate this distance that enables rationality. Yet he cannot maintain this position and remain logically consistent since his theory of art appreciation requires the *decrease* of distance (234). To view a work of art with utter detachment would be to remain unaffected by it and to deny its special artistic quality, which is to evoke emotion.

Finnis relates his reason-passion opposition to the Court's three-part test for obscenity.[2] The first part of the test deals with materials appealing to the prurient interest. Finnis argues that the reason-passion distinction presents a simple option: "Does the reader look for 'titillation' or for '*intellectual* content'?" But this question is not so simple considering how his discussion of art disrupts the "clear" reason-passion dualism. Strike one. Finnis suggests that his theory connects with the part of the obscenity test that looks for "offensiveness" through the importance of distance to the maintenance of rational control. Offensiveness, according to Finnis, is the feeling of threat or shock when distance is overcome. But distance cannot distinguish art from pornography. Strike two. This leaves the last part of the obscenity test: the question of social importance or value. At first, Finnis states that social importance "derives from connection, indirect or direct, with the intellectual realm." But he goes on to say that "assuming some consensus in the relevant levels of American culture, this . . . defining element provides courts with a broad common-sense criterion" (240). Strike three. Finnis and formalism have lost the game.

Finnis's argument shows that neat and objective-sounding decision rules such as reason or "distance" versus passion, which are meant to ensure the legitimacy of law as based on reason, rather than social factors such as bias, power, politics, or desire fail to do the work that is demanded of them. In the end, Finnis refers outside law to "American culture" in order to supplement what is lacking in his formalist model by relying on the way that individuals make sense in common as Americans. Thus, Finnis presumes sufficient unity within American society to create a basis on which to rebuild the legitimacy of the legal distinction between art and protected speech on one side and obscenity on the other. The failure of Finnis's liberal legal formalism is significant because the Court also argues that regulating obscenity is distinct from "a control of reason or the intellect." In addition to citing Finnis as support for this proposition, the Court also traces this distinction's genealogy back through a series of cases that reaches ultimately to *Roth* and to *Chaplinsky v. New Hampshire* (1942), which creates the framework for the twentieth century's free-speech jurisprudence (*Paris Adult Theatre I v. Slaton* [1973], 61, 67). In this way, we can see how central to modern First Amendment doctrine creating formalistic legal tests, based on a distinction between reason and passion to distinguish protected speech from that which is without value, has been. We can also apprehend how obscenity brings to the surface the fragility of this project.

We have seen how legal positivism relies on a cultural supplement, leading to a search into American society for the principles lacking in the law. Shifting grounds in the search for foundations, however, merely opens a new set of questions. Now, we must ask, is

American identity cohesive enough to anchor a definition of obscenity? Because of social pluralism that lacks a common denominator, when the justices claim to *represent* America through their legal decisions, they should be understood as really *constituting* "America."

American Identity: Decency

The law and politics of regulating sexuality, including defining deviant expressions of sexuality and outlining what is gained by their regulation, rest on America's identity as a "Western" nation. I will focus on two dimensions of this identity formation that conflict when sexual expression is adjudicated in the context of U.S. obscenity law. Americans identify as part of the West vis-à-vis the governance of their sexuality according to the social norms of civility or decency and a capacity to be governed by the rule of law.[3]

Since at least the early modern period, the terms "decent" and "civilized" have been used interchangeably to refer to the social significance of bodily propriety that is taken to represent the "inner" individual (Elias 1994, 44–45). Treatises on manners describe how every aspect of bodily comportment, such as how to fart, eat, and deal with nudity and sexuality, should be molded in order to conform to norms of civility and decency. To be decent or civilized requires the cultivation of forms of public self-governance that are different from nonpublic identities (156). Although a sixteenth-century treatise on manners such as Erasmus's might refer to wolves or peasants as negative points of reference to inspire self-discipline, by the eighteenth and nineteenth centuries, the term "civilized" is defined in relation to the racial difference of non-Western "savages" and "barbarians" who are not self-governed but must be tamed by despotism (Mill 1975a, 15–16; 1975b, 149, 175). Unfortunately, the constitution of U.S. national identity still requires such distinctions.

For example, contemporary observers like Robert Bork who warn of American decline frequently inscribe this degeneration within a racial narrative. Bork, for instance, refers to the enemies of the United States as "savages" or "barbarians" and describes a socialization function of families, schools, and churches as a process by which "savages" are "civilized" (Bork 1996, 21). He also calls the challenge multiculturalism presents to presently hegemonic conceptions of American identity "barbarism" (311–13). Others describe the failure to impeach Bill Clinton as an indication that American culture has decayed from "Western, Judeo-Christian culture" to "barbarism" (Weyrich 1999). Those continuing the culture wars advocate censorship of many aspects of popular culture, including pornography, to maintain "standards of decency" (Bork 1996, 147).

America's identity as a civilized Western nation justifies the distinction between protected speech and obscenity. Just as any social identity is constituted through relations of difference, Americanness and the "obscene" are defined by their mutual opposition. For example, in *Ex Parte Jackson* (1877), the Court finds that free speech is one of the "rights reserved to *the people*" (732) (italics added). In *Roth v. U.S.* (1957), Brennan argues that this right embraces "the liberty to discuss publicly and truthfully *all matters of public concern*" (488, citation omitted). All ideas having "even the slightest social importance . . . have the full protection of the [free speech and press] guaranties." But, Brennan also states, "implicit in the history of the First Amendment is the rejection of obscenity as utterly without *social* importance" (484; italics added). Obscenity is by definition without *social* importance, and Chief Justice Warren describes it as a "social problem" (495). The First

Amendment protects expression valuable to American society, while "obscenity" describes what troubles the norms and values of this society.

In order to draw the line between a right to free speech and the social problem of obscenity, one must be able to discern the identity of the American people so that those problems that must be regulated for its welfare can be separated from that which has value for this society. In *Jacobellis v. Ohio* (1964), Warren defines these norms in a frequently quoted passage when he defends the right of "the Nation and of the States to maintain a decent society" (199). "Decency" is a key element of the normative framework defining American identity, and recognizing its opposite, "indecency," enables the identification of social problems.

If American national identity is given content through the norms of decency, then sexual expression is invested with national significance: "Sex . . . is one of the vital problems of human interest and public concern" (*Roth,* 487). Sexuality properly expressed can signify the civility indicative of the American people, while improper forms of sexual expression indicate social difference. Thus, America is represented by a particular brand of sexuality. The nation reproduces itself through certain sociosexual relations, while other sexual relations signify social formations that are nonidentical with the nation, allowing America to maintain a *distinct* existence. The right of U.S. citizens to a "decent society" is sustained by obscenity laws and the opposition of Western civilization and the savage or barbarian that governs their meaning. In *Ginzburg v. U.S.* (1966), the Court describes this problem of improperly governed sexual expression for the nation.

In *Ginzburg,* the Supreme Court upheld the obscenity conviction of Ralph Ginzburg for selling and promoting various publications with sexual themes. While the Court conceded the educational or therapeutic value of the publications, the justices objected to the fact that the audience to which Ginzburg advertised went beyond the medical or psychiatric professions. Furthermore, the Court objected to the way that the publications are *represented* in the advertisements as "erotically arousing . . . stimulating the reader to accept them as prurient" (472). Ginzburg's conviction was upheld because the materials are disseminated "without restraint of any kind" (470) and not because the materials are obscene.

Citing Judge Learned Hand, Brennan states,

> The works themselves had a place, though a limited one, in anthropology, and in psychotherapy. They might also have been lawfully sold to laymen who wished seriously to study the *sexual practices of savage or barbarous peoples, or sexual aberrations;* in other words most of them were not obscene per se. . . . However, in the case at bar, the prosecution succeeded . . . when it showed that the defendants indiscriminately flooded the mails. (*Ginzburg,* 467–73; italics added)

Brennan understands that a text receives its meaning and value through the economy of its circulation and use. Ginzburg's lack of discrimination constitutes a social problem, one threatening to erode the difference that constitutes American identity. The circulation of the texts incites a sexuality inconsistent with civilized norms. The Court would not have found the materials obscene if they had been circulated in a way that represented the sexual difference of savages or barbarians as a deviation from the norms of decency that mark the progress of Western civilization. Obscenity is the failure to articulate sexual "aberration" with savage or barbarous behavior. The Court restores decency and thus American identity by expelling indecent sexuality from the body politic and linking sexual difference to the savage.

Even as the Supreme Court bases its obscenity decision on the differences between norms of Western civilization and those of a "savage" or "barbarian," such norms apparently fail to govern American society. Indeed, the very occasion for a finding of obscenity by Brennan is the *absence* of decency, as exemplified by the popularity of Ginzburg's materials. Obscenity law does not rest securely on America's civility; rather, the law of obscenity *constitutes* America as a civilized nation by representing the United States as part of Western civilization and then by enforcing the requirements of this identity against manifest transgressions. The law supplements a lack in the social by constituting the authority in whose name the law speaks.

American Identity: The Rule of Law

Historically, the story of modern law centers on the state flattening the diversity of minor jurisdictions, "customs," and centers of power and unifying them under the law of one territorial sovereign (Goodrich 1996). The state's legitimacy rests on the law's ability to adjudicate the conflicting claims generated by a plurality of values in a neutral manner. If it should fail, then the law's authority is undermined, and it becomes a source of domination. When law's legitimacy is undermined, so is the state's, which is based on the formal rationality of the law.

Legal scholars exhort judges to conform to the image of legal impartiality. The legal literature prescribes a role for judges that is "value free," "impartial," and obedient to "neutral principles." Judges are told to maintain their "abstinence" in the face of temptation to do justice (cf. Fiss 1979, 13–14; McKay 1983, 123; Bork 1990, 1–2). Judges must control themselves in order to perform in accordance with the rule of law.

The modern West's confidence in its civilized identity is constituted through endless representations of the chasm separating the West from the Rest. The articulation of civilization and law, which is set against the savage and the lack of law, pervades the discourses of the Enlightenment and modernity. Uncivilized, the savage lacking self-government is represented as without law (Fitzpatrick 1992). To progress toward (Western) civilization and (Western) modernity, the savage must submit to (what the West recognizes as) law. Linking civilization and law, Walter Bagehot (1948), a Social Darwinist and editor of the *Economist,* notes, "If human nature was to be gradually improved, each generation must be born better tamed, more calm, more capable of civilization—in a word, more *legal* than the one before it" (225).[4] Such a statement conforms to a long pattern in Western mythology (Fitzpatrick 1992).

Unfortunately, there has been a recurring temptation to understand the rule of law within the racial frame of Western civilization versus the savage or barbarian even during more recent times. In the United States during the late 1960s, one response to unrest in urban areas was to evoke the rule of law and to compare the uprisings to savage lawlessness. For example, former Supreme Court Justice Whittaker urged "our governments" to discharge their duties by "protecting the people against lawless invasions upon their persons and property by the impartial and vigorous enforcement of our criminal laws." Such a response is "fundamental and vital, as every thinking man should see, to the survival of our civilized and cultured society" (Whittaker 1967, 27). The identity of "our," which defines whose "society" and "law" Whittaker references, is not categorically different from Georgia Governor Lester Maddox's American imaginary that he invokes while commenting on the Newark and Detroit disturbances: "You can't say 'please' to a bunch of savages, rapists and murderers" ("The Nation," 1967, 17). In fact, even today Bork can assert that among the benefits Europe bestowed on the world is the "rule of law" (Bork 1996, 312).

Decency and the rule of law, both informed by the norms of Western civilization, constitute different dimensions of American national identity. Both were recently on prominent display during President Clinton's impeachment proceedings. Attempts to distinguish constitutionally between a right to free speech and the social problem of obscenity create conflict between these two dimensions of American identity as civilized, leading to the following paradox. If America is to maintain one aspect of this civilized identity, it must police the most extreme indecencies using the legal category of obscenity. Yet the nation's most publicly visible representative of law, the Supreme Court, cannot actually find materials obscene without eroding the image of a nation governed by the rule of law. Sexual decency is one central aspect to America's civilized national identity. Obedience to the rule of law is another. Paradoxically, governing according to one aspect of America's civilized identity conflicts with the requirements of the other, as we will now see.

The Paradox of Obscenity Law

In reviewing obscenity cases, the justices make comments symptomatic of the challenges facing them. They refer to the materials' lack of worth or the process of review as unedifying or announce their refusal to look at them. In other words, they *distance* themselves from the materials involved. In so doing, they are presenting themselves as detached, unbiased, and not likely to be overcome by desire. The justices perform their role requirements as prescribed by Finnis and the rest of the legal literature.

In *Jacobellis v. Ohio* (1964), Justice Brennan, announcing the judgment of the Court, describes the process of reviewing the materials as a "difficult, recurring, and unpleasant task" (187). Dissenting from Brennan's opinion for the Court in *Ginzburg v. U.S.* (1966), which upheld the conviction of Ginzburg under a federal obscenity statute, Justice Stewart, referring to testimony regarding artistic and social merit, notes, "*Personally,* I have a hard time discerning any. Most of the material strikes me as vulgar and unedifying. But if the First Amendment means anything, it means that a man cannot be sent to prison merely for distributing publications which offend a judge's esthetic sensibilities, mine or any other's" (498; italics added). Justice Black, dissenting from conviction in *Mishkin v. New York* (1966), argues, "Neither in this case nor in Ginzburg have I read the alleged obscene matter. This is because I believe . . . that this Court is without constitutional power to censor speech or press regardless of the particular subject discussed." He continues,

> I wish once more to express my objections to saddling this Court with the irksome and inevitably unpopular and unwholesome task of finally deciding by a case-by-case, sight-by-sight *personal* judgment of the members of this Court what pornography (whatever that means) is too hardcore for people to see or read. If censorship of views about sex or

> any other subject is constitutional then I am reluctantly compelled to say that I believe the tedious, time-consuming and unwelcome responsibility for finally deciding what particular discussions of opinion must be suppressed in this country, should, *for the good of this Court and of the Nation,* be vested in some governmental institution or institutions *other than this Court.* (516–17; italics added)

Justice Douglas, dissenting from the majority ruling in *Paris Adult Theatre I v. Slaton* (1973), concedes that the "materials before us may be garbage" but goes on to suggest that "[w]e deal with highly emotional, not rational, questions" when addressing the question of obscenity. The Court, he asserts, has no business involving itself with the issue at the present time (45–46).

Why must justices distance themselves from the materials put before them in obscenity cases? Why must they insert asides describing the materials as "garbage" or note their lack of enjoyment when reviewing the materials? In light of Black's and Douglas's comments, why do potentially "obscene" materials pose a serious threat to the highest judicial body and hence the nation?

In addition to the questions of social value and offensiveness, the legal test for obscenity involves the question of prurience. Brennan's opinion in *Roth* cautions that sex and obscenity are not synonymous. Obscene material "deals with sex in a manner appealing to the prurient interest" (487). Footnote 20, following this sentence, attempts to define "prurient" by suggesting that such material has a "tendency to excite lustful thoughts." Brennan continues by quoting from *Webster's New International Dictionary* (1949 ed.) to describe the effects of prurience as "[i]tching; longing; uneasy with desire or longing . . . lewd." He then quotes the ALI (American Law Institute) Model Penal Code (tentative draft no. 6 of 1957): "A thing is obscene if, taken as a whole, its predominant appeal is to prurient interest, i.e. a shameful or morbid interest in nudity, sex, or excretion, and if it goes substantially beyond customary limits of candor in description or representation of such matters" (487, n. 20). Brennan's opinion intimates that a normal sexual interest is permissible but that which excites an excessive or deviant sexual interest is not.

In order to judge materials as obscene, the justices must recognize the excessive desire the materials incite, one deviating from normal and healthy sexual desire (*Mishkin v. U.S.* [1966]). Such recognition may occur because they may experience "excessive desire" in the process of judging. In a rare confession, Justice Clark concedes having been affected when reviewing materials in the *Memoirs* case. Clark confesses, "Though I am not known to be a purist—or a shrinking violet—this book is too much even for me. . . . In order to give my remarks the proper setting I have been obliged to portray the book's contents, which causes me embarrassment. However, quotations from typical episodes would so debase our Reports that I will not follow that course" (*A Book . . . v. Att'y General of Mass.* [1966], 441). Clark's remarks are exceedingly personal. He admits that he has been affected by the book. To find something "prurient," hence obscene, requires an admission that one's passions and desires have been set in motion toward deviant ends and that they have transgressed the bounds of decency and self-control. One feels desire because one is seduced. Obscenity is the song of the tempters, and a finding of prurience is an admission that the song is an effective and affecting one.

In conjunction with the remarks of his brethren, Clark demonstrates the double bind of obscenity law. A finding of obscenity requires prurience, which refers to desire, passion, deviance, and seduction. Prurience evokes bias. Law, however, is defined against the passions in order to preserve its identity as impartial and as a constraint on naked interests and the temptations of illicit desires. Although a ruling of obscenity occurs when constraints fail, modern law draws its legitimacy from neutrality, detachment, and the maintenance of abstinence. According to Justice Black, if the nation persists in addressing these questions, then some other institution should be responsible not only to preserve the Court's legitimacy but also to preserve the nation, which relies on the rule of modern law as the foundation for its identity. *A decision finding obscenity can occur only at the price of law's legitimacy.*

A determination of obscenity threatens to unmask judicial passions. To the extent that America imagines itself as part of the West, however, the nation cannot forgo the regulation of decency. Obscenity rulings threaten one boundary between Western civilization and the savage as judicial desire determines the rule of law, while a refusal to defend decency would threaten another. This is the paradox that obscenity presents the *constitution* of America.

Law's Crisis

In the late 1960s, obscenity law was exceedingly unstable because the justices could not agree on an objective standard to define obscenity. Beginning in 1967, the Court entered a period of ad hoc judgments, either denying writs of certiorari or, when it heard such cases (which it did frequently because of the confusion surrounding obscenity), disposing of them on a per curiam basis. The Court decided thirty-one cases during this period in such a manner (*Paris Adult Theatre I v. Slaton* [1973], Brennan dissenting at 82, n. 8). In a long dissenting opinion where he reconsiders the Court's approach to obscenity, Brennan describes this period as undermining law's legitimacy (73).

Brennan states that the meanings of the key concepts in the test for obscenity "necessarily [vary] with the experience, outlook, and even idiosyncracies of the person defining them" (84). Recognizing the instability at the heart of obscenity, Brennan finds obscenity law unconstitutionally vague. The reality of the Court's obscenity jurisprudence is that "no person, not even the most learned judge much less a layman, is capable of knowing in advance of an ultimate decision in his particular case by this Court whether certain material comes within the area of 'obscenity'" (87, quotation and citation removed). Such vagueness "invites arbitrary and erratic enforcement of the law" (88). The failure to "define standards with predictable application to any given piece of material [means] there is no probability of regularity in obscenity decisions by state and lower federal courts." Lack of consistency is not due to the courts' shortcomings. Rather, it stems from a consequence of the fact that "one cannot say with certainty that material is obscene until at least five members of this Court . . . have pronounced it so." A sign of this crisis is the large number of obscenity cases on the Court's docket (92). Brennan recognizes the threat that obscenity poses to the rule of law. Basing judicial determinations on how the materials in question affect a majority of the justices gives "the appearance of arbitrary action" motivated by desire rather than the rule of law. Therefore, Brennan argues that the Court should give up trying to police obscenity in the absence of distribution to minors or to unconsenting adults (92–93, 112–13).[5]

The Court has not followed Brennan's suggestion. Instead, it issued its most recent legal test for obscenity in *Miller* and then has put the problem of creating an overarching definition for obscenity to one side. The Court, however, has not ended its efforts at sexual governance. Rather, it has largely pursued these interests through a different strategy since 1973.

Social Law

Obscenity jurisprudence demonstrates the incompletion of both "law" and "society": The identity of each is supplemented by the other. In the face of unrelenting pluralism in the law of desire, attempts to regulate decency through obscenity law imploded under the weight of inappropriate assumptions. These assumptions include the existence of "law" and "society" as mutually opposed and coherent categories and the assumption that the underlying principles of both categories are susceptible to positive specification. The goals of obscenity law are to regulate social problems associated with excessive sexual deviance while not burdening "speech." The Court pursued these goals, however, by techniques ill suited to their achievement. Since the 1970s, the Supreme Court has legitimized policies to *contain* indecency and the social problems ostensibly associated with it instead of seeking to *censor* obscenity. The present approach diverges from the juridical model of law and more closely approximates a concept of "social law," which is a form of law that reflects society's focus on normalization.

Social law does not refer to abstract principles of justice or law as does juridical law, which is implied by the attempt to discover formal legal tests to distinguish speech from obscenity. Social law balances conflicting interests in "society." Social law governs a population in relation to itself (Ewald 1986, 58). The standard of legal judgment is the social norm that varies in relation to its referential population rather than essential and transcendent principles of law or justice (70). Superficiality and relativity, rather than original causes and absolutism, characterize social law and its basis in normalization (Ewald 1991, 156).

Scholarship on governmentality suggests that a new political space has opened up during modernity—the space of the social. The literature, however, presents this space ambiguously (cf. Rose 1996). On the one hand, society is opaque. Its principles are not fully transparent to state officials. Moreover, the social is a complex of interacting variables without a singular point of unification. Any attempt to conform the social completely to state rules is likely to produce unintended consequences either because of the limits of state knowledge or because an intervention at one point in the social may engender effects in a different area. Thus, excessive state governance, exemplified by the police state, is likely to be self-defeating (Barry, Osborne, and Rose 1996, 9). As a consequence, policymakers come to recognize that forms of freedom can produce good government.

On the other hand, a modern form of political reason generates the concept of a population as the exercise of power aims at normalization (Foucault 1978). In particular, the nation is modernity's ultimate political and legal referent. Rebels resist colonial and imperial power in the name of national self-determination. The state appropriates citizens' lives and regulates the movements of persons through immigration and naturalization laws for "national security." Citizens demand, and states provide, policies for the biological, economic, and cultural health of the nation that are known broadly as serving the ends of "social security." In sum, the national people becomes the condition that enables both political and legal claims for freedom (freedom from imperial domination, disease, or hunger) and highly intrusive and inhumane forms of oppression (laws controlling movement, birth, sex, marriage, and death). The U.S. Constitution and subsequent legal developments, by making the "American people" the ultimate constitutional authority, referent of rights, and purpose of government, exemplifies these sociolegal tendencies. It makes the preservation of the American people the fundamental interest of law and politics.

Socialized law is double sided. Playing a more limited role of a tactic in the ongoing practice of social balancing that presumes a lack of unity, sociolegal understanding acknowledges conflict and the limits of its own knowledge (Foucault 1991). This may translate politically into policies promoting tolerance and freedom. Yet the entity of a population fills the space of the social.[6] From this perspective, sociolegal practice may seek to cultivate the population's normal tendencies and may display hostility toward social deviance.

Governing Decency, Containing Indecency

Legal developments since 1973 in the area of sexual speech conform to the model of social law. These developments display the dangerously normalizing tendencies of this model as well as the forms of toleration permitted under this model. The emergence of the legal category "indecent speech," a category of expression that is not as extreme or deviant as the legal definition of "obscenity," permits a more sensitive governance of the social body than obscenity jurisprudence allowed and thus provides policymakers with a tool that has greater normalizing potential. The racially inflected discourse of Western civilization continues to supply the content for the norms enforced by these regulations of public decency. Therefore, the changed legal environment threatens to implant these racially informed concerns with the proper governance of sexuality more deeply into American self consciousness.[7] The forms of toleration enabled by the model of social law include speech rights for decent American subjects on the one hand and narrow spaces for contained indecencies on the other.

While maintaining the absolute boundary of obscenity, the Supreme Court has lowered the threshold for regulating sexual expression by creating a legal category of nonobscene yet indecent speech. While indecent, nonobscene speech may not be censored completely, its detrimental effects may be regulated and contained through various zoning strategies. For example, in *FCC v. Pacifica Foundation* (1978), the Court found that prohibiting indecent but nonobscene speech during hours when children were likely to be listening to the radio did not violate the First Amendment. By lowering the threshold of speech that may be regulated but not permitting its total censorship, Stevens's majority opinion avoided the lure of positivism. He resisted defining indecency or the nature of the nuisance posed by indecent speech in the public sphere. Instead, he argued that a nuisance can be merely the right thing in the wrong place, like a pig in the parlor instead of the barnyard. Stevens states, "We simply hold that when the Commission finds that a pig has entered the parlor, the exercise of its regulatory power does not depend on proof that the pig is obscene" (*FCC v. Pacifica* [1978], 751). Thus, Stevens evades a formalistic approach to indecency by asserting the importance of a contextual evaluation of "a host of variables" and by highlighting the fact that the speech at issue was being channeled and not censored.

The Court's post-1973 legal strategy for regulating sexuality is based on a distinct form of political reason. That is, the Court's new legal strategy is underwritten by a different form of logic than its obscenity jurisprudence, one that is satisfied with contextual correlations rather than absolute definitions and underlying causes. For example, the Court has created a new rationale for regulating sexual speech called "secondary effects." In a series of cases that include *Young v. American Mini Theatres* (1976), *Renton v. Playtime Theatres* (1986), and *Barnes v. Glen Theatre* (1991), the Court has allowed the regulation of nude dancing and other "adult"-oriented businesses through restrictive zoning laws. This strategy either disperses such businesses, clusters them, and/or regulates their proximity to churches, schools, or homes.[8] Sexual expression is not directly censored. Instead, the Court permits zoning to contain "secondary effects," such as crime, that are claimed to be *correlated* with adult businesses. Recognizing the complexity and opacity of the social, the Court permits these regulations because there is no claim that the secondary effects associated with the sex industry are caused by sexual expression itself. Ironically, if these effects were caused by sexual expression, then legal support for their regulation would vanish, and the law or ordinance in question would be a form of censorship and therefore unconstitutional under the First Amendment. Secondary effects are simply and mysteriously *correlated* with sexual materials (*Barnes v. Glen Theatre* [1991], Souter concurring at 524). In the words of Justice Souter, men are not led by sexual expression to commit crime. It just so happens that a "concentration of crowds of men predisposed to such activities" tends to congregate in the vicinity of such establishments (524). The Court, in the interest of containing the ill effects associated with indecent speech, while not censoring such expression outright, permits governments to utilize spatial strategies such as zoning to mitigate the deleterious consequences of indecent expressions of sexuality.[9]

These secondary-effects cases negotiate the opacity and the lack of unity of the social through the lenient judicial burden that state regulations face. Governments need not justify restrictive laws according to impossibly rigorous standards of positivism or proof of causation. Mere correlations between sexual expression and social problems will suffice for Supreme Court approval. The social norms that motivate such decency regulations, however, are borne out of the racial opposition of Western civilization and the savage or barbarian. Thus, the more sensitive measure of social problems exemplified by the susceptibility to regulation of nonobscene indecent expression indicates the possibility of implanting a racialized self-surveillance more extensively within the social body.

In *Barnes v. Glen Theatre* (1991), the Supreme Court overturned two federal appellate decisions declaring Indiana's public decency statute in violation of the First Amendment. The state defended the statute on the grounds that it was targeted at the offense, traditional in "*Western* culture," of "public indecency" (Oral Argument 1992, 388; italics added). In order to discern a legitimate state interest in "societal order and morality," Chief Justice Rehnquist's opinion referenced an Indiana Supreme Court decision, *Ardery v. State* (1877).

Henry Ardery ran afoul of the law by exposing himself in a public place. According to

Indiana's supreme court, decency involves concealing one's "privates" from public gaze. Adam and Eve's example of "covering their privates," the court argued, "has been imitated by all mankind since that time except, perhaps, by some of the lowest grades of savages" (*Ardery v. State* [1877], 329–30). By contrasting the requirements of public decency to the habits of savages, both Indiana and the U.S. Supreme Court understand the question of decency in the discursive context of the civilized versus the savage and rely on these racially derived norms to pass legal judgment on public behavior. Moreover, by permitting the human genitals, pubic areas, buttocks, any part of the female nipple, male genitals in a "discernibly turgid state," and "deviate sexual conduct" to come within the view of the law *(Barnes),* the Court's secondary-effects jurisprudence provides a more sensitive technique than obscenity for policing the decency of America's body politic.

More recently, the logic of governmentality centered on racially derived norms has defined the context within which the Communications Decency Act (CDA) of 1996, which attempted to regulate decency on the Internet, was adjudicated in *Reno v. ACLU* (1997). In *Young v. American Mini Theatres,* Justice Powell described how unregulated sexual expression can foster urban decline: "[A] *modern* city can deteriorate into an urban *jungle* with tragic consequences to social, environmental, and economic values" (2457). Echoing these sentiments, an amicus brief in *Reno* argued that the current disorder in cyberspace leaves "children unprotected in the Internet *jungle*" (*Enough is Enough et al.* [1997]; italics added). According to the Department of Justice, the CDA protects the speech rights of Americans by creating decent cyberspace through the containment of indecency. The government seeks "to ensure that the Internet will not become a wasteland visited by a small segment of the population, but will instead thrive and flourish as a gathering place for all Americans" (*Reno et al.* [1997]). Distinguishing sexual wastelands from public fora where "all" Americans can come together, the Department of Justice suggests that decency is constitutive of American identity. The Court ruled in *Reno,* however, that the CDA was a blanket, vague, content-based regulation rather than a regulation zoning secondary effects. The *Reno* Court found that the CDA conformed too closely to the censorship model despite the government's justification of the legislation based on a containment model.

Zoning indecency permits a more subtle regulation of sexually expressive practices than the censorship of obscenity. The containment model, however, does appear to leave some room for incommensurate practices. For example, because the Court's secondary-effects jurisprudence is built on a narrative of racialized urban decline, its applicability to rural settings is contestable. The Wisconsin Supreme Court argues in a recent case that a secondary-effects justification for a public decency law in a rural locality is illegitimate and violates the First Amendment (*Lounge Management v. Town of Trenton* [1998]). Even in New York City, where Mayor Rudolph Giuliani sought to eradicate substantial portions of the sex industry from that city, estimates suggest that these regulations will not completely remove all alternative sexual fora. Forced closings of sexually oriented businesses will expose many, particularly gays, to increased danger and violence and is one reason why this policy should be condemned. Yet spaces for alternative sexual modalities will continue to exist, however precariously.[10]

The primary form of freedom enabled by the Court's secondary-effects jurisprudence is not the narrowly tolerated indecencies exemplified by New York City sex policy but is the freedom protected for decent and civilized American subjects. In secondary-effects cases, the Court paradoxically valorizes both decency and robust national debate. Although the U.S. government's legal arguments did not sway the Supreme Court in *Reno v. ACLU,* Attorney General Janet Reno's argument that decency regulations promote the First Amendment interests of Americans is reflected in cases preceding and following the Court's ruling on the CDA. For example, in *Young v. American Mini Theatres* (1976), Justice Stevens argues,

> To permit the continued building of our politics and culture, and to assure self-fulfillment for each individual, our people are guaranteed to express any thought, free from government censorship. The essence of this forbidden censorship is content control. Any restriction on expressive activity because of its content would completely undercut the "profound national commitment to the principle that debate on public issues should be uninhibited, robust, and wide-open." (2449)

Yet Stevens also argues that society's interest in protecting indecent sexual expression is of a "wholly different, and lesser, magnitude than the interest in untrammeled political debate" (2452). The contradiction between the regulation of sexual expression and the right to free speech vanishes with the recognition that decency and civility secure the social identity from which a national commitment to public debate can be made. Civility and decency identify the people whose speech rights are inscribed within the First Amendment. Governing subjects according to these norms establishes a position from which American rights can be claimed and from which *national* deliberation can proceed (Passavant 2000).

More recently, in *National Endowment for the Arts v. Finley* (1998), the Supreme Court finds that promoting decency is completely consistent with protecting the speech rights reserved to the people in the First Amendment. According to the Court, the decency requirement appended to NEA money is not a form of viewpoint discrimination.[11] Regulating sexuality to promote civility constitutes a subject position from which points of view can be expressed.

The containment model and the censorship model display distinctive forms of political reason. Assessing which model permits more freedom or which is more oppressive, however, is a more complex question. On the one hand, the containment model is a more sensitive regulatory tool, but on the other hand it also tolerates some "indecent" sexual practices, however narrowly construed. The containment model, based on the logic of social law, is totalizing in that it makes room for difference, but such tolerance comes at the price of constant comparison of differing sexual practices to social norms, thereby contributing to the reintegration of the social formation. The obscenity model is totalizing in the sense that it governs social space according to an absolute rule of law or homogeneous community identity. Thus, it deals poorly with conflict and difference. The obscenity model, however, by focusing on the dichotomy between speech and obscenity, is not as sensitive a regulatory tool as the containment model of decency when it comes to more subtle deviations from social norms. The containment model "picks up" these less-than-obscene deviations from the social norms of civility and decency on its more finely tuned radar screen.

Conclusion

The Supreme Court's obscenity jurisprudence failed to locate a foundation in either law or society to justify the regulation of obscenity. Preoccupation with this ultimately unresolvable quest led to a legitimation crisis for the Court as it failed to discover a solution to the problem of obscenity within the context of a law-versus-society paradigm. Since 1973, the Court has encouraged and legitimized practices of governance seeking to contain the perceived ill effects of indecent sexual expression. These developments indicate a shift of emphasis from censorship to containment. The emerging containment model of sexual regulation shares certain tendencies attributed to the concept of "social law."

The Supreme Court's jurisprudence also opens up the ethical ambivalences immanent in the question of governmentality. As a form of power, one is rightly suspicious of governmentality, particularly with its openness to biopolitics and the ease with which populations can become subjects or objects of "ethnic cleansing." The shift in regulatory rationales from causation and positivism to correlation and contextual evaluation lightens the burden governments have to bear in order to justify their policies. Yet the epistemic shift coincident with the rise of social law can justify limited forms of toleration for deviance through a liberal admission that complete social knowledge necessary to legitimize more absolute legal regulation is lacking. Thus, any simple evaluation of the Court's post-1973 jurisprudence is foreclosed by the complex mix of oppression and freedom that it enables.

Notes

The author would like to thank Lisa Bower and Jodi Dean for reading proof drafts of this chapter.

1. In making this argument, I am influenced by Derrida (1976).
2. Obscenity was defined in the 1960s under the Memoirs test: "(a) the dominant theme of the material taken as a whole appeals to a prurient interest in sex; (b) the material is patently offensive because it affronts contemporary community standards relating to the description or representation of sexual matters; and (c) the material is utterly without redeeming social value" (*A Book . . . v. Attorney General of Mass. 383 U.S.* [1966] at 418).
3. Peter Fitzpatrick (1992) discusses how the rule of law is an integral mythology for the modern West.
4. Bagehot has experienced something of a minirevival in the 1990s as his concepts have seeped back into contemporary constitutional discourse. See Beer (1993) and Sunstein (1993).
5. Brennan's position converges with the conclusions of the Commission on Obscenity and Pornography created by Congress in 1967 (Commission on Obscenity and Pornography 1970).
6. On the rise of the space of the social, see Donzelot (1979).
7. Elsewhere I suggest that American national identity has become more racially defined since the end of the Cold War (Passavant 1998).
8. This is the tactic employed by Rudolph Giuliani to "clean up" New York City, or, in the words of the *New York Times,* to balance free speech with "civility" (Sachs 1998). This chapter was written prior to the Supreme Court's decision in *City of Erie v. Pap's A.M.* (2000), a case that extends the logic of the Court's secondary-effects jurisprudence to its breaking point.
9. On spatial strategies as a tactic of governmentality, see Valverde (1996).

10. See Berlant and Warner (1998). On the articulation of sexual practice and national identity, see also Berlant (1997).

11. Viewpoint discrimination is a particularly unjustified form of First Amendment regulation. This is when the government chooses which points of view to promote and which to burden. This is understood by the Supreme Court and First Amendment scholars to be one of the exemplary evils the First Amendment is meant to prohibit. See Sunstein (1993, 173–93).

References

Bagehot, W. 1948. *Physics and Politics.* New York: Knopf.

Barry, A., T. Osborne, and N. Rose. 1996. "Introduction." In A. Barry, T. Osborne, and N. Rose, eds., *Foucault and Political Reason* (1–17). Chicago: University of Chicago Press.

Beer, S. 1993. *To Make a Nation.* Cambridge, Mass.: Harvard University Press.

Berlant, L. 1997. *The Queen of America Goes to Washington City.* Durham, N.C.: Duke University Press.

Berlant, L., and M. Warner. 1998. "Sex in Public." *Critical Inquiry* 24: 547–66.

Bork, R. 1990. *The Tempting of America.* New York: Simon and Schuster.

———. 1996. *Slouching towards Gomorrah.* New York: Regan Books.

Commission on Obscenity and Pornography. 1970. *The Report of the Commission on Obscenity and Pornography.* New York: Bantam Books.

Derrida, J. 1976. *Of Grammatology.* Baltimore: The Johns Hopkins University Press.

Donzelot, J. 1979. *The Policing of Families.* Baltimore: The Johns Hopkins University Press.

Elias, N. [1939] 1994. *The Civilizing Process.* Cambridge, Mass.: Basil Blackwell.

Ewald, F. 1986. "A Concept of Social Law." In G. Teubner, ed., *Dilemmas of Law in the Welfare State* (40–75). New York: Walter de Gruyter.

———. 1987. "Justice, Equality, Judgement: On 'Social Justice.'" In G. Teubner, ed., *Juridification of Social Spheres* (91–110). New York: Walter de Gruyter.

———. 1991. "Norms, Discipline, and the Law." In R. Post, ed., *Law and the Order of Culture* (138–61). Berkeley and Los Angeles: University of California Press.

Finnis, J. 1967. "'Reason and Passion': The Constitutional Dialectic of Free Speech and Obscenity." *University of Pennsylvania Law Review* 116: 222–43.

Fiss, O. 1979. "Foreword: The Forms of Justice." *Harvard Law Review* 93: 1–58.

———. 1982. "Objectivity and Interpretation." *Stanford Law Review* 34: 739–63.

Fitzpatrick, P. 1992. *The Mythology of Modern Law.* New York: Routledge.

Foucault, M. 1977. *Discipline and Punish.* New York: Vintage.

———. 1978. *The History of Sexuality: An Introduction.* New York: Vintage.

———. 1991. "Governmentality." In G. Burchell, C. Gordon, and P. Miller, eds., *The Foucault Effect* (87–104). Chicago: University of Chicago Press.

Goodrich, P. 1996. *Law in the Courts of Love.* New York: Routledge.

Gunther, G., and K. Sullivan. 1997 *Constitutional Law.* New York: Foundation Press.

Horwitz, M. 1992. *The Transformation of American Law 1870–1960.* New York: Oxford University Press.

McKay, R. 1983. "Judicial Review in a Liberal Democracy." In J. R. Pennock and J. Chapman, eds., *Liberal Democracy NOMOS XXV* (121–52). New York: New York University Press.

Mill, J. S. [1859] 1975a. "On Liberty." In R. Wollheim, ed., *Three Essays* (5–141). New York: Oxford University Press.

———. [1861] 1975b. "Considerations on Representative Government." In R. Wollheim, ed., *Three Essays* (145–423). New York: Oxford University Press.

"The Nation." 1967. *Time,* August 4, 12.

Passavant, P. A. 1998. "The Landscape of Rights Claiming: The Shift to a Post-Cold War American National Formation." *Studies in Law, Politics, and Society* 18: 79–114.

———. 2000. "The Governmentality of Discussion." In J. Dean, ed., *Cultural Studies and Political Theory* (115–31). Ithaca, N.Y.: Cornell University Press.

Rose, N. 1996. "Governing 'Advanced' Liberal Democracies." In A. Barry, T. Osborne, and N. Rose, eds., *Foucault and Political Reason* (37–64). Chicago: University of Chicago Press.

Sachs, Susan. 1998. "Civility vs. Civil Liberties." *New York Times,* July 6, A12.

Sunstein, C. 1993. *Democracy and the Problem of Free Speech.* New York: The Free Press.

Valverde, M. 1996. "'Despotism' and Ethical Governance." *Economy and Society* 25: 357–72.

Weyrich, P. 1999. "A Moral Minority." www.freecongress.org (February 18, 1999).

Whittaker, C. 1967. "Can a Disorderly Society Survive?" *U.S. News and World Report,* July 31, 27.

CASES AND BRIEFS CITED

A Book Named "John Cleland's Memoirs of a Woman of Pleasure" v. Attorney General of Massachusetts 383 U.S. 415 (1966).

Ardery v. The State 56 Ind. 328 (1877).

Barnes v. Glen Theatre 115 L. Ed. 2d 504 (1991).

Brief for Amici Curiae Enough is Enough et al., Reno v. ACLU 1996 U.S. Briefs 511 (1997).

Brief for Appellants Janet Reno et al., Reno v. ACLU 1996 U.S. Briefs 511 (1997).

City of Erie v. Pap's A.M. 120 S. Ct. 1382 (2000).

Ex Parte Jackson 96 U.S. 727 (1877).

Federal Communications Commission v. Pacifica 438 U.S. 726 (1978).

Ginzburg v. U.S. 383 U.S. 463 (1966).

Jacobellis v. Ohio 378 U.S. 184 (1964).

Lounge Management v. Town of Trenton 219 Wisc. 2d 13 (1998).

Miller v. California 413 U.S. 15 (1973).

Mishkin v. New York 383 U.S. 501 (1966).

National Endowment for the Arts v. Finley 118 S. Ct. 2168 (1998).

Oral Arguments, *Barnes v. Glen Theatre* (1991). In P. Kurland and G. Casper, eds., *Landmark Briefs and Arguments of the Supreme Court of the United States: Constitutional Law,* Vol. 201 (377–406). Bethesda, Md.: University Publications of America.

Paris Adult Theatre I v. Slaton 413 U.S. 49 (1973).

Reno v. American Civil Liberties Union 521 U.S. 844 (1997).

Renton v. Playtime Theatres, Inc. 475 U.S. 41 (1986).

Roth v. United States 354 U.S. 476 (1957).

Young v. American Mini Theatres Inc. 427 U.S. 791 (1976).

Contributors

LISA C. BOWER is an independent scholar who has published numerous articles and book chapters on the diacritical relationships among law, culture, community, and social transformation. She currently resides in San Francisco.

ROSEMARY J. COOMBE is professor of law at the University of Toronto. She is author of *The Cultural Life of Intellectual Properties: Authorship, Appropriation, and the Law.*

DAVID M. ENGEL is professor and vice dean in the School of Law at the State University of New York at Buffalo, where he also serves as director of the Christopher Baldy Center for Law and Social Policy. He is coauthor (with Carol J. Greenhouse and Barbara Yngvesson) of *Law and Community in Three American Towns.*

MARJORIE GARBER is William R. Kenan Jr. Professor of English and director of the Center for Literary and Cultural Studies at Harvard University. A writer and critic, she is author of *Vested Interests: Cross-Dressing and Cultural Anxiety, Vice Versa: Bisexuality and the Erotics of Everyday Life, Symptoms of Culture,* and *Dog Love.*

DAVID THEO GOLDBERG is director of the University of California Humanities Research Institute and professor of African American Studies and Criminology, Law, and Society at the University of California, Irvine. He is author of *Racist Culture: Philosophy and the Politics of Meaning, Racial Subjects: Writing on Race in America,* and *Ethical Theory and Social Issues* and editor of *Anatomy of Racism* (Minnesota, 1990). He is also founding coeditor of *Social Identities: Journal for the Study of Race, Nation, and Culture.*

HERMAN GRAY is associate professor of sociology at the University of California, Santa Cruz. He is author of *Watching Race: Television and the Struggle for "Blackness"* (Minnesota, 1995) and *Producing Jazz.* He has appeared in the documentaries *Color Adjustment* and *Signal to Noise.*

RONA TAMIKO HALUALANI is assistant professor of communications studies at San Jose State University. Her interests revolve around the construction of the social subject through historical memory, law, tourism, and popular culture. Her book *In the Name of Hawaiians: Native Identities and Cultural Politics* is forthcoming from the University of Minnesota Press.

DAVID HARVEY is professor of geography at City University of New York and Miliband Fellow at the London School of Economics. His books include *Justice, Nature, and the Geography of Difference, The Condition of Postmodernity: An Enquiry into the Origins of Cultural Change, The Urban Experience, The Limits to Capital,* and *Social Justice and the City.*

DEBORAH HENDERSON is a graduate student in sociology at Arizona State University.

YUEN J. HUO is assistant professor of psychology at the University of California, Los Angeles. She has also been a research fellow at the Public Policy Institute of California. Her research focuses on the influence of identification processes and justice concerns on social relations within groups and institutions. She is coauthor (with Tom R. Tyler) of *How Different Ethnic Groups React to Legal Authority.*

S. LILY MENDOZA is assistant professor in the School of Communication at the University of Denver. She also teaches critical intercultural communication at the Women's College in Denver. She is the author of *Between the Homeland and the Diaspora: The Politics of Theorizing Filipino and Filipino American Identities.* Her current work concerns the translocal narratives of Filipino women in intercultural relationships, and she also is involved in a collaborative project mapping out the critical turn in intercultural communication.

MICHAEL MUSHENO is professor of justice studies at Arizona State University. His articles have appeared in *Law and Society Review, Law and Policy, Law and Social Inquiry,* and *Identities: Global Studies in Culture and Power.*

TRISH OBERWEIS is project manager at the American Justice Institute in San Francisco and lecturer at California State University at Hayward. She earned her Ph.D. in justice studies at Arizona State University. Her work has appeared in *Law and Social Inquiry,* and she is lead author of the forthcoming book *On Knowing Rights: State Workers' Stories of Power, Identity, and Morality.*

PAUL A. PASSAVANT teaches political science at Hobart and William Smith Colleges. He has published essays on the subjects of rights, culture, nationalism, and free speech.

LISA E. SANCHEZ is assistant professor of criminology at the University of Illinois, Chicago.

CARL F. STYCHIN is professor of law at the University of Reading, United Kingdom. He is author of *Law's Desire: Sexuality and the Limits of Justice, A Nation by Rights: National Cultures, Sexual Identity Politics, and the Discourse of Rights,* and *Legal Method* as well as numerous journal articles. He is also the coeditor (with Didi Herman) of *Law and Sexuality: The Global Arena* (Minnesota, 2001) and general editor of *Social and Legal Studies: An International Journal.* He is secretary of the British Socio-Legal Studies Association.

TOM R. TYLER is professor of psychology at New York University. He is coeditor (with Roderick M. Kramer and Oliver P. John) of *The Psychology of the Social Self* and coauthor (with Yuen J. Huo) of *How Different Ethnic Groups React to Legal Authority.*

CHRISTINE A. YALDA is a graduate student of law and the social sciences at Arizona State University. Her research interests include representation, identity, community, and deviance in contemporary urban space. She has served as a civil rights attorney representing individual clients, nonprofit organizations, tribal governments, and the federal Equal Employment Opportunity Commission.

Index